MANAGEMENT INFORMATION SYSTEMS

1st Australasian edition

MANAGEMENT INFORMATION SYSTEMS

1st Australasian edition

GRAY
ISSA
PYE
TROSHANI

RAINER
PRINCE
WATSON

WILEY

First published 2015 by
John Wiley & Sons Australia, Ltd
42 McDougall Street, Milton Qld 4064

Typeset in 10/12 pt Minion Pro

National Library of Australia
Cataloguing-in-Publication entry

Author:	Gray, Heather, author.
Title:	Management information systems / Heather Gray, Tomayess Issa, Graeme Pye, Indrit Troshani, R. Kelly Rainer, Brad Prince, Hugh Watson.
Edition:	First Australasian edition.
ISBN:	9781118646021 (pbk.)
Notes:	Includes bibliographical references and index.
Subjects:	Management information systems—Australia. Management—Communication systems. Information retrieval—Australia
Other Authors/Contributors:	Issa, Tomayess, 1965– author. Pye, Graeme, author. Troshani, Indrit, author. Rainer, R. Kelly (Rex Kelly), author. Prince, Brad, author. Watson, Hugh J. (Hugh James), 1950– author.
Dewey Number:	658.4038

Typeset in India by DiacriTech

Printed in Singapore by
C.O.S. Printers Pte Ltd

10 9 8 7 6 5 4 3 2

BRIEF CONTENTS

CONTENTS

PREFACE

To me, this is not an information age. It's an age of networked intelligence; it's an age of vast promise.

—Don Tapscott

Information systems are at the forefront of business innovation in the Asia–Pacific region. In today's dynamic digital business environment, rapid advances in information systems mean that change will be the only constant. Information systems are transforming the world into a very small place and are contributing to increased global competition. As a result, Australian and New Zealand organisations are constantly searching for ways to gain a competitive advantage by achieving operational excellence; developing new products, services and business models; providing superb customer service; and improving decision-making capabilities.

Although immersed in technology, many first-year students initially struggle to see the relevance of information systems to their future professions. We wrote this resource to specifically cater for the needs of business students from all majors who will soon embark on professional careers, with three goals in mind:

1 to enable students to be immediately successful when joining an organisation
2 to help students understand the importance of information systems for individuals, organisations and society as a whole
3 to empower students to become informed users of any given organisation's information systems.

To accomplish these goals, we aim to provide the essential, relevant knowledge students require to understand how to become adaptable business professionals and effectively use information systems in their careers.

Management Information Systems, First Australasian Edition is interwoven with contemporary themes such as business ethics and culture, green IT, cloud computing, IT risk and security, and the impact of social media on e-commerce. We have provided a platform for students to develop their strategic thinking skills along with frequent opportunities to practise developing systems that support and improve businesses' organisational processes.

Our resource draws on diverse, vivid examples from large corporations, small- and medium-sized enterprises, and government and not-for-profit sectors in Australia and New Zealand. Through our series of 'IT's About Business' case studies in every chapter, we provide a strong pedagogical balance of grounding theory and real-world applications. We have adopted a cross-functional approach that considers the perspectives of all majors within the business degree, with extensive hands-on exercises to encourage creative thinking, problem solving and industry best practice.

Critically, we recognise that despite the increasingly automated nature of modern workplaces, *people* continue to play a crucial role in systems.

We would like to extend a most sincere thank you to the scores of business information systems academics whose invaluable advice helped shape our manuscript. Special thanks go to Lubna Alam (University of Canberra), Christine Bruff (University of Newcastle), Peter Clutterbuck (University of Queensland), Paul Darbyshire (Victoria University), Kristy de Salas (University of Tasmania), Rohan Genrich (University of Southern Queensland), Marta Indulska (University of Queensland), Dale MacKrell (University of Canberra), Matthew Mansour (Macquarie University), Nigel Martin (Australian National University), Peter Radoll (University of Canberra) and Jian Yang (Macquarie University) for their time and consultation at the conception of the project. We would also like to thank Marie van der Klooster in addition to our other academic colleagues who authored the comprehensive resources that accompany the text.

Our appreciation goes to the John Wiley & Sons team for their contribution to this book: Terry Burkitt (Publishing Editor), Kylie Challenor (Managing Content Editor), Tara Seeto (Publishing Assistant), Catherine Spedding (Content Editor), Renee Bryon (Copyright and Image Research Supervisor), Delia Sala (Graphic Designer), Tony Dwyer

(Production Controller), Rebecca Cam (Digital Content Editor) and Beth Klan (Editorial Assistant).

We hope you will enjoy our active approach in *Management Information Systems, First Australasian Edition*. We are confident your learning experience will position you as a highly valued future employee within a broad range of professions as you form a deeper understanding of 'what's in IT for you'.

Heather Gray
Tomayess Issa
Graeme Pye
Indrit Troshani
July 2014

ABOUT THE AUTHORS

HEATHER GRAY

Dr Heather Gray's research interests include using emerging technologies to bridge the digital divide in developing countries. Dr Gray is also actively pursuing the use of technology in online delivery of tertiary courses. She has experience with teaching large classes in an online environment where she is responsible for designing and delivering subjects for Open Universities Australia where some subjects have thousands of students. Dr Gray has published her learning and teaching research as book chapters and journal articles.

Dr Gray's industry background includes short- and long-term contracts with governments in Queensland and South Korea, as well as Australian national and international corporations in roles that included business systems analysis, project management and business process coaching. With a keen interest in online education supported by social networking and cloud computing tools, she uses innovative approaches in learning and teaching that saw her ranked in the top 20 'UniJobs Lecturers of the Year' in 2012. By keeping business and education capacity building at the forefront of her learning and teaching approaches, Dr Gray is focussed on supporting and enabling the development of business leaders for the future.

As the Outreach and Internationalisation Project Officer in Griffith Sciences for the Griffith School of Information and Communication Technology, Dr Gray is involved in the development of education research and programs, staff development and curriculum design in the Australasian region. She is also heavily involved in the development of online education courses and programs that bring together a scaffolded approach to learning and teaching to enable students to engage with real world tools, technologies and problem solving. As a digital divide researcher she explores technology leapfrogging and mobile technology use in business and education in the Australasian region, bringing this knowledge into her educational learning and teaching approaches.

TOMAYESS ISSA

Dr Tomayess Issa is a Senior Lecturer at the School of Information Systems at Curtin University, Australia. Tomayess completed her doctoral research in web development and human factors. As an academic, she is also interested in establishing teaching methods and styles to enhance students' learning experiences and resolve problems that students face. Dr Issa is a Conference and Program Co-Chair of the IADIS International Conference on Internet Technologies and Society and IADIS International Conference on International Higher Education.

Furthermore she initiated the IADIS conference for Sustainability, Green IT and Education. Currently, she conducts research locally and globally in information systems, human-computer interaction, usability, social networking, teaching and learning, sustainability, green IT, and cloud computing.

Dr Issa has participated in conferences and published her work in several peer-reviewed journals, books, book chapters, papers and research reports. Dr Issa is a Project Leader in the International Research Network (IRNet-EU, 2014–2016) for study and development of new tools and methods for advanced pedagogical science in the field of ICT instruments, e-learning and intercultural competences.

GRAEME PYE

Dr Graeme Pye received his PhD in information systems security analysis and modelling in 2009 and has been a Lecturer with the School of Information and Business Analytics, Deakin University, Victoria, Australia, since 2004. His research is widely published and focuses primarily on security analysis and modelling of systems, and is continuing to investigate the security and risk aspects of Australian critical infrastructure systems, their resilience, and the human and social networking relationships associated with emergency management and disaster recovery. Dr Pye is also interested in information warfare;

human and social communication networks; and computer ethics, privacy and governance of information systems.

Dr Pye has taught a variety of information systems subjects including systems analysis and design, advanced database, information security and risk management, business information systems, business intelligence, and information systems management.

INDRIT TROSHANI

Dr Indrit Troshani is a Senior Lecturer at the University of Adelaide Business School. He holds a PhD (Computer Science) from Edith Cowan University (Western Australia) and an MSc (Computer-based Information Systems) from the University of Sunderland (UK). Dr Troshani teaches accounting information systems to both undergraduate and postgraduate students. He also teaches information systems, internet commerce and electronic commerce.

Dr Troshani is an active researcher and his research interests include information technology adoption and diffusion (e.g. digital business reporting, mobile technology in healthcare and e-health, public sector adoption of social media, green IS/IT), accounting information systems, and social construction of technology. His work has been published in several journals including *Information Technology & People*, *Electronic Markets*, *Journal of Computer Information Systems*, *Journal of Engineering and Technology Management*, *European Journal of Innovation Management*, and *Industrial Management & Data Systems*. Dr Troshani has also provided consulting services in his areas of expertise to various public and private sector organisations on an adhoc basis.

APPLICATIONS AT A GLANCE

IT'S ABOUT BUSINESS	OPENING CASE >	CLOSING CASE >
CHAPTER 1 Introduction to information systems		
Driving business-driven mobile apps IS in SA agriculture Telepresence robots	Kogan Technologies	1 Today, every company is a technology company 2 The Arab Spring
CHAPTER 2 Organisational strategy, competitive advantage and information systems		
Kennards Hire BI systems The Surui tribe of the Amazon Two strategic information systems Rewards and recognition to increase user adoption and engagement	M2M: the case of Coca-Cola Amatil	1 IT behind the Asia–Pacific's largest low-cost airline 2 A tool to combat terrorism and fight crime
CHAPTER 3 Data and knowledge management		
Cloud accounting: the case of MYOB's AccountRight Live for SMEs How data warehousing is supporting tourism business in Australia A website for gathering subjective knowledge	Loyalty New Zealand — reaping the big data rewards	1 Big data 2 How Nimble is affecting the short-term micro lending industry in Australia
CHAPTER 4 Telecommunications and networking		
Browser competition heats up All hail Taxi Pro? Massive open online courses	Studio G	1 Managing information flow 2 Marriott's corporate portal
CHAPTER 5 Business intelligence		
Virgin Australia's BI performance Using analytics to save Grevy's zebra Australian cardiologists using GIS technology	Farmer wants an app	1 Procter & Gamble uses analytics in novel ways 2 North East Water
CHAPTER 6 Ethics and privacy		
Know thy customer AFP and Australians' private data	Big brother watching you work	1 Dunedin City Council blocks hate site 2 Google and China
CHAPTER 7 Information security		
Hacktivists 'Anonymous' attack Australian government websites Melbourne IT: an Australian internet success SaaS and Cancer Council SA	Small businesses in danger	1 An inside look at the Australian government's cyber security plans 2 Compliance
CHAPTER 8 Social computing		
Pinterest How tweeting has grown our wine business Buying a vehicle takes work! So you want to find a job Scientific discoveries via crowdsourcing and online gamers	La Casa Ristorante's Twitter dream	1 Facebook commerce 2 Tourism Australia's social strategy

APPLICATIONS AT A GLANCE *(continued)*

IT'S ABOUT BUSINESS	OPENING CASE >	CLOSING CASE >
CHAPTER 9 E-business and e-commerce		
Sydney app 'Ingogo' David Jones building an online shopping presence What to do about customer 'showrooming' practices? New Zealander starting a wildfire	Matt Barrie's Freelancer.com	1 The new virtual economy of Bitcoin 2 Two Australians on the 'up and up'
CHAPTER 10 Wireless, mobile computing and mobile commerce		
Near-field communications helps travellers in Japan Free municipal wi-fi in Brisbane parks Xero to hero — floating on a NZ cloud Eco IT in Aus — animal telemetry data collection BP uses wireless technologies Brazil uses smart meters	Mobile technology changing IT service delivery in Queensland's outback	1 A paperless airport 2 The battle for the mobile wallet
CHAPTER 11 Information systems within the organisation		
Burra Foods expansion required revamped ERP solution	Hog's Breath Cafe and Imagatec	1 Information systems helping farmers manage emissions 2 Hilton embraces collaboration with information technology partners
CHAPTER 12 Extending the organisation to customers		
7-Eleven social media strategy Tweet for immediate customer service Google Helpout: real time customer relationship support CRM risk/return	Business consultant CRM in the cloud	1 Competitive advantage using a concierge app 2 British Gymnastics
CHAPTER 13 Extending the organisation along the supply chain		
Energizer supply chain and technology Airbus moves to a smart supply chain Concrete ideas for sustainable business	The Kimberly Clark Australia supply chain story	1 The computer that could cut fatality rates for truckies 2 IT helps Cannondale manage its complex supply chain
CHAPTER 14 Acquiring information systems and applications		
Atlassian helps manage large software projects Virgin Australia's reservation system GE Healthcare switches from Waterfall to Agile	Learning from the Queensland Health payroll fiasco	1 Tweak or trash? 2 Smart technology in Western Australia information security group

HOW TO USE THIS RESOURCE

CHAPTER OUTLINE/LEARNING OBJECTIVES

The chapter outline lists the major concepts covered in each chapter, while the learning objectives provide an overview of the key learning goals that students should achieve after reading the chapter.

OPENING CASE

A short, real-world case focuses on a company from our local region using information systems to solve a business problem. Cases in introductory information systems textbooks typically focus on multinational corporations. In contrast, our chapter opening cases also demonstrate how small- and medium-sized enterprises address business problems using information systems. The cases add an entrepreneurial flavour to each chapter for students considering their own start-up business.

THE NOOK

At the beginning of each chapter is a recurring case focusing on 'The Nook', a small Sydney cocktail bar run by university graduates Malakai and Abbie. The Nook needs help redesigning its online presence and overhauling its technological infrastructure. Throughout the course of the book, students are presented with a series of related business problems for them to solve as if they were on work experience at The Nook. Each chapter-opening scenario poses a business challenge that students will be able overcome after reading the chapter content.

IT'S ABOUT BUSINESS

Short cases that demonstrate real-world applications of IT to business in Australia and New Zealand. Each case is accompanied by a series of critical thinking questions.

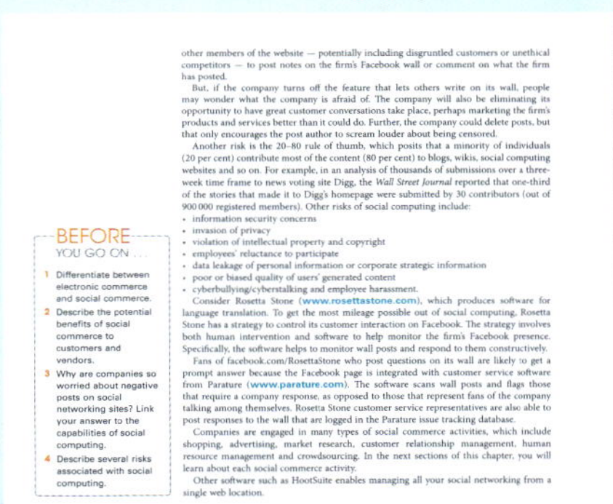

BEFORE YOU GO ON...

These end-of-section reviews prompt students to pause and test their understanding of concepts before moving on to the next section.

APPLY THE CONCEPT

This book's unique pedagogical structure is designed to keep students actively engaged with the course material. Reading content in each section is followed by an 'Apply the Concept' activity. These are a hands-on opportunity for students to immediately apply what they have learned. Each feature has the following progression: background (places the activity in the context of relevant reading material), activity (a hands-on exercise) and deliverable (various tasks for students to complete as they perform the activity).

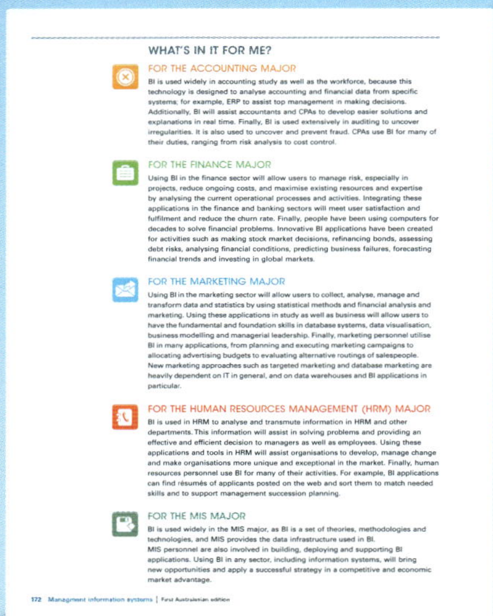

WHAT'S IN IT FOR ME?

FOR THE ACCOUNTING MAJOR

BI is used widely in accounting study as well as the workforce, because this technology is designed to analyse accounting and financial data from specific systems; for example, ERP to assist top management in making decisions. Additionally, BI will assist accountants and CPAs to develop easier solutions and explanations in real time. Finally, BI is used extensively in auditing to uncover irregularities. It is also used to uncover and prevent fraud. CPAs use BI for many of their duties, ranging from risk analysis to cost control.

FOR THE FINANCE MAJOR

Using BI in the finance sector will allow users to manage risk, especially in projects, reduce ongoing costs, and maximise existing resources and expertise by analysing the current operational processes and activities. Integrating these applications in the finance and banking sectors will meet user satisfaction and fulfilment and reduce the churn rate. Finally, people have been using computers for decades to solve financial problems. Innovative BI applications have been created for activities such as making stock market decisions, refinancing bonds, assessing debt risks, analysing financial conditions, predicting business failures, forecasting financial trends and investing in global markets.

FOR THE MARKETING MAJOR

Using BI in the marketing sector will allow users to collect, analyse, manage and transform data and statistics by using statistical methods and financial analysis and marketing. Using these applications in study as well as business will allow users to have the fundamental and foundation skills in database systems, data visualisation, business modelling and managerial leadership. Finally, marketing personnel utilise BI in many applications, from planning and executing marketing campaigns to allocating advertising budgets to evaluating alternative routings of salespeople. New marketing approaches such as targeted marketing and database marketing are heavily dependent on IT in general, and on data warehouses and BI applications in particular.

FOR THE HUMAN RESOURCES MANAGEMENT (HRM) MAJOR

BI is used in HRM to analyse and transmute information in HRM and other departments. This information will assist in solving problems and providing an effective and efficient decision to managers as well as employees. Using these applications and tools in HRM will assist organisations to develop, manage change and make organisations more unique and exceptional in the market. Finally, human resources personnel use BI for many of their activities. For example, BI applications can find résumés of applicants posted on the web and sort them to match needed skills and to support management succession planning.

FOR THE MIS MAJOR

BI is used widely in the MIS major, as BI is a set of theories, methodologies and technologies, and MIS provides the data infrastructure used in BI.
MIS personnel are also involved in building, deploying and supporting BI applications. Using BI in any sector, including information systems, will bring new opportunities and apply a successful strategy in a competitive and economic market advantage.

172 Managment information systems | First Australasian edition

WHAT'S IN IT FOR ME?

This unique end-of-chapter summary demonstrates the relevance of each key chapter topic to different functional areas of a business degree, including accounting, finance, marketing, human resources management and management information systems. This cross-functional focus makes the book accessible for students from any major.

SUMMARY

Aligned to the learning objectives listed at the beginning of the chapter, the summary enables students to review the major concepts covered.

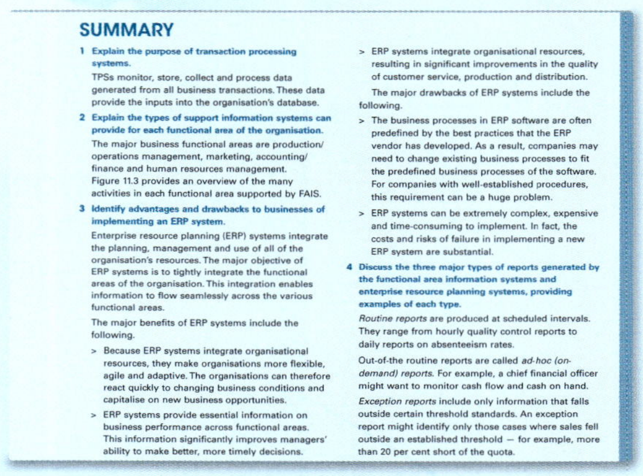

SUMMARY

1 **Explain the purpose of transaction processing systems.**
TPSs monitor, store, collect and process data generated from all business transactions. These data provide the inputs into the organisation's database.

2 **Explain the types of support information systems can provide for each functional area of the organisation.**
The major business functional areas are production/operations management, marketing, accounting/finance and human resources management. Figure 11.3 provides an overview of the many activities in each functional area supported by FAIS.

3 **Identify advantages and drawbacks to businesses of implementing an ERP system.**
Enterprise resource planning (ERP) systems integrate the planning, management and use of all of the organisation's resources. The major objective of ERP systems is to tightly integrate the functional areas of the organisation. This integration enables information to flow seamlessly across the various functional areas.
The major benefits of ERP systems include the following.
> Because ERP systems integrate organisational resources, they make organisations more flexible, agile and adaptive. The organisations can therefore react quickly to changing business conditions and capitalise on new business opportunities.
> ERP systems provide essential information on business performance across functional areas. This information significantly improves managers' ability to make better, more timely decisions.
> ERP systems integrate organisational resources, resulting in significant improvements in the quality of customer service, production and distribution.
The major drawbacks of ERP systems include the following.
> The business processes in ERP software are often predefined by the best practices that the ERP vendor has developed. As a result, companies may need to change existing business processes to fit the predefined business processes of the software. For companies with well-established procedures, this requirement can be a huge problem.
> ERP systems can be extremely complex, expensive and time-consuming to implement. In fact, the costs and risks of failure in implementing a new ERP system are substantial.

4 **Discuss the three major types of reports generated by the functional area information systems and enterprise resource planning systems, providing examples of each type.**
Routine reports are produced at scheduled intervals. They range from hourly quality control reports to daily reports on absenteeism rates.
Out-of-the routine reports are called *ad-hoc (on-demand) reports*. For example, a chief financial officer might want to monitor cash flow and cash on hand.
Exception reports include only information that falls outside certain threshold standards. An exception report might identify only those cases where sales fell outside an established threshold — for example, more than 20 per cent short of the quota.

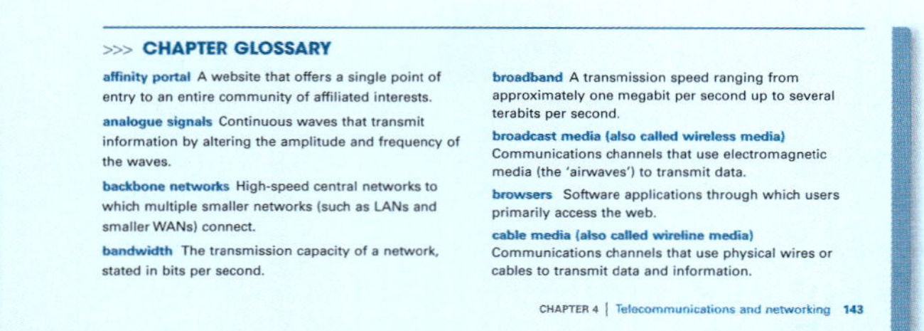

>>> CHAPTER GLOSSARY

affinity portal A website that offers a single point of entry to an entire community of affiliated interests.

analogue signals Continuous waves that transmit information by altering the amplitude and frequency of the waves.

backbone networks High-speed central networks to which multiple smaller networks (such as LANs and smaller WANs) connect.

bandwidth The transmission capacity of a network, stated in bits per second.

broadband A transmission speed ranging from approximately one megabit per second up to several terabits per second.

broadcast media (also called wireless media) Communications channels that use electromagnetic media (the 'airwaves') to transmit data.

browsers Software applications through which users primarily access the web.

cable media (also called wireline media) Communications channels that use physical wires or cables to transmit data and information.

CHAPTER 4 | Telecommunications and networking 143

CHAPTER GLOSSARY

This study tool highlights vocabulary within the chapters and facilitates student revision.

DISCUSSION QUESTIONS AND PROBLEM-SOLVING ACTIVITIES

These features provide practice through active learning. The exercises are hands-on opportunities to apply the concepts discussed in the chapter.

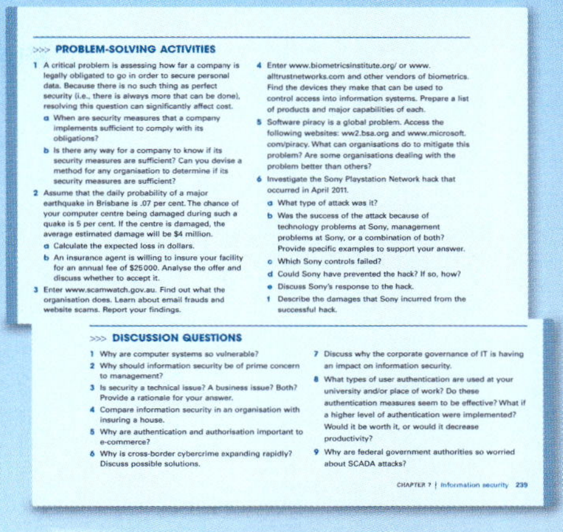

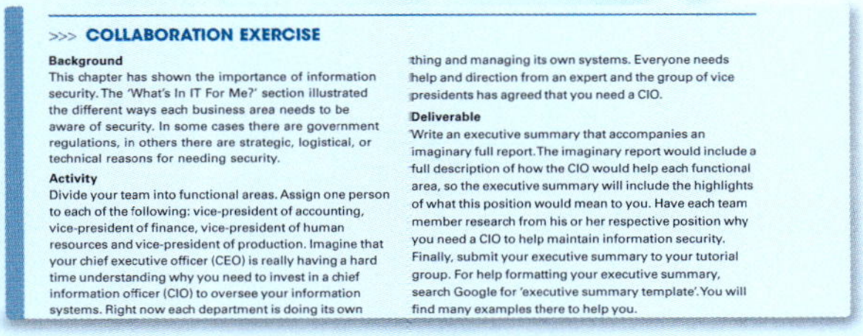

COLLABORATION EXERCISES

These are team exercises that require students to take on different functional roles and collaborate to solve business problems. The activities give students first-hand experience solving business problems using IS tools while also experiencing an authentic team environment.

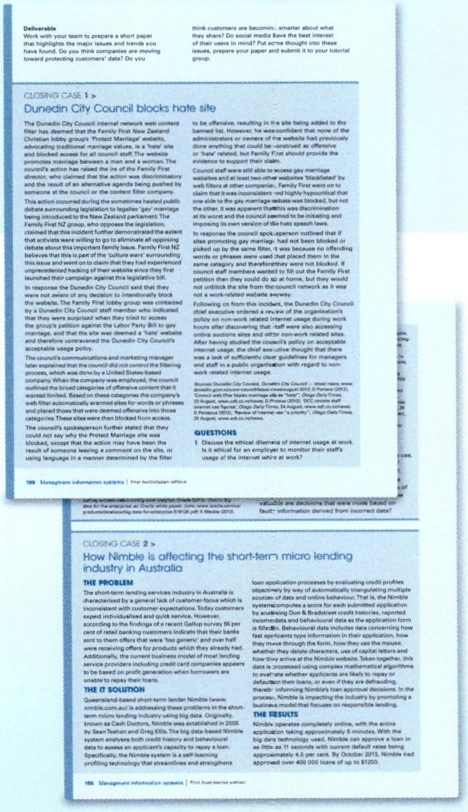

CLOSING CASES

Each chapter concludes with two cases about business problems faced by actual Australian, New Zealand and global companies, outlining how they have used IS tools to solve those issues. The cases are broken down into four parts: a description of the problem, an overview of the IS solution implemented, a presentation of the results of the implementation and an analysis of the key take-aways from the case. Each case is followed by discussion questions so that students can further explore the concepts presented in the case.

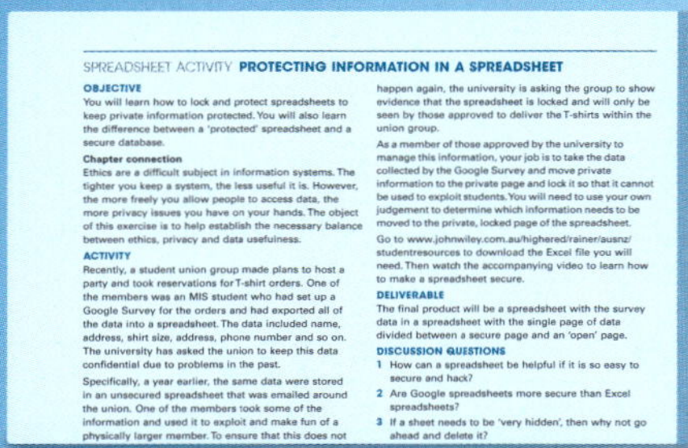
SPREADSHEET ACTIVITY **PROTECTING INFORMATION IN A SPREADSHEET**

OBJECTIVE

You will learn how to lock and protect spreadsheets to keep private information protected. You will also learn the difference between a 'protected' spreadsheet and a secure database.

Chapter connection

Ethics are a difficult subject in information systems. The tighter you keep a system, the less useful it is. However, the more freely you allow people to access data, the more privacy issues you have on your hands. The object of this exercise is to help establish the necessary balance between ethics, privacy and data usefulness.

ACTIVITY

Recently, a student union group made plans to host a party and took reservations for T-shirt orders. One of the members was an MIS student who had set up a Google Survey for the orders and had exported all of the data into a spreadsheet. The data included name, address, shirt size, address, phone number and so on. The university has asked the union to keep this data confidential due to problems in the past.

Specifically, a year earlier, the same data were stored in an unsecured spreadsheet that was emailed around the union. One of the members took some of the information and used it to exploit and make fun of a physically larger member. To ensure that this does not happen again, the university is asking the group to show evidence that the spreadsheet is locked and will only be seen by those approved to deliver the T-shirts within the union group.

As a member of those approved by the university to manage this information, your job is to take the data collected by the Google Survey and move private information to the private page and lock it so that it cannot be used to exploit students. You will need to use your own judgement to determine which information needs to be moved to the private, locked page of the spreadsheet.

Go to www.johnwiley.com.au/highered/rainer/ausnz/studentresources to download the Excel file you will need. Then watch the accompanying video to learn how to make a spreadsheet secure.

DELIVERABLE

The final product will be a spreadsheet with the survey data in a spreadsheet with the single page of data divided between a secure page and an 'open' page.

DISCUSSION QUESTIONS

1 How can a spreadsheet be helpful if it is so easy to secure and hack?
2 Are Google spreadsheets more secure than Excel spreadsheets?
3 If a sheet needs to be 'very hidden', then why not go ahead and delete it?

SPREADSHEET ACTIVITY

Every chapter contains a hands-on spreadsheet project that requires students to practise their Excel skills while using the concepts learned in the chapter. Each activity includes deliverables and discussion questions.

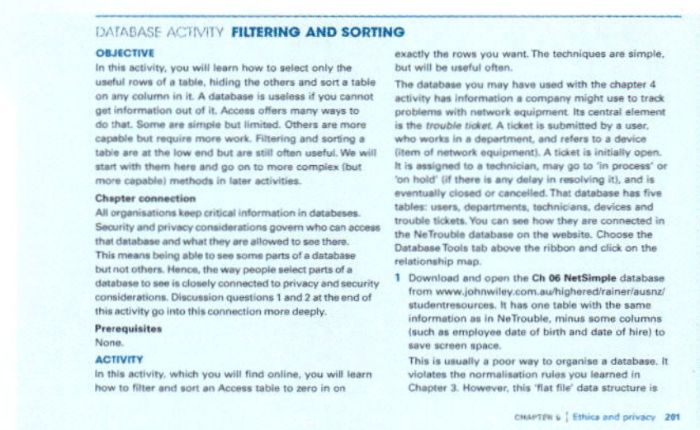
DATABASE ACTIVITY **FILTERING AND SORTING**

OBJECTIVE

In this activity, you will learn how to select only the useful rows of a table, hiding the others and sort a table on any column in it. A database is useless if you cannot get information out of it. Access offers many ways to do that. Some are simple but limited. Others are more capable but require more work. Filtering and sorting a table are at the low end but are still often useful. We will start with them here and go on to more complex (but more capable) methods in later activities.

Chapter connection

All organisations keep critical information in databases. Security and privacy considerations govern who can access that database and what they are allowed to see there. This means being able to see some parts of a database but not others. Hence, the way people select parts of a database to see is closely connected to privacy and security considerations. Discussion questions 1 and 2 at the end of this activity go into this connection more deeply.

Prerequisites

None.

ACTIVITY

In this activity, which you will find online, you will learn how to filter and sort an Access table to zero in on exactly the rows you want. The techniques are simple, but will be useful often.

The database you may have used with the chapter 4 activity has information a company might use to track problems with network equipment. Its central element is the *trouble ticket*. A ticket is submitted by a user, who works in a department, and refers to a device (item of network equipment). A ticket is initially open. It is assigned to a technician, may go to 'in process' or 'on hold' (if there is any delay in resolving it), and is eventually closed or cancelled. That database has five tables: users, departments, technicians, devices and trouble tickets. You can see how they are connected in the NeTrouble database on the website. Choose the Database Tools tab above the ribbon and click on the relationship map.

1 Download and open the **Ch 06 NetSimple** database from www.johnwiley.com.au/highered/rainer/ausnz/studentresources. It has one table with the same information as in NeTrouble, minus some columns (such as employee date of birth and date of hire) to save screen space.

This is usually a poor way to organise a database. It violates the normalisation rules you learned in Chapter 3. However, this 'flat file' data structure is

CHAPTER 6 | Ethics and privacy 201

DATABASE ACTIVITY

Every chapter includes a hands-on database project that requires students to practise their Access skills while using concepts learned in the chapter. Each activity includes deliverables, quiz questions and discussion questions.

DIGITAL SELF-STUDY RESOURCES

'PLUG IT IN' LEARNING EXTENSIONS

Comprising additional mini chapters relating to effective use of information systems in contemporary business, the 'Plug IT In' learning extensions enable a high level of flexible learning. Students can access these in digital format.

1. Business processes and business process management
2. Hardware and software
3. Cloud computing
4. Intelligent systems
5. Project management
6. Protecting your information assets

BASE FILES ACCOMPANYING THE SPREADSHEET AND DATABASE ACTIVITIES

Every chapter contains a hands-on spreadsheet and database project activity that enables students to practise their Excel and Access skills respectively.

The base files for these activities can be downloaded from Wiley's student resource site: www.johnwiley.com.au/highered/rainer/ausnz/studentresources

1
Introduction to information systems

CHAPTER OUTLINE

1.1 Why should I study information systems?

1.2 Overview of computer-based information systems

1.3 How does IT impact organisations?

1.4 Why are information systems important to society?

LEARNING OBJECTIVES

1 Identify the reasons why being an informed user of information systems is important in today's world.

2 Describe the various types of computer-based information systems in an organisation.

3 Discuss ways in which information technology can affect managers and non-managerial workers.

4 Identify positive and negative societal effects of the increased use of information technology.

OPENING CASE >

Kogan Technologies (www.kogan.com.au)

Founded in 2006 and led by CEO Ruslan Kogan, Kogan Technologies is a Melbourne-based, Australian-owned consumer electronics online retailer that sells products from Asian manufacturers to consumers in Australia and the UK. Starting with zero external capital, Kogan Technologies has grown to a A$250 million business, becoming the fastest growing business in Australia. In 2013, Kogan Technologies was listed as one of the top 20 Australian online retailers. At this pace, and with global expansion plans, Kogan Technologies are expected to overtake long-established leading Australian consumer retailers such as Harvey Norman. In addition to the strong entrepreneurial sense that characterises its CEO, Kogan Technologies' success is also attributed to the innovative ways in which the advantages offered by the internet have been capitalised. These advantages include availability of and access to inexpensive internet and related technologies, and reduced financial barriers and reliance on brick and mortar for starting up and developing Kogan Technologies. In an interview with *InTheBlack's* Mark Phillips, Ruslan Kogan argues that online channels lower the barriers to entry to almost every industry. In his case, internet technologies offered enormous efficiencies in relation to product sourcing, business intelligence, targeted marketing, email marketing and administration (e.g. paperless office).

By adopting advanced analytics including Google searches (e.g. using Google and Google Adwords to search the number of times key words are searched for), Kogan Technologies can determine the types of products that are in demand. Subsequently, they use electronic commerce channels to cut out middle men in supply chains, including agents, importers, wholesalers and retailers. In doing so, Kogan Technologies have created efficiencies in the supply chain and business processes that have enabled products to be sourced directly to Australian and UK customers inexpensively from leading manufacturers in Asia such as Samsung and LG. In this way, Kogan Technologies have achieved price leadership in the competitive consumer electronics retail industry. For example, in April 2013 Kogan Technologies was one of the cheapest consumer electronics providers, leaving behind competitors such as Harvey Norman, JB Hi-Fi and Dick Smith.

Stemming from the understanding that consumers of commoditised products (such as consumer electronics) are price sensitive, Kogan Technologies have adopted effective targeted price marketing strategies by offering products at the 'world's best price', creating a source of unmatched competitive advantage. Specifically, leveraging the power of internet technologies for implementing their targeted marketing strategies, Kogan Technologies are using viral marketing and online reviews which, in addition to contributing to their positioning in the market relative to competitors, has also helped realise enormous savings in their marketing budget. For example, given the increasing sophistication of consumers, Ruslan Kogan is cited by AdNews to have said that 'customers are too smart to believe the ads now', suggesting that traditional Australian electronic retailers may have to spend their marketing dollars more effectively both online and offline if they are to crystallise their value proposition.

Additionally, Kogan Technologies are harnessing the power of internet technologies to create and build the Kogan community which includes individuals that have opted in because they feel connected to the Kogan brand. Using email marketing, members of the Kogan community are engaged in a two-way conversation with the company. That is, they are the first to learn about upcoming specials and new products while also offering feedback to Kogan Technologies in relation to existing products, services and business practices, offering a cost-effective market research tool which has both enhanced the loyalty of existing customers and interest by prospective customers to become part of this community. Taken together, these approaches have increased Kogan's conversions and retention rates, thereby contributing to its spectacular growth.

Sources: Adnews (2013), 'Kogan warns Harvey: the ads won't fool anyone', *AdNews*, 30 April, www.adnews.com.au/adnews/kogan-warns-harvey-the-ads-won-t-fool-anyone; G Cassar (2012), 'Supply chain & ecommerce master class', *Internet Marketing Magazine*, August, pp. 7–13, media.kogan.com/files/newsroom/attachments/20120801-internet-marketing-mag2.pdf; CDN (2013), 'Harvey priciest chain: report', *Computer Daily News*, 1 May, media.kogan.com/files/newsroom/attachments/20130501_-_computer_daily_news_-_price_chain.pdf; K Cincotta (2013), 'Microsoft takes stock of strategy', *The Age*, Digital Life, www.theage.com.au/digital-life/tablets/microsoft-takes-stock-of-strategy-20130403-2h5l1.html; N Clark (2013), 'The mini moguls: armed with the latest technology, four Australian teenage entrepreneurs are turning bright ideas into dollars', *VirginAustralia Inflight Magazine*, 5 April, media.kogan.com/files/newsroom/attachments/20130401_-_virgins_inflight_magazine_-_mini_moguls.pdf; Kogan (2013), 'About Kogan', www.kogan.com/au/about/; M Phillips (2013), 'Kogan Technologies' CEO and founder, Ruslan Kogan: how a computer geek started a business in his parents' garage and became Australia's richest 20-something', *InTheBlack*, 9 April, newsle.com/article/0/68934534/'; P Stafford (2013), 'The top 20 Australian online retailers of 2013', *Smart Company*, 25 March, www.smartcompany.com.au/retail/054778-the-top-20-australian-online-retailers-of-2013-5.html; P Stafford (2013), 'Kogan's prank a lesson — don't ignore offline', *Smart Company*, 4 April, www.smartcompany.com.au/tech-head/054913-kogan-s-prank-a-lesson-don-t-ignore-offline-6.html.

Introduction

Before you proceed, it is important to define information technology and information systems. **Information technology (IT)** relates to any computer-based tool that people use to work with information and to support the information and information-processing needs of an organisation. An **information system (IS)** collects, processes, stores, analyses and disseminates information for a specific purpose.

IT has far-reaching effects on us as individuals, on organisations and on our planet. Although this book is largely devoted to the many ways in which IT has transformed modern organisations, you will also learn about the significant impacts of IT on individuals and societies, the global economy and our physical environment. In addition, IT is making our world smaller, enabling more and more people to communicate, collaborate and compete, thereby levelling the digital playing field.

THE NOOK

The Nook is a small cocktail bar that opened in 2005 after its owners, Malakai and Abbie, graduated from university. Throughout their college years, they DJed together and earned business degrees in management and marketing, respectively. They decided to put their collective knowledge together and open their own venue in Paddington, Sydney.

The Nook has been very successful. However, the pair realise that they can now be more successful by collecting, analysing and using the data that is available to them. To do this, they need to upgrade their infrastructure. This is the perfect time to upgrade everything because they have recently closed for renovation.

Information technology (IT) was not even part of their degree structure when they were in university, so they have not used much (if any) technology in their bar. While they are considering its use as they restructure, they are not sure how much and in what ways they should pursue the use of IT.

To help them with the use of IT in The Nook, Malakai and Abbie have hired you as an IT apprentice to help answer many of their questions about technology. They have teamed up with your IT lecturer and designed questions to go along with the topics you will be learning about in your information systems course.

This apprenticeship is designed to accomplish two things. First, it will give Malakai and Abbie the benefit of learning technology in a class that was not offered when they were in university. Second, it will give you the benefit of applying the textbook knowledge you learn to the real world.

As this chapter states, your generation is considered *Homo conexus*. This constant connectivity has to play a role in the restructuring of The Nook. It is your job to help Malakai and Abbie understand exactly how this will look. As you read through the chapters, you will be provided with some discussion questions to help you consider the impact of ISs on The Nook.

When you graduate, either you will start your own business or you will go to work for an organisation, whether it is public sector, private sector, for profit, or not for profit. Your organisation will have to survive and compete in an environment that has been radically changed by information technology. This environment is global, massively interconnected, intensely competitive, 24/7/365, real time, rapidly changing and information intensive. To compete successfully, your organisation must use IT and IS effectively.

As the case illustrates, the core competency of business is not technology. Rather, it is the company's business model. However, the company is effectively using IT to support its business model and thus to create a successful business.

As you read this chapter and this book, keep in mind that the information technologies you will learn about are important to businesses of all sizes. No matter what area of business you major in, what industry you work for, or the size of your company, you will benefit from learning about IT. Who knows? Maybe you will have a great idea and use the tools you learn about in this class to make your dream a reality, much the way Ruslan Kogan has!

The modern environment is not only intensely competitive for your organisation, but for you as well. You must compete with human talent from around the world. Therefore, you will also have to make effective use of IT.

Accordingly, this chapter begins with a discussion of why you should become knowledgeable about IT. It also distinguishes among data, information and knowledge, and it differentiates computer-based information systems from application programs. Finally, it considers the impacts of information systems on organisations and on society in general.

1.1 Why should I study information systems?

You are the most connected generation in history. You have grown up online. You are, quite literally, never out of touch. You use more information technologies (in the form of digital devices) for more tasks and are bombarded with more information, than any generation in history. The *MIT Technology Review* refers to you as *Homo conexus*. Information technologies are so deeply embedded in your life that your daily routines would be almost unrecognisable to a university student just 20 years ago.

Essentially, you are practising continuous computing, where you are surrounded with a movable and fluid information network. Your network is created by constant cooperation between the digital devices you carry (for example, smart phones, tablets, laptops and media players); the wireline and wireless networks that you access as you move about; and web-based tools for finding information and communicating and collaborating with other people. Your network enables you to pull information about virtually anything from anywhere, at any time and to push your own ideas back to the web, from wherever you are, via a mobile device. Think of everything you do online, often with your phone: register for classes; take classes (and not just at your university); access class syllabi, information, PowerPoints and lectures; research class papers and presentations; conduct banking; pay your bills; research, shop and buy products from companies or other people; sell your 'stuff'; search for, and apply for, jobs; make your travel reservations (hotel, airline, rental car); have your own blog and post your own podcasts and videocasts to it; have your own page on Facebook; make and upload videos to YouTube; take, edit and print your own digital photographs; burn your own custom-music CDs and DVDs; use RSS feeds to create your personal electronic newspaper; text and tweet your friends and family throughout your day; and many other activities. (*Note:* If any of these terms are unfamiliar to you, do not worry. You will learn about everything mentioned here in detail later in this book.)

The informed user — you!

So, the question is, Why should you learn about ISs and ITs? After all, you can comfortably use a computer (or other electronic device) to perform many activities, you have been surfing the web for years and you may feel confident that you can manage any IT application that your organisation's management information systems (MIS) department installs. The answer lies in your becoming an **informed user** — that is, a person knowledgeable about information systems and information technology. There are several reasons why you should be an informed user.

Students today are connected by many devices — almost all are wireless.

In general, informed users tend to get more value from whatever technologies they use. You will enjoy many benefits from being an informed user of IT. First, you will benefit more from your organisation's IT applications because you will understand what is 'behind' those applications (see figure 1.1). That is, what you see on your computer screen is brought to you by your MIS department operating 'behind' your screen. Second, you will be in a position to enhance the quality of your organisation's IT applications with your input. Third, even as a new graduate, you will quickly be in a position to recommend — and perhaps help select — the IT applications that your organisation will use. Fourth, being an informed user will enable you to keep abreast of both new information technologies and rapid developments in existing technologies. In fact, as you will see in the chapter's Closing Case 1, every company today is a technology company, making it even more important for you to be an informed user of information technologies.

Remaining 'on top of things' will help you to anticipate the impacts that 'new and improved' technologies will have on your organisation and to make recommendations on the adoption and use of these technologies. Finally, you will understand how IT can be used to improve your organisation's performance and teamwork as well as your own productivity.

Managing the IS function within an organisation is no longer the exclusive responsibility of the IS department. Rather, users now play key roles in every step of this process. Our overall objective in this book is for you to be able to immediately contribute to managing the IS function in your organisation from your user's perspective. In short, we want to help you become a very informed user!

In addition, if you wish to become an entrepreneur, then being an informed user will help you use IT when you start your own business. IT's About Business (overleaf) illustrates how you can build your own apps for your startup company or small business.

IT offers career opportunities

Because IT is vital to the operation of modern businesses, it offers many employment opportunities. The demand for traditional IT staff — programmers, business analysts, systems analysts and designers — is substantial. In addition, many well-paid jobs exist in areas such as the internet and electronic commerce (e-commerce), mobile commerce, network security, telecommunications and multimedia design.

The ISs field includes the people in organisations who design and build information systems, the people who use those systems and the people responsible for managing those systems. At the top of the list is the chief information officer (CIO).

FIGURE 1.1 IT skills open many doors because IT is so widely used.

The CIO is the executive who is in charge of the IS function. In most modern organisations, the CIO works with the chief executive officer (CEO), the chief financial officer (CFO) and other senior executives. Therefore, he or she actively participates in the organisation's strategic planning process. In today's digital environment, the IS function has become increasingly important and strategic within organisations. As a result, although the majority of CIOs still rise from the IS department, a growing number are coming up through the ranks in the business units (e.g. marketing and finance). So, regardless of your university major, you could become the CIO of your organisation one day. This is another reason to be an informed user of information systems!

Figure 1.2 provides a list of IT jobs along with a description of each one.

Career opportunities in IS are strong and are projected to remain strong in the future.[1] A report from Hudson ICT for ICT salary and employment insights for Australia and New Zealand found that cheap hires are in fact dearer to Australian and New Zealand organisations, suggesting that employers will now be attempting to attract high performers

Position	Job description
Chief information officer (CIO)	Highest ranking IS manager; is responsible for all strategic planning in the organisation
IS director	Manages all systems throughout the organisation and day-to-day operations of the entire IS organisation
Information centre manager	Manages IS services such as help desks, hot lines, training and consulting
Applications development manager	Coordinates and manages new systems development projects
Project manager	Manages a particular new systems development project
Systems manager	Manages a particular existing system
Operations manager	Supervises the day-to-day operations of the data and/or computer centre
Programming manager	Coordinates all applications programming efforts
Systems analyst	Interfaces between users and programmers; determines information requirements and technical specifications for new applications
Business analyst	Focuses on designing solutions for business problems; interfaces closely with users to demonstrate how IT can be used innovatively
Systems programmer	Creates the computer code for developing new systems software or maintaining existing systems software
Applications programmer	Creates the computer code for developing new applications or maintaining existing applications
Emerging technologies manager	Forecasts technology trends and evaluates and experiments with new technologies
Network manager	Coordinates and manages the organisation's voice and data networks
Database administrator	Manages the organisation's databases and oversees the use of database-management software
Auditing or computer security manager	Oversees the ethical and legal use of information systems
Webmaster	Manages the organisation's world wide web (www) site
Web designer	Creates world wide websites and pages

FIGURE 1.2 IT jobs.

IT's not just for students. Today's professionals must be able to use computing technologies to do their jobs.

who can offer the greatest worth to their organisations.[2] In particular, individuals who possess combined skills enabling them to carry out roles for liaising between business management and leadership and technologists can command annual salaries of up to \$170K.[3] Additionally, based on the Hudson ICT report the roles that are expected to be most in demand in the future include:

- development consultant
- IT management
- data centre manager
- business analysts
- architects
- systems engineers (including virtualisation and cloud computing)
- business intelligence consultant
- application developers
- security consultants
- database administration
- web designers.

Managing information resources

Managing information systems in modern organisations is a difficult, complex task. Several factors contribute to this complexity. First, information systems have enormous strategic value to organisations. Firms rely on them so heavily that, in some cases, when these systems are not working (even for a short time), the firm cannot function. (This situation is called 'being hostage to information systems'.) Second, information systems are very expensive to acquire, operate and maintain.

IT'S ABOUT BUSINESS

Driving business-driven mobile apps

The use of mobile applications (apps) is in its infancy both in Australia and internationally. Yet, the mobile apps industry has been growing and thriving at an unprecedented rate. For example, in Australia there are over 30 million apps downloads per annum.[4] Mobile apps therefore constitute an important part of the trend towards online productivity and services delivery. In fact, mobile apps need to be understood to cover areas beyond games that encompass business applications, health and disability applications. A 2012 survey[5] by the Australian Interactive Multimedia Industry Association (AIMIA) concerning the use of mobile apps and websites found the following.

- Overall, 77 per cent of all respondents access websites and/or applications on their mobile phone.
- Social networking websites and mobile apps were found to be almost equally popular with a little over 40 per cent of respondents considering themselves as high-level users.
- Approximately 69 per cent of the respondents indicated that they had installed mobile apps, representing a sharp rise from 55 per cent in 2011 and 41 per cent in 2010.
- Approximately half of the respondents indicated that they were using between 2 and 5 mobile apps weekly on average, while just over one-third of respondents indicated that they were using more than 6 mobile apps.

In this context, business owners are becoming increasingly dependent on mobile apps. Many Australian businesses envisage many emerging opportunities by using mobile apps to better connect and engage with their customers. Australia Post, for example, is facing a significant decline in its traditional business. In response to the new environment, they are now using mobile apps to invigorate their value proposition by enhancing the manner in which their customers interact with Australia Post in relation to their services. For example, Australia Post customers can use mobile apps to send postcards or pay their bills or even for personalised real-time tracking of parcels. In relation to this, Australia Post CIO Andrew Walduck is quoted saying that 'mobile is the new front door for our organisation'.[6] Likewise, Westfield is identifying mobile apps as opportunities for assisting customers in their visits at Westfield shopping centres, including assisting them with product research prior to the visit, planning the trip to the centre and even in looking for parking.[7] Additional examples of the use of mobile apps include:

- Andrew Campbell and GoCatch — developed a smartphone app that allows passengers to directly book taxis with taxi drivers, bypassing the networks and their booking fees
- Steve Fanale and AppVillage — set up an incubator for would-be 'app entrepreneurs'. Developers pitch their ideas to AppVillage and if it is approved, its community, or 'villagers' and 'innovators' can get involved in the process, offering everything from professional services to funding
- CliMate — a free app available through the iTunes store that provides localised information for rainfall, temperature and sunlight radiation data for the past 60 years, based on data collated by the Bureau of Meteorology for farmers.

Small business owners who want to create mobile apps — whether to market their products and services to customers or to improve internal productivity — are finding many alternatives to hiring professional programmers. These alternatives include:

- Appsbar (www.appsbar.com)
- MyAppBuilder (myappbuilder.com)
- AppBreeder (www.appbreeder.com)
- AppsGeyser (www.appsgeyser.com)
- Mobile Roadie (www.mobileroadie.com)
- AppMakr (www.appmakr.com).

The Queensland Government also offers tips about how mobile apps can be used to build and consolidate their business.[8]

Do-it-yourself apps can be used to create more complex applications for businesses. Greg Taylor, who runs an investment advisory firm called Powerline Advisors, created an app that brings together a wide range of data from five different online sources that could not be found in a single location. These include easily accessible sources such as Yahoo! Finance, in

➜

addition to harder-to-find information such as company balance sheets and cash flow statements. He paid programmers about $700 to implement his app and put about 200 hours of 'sweat equity' into the app.

Taylor updates the data in his app every night and pays a provider called Xignite (www.xignite.com) about $100 per month for corporate financial data. The app integrates the data from different sources, allowing Taylor to gain investment insights because he can more easily see relationships among the different types of financial data. These insights enable him to provide his clients with better investment advice.

Sources: Compiled from K Casey (2011), 'Appsbar helps SMBs build mobile apps', *InformationWeek*, 28 April; S Gerber (2011), 'Mobile app development: 10 tips for small business owners', *Mashable*, 7 April; 'AT&T survey shows mobile apps integral to small business operations, remote workers on the rise, Facebook use growing rapidly' (2001), www.att.com, 15 March; R King (2012), 'DIY apps save small businesses time, money', *Bloomberg BusinessWeek*, 6 February; T Kuittinen (2012), 'US consumers shun games — mobile apps triumphant', *Forbes*, 13 January; B Tinker (2012), '2011: the year mobile figured out IT and vice versa', *Forbes*, 2 January; www.att.com; www.zoho.com.

QUESTIONS

1. Why are mobile apps becoming increasingly important?
2. Why are businesses becoming so dependent on mobile applications? Provide specific examples to support your answer.
3. In what ways would smaller businesses and larger businesses benefit from mobile applications? Explain your answer.
4. Identify and evaluate the advantages and disadvantages of do-it-yourself mobile apps.

A third factor contributing to the difficulty in managing information systems is the evolution of the MIS function within the organisation. When businesses first began to use computers in the early 1950s, the MIS department 'owned' the only computing resource in the organisation: the mainframe. At that time, end users did not interact directly with the mainframe.

In contrast, in the modern organisation, computers are located in all departments and almost all employees use computers in their work. This situation, known as *end user computing*, has led to a partnership between the MIS department and the end users. The MIS department now acts as more of a consultant to end users, viewing them as customers. In fact, the main function of the MIS department is to use IT to solve end users' business problems.

As a result of these developments, the responsibility for managing information resources is now divided between the MIS department and the end users. This arrangement raises several important questions: Which resources are managed by whom? What is the role of the MIS department, its structure and its place within the organisation? What is the appropriate relationship between the MIS department and the end users? Regardless of who is doing what, it is essential that the MIS department and the end users work in close cooperation.

There is no standard set of choices for how to regulate and divide responsibility for developing and maintaining information resources between the MIS department and end users. Instead, that division depends on several factors:

- the size and nature of the organisation (e.g. public versus private)
- the industry in which it operates (e.g. education, mining, healthcare)
- the amount and type of IT resources
- the organisation's attitudes toward computing
- the attitudes of top management toward computing
- the maturity level of the technology
- the amount and nature of outsourced IT work
- the countries in which the company operates.

Generally speaking, the MIS department is responsible for corporate-level and shared resources, and the end users are responsible for departmental resources. Figure 1.3 identifies both the traditional functions and various new, consultative functions of the MIS department.

BEFORE YOU GO ON . . .

1. Rate yourself as an informed user. (Be honest; this is not a test!)
2. Explain the benefits of being an informed user of information systems.
3. Discuss the various career opportunities offered in the IT field.

So, where do the end users come in? Take a close look at figure 1.3. Under the traditional MIS functions, you will see two functions for which you provide vital input. Under the consultative MIS functions, you will see how the primary responsibility for each function is exercised and how the MIS department acts as an adviser.

Traditional functions of the MIS department
• Managing systems development and systems project management ○ As an end user, you will have critical input into the systems development process. You will learn about systems development in chapter 14.
• Managing computer operations, including the computer centre
• Staffing, training and developing IS skills
• Providing technical services
• Infrastructure planning, development and control ○ As an end user, you will provide critical input about the IS infrastructure needs of your department.
New (consultative) functions of the MIS department
• Initiating and designing specific strategic information systems ○ As an end user, your information needs will often mandate the development of new strategic information systems. You will decide which strategic systems you need (because you know your business needs better than the MIS department) and you will provide input into developing these systems.
• Incorporating the internet and electronic commerce into the business ○ As an end user, you will be primarily responsible for effectively using the internet and electronic commerce in your business. You will work with the MIS department to accomplish this task.
• Managing system integration including the internet, intranets and extranets ○ As an end user, your business needs will determine how you want to use the internet, your corporate intranets and extranets to accomplish your goals. You will be primarily responsible for advising the MIS department on the most effective use of the internet, your corporate intranets and extranets.
• Educating the non-MIS managers about IT ○ Your department will be primarily responsible for advising the MIS department on how best to educate and train your employees about IT.
• Educating the MIS staff about the business ○ Communication between the MIS department and the business units is a two-way street. You will be responsible for educating the MIS staff on your business, its needs and its goals.
• Partnering with business-unit executives ○ Essentially, you will be in a partnership with the MIS department. You will be responsible for seeing that this partnership is one 'between equals' and ensuring its success.
• Managing outsourcing ○ Outsourcing is driven by business needs. Therefore, the outsourcing decision largely resides with the business units (i.e. with you). The MIS department, working closely with you, will advise you on technical issues such as communications bandwidth, security and so on.
• Proactively using business and technical knowledge to seed innovative ideas about IT ○ Your business needs will often drive innovative ideas about how to effectively use information systems to accomplish your goals. The best way to bring these innovative uses of IS to life is to partner closely with your MIS department. Such close partnerships have amazing synergies!
• Creating business alliances with business partners ○ The needs of your business unit will drive these alliances, typically along your supply chain. Again, your MIS department will act as your adviser on various issues, including hardware and software compatibility, implementing extranets, communications and security.

FIGURE 1.3 The changing role of the IS department.

THE NOOK

QUESTIONS

1 Given that The Nook's customers are university-aged *Homo conexus* users of technology, do you think it will be possible for them to be successful moving into the future without a strong IT strategy?

2 If 'informed users' provide more value to a company, can the same be said of 'informed customers'?

1.2 Overview of computer-based information systems

Organisations refer to their MIS functional area by several names, including the MIS department, the information systems department, the information technology department and the information services department. Regardless of the name, however, this functional area deals with the planning for — and the development, management and use of — IT tools to help people perform all of the tasks related to information processing and management. IT relates to any computer-based tool that people use to work with information and to support the information and information-processing needs of an organisation.

An IS collects, processes, stores, analyses and disseminates information for a specific purpose. In fact, the purpose of ISs is to get the right information to the right people at the right time in the right amount and in the right format. Because ISs are intended to supply useful information, we need to differentiate between information and two closely related terms: *data* and *knowledge* (see figure 1.4).

Data items refer to an elementary description of things, events, activities and transactions that are recorded, classified and stored but are not organised to convey any specific meaning. Data items can be numbers, letters, figures, sounds and images. Examples of data items are a collection of numbers (e.g. 3.11, 2.96, 3.95, 1.99, 2.08) and characters (e.g. B, A, C, A, B, D, F, C).

FIGURE 1.4 Binary code, the foundation of information and knowledge, is the key to making complex decisions.

Information refers to data that have been organised so that they have meaning and value to the recipient. For example, a grade point average (GPA) by itself is data, but a student's name coupled with his or her GPA is information. The recipient interprets the meaning and draws conclusions and implications from the information. Consider the examples of data provided in the preceding paragraph. Within the context of a university, the numbers could be GPAs and the letters could be grades in an Introduction to MIS class.

Knowledge consists of data and/or information that have been organised and processed to convey understanding, experience, accumulated learning and expertise as they apply to a current business problem. For example, a company recruiting at your school has found over time that students who average a high distinction or higher have experienced the greatest success in its management program. Based on this accumulated knowledge, that company may decide to interview only those students with GPAs over 5.0. Organisational knowledge, which reflects the experience and expertise of many people, has great value to all employees.

Data [no context]	Information [university context]	Knowledge
5.16	5.16 + John Jones = GPA	*Job prospects
4.92	4.92 + Sue Smith = GPA	*Graduate school prospects
3.39	3.39 + Kyle Owens = GPA	*Scholarship prospects
5.95	5.95 + Tom Elias = GPA	

GPA = grade point average (higher is better)

You see that the same data items, with no context, can mean entirely different things in different contexts.

Now that you have a clearer understanding of data, information and knowledge, we shift our focus to computer-based information systems. As we noted, these systems process data into information and knowledge that you can use.

A **computer-based information system (CBIS)** is an information system that uses computer technology to perform some or all of its intended tasks. Although not all information systems are computerised, today most are. For this reason, the term *information system* is typically used synonymously with *computer-based information system*. The following are the basic components of computer-based information systems. The first four are called **information technology (IT) components**. Figure 1.5 shows how these four components interact to form a CBIS.

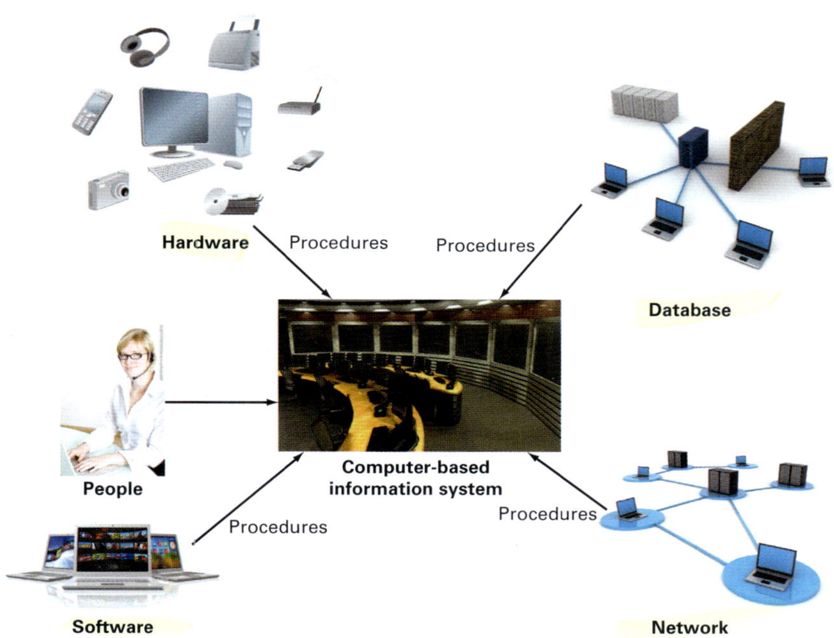

FIGURE 1.5 It takes technology (hardware, software, databases and networks) with appropriate procedures to make a CBIS useful for people.

- **Hardware** is a device such as a processor, monitor, keyboard, or printer. Together, these devices accept data and information, process them and display them.
- **Software** is a program or collection of programs that enable the hardware to process data.
- A **database** is a collection of related files or tables containing data.
- A **network** is a connecting system (wireline or wireless) that permits different computers to share resources.
- **Procedures** are the set of instructions about how to combine hardware, software, databases and networks in order to process information and generate the desired output.
- *Users* are those individuals who use the hardware and software, interface with it, or utilise its output.

Computer-based information systems have many capabilities. Figure 1.6 summarises the most important ones.

Figure 1.7 shows how components are integrated to form the wide variety of information systems in an organisation. Starting at the bottom of the figure, you see that the IT components of hardware, software, networks (wired and wireless) and databases form the **information technology (IT) platform**. IT personnel use these components to develop information systems, oversee security and risk, and manage data. These activities cumulatively are called **information technology (IT) services**. The IT components plus IT services comprise the organisation's **information technology (IT) infrastructure**. At the top of the pyramid are the various organisational information systems.

Information systems perform these various tasks via a wide spectrum of applications. An **application (app)** is a computer program designed to support a specific task or business process. (A synonymous term is *application program*.) Each functional area or department within a business organisation uses dozens of application programs. For instance, the human resources department sometimes uses one application for screening job applicants and another for monitoring employee turnover. The collection of application programs in a single department is usually referred to as a *departmental information system* (also known as a *functional area information system*). For example, the collection of application programs in the human resources area is called the *human resources information system* (*HRIS*). Collections of application programs — that is, departmental information systems — are used in other functional areas as well, such as accounting, finance, marketing and production/operations. IT's About Business (opposite) illustrates how the Department of Primary Industries and Regions in South Australia (PIRSA), a key Government of South Australia agency, is using information systems to improve their regulatory monitoring operations.

Types of computer-based information systems

Modern organisations employ many different types of information systems. Figure 1.7 illustrates the different types of information systems that function *within* a single organisation and figure 1.8 (overleaf) shows the different types of information systems that function *among* multiple organisations. You will study transaction processing systems, management information systems and enterprise resource planning systems in chapter 11. You will learn about customer relationship management (CRM) systems in chapter 12 and supply chain management (SCM) systems in chapter 13.

- Perform high-speed, high-volume, numerical computations
- Provide fast, accurate communication and collaboration within and among organisations
- Store huge amounts of information in an easy-to-access yet small space
- Allow quick and inexpensive access to vast amounts of information, worldwide
- Interpret vast amounts of data quickly and efficiently
- Automate both semiautomatic business processes and manual tasks

FIGURE 1.6 Major capabilities of information systems.

IT'S ABOUT BUSINESS

IS in SA agriculture

The Department of Primary Industries and Regions in South Australia (PIRSA) is a key Government of South Australia agency that aims at growing sustainable and competitive regions in South Australia. PIRSA focuses on the sustainable development SA's agriculture, wine, seafood, forestry and food industry by providing relevant research, policy development, regulation and biosecurity imperatives.[9] In order to proactively deal with SA's diverse communities, industries and natural resourses, PIRSA employees require information tools to assist them with planning and monitoring activities. PIRSA partnered with Fujitsu to develop the Primary Industries Information Management System (PIIMS), which integrates 23 legacy systems. PIIMS offers a single geospatial reference point in relation to activities concerning registration, management and ongoing monitoring of all types of resources that are covered by PIRSA such as:[10]

- land operation and animal registration
- disease outbreak and control
- livestock tagging and tracking through the value chain
- monitoring of rural chemical usage
- support for fisheries and aquaculture industries
- licensing and associated financial processes
- plant produce accreditations held by plant produce facilities that supply fruit and vegetable markets/ supermarkets
- opal mining permits and claims
- recording regulatory compliance activities.

Specifically, PIIMS can support PIRSA in managing natural, industrial and community resources with geospatial representation and mapping and in doing so assist PIRSA to meet its strategic environmental sustainability objectives. For example, PIIMS offers a web-based interface that can be used by all PIRSA departments to record all licensing details as required under the law (e.g. Fisheries Management Act).[11] Additionally, PIIMS can offer PIRSA staff (e.g. Fisheries compliance officers), with complete information in relation to a license or license holder in real time via personal digital assistants (PDA) or smartphones when they are out in the field. Additionally, PIIMS helps with the management of animal health programs in South Australia which includes (but is not limited to):

- generic registration processes
- availability of both textual and spatial representations of all properties and associated managers, owners and relevant stakeholders
- capability for mapping of animal health zones and restricted and control areas
- capability of recording, managing and reporting of various events including inspections (e.g. livestock properties and abattoir surveillance).

PIIMS also supports the planning of rapid responses to disease outbreak detection and coordination of containment activities while offering greater visibility, management and control for ensuring the enhancement of South Australia's key resources.

QUESTIONS

1. Describe how PIRSA is using PIIMS to accomplish its operational and strategic objectives.
2. Explain how information systems could be used by regulators for monitoring of regulatory compliance and intervention.

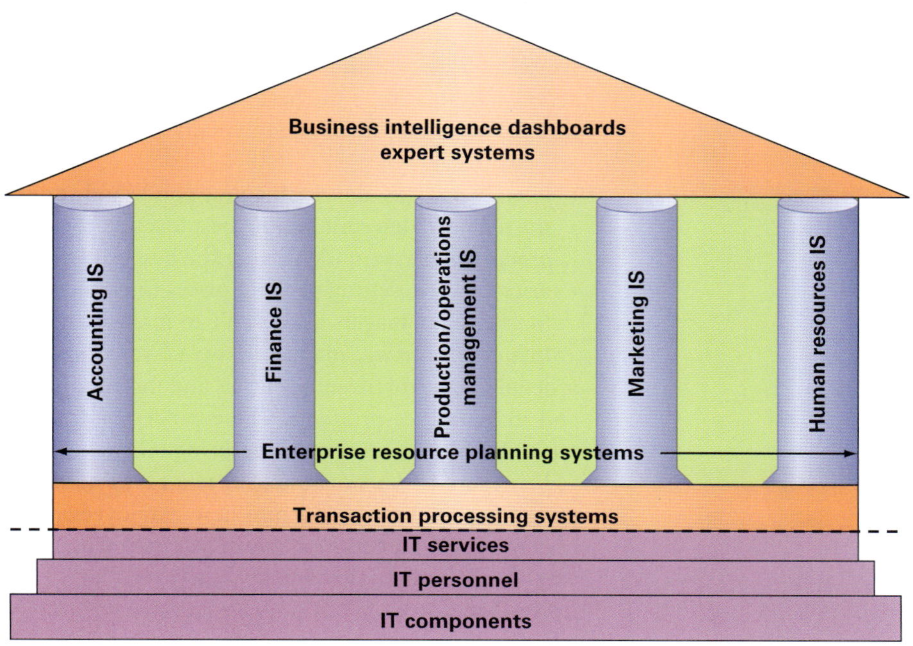

FIGURE 1.7 How IT components are integrated to form the wide variety of information systems within a single organisation.

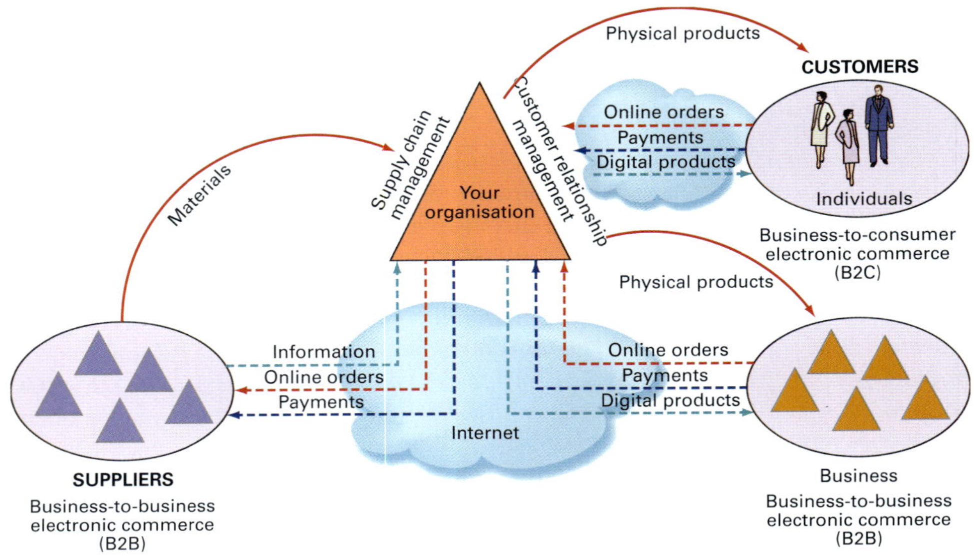

FIGURE 1.8 The different types of information systems that function among multiple organisations.

In the next section, you will learn about the numerous and diverse types of information systems employed by modern organisations. You will also read about the types of support these systems provide.

Breadth of support for information systems

Certain information systems support parts of organisations, others support entire organisations and still others support groups of organisations. This section addresses all of these systems.

Recall that each department or functional area within an organisation has its own collection of application programs, or information systems. These **functional area information systems (FAISs)** are supporting pillars for the information systems located at the top of figure 1.7: business intelligence systems and dashboards. As the name suggests, each FAIS supports a particular functional area within the organisation. Examples are accounting IS, finance IS, production/operations management (POM) IS, marketing IS and human resources IS.

Consider these examples of IT systems in the various functional areas of an organisation. In *finance* and *accounting*, managers use IT systems to forecast revenues and business activity, to determine the best sources and uses of funds, and to perform audits to ensure that the organisation is fundamentally sound and that all financial reports and documents are accurate:

- *product analysis*: developing new goods and services
- *site analysis*: determining the best location for production and distribution facilities
- *promotion analysis*: identifying the best advertising channels
- *price analysis*: setting product prices to obtain the highest total revenues.

Marketing managers also use IT to manage their relationships with their customers.

In *manufacturing*, managers use IT to process customer orders, develop production schedules, control inventory levels and monitor product quality. They also use IT to design and manufacture products. These processes are called computer-assisted design (CAD) and computer-assisted manufacturing (CAM).

Managers in *human resources* use IT to manage the recruiting process, analyse and screen job applicants and hire new employees. They also employ IT to help employees manage their careers, to administer performance tests to employees and to monitor employee productivity. Finally, they rely on IT to manage compensation and benefits packages.

Two information systems support the entire organisation: enterprise resource planning systems and transaction processing systems.

Enterprise resource planning (ERP) systems are cross-functional systems that are designed to correct a lack of communication among the FAISs. As a result, figure 1.7 shows ERP systems spanning the FAIS.

ERP systems were an important innovation because the various FAISs were often developed as stand-alone systems and did not communicate effectively (if at all) with one another. ERP systems resolve this problem by tightly integrating the FAISs via a common database. In doing so, they enhance communications among the functional areas of an organisation. For this reason, experts credit ERP systems with greatly increasing organisational productivity.

A **transaction processing system (TPS)** supports the monitoring, collection, storage and processing of data from the organisation's basic business transactions, each of which generates data. For example, when you are checking out of Target or Coles, each time the cashier swipes an item across the bar code reader, that is one transaction.

Definitions of a transaction differ throughout an organisation. In accounting, for example, a transaction is anything that changes a firm's chart of accounts. The information system definition of a transaction is broader: A transaction is anything that changes the firm's database. The chart of accounts is only part of the firm's database. Consider a scenario in which a student transfers from one section of an Introduction to MIS course to another section. This move would be a transaction in the university's information system, but not a transaction in the university's accounting department.

The TPS collects data continuously, typically in *real time* — that is, as soon as the data are generated — and provides the input data for the corporate databases. TPSs are considered critical to the success of any enterprise because they support core operations. Significantly, nearly all ERP systems are also TPSs, but not all TPSs are ERP systems. In fact, modern ERP systems incorporate many functions that have previously been handled by the organisation's functional area information systems. You study both TPSs and ERP systems in detail in chapter 11.

ERP systems and TPS function primarily within a single organisation. Information systems that connect two or more organisations are referred to as **interorganisational information systems (IOSs)**. IOSs support many interorganisational operations, of which supply chain management is the best known. An organisation's **supply chain** is the flow of materials, information, money and services from suppliers of raw materials through factories and warehouses to the end customers.

Note that the supply chain in figure 1.8 shows physical flows, information flows and financial flows. Digitisable products are those that can be represented in electronic form, such as music and software. Information flows, financial flows and digitisable products go through the internet, whereas physical products are shipped. For example, when you order a computer from **www.dell.com.au**, your information goes to Dell via the internet. When your transaction is completed (i.e. your credit card is approved and your order is processed), Dell ships your computer to you.

Electronic commerce systems are another type of interorganisational information system. An **electronic commerce (e-commerce) system** enables organisations to conduct transactions, called business-to-business (B2B) electronic commerce and customers to conduct transactions with businesses, called business-to-consumer (B2C) electronic commerce. (*Note*: You will learn about other types of e-commerce systems in chapter 9.) E-commerce systems are typically internet based. Figure 1.8 illustrates B2B and B2C electronic commerce.

Support for organisational employees

So far you have been concentrating on information systems that support specific functional areas and operations. Now you will learn about information systems that typically support particular employees within the organisation.

Clerical workers, who support managers at all levels of the organisation, include bookkeepers, secretaries, administration officers and insurance claim processors. *Lower-level managers* handle the day-to-day operations of the organisation, making routine decisions such as assigning tasks to employees and placing purchase orders. *Middle managers* make tactical decisions, which deal with activities such as short-term planning, organising and control.

Knowledge workers are professional employees, such as financial and marketing analysts, engineers, lawyers and accountants. All knowledge workers are experts in a particular subject area. They create information and knowledge, which they integrate into the business. Knowledge workers act as advisers to middle managers and executives. Finally, *executives* make decisions that deal with situations that can significantly change the manner in which business is done. Examples of executive decisions are introducing a new product line, acquiring other businesses and relocating operations to a foreign country.

Office automation systems (OASs) typically support the clerical staff, lower and middle managers, and knowledge workers. These employees use OASs to develop documents (word processing and desktop publishing software), schedule resources (electronic calendars) and communicate (email, voice mail, videoconferencing and groupware).

FAISs summarise data and prepare reports, primarily for middle managers, but sometimes for lower-level managers as well. Because these reports typically concern a specific functional area, report generators (RPGs) are an important type of functional area IS.

Business intelligence (BI) systems provide computer-based support for complex, non-routine decisions, primarily for middle managers and knowledge workers. (They also support lower-level managers, but to a lesser extent.) These systems are typically used with a data warehouse and they enable users to perform their own data analysis. You learn about BI systems in chapter 5.

Expert systems (ESs) attempt to duplicate the work of human experts by applying reasoning capabilities, knowledge and expertise within a specific domain. They have become valuable in many application areas, primarily but not exclusively areas involving decision making. For example, navigation systems use rules to select routes, but we do not typically think of these systems as expert systems. Significantly, expert systems can operate as stand-alone systems or be embedded in other applications. We examine ESs in greater detail in Plug IT In 4.

Dashboards (also called **digital dashboards**) are a special form of IS that support all managers of the organisation. They provide rapid access to timely information and direct access to structured information in the form of reports. Dashboards that are tailored to the information needs of executives are called *executive dashboards*. Chapter 5 provides a thorough discussion of dashboards.

Table 1.1 provides an overview of the different types of organisational information systems.

BEFORE YOU GO ON . . .

1. What is a computer-based information system?
2. Describe the components of computer-based information systems.
3. What is an application program?
4. Explain how information systems provide support for knowledge workers.
5. As we move up the organisation's hierarchy from clerical workers to executives, how does the type of support provided by information systems change?

TABLE 1.1 Types of organisational information systems

Type of system	Function	Example
Functional area IS	Supports the activities within specific functional area	System for processing payroll
Transaction processing system	Processes transaction data from business events	Target or Coles checkout point-of-sale terminal
Enterprise resource planning system	Integrates all functional areas of the organisation	Oracle, SAP
Office automation system	Supports daily work activities of individuals and groups	Microsoft Office
Management information system	Produces reports summarised from transaction data, usually in one functional area	Report on total sales for each customer
Decision support system	Provides access to data and analysis tools	'What-if' analysis of changes in budget
Expert system	Mimics human expert in a particular area and makes decisions	Credit card approval analysis
Executive dashboard	Presents structured, summarised information about aspects of business important to executives	Status of sales by product
Supply chain management system	Manages flows of products, services and information among organisations	Woolworths or Coles supply chain management systems connecting suppliers to Woolworths or Coles
Electronic commerce system	Enables transactions among organisations and between organisations and customers	www.dell.com.au

Apply the Concept

Background

This section discusses the various functional areas that you will most likely work in and the different systems that support them. It should be no surprise that these are the very majors you can choose from in most business programs. These four major functional areas are:

- marketing/sales
- finance/accounting
- manufacturing
- human resources.

Often, these different functional areas will use the same database and networks within a company, but they will all use them to support their specific needs. This activity will help you develop a solid understanding of the role of information systems within the different functional areas.

Activity

Review the section material that describes the major function of the following departments in most companies: marketing/sales, finance/accounting, manufacturing and human resources. Then review the basic function of the following types of information systems: transaction processing, management information and decision support. Once you have a solid understanding of the functional areas and information systems that support them you are ready to move forward with the activity!

Deliverable

Rebuild and complete the chart shown below with the activities that may be completed by each system for each department. To help out, we have pre-filled one item in each type of system. Once you complete your chart, submit it to your tutorial group.

	Transaction processing	Management information	Decision support
Marketing/sales	Enter sales data		
Accounting/finance			
Human resources			Comply with EEOC
Manufacturing		Inventory reporting	

THE NOOK

QUESTIONS

1 Given that The Nook is a bar with a small food menu, what type of data do you think this establishment should collect from a single transaction (such as an order for food)?

2 How can The Nook use data from transactions over a month to help manage inventory?

3 If Malakai and Abbie have transactional data that is organised to create information regarding their customer base, why could knowledge be gained from this that would help them develop a marketing plan?

1.3 How does IT impact organisations?

Throughout this book, you will encounter numerous examples of how IT affects various types of organisations. This section provides an overview of the impact of IT on modern organisations. As you read this section, you will learn how each of these impacts will affect you as well.

IT will reduce the number of middle managers

IT makes managers more productive and it increases the number of employees who can report to a single manager. In these ways, IT ultimately decreases the number of managers and experts. It is reasonable to assume, therefore, that in the coming years organisations will have fewer managerial levels and fewer staff and line managers. If this trend materialises, then promotional opportunities will decrease, making promotions much more competitive. Bottom line: pay attention in class!

IT will change the manager's job

One of the most important tasks of managers is making decisions. One of the major consequences of IT has been to change the manner in which managers make many of their decisions. In this way, IT ultimately has changed managers' jobs.

IT often provides managers with near real-time information, meaning that managers have less time to make decisions, making their jobs even more stressful. Fortunately, IT also provides many tools — for example, business intelligence applications such as dashboards, search engines and intranets — to help managers handle the volumes of information they must deal with on an ongoing basis.

We have been focusing on managers in general in this section. Now, let's focus on you. Because of advances in IT, you will increasingly supervise employees and teams who are geographically dispersed. Employees can work from anywhere at any time and teams can consist of employees who are literally dispersed throughout the world. Information technologies such as telepresence systems (discussed in chapter 4) can help you manage these employees even though you do not often see them face to face. For these employees, electronic or 'remote' supervision will become the norm. Remote supervision places greater emphasis on completed work and less emphasis on personal contacts and office politics. You will have to reassure your employees that they are valued members of the organisation, thereby diminishing any feelings they might have of being isolated and 'out of the loop'.

Will IT eliminate jobs?

One of the major concerns of every employee, part time or full time, is job security. Relentless cost-cutting measures in modern organisations often lead to large-scale layoffs. Put simply, organisations are responding to today's highly competitive environment by doing more with less. Regardless of your position, then, you will consistently have to add value to your organisation and ensure your superiors are aware of this value.

Many companies have responded to difficult economic times, increased global competition, demands for customisation and increased consumer sophistication by increasing their investments in IT. In fact, as computers continue to advance in terms of intelligence and capabilities, the competitive advantage of replacing people with machines is increasing rapidly. This process frequently leads to layoffs. At the same time, however, IT creates entirely new categories of jobs, such as electronic medical record keeping and nanotechnology.

IT impacts employees at work

Many people have experienced a loss of identity because of computerisation. They feel like 'just another number' because computers reduce or eliminate the human element that was present in non-computerised systems.

The internet threatens to exert an even more isolating influence than computers and television. Encouraging people to work and shop from their living rooms could produce some unfortunate psychological effects, such as depression and loneliness.

IT impacts employees' health and safety

Although computers and information systems are generally regarded as agents of 'progress', they can adversely affect individuals' health and safety. To illustrate this point, we consider two issues associated with IT: job stress and long-term use of the keyboard.

An increase in an employee's workload and/or responsibilities can trigger *job stress*. Although computerisation has benefited organisations by increasing productivity, it has also created an ever-expanding workload for some employees. Some workers feel overwhelmed and have become increasingly anxious about their job performance. These feelings of stress and anxiety can actually diminish rather than improve workers' productivity while jeopardising their physical and mental health. Management can help to alleviate these problems by providing training, redistributing the workload among workers and hiring more workers.

On a more specific level, the long-term use of keyboards can lead to *repetitive strain injuries* such as backaches and muscle tension in the wrists and fingers. *Carpal tunnel syndrome* is a particularly painful form of repetitive strain injury that affects the wrists and hands.

Designers are aware of the potential problems associated with the prolonged use of computers. To address these problems, they continually attempt to design a better computing environment. The science of designing machines and work settings that minimise injury and illness is called **ergonomics**. The goal of ergonomics is to create an environment that is safe, well lit and comfortable. Examples of ergonomically designed products are antiglare screens that alleviate problems of fatigued or damaged eyesight and chairs that contour the human body to decrease backaches. Figure 1.9 on the next page displays some sample ergonomic products.

(a)

(b)

FIGURE 1.9 Ergonomic products protect computer users.
(a) Ergonomic keyboard
(b) Ergonomic office chair

BEFORE YOU GO ON . . .

1. Why should employees in all functional areas become knowledgeable about IT?
2. Describe how IT might change the manager's job.
3. Discuss several ways in which IT impacts employees at work.

IT provides opportunities for people with disabilities

Computers can create new employment opportunities for people with disabilities by integrating speech- and vision-recognition capabilities. For example, individuals who cannot type are able to use a voice-operated keyboard and individuals who cannot travel can work at home.

Going further, adaptive equipment for computers permits people with disabilities to perform tasks they would not normally be able to do. You should note that the web and graphical user interfaces (e.g. Microsoft Windows) can still make life difficult for people with impaired vision. Adding audible screen tips and voice interfaces to deal with this problem essentially restores functionality to the way it was before rich, graphical interfaces became standard.

Other devices help improve the quality of life for people with disabilities in more mundane, but useful, ways. Examples are a two-way writing telephone, a robotic page turner, a hair brusher and a hospital-bedside video trip to the zoo or the museum. Several organisations specialise in IT designed for people with disabilities.

THE NOOK

QUESTIONS

1. Malakai and Abbie have always spent hours going through paper receipts trying to determine past sales. They need these figures to know purchase quantities for the products they sell. Given that some of their products have a short shelf life (perishable foods), this needs to be very accurate. In what ways could the capabilities of ISs help them accomplish this task?
2. What type of procedures would Malakai and Abbie need to ensure that the people interacting with the ISs are doing so in an appropriate manner (i.e. correctly inputting data, not using customer data, etc.)?

1.4 Why are information systems important to society?

This section explains in greater detail why IT is important to society as a whole. Other examples of the impacts of IT on society appear throughout the book.

IT affects our quality of life

IT has significant implications for our quality of life. The workplace can be expanded from the traditional 9-to-5 job at a central location to 24 hours a day at any location. IT can provide employees with flexibility that can significantly improve the quality of leisure time, even if it does not increase the total amount of leisure time.

From the opposite perspective, however, IT can also place employees on 'constant call' where they are never truly away from the office, even when they are on holiday. In fact, a recent poll revealed that 80 per cent of respondents took their laptop computers on their most recent holidays and 100 per cent took their mobile phones. Going further, 80 per cent did some work while on holiday and almost all of them checked their email.

Robot revolution on the way

Once restricted largely to science fiction movies, robots that can perform practical tasks are becoming more common. In fact, 'cyberpooches', nursebots and other mechanical beings may be our companions before we know it. Around the world, quasi-autonomous devices have become increasingly common on factory floors, in hospital corridors and in farm paddocks. In our homes, iRobot (**www.irobot.com**) produces the Roomba to vacuum our floors, the Scooba to wash our floors, the Dirt Dog to sweep our garages, the Verro to clean our pools and the Looj to clean our gutters.

Telepresence robots are a recent development in the field of robotics. IT's About Business (overleaf) illustrates how organisations use these robots.

The telepresence robot provides a solution to all of the issues listed earlier.

IT'S ABOUT BUSINESS

Telepresence robots

The business problem

In our modern digital world, knowledge workers can work from anywhere via a process called *telecommuting*. In fact, a new term, *digital nomad*, has appeared that refers to someone who uses a variety of information technologies such as smartphones, wireless internet access and web-based applications to work remotely from a home, coffee shop, restaurant, airport, aeroplane, internet café or other location.

Digital nomads present a couple of issues for the offices that employ them. First, digital nomads lack a 'presence' in their respective offices. Second, it is typically expensive and time-consuming for them to travel to their offices for example, to attend meetings.

Yet another business issue occurs when a person with a highly desirable skill is needed at a distant location. Examples of individuals with such desirable skills include surgeons, consultants with expertise in a specific industry, salespeople who are well known to high-value clients and many others.

The IT solution

Telepresence robots have been humorously described as a cross between a Segway and Wall-E. These robots are designed to help companies save money on travel and on expensive teleconferencing technology. The robots enable people in remote offices or locations to have a rich communications experience without having to use a complicated videoconferencing system.

A telepresence robot has both a video camera and a video screen embedded in its 'head'. It also has wheels and can be moved around remotely by computer. It is designed to steer its way clear of obstacles or people.

The robots let a person maintain a consistent connection with co-workers, customers, or clients. The human user controls the robot, located at a remote location and directs it to move around — for example, around a conference room during a meeting — while broadcasting what is going on to the human it represents. Interestingly, the robots actually break down barriers of awkwardness that people sometimes feel in person-to-person meetings.

Organisations are using telepresence robots for a variety of applications. Consider the following examples.

- Dr Johns was paged because a man had suffered a stroke and someone had to quickly decide which drug to give him. She hurried, not to the emergency room 200 kilometres away where the man had been admitted, but to a room in her local hospital. She sat in front of computer monitors, a keyboard and a joystick that controlled her assistant in the remote emergency room: a telepresence robot.

  She acknowledged the nurse and introduced herself to the patient's grandson, explaining that she would question the patient to determine what drug to give him. The robot's stereophonic hearing conveyed the answers and its hypersensitive camera allowed her to zoom her view of the room in and out, and swing the display left and right.

  By speaking directly with the patient, examining his face and how he controlled his hands and looking at the cardiac monitor in the emergency room, Dr Johns was able to assess the stroke with the same accuracy as if she had been physically present. She instructed the nurse to give the patient a particular drug.
- Telepresence robot technology is being used at the National Museum of Australia to enable students from regional and remote Australia to visit the museum virtually. Students can control the telepresence robots which are equipped with cameras, allowing them to control their own view of the items in the museum as well as to interact with museum educators.[12]
- Chad Evans, a software designer for Phillips Healthcare, is located at his home in Atlanta, Georgia, and his telepresence robot works at the company's headquarters in Santa Monica, California. While he works at his desk in Atlanta, he is visible on the monitor of his robot. His colleagues can see at a glance whether he is available for a chat. When Chad needs to go to a meeting in California or visit a colleague, he drives his robot to a desk or meeting room. If he needs to go to a different floor, someone has to press the elevator buttons for his robot. His robot enables Chad to be as available and transparent to his colleagues as though he were physically present in the office.
- Tom Serani's boss was frustrated that while Tom was on the road, his 20-person sales team working the phones back at company headquarters did not have the same 'energy' as when Tom was in the office. As a result, Tom now has a telepresence robot at company headquarters. When he is travelling, Tom can roll his robot up to an office cubicle at headquarters, listen in on a telephone sales pitch and offer advice. Interestingly, Tom's boss noted that the telepresence robot increased the sales team's energy level to the same level as when Tom was physically in the office.

The results

Telepresence robots allow much greater flexibility for digital nomads. They provide a flexible view into what is happening in their offices, without requiring money and time to be spent on travel. As you saw in the previous examples, companies benefit from valuable employees having a 'presence' in the office. Companies also use telepresence robots to connect with people having specialised skills in remote locations.

In the near future, telepresence robots will have artificial intelligence that allows them to do some things on their own. Inevitably, these robots will become 'smarter' and more agile. They will not only represent their human users, they will augment them.

Sources: Compiled from K Terry (2012), 'Roomba maker sets sights on telemedicine', *InformationWeek*, 2 February; D Bennett (2011), 'I'll have my robots talk to your robots', *Bloomberg BusinessWeek*, 21–27 February; A Diana (2011), '12 advances in medical robotics', *InformationWeek*, 29 January; D Terdiman (2010), 'The telepresence robots are coming', CNET.com, 18 May; J Markoff (2010), 'The boss is robotic, and rolling up behind you', *The New York Times*, 4 September; www.anybots.com.

QUESTIONS

1 What are the advantages of a telepresence robot representing you at your office? Provide specific examples to support your answer.
2 What are the disadvantages of a telepresence robot representing you at your office? Provide specific examples to support your answer.

University of Sydney is developing and trialling robotic systems, sensors and intelligent devices that are capable of identifying individual fruits on a tree and their ripeness. They can also diagnose the health state of trees. These robotic systems are currently being trialled on an almond farm in Mildura, Victoria, and an apple orchard near Melbourne.[13]

Many robotic devices are also being developed for military purposes. For example, the Pentagon is researching self-driving vehicles and bee like swarms of small surveillance robots, each of which would contribute a different view or angle of a combat zone. The Predator, an unmanned aerial vehicle (UAV), is being used in Iraq, Libya, Pakistan and Afghanistan.

It probably will be a long time before we see robots making decisions by themselves, handling unfamiliar situations and interacting with people. Nevertheless, robots are extremely helpful in various environments, particularly environments that are repetitive, harsh, or dangerous to humans.

Improvements in health care

IT has brought about major improvements in health care delivery. Medical personnel use IT to make better and faster diagnoses and to monitor critically ill patients more accurately. IT also has streamlined the process of researching and developing new drugs. Expert systems now help doctors diagnose diseases and machine vision is enhancing the work of radiologists. Surgeons use virtual reality to plan complex surgeries. They also have used a surgical robot to perform long-distance surgery by controlling the robot's movements. In addition, doctors discuss complex medical cases via videoconferencing and new computer simulations re-create the sense of touch, allowing doctors in training to perform virtual procedures without risking harm to an actual patient.

Of the thousands of other applications related to health care, administrative systems are critically important. These systems range from detecting insurance fraud to creating nursing schedules to financial and marketing management.

The internet contains vast amounts of useful medical information (see **www.mydr.com.au**, for example). In an interesting study, researchers at the Princess Alexandra Hospital in Brisbane, Australia, identified 26 difficult diagnostic cases published in the *New England Journal of Medicine*. They selected three to five search terms from each case and then conducted a Google search. The researchers selected and recorded the three diagnoses that Google ranked most prominently and that appeared to fit the symptoms and signs. They then compared these results with the correct diagnoses as published in the journal. They discovered that their Google searches had found the correct diagnosis in 15 of the 26 cases, a success rate of 57 per cent. The researchers caution, however, against the dangers of self-diagnosis. They maintain that people should use the information gained from Google and medical websites such as myDr only to participate in their health care by asking questions of their doctor.

BEFORE YOU GO ON . . .

1 What are some of the quality-of-life improvements made possible by IT? Has IT had any negative effects on our quality of life?
2 Describe the robotic revolution and consider its possible implications for humans.
3 Explain how IT has improved health care practices.

Apply the Concept

Background

As you have read in this chapter, ISs have made a very significant impact on society. In fact, most of us now use the internet to communicate with friends, family and colleagues. Email, Facebook, Twitter, text messages, Skype and all other communication technologies run on and are supported by IS. We can also collaborate in ways that have never before been possible.

For example, what if you needed to plan a holiday with some friends for a long weekend? Although this may seem simple, you will use search tools, post links, take notes, etc. Why not give it a try?

Activity

If you do not have a Google account (that provides access to Gmail, Calendars, Drive, YouTube, etc.), you will need to set one up for this activity. Have your friends do the same and share your usernames (not passwords) with each other.

Now sign into Google Drive (drive.google.com) and create a new document. Towards the right-hand side, you will see a 'share' button. Click this and add your friends' Google email addresses in the share box. Be sure to give the rights to edit.

Coordinate with them for all of you to sign on at the same time and use the document to type, share links, notes, ideas, etc. and plan your trip! Look up hotels, activities, restaurants and so on.

Deliverable

Download the document as a PDF when you have your trip planned out (and are a bit disappointed that you are not actually going). Be prepared to discuss some of the benefits of using of Google Drive (or any tool that may become available that would be similar to it). What are some ways in which you could use this tool at university, at home, or at work?

THE NOOK

QUESTIONS

1 How might a well-designed information system impact The Nook's employees? Specifically, how might it impact Malakai and Abbie? What aspects of running a club would be easier on a computer than on paper?

2 Do you think the addition of an IS would create or eliminate jobs at The Nook?

WHAT'S IN IT FOR ME?

In a previous section of this chapter, we discussed how IT supports each of the functional areas of the organisation. Here we examine the MIS function.

FOR THE MIS MAJOR

The MIS function directly supports all other functional areas in an organisation. That is, the MIS function is responsible for providing the information that each functional area needs in order to make decisions. The overall objective of MIS personnel is to help users improve performance and solve business problems using IT. To accomplish this objective, MIS personnel must understand both the information requirements and the technology associated with each functional area. Given their position, however, while MIS personnel must think 'business needs' first and 'technology' second, they must also consider the ways in which technology restricts or enhances the ability of MIS personnel to address business needs.

SUMMARY

1 Identify the reasons why being an informed user of information systems is important in today's world.

You will benefit more from your organisation's IT applications because you will understand what is 'behind' those applications.

- You will be able to provide input into your organisation's IT applications, therefore improving the quality of those applications.
- You will quickly be in a position to recommend, or participate in, the selection of IT applications that your organisation will use.
- You will be able to keep up with rapid developments in existing information technologies, as well as the introduction of new technologies.
- You will understand the potential impacts that 'new and improved' technologies will have on your organisation and, therefore, will be qualified to make recommendations concerning their adoption and use.
- You will play a key role in managing the information systems in your organisation.
- You will be in a position to use IT if you decide to start your own business.

2 Describe the various types of computer-based information systems in an organisation.

- Transaction processing systems (TPS) support the monitoring, collection, storage and processing of data from the organisation's basic business transactions, each of which generates data.
- Functional area information systems (FAISs) support a particular functional area within the organisation.
- Interorganisational information systems (IOSs) support many interorganisational operations, of which supply chain management is the best known.
- Enterprise resource planning (ERP) systems correct a lack of communication among the FAISs by tightly integrating the functional area ISs via a common database.
- Electronic commerce (e-commerce) systems enable organisations to conduct transactions with other organisations (called business-to-business (B2B) electronic commerce) and with customers (called business-to-consumer (B2C) electronic commerce).
- Office automation systems (OASs) typically support the clerical staff, lower and middle managers, and knowledge workers, by enabling them to develop documents (word processing and desktop publishing software), schedule resources (electronic calendars) and communicate (email, voice mail, videoconferencing and groupware).
- Business intelligence (BI) systems provide computer-based support for complex, non-routine decisions, primarily for middle managers and knowledge workers.
- Expert systems (ESs) attempt to duplicate the work of human experts by applying reasoning capabilities, knowledge and expertise within a specific domain.

3 Discuss ways in which information technology can affect managers and non-managerial workers.

Potential IT impacts on managers

- IT may reduce the number of middle managers.
- IT will provide managers with real-time or near real-time information, meaning that managers will have less time to make decisions.
- IT will increase the likelihood that managers will have to supervise geographically dispersed employees and teams.

Potential IT impacts on non-managerial workers

- IT may eliminate jobs.
- IT may cause employees to experience a loss of identity.
- IT may cause job stress and physical problems, such as repetitive stress injury.

4 Identify positive and negative societal effects of the increased use of information technology.

Positive societal effects

- IT can provide opportunities for people with disabilities.
- IT can provide people with flexibility in their work (e.g. work from anywhere, anytime).
- Robots can take over mundane chores.
- IT can enable improvements in health care.

Negative societal effects

- IT can cause health problems for individuals.
- IT can place employees on constant call.
- IT can potentially misinform patients about their health problems.

>>> CHAPTER GLOSSARY

application (app) A computer program designed to support a specific task or business process.

business intelligence (BI) systems Provide computer-based support for complex, non-routine decisions, primarily for middle managers and knowledge workers.

computer-based information system (CBIS) An information system that uses computer technology to perform some or all of its intended tasks.

dashboards (or digital dashboards) A special form of IS that supports all managers of the organisation by providing rapid access to timely information and direct access to structured information in the form of reports.

data items Elementary descriptions of things, events, activities and transactions that are recorded, classified and stored but are not organised to convey any specific meaning.

database A collection of related files or tables containing data.

electronic commerce (e-commerce) system A type of interorganisational information system that enables organisations to conduct transactions, called business-to-business (B2B) electronic commerce and customers to conduct transactions with businesses, called business-to-consumer (B2C) electronic commerce.

enterprise resource planning (ERP) systems ISs that correct a lack of communication among the FAISs by tightly integrating the functional area ISs via a common database.

ergonomics The science of adapting machines and work environments to people with the goal of creating an environment that is safe, well lit and comfortable.

expert systems (ESs) Attempt to duplicate the work of human experts by applying reasoning capabilities, knowledge and expertise within a specific domain.

functional area information systems (FAISs) ISs that support a particular functional area within the organisation.

hardware A device such as a processor, monitor, keyboard, or printer. Together, these devices accept data and information, process them and display them.

information Data that have been organised so that they have meaning and value to the recipient.

information system (IS) Collects, processes, stores, analyses and disseminates information for a specific purpose.

information technology (IT) Relates to any computer-based tool that people use to work with information and support the information and information processing needs of an organisation.

information technology (IT) services IT personnel use IT components to perform these IT services: develop information systems, oversee security and risk, and manage data.

informed user A person knowledgeable about information systems and information technology.

interorganisational information systems (IOSs) Information systems that connect two or more organisations.

knowledge Data and/or information that have been organised and processed to convey understanding, experience, accumulated learning and expertise as they apply to a current problem or activity.

knowledge workers Professional employees, such as financial and marketing analysts, engineers, lawyers and accountants, who are experts in a particular subject area and create information and knowledge, which they integrate into the business.

network A connecting system (wireline or wireless) that permits different computers to share resources.

office automation systems (OASs) Typically support clerical staff, lower and middle managers, and knowledge workers to develop documents, schedule resources and communicate.

procedures The set of instructions about how to combine the components of information technology in order to process information and generate the desired output.

software A program or collection of programs that enable the hardware to process data.

supply chain The flow of materials, information, money and services from suppliers of raw materials through factories and warehouses to the end customers.

transaction processing system (TPS) Supports the monitoring, collection, storage and processing of data from the organisation's basic business transactions, each of which generates data.

>>> DISCUSSION QUESTIONS

1 Describe a business that you would like to start. Discuss how you would use outsourcing to accomplish your goals.

2 Your university wants to recruit high-quality high school students from your state. Provide examples of (a) the data that your recruiters would gather in this process, (b) the information that your recruiters would process from these data and (c) the types of knowledge that your recruiters would infer from this information.

3 Can the terms *data, information* and *knowledge* have different meanings for different people? Support your answer with examples.

4 Information technology makes it possible to 'never be out of touch'. Discuss the pros and cons of always being available to your employers and clients (regardless of where you are or what you are doing).

5 Robots have the positive impact of being able to relieve humans from working in dangerous conditions. What are some negative impacts of robots in the workplace?

6 Is it possible to endanger yourself by accessing too much medical information on the web? Why or why not? Support your answer.

7 Is the vast amount of medical information on the web a good thing? Answer from the standpoint of a patient and from the standpoint of a doctor.

8 Describe other potential impacts of IT on societies as a whole.

9 What are the major reasons why it is important for employees in all functional areas to become familiar with IT?

10 Refer to the study at Princess Alexandra Hospital (see p. 25). How do you feel about Google searches finding the correct diagnosis in 57 per cent of the cases? Are you impressed with these results? Why or why not? What are the implications of this study for self-diagnosis?

>>> PROBLEM-SOLVING ACTIVITIES

1 Visit some websites that offer employment opportunities in IT. Prominent examples are www.seek.com.au, www.unijobs.com.au, www.recruitshop.com.au, www.hays.com.au, www.recruitmentdirectory.com.au and www.recruitloop.com.au. Compare the IT salaries to salaries offered to accountants, marketing personnel, financial personnel, operations personnel and human resources personnel. For other information on IT salaries, check www.computerworld.com.au or www.acs.org.au for annual salary information data.

2 Enter the website of Australia Post (auspost.com.au/index.html).

a Find out what information is available to customers before they send a package.

b Find out about the package tracking system.

3 Surf the internet for information about the Australian Taxation Office (ATO). Examine the available information and comment on the role of information technologies in the ATO.

4 Access www.irobot.com and investigate the company's robots for education and research. Surf the web for other companies that manufacture robots and compare their products with those of iRobot.

>>> COLLABORATION EXERCISE

Background

This chapter has shown the many ways ISs have changed business. As you will learn through this course, many jobs have been created as a result of the growth of IS. Although many positions have been eliminated (such as the typist), others have been created (software developers who write word processing programs).

Activity

Divide your team into the following functional areas: marketing, accounting, finance, human relations, logistics. Do some research as individuals to find out what type of jobs are related to IT for each area. Find some software companies that provide the systems (such as Frontier Technologies for human resources) and learn about the IT people involved in the organisation who support the various departments.

Once everyone has completed the research, meet as a team and have a conversation about the current job market. Work as a team to find open positions related to the areas you have found.

Deliverable

Build a short table that has four columns as shown in the example below. Submit work to your tutor.

Department	IS that supports	Related IS positions	Current job opening

CLOSING CASE **1** >

Today, every company is a technology company

THE BUSINESS PROBLEM

Sixty years into the computer revolution, forty years into the age of the microprocessor and twenty years into the rise of the modern internet, all of the technology required to transform industries through software has been developed and integrated and can be delivered globally. Over two billion people now access the internet via broadband connections. Worldwide, over five billion people use mobile phones. One billion of those five billion mobile phone users have smartphones that provide them with instant access to the internet at all times.

In addition, software programming tools and internet-based services allow companies in many industries to launch new software-powered startups without investing in new infrastructure or training existing or new employees. For example, in the year 2000 the cost of a business operating a basic internet application was approximately $150 000 per month. Operating that same application today in Amazon's cloud (discussed in detail in Plug IT In 3) costs approximately $1500 per month.

In essence, software is disrupting every industry and every organisation must prepare for this disruption. Numerous companies have attempted to meet the disruption challenge; some have succeeded and some have failed.

SOFTWARE DISRUPTIONS

Let's look at examples of software disruption across several industries. In many of these examples, you can first see where software disrupted the previous market leading companies and then where a new company (or companies) used software to gain a competitive advantage.

- *The book industry:* Booktopia is one of Australia's few online booksellers and is one of the few companies partnering with Google to sell its eBooks alongside physical copies.[14] In 2012 Booktopia won the Telstra Business Awards People's Choice Award. They were also listed in the BRW Fast 100 in 2009, 2010, 2011 and 2012. In 2012 the Australian Institute of Management's publication, *Management Today*, ranked Booktopia in the Top 10 of all retailers operating online in Australia.[15]
- *The music industry:* Today's dominant music companies are software companies, such as Apple's iTunes (www.apple.com/itunes). Traditional record labels today exist largely to provide those software companies with content. In Australia and New Zealand, APRA|AMCOS endeavour to ensure that composers, songwriters and publishers are rewarded adequately when their works are played, performed or reproduced in any shape or form via any media (www.apra-amcos.com.au).
- *The video industry:* Movie rental kiosks operated by companies such as Oovie are replacing traditional movie rental businesses, as are online rental and download companies such as Quickflix (www.quickflix.com.au) and BigPond (bigpondmovies.com).
- *The software industry:* Incumbent software companies such as Oracle and Microsoft are increasingly threatened by software-as-a-service products (e.g. Salesforce.com) and Android, an open-source operating system developed by the Open Handset Alliance (www.openhandsetalliance.com) and led by Google. (We discuss operating systems in Plug IT In 2 and software-as-a-service in Plug IT In 3).
- *The videogame industry:* Today, the fastest growing entertainment companies are videogame makers — again, software. Examples of fast-growing videogame companies include the following.
    - Electronic Arts (www.electronicarts.com.au) develops and distributes interactive

software worldwide for internet-connected consoles, personal computers, mobile phones and social networks. In 2012, EA reported a net revenue of $4.1 billion. Electronic Arts is known for high-quality blockbuster franchises including The Sims™, Madden NFL, FIFA Soccer, Need for Speed™, Battlefield™ and Mass Effect™.
    - Rovio (www.rovio.com), the maker of Angry Birds, made almost $100 million in revenue in 2011. The company was nearly bankrupt when it launched Angry Birds on the iPhone in late 2009.
    - Minecraft (www.minecraft.net), another video game delivered only online over the internet, was first released in 2009. By February 2012, over 5 million people had downloaded it. Interestingly, the creator of Minecraft, Markus Persson, has never spent any money to market his game. Sales grew only by word of mouth.
- *The photography industry:* This industry was disrupted by software years ago. Today it is virtually impossible to buy a mobile phone that does not include a software-powered camera and photos can be uploaded automatically to the internet for permanent archiving and global sharing. The previous market leader, Kodak, has been replaced by companies such as Shutterfly (www.shutterfly.com), Snapfish (www.snapfish.com), Flickr (www.flickr.com) and Instagram (www.instagram.com). Kodak declared bankruptcy in January 2012.
- *The marketing industry:* Today's largest direct marketing companies are Facebook (www.facebook.com), Google (www.google.com), Groupon (www.groupon.com.au), Living Social (www.livingsocial.com), DealsDirect (www.dealsdirect.com.au), Orchard Marketing (www.orchard.com.au), iMarketing (www.imarketingsolutions.com.au), Tapjoy (www.tapjoy.com.au) and others. These companies are using software to disrupt the retail marketing industry.
- *The recruiting industry:* LinkedIn (www.linkedin.com) is a fast-growing recruiting company. For the first time, employees can maintain their own résumés on LinkedIn for recruiters to search in real time. Another example is Seek (www.seek.com.au).
- *The financial services industry:* Software has transformed the financial services industry. Practically every financial transaction is performed by software. And many of the leading innovators in financial services are software companies. For example, Financial Services Online (www.financialservicesonlin.com.au) assists Australian residents source financial services, products and information online. Almost all major banks operating in Australia offer financial services online at different levels.

Software is also disrupting industries that operate primarily in the physical world. Consider these examples.

- *The motor vehicle industry:* In modern cars, software is responsible for running the engines, controlling safety features, entertaining passengers, guiding drivers to their destinations and connecting the car to mobile, satellite and GPS networks. Other software functions in modern cars include wi-fi receivers, which turn your car into a mobile hot spot, software, which helps maximise fuel efficiency and ultrasonic sensors, which enable automatic parallel parking.

The next step is to network all vehicles together. The creation of software-powered driverless cars is already being undertaken at Google and major car companies.

THE RESULTS

As you have seen, an increasing number of major businesses and industries are being run on software and delivered as online services — from motion pictures to agriculture to national defence. Regardless of the industry, companies face constant competitive threats from established rivals and entrepreneurial technology companies that are developing disruptive software. These threats will force companies to become more agile in the future and respond to competitive threats more quickly, efficiently and effectively.

Sources: Compiled from M De La Merced (2012), 'Eastman Kodak files for bankruptcy', *The Wall Street Journal*, 19 January; J Trachtenberg and M Peers (2012), 'Barnes & Noble seeks next chapter', *The Wall Street Journal*, 6 January; 'Driverless car: Google awarded US patent for technology' (2011), *BBC News*, 15 December; J McKendrick (2011), 'Five non-IT companies that are now indistinguishable from software companies', *ZDNet*, 7 December; A Bleicher (2011), 'Five reasons every company should act like a software startup', *Forbes*, 14 November; B Austen (2011), 'The end of Borders and the future of books', *Bloomberg BusinessWeek*, 10 November; M Andreessen (2011), 'Why software is eating the world', *The Wall Street Journal*, 20 August; J Knee (2011), 'Why content isn't king', *The Atlantic*, July/August; J Checkler and J Trachtenberg (2011), 'Bookseller Borders begins a new chapter...11', *The Wall Street Journal*, 17 February.

QUESTIONS

1. If every company is now a technology company, then what does this mean for the company's employees? Discuss your answer and provide specific examples to support your answer.
2. If every company is now a technology company, then what does this mean for every person majoring in business at university? Discuss your answer and provide specific examples to support your answer.

CLOSING CASE 2 >

The Arab Spring

THE PROBLEM

The Arab Spring is a wave of demonstrations and protests occurring in the Arab world. Demonstrators have been demanding greater political freedom and an end to autocracy. By mid 2012, there were revolutions in Tunisia and Egypt, a civil war in Libya, civil uprisings in Bahrain, Syria and Yemen, major protests in Algeria, Iraq, Jordan, Kuwait, Morocco and Oman, and minor protests in Lebanon, Mauritania, Saudi Arabia and Sudan. Protesters have made use of mobile communications, the internet and social media to organise, communicate and raise awareness in the face of state repression and internet censorship. In this case, we will look at three examples: Tunisia, Egypt and Syria.

Tunisia

In December 2010, the modern Arab world's first successful popular uprising, called the Jasmine Revolution (named for the national flower), erupted in Tunisia when Mohamed Bouazizi set himself on fire. When he died 18 days later, his story went viral, providing millions of angry young Tunisians with a martyr. Vast numbers of protesters took to the streets, sparking the Jasmine Revolution.

Egypt

In January 2011, another popular uprising broke out in Egypt. In 2010, Khaled Said, a young man from Alexandria, was beaten to death by the police. Protesters rallied around a Facebook page entitled 'We Are All Khaled Said'. Mr Said's death became the focal point for Egyptians who had not previously been involved in the protest movement. Beginning on 25 January 2011, millions of protesters from a variety of backgrounds and religions demanded the overthrow of Egyptian President Hosni Mubarak, who had held office since 1981.

Syria

An uprising began in Syria on 26 January 2011, when Hasan Ali Akleh set himself on fire, protesting against the Syrian government. Since that date, the protests have become more widespread and violent. According to the United Nations, by mid-2013 between 92 900 and 100 000 people were estimated to have been killed and the conflict was ongoing.

THE ROLE OF INFORMATION TECHNOLOGY

Tunisia

The Jasmine Revolution did not need any prominent leaders to rally the protesters or organise the demonstrations. Instead, the revolution was fuelled by a steady stream of anonymous text messages and Twitter and Facebook updates. Documents posted on WikiLeaks (see chapter 6), in which US diplomats had catalogued the corruption at the highest levels of the Tunisian government, deepened the popular rage. Mobile phone videos posted online documented the government's brutal response, including images of police beating and shooting protesters, resulting in at least 100 deaths. The protesters used the one weapon they understood much better than the government: the internet. Young Tunisians — educated, multilingual and knowledgeable about the internet and social media — devised strategies to evade the government's crude firewalls. Protestors spent several hours each day on Facebook and other social networks. By rendering the state television and radio stations irrelevant, they were able to undermine the regime's propaganda for the first time in many years.

Egypt

In an effort to silence demonstrators, President Mubarak 'turned off the internet'. At 12.34 am on 28 January 2011, Egypt's four primary internet providers — Link Egypt, Vodafone/Raya, Telecom Egypt and Etisalat Misr — all went 'dark'. That is, the four providers stopped transmitting all internet traffic into and out of Egypt. The blackout appeared to be designed to disrupt the organisation of the country's protest movement.

'When countries block, we evolve', wrote one activist from the group We Rebuild in a Twitter message on 28 January. We Rebuild and other activist groups scrambled to keep the country connected to the outside world, turning to landline telephones, fax machines and even ham radios to keep information flowing in and out of Egypt.

The activists were successful. On 2 February Egypt's embattled leaders realised that the communications blockage was largely ineffective and indeed counterproductive. The shutdown proved to be more a source of fresh anger than an impediment to the protest movement. Protesters had no trouble gathering larger and larger crowds, culminating with an estimated 250 000 people who assembled in central Cairo on 29 January to demand an end to Mubarak's rule.

Syria

The internet is playing a major role in the organisation and coverage of the protests in Syria. The largest Facebook page in support of the Syrian uprising, called 'The Syrian Revolution 2011', has more than 380 000 followers. The page reports on news related to the uprising.

Because the international news media were banned in Syria, the main source of information to the outside world has been private videos, usually taken with mobile phone cameras and uploaded to YouTube and Flickr. Such videos are difficult to verify independently.

To add credibility to the videos, protesters often explicitly mention the date and location of the scene and show current newspaper issues.

Activists are organising protests via Twitter and Facebook and are using Skype and Twitter to communicate because the regime often blocks mobile phone transmissions.

For example, Syrian activists are using an iPhone app called 'Souria Wa Bas' to disseminate news and information about the conflict. The app, which works on both iPhone and iPad, includes recent news about opposition groups and their activities, as well as videos, maps and photos.

THE RESULT

Tunisia

On 14 January 2011, President Ben Ali was forced into exile.

Egypt

On 11 February 2011, following weeks of determined popular protest and pressures, President Mubarak resigned from office. On 24 June 2012, Egypt's election commission announced that Muslim Brotherhood candidate Mohamed Morsi had won Egypt's presidential election. In 2013 there was a coup and interim Prime Minister Adly Mansour was appointed.

SYRIA

The conflict continues. Some countries have cut ties with the Assad regime including the Gulf States, Libya, Tunisia, Britain, Spain, Turkey, the United States and Belgium. In addition, the Arab League, Turkey and most Western powers have imposed severe sanctions on Syria, including bans on trade and transportation, isolating the Assad regime.

Sources: Compiled from J Peterson (2011), 'The Facebook revolutions: one year on', *The Daily Caller*, 18 December; J Harris (2011), 'The year of the networked revolution', *The Guardian*, 13 December; A Hauslohner (2011), 'The revolution's second act', *Time*, 5 December; J Titlow (2011), 'How Syrian protesters are using the iPhone to fuel an uprising', *ReadWriteWeb*, 18 November; A Flamand and H Macleod (2011), 'Syria's protesters turn to Facebook to expose "citizen spies"', *The Guardian*, 8 October; R Ratnesar (2011), 'Not just the Facebook revolution', *Bloomberg BusinessWeek*, 6–12 June; R Mackey (2011), 'Social media accounts of protests in Syria', *The New York Times*, 23 April; N Blanford (2011), 'On Facebook and Twitter, spreading revolution in Syria', *The Christian Science Monitor*, 8 April; J Solomon and C Levinson (2011), 'West to isolate Gadhafi', *Wall Street Journal*, 26–27 February; 'The faces of Egypt's "Revolution 2.0"' (2011), *CNN.com*, 21 February; 'After Egypt, people power hits like a tsunami' (2011), *CNN.com*, 15 February; 'Egyptian president steps down amidst groundbreaking digital revolution' (2011), *CNN.com*, 11 February; C Levinson, M Coker and J Solomon (2011), 'How Cairo, US were blindsided by revolution', *Wall Street Journal*, 2 February; P McNamara (2011), 'Egypt lifts blockade on internet service', *Network World*, 2 February; V Blue (2011), '#Egypt blocked in China: is internet access a human right?', *ZDNet.com*, 31 January; V Walt (2011), 'Tunisia's nervous neighbors watch the Jasmine Revolution', *Time*, 31 January; N Gohring and R McMillan (2011), 'Without internet, Egyptians find new ways to get online', *Computerworld*, 28 January; J Robertson (2011), 'The day part of the internet died: Egypt goes dark', *USA Today*, 28 January; 'Tunisia's revolution should be wake-up call to Middle East autocrats' (2011), *Washington Post*, 15 January.

QUESTIONS

1. Describe how information technology enabled the Jasmine and Egyptian revolutions.
2. Describe efforts by the Tunisian and Egyptian governments to quell the revolutions. In particular, describe the efforts that were directed at information technology.
3. Discuss how information technology contributed to higher oil prices and higher prices you pay for petrol.

SPREADSHEET ACTIVITY

OBJECTIVE

A spreadsheet is a software tool that allows large amounts of data to be stored, organised, analysed and presented in graphical form. A spreadsheet is extremely useful because of its ability to make simple work of a mundane task (such as calculating the average inventory turnover time for 1000 products). Although it is not difficult to calculate averages, the sheer volume of the work makes it very time-consuming. A spreadsheet allows you to create your own 'formula' and then apply that formula to all 1000 products at the same time, reducing the amount of work necessary dramatically.

Given these possibilities, you need to take some time to consider the possible applications of a spreadsheet. It is the endless application of the spreadsheet that makes it so powerful. This activity will show you that this tool can be used for a variety of situations and purposes.

Chapter connection

Data, information and knowledge are the main focus of this chapter. Spreadsheets are just one of many tools (albeit the most widespread and easily accessible) that can be used to manage data, information and knowledge.

Activity

As the text introduces the concepts of data, information and knowledge, this activity will introduce you to the vast possibilities of using spreadsheets to help manage and control data. Unmanaged data will never provide information or knowledge, so it is imperative to understand not only how to use a spreadsheet but the possibilities of when to use it. Consider the following three examples, then develop your own ideas about how spreadsheets can be used.

- *Individual:* Money is something everyone has to deal with. A spreadsheet is a great tool to help track and manage personal finances. Someone with a spreadsheet budget can quickly see where his or her money is being spent and make plans for where it will go in the future. With a little creativity and experience, one can quickly create a personal spreadsheet that will help track finances without purchasing a boxed program.

- *Organisations:* It is still the simple things that make a big difference. Companies continue to seek better ways to manage inventory and often these systems incorporate a spreadsheet. Many supply chain management tools will export data into spreadsheets for analysis. Once in a spreadsheet, charts and graphs can be used to easily display how inventory is being handled.
- *Society:* The Australian Bureau of Statistics (ABS) performs a census regularly. Much of this information is available to the public. A good deal of interesting information can be gained by placing these data in a spreadsheet. Charts and graphs can be used to analyse population changes, employment rates, demographic information and trends over time. Spreadsheets can be used to tell a story with this information.

Having read these descriptions, describe to your tutorial group how you might use a spreadsheet to help manage the required maintenance on your vehicle. Think about things like petrol mileage, oil changes, expenses, etc. What 'maths formulas' would you use that a spreadsheet could help with? If it will help, search the web for 'vehicle maintenance spreadsheets' to see what other people do with it!

Deliverable

You will provide a written description that demonstrates the ways a spreadsheet can be used to help keep up with routine maintenance on a vehicle.

DISCUSSION QUESTIONS

1. For data to be turned into information, they often need to be cleaned, organised, calculated and ultimately presented in some graphical format. Spreadsheets are excellent at all of these. Discuss three tools that help spreadsheets accomplish all of these goals.
2. Students have generated their own ideas for using spreadsheets. Be prepared to discuss your ideas with the class at large. Hopefully, you did not all come up with the same possibilities as other students and this will help broaden their horizons even more.

Suggested solution: There is no suggested solution. There is no end to the possible applications of spreadsheet tools. This is the major point of this exercise. It does not teach you anything in particular (although you may learn something); it simply opens your eyes to see that this tool will apply to you sometime. We hope it will make these concepts more real to you as you work through the following exercises.

DATABASE ACTIVITY **INTRODUCTION TO THE DATABASE PROJECT**

OBJECTIVE

How to open and use an existing Access 2010 database, even if you have never done it before.

Chapter connection

All aspects of modern information systems depend on shared databases. Being able to work with them is essential to any manager or knowledge worker of the 21st century. In this chapter, you saw how every department in a modern organisation uses information systems. You saw how different departments use them differently: HR staff to recruit, marketing managers to select marketing channels, manufacturing coordinators to develop production schedules. Much of this information is not just for one part of the organisation. Order information from sales, for example, goes to manufacturing (if you sell something, it must be produced), purchasing (materials come from suppliers) and accounting (payments, adjustments to inventory values). Linking an organisation through a shared database is a major benefit of today's systems.

These uses depend on *data*. You will read more about that later in this course. However, it is never too early to start thinking about ISs in terms of the data they use. Computers can only work with the data they have. Having the right data is vital to any IS.

Prerequisites

None.

ACTIVITY

1. Download the **Ch 01 NeTrouble** database from www.johnwiley.com/au/highered/rainer/ausnz/studentresources and double-click to open it.
2. Familiarise yourself with the parts of the Access window you see. The main ones are shown in figure 1A.1. (It is from a different database, but the window has the same parts.)

   The ribbon, A, provides tools to manipulate your database. The tools depend on the object you are working with and are organised into groups accessed via tabs (B). The tabs vary with object type, but there will always be a Home tab at the left and a Create tab next to it.

   The arrangement of the icons on the ribbon depends on how much space Access has to spread them out. Vary the width of your window to see how the icons rearrange as it becomes narrower. (On most displays, it starts out wide enough for a full array, so making it wider will not change anything.) The sections stay the same, but some tools may lose their labels or disappear under an arrow indicating a pull-down menu when space is tight.

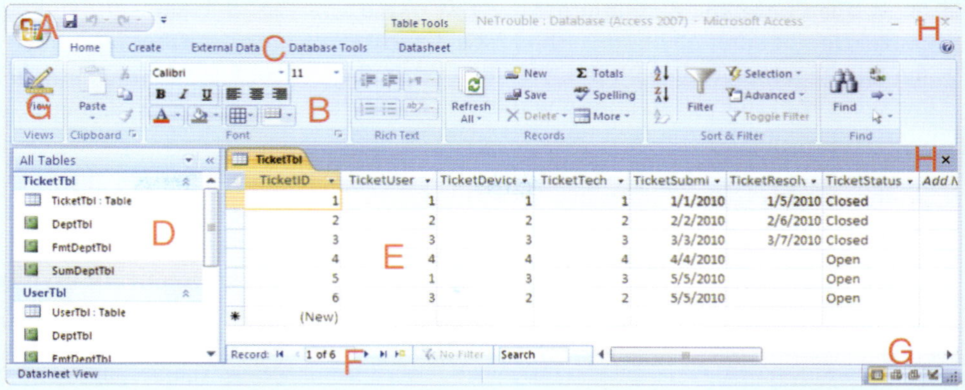

FIGURE 1A.1 Microsoft Access: Screen shot 1.

The File tab, letter C, controls the database as a file. You open, close and save your work here. In Office 2010, this was done via the Office button. Prior releases used a File menu.

The navigation pane, D, lists the objects in the current database. You can choose which types of objects it lists via the pull-down menu that opens when you click the down arrow to the right of 'AllTables'. Each object type has its own icon. In the screen shot, the spreadsheets represent tables; the green booklets, reports.

Usage hint: If you see just 'Navigation Pane' vertically at the left of the window, click on that text or the » above to expand it. The « at the top of the navigation pane in the screen shot shrinks the pane. That leaves more space for other items.

The main part of the window, E, houses all open objects. The screen shot shows a data table. Each object has a tab with its name at the top. Clicking a tab brings that object to the front. You probably do not see any open tables in your database yet.

The navigation area, F, lets you move through individual records in a database. Here, it shows '1 of 19', corresponding to the highlighted first record of 19 in the table.

Most Access objects can be manipulated in several *views*. A table, for example, has one view (Datasheet view) for reading and editing data, another (Design view) for designing the table itself. You can switch views by clicking the icon at the left of the ribbon (G), by pulling down the menu there, or via the icons at the lower right of the window (also G).

The Access window has two Close boxes (H). The one at the top right of the object area closes the object in front (here, the table TicketTbl). If other objects are open, one of them will now be in front. The Close box at the top right of the window closes the application and exits Access. (It prompts you to save unsaved work first.)

3 Open UserTbl (short for 'User Table'). How many records are in it?

Usage hint: Access can be set to open objects with a single or double click in the navigation pane. If you are using a personal copy, you can set this preference via Options under the File ribbon tab. Click Current Database, then Navigation Options.

4 Sort this table by date of birth: Click in the UserDOB column to select it, then click the top (A to Z) sorting icon in the Sort & Filter section under the ribbon. Who is the oldest user? How old is he or she?

5 Look at the UserDept (User Department) column of the User table. It does not have department names. Instead, it has numbers. Adam is from Department 1 and so on.

6 Open DeptTbl (Department Table). What is the name of Department 1?

7 Open UserRpt (User Report). Adam is listed under that department. Access used his department number to connect his name in the user table with the department name in the department table. This is how relational databases link different types of data. How many users in the Marketing department submitted network trouble tickets? After you find the answer, close the report. Be sure to click the X at the top right of the object area, below the ribbon — not the one at the top right of the entire Access window. Clicking the X at the top right of the entire Access window will exit the Access application.

8 Open UserFrm (User Form). You will see information about the first user, Adam. In the navigation area at the bottom of the window, F in the figure, click on the far right icon to insert a new record. Enter reasonable data. For the user's department, pick any department from the list to the right of the legend 'Select department.' What department did you pick? Note the User ID number of your new user. Click the New Record icon again to save your work.

Usage hint: Access saves new data in the database as soon as you exit a record. Changes to the design of the database, however, are saved only when you tell it to.

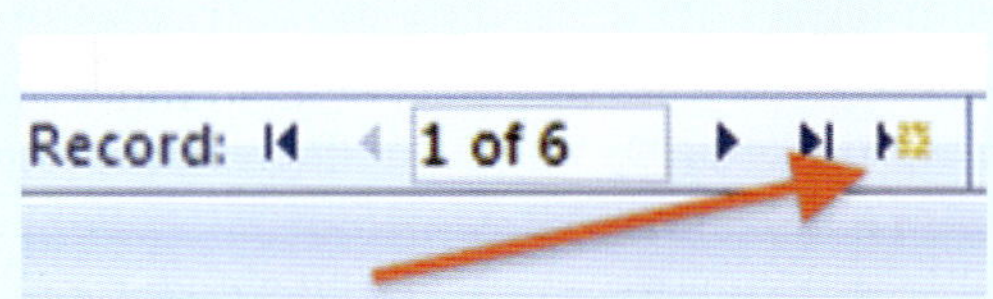

FIGURE 1A.2 Microsoft Access: Screen shot 2.

9 Now open TicketTbl. Click in the 'New' row of the table. Do not enter anything in the first column; it will be filled automatically with the next number. In the next column, TicketUser, enter the number of the user you just created. In the next two, TicketDevice and TicketTech, fill in any numbers that are already used in the existing rows of the table. In the next two, enter any dates you want. (If you click on the calendar icon that appears when you select either of those fields, you can use a built-in calendar to select dates.) In the last column, enter any data you want.

10 Open UserRpt again. How many users are in that department now?

Usage hint: Reports are not automatically updated when data they are based on change. You have to close and reopen them.

Usage hint: The reason you created a ticket for your new user is that this report shows only users who have submitted trouble tickets. It could have been designed to show all users, whether or not they submitted tickets, but it was not.

11 Open UserQry (User Query) to find all users born after a certain date. Key in 6/6/1986 (June 6, 1986) and click OK. How many users were born after that date?

DELIVERABLE

Submit answers to the eight questions posed in the activity above and on the previous page:

In step 3: 1 question
In step 4: 2 questions
In step 6: 1 question
In step 7: 1 question
In step 8: 2 questions
In step 11: 1 question

(Steps not listed have no questions.)

QUIZ QUESTIONS

1 True or false: Access puts all the information about something of interest (such as an employee) into a single table.

2 Which of the following information items about a user is *not* given in UserTbl?

a The user's name.
b The user's date of birth.
c The user's email address.
d The user's blood type.

3 If you want to find out a user's age from UserTbl, which of the following is correct?

a There is insufficient information here to determine it.
b It can be found by subtracting the date of birth from today's date, dividing the difference in days by 365 and deleting any fractional remainder.
c It can be found by subtracting the date of hire from today's date, dividing the difference in days by 365 and deleting any fractional remainder.
d It can be found by asking the user or a member of his/her family.

4 The report you looked at in step 7 had all of the following elements, except:

a An overall header at the top, to identify it.
b Number of trouble tickets submitted by each department, below the list of that department's employees.
c Number of trouble tickets submitted by each department, above the list of that department's employees.
d Detail rows with information about each user.

DISCUSSION QUESTIONS

1 In step 9 of this activity, you entered a birth date cut-off for the query. User input like this, that determines what data a query returns, is called a *parameter*. Now, suppose you want to book a round trip on an air travel reservation system. List three parameters you must enter into such a system before it can tell you about available flights.

2 The report you used in steps 7 and 8 of this activity included a summary field after each department. It was a simple summary, just a count of users in that department. Suppose this report also contained numeric data, such as user salaries. What other types of department summaries could you have? Are there any summaries, other than the employee count, that you could possibly create from this table as it exists here? (Be creative. Do not worry about whether or not it would make sense to create them. Just ask: Would it be possible?)

3 A university cafeteria checkout system reads the barcode on each item, looks it up in a table and finds the product description and price. Using this information, it keeps track of the running total. At the end it calculates the total due and compares it to the student's account balance. If the balance is insufficient, it calls a supervisor. Otherwise, it subtracts the cost of the meal from the balance and prints an itemised receipt showing the remaining balance.

a What tables does this database need? (One was mentioned in the description.)
b Using paper and pencil or any other tools your instructor specifies, draw the tables as in TicketTbl in the Figure 1A.1. Show columns for all the data in them. Show a few sample rows. Also draw a sample itemised receipt as it might be printed for a student. For each different kind of data item on the receipt, say where it comes from: in the database or as the result of some other calculation.

4 The technician table (TechTbl) lists all the technicians, with their names and other information such as their pay grade (job title). Describe in words how you could find, using the tables in this database, the names of all the users whose problems a given technician worked with.

2 Organisational strategy, competitive advantage and information systems

CHAPTER OUTLINE

2.1 Business pressures, organisational responses and IT support

2.2 Competitive advantage and strategic information systems

2.3 Business–IT alignment

LEARNING OBJECTIVES

1 Identify effective IT responses to different kinds of business pressures.

2 Describe the strategies that organisations typically adopt to counter Porter's five competitive forces.

3 Describe the characteristics of effective business–IT alignment.

OPENING CASE >

M2M: the case of Coca-Cola Amatil

Machine-to-machine (M2M) technology enables machines to 'talk' to each other, which requires sensors and communication modules (e.g. SIM cards) to be embedded within devices. This enables data to be transferred between them by way of both wireless and wired networks. M2M technology has the potential to connect billions of physical devices in different industries including retail and supply chains, thereby enabling smarter infrastructures and enhanced connectedness. With a huge growth potential in Australia, nearly 35 per cent of Australian businesses are considering adopting M2M technology. Cisco, one of the world's leading internet equipment makers, has forecast that by 2016, Australia is expected to have approximately 142 million connected devices, which is approximately six for each Australian.

Coca-Cola Amatil (CCA) is one of the early adopters of this technology in Australia that are strategically using M2M to increase productivity and profitability. CCA is one of the largest bottlers of non-alcoholic drinks in the Asia–Pacific and is investing in M2M to better enable them to manage vending machines. CCA has equipped nearly 30 000 vending machines with SIM cards, enabling them to communicate directly with automated systems using Telstra's Next G® network. In doing so, M2M technology enables CCA to have real-time access to, and control of, their vending machines, achieving the following benefits.

- Vending machines can be serviced proactively and stocks replenished as required, thereby increasing productivity of technicians and reducing operational business costs.
- Collected data can be used to generate valuable business intelligence which CCA employs to better understand the behaviour of their customers by geographic location.
- With cashless vending (e.g. payment using credit, debit and even staff cards) becoming increasingly more popular, M2M technology can help identify returning customers, enabling CCA to reward their loyalty through personalised bonus offers.

Sources: M Bingemann (2013), *Get smart and build digital today: Telstra*, www.theaustralian.com.au/business/in-depth/get-smart-and-build-digital-today-telstra/story-fni4k1kl-1226627378895; F Fadaghi and A Lee (2013), *Australian mobile services market study 2011–15*, www.telsyte.com.au/?page_id=697; T Herrmann (2013), *The great potential of machine to machine*, www.abc.net.au/technology/articles/2013/08/08/3821104.htm,

ABC (Technology + Games); Telstra (2013), *Telstra case study: Coca-Cola Amatil M2M*, www.telstra.com.au/business-enterprise/download/document/business-case-study-transcript-cocacola-m2m.pdf; Telstra (2013), *Turn on a smart business*, www.telstra.com.au/business-enterprise/download/document/business-m2m-brochure.pdf; TelstraEnterprise (2013), *Telstra case study: Coca-Cola Amatil M2M*, tech.smashpipe.com/?f=KRYRxYz3uFE#play/KRYRxYz3uFE.

Introduction

Information systems are critically important in helping organisations respond to business pressures and in supporting organisations' global strategy. As you study this chapter, you will see that any information system can be *strategic*, meaning that it can provide a competitive advantage — if it is used properly.

This chapter also demonstrates the incredible complexity of the information systems employed by a large international company.

Competitive advantage is an advantage in some measure such as cost, quality, or speed that is not easily imitable by competitors; it leads to control of a market and to larger than average profits. Strategy and competitive advantage come in many forms. For example, Coca-Cola Amatil is using M2M technology to improve productivity in its vending machine operations and better service to customers through business intelligence. M2M technology has lowered operating costs and contributed to improved profitability.

This chapter is important for you for several reasons. First, the business pressures addressed here will affect your organisation, but they will also affect you. As a result, you must understand how information systems can help you, and eventually your organisation, respond to these pressures.

In addition, acquiring competitive advantage is essential for your organisation's survival. Many organisations achieve competitive advantage through the efforts of their employees. Therefore, becoming knowledgeable about strategy and how information systems affect strategy and competitive position will help you throughout your career.

This chapter encourages you to become familiar with your organisation's strategy, mission and goals, and to understand its business problems and how it makes (or loses) money. It will help you understand how IT contributes to organisational strategy. Further, it is likely that you will be a member of business–IT committees that decide (among many other things) whether to adopt new technologies and how to use existing technologies more effectively. After studying this chapter, you will be able to make immediate contributions in these committees when you join your organisations.

THE NOOK

Malakai and Abbie have a vision that their club will provide a relaxed community atmosphere, with good drinks and good music. However, they operate in a very competitive business environment and feel market pressure to be everything to everyone, even though that is not what they want to be. They feel pressure from their customers to be more technologically advanced, even though they do not see any competitive advantage from it. They also feel a tremendous responsibility (legal and societal pressure) to manage underage consumption of alcohol. However, they are not sure how to respond to these pressures while maintaining their desired atmosphere.

Over the years, they have learned that they not only compete with other clubs and local restaurants, but with the threat of substitute products or services including theatres, athletic events, parties and anything else patrons choose to do for entertainment. To gain and maintain a solid customer base, they feel they really want a community feel to their club. To achieve this, they are not quite sure what mix of music, drinks, information, networks, data, advertisements, controls, policies and procedures would position them where they want to be in the marketplace. Malakai and Abbie need a solid strategy to help accomplish their vision.

In this chapter, you will see how information systems enable organisations to respond to business pressures. Next, you will learn how information systems help organisations gain competitive advantages in the marketplace. The chapter concludes with a discussion of business–IT alignment — in other words, how the IT function in an organisation supports its strategy.

2.1 Business pressures, organisational responses and IT support

Modern organisations compete in a challenging environment. To remain competitive, they must react rapidly to problems and opportunities that arise from extremely dynamic conditions. In this section you examine some of the major pressures confronting modern organisations and the strategies that organisations employ to respond to these pressures.

Business pressures

The **business environment** is the combination of social, legal, economic, physical and political factors in which businesses conduct their operations. Significant changes in any of these factors are likely to create business pressures on organisations. Organisations typically respond to these pressures with activities supported by IT. Figure 2.1 illustrates the relationships among business pressures, organisational performance and responses, and IT support. You will learn about three major types of business pressures: market, technology and societal pressures.

Market pressures

Market pressures are generated by the global economy, intense competition, the changing nature of the workforce and powerful customers. Let's look more closely at each of these factors.

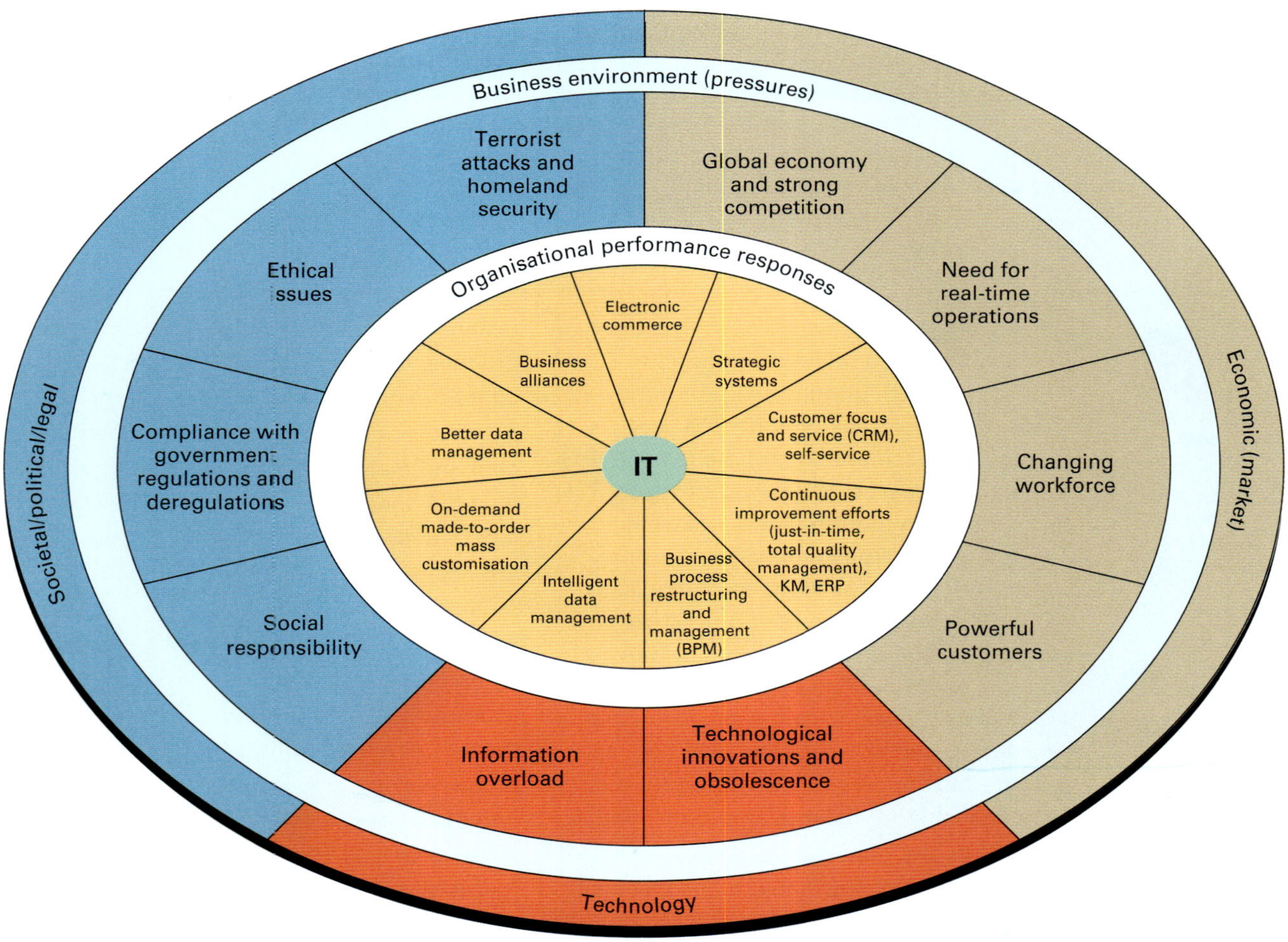

FIGURE 2.1 Business pressures, organisational performance and responses, and IT support.

Globalisation

Globalisation is the integration and interdependence of economic, social, cultural and ecological facets of life, made possible by rapid advances in IT. In his book *The world is flat*, Pulitzer Prize–winning author Thomas Friedman argues that technology is levelling the global competitive playing field, thereby making it 'flat'.

Friedman identifies three eras of globalisation. The first era, Globalisation 1.0, lasted from 1492 to 1800. During this era, the force behind globalisation was how much muscle, horsepower, or wind power a country could deploy.

The second era, Globalisation 2.0, lasted from 1800 to 2000. In this era, the force behind globalisation was the emergence of multinational companies — that is, companies that had their headquarters in one country but operated in several countries. In the first half of this era, globalisation was driven by falling transportation costs, generated by the development of the steam engine and the railroads. In the second half, the driving force was falling telecommunications costs resulting from the telegraph, telephones, computers, satellites, fibre-optic cable, and the internet and world wide web. The modern global economy began to evolve during this era.

Around the year 2000, the world entered Globalisation 3.0. In this era globalisation has been driven by the convergence of ten forces that Friedman calls 'flatteners'. Figure 2.2 identifies these forces.

- Fall of the Berlin Wall on 9 November 1989
  - Shifted the world toward free-market economies and away from centrally planned economies
  - Led to the emergence of the European Union and early thinking about the world as a single, global market
- Netscape goes public on 9 August 1995
  - Popularised the internet and the world wide web
- Development of workflow software
  - Enabled computer applications to work with one another without human intervention
  - Enabled faster, closer collaboration and coordination among employees, regardless of their location
- Uploading
  - Empowered all internet users to create content and put it on the web
  - Led the transition from a passive approach to content to an active, participatory, collaborative approach
- Outsourcing
  - Contracting with an outside company to perform a specific function that your company was doing itself and then integrating that work back into your operation (e.g. moving customer call centres to India)
- Offshoring
  - Relocating an entire operation, or certain tasks, to another country (e.g. moving an entire manufacturing operation to China)
- Supply chaining
  - Technological revolution that led to the creation of networks comprised of companies, their suppliers and their customers, all of which could collaborate and share information for increased efficiency
- Insourcing
  - Delegating operations or jobs within a business to another company that specialises in those operations (e.g. Yarra Valley Water has used IT outsourcing since it separated from Melbourne Water in 1995. First it relied on MITS, then Logica and then Fujitsu since 2005. By insourcing IT, the utility has generated approximately $2 million savings in its annual expenditure.[1])
- Informing
  - The ability to search for information, best illustrated by search engines
- The steroids
  - Technologies that amplify the other flatteners
  - Enable all forms of computing and collaboration to be digital, mobile and personal

FIGURE 2.2 Friedman's ten flatteners.

According to Friedman, each era has been characterised by a distinctive focus. The focus of Globalisation 1.0 was on countries, the focus of Globalisation 2.0 was on companies, and the focus of Globalisation 3.0 is on groups and individuals.

As you look at figure 2.2, note that nine of Friedman's ten flatteners directly relate to IT (all except the fall of the Berlin Wall). These flatteners enable individuals to connect, compute, communicate, collaborate and compete everywhere and anywhere, anytime and all the time; to access limitless amounts of information, services and entertainment; to exchange knowledge; and to produce and sell goods and services. People and organisations can now operate without regard to geography, time, distance, or even language barriers. The bottom line? Globalisation is markedly increasing competition.

These observations make our discussion all the more important for you. Simply put, you and the organisations you join will be competing with people and organisations from all over a flat world.

Let's consider some examples of globalisation. Regional agreements such as the North American Free Trade Agreement (NAFTA), which includes the United States, Canada and Mexico, have contributed to increased world trade and increased competition. Further, the rise of India and China as economic powerhouses has increased global competition.

One important pressure that businesses in a global market must contend with is the cost of labour, which varies widely among countries. In general, labour costs are higher in developed countries like Australia and Japan than in developing countries such as China. Also, developed countries usually offer greater benefits, such as healthcare, to employees, driving the cost of doing business even higher. Therefore, many labour-intensive industries have moved their operations to countries with low labour costs. IT has made such moves much easier to implement.

However, manufacturing overseas is no longer the bargain it once was. For example, manufacturing wages in China tripled between 2004 and 2013,[2] and the value of China's currency has steadily risen.

The changing nature of the workforce

The workforce, particularly in developed countries, is becoming more diversified. Increasing numbers of women, single parents and people with disabilities are now employed in all types of positions. IT is easing the integration of these employees into the traditional workforce. IT is also enabling people to work from home, which can be a major benefit for parents with young children and for people confronted with mobility and/or transportation issues.

Powerful customers

Consumer sophistication and expectations increase as customers become more knowledgeable about the products and services they acquire. Customers can use the internet to find detailed information about products and services, to compare prices and to purchase items at electronic auctions.

Organisations recognise the importance of customers and have increased their efforts to acquire and retain them. Modern firms strive to learn as much as possible about their customers to better anticipate and address their needs. This process, called *customer intimacy*, is an important component of *customer relationship management* (CRM), an organisation-wide effort toward maximising the customer experience. You will learn about CRM in chapter 12.

Technology pressures

The second category of business pressures consists of those pressures related to technology. Two major technology-related pressures are technological innovation and information overload.

Technological innovation and obsolescence

New and improved technologies rapidly create or support substitutes for products and alternative service options, as you see in IT's About Business. As a result, today's state-of-the-art products may be obsolete tomorrow. For example, how fast are new versions of your smartphone being released? How quickly are electronic versions of books, magazines and newspapers replacing traditional hard-copy versions? These changes force businesses to keep up with consumer demands.

Consider the Apple iPad (www.apple.com/ipad). Apple released the first iPad in April 2010 and sold 3 million of the devices in 80 days. Rather than taking time to enjoy its success, Apple made its iPad2 available for sale on 11 March 2011, only 11 months later. Apple then released the iPad3 in March 2012 and iPad4 in November 2012.[10] The iPad5, called the iPad Air, was released in November 2013.[11]

IT'S ABOUT BUSINESS

Kennards Hire BI systems

Established in 1948, Kennards Hire (www.kennardshire.com.au) is one of the largest family-owned tool and equipment hire companies in Australia. Headquartered in Sydney, Kennards Hire operates through over 120 branches and employs almost 1000 employees across Australia. In the last few years Kennards Hire has experienced rapid growth, with revenue increasing by approximately 50 per cent. This growth was also associated with large volumes of data concerning Kennard Hire operations. For example, at the time of this growth Kennards Hire was handling more than 7 million transactions annually and servicing over 36 000 accounting customers.[3]

To manage their operations Kennards Hire originally used many fragmented legacy systems which could not interface with each other, although they worked well in isolation. These systems are often interdependent, with data generated by one often required as input by another.[4] Consequently, extensive manual intervention and repurposing of data was often required as data were transferred between systems, which made business data analysis and integration (e.g. historical trends and financial outcomes analyses) and reporting challenging and inefficient, thereby constraining the ability of Kennards managers to manage business operations (e.g. financial performance of branches and customer activity). As a result, Kennards Hire managers often had to rely on personal experience and guesswork, rather than evidence, to make decisions.

Recently, Kennards Hire implemented a business intelligence (BI) system (Microsoft BI and data warehouse solution based on Microsoft SQL Server 2008 R2, SharePoint Server 2010 and Excel 2010[5]) which enabled them to address many of the challenges and issues of the previously fragmented legacy systems.[6] Specifically, BI systems are used to systematically analyse raw data in organisations and comprise many activities, including data mining, online analytical processing (OLAP), querying and reporting.[7] First the Kennards Hire BI system contributed towards improving decision making.[8] With the new BI system, Kennards Hire managers are able to access up-to-date data and generate both customised and ad-hoc reports easily and quickly, which has increased visibility of various operational aspects of the company and branch operations, including financial outcomes, sales, hire history of products and customers. With enhanced visibility and accessibility to this information, Kennards Hire managers now have a better understanding of the types of hire products they need to invest in, the geographical locations where these should be offered and the manner in which customer preferences can change. Taken together, these enhancements have enabled Kennards Hire branch managers to both monitor and control performance while also empowering them to make better decisions.

Second,[9] the Kennards Hire BI system contributed towards improving customer service. The new BI system has significantly enhanced the quality of the data collected and held by Kennards Hire. For example, the new system has improved the management of fleet and customer hire history. With fleet hire history data, Kennards Hire can quickly identify popular and unpopular products and adjust offerings accordingly. With customer history data, Kennards Hire can now analyse and correlate their customers' product hire preferences, location information and problems encountered. This enables Kennards Hire to offer better and more personalised service to customers while also creating growth opportunities for cross-selling and up-selling of hire services.

QUESTIONS

1. What are potential disadvantages of using fragmented applications in a distributed business such as Kennards Hire? Provide specific examples to support your answer.
2. Provide examples of how BI helps Kennards Hire gain competitive advantage in the tool and equipment hire industry.
3. Look ahead in this chapter to the discussion of five strategies for competitive advantage. Which strategy (or strategies) does BI use to help Kennards Hire address decision making? Provide examples to support your answer.

Information overload

The amount of information available on the internet doubles approximately every year and much of it is free. The internet and other telecommunications networks are bringing a flood of information to managers. To make decisions effectively and efficiently, managers must be able to access, navigate and utilise these vast stores of data, information and knowledge. Information technologies, such as search engines (discussed in chapter 4) and data mining (discussed in chapter 5), provide valuable support in these efforts.

Societal/political/legal pressures

The third category of business pressures includes social responsibility, government regulation/deregulation, spending for social programs, spending to protect against terrorism and ethics. This section will explain how all of these elements affect modern businesses.

Social responsibility

Social issues that affect businesses and individuals range from the state of the physical environment, to company and individual philanthropy, to education. Some corporations and individuals are willing to spend time and/or money to address various social problems. These efforts are known as corporate **organisational social responsibility** or **individual social responsibility**.

One critical social problem is the state of the physical environment. A growing IT initiative, called *green IT*, is addressing some of the most pressing environmental concerns. IT is instrumental in organisational efforts to 'go green' in at least four areas.

- Facilities design and management. Organisations are creating more sustainable work environments. Many organisations are pursuing the guidance of the Green Building Council Australia (GBCA) (www.gbca.org.au) in building, facilities design and management. GBCA is a national, not-for-profit organisation which aims at developing a sustainable property industry in Australia and is supported by both industry and governments across the country. GBCA aims to achieve this by encouraging the adoption of green building practices through market-based solutions including green building programs and technologies, building design practices and construction and their integration with mainstream building practices. One impact of this development is that IT professionals are expected to help create green facilities. Consequently, IT personnel have to consider how their computing decisions influence sustainable design and, in turn, how the building's design influences the IT infrastructure. Green design influences the type of IT devices used and the locations where IT clusters personal computers, people and servers. IT must become familiar with the metering and monitoring systems used in green buildings and the requirements of buildings' computerised infrastructure.
- Carbon management. As companies try to reduce their carbon footprints, they are turning to IT executives to develop the systems needed to monitor carbon throughout the organisation and its supply chain, which can be global in scope. Therefore, IT employees need to become knowledgeable about embedded carbon and how to measure it in the company's products and processes.

  Consider, for example, application development. IT managers will have to ask whether an application will require new hardware to test and run, or how much additional server space (and thus energy) it will require — and how these issues translate into carbon output. In relation to this, the Australian Federal Government has undertaken initiatives to improve IT energy and carbon management. For example, in their ICT Sustainability plan 2010–15,[12] the Australian Federal Government attempts to improve IT energy and carbon performance within its own public sector operations by way of:[13]

  i specifying ICT energy consumption targets for Australian Government operations supported by systematic performance measures

  ii isolating energy intensity measures and targets for use across Australian Government agencies and departments

  iii developing ICT energy management plans in agencies that have an annual ICT spend exceeding $20 million.

When considering application development, IT managers will have to ask how much additional server space (and thus energy) it will require and how it will translate into carbon output.

- National and state environmental laws and policies. IT executives must deal with state laws and national regulations that impact everything from the IT products they buy, to how they dispose of them, to their company's carbon footprint. IT managers must understand environmental compliance issues so they can ask their vendors the right questions regarding specific state, national, and international environmental standards before buying, deploying and disposing of equipment.[14] For example, using the Product Stewardship Bill 2011[15] as a basis, Australian environment ministers have approved an industry-led scheme for the collection and recycling of end-of-life ICT equipment including computers and computer peripherals across Australia.[16] States have developed similar policies. For example, South Australia's Environment Protection Authority (EPA) issued legislation banning e-waste from direct landfill disposal across all of South Australia, under the Environment Protection (Waste to Resources) Policy 2010 (W2R EPP). This legislation became effective on 1 September 2013.[17]
- Energy management. IT executives must understand their entire organisation's energy needs for several reasons. First, energy management systems are becoming increasingly sophisticated. To employ these systems effectively and make intelligent consumption decisions, IT personnel must understand the system's complex monitors and sensors. Second, utilities are offering incentives to commercial customers who take certain energy conservation steps, such as enabling computer power management across their networks and designing energy-efficient data centres. Finally, utilities are offering variable rate incentives depending on when companies use electricity and how much they use. These issues require IT systems that can regulate electricity use. In Australia, the Energy Efficiency Council (**www.eec.org.au**) encourages investment in energy efficiency and cogeneration to help companies to cut carbon emissions while increasing their profits and lowering costs through best-practice guides, case studies and service directories to locate facilitators and suppliers of services and products.

Continuing our discussion of social responsibility, social problems all over the world may be addressed through corporate and individual philanthropy. In some cases, questions arise as to what percentage of contributions actually goes to the intended causes and recipients and what percentage goes to the charity's overhead. Another problem that concerns contributors is that they often exert little influence over the selection of projects their contributions will support. The internet can help address these concerns and facilitate generosity and connection. Consider the following local examples:

- dNet (depressionet.org.au) offers a website and an online community for Australians from different backgrounds who have had personal experiences with depression. They also provide comprehensive information for people living with depression.

- University of the Third Age Online (U3A Online) (**www.u3aonline.org.au**) represents an example of an Australian online community of practice that promotes the use of internet technology by and for the benefit of older people. For example, U3A Online provides short courses for older or younger disabled individuals who are isolated either through physical or social circumstances and who prefer the freedom to study where and when they choose.
- Australian Chess Federation (ACF) (auschess.org.au) is an online community of interest whose objective is to promote the game of chess in Australia. It includes chess news, tournament games and details of upcoming tournaments and events, as well as disseminating a free and comprehensive newsletter.
- Givit (**www.givit.org.au**) is a charitable foundation dedicated to connecting the community and contributing towards improving the quality of people's lives by matching individuals in need with individuals who are willing to give.
- Freestuff (**www.freestuff.co.nz**) represents a convenient way for people in New Zealand to give away items they no longer want.
- Australian Volunteers International (**www.australianvolunteers.com**) is funded by AusAid, an Australian Government agency, and donations in order to place and manage volunteers overseas.
- Volunteering New Zealand (VNZ) (**www.volunteeringnz.org.nz**) fosters and encourages volunteering and volunteering management in New Zealand.

International examples include:

- PatientsLikeMe (**www.patientslikeme.com**), or any of the thousands of message boards dedicated to infertility, cancer and various other ailments. People use these sites and message boards to obtain information about life-and-death decisions based on volunteered information, while also receiving much-needed emotional support from strangers.
- GiftFlow (**www.giftflow.org**): GiftFlow is a virtual community where you can obtain things you need for free and find people who need the 'stuff' you have to give away. GiftFlow connects community organisations, businesses, governments and neighbours in a network of reciprocity.
- Kiva (**www.kiva.org**): Kiva is a non-profit enterprise that provides a link between lenders in developed countries and entrepreneurs in developing countries. Users pledge interest-free loans rather than tax-deductible donations. Kiva directs 100 per cent of the loans to borrowers.

Still another social problem that affects modern business is the **digital divide**. The digital divide refers to the wide gap between those who have access to information and communications technology and those who do not. This gap exists both within and among countries. IT's About Business (opposite) provides an example of how modern information technologies are enabling the Surui people of the Amazon region in Brazil to bridge the digital divide.

Many government organisations are trying to close the digital divide in Australia through various initiatives. As technologies develop and become less expensive, the speed at which the gap can be closed is expected to accelerate. For example, the $60 million Australian Government Digital Regions Initiative was concluded in June 2013. It attempted to close the digital divide between rural and remote regions and metropolitan Australia, with various projects including education and health.[18] Additionally, the Australian Government has committed over $25 million for the Broadband for Seniors initiative over seven years until 2015. As part of this initiative, approximately 2000 Broadband for Seniors kiosks have been set up across Australia since 2008, where Australian seniors can receive free and personalised training concerning how to use computers, various applications and surf the internet. While this initiative is part of the Australian Government's National Digital Economy Strategy, it also attempts to bridge the digital divide between older and younger Australians.[19] A similar program was developed for addressing the digital divide between Aboriginal and non-Aboriginal Australians.[20]

IT'S ABOUT BUSINESS

The Surui tribe of the Amazon

Chief Almir of the Surui tribe of the Brazilian Amazon is using Google to help his tribe maintain its traditional way of life. In 1969, the Surui had their first contact with outsiders, who brought with them disease, violence and death. Then, loggers arrived and laid waste to the Surui's homeland.

Chief Almir took a leadership role in his tribe at 17 and became the tribe's first member to attend college. In 2006, he fled briefly to the United States when loggers put a bounty on his head. He stumbled upon Google Earth in an internet café in 2007.

Chief Almir decided that his tribe's survival depended on outreach. His partnership with Google has enabled the tribe to create an online 'cultural map' of the Surui with stories from the tribe's elders that are uploaded onto YouTube, as well as a geographical map of their territory created with GPS-equipped smartphones from Google. In 2009, Google employees taught the Surui to use cell phones to record illegal logging on their land. Tribal members can now take photos and videos that are geo-tagged and immediately upload the images to Google Earth. Law enforcement officials can no longer claim ignorance of the problem when evidence of the deforestation is publicly available online. Satellite pictures show that the Surui use of technology is highly effective as the Surui territory is the only remaining intact piece of rainforest in the area.

Chief Almir views his partnership with Google not only as a way to sustain his traditions and his land, but also as an opportunity to teach others about the Surui. Furthermore, the tribe has mounted an ambitious reforestation plan to combat the aggressive logging that is destroying the Surui's 98 257 hectares of land. Smartphones have enabled the tribe to document cleared areas in the forest and form planting plans. The Surui plan to plant 100 million saplings in the next decade. They hope to raise millions of dollars through a United Nations program that gives carbon credits, which can be traded for cash, to countries and tribes that maintain their forests. The money would fund new homes, a hospital and a school. The Surui have created a word for Google in their language: *ragogmakann*, meaning 'the messenger'.

The Amazonian rainforest is being destroyed by burning and logging.

Sources: Compiled from 'The most creative people in business 2011' (2011), *FastCompany*, June; S Zwick (2010), 'Brazil's Surui establish first indigenous carbon fund', *Ecosystem Marketplace*, 3 December; R Butler (2009), 'Brazilian tribe owns carbon rights to Amazon rainforest land', *Mongabay.com*, 9 December; R Butler (2009), 'Big REDD', *Washington Monthly*, 7 September; R Butler (2006), 'Amazon conservation team puts Indians on Google Earth to save the Amazon', *Mongabay.com*, 14 November.

QUESTIONS

1 Describe the benefits that all of us gain from the Surui's use of IT.

2 Provide specific examples of how the Surui could make further use of IT to improve their lives.

Compliance with government regulations

Another major source of business pressures is government regulations regarding health, safety, environmental protection and equal opportunity. Businesses tend to view government regulations as expensive constraints on their activities. In general, government deregulation intensifies competition. For example, Australia's *Spam Act 2003* regulates the sending of commercial electronic messages (e.g. email, short-message service (SMS), multimedia message services (MMS) and instant messaging (iM)).[21] Specifically the Spam Act prohibits the sending of unsolicited commercial electronic messages with an Australian link. A link is considered to be Australian if it originates or is commissioned in Australia, or even if it originates from another country but was sent to an address accessed in Australia. Examples of commercial messages include offers and advertisements that promote supplying of goods and services or investment opportunities.[22] Organisations must be in compliance with the regulations contained in these statutes. The process of becoming and remaining compliant is expensive and time consuming. In almost all cases, organisations rely on IT support to provide the necessary controls and information for compliance.

Protection against terrorist attacks

IT can help protect businesses by providing security systems and possibly identifying patterns of behaviour associated with terrorist activities, including cyberattacks (discussed in chapter 7). See Chapter Closing Case 2 for a look at a software tool developed to combat terrorism. Part of the Australian Government's Attorney-General's Department, CERT Australia (**www.cert.gov.au**), has been established as Australia's national computer emergency response team. CERT is an important point of contact that can help defend Australian businesses against cyber security issues, including cyberattacks.

Ethical issues

Ethics relates to general standards of right and wrong. Information ethics relates specifically to standards of right and wrong in information-processing practices. Ethical issues are very important because, if handled poorly, they can damage an organisation's image and destroy its employees' morale. The use of IT raises many ethical issues, ranging from monitoring email to invading the privacy of millions of customers whose data are stored in private and public databases. (Chapter 6 covers ethical issues in detail.)

Clearly, then, the pressures on organisations are increasing and organisations must be prepared to take responsive actions if they are to succeed. You will learn about these organisational responses in the next section.

Organisational responses

Organisations are responding to the various pressures just discussed by implementing IT such as strategic systems, customer focus, make-to-order and mass customisation, and e-business. This section explores each of these responses.

Strategic systems

Strategic systems provide organisations with advantages that enable them to increase their market share and/or profits, to better negotiate with suppliers, and to prevent competitors from entering their markets. As an example, the IT department at Procter & Gamble (P&G; **www.pg.com/en_ANZ**) developed a virtualised environment that the company uses for product design work, product placement research and consumer feedback studies. P&G utilises virtual reality models to test design ideas for the next breakthroughs in products such as nappies and cosmetics. Within these 'cyberworlds', P&G can rapidly test product performance as well as consumer responses to various kinds of ingredient and packaging choices. Consider how the organisations in IT's About Business (opposite) rely on strategic information systems to carry out their missions more effectively. Pay particular attention to how a strategic information system in one group of organisations can actually harm another group of organisations (see Small theatres may go dark).

Customer focus

Organisational attempts to provide superb customer service can make the difference between attracting and keeping customers and losing them to competitors. Numerous IT tools and business processes have been designed to keep customers happy. Consider Amazon, for example. When you visit Amazon's website any time after your first visit, the site welcomes you back by name and presents you with information on books that you might like, based on your previous purchases. In another example, Dell guides you through the process of buying a computer by providing information and choices that help you make an informed buying decision.

Make-to-order and mass customisation

Make-to-order is a strategy of producing customised (made to individual specifications) products and services. The business problem is how to manufacture customised goods efficiently and at a reasonably low cost. Part of the solution is to change manufacturing processes from mass production to mass customisation. In **mass production**, a company produces a large quantity of identical items. In mass customisation, it also produces a large quantity of items, but it customises them to fit the needs and preferences of individual customers.

IT'S ABOUT BUSINESS

Two strategic information systems

Sustainability for Hilton Worldwide

Hilton Worldwide is the first major multibrand hospitality company to make sustainability measurement a brand standard. Company management decided to require all of its 3750 properties to implement LightStay, Hilton's sustainability measurement system, by December 2011.

The LightStay system analyses performance across 200 operational practices, such as housekeeping, paper-product usage, food waste, chemical storage, air quality and transportation. LightStay also provides a 'meeting impact calculator' that calculates the sustainability impact of any meeting or conference held at any Hilton property. Finally, LightStay also allows Hilton hotels to track sustainability projects, share best practices and communicate with one another through a dashboard.

Hilton Worldwide has made significant savings since the introduction of LightStay.

Since the introduction of LightStay, Hilton has continuously improved its sustainability and economic performance and has saved more than $74 million in utility costs as a result of the following reductions:

- 6.6 per cent reduction in energy use
- 7.8 per cent reduction in carbon output
- 19 per cent reduction in waste output
- 3.8 per cent reduction in water use.

Small theatres may go dark

A strategic information system in one industry may not benefit another industry. In fact, some strategic information systems may have the effect of damaging businesses that cannot keep up.

For the past decade, Hollywood's largest studios have been working on a new production standard for digital motion pictures that could save them $1 billion annually in printmaking fees and shipping costs. Movies in this new format are shipped on hard drives that can hold hundreds of gigabytes of data and are connected to extremely high-definition projectors. To unlock a movie, a distributor sends the theatre a code that controls where, when and how long the theatre can play the particular movie.

Unfortunately, many small theatre owners cannot afford the expensive new projectors and other equipment that major studios want them to buy. The cost for each theatre to play movies in this format is $65 000 to $70 000. Small theatre owners note that they would be spending this additional money without incurring any additional revenue. That is, they feel that they cannot pass the cost along to their customers in the form of increased ticket prices.

To induce theatres to purchase the new equipment, celluloid prints (actual hard-copy film) of new movies from major studios will no longer be available in the United States by the end of 2013, according to John Fithian, president of the National Association of Theater Owners.

The largest motion picture chains — Regal Entertainment, AMC Entertainment and Cinemark Theaters, which account for about half of the $10.2 billion annual revenue pulled in by the US box office — expect to complete the conversion by early 2013. However, Fithian predicts that the United States will lose several thousand screens in small theatres.

Sources: Compiled from N Leiber (2012), 'For small theaters, the digital future is dark', *Bloomberg BusinessWeek*, 20–26 February; 'Hilton Worldwide quantifies product sustainability for global procurement operations' (2012), *IBM Customer Success Case Study*, 30 January; J Bruner (2011), 'River of information', *Forbes*, 7 November; G Hasek (2011), 'Hilton LightStay program cuts hotel energy use by 6.6%, saves $74M', *Greenbiz.com*, 25 October; M Mills (2011), 'Entertainment's tech boom: the internet has been assimilated', *Forbes*, 10 May; www.ibm.com, www.hiltonworldwide.com.

QUESTIONS

1. How does the LightStay system contribute to Hilton's sustainability efforts?
2. Is 'going digital' in motion picture production a strategic information system for the motion picture industry? Why or why not? Provide examples to support your answer.
3. Is 'going digital' in the motion picture industry a strategic information system for the National Association for Theater Owners? Why or why not? Provide examples to support your answer.
4. Given your answers to questions 3 and 4 above, what should the motion picture industry do?
5. Can you think of another example where a strategic information system in one company (or industry) can harm another company (or industry)?

Mass customisation is simply an attempt to perform make-to-order on a large scale. For example, IKEA Australia (**www.ikea.com.au**) uses the PAX wardrobe planning tool to assist their customers to customise their wardrobe products online.[23]

EXAMPLE

Well-fitting jeans are notoriously difficult to find. To address this problem, Bodymetrics has partnered with PrimeSense to develop a three-dimensional body-mapping product. The product uses PrimeSense 3D sensors to scan the shapes and curves that make each body unique. The scanner produces a digital replica of each user's size and shape. Customers can try on clothes virtually at a store or in their homes. This scan is then used to provide three services: made-to-measure jeans, body-shape jeans and online virtual try-on.

With made-to-measure jeans, the scan is used to create a pattern for the jeans, which are hand tailored to the exact lines and contours of the customer's body. The jeans are ready in 3 to 6 weeks, at which time the customer has a final fitting with a Bodymetrics tailor.

Based on its experience with made-to-measure jeans, Bodymetrics has identified three body shapes: straight, semi-curvy and curvy. Body-shape jeans are specifically designed to fit these different body shapes. After customers are scanned, a Bodymetrics jeans expert helps them determine their body shapes. Customers can then instantly purchase jeans matching their body shapes off the rack in the store.

The online virtual try-on allows customers who have been scanned to try on jeans virtually on their own bodies without physically trying on jeans in a dressing room. The service creates an *avatar* (a three-dimensional graphical representation), which has an amazing resemblance to the customer. Then, the customer can pick various styles of jeans and 'virtually see' what the jeans look like on her or his avatar.

Sources: Compiled from S Laird (2012), 'Clothes shopping with Bodymetrics lets you try it on for virtual size', *Mashable*, 9 January; 'The first time I had a Bodymetrics scan' (2011), howfayeseesit.wordpress.com, 23 March; L Talbot (2011), 'Bodymetrics: what's your jean shape?', lisatalbot.blogspot.com, 2 February; Asmita (2007), 'Custom-fit jeans with Bodymetrics', www.styleguru.com, 18 January (*Note:* StyleGuru is a promotional blog.); R Young (2007), 'Turning tailoring over to a computer', *International Herald Tribune*, 15 January; www.bodymetrics.com; www.primesense.com.

BEFORE YOU GO ON . . .

1 What are the characteristics of the modern business environment?
2 Discuss some of the pressures that characterise the modern global business environment.
3 Identify some of the organisational responses to these pressures. Are any of these responses specific to a particular pressure? If so, which ones?

E-business and e-commerce

Doing business electronically is an essential strategy for companies that are competing in today's business environment. **Electronic commerce (EC or e-commerce)** describes the process of buying, selling, transferring, or exchanging products, services, or information via computer networks, including the internet. **E-business** is a somewhat broader concept. In addition to the buying and selling of goods and services, e-business also refers to servicing customers, collaborating with business partners and performing electronic transactions within an organisation. (Chapter 9 focuses extensively on this topic. In addition, e-commerce applications appear throughout the book.)

You now have a general overview of the pressures that affect companies in today's business environment and the responses that organisations choose to manage these pressures. To plan for the most effective responses, companies formulate strategies. In the new digital economy, these strategies rely heavily on IT, especially strategic information systems. These topics are examined in the next section.

Apply the Concept

Background

This chapter has described many theories and pointed out that information overload is a very real problem today. The amount of data we can now collect is amazing. Did you know that even your Facebook posts and tweets are data? What about organisational data? Soon mobile commerce will allow companies to store GPS location, demographic data and purchase data to create customer profiles that will provide tonnes of digital data. Businesses will be able to use this in ways that we cannot even imagine today. Companies like IBM, Oracle, SAP and SAS are leading the way into this world by designing software to help manage this data.

Activity

Go to YouTube and search for 'IBM why data matters'.

Deliverable

As a consumer, how do you feel about your own privacy given that businesses collect massive amounts of data on your spending habits? How much is too much? At what point would you like to disconnect? Could you? Do you think that people in general have become too dependent on data? Could businesses go back to operating with less knowledge?

Imagine that you were asked to provide a report about this issue to your local member of parliament explaining the direction we are going and whether it is a good thing or not.

QUESTIONS

THE NOOK

1. How could IT help The Nook comply with legal requirements and social responsibilities surrounding the sale of alcohol?
2. Drinks and music never become obsolete, right? How could The Nook's lack of IT create the environment that makes them appear obsolete?
3. The sheer number of possibilities are creating overload for Malakai and Abbie before they even adopt any specific IT. How can technology be used to help them make a decision about the IT they choose to adopt?

2.2 Competitive advantage and strategic information systems

A *competitive strategy* is a statement that identifies a business's approach to compete, its goals and the plans and policies that will be required to carry out those goals.[24] A strategy, in general, can apply to a desired outcome, such as gaining market share. A competitive strategy focuses on achieving a desired outcome when competitors want to prevent you from reaching your goal. Therefore, when you create a competitive strategy, you must plan your own moves, but you must also anticipate and counter your competitors' moves.

Through its competitive strategy, an organisation seeks a competitive advantage in the industry in which it operates. That is, it seeks to outperform its competitors in a critical measure such as cost, quality, and time-to-market. Competitive advantage helps a company function profitably within its market and generate larger-than-average profits.

Competitive advantage is increasingly important in today's business environment, as you will note throughout the book. In general, the *core business* of companies has remained the same. That is, information technologies simply offer tools that can enhance an organisation's success through its traditional sources of competitive advantage, such as low cost, excellent customer service, and superior supply chain management. **Strategic information systems (SISs)** provide a competitive advantage by helping an organisation to implement its strategic goals and to improve its performance and productivity. Any information system that helps an organisation gain a competitive advantage or reduce a competitive disadvantage, therefore, qualifies as an SIS.

Porter's competitive forces model

The best-known framework for analysing competitiveness is Michael Porter's **competitive forces model**.[25] Companies use Porter's model to develop strategies to increase their competitive edge. Porter's model also demonstrates how IT can make a company more competitive.

Porter's model identifies five major forces that can endanger or enhance a company's position in a given industry. Figure 2.3 highlights these forces. Although the web has changed the nature of competition, Porter's five fundamental forces remain applicable. In fact, what makes these forces so valuable as analytical tools is that they have not changed for centuries. Every competitive organisation, no matter how large or small, or what business it is in, is affected by these forces. This observation applies even to organisations that you might not consider competitive, such as public sector organisations (e.g. local government). Although local governments are not-for-profit enterprises, they compete for businesses to locate in their districts, for funding from higher levels of government, for employees and for many other things.

Significantly, Porter concludes that the *overall* impact of the web is to increase competition, which generally diminishes a firm's profitability.[26] Let's examine Porter's five forces and the ways that the web influences them.

1 ***The threat of entry of new competitors.*** The threat that new competitors will enter your market is high when entry is easy and low when there are significant barriers to entry. An **entry barrier** is a product or service feature that customers have learned to expect from organisations in a certain industry. A competing organisation must offer this feature in order to survive in the marketplace. There are many types of entry barriers. Consider, for example, legal requirements to complete a law degree and complete the practical legal training requirements to practise law in Australia,[27] or a license to serve liquor, where only a certain number of licenses are available.

   Suppose you want to open a petrol station. To compete in that industry, you would have to offer pay-at-the-pump service to your customers. Pay-at-the-pump is an IT-based barrier to entering this market because you must offer it for free. The first petrol station that offered this service gained first-move advantage and established barriers to entry. This advantage did not last, however, because competitors quickly offered the same service and thus overcame the entry barrier.

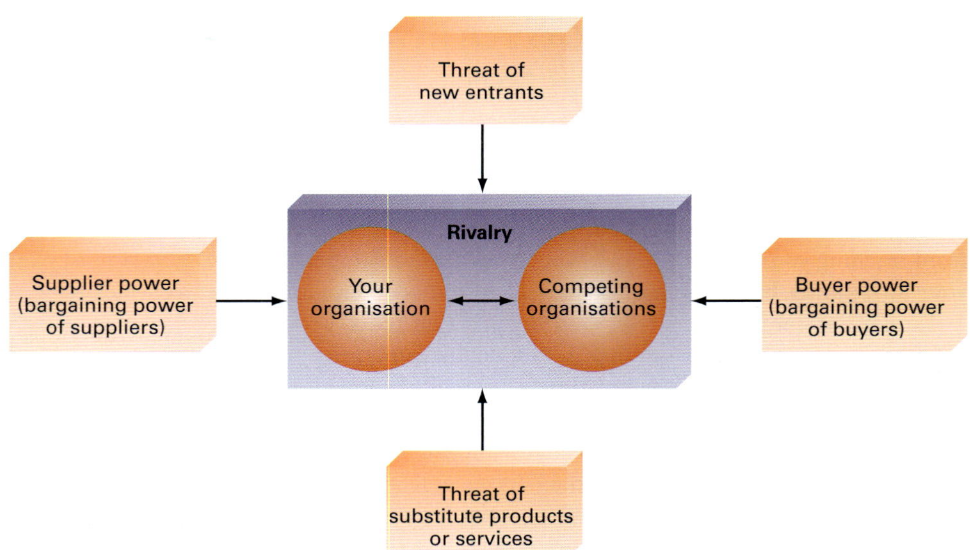

FIGURE 2.3 Porter's competitive forces model.

For most firms, the web *increases* the threat that new competitors will enter the market because it sharply reduces traditional barriers to entry, such as the need for a sales force or a physical storefront. Today, competitors frequently need only to set up a website. This threat of increased competition is particularly acute in industries that perform an *intermediation role*, which is a link between buyers and sellers (for example, stock brokers and travel agents), as well as in industries where the primary product or service is digital (for example, the music industry). In addition, the geographical reach of the web enables distant competitors to compete more directly with an existing firm.

In some cases the web increases barriers to entry. This scenario occurs primarily when customers have come to expect a nontrivial capability from their suppliers. For example, the first company to offer web-based package tracking gained a competitive advantage from that service. Competitors were forced to follow.

2 ***The bargaining power of suppliers.*** Supplier power is high when buyers have few choices from whom to buy and low when buyers have many choices. Therefore, organisations would rather have more potential suppliers so they will be in a stronger position to negotiate price, quality and delivery terms.

The internet's impact on suppliers is mixed. On the one hand, it enables buyers to find alternative suppliers and to compare prices more easily, thereby reducing the supplier's bargaining power. On the other hand, as companies use the internet to integrate their supply chains, participating suppliers prosper by locking in customers.

3 ***The bargaining power of customers (buyers).*** Buyer power is high when buyers have many choices from whom to buy and low when buyers have few choices. For example, in the past, there were few locations where students could purchase textbooks (typically, one or two campus bookstores). In this situation, students had low buyer power. Today, the web provides students with access to a multitude of potential suppliers as well as detailed information about textbooks. As a result, student buyer power has increased dramatically.

In contrast, *loyalty programs* reduce buyer power. As their name suggests, loyalty programs reward customers based on the amount of business they conduct with a particular organisation (e.g. airlines, hotels and rental car companies). IT enables companies to track the activities and accounts of millions of customers, thereby reducing buyer power. That is, customers who receive rewards from loyalty programs are less likely to do business with competitors. (Loyalty programs are associated with customer relationship management, which you will study in chapter 12.)

4 ***The threat of substitute products or services.*** If there are many alternatives to an organisation's products or services, then the threat of substitutes is high. If there are few alternatives, then the threat is low. Today, new technologies create substitute products very rapidly. For example, customers today can purchase wireless telephones instead of landline telephones, internet music services instead of traditional CDs and LPG instead of petrol in cars.

Information-based industries experience the greatest threat from substitutes. Any industry in which digitised information can replace material goods (e.g. music, books and software) must view the internet as a threat because the internet can convey this information efficiently and at low cost and high quality.

Even when there are many substitutes for their products, however, companies can create a competitive advantage by increasing switching costs. *Switching costs* are the costs, in money and time, of a decision to buy elsewhere. For example, contracts with smart phone providers typically include a substantial penalty for switching to another provider until the term of the contract expires (quite often, two years or eighteen months). This switching cost is financial in nature.

As another example, when you buy products from Amazon, the company develops a profile of your shopping habits and recommends products targeted to your preferences. If you switch to another online vendor, it will take time for that company to develop a profile of your wants and needs. In this case, the switching cost involves time rather than money.

5 ***The rivalry among existing firms in the industry.*** The threat from rivalry is high when there is intense competition among many firms in an industry. The threat is low when the competition is among fewer firms and is not as intense.

In the past, proprietary information systems — systems that belong exclusively to a single organisation — have provided strategic advantage to firms in highly competitive industries. Today, however, the visibility of internet applications on the web makes proprietary systems more difficult to keep secret. In simple terms, when a businessperson sees a competitor's new system online, he or she will rapidly match its features in order to remain competitive. The result is fewer differences among competitors, which leads to more intense competition in an industry.

To understand this concept, consider the highly competitive grocery industry, where Coles and Woolworths and other companies compete essentially on price. Some of these companies have IT-enabled loyalty programs in which customers can receive rewards and the store gains valuable business intelligence on customers' buying preferences. Stores use this business intelligence in their marketing and promotional campaigns. (You will learn about business intelligence in chapter 5.)

According to Mark Coombes, Cotton On's marketing manager, Cotton On, an Australian fashion clothing retailer targeting teenagers to young adults, has implemented RFID technology in its store in the Brisbane suburb of Carindale in an attempt to offer customers a 'mini gig' experience while they are trying on clothing in fitting rooms. Cotton On customers trying on clothing in the Carindale store can listen to music specifically selected to suit the style of a particular garment selected by the customer which is automatically triggered by the RFID tags placed in these garments.[28] Cotton On is therefore using IT to enhance overall customer experience while shopping at its stores with the hope that they will return.

Competition is also being affected by the extremely low variable cost of digital products. That is, once a digital product has been developed, the cost of producing additional 'units' approaches zero. Consider the music industry as an example. When artists record music, their songs are captured in digital format. Producing physical products, such as CDs or DVDs, with the songs on them for sale in music stores involves costs. The costs in a physical distribution channel are much higher than the costs involved in delivering the songs over the internet in digital form.

In fact, in the future companies might give away some products for free. For example, some analysts predict that commissions for online stock trading will approach zero because investors can access the necessary information via the internet to make their own decisions regarding buying and selling stocks. At that point, consumers will no longer need brokers to give them information that they can obtain themselves, virtually for free.

Porter's value chain model

Organisations use the Porter competitive forces model to design general strategies. To identify specific activities in which they can use competitive strategies for greatest impact, they use Porter's **value chain model** (1985). The value chain model also identifies points where an organisation can use IT to achieve competitive advantage (see figure 2.4).

According to Porter's value chain model, the activities conducted in any organisation can be divided into two categories: primary activities and support activities. **Primary activities** relate to the production and distribution of the firm's products and services. These activities create value for which customers are willing to pay. Next, you are going to learn about the value chain of a manufacturing company. Keep in mind that other types of firms, such as transportation, health care, education and retail, have different value chains. The key point is that every organisation has a value chain: a sequence of activities through which the organisation's inputs, whatever they are, are transformed into more valuable outputs, whatever they are.

In a manufacturing company, for example, primary activities involve purchasing materials, processing the materials into products and delivering the products to customers. Companies typically perform five primary activities:

- inbound logistics (inputs)
- operations (manufacturing and testing)
- outbound logistics (storage and distribution)
- marketing and sales
- services.

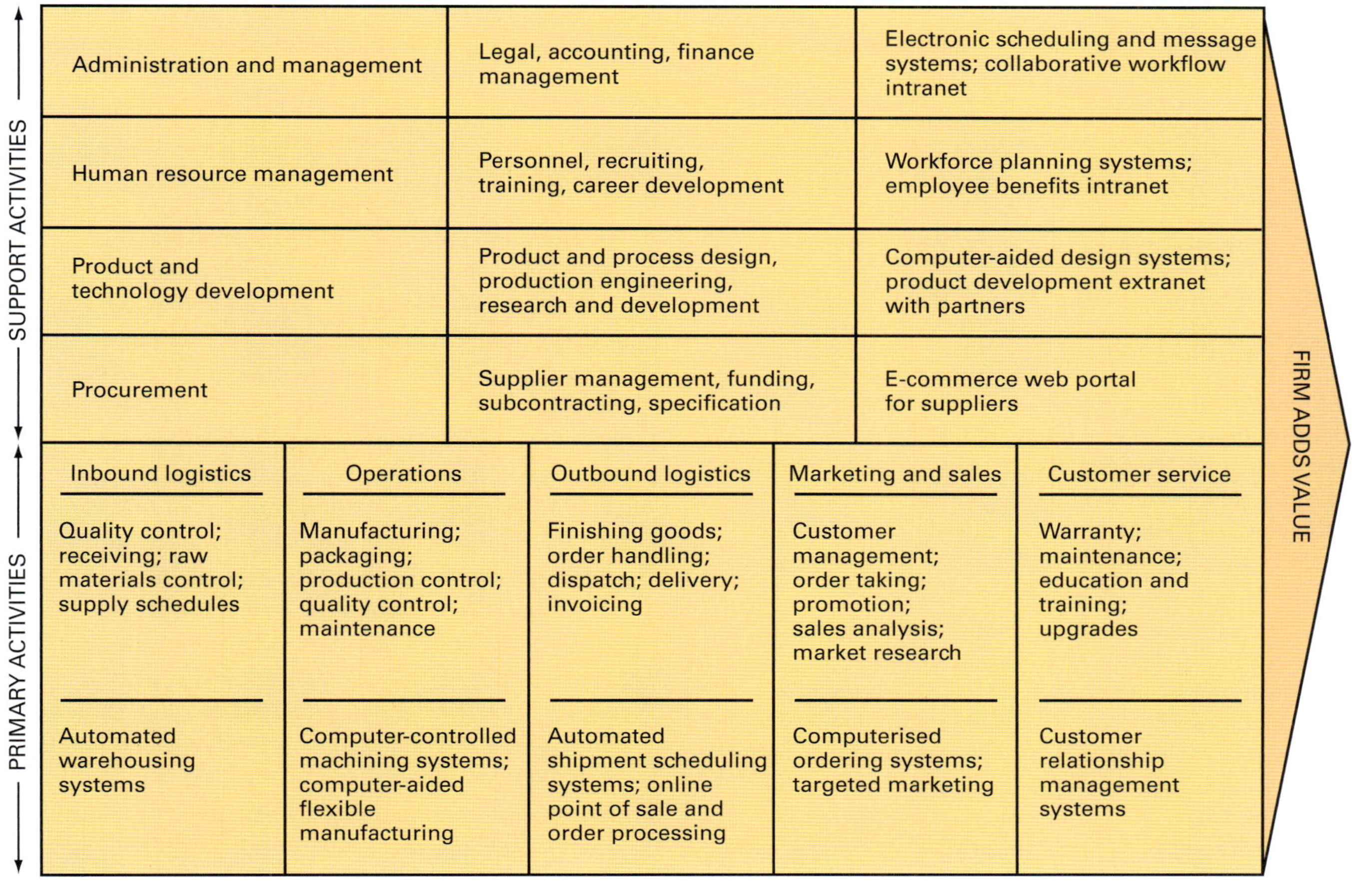

FIGURE 2.4 Porter's value chain model.

Primary activities usually take place in a sequence from 1 to 5. As work progresses in the sequence, value is added to the product in each activity. Specifically, the following steps occur.

1 The incoming materials are processed (in receiving, storage, and so on) in activities called inbound logistics.
2 The materials are used in operations, where value is added by turning raw materials into products.
3 These products are prepared for delivery (packaging, storing and shipping) in the outbound logistics activities.
4 Marketing and sales sell the products to customers, increasing product value by creating demand for the company's products.
5 Finally, the company performs after-sales service, such as warranty service or upgrade notification, for the customer, adding further value.

The primary activities are buttressed by **support activities**. Unlike primary activities, support activities do not add value directly to the firm's products or services. Rather, as their name suggests, they contribute to the firm's competitive advantage by supporting the primary activities. Support activities consist of the following:

1 the firm's infrastructure (accounting, finance, management)
2 human resources management
3 product and technology development (R & D)
4 procurement.

Each support activity can be applied to any or all of the primary activities. In addition, the support activities can also support one another.

A firm's value chain is part of a larger stream of activities, which Porter calls a value system. A **value system**, or an *industry value chain*, includes the suppliers that provide the inputs necessary to the firm along with their value chains. After the firm creates products, these products pass through the value chains of distributors (which also have their own value chains), all the way to the customers. All parts of these chains are included in the value system. To achieve and sustain a competitive advantage, and to support that advantage with information technologies, a firm must understand every component of this value system.

IT'S ABOUT BUSINESS

Rewards and recognition to increase user adoption and engagement

IBM award-winning Premier Business Partner ISW delivers innovative and intelligent business technology solutions to its clients across a wide range of industries. ISW is a small Australian company committed to achieving excellence in the design, development, implementation, training and support of IT software and services.

ISW has performed many implementations of IBM Connections, a social software platform that provides organisations of all sizes with a web 2.0 collaborative work environment. However, during implementation it was observed that despite the obvious business benefits of the solution, many employees continued to work around it. This lack of uptake was a problem for ISW given that a significant factor in organisations deriving business value from IBM Connections was ensuring strong user adoption and helping users understand why they should leverage social software to work better.

ISW solved this problem through the introduction of Kudos Badges, which is a flexible gamification engine that incorporates achievements, rewards and recognition, rank and leader boards, and missions. This solution both increased user engagement with IBM Connections and helped guide users on how they can improve their usage of it.

Adam Brown, Director of Technology and Business Development for ISW, indicates that Kudos Badges was designed with the following goals in mind.

1 Leverage Gamification to drive user participation and adoption of IBM Connections.

We wanted to reward users that contribute valuable content ... to provide users with status and recognition as a direct result of not only their actions in Connections but also the actions of others around the content that they create. For example, ... you create a blog post in Connections: that is great! You earn a Kudos Point. However if a heap of people comment on that blog post, or recommend the blog post, then that content you created has higher value, and hence you might receive 5 or 10 Kudos Points.

2 Leverage Game Mechanics to guide users towards using the more advanced features of IBM Connections.

We often find with our Connections clients that users focus on one or two particular areas. Through Kudos Badges we wanted to expand their understanding of both the business value of using Connections, but also guide them to use more advanced features of Connections. When users 'win' rewards such as badges, these badges are designed to not only recognise the good work a person has done, but also to show them the business value of what they have done and to encourage them to expand their usage of Connections with more advanced features. For example, when you complete an activity you might receive an 'Activity Done!' badge. This is neat of course, however the message that accompanies the badge might then encourage you to consider creating an Activity Template.

3 Ensuring that Kudos Badges was both customisable as well as extensible.

We know that every organisation is different and that the Kudos Point value of some Connections actions would be different for different organisations and business objectives, so we allow clients to build their own badges and rewards that drive users to deliver on their business objectives or goals. We made Kudos Badges extensible so that organisations can leverage it to drive behaviour in other applications, so it allows organisations to integrate external applications such as their Sales Force Automation, CRMs, HR Systems, etc.

The overwhelming response to *Kudos Badges* from clients of ISW has been positive: they quickly understand how gamification can help them drive adoption of IBM Connections and ultimately increase the business value from it.

Source: Kristy de Salas and Ben Geelan, University of Tasmania.

QUESTIONS

1 How does ISW seek to develop and maintain engagement through the Kudos Badge gamification solution?

2 Does gamification suit all businesses? Discuss the elements of organisational culture that might facilitate the adoption and use of gamification. What elements might inhibit it?

Strategies for competitive advantage

Organisations continually try to develop strategies to counter the five competitive forces identified by Porter. You will learn about five of those strategies here. Before we go into specifics, however, it is important to note that an organisation's choice of strategy involves trade-offs. For example, a firm that concentrates only on cost leadership might not have the resources available for research and development, leaving the firm unable to innovate. As another example, a company that invests in customer happiness (customer-orientation strategy) will experience increased costs.

Companies must select a strategy and then stay with it, because a confused strategy cannot succeed. This selection, in turn, decides how a company will utilise its information systems. A new information system that can improve customer service but will increase costs slightly will be welcomed at a high-end retailer such as David Jones but not at a discount store like the Reject Shop or Cheap As Chips. You learn about the most commonly used strategies in the following paragraphs. Figure 2.5 provides an overview of these strategies.

1 ***Cost leadership strategy.*** Produce products and/or services at the lowest cost in the industry. An example is Super Cheap Auto's (**www.supercheapauto.com.au**) automatic inventory replenishment system, which enables Super Cheap Auto to reduce inventory storage requirements. As a result, Super Cheap Auto stores have improved inventory management and realised significant savings in inventory costs.[29]
2 ***Differentiation strategy.*** Offer products, services, or product features that are different from those of your competitor. Jetstar, for example, has differentiated itself as a low-cost airline that has a close relationship with Qantas, which is important to Jetstar as Qantas has an excellent reputation for safety. At least in part, this has proved to be a winning strategy for competing in the highly competitive airline industry. Also, Dell has differentiated itself in the personal computer market through its mass-customisation strategy.
3 ***Innovation strategy.*** Introduce new products and services, add new features to existing products and services, or develop new ways to produce them. A classic example is the introduction of automated teller machines (ATMs) in 1977 in Australia by the Queensland Teachers' Credit Union (QTCU),[30] known since 2011 as the QT Mutual Bank Limited.[31] The convenience and cost-cutting features of this innovation gave QTCU/ QT Mutual Bank Ltd an advantage over its competitors. Like many innovative products, the ATM changed the nature of competition in the banking industry. Today an ATM is a competitive *necessity* for any bank.
4 ***Operational effectiveness strategy.*** Improve the manner in which internal **business processes** are executed so that a firm performs these activities better than its rivals. Such improvements increase quality, productivity, and employee and customer satisfaction while decreasing time to market.
5 ***Customer-orientation strategy.*** Concentrate on making customers happy. Web-based systems are particularly effective in this area because they can provide a personalised, one-to-one relationship with each customer.

BEFORE YOU GO ON . . .

1 What are strategic information systems?
2 According to Porter, what are the five forces that could endanger a firm's position in its industry or marketplaces?
3 Describe Porter's value chain model. Differentiate Porter's competitive forces model and his value chain model.
4 What strategies can companies use to gain competitive advantage?

FIGURE 2.5 Strategies for competitive advantage.

Apply the Concept

Background

This section has exposed you to Porter's five forces model. This demonstrates the ways that different things influence an organisation. The threat of entry of new competitors, bargaining power of suppliers, bargaining power of customers, threat of substitute products or services, and rivalry among existing firms in the industry all have an impact on the outcome of the organisation and its ultimate success. Based on this strategic model, there are five strategies presented for competitive advantage: cost leadership, differentiation, innovation, operational effectiveness and customer orientation.

Aldi (**www.aldi.com.au**) is a German-based supermarket chain that began its operations in Australia in 2001. Since then, Aldi has established and operates over 300 stores in New South Wales, Victoria, Queensland and the Australian Capital Territory.[32] Aldi focuses on a cost-leadership strategy[33] that is also reflected in its mission statement: 'Our philosophy still stands. All people, wherever they live, should have the opportunity to buy everyday groceries of the highest quality at the lowest possible price'.[34] Aldi is now an established player in the supermarket industry with over 1 million customers weekly and sales revenues understood to be approximately $5 billion.[35] Go back and review the ways Aldi uses the five forces (or controls them) so that they maintain their position as a cost leader.

Activity

Visit your favourite restaurant and ask to speak to the manager. In just a few questions, see if the manager has a grasp of the five forces model. Do not ask anything about Porter, but ask about rivals, substitutes, bargaining power of customers, supplier power, etc. A good manager should be familiar with these concepts whether he or she uses the term *Porter's five forces* or not. Finally, ask what strategy the manager uses and see if you can classify it as a cost leadership, differentiation, innovation, operational effectiveness and customer orientation strategy.

Deliverable

After your meal is over, write a summary that answers the following questions: Does the manager understand all of the forces that impact the business? Are there some forces that the manager needs a better understanding of? Do you see any additional forces at play here? What did you determine the manager's strategy to be?

THE NOOK

QUESTIONS

1. In suburbs with a high concentration of student housing, how strong is the threat of substitute entertainment?
2. Malakai and Abbie's vision for The Nook is to create a relaxing, community atmosphere. Which strategy do you think best suits their desire — cost leader, differentiator, innovator, operational effectiveness, or customer orientation?
3. Which is more powerful for The Nook? The bargaining power of suppliers or the bargaining power of customers?

2.3 Business–IT alignment

The 'holy grail' of organisations is business–IT alignment, or strategic alignment. **Business–IT alignment** (which we will call 'alignment') is the tight integration of the IT function with the strategy, mission and goals of the organisation. That is, the IT function directly supports the business objectives of the organisation. There are six characteristics of excellent alignment.

- Organisations view IT as an engine of innovation that continually transforms the business, often creating new revenue streams.
- Organisations view their internal and external customers and their customer service function as supremely important.
- Organisations rotate business and IT professionals across departments and job functions.
- Organisations provide overarching goals that are completely clear to each IT and business employee.
- Organisations ensure that IT employees understand how the company makes (or loses) money.
- Organisations create a vibrant and inclusive company culture.

Unfortunately, many organisations fail to achieve this type of close alignment. In fact, according to a McKinsey & Company survey on IT strategy and spending, only 16 per cent of the IT and business executives who participated agreed that their organisation had adequate alignment between IT and the business.[36] Given the importance of alignment, why do so many organisations fail to implement this policy? The major reasons are as follows.

- Business managers and IT managers have different objectives.
- The business and IT departments are ignorant of each other's expertise.
- Communication is lacking.

Put simply, business executives know little about IT and IT executives understand the technology but do not understand the real needs of the business.

BEFORE YOU GO ON . . .

1 What is alignment?
2 Give examples of alignment regarding student systems at your university. (*Hint:* What are the 'business' goals of your university with regard to student registration, fee payment, grade posting, etc.?)

Apply the Concept

Background

As this section has illustrated, corporate strategy and IT strategy must be tightly aligned. For example, if a manager determines that better inventory management is needed, he or she does not necessarily need to go looking for a new point-of-sale system. The manager needs to look for an inventory management system. If you operate in a manufacturing industry, you do not need to implement an electronic health records (EHR) system. Although those are simple examples when you are making these decisions, it becomes imperative that you are very familiar with corporate strategy and available technology to make sure they match up.

Visit **garmin.com.au** and consider the many options Garmin offers for GPS devices. There are product options that are designed for pilots, cars, motorcycles, hikers, anglers and more. If this is all the same technology (GPS), then why can't the company just build one device and sell it to everyone? It is simply because the way the company needs the product to work and the information that the customer needs from it is different depending on what the customer plans to do with it. Although this may be a simple answer, it brings out an important point. Business applications of technology are much the same. Implemented IT must align with business need or it will only be 'pretty' technology with no real purpose.

Activity

SAP is a global enterprise resource planning (ERP) software provider. Visit **sap.com** and have a look at the various industries and solutions that the company offers. Specifically, choose three industries to review. Look for similarities and differences.

Deliverable

Write a small summary for your tutorial group detailing how this single company provides so many solutions based on its single platform. Be sure to bring IT alignment into your thoughts for your summary.

THE NOOK

QUESTIONS

1 It seems like The Nook is in a good position to create strategic IT alignment since the club can build its IT from the ground up to support its strategy. Do you think it is better to build from scratch, or is it better to have an existing system that you are just updating?

2 How do you think IT alignment could play a role in creating the desired atmosphere for The Nook?

WHAT'S IN IT FOR ME?

FOR ALL MAJORS

All of the functional areas of any organisation are literally composed of a variety of business processes. Regardless of your major, you will be involved in a variety of business processes from your first day on the job. Some of these processes you will perform by yourself, some will involve only your group or department and others will involve several (or all) of the organisation's functional areas.

It is important for you to be able to visualise processes, understand the inputs and outputs of each process and identify the 'customer' of each process. These capabilities will enable you to make the organisation's business processes more efficient and effective. This task generally involves incorporating IT in the process. It is also important for you to appreciate how each process fits into your organisation's strategy.

All functional areas in any organisation must work together in an integrated fashion in order for the firm to respond adequately to business pressures. These responses typically require each functional area to utilise a variety of information systems. In today's competitive global marketplace, the timeliness and accuracy of these responses is even more critical.

Closely following this discussion, all functional areas must work together for the organisation to gain competitive advantage in its marketplace. Again, the functional areas use a variety of strategic information systems to achieve this goal.

You have seen why companies must be concerned with strategic advantage. However, this chapter is particularly important for you for several reasons. First, the business pressures you have learned about affect your organisation, but they also affect you as an individual. Thus, it is critical that you understand how information systems can help you, and eventually your organisations, respond to these pressures.

In addition, achieving competitive advantage is essential for your organisation's survival. In many cases, you, your team and all your colleagues will be responsible for creating a competitive advantage. Therefore, having general knowledge about strategy and about how information systems impact the organisation's strategy and competitive position will help you in your career.

You also need a basic knowledge of your organisation's strategy, mission and goals, as well as its business problems and how it makes (or loses) money. You now know how to analyse your organisation's strategy and value chain, as well as the strategies and value chains of your competitors. You have also acquired a general knowledge of how IT contributes to organisational strategy. This knowledge will help you to do your job better, to be promoted more quickly and to contribute significantly to the success of your organisation.

SUMMARY

1 Identify effective IT responses to different kinds of business pressures.

> *Market pressures:* An example of a market pressure is powerful customers. Customer relationship management systems are an effective IT response that helps companies achieve customer intimacy.

> *Technology pressures:* An example of a technology pressure is information overload. Search engines and business intelligence applications enable managers to access, navigate and utilise vast amounts of information.

> *Societal/political/legal pressures:* An example of a societal/political/legal pressure is social responsibility, such as the state of the physical environment. Green IT is one response that is intended to improve the environment.

2 Describe the strategies that organisations typically adopt to counter Porter's five competitive forces.

Porter's five competitive forces are:

> *the threat of entry of new competitors*

> *the bargaining power of suppliers*

> *the bargaining power of customers (buyers)*

> *the threat of substitute products or services*

> *the rivalry among existing firms in the industry.*

Organisations typically use five strategies to combat Porter's five competitive forces and achieve a competitive advantage.

> *Cost leadership strategy*: Produce products and/or services at the lowest cost in the industry.

> *Differentiation strategy*: Offer different products, services, or product features.

> *Innovation strategy*: Introduce new products and services, put new features in existing products and services, or develop new ways to produce them.

> *Operational effectiveness strategy*: Improve the manner in which internal business processes are executed so that a firm performs similar activities better than its rivals.

> *Customer-orientation strategy*: Concentrate on making customers happy.

Keep in mind that organisations may use more than one strategy to combat each competitive force. For example, to raise barriers to entry for a competitor, an organisation might adopt all five of these strategies to make it more difficult for a potential competitor to enter a market.

3 Describe the characteristics of effective business—IT alignment.

Alignment is the tight integration of the IT function with the strategy, mission and goals of the organisation. There are six characteristics of effective alignment.

> Organisations view IT as an engine of innovation that continually transforms the business.

> Organisations view customers and customer service as supremely important.

> Organisations rotate business and IT professionals across departments and job functions.

> Organisations provide clear, overarching goals for all employees.

> Organisations ensure that IT employees understand how the company makes (or loses) money.

> Organisations create a vibrant and inclusive company culture.

>>> CHAPTER GLOSSARY

business environment The combination of social, legal, economic, physical and political factors in which businesses conduct their operations.

business–IT alignment The tight integration of the IT function with the strategy, mission and goals of the organisation.

business processes Related activities that produce a product or a service of value to the organisation, its business partners and/or its customers.

competitive advantage An advantage over competitors in some measure such as cost, quality, or speed; leads to control of a market and to larger-than-average profits.

competitive forces model A business framework devised by Michael Porter that analyses competitiveness by recognising five major forces that could endanger a company's position.

digital divide The gap between those who have access to information and communications technology and those who do not.

e-business Buying and selling of goods and services as well as servicing customers, collaborating with business partners and performing electronic transactions within an organisation.

electronic commerce (EC or e-commerce) The process of buying, selling, transferring, or exchanging products, services, or information via computer networks, including the internet.

entry barrier Product or service feature that customers expect from organisations in a certain industry; an organisation trying to enter this market must provide this product or service at a minimum to be able to compete.

globalisation The integration and interdependence of economic, social, cultural and ecological facets of life, enabled by rapid advances in information technology.

individual social responsibility See organisational social responsibility.

make-to-order The strategy of producing customised products and services.

mass customisation A production process in which items are produced in large quantities but are customised to fit the desires of each customer.

organisational social responsibility (also called individual social responsibility) Efforts by organisations to solve various social problems.

primary activities Business activities related to the production and distribution of the firm's products and services, thus creating value.

strategic information systems (SISs) Systems that help an organisation gain a competitive advantage by supporting its strategic goals and/or increasing performance and productivity.

support activities Business activities that do not add value directly to a firm's product or service under consideration but support the primary activities that do add value.

value chain model Model that shows the primary activities that sequentially add value to the profit margin; also shows the support activities.

value system Includes the producers, suppliers, distributors, and buyers, all with their value chains.

>>> DISCUSSION QUESTIONS

1 Explain why IT is both a business pressure and an enabler of response activities that counter business pressures.
2 What does a flat world mean to you in your choice of a major? In your choice of a career? Will you have to be a lifelong learner? Why or why not?
3 What might the impact of a flat world be on your standard of living?
4 Is IT a strategic weapon or a survival tool? Discuss.
5 Why might it be difficult to justify a strategic information system?
6 Describe the five forces in Porter's competitive forces model and explain how the internet has affected each one.
7 Describe Porter's value chain model. What is the relationship between the competitive forces model and the value chain model?
8 Discuss the idea that an information system by itself can rarely provide a sustainable competitive advantage.

>>> PROBLEM-SOLVING ACTIVITIES

1 Surf the internet for information about the Australian Security Intelligence Organisation (www.asio.gov.au) or the Department of Defence (www.defence.gov.au). Examine the available information and comment on the role of information technologies in the department.
2 Experience customisation by designing your own shoes at www.nike.com, your car at www.jaguar.com, your CD at www.easternrecording.com, your business card at www.iprint.com, and your diamond ring at www.bluenile.com. Summarise your experiences.
3 Access www.go4customer.com. What does this company do and where is it located? Who are its customers? Which of Friedman's flatteners does this company fit? Provide examples of how an Australian company would use its services.
4 Enter Harvey Norman Malaysia (www.harveynorman.com.my). How does Harvey Norman Malaysia differ from your local Harvey Norman (consider products, prices, services, etc.)? Describe these differences.
5 Apply Porter's value chain model to Big W (www.bigw.com.au). What is Big W's competitive strategy? Who are Big W's major competitors? Describe Big W's business model. Describe the tasks that Big W must accomplish for each primary value chain activity. How would Big W's information systems contribute to Big W's competitive strategy, given the nature of its business?
6 Apply Porter's value chain model to Dell (www.dell.com.au). What is Dell's competitive strategy? Who are Dell's major competitors? Describe Dell's business model. Describe the tasks that Dell must accomplish for each primary value chain activity. How would Dell's information systems contribute to Costco's competitive strategy, given the nature of its business?
7 The market for optical copiers is shrinking rapidly. As documents are duplicated increasingly on computer printers, can a company such as Xerox Corporation survive?
   a Read about the problems and solutions of Xerox from 2000 to 2013 at www.fortune.com, www.findarticles.com and www.google.com.
   b Identify all the business pressures on Xerox.
   c Find some of Xerox's response strategies (see www.xerox.com, www.yahoo.com and www.google.com).
   d Identify the role of IT as a contributor to the business technology pressures (e.g. obsolescence).
   e Identify the role of IT as a facilitator of Xerox's critical response activities.

>>> COLLABORATION EXERCISE

Background

Imagine that you work for a company based in Perth, Western Australia. Recent significant growth on the west coast has made it necessary to open an office there. Because of the time lost in travelling across the country, it has been decided that web meetings will suffice for 95 per cent of the meetings that take place.

You and a few colleagues from other departments are given the job of determining which platform would be the best to support your company's upcoming web meetings. There are many companies (Adobe Connect, Webex, Fuze Meeting, etc.) that offer web-casting type technologies, but each vary in some ways. Obviously, they offer different price packages, but is the one with the lowest cost the best option?

Activity

Work with a team of classmates who are majoring in other areas to determine which online tool will serve the purposes your company has requested. Based on your experiences, what tools will be needed for meetings that each area may have? Are the meeting requirements from Accounting different from HR? What about Finance and Operations?

To accomplish your task, create a new Google document (this will require a Gmail account) and share it with your team members. Be sure that everyone is online at the same time and working together to determine which webcasting solution is the best to meet the needs of your company. Be creative in your document with the use of tables or colours or something to help your reader see how the solution you have chosen fits the criteria requested by your company.

Deliverable

You will now need to submit your work. At the bottom of your report that shows which webcasting solution you have chosen, write a short paragraph explaining how you think this particular online meeting program will support your company. Export the Google Document you created to a pdf and submit this however your instructor has required. Be sure to include all the names of group members and the role that each played (which department they represented).

CLOSING CASE **1** >

The information technology behind the Asia–Pacific's largest low-cost airline

THE BUSINESS PROBLEM

Established in 2004 and headquartered in Melbourne, Australia, Jetstar Airways is one of Australia's value-based low-cost airlines and is wholly owned by the Qantas Group. With Jetstar the Qantas Group has established a two-brand strategy, with Qantas Airways servicing the premium full-service market and Jetstar servicing the low-cost market. This is the Qantas response to the threat posed by the launch of Virgin Australia in 2000, another low-cost airline that operates in Australia. Since its launch Jetstar has become the largest low-cost airline in the Asia–Pacific region. With over 100 aircraft servicing 62 destinations, Jetstar has flown over 100 million passengers, 20 per cent of whom were flown in 2012. Currently Jetstar employs over 7000 employees, a substantial increase from the 400 it employed when it commenced its operations. Much of this growth has come from Jetstar's international expansion, which entailed ensuring that Jetstar's team working and communication culture was maintained. Communication was also imperative for ensuring international collaboration as Jetstar refocused its business from just servicing domestic Australian routes to servicing international routes in the Asia–Pacific region as well as running operations effectively and efficiently from multiple locations internationally. In order to facilitate international communication and collaboration Jetstar employees needed access to resilient and ubiquitous IT that would enable them to make low-cost calls, videoconferencing and easy document-sharing.

THE IT SOLUTION

The Microsoft Lync Server, a solution which Jetstar deployed in its Tokyo and Hong Kong offices, offered its employees local phone numbers without having to invest in expensive organisational phone systems (e.g. private branch exchange or PBX). This solution enabled dynamic multi-party video-conferencing features that enhanced collaboration amongst the Jetstar teams internationally using both desktops and mobile devices. Integrating Microsoft Lync with Microsoft Office application enabled Jetstar employees to easily share corporate documents.

THE RESULTS

Using this 'top-grade communication technology' as a solution has enabled Jetstar to achieve numerous benefits. First, it provided seamless international collaboration. Jetstar's Chief Information Officer (CIO), Stephen Tame, argues that while the Jetstar IT, finance and operations are located in and operate from five countries, they have been able to operate single unified centres of excellence, which to a large extent is attributed to the collaborative environment offered by the adopted solution. Second, it offered enhanced mobility. Both Jetstar executives and cabin crew employees can connect easily with the Jetstar contact centre ubiquitously; that is, anytime, anywhere. Third, it has provided resilience. As the Jetstar communications infrastructure operates from distributed data centres, business resilience has increased. In fact, the Jetstar CIO is quoted to have said that, 'If our head office became inoperable, we could relocate our core operations within a matter of hours. . . . This is because each person's contact point is whatever device they are working from.'

Sources: 'Our company', Jetstar website, www.jetstar.com/au/en/about-us/our-company; 'QANTAS: The Australian flag carrier undergoes a metamorphosis as it attains 90 years of operations', Airline Leader website, www.airlineleader.com/airline-of-the-month/qantas; Microsoft (2013), 'Jetstar takes off in Asia with network-based telephony and multi-party desktop video', *Microsoft case studies*, www.microsoft.com/casestudies/Microsoft-Lync-Server-2010/The-Jetstar-Group/Jetstar-Takes-off-in-Asia-with-Network-based-Telephony-and-Multiparty-Desktop-Video/710000003029; R LeMay (2010), 'Jetstar jumps on Microsoft's Lync', *ZD Net*, 18 November, www.zdnet.com/jetstar-jumps-on-microsofts-lync-1339307354/; L Banks (2010), 'Jetstar upgrades unified communications platform', *CIO*, 18 November, www.cio.com.au/article/368501/jetstar_upgrades_unified_communications_platform; R Crozier (2010), 'Jetstar adopts Microsoft Lync', *iTnews*, 18 November, www.itnews.com.au/News/238950,jetstar-adopts-microsoft-lync.aspx.

QUESTIONS

1 Provide two specific examples of why it was so important for Jetstar to adopt an information and communication technology such as Microsoft Lync.

2 Provide two specific benefits that companies like Jetstar can experience by using information and communication technologies.

CLOSING CASE **2 >**

A tool to combat terrorism and fight crime

THE PROBLEM

In the months leading up to the terrorist attacks of 11 September 2001 the US government had all the necessary clues to stop al Qaeda perpetrators. The perpetrators were from countries known to harbour terrorists, they entered the United States on temporary visas, they had trained to fly civilian airliners and they purchased one-way aeroplane tickets on 11 September.

Unfortunately for the workers in the World Trade Center, those clues were located in different databases across many government agencies. An organisation like the CIA or FBI has thousands of different databases, each with its own data: financial records, DNA samples, voice and other sound samples, video clips, maps, floor plans, human intelligence reports from all over the world and many other types of data. Integrating all that data into a coherent whole is extremely difficult. At that time, there was no tool available that enabled government analysts to integrate different types of data located in so many different places.

THE IT SOLUTION

The origins of Palantir go back to PayPal. Because PayPal was so successful, it attracted criminals who used it to enable money laundering and fraud. By 2000, it was in financial trouble because the antifraud software tools of the time could not keep up with the criminal activity. Each time PayPal analysts caught onto one ploy, the perpetrators changed tactics.

To deal with these issues, PayPal's analysts built software that could view each transaction as a part of a pattern, rather than as just an entry in a database. This process enabled analysts to spot networks of suspicious accounts and discover patterns missed by the computers. PayPal was then able to freeze suspicious payments before they were processed. The software saved the company hundreds of millions of dollars.

After Ebay acquired PayPal in 2002, PayPal engineers decided to turn PayPal's fraud detection tool into a data analysis system that integrated pattern recognition, artificial intelligence software and human skills. Palantir (www.palantir.com) was named for the 'seeing stones' in the *Lord of the Rings* and was initially developed as a software tool employed by the US intelligence community in the war on terrorism. Palantir technology essentially solves intelligence problems that allowed September 11 to take place. That is, Palantir helps law enforcement agencies spot patterns in the huge amounts of data they must analyse every day. Palantir software combs through all available databases, identifies related pieces of information and integrates everything in one place.

THE RESULTS

Palantir has a customer list that includes the US Department of Defense, the CIA, the FBI, the Army, the Marines, the Air Force, the police departments of New York and Los Angeles, and an increasing number of financial institutions with an interest in detecting bank fraud. Most of Palantir's government work remains classified, but information on some cases has leaked out. In April 2010, security researchers in Canada used Palantir software to crack a spy operation called the

Shadow Network that had, among other things, broken into the Indian Defense Ministry and infiltrated the Dalai Lama's email account. Palantir has also been used to unravel child abuse and abduction cases, to find suspects for the murder of a US Immigration and Customs Enforcement special agent, and to uncover bombing networks in Syria, Afghanistan and Pakistan.

In Afghanistan, the US Special Operations Forces use Palantir to plan assaults. They type a village's name into the system and a map of the village appears, detailing the locations of all reported shooting skirmishes and improvised explosive device (IED) incidents. Using the timeline function, the soldiers can see where the most recent attacks occurred and plot their mission in the village accordingly.

Another good example of Palantir's usefulness comes from the US Marines. They used to spend years gathering fingerprint and DNA evidence from IEDs and trying to match that data against a database of similar information collected from villagers. Usually, by the time they obtained any results, the bombers had disappeared. In contrast, field operatives can now upload fingerprint/DNA evidence from villagers into Palantir and instantly find matches from past attacks.

Wall Street banks are also making good use of Palantir. They are using Palantir technology to search their transaction databases for criminal fraud, trading insights and even new ways to price mortgages. One of the world's largest banks uses Palantir software to break up a popular scam called BustOut. BustOut involves criminals who steal or purchase access to thousands of people's online identities, and then break into their bank and credit card accounts. After breaking in, the criminals spend weeks biding their time. Once someone on their radar purchases a plane ticket or leaves on holiday, they siphon money out of the accounts as fast as they can while the victim is in transit. The criminals hide their trails by anonymising their computing activity and disabling alert systems in the bank and credit card accounts. When the bank identifies a small number of compromised accounts, it uses Palantir to uncover the network of thousands of other accounts that have not yet been tapped.

Using Palantir technology, the FBI can now instantly compile thorough dossiers on US citizens. For example, they can integrate surveillance videos with credit card transactions, cell phone records, emails, air itineraries and web search information. Privacy advocates worry that Palantir will make the FBI and other government agencies even more intrusive consumers of personal data. Another event that caused concern for privacy advocates occurred when a Palantir engineer, exposed by the hacker collective Anonymous for participating in a plot to break into the personal computers of WikiLeaks supporters, was quietly rehired by Palantir after being placed on leave.

Palantir likes to emphasise that the company has developed very sophisticated privacy protection technology. Its software creates audit trails that detail who is privy to certain pieces of information and what they have done with the information. Palantir also has a permission system that ensures that agency workers using their software can access only the data allowed by their clearance level.

Sources: Compiled from A Vance and B Stone (2011), 'Palantir, the war on terror's secret weapon', *Bloomberg BusinessWeek*, 22 November; 'Husky names Palantir as software and consulting partner' (2011), *Oil & Gas Financial Journal*, 4 November; P Gobry (2011), 'Secretive spy tech company Palantir Technologies raises another $50 million', *Business Insider*, 11 May; D Primack (2011), 'Analyse this: Palantir worth more than $2 billion', *CNN Money*, 6 May; A Greenberg (2011), 'Palantir apologizes for WikiLeaks attack proposal, cuts ties with HBGary', *Forbes*, 11 February; D Storm (2011), 'Bank of America using three intelligence firms to attack WikiLeaks', *Computerworld*, 9 February; S Gorman (2009), 'How team of geeks cracked the spy trade', *Wall Street Journal*, 4 September; www.palantir.com.

QUESTIONS

1 Palantir states that it has privacy protection technology. Is this technology sufficient to protect against the misuse of Palantir technology? Why or why not? Provide specific examples to support your answer.

2 Describe possible applications of Palantir in the health care industry.

SPREADSHEET ACTIVITY

OBJECTIVE

Strategic information systems are designed to help create some type of competitive advantage. This activity teaches you that something as simple as sorting and filtering within a spreadsheet can be a form of a strategic information system in that it will help make strategic decisions.

Chapter connection

Porter's five forces are demonstrated in this activity. The two most focused on are the bargaining power of customers and industry rivalry. These will be evaluated in the activity by working with multiple pages within one workbook. Each page will provide a different comparison that will provide new/different information.

ACTIVITY

Many factors play a role in determining the final cost of a product. Even more decisions play into which options are chosen for a given product. Often, strategic information systems are used to help create competitive advantage. The recreational vehicle (RV) industry is no exception. Companies try to fit as many options into a camper as they can without dramatically increasing the weight, sacrificing the durability of the unit, or driving manufacturing costs so high that the price is uncompetitive. Industry innovations quickly become standard, customer desires change as petrol prices go up and down and businesses are left to sort everything out.

Visit www.johnwiley.com.au/highered/rainer/ausnz/studentresources and find the links provided for chapter 2. The first link will be a video about sorting and filtering within spreadsheets. It will explain the process and how something this simple can be used to help make strategic decisions. Then click on the second link to download the file for this activity, 'MIS–Chapter 2.xlsx'. It includes a customer survey regarding RV options and customer preferences as well as a list of competitive offerings and prices.

Then sort and filter the information based on criteria given to you by your instructor. By sorting and filtering, you are creating information from your data (the raw facts). You will then use this information to make strategic business decisions to help your RV company create a competitive advantage within the marketplace.

DELIVERABLE

The final product will be a spreadsheet filtered to show rank of the organisation among different criteria relative to their competition. Once you have filtered and ranked the data, you will make suggestions as to the best course of action that will provide the strongest possible competitive advantage for the company. This recommendation will come in the form of a business letter.

DISCUSSION QUESTIONS

1. Too often, information systems are viewed as complicated computer programs that are difficult to understand. However, spreadsheets can provide much of the needed functionality. At what point is it cost-effective to purchase a more legitimate program than to use simple tools found within a spreadsheet?
2. Given the fact that information systems are there to support decisions, why do you think many opt for more expensive systems than the relatively easy-to-use spreadsheet?

DATABASE ACTIVITY **CREATING TABLES**

OBJECTIVE

In this activity, you will learn how to create Access tables from an existing design. The construction of any database begins with creating its data tables. If you cannot create tables, you cannot create a database. Even if you use a database that someone else has created, knowing where the tables come from will help you understand what you can do with it and why it sometimes behaves in ways that you might otherwise not expect.

The database has to be designed first, of course. You will do that in the chapter 3 activity if your instructor assigns it. Here we have done the design for you, so you can 'get your hands dirty' early in the course.

Chapter connection

Competitive advantage and strategic information systems depend on high-quality data. The tables in a database determine what can be done with it. Understanding how its tables determine what a database can do will help you figure out what strategic systems your company can develop or how its databases must change to support the systems it needs.

Prerequisites

None.

ACTIVITY

1. In this activity, you will create a database of university departments and courses from scratch. You will create database tables, tell Access how they are related to each other and enter data into them. You will use similar tables in future Access activities.

The following database diagram (a type of diagram called an entity-relationship diagram or *ERD*, as you will learn in Chapter 3) describes part of the data for a university. Specifically, this part of the database will store data about four *entities*: departments, courses, students and grades.

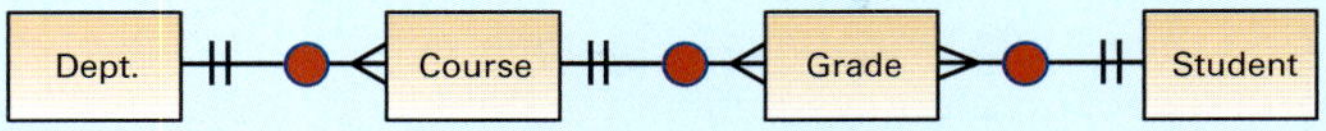

The lines in the diagram tell us that:

- each department can have several courses, but might not have any
- each course belongs to exactly one department
- each course can have several students, but might not have any (this would be a temporary situation when registration starts)
- each student in the course receives one grade
- each student can take several courses, but might not be registered for any (yet)
- each course gives that student one grade.

This information is contained in four tables. You will create the two on the left of the ERD, the Department and Course tables. The first, the department table, will contain the same data that we see here on a spreadsheet:

	A	B	C	D
1	**Name**	**Prefix**	**Space**	**Created On**
2	English	ENL	2500	2/9/1894
3	History	HIS	3500	8/1/1892
4	Physics	PHY	4000	9/1/1892
5	Economics	ECO	2000	3/1/1926
6	Languages	LAN	2300	4/15/1918
7				

2 To create the department table, start by launching Access. Click 'Blank database' at the upper left of the 'Available Templates' section of its opening window. At the lower right, name this database Activity2.accdb (or as your instructor specifies). Then click Create.

3 You will see the *Datasheet view* of the new table, with no data. You could start by entering column names and data in this view. If you do this, Access will make assumptions about your data. Its assumptions are usually correct, but they are wrong often enough to cause problems that are easier to avoid now than fix later. There are also things you cannot do in this view. So, switch to *Design view* by clicking the 'drafting tools' icon at the top left corner.

Usage hint: Most Access objects can be manipulated in three, four, or more views. The icon shows the view that Access designers thought you are most likely to want next. If you want a different view, you can click the triangle under the drafting tools icon to drop down a menu of icons or click on one of the icons at the bottom right corner of the window, which shows all available views.

4 Before changing views, Access requires you to name your new table. Name it DeptTbl and click 'OK'. The ending 'Tbl' identifies it as a table, distinguishing it from other things called 'Dept' (such as, for example, a department list) that you might create later.

Usage hint: Some people put the letters that identify the object type at the start of its name: TblDept, for example. That groups objects of each type in an alphabetical list. Here, it is a matter of personal preference unless your instructor specifies otherwise. This project will put the letters that identify the object type at the end of its name.

5 Access has already created the first field of your table, a unique identifier called 'ID'. It was not on the spreadsheet, but a true database needs it. The *AutoNumber* data type will assign a different number to every department, ensuring you will be able to tell them apart even if two have the same name. (This is why universities give students unique ID numbers.) In a database, such a unique identifier is called a *primary key*. Access indicates primary keys by key icons to the left of their names in Design view. Change the name of this field from ID to DeptID, to avoid later confusion with primary keys of other tables.

6 Enter the name of the next column, DeptName, below DeptID. If you tab to the next field, you will see that Access automatically sets its data type to Text. Because department names are text strings, leave that alone. You can describe it in the third column if you want. (Your instructor may have requirements for this.)

Usage hint: Both these names begin with 'Dept'. This helps us tell department names from student or instructor names outside the context of their tables.

7 The next row, which will become the next column of the table in Datasheet view, gives the three-letter prefix that applies to that department's courses. Call it DeptPrefix. It is of data type Text too. In the Description column, enter 'Three upper-case letters'. This will help people who use the database know what to enter there.

8 The fourth column of the database table will say how many square metres of office space the department uses. So, in the fourth row, enter the name DeptSpace. This time, click the down arrow at the right of its Data Type field to drop down a menu of data types. Select Number.

Usage hint: You can also key in the word 'Number'. As soon as you enter 'n' Access will complete the word because no other data types start with that letter.

9 The fifth data column will say when the department was created. (This is needed because university tradition calls for departments to march into graduation ceremonies in order of creation, oldest first.) Call this field DeptCreated. Change its data type to Date/Time. In the Field Properties pane in the lower part of the window, click the blank area to the right of the word 'Format'. In the menu of date/time formats that drops down, select Medium Date.

At this point your table definition should look like this:

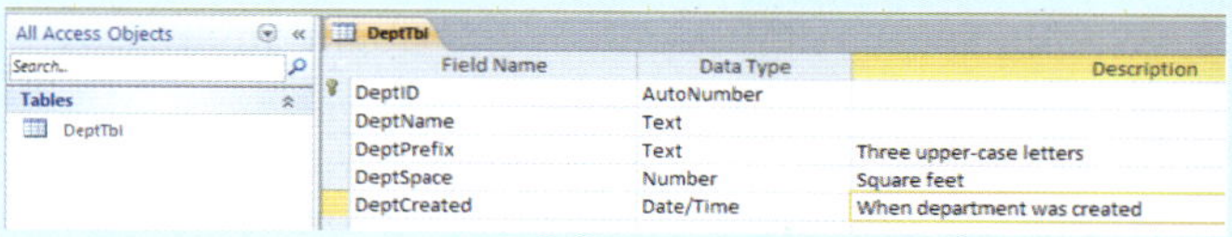

10 Now, click on the Datasheet icon at the top left of the window to return to Datasheet view and enter data. Access will prompt you to save the table. Answer 'Yes'. (Answering 'No' would leave the table in Design view.)

Usage hint: If you are defining a large data table, do not wait until it is all done to save your work. Click the File ribbon tab and choose Save, or click the diskette icon at the top left of the window, every few minutes.

11 In Datasheet view, click in the first row under DeptName to begin entering data for the first department. Enter the name 'English', the prefix 'ENG', an area of 2500 square metres and a creation date of 2 September 1894. Access automatically gave the first department a DeptID of 1. Your table should now look like this:

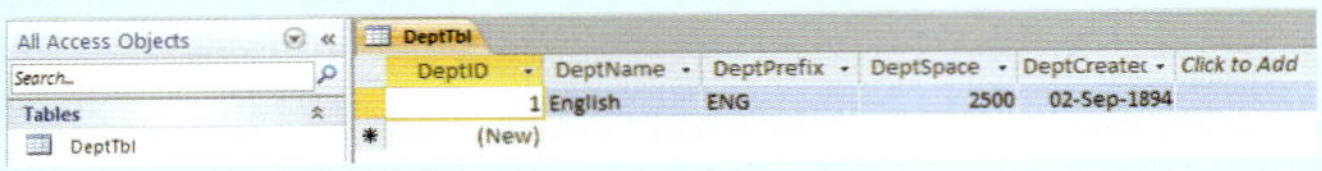

12 When you see this, you realise that the area should be formatted with a comma after the thousands digit. Select the DeptSpace column, or any data in it. Make the Fields ribbon tab active and select Standard format from the Format pull-down menu in the Formatting section.

Usage hint: Another way to do this is to click the Apply Comma Number Format icon (looks like a comma) in the Formatting section. That format also puts two decimal places after the integer part of the number. We do not want decimal places here, so click the Decrease Decimals icon (shows two zeroes with an arrow pointing to one zero) twice to get rid of them.

Usage hint: A third option is to return to Design view, select DeptSpace, click in the Format row of the Field Properties panel, click the down arrow at the far right of that row to pull down the menu of formats and select Standard format. Then return to Datasheet view. That is overkill for comma formatting, but you need to do it if the option you want is not in the ribbon.

13 Continue to add the remainder of the data shown in the above spreadsheet. If your instructor gives you different or additional requirements, follow them.

14 Now create the Course table, as shown in the following spreadsheet. Start by clicking the Create tab above the ribbon. In that ribbon click the leftmost icon, Table. Then continue as before, naming this table CourseTbl. Include a primary key, even though it is not shown in the spreadsheet. Be sure to give the CourseDept field data type Number, to match the AutoNumber data type of the primary key in DeptTbl. Select data types for the other fields based on your understanding of their content. (A real database, rather than showing the instructor's name here, would have a link to a faculty table.)

15 The key characteristic of a database, which differentiates it from a file with information about one real-world entity, is that the tables in it are associated with each other. Look at the Course table. It does not show directly that the first course is taught by the English department. It does contain, however, the department key '1'. That key identifies a row in the Department table. That row gives us the prefix ENG to create the complete identifier 'ENG 307', the full name of the department ('English') if we need it and anything else we want to know about the department.

	A	B	C	D	E	F	G
1	**CrsDept**	**CrsNum**	**CrsTitle**	**CrsProf**	**CrsRoom**	**CrsDays**	**CrsStart**
2	1	101	English Literature	Barker	McCosh 150	MWF	9:00
3	1	307	Chaucer	Robertson	Mahoney 301	MW	1:00
4	2	131	Asian History	Zhang	Healey 310	TR	1:00
5	2	225	World War II	Freedman	Healey 312	MWF	10:00
6	3	215	Quantum Mechanics	Wheeler	Palmer 242	MWF	11:00
7	4	101	Macroeconomics	Doody	Higgins 120	W	6:00
8	5	207	French Short Story	Malraux	Charlton 202	TR	11:30
9	5	321	Spanish Poetry	Garcia	Wexler 431	TR	8:30
10							

Creating a column with department codes in the Courses table makes it possible for Access to connect the two tables. But what if we enter, say, 55, into a CourseDept field when we mean 5? Access will accept the data, but later it will not be able to find a department to match it. That is because it does not know, yet, that these two fields are meant to match.

Now we have to tell it to make that connection. To do that, first close the tables, saving them if prompted. Then, click the Database Tools tab on the ribbon. On that ribbon click 'Relationships', left of centre. In the Show Tables dialogue box, shift-click the unselected table to select both of them, click Add and close the box.

16 To tell Access about the connection, drag CourseDept in the Course table onto DeptID in the Department table. You will see a dialogue box with a check-box to 'Enforce Referential Integrity'. This means that Access will check that every CourseDept in the Course table matches an existing DeptID in the Department table: it will not let you assign a course to Department 55 unless Department 55 exists. Check this box and click Create.

If you carried out the previous steps correctly, you will see a line between these two data fields. It will have a '1' by DeptTbl and a ∞ (infinity) symbol by CourseTbl. This means the two are in a many-to-one relationship: a department can have many courses, but each course is in only one department. It should look like this:

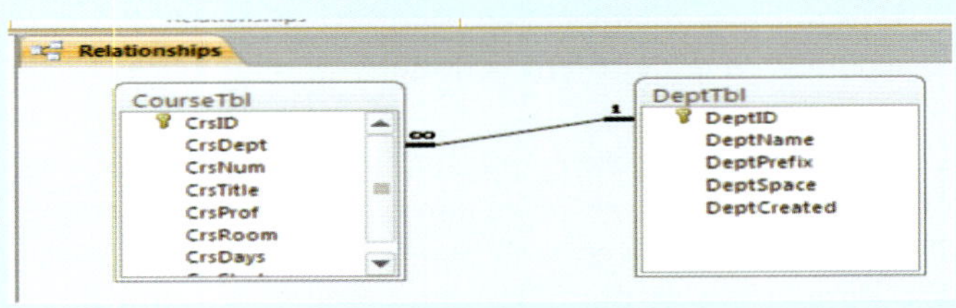

If this did not happen, the most common reasons are:

- **You got a line between the two, but there are no symbols at its ends.** You did not check 'Enforce Referential Integrity'. Double-click the line to edit it (or right-click and select Edit Relationship), check the box and OK the change.
- **'The database engine could not lock table [name] because it is already in use by another person or process.'** A table is still open. Cancel the request, bring the open table to the front by clicking its tab, close it (saving if asked) and repeat.
- **'Microsoft Office Access can't create this relationship and enforce referential integrity.'** At least one CourseDept does not match a DeptID.

Check that CourseDept is of data type Number and all values in that column are correct. If you used data from this activity, check your tables against the data here. If you used other data, such as your instructor's, check the tables against that data. If you used your own, confirm that all CourseDept values match DeptID values. Then repeat the process.

DELIVERABLE

Your database file with the two tables from the previous page, their data and the relationship.

QUIZ QUESTIONS

1 True or false: If a field has data type AutoNumber, it will never have the same value in two rows of the table.

2 Which of the following is *not* a valid Access data type?

a Text

b Date/Time

c Colour

d Number

3 True or false: You must use the Description field in a table's Design view to describe what each field of the table is for.

4 True or false: To enter data into a table, you use Datasheet view.

DISCUSSION QUESTIONS

1 A primary key, such as DeptID in this activity, identifies a single row of a database table uniquely. It must meet two conditions: every row of the table has to have one and they must all be different. Would the three-letter prefix that a department uses for its courses be a suitable primary key? Why or why not?

2 Use Access online help and/or the search engine of your choice to learn the difference between Text and Memo data types. Explain, to a nontechnical reader, when to use each.

3 Suppose the English department changes its name to English Literature and its course prefix to ENL. The Department table is updated to reflect these changes. What changes must be made to the Course table in order to update all the course listings?

3 Data and knowledge management

CHAPTER OUTLINE

LEARNING OBJECTIVES

1. Discuss ways that common challenges in managing data can be addressed using data governance.
2. Explain how to interpret relationships depicted in an entity–relationship diagram.
3. Discuss the advantages and disadvantages of relational databases.
4. Explain the elements necessary to successfully implement and maintain data warehouses.
5. Describe the benefits and challenges of implementing knowledge management systems in organisations.

OPENING CASE >

Loyalty New Zealand — reaping the big data rewards

Established in 1996 and based in Wellington and Auckland, Loyalty New Zealand operates a FlyBuys loyalty program that recognises and rewards customers while also offering over 50 participating businesses vital information concerning their customers. The vision of Loyalty New Zealand is to create, maintain and motivate loyal customers for their business partners. With 75 per cent of New Zealand households being active members of the FlyBuys program, transactional information is systematically recorded at point-of-sale (POS) terminals when customers use their FlyBuys card. This gives Loyalty New Zealand access to rapidly growing, vast amounts of customer behaviour data. Loyalty New Zealand is currently using big data to enhance the benefits and the value customers get by using their cards. Big data refers to vast amounts of generally unstructured and distributed customer information collected from various sources such as transactional histories, customer feedback and surveys, social media applications, mobile device activity and software logs which can be processed by using special application software in order to obtain new insight concerning customer behaviour.

Using SAS software, Loyalty New Zealand are enhancing their ability to better understand their customers by way of profiling, segmenting and analysing data in order to target customers with meaningful offers and campaigns that aim at providing the right offer to the right consumer at the right time. With SAS, Loyalty New Zealand now can develop, scale and launch campaigns within a single day which is almost 20 times faster than before. Specifically, Loyalty New Zealand now has many new capabilities, including the ability to carry out highly targeted campaigns, the ability to model behavioural propensity of consumers and the ability to profile them on the basis of the geographical area of residence and proximity to business outlets. Customised recommendations can also be provided in real time to customers based on continuously evolving individual product preferences. For example, recurring patterns of purchases of baby products could be indicative of a new baby in the family of the cardholder, which can be used as a basis to offer types of complementary baby products or even information related to relevant promotional campaigns of businesses that are partners of Loyalty New Zealand in the cardholder's geographical area of residence. Recurring patterns of past purchases can also be used as a basis to anticipate the types of products or services that customers might be likely to purchase into the future. For example, big data applications can analyse present purchases of toddler products and use findings as a basis to provide insight into the types of school-aged children's products that the household is likely to be purchasing in the near future. Integrating transaction histories from multiple business partners and past customer preferences can also provide insight into *what else and from where* customers might be likely to purchase in the future. Taken together, this information can be invaluable to help predict the manner in which customers will behave and address it accordingly.

Sources: www.loyalty.co.nz/aboutus; V Morder (2013), 'Insight on Loyalty's approach to big data', www.sas.com/offices/asiapacific/sp/usergroups/sunz/Vince_Morder.pdf; www.sas.com/success/loyaltynz.html; www.loyalty.co.nz/whatwedo/loyaltyprogrammes; B Bennett (2013), 'Big data big rewards', *New Zealand Management*, vol. 60, no. 3, pp. 28–36; K Jackson (2013), 'Big data key for small business', www.stuff.co.nz/business/small-business/8987045/Big-data-key-for-small-business; D Paredes (2013), 'Big data demystified', www.cio.co.nz/article/439724/big_data_demystified; www.sas.com/success/loyaltynz.html.

QUESTIONS

1 How is Loyalty New Zealand using big data?
2 Why is Loyalty New Zealand using big data and what business outcomes are likely to be achieved for both business partners and consumers?

Introduction

The opening case describes the opportunities that big data can create and the solutions that organisations are employing to manage these data with potentially several good results. The important idea to realise here is that big data will continue to get bigger and organisations will have to find ever-more creative solutions to manage it.

Big data is growing exponentially. Currently, big data is generated at the rate of 2.5 exabytes per day.[1] According to Reuters, big data is expected to grow by 45 per cent annually[2] and by 2019 big data revenues are expected to exceed $135 billion.[3] Images captured by billions of devices around the world, from digital cameras and camera phones to medical scanners and security cameras, comprise the largest component of this digital information. Big data is becoming so important that around 4.4 million jobs are expected to be created around big data by 2015.[4]

We are accumulating data and information at a frenzied pace from such diverse sources as company documents, emails, web pages, credit card swipes, phone messages, stock trades, memos, address books and radiology scans. New sources of data and information include blogs, podcasts, videocasts (think of YouTube), digital video surveillance and radio frequency identification (RFID) tags and other wireless sensors (discussed in chapter 10). We are awash in data that we have to make sense of and manage. To deal with the growth and the diverse nature of digital data, organisations must employ sophisticated techniques for information management.

THE NOOK

Data collection has always been important to Malakai and Abbie. However, their form of data collection was to keep up with paper receipts from cover charges, drinks, food, etc. They mainly did this to create financial statements. However, they also know that their data collection is incomplete because many people pay with cash and no itemised receipt is printed. Therefore, often the best they can do is a general statement of costs and sales. They have no way to measure and track individual sales, customers, products and the like.

In fact, they have never been able to track sales to customers, night of the week, band (type of music playing) and so on. Even more important, they do not know very much about their customers. Why do they come? What do they like? What do they wish was better? What are the most popular drink items? How do people rate their overall experience? Which drink and food items are most popular and at what time of the night? How can they best reach their customer base? Facebook? Twitter? Email?

The only way to answer these questions is to have data that can be analysed to create information. The only way to capture the data in an organised format is to use a database. And the only way to have a structured database is to start by laying out the outline of that database. This process is called normalisation and entity relationship modelling.

Information technologies and systems support organisations in managing — that is, acquiring, organising, storing, accessing, analysing and interpreting — data. As you noted in chapter 1, when these data are managed properly, they become *information* and then *knowledge*. Information and knowledge are valuable organisational resources that can provide a competitive advantage. This chapter examines the processes whereby data are transformed first into information and then into knowledge.

Few business professionals are comfortable making or justifying business decisions that are not based on solid information. This is especially true today, when modern information systems make access to that information quick and easy. For example, we have technology that formats data in a way that managers and analysts can easily understand. Consequently, these professionals can access these data themselves and analyse them according to their needs, using a variety of tools. The result is useful information. Executives can then apply their experience to use this information to address a business problem, thereby producing knowledge. Knowledge management, enabled by information technology, captures and stores knowledge in forms that all organisational employees can access and apply, thereby creating the flexible, powerful 'learning organisation'.

Clearly, data and knowledge management are vital to modern organisations. But, why should *you* learn about them? The reason is that you will have an important role in the development of database applications. The structure and content of your organisation's **database**, a group of logically related files that stores data and the associations among them, depends on how users (you) look at your business activities. For example, when database developers in the firm's MIS group build a database, they use a tool called entity-relationship (ER) modelling. This tool creates a model of how users view a business activity. When you understand how to create and interpret an ER model, then you can evaluate whether the developers have captured your business activity correctly.

Keep in mind that decisions about data last longer, and have a broader impact, than decisions about hardware or software. If decisions concerning hardware are wrong, then the equipment can be replaced relatively easily. If software decisions turn out to be incorrect, they can be modified, though not always painlessly or inexpensively. Database decisions, in contrast, are much harder to undo. Database design constrains what the organisation can do with its data for a long time. Remember that business users will be stuck with a bad database design, and not the database programmers, who will quickly move on to their next projects. This is why it is so important to get database designs right the first time — and you will be playing a key role in these designs.

Regarding relational databases, when you know how data are stored in tables, then you know what types of data you have available for analysis and decision making. Of course, your familiarity with data warehouses will serve the same purpose. Also, understanding relational databases will help you work with database developers in defining a new database or suggesting improvements to an existing one. It is one thing for you to say to a database developer, 'I wish I could get this information from the database'. It is quite another thing to say, 'If you could add this column of data to table A and this other column of data to table B, then I could get this information from the database'. Database developers enjoy responding to specific, knowledgeable requests from users!

In addition, you might want to create a small, personal database using a software product such as Microsoft Access. In that case, you will want to know at least the basics of the product.

After the data are stored in your organisation's databases, they must be accessible to users in a form that helps users make decisions. Organisations accomplish this objective by developing data warehouses. You should become familiar with data warehouses because they are invaluable decision-making tools.

You will also make extensive use of your organisation's knowledge base to perform your job. For example, when you are assigned a new project, you will likely research your firm's knowledge base to identify factors that contributed to the success of previous, similar projects.

You begin this chapter by examining the multiple problems involved in managing data and the database approach that organisations use to solve those problems. You will then see how database management systems enable organisations to access and use the data stored in the databases. Next, you study data warehouses and data marts and how you use them for decision making. You finish the chapter by taking a look at knowledge management.

3.1 Managing data

IT applications require data. Data should be of high quality, meaning that they should be accurate, complete, timely, consistent, accessible, relevant and concise. Unfortunately, however, the process of acquiring, keeping and managing data is becoming increasingly difficult.

The difficulties of managing data

Because data are processed in several stages and often in several places, they are frequently subject to problems and difficulties. Managing data in organisations is difficult for many reasons.

First, the amount of data increases exponentially with time. Much historical data must be kept for a long time and new data are added rapidly. For example, to support millions of customers, large retailers such as Coles or Woolworths have to manage many terabytes of data. IT's About Business illustrates how cloud accounting helps small businesses manage their accounting data storage and processing needs.

IT'S ABOUT BUSINESS

Cloud accounting: the case of MYOB's AccountRight Live for SMEs

Cloud accounting offers organisations the tools to prepare, publish and automatically exchange financial reports online. With cloud accounting, accounting software is executed using web browsers, and accounting data is securely stored and processed on the servers of cloud accounting providers. This offers flexibility of accessing data ubiquitously.[5] Cloud accounting benefits are expected to realise significant savings in relation to financial and human resources required to fulfil accounting services. For example, Cloud Accounting Australia estimates $625 billion in savings over the next 5 years.[6] In fact, there is widespread agreement in both academia and industry that cloud accounting is poised for strong growth into the future.

As traditional practices of capturing financial data in SMEs can be tedious and onerous, industry experts warn that Australian small business owners are forgoing business growth and significant cost-saving opportunities by not adopting cloud accounting. Industry experts also indicate that time and cost savings generated by using cloud accounting can be otherwise used for critical value-adding aspects of the business including innovation and growth.[7] For example, many small business owners enter receipts into their accounting systems at the end of the month which indicates that information used to make decisions is usually generated late after expenses have been incurred. With cloud accounting business owners can enter expenses data immediately through a variety of devices including smart phones, tables and traditional computers and assess purchase and investment decisions more frequently.[8] Additionally, using cloud accounting reduces the need for software and hardware upgrades which results in high cost savings for small businesses.

MYOB's AccountRight Live is an example of an application that caters for small to medium business accounting needs, allowing them to pay only for software features they need to use.[9] MYOB's AccountRight Live facilitates cloud accounting by offering accounting including inventory payroll ubiquitously either on a local PC or on the cloud via the internet. Accounts can, as a result, be accessed live and reports generated flexibly as required. Operating AccountRight Live on the cloud means that users can use the program online as data is stored online. This can be useful as it allows users to access their MYOB data ubiquitously from any device. For instance, external accountants who carry out processing and reporting can have access to live up-to-date accounting data without having to rely on backups to be sent to them by data entry officers and bookkepeers. In addition to allowing multiple users and the ability to use required features, MYOB's AccountRight Live also enables users to automatically update live bank transactions, thereby eliminating time-consuming manual data entry.[10]

Many Australian SMEs have begun to experience cloud accounting benefits using MYOB's AccountRight Live.[11] For example, using MYOB's cloud accounting software that includes real-time management of operating

➜

expenses at a bakery in Victoria,[12] the owners quickly realised that they were baking twice as many loaves as they were selling. This helped them turn their business around by better managing both their stock and expenses. In another case concerning the management of a caravan park, MYOB's cloud accounting software helped owners with real-time business reporting, enabling business owners to identify issues before they grew to become major harder-to-solve problems.[13]

QUESTIONS

1. What are some of the advantages that cloud accounting can offer to small and medium enterprises?
2. What are some of the risks that cloud accounting users can face?

In addition, data are also scattered throughout organisations and are collected by many individuals using various methods and devices. These data are frequently stored in numerous servers and locations and in different computing systems, databases, formats, and human and computer languages.

Another problem is that data come from multiple sources: internal sources (for example, corporate databases and company documents), personal sources (for example, personal thoughts, opinions and experiences) and external sources (for example, commercial databases, government reports and corporate websites). Data also come from the web, in the form of clickstream data. **Clickstream data** are those data that visitors and customers produce when they visit a website and click on hyperlinks (described in chapter 4). Clickstream data provide a trail of the users' activities in the website, including user behaviour and browsing patterns.

Adding to these problems is the fact that new sources of data, such as blogs, podcasts, videocasts, and RFID tags and other wireless sensors, are constantly being developed. Data can degrade over time. For example, customers move to new addresses or change their names, companies go out of business or are bought, new products are developed, employees are hired or fired, and companies expand into new countries.

Data are also subject to **data rot**. Data rot refers primarily to problems with the media on which the data are stored. Over time, temperature, humidity and exposure to light can cause physical problems with storage media and make it difficult to access the data. The second aspect of data rot is that finding the machines needed to access the data can be difficult. For example, it is almost impossible today to find 8-track players. This means that a library of 8-track tapes has become relatively worthless, unless you have a functioning 8-track player or you convert the tapes to a modern medium such as CD.

Data security, quality and integrity are critical, yet they are easily jeopardised. In addition, legal requirements relating to data differ among countries as well as industries and they change frequently.

Another problem arises from the fact that, over time, organisations have developed information systems for specific business processes, such as transaction processing, supply chain management, customer relationship management and other processes. Information systems that specifically support these processes impose unique requirements on data, which results in repetition and conflicts across an organisation. For example, the marketing function might maintain information on customers, sales territories and markets that duplicates data within the billing or customer service functions. This situation produces inconsistent data in the enterprise. Inconsistent data prevent a company from developing a unified view of core business information — data concerning customers, products, finances and so on — across the organisation and its information systems.

Two other factors complicate data management. First, federal regulations have made it a top priority for companies to better account for how information is being managed within their organisations. For example, Australia's *Privacy Act 1988* regulates the handling of personal information about individuals including collection, use, storage and disclosure of personal information.[14] Second, companies are drowning in data, much of which is unstructured. As you have seen, the amount of data is increasing exponentially. To be profitable, companies must develop a strategy for managing these data effectively.

Because of these numerous problems, data are difficult to manage. As a result, organisations are turning to data governance.

Data governance

Data governance is an approach to managing information across an entire organisation. It involves a formal set of business processes and policies that are designed to ensure that data are handled in a certain, well-defined fashion. That is, the organisation follows unambiguous rules for creating, collecting, handling and protecting its information. The objective is to make information available, transparent and useful for the people authorised to access it, from the moment it enters an organisation, until it is outdated and deleted.

One strategy for implementing data governance is master data management. **Master data management** is a process that spans all organisational business processes and applications. It provides companies with the ability to store, maintain, exchange and synchronise a consistent, accurate and timely 'single version of the truth' for the company's core master data.

Master data are a set of core data, such as customer, product, employee, vendor, geographic location and so on, that span the enterprise information systems. It is important to distinguish between master data and transaction data. *Transaction data*, which are generated and captured by operational systems, describe the activities, or transactions, of the business. In contrast, master data are applied to multiple transactions and are used to categorise, aggregate and evaluate the transaction data.

Let's look at an example of a transaction: you (Jameela Yousafzai) purchase one Samsung 55-inch full HD 3D television, part number 1234, from Bill Roberts at JB Hi-Fi, for $1996, on 20 November 2014. In this example, the master data are 'product sold', 'vendor', 'salesperson', 'store', 'part number', 'purchase price' and 'date'. When specific values are applied to the master data, then a transaction is represented. Therefore, transaction data would be, respectively, '55-inch full HD 3D television', 'Samsung', 'Bill Roberts', 'JB Hi-Fi', '1234', '$1996' and '20 November 2014'.

An example of master data management is the NSW Police Force business process digitisation program for accounting payments.[15] The main aim of this program was to remove inefficiencies and introduce process improvement for accounts payable. It also aimed at ensuring that data and records within existing systems would not create ongoing storage and legacy problems for the NSW Police. Digitisation and integration would also help NSW Police be compliant with State Records' standards on digital recordkeeping where suitable and compliant protections and metadata were applied. Digitisation master data was necessary for a number of reasons. First, there were many inefficiencies in existing manual accounts payable management processes, where invoices could be lost and payments delayed. For example, the NSW Police receive over 120 000 invoices annually. Invoices were typically received in paper form from local commands and were distributed for approval across different roles in the NSW Police hierarchy before being forwarded to police headquarters for payment. This situation was prone to inefficiencies whereby invoices could be lost and payments delayed. Additionally, at the end of the financial year, paper invoices were batched and boxed, resulting in approximately 150 to 200 boxes annually that had to be retained for a number of years before being disposed of using legally compliant processes. By streamlining processes, the digitisation of the NSW Police accounts payable enhanced the efficiency of accounting payable processes. Also, in addition to improving invoice disposal, the NSW Police Force also realised paper storage cost savings and savings in staff time previously committed to manually manage paper invoices and their disposal.

Along with data governance, organisations use the database approach to efficiently and effectively manage their data. You turn your attention to the database approach in the next section.

BEFORE YOU GO ON . . .

1. What are some of the difficulties involved in managing data?
2. Define *data governance, master data* and *transactional data.*

QUESTIONS

1. How many sources of information can you think of for The Nook?
2. Even though The Nook is not subject to Sarbanes-Oxley legal documentation requirements, can you think of any reasons why it would be a good idea for the club to operate up to these standards?

3.2 The database approach

From the time of the first computer applications in business (mid 1950s) until the early 1970s, organisations managed their data in a *file management environment*. This environment evolved because organisations typically began automating one application at a time. These systems grew independently from one another, without overall planning. Each application required its own data, which were organised in a data file.

A data file is a collection of logically related records. Therefore, in a file management environment, each application has a specific data file related to it, containing all the data records needed by the application. Over time, organisations developed numerous applications, each with an associated, application-specific data file.

For example, you can relate to a situation where most of your information is in your university's central database, but a club to which you belong has its own files, the student union has separate files for student members and your instructors may maintain grade data on their personal computers. It is easy for your name to be misspelled in one of these databases or files but not in others. If you move, your address might be updated correctly in one database or file but not in others.

Using databases eliminates many problems that arose from previous methods of storing and accessing data, such as file management systems. Databases are arranged so that one set of software programs — the database management system — provides all users with access to all the data. (You will study database management systems later in this chapter.) This system minimises the following problems:

- *data redundancy:* the same data are stored in many places
- *data isolation:* applications cannot access data associated with other applications
- *data inconsistency:* various copies of the data do not agree.

In addition, database systems maximise the following issues:

- *data security:* because data are 'put in one place' in databases, there is a potential for losing a lot of data at once. Therefore, databases have extremely high security measures in place to deter mistakes and attacks (you will learn about information security in chapter 7)
- *data integrity:* data meet certain constraints, such as no alphabetic characters in a tax file number (TFN) number field
- *data independence:* applications and data are independent of one another (that is, applications and data are not linked to each other, meaning that all applications are able to access the same data).

Figure 3.1 illustrates a university database. Note that university applications from the registrar's office, the accounting department and the student union access data through the database management system.

FIGURE 3.1 A database management system (DBMS) provides access to all data in the database.

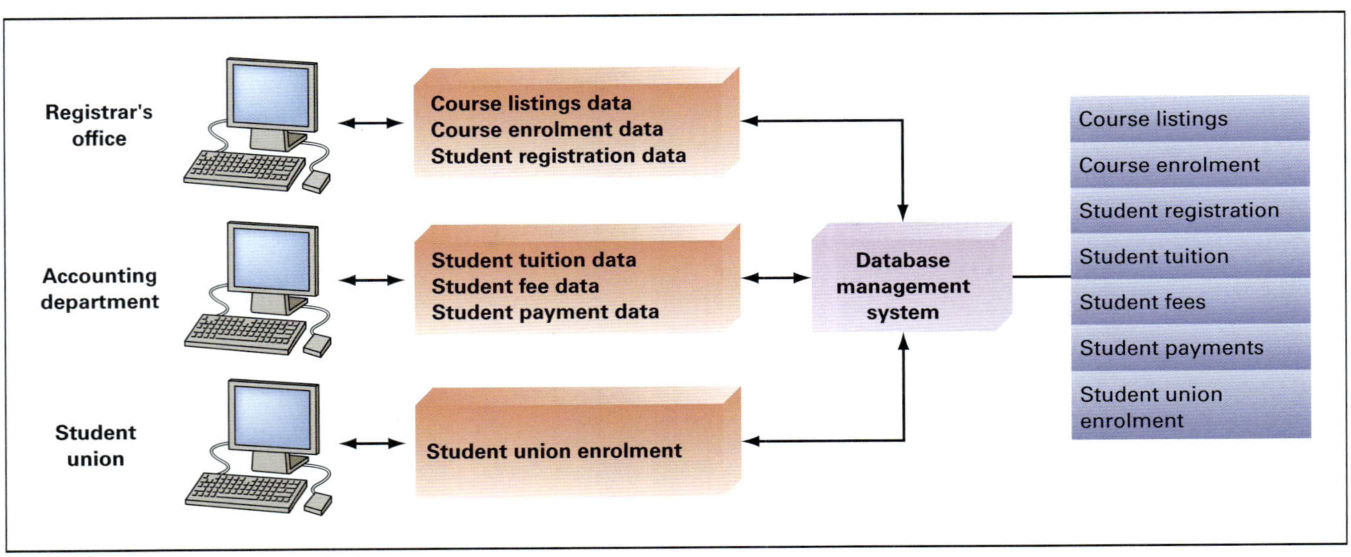

A database can contain vast amounts of data. To make these data more understandable and useful, they are arranged in a hierarchy. In the next section, you will become familiar with the data hierarchy. You will then see how databases are designed.

The data hierarchy

Data are organised in a hierarchy that begins with bits and proceeds all the way to databases (see figure 3.2). A **bit** (*b*inary dig*it*) represents the smallest unit of data a computer can process. The term *binary* means that a bit can consist only of a 0 or a 1. A group of eight bits, called a **byte**, represents a single character. A byte can be a letter, a number, or a symbol. A logical grouping of characters into a word, a small group of words, or an identification number is called a **field**. For example, a student's name in a university's computer files would appear in the 'name' field and her or his date of birth number would appear in the 'Date of Birth' field. Fields can also contain data other than text and numbers. A field can contain an image, or any other type of multimedia. Examples are a motor vehicle department's licensing database containing a person's photograph and a field containing a voice sample to authorise access to a secure facility; and in the Apple iTunes Store, a song is a field in a record, with other fields giving the song's title, its price and the album of which it is part.

A logical grouping of related fields, such as the student's name, the courses taken, the date and the grade, comprises a *record*. A logical grouping of related records is called a **file** or a **table**. For example, the records from a particular course, consisting of course number, lecturer and students' grades, would constitute a *data file* for that course. A logical grouping of related files would constitute a *database*. Using the same example, the student course file could be grouped with files on students' personal histories and financial backgrounds to create a student database.

Now that you have seen how data are arranged in a database, you will learn about how today's organisations design their databases. You will focus on entity–relationship (ER) modelling and normalisation procedures.

Designing the database

To be valuable, a database must be organised so that users can retrieve, analyse and understand the data they need. A key to designing an effective database is the data model. A **data model** is a diagram that represents entities in the database and their relationships. An entity is a person, place, thing, or event — such as a customer, an employee, or a product — about which information is maintained. Entities can typically be identified in the user's work environment. A **record** generally describes an entity. An instance of an entity is a specific, unique representation of the entity. For example, an instance of the entity STUDENT would be a particular student.

FIGURE 3.2 Hierarchy of data for a computer-based file.

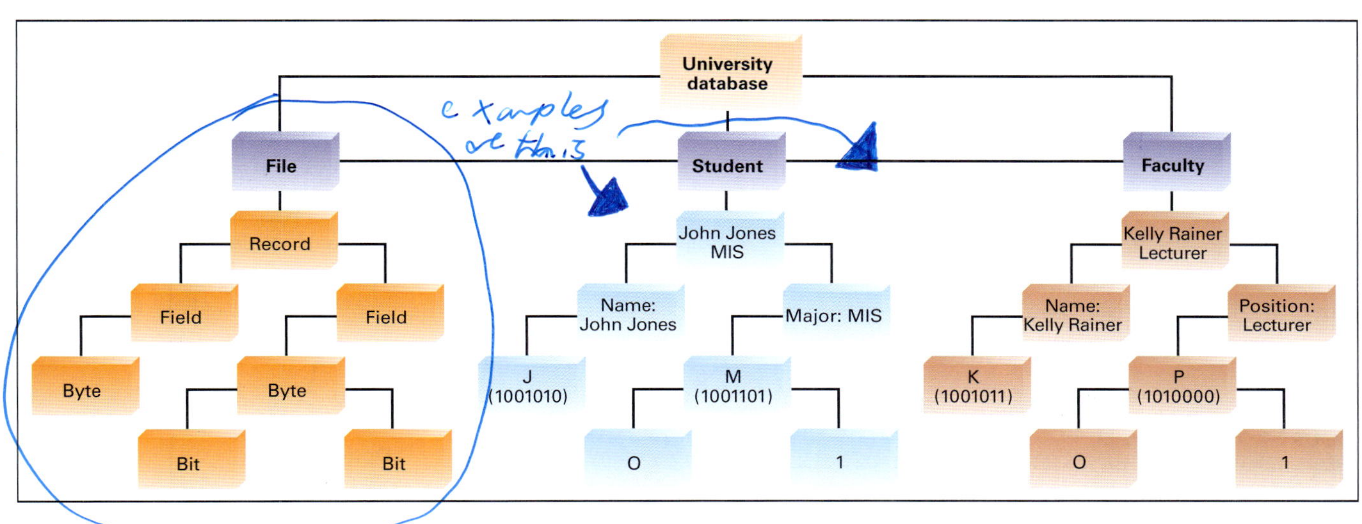

Each characteristic or quality of a particular entity is called an *attribute*. For example, if our entities were a customer, an employee and a product, entity attributes would include customer name, employee number and product colour.

Every record in a file must contain at least one field that uniquely identifies that record so that it can be retrieved, updated and sorted. This identifier field is called the **primary key**. For example, a student record in an Australian university would use a unique student number as its primary key. In some cases, locating a particular record requires the use of secondary keys. A **secondary key** is another field that has some identifying information but typically does not identify the file with complete accuracy. For example, the student's major might be a secondary key if a user wanted to find all students in a particular major field of study. It should not be the primary key, however, because many students can have the same major.

Entity–relationship modelling

Designers plan and create the database through the process of **entity–relationship modelling**, using an **entity–relationship (ER) diagram**. There are many approaches to ER diagramming. You will see one particular approach here, but there are others. The good news is that if you are familiar with one version of ER diagramming, then you will be able to easily adapt to any other type of ER diagramming.

ER diagrams consist of entities, attributes and relationships. Entities are pictured in boxes and relationships are shown in diamonds. The attributes for each entity are listed and the primary key is underlined.

Relationships illustrate an association between two entities. A relationship has a name that is a verb. Cardinality and modality are the indicators of the business rules in a relationship. *Cardinality* refers to the maximum number of times an instance of one entity can be associated with an instance in the related entity. *Modality* refers to the minimum number of times an instance of one entity can be associated with an instance in the related entity. Cardinality can be 1 or many and its symbol is placed on the outside of the relationship line, closest to the entity. Modality can be 1 or 0 and its symbol is placed on the inside of the relationship line, next to the cardinality symbol. Figure 3.3 shows the cardinality and modality symbols. Figure 3.4 shows an ER diagram.

As defined earlier, an **entity** is something that can be identified in the users' work environment. For example, consider student registration at a university. Students register for courses and register their cars for parking permits. In this example, STUDENT, PARKING PERMIT, CLASS and LECTURER are entities, as shown in figure 3.4.

Entities of a given type are grouped in **entity classes**. In our example, STUDENT, PARKING PERMIT, CLASS and LECTURER are entity classes. An **instance** of an entity class is the representation of a particular entity. Therefore, a particular STUDENT (James Smythe, 145-89-7123) is an instance of the STUDENT entity class; a particular parking permit (91778) is an instance of the PARKING PERMIT entity class; a particular

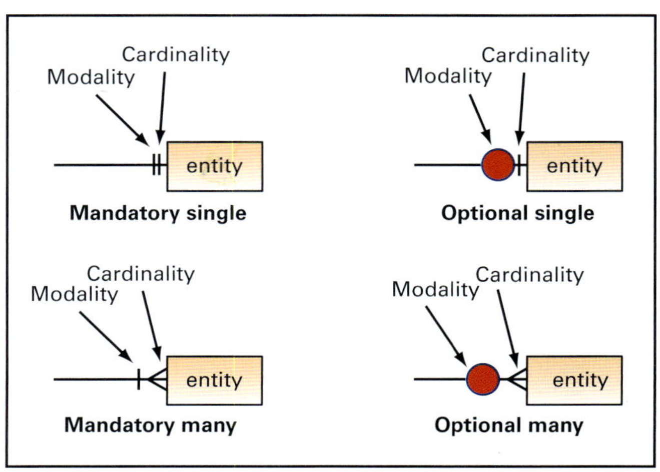

FIGURE 3.3 Relationships between entities reflecting business rules.

class (76890) is an instance of the CLASS entity class; and a particular lecturer (Margaret Wilson, 115-65-7632) is an instance of the LECTURER entity class.

Entity instances have **identifiers**, which are attributes that are unique to that entity instance. For example, STUDENT instances can be identified with Student Identification Number; PARKING PERMIT instances can be identified with Permit Number; CLASS instances can be identified with Class Number; and LECTURER instances can be identified with Lecturer Identification Number. These identifiers (or primary keys) are underlined on ER diagrams, as in part (b) of figure 3.4.

FIGURE 3.4 Entity–relationship diagram model.

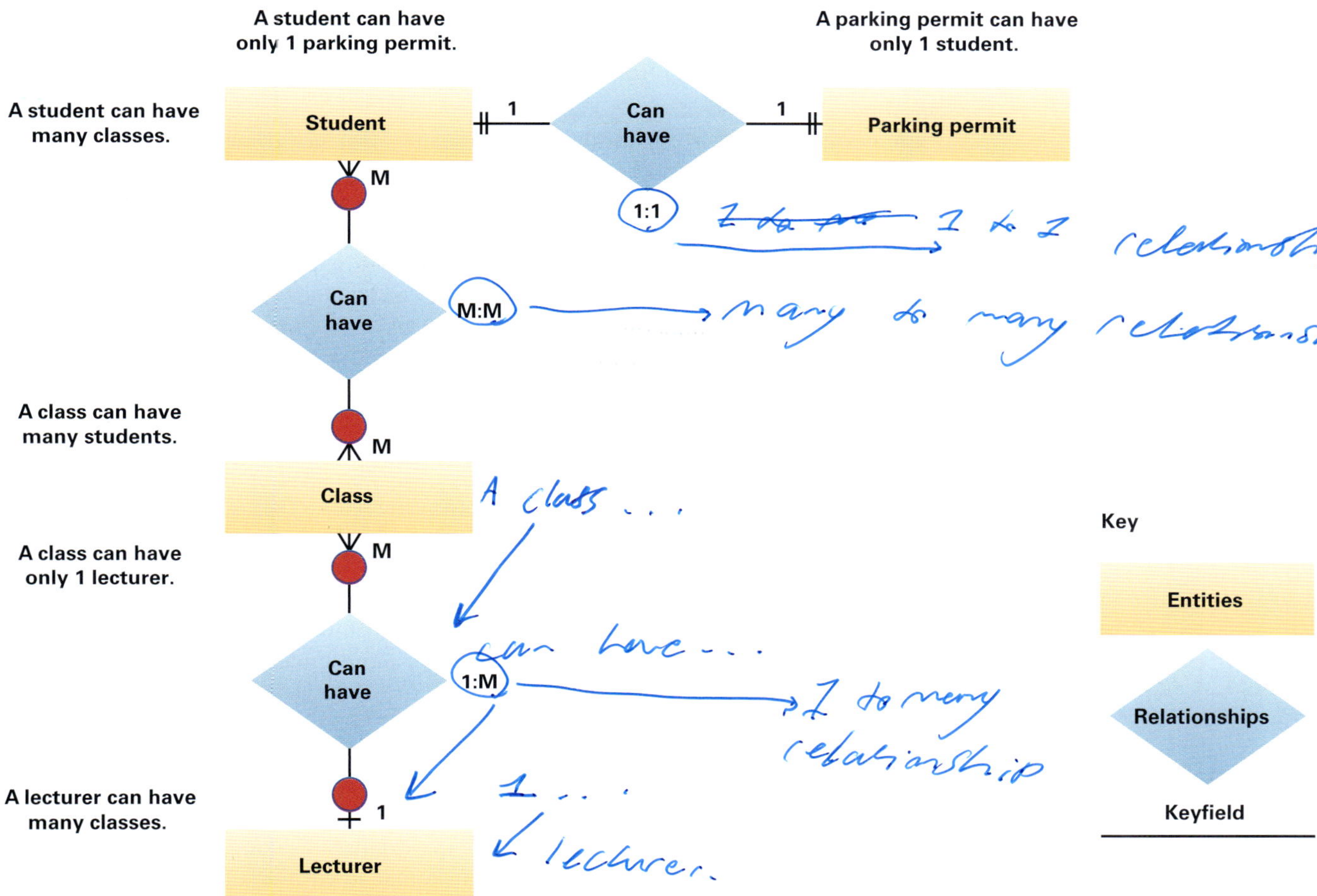

(a) ER diagram

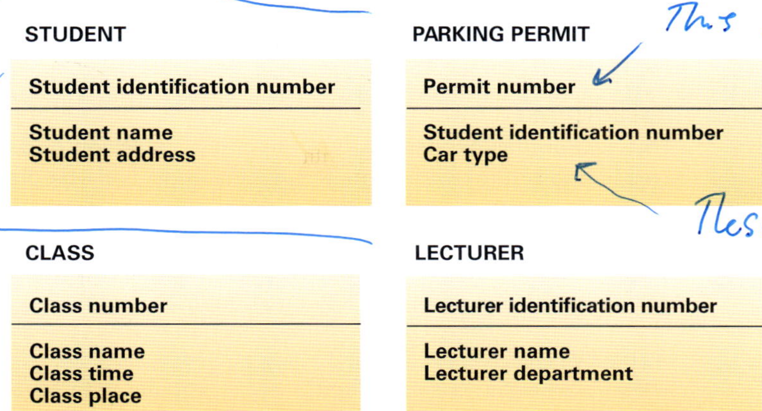

(b) Entities, attributes and identifiers

Entities have **attributes**, or properties, that describe the entity's characteristics. In our example, examples of attributes for STUDENT are Student Name and Student Address. Examples of attributes for PARKING PERMIT are Student Identification Number and Car Type. Examples of attributes for CLASS are Class Name, Class Time and Class Place. Examples of attributes for LECTURER are Lecturer Name and Lecturer Department. (Note that each course at this university has one lecturer — no team teaching.)

Why is Student Identification Number an attribute of both the STUDENT and PARKING PERMIT entity classes? That is, why do we need the PARKING PERMIT entity class? If you consider all interlinked university systems, the PARKING PERMIT entity class is needed for other applications, such as fee payments, parking tickets and external links to the state Department of Transport.

Entities are associated with one another in relationships, which can include many entities. (Remember that relationships are noted by diamonds on ER diagrams.) The number of entities in a relationship is the degree of the relationship. Relationships between two items are called *binary relationships*. There are three types of binary relationships: one-to-one, one-to-many and many-to-many.

In a *one-to-one (1:1)* relationship, a single-entity instance of one type is related to a single-entity instance of another type. Figure 3.4(a) shows STUDENT–PARKING PERMIT as a 1:1 relationship. The relationship means that a student can have a parking permit, but does not need to have to have one. (Clearly, if a student does not have a car, then he or she will not need a parking permit.) Note that the relationship line on the PARKING PERMIT side shows zero or one — that is, a cardinality of 1 and a modality of 0. On the STUDENT side of the relationship, only one parking permit can be assigned to one student. Note that the relationship line on the STUDENT side shows one and only one — that is, a cardinality of 1 and a modality of 1.

The second type of relationship, *one-to-many (1:M)*, is represented by the CLASS–LECTURER relationship in figure 3.4(a). This relationship means that a lecturer can have one or more courses, but each course can have only one lecturer. Note that the relationship line on the LECTURER side shows one and only one — that is, a cardinality of 1 and a modality of 1. The relationship line on the CLASS side shows 1 or many — that is, a cardinality of many and a modality of 1.

The third type of relationship, *many-to-many (M:M)*, is represented by the STUDENT–CLASS relationship in figure 3.4(a). This M:M relationship means that a student can have one or more courses and a course can have one or more students. Note that the relationship line on the STUDENT side shows one or more — that is, a cardinality of Many and a modality of 1. Further, the relationship line of the CLASS side shows one or more — that is, a cardinality of Many and a modality of 1.

ER modelling is valuable because it allows database designers to talk with users throughout the organisation to ensure that all entities and the relationships among them are represented. This process underscores the importance of taking all users into account when designing organisational databases. Notice that all entities and relationships in our example are labelled in terms that users can understand. Now that you understand how a database is designed, you can turn your attention to database management systems.

BEFORE YOU GO ON . . .

1. What is a data model?
2. What is a primary key? A secondary key?
3. What is an entity? An attribute?

Apply the Concept

Background

This section has exposed you to the complicated job of designing a database. This is one of those concepts that just cannot really be grasped until you work through a problem. Even though very few people go on to become database administrators, it is still good to have some understanding of how a database is built and administered. This activity will present you with a scenario and then you will apply the concepts you have just learned about.

Activity

Imagine working as a coordinator of a company with several ongoing projects. As part of your job, you are supposed to keep track of its commercial projects, employees and the employees' participation in each project. Usually, a project will have multiple team members, but some projects have not been assigned to any team member. For each project, the company must keep track of the project's title, description, location, estimated budget and due date.

Each employee can be assigned to one or more projects. Some employees can also be on leave and will not be working on any particular assignment. Project leaders usually need to know the following information about their team members: name, address, phone number, highest degree attained and his/her expertise (for example, IS, accounting, marketing and finance).

You have been asked by your manager to conceptually design a database that can help the company keep track of the information described in this scenario. To begin, you need to identify entity classes and their attributes and determine (or create) primary key attribute(s) for each entity class. In addition, you will need to identify foreign key attribute(s) and establish relationships among the entity classes you have identified.

Deliverable

Develop your conceptual design and present your tutor with your entity classes and their attributes. Also be sure to identify the primary key attribute(s). Present a drawing similar to the one in the text if your instructor requires it.

THE NOOK

QUESTIONS

1. If the bartender, door attendant and chef all kept separate spreadsheets to keep up with customers, purchases and payments, what type of data problems do you see they could have?
2. How could a networked database help to alleviate some of the problems in the first question?

3.3 Database management systems

A **database management system (DBMS)** is a set of programs that provide users with tools to add, delete, access, modify and analyse data stored in one location. An organisation can access the data by using query and reporting tools that are part of the DBMS or by using application programs specifically written to access the data. DBMSs also provide the mechanisms for maintaining the integrity of stored data, managing security and user access, and recovering information if the system fails. Databases and DBMSs are essential to all areas of business so they must be carefully managed.

There are a number of different database architectures, but we focus on the relational database model because it is popular and easy to use. Other database models (for example, the hierarchical and network models) are the responsibility of the MIS function and are not used by organisational employees. Popular examples of relational databases are Microsoft Access and Oracle.

The relational database model

Most business data — especially accounting and financial data — traditionally were organised into simple tables consisting of columns and rows. Tables allow people to compare information quickly by row or column. In addition, items are easy to retrieve by finding the point of intersection of a particular row and column.

The **relational database model** is based on the concept of two-dimensional tables. A relational database generally is not one big table — usually called a *flat file* — that contains all of the records and attributes. Such a design would entail far too much data redundancy. Instead, a relational database is usually designed with a number of related tables. Each of these tables contains records (listed in rows) and attributes (listed in columns).

These related tables can be joined when they contain common columns. The uniqueness of the primary key tells the DBMS which records are joined with others in related tables. This feature allows users great flexibility in the variety of queries they can make. Despite these features, however, this model has some disadvantages. Because large-scale databases can be composed of many interrelated tables, the overall design can be complex and therefore have slow search and access times.

Consider the relational database example about students shown in figure 3.5. The table contains data about the entity called students. Attributes of the entity are student name, undergraduate major, grade point average and graduation date. The rows are the records on Sally Adams, John Jones, Jane Lee, Kevin Durham, Juan Rodriguez, Stella Zubnicki and Ben Jones. Of course, your university keeps much more data on you than our example shows. In fact, your university's student database probably keeps hundreds of attributes on each student.

Query languages

Requesting information from a database is the most commonly performed operation. **Structured query language (SQL)** is the most popular query language used to request information. SQL allows people to perform complicated searches by using relatively simple statements or key words. Typical key words are SELECT (to specify a desired attribute), FROM (to specify the table to be used) and WHERE (to specify conditions to apply in the query).

To understand how SQL works, imagine that a university wants to know the names of students who will graduate with distinction in December 2015. The university IS staff would query the student relational database with an SQL statement such as SELECT Student Name, FROM Student Database, WHERE Grade Point Average < 85 and Grade Point Average > 74. The SQL query would return: John Jones and Juan Rodriguez.

Another way to find information in a database is to use **query by example (QBE)**. In QBE, the user fills out a grid or template (also known as a *form*) to construct a sample or description of the data desired. Users can construct a query quickly and easily by using drag-and-drop features in a DBMS such as Microsoft Access. Conducting queries in this manner is simpler than keying in SQL commands.

Data dictionary

When a relational model is created, the **data dictionary** defines the format necessary to enter the data into the database. The data dictionary provides information on each

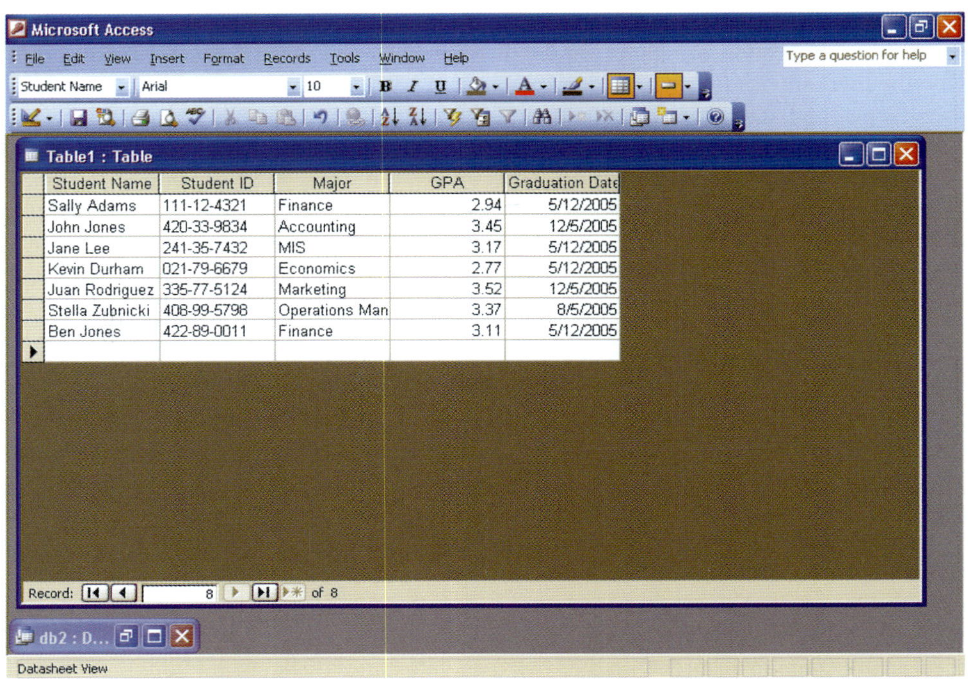

FIGURE 3.5 Example of a student database.

attribute, such as its name, whether it is a key or part of a key, the type of data expected (alphanumeric, numeric, dates and so on) and valid values. Data dictionaries can also provide information on how often the attribute should be updated; why it is needed in the database; and which business functions, applications, forms and reports use the attribute.

Data dictionaries provide many advantages to the organisation. Because they provide names and standard definitions for all attributes, they reduce the chances that the same attribute will be used in different applications but with a different name. In addition, data dictionaries give organisations an inventory of their data resources, making it possible to manage that resource more effectively.

Normalisation

To use a relational database management system effectively, the data must be analysed to eliminate redundant data elements. **Normalisation** is a method for analysing and reducing a relational database to its most streamlined form for minimum redundancy, maximum data integrity and best processing performance. When data are *normalised*, attributes in the table depend only on the primary key.

As an example of normalisation, consider a motor vehicle repair garage. This business takes orders from customers who want to have their cars repaired. In this example, ORDER, PART, SUPPLIER and CUSTOMER are entities. There can be many PARTS in an ORDER, but each PART can come from only one SUPPLIER. In a non-normalised relation called ORDER (see figure 3.6), each ORDER would have to repeat the name, description and price of each PART needed to complete the ORDER, as well as the name and address of each SUPPLIER. This relation contains repeating groups and describes multiple entities.

For example, consider the table in figure 3.6 and notice the very first column (labelled Order). This column contains multiple entries for each order — four rows for Order 11, six rows for Order 12 and so on. These multiple rows for an order are called repeating groups. The table in figure 3.6 also contains multiple entities:

- ORDER
- PART
- SUPPLIER
- CUSTOMER.

When you normalise the data, you want to eliminate repeating groups and have normalised tables, each containing only one entity.

You might think that four entities would mean four normalised tables. (The ORDER, SUPPLIER and CUSTOMER tables are shown in figure 3.7(a), and the PART table is

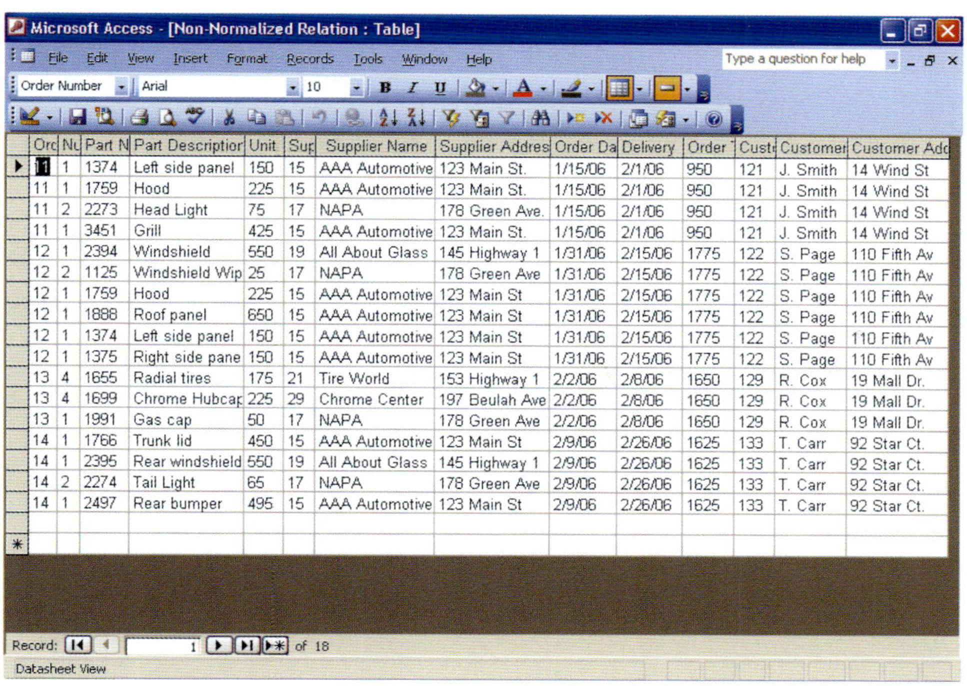

Microsoft Access - [Non-Normalized Relation : Table]

Orc	Nu	Part N	Part Descriptior	Unit	Sup	Supplier Name	Supplier Addres	Order Da	Delivery	Order T	Cust	Customer	Customer Add
11	1	1374	Left side panel	150	15	AAA Automotive	123 Main St.	1/15/06	2/1/06	950	121	J. Smith	14 Wind St
11	1	1759	Hood	225	15	AAA Automotive	123 Main St.	1/15/06	2/1/06	950	121	J. Smith	14 Wind St
11	2	2273	Head Light	75	17	NAPA	178 Green Ave.	1/15/06	2/1/06	950	121	J. Smith	14 Wind St
11	1	3451	Grill	425	15	AAA Automotive	123 Main St.	1/15/06	2/1/06	950	121	J. Smith	14 Wind St
12	1	2394	Windshield	550	19	All About Glass	145 Highway 1	1/31/06	2/15/06	1775	122	S. Page	110 Fifth Av
12	2	1125	Windshield Wip	25	17	NAPA	178 Green Ave	1/31/06	2/15/06	1775	122	S. Page	110 Fifth Av
12	1	1759	Hood	225	15	AAA Automotive	123 Main St	1/31/06	2/15/06	1775	122	S. Page	110 Fifth Av
12	1	1888	Roof panel	650	15	AAA Automotive	123 Main St	1/31/06	2/15/06	1775	122	S. Page	110 Fifth Av
12	1	1374	Left side panel	150	15	AAA Automotive	123 Main St	1/31/06	2/15/06	1775	122	S. Page	110 Fifth Av
12	1	1375	Right side pane	150	15	AAA Automotive	123 Main St	1/31/06	2/15/06	1775	122	S. Page	110 Fifth Av
13	4	1655	Radial tires	175	21	Tire World	153 Highway 1	2/2/06	2/8/06	1650	129	R. Cox	19 Mall Dr.
13	4	1699	Chrome Hubcap	225	29	Chrome Center	197 Beulah Ave	2/2/06	2/8/06	1650	129	R. Cox	19 Mall Dr.
13	1	1991	Gas cap	50	17	NAPA	178 Green Ave	2/2/06	2/8/06	1650	129	R. Cox	19 Mall Dr.
14	1	1766	Trunk lid	450	15	AAA Automotive	123 Main St	2/9/06	2/26/06	1625	133	T. Carr	92 Star Ct.
14	1	2395	Rear windshield	550	19	All About Glass	145 Highway 1	2/9/06	2/26/06	1625	133	T. Carr	92 Star Ct.
14	2	2274	Tail Light	65	17	NAPA	178 Green Ave	2/9/06	2/26/06	1625	133	T. Carr	92 Star Ct.
14	1	2497	Rear bumper	495	15	AAA Automotive	123 Main St	2/9/06	2/26/06	1625	133	T. Carr	92 Star Ct.

Record: 1 of 18

Datasheet View

FIGURE 3.6 Non-normalised relation.

shown in figure 3.7(b).) But, to fully normalise the data in this example, you must create an extra table, called ORDERED-PARTS. This table (see figure 3.7(b)) contains the particular parts and how many of each part are in a particular order.

The normalisation process, illustrated in figure 3.8, breaks down the relation, ORDER, into smaller relations: ORDER, SUPPLIER and CUSTOMER (figure 3.7(a)) and ORDERED PARTS and PART (figure 3.7(b)). Each of these relations describes a single entity. This process is conceptually simpler and it eliminates repeating groups. For example, consider an order at the automobile repair shop. The normalised relations can produce the order in the following manner (see figure 3.8).

- The ORDER relation provides the Order Number (the primary key), Order Date, Delivery Date, Order Total and Customer Number.

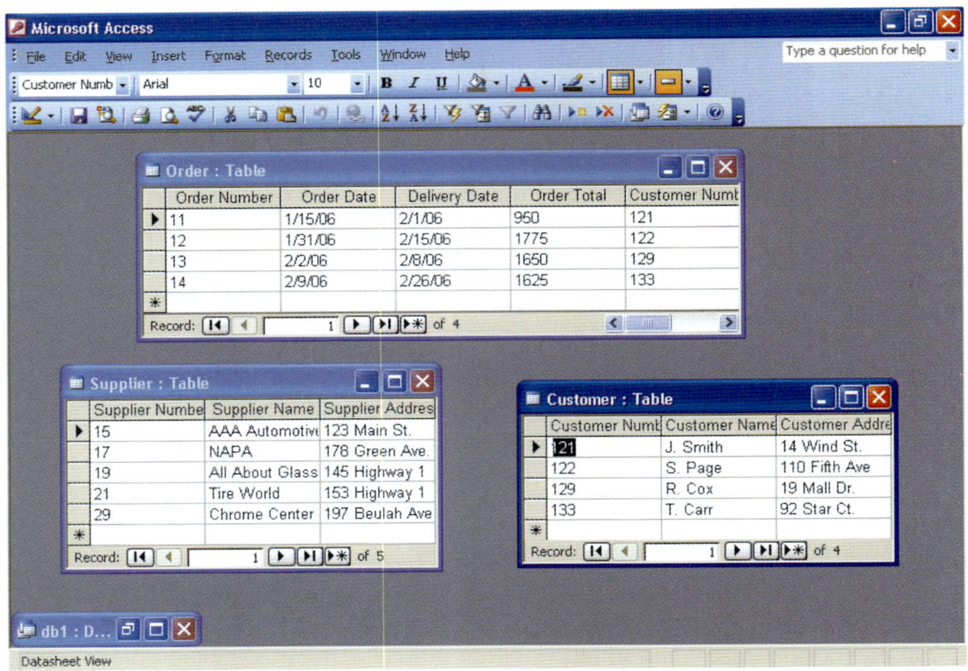

Order : Table

Order Number	Order Date	Delivery Date	Order Total	Customer Numt
11	1/15/06	2/1/06	950	121
12	1/31/06	2/15/06	1775	122
13	2/2/06	2/8/06	1650	129
14	2/9/06	2/26/06	1625	133

Supplier : Table

Supplier Numbe	Supplier Name	Supplier Addres
15	AAA Automotiv	123 Main St.
17	NAPA	178 Green Ave.
19	All About Glass	145 Highway 1
21	Tire World	153 Highway 1
29	Chrome Center	197 Beulah Ave

Customer : Table

Customer Numt	Customer Name	Customer Addre
121	J. Smith	14 Wind St.
122	S. Page	110 Fifth Ave
129	R. Cox	19 Mall Dr.
133	T. Carr	92 Star Ct.

(a)

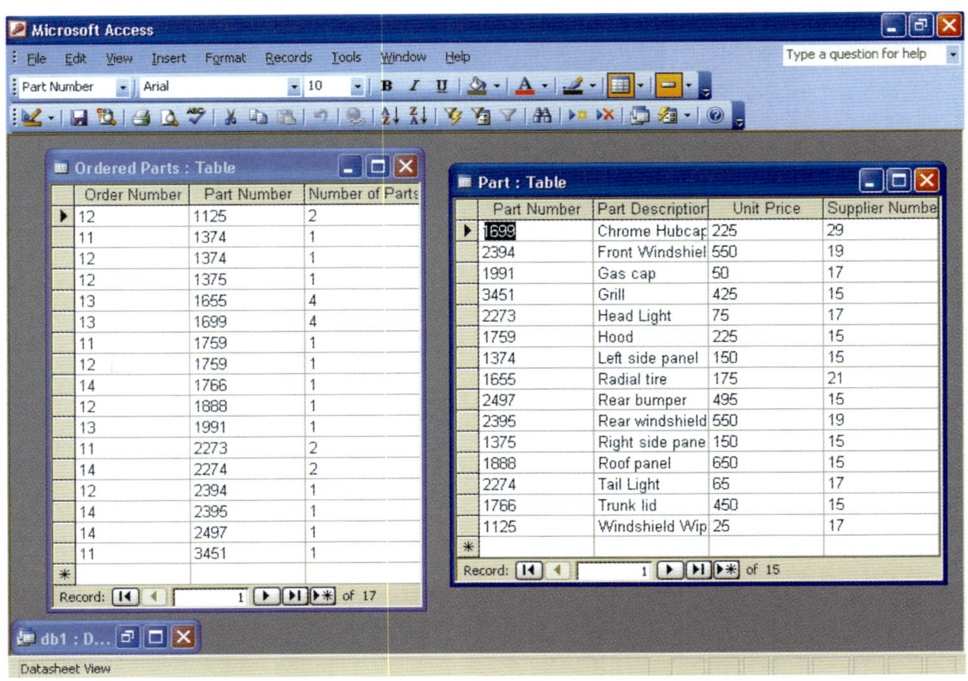

Ordered Parts : Table

Order Number	Part Number	Number of Parts
12	1125	2
11	1374	1
12	1374	1
12	1375	1
13	1655	4
13	1699	4
11	1759	1
12	1759	1
14	1766	1
12	1888	1
13	1991	1
11	2273	2
14	2274	2
12	2394	1
14	2395	1
14	2497	1
11	3451	1

Part : Table

Part Number	Part Descriptior	Unit Price	Supplier Numbe
1699	Chrome Hubcap	225	29
2394	Front Windshiel	550	19
1991	Gas cap	50	17
3451	Grill	425	15
2273	Head Light	75	17
1759	Hood	225	15
1374	Left side panel	150	15
1655	Radial tire	175	21
2497	Rear bumper	495	15
2395	Rear windshield	550	19
1375	Right side pane	150	15
1888	Roof panel	650	15
2274	Tail Light	65	17
1766	Trunk lid	450	15
1125	Windshield Wip	25	17

(b)

FIGURE 3.7 Smaller relationships broken down from the non-normal relations. (a) Order, Supplier, Customer. (b) Ordered Parts, Part.

- The primary key of the ORDER relation (Order Number) provides a link to the ORDERED PARTS relation (the link numbered 1 in figure 3.8).
- The ORDERED PARTS relation supplies the Number of Parts information to ORDER.

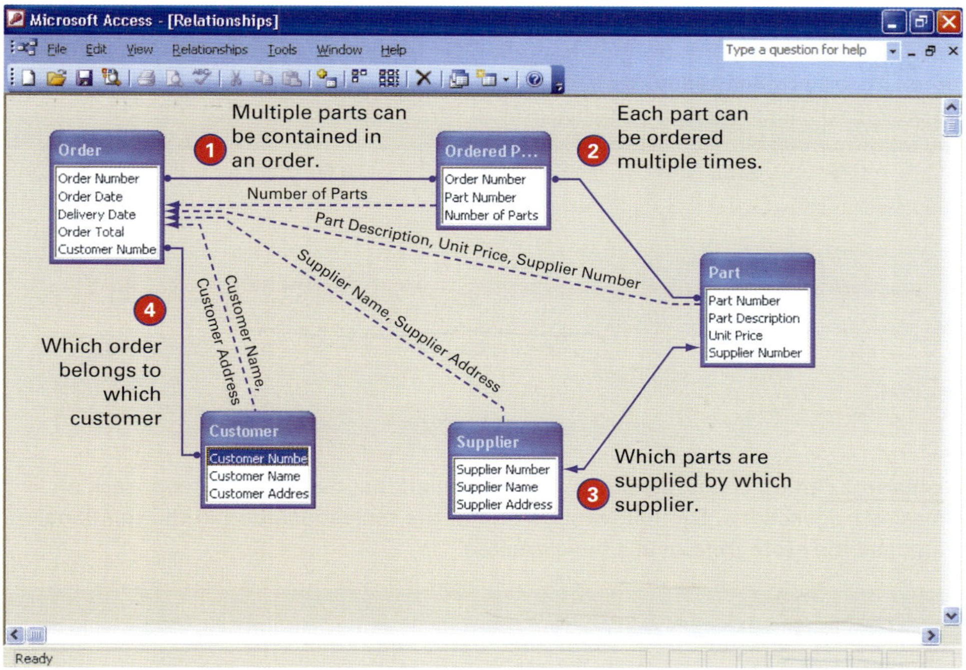

FIGURE 3.8 How normalised relations produce the order.

- The primary key of the ORDERED PARTS relation is a composite key that consists of Order Number and Part Number. Therefore, the Part Number component of the primary key provides a link to the PART relation (the link numbered 2 in figure 3.8).
- The PART relation supplies the Part Description, Unit Price and Supplier Number to ORDER.
- The Supplier Number in the PART relation provides a link to the SUPPLIER relation (the link numbered 3 in figure 3.8).
- The SUPPLIER relation provides the Supplier Name and Supplier Address to ORDER.
- The Customer Number in ORDER provides a link to the CUSTOMER relation (the link numbered 4 in figure 3.8).
- The CUSTOMER relation supplies the Customer Name and Customer Address to ORDER.

Databases in action

It is safe to say that almost all organisations have one or more databases. Further, there are numerous interesting database applications. Organisations implement databases to efficiently and effectively manage their data. However, because databases typically process data in real time (or near real time), it is not practical to allow users access to the databases. After all, the data will change while the user is looking at it! As a result, data warehouses have been developed that allow users to access data for decision making. You will learn about data warehouses in the next section.

BEFORE YOU GO ON . . .

1. What are the advantages and disadvantages of relational databases?
2. What are the benefits of data dictionaries?
3. Describe how structured query language works.

Apply the Concept

Background

This section has shown some of the issues with traditional filing systems. Redundancy is one of them and is a huge problem in data management because any time there is redundancy there is a possibility to introduce error. If you have one customer listed two ways in your database, how do you know it is not two separate people? What would it do to your data analysis to have incorrect data?

Activity

As was stated in Apply the Concept (p. 82), there are times when the best way to learn something is to do it. Consider the following tables and scenarios and see if you can find the problems based on what you have learned in this section about normalisation and problems within databases.

Scenario 1. A retail store decides to create a relational database to help keep track of its customers. The following is one of the tables included in this database.

Customer ID	First name	Last name	Income	Phones
1	John	Smith	$20 000	08 7561 1111, 08 7562 9111, 08 7569 8400
2	Jane	Summers	$35 000	08 7565 1000, 08 7561 4567
3	Joe	Saunders	$30 000	08 7565 6111
4	Jen	Smithson	$45 000	08 7565 0094, 08 7562 0924

Scenario 2. An office supply store creates a relational database to keep track of its sales transactions. The following is one of the tables included in the relational database the store employees have created.

Customer ID	First name	Last name	Customer phone	Order number	Order date	Item description	Quantity	Unit price	Shipped
1	Kara	Liu	08 7562 1111	1	01/02/2015	Staplers	2	$18.99	Y
1	Kara	Liu	08 7562 1111	1	01/02/2015	Pens	20	$5.79	N
2	Kevin	Lawrence	08 7563 1000	2	01/03/2015	Staplers	5	$18.99	N
3	Kimberly	Long	08 7569 6111	3	01/05/2015	Pens	35	$5.79	Y

Deliverable

For Scenario 1, describe what potential problems might arise if the store continues to store its customer information in this table. Be sure to use the terminology presented in this section with your answer. What changes would you make to improve the design of this table?

For Scenario 2, describe any potential problems that may arise if the store continues to store its sales information in this table. Again, look through the terms presented in this section for your answer. What changes would you recommend to this business owner in regard to this database design?

THE NOOK

QUESTIONS

1 Given the type of information Malakai and Abbie want to find in their data, what advantages would they find in a relational database over multiple flat files (spreadsheets)?

2 What safety precautions could Malakai and Abbie implement for customers with a relational database? For example, a bartender may recognise that he has sold five shots to a particular customer and refuse to serve that person more out of concern for his or her health. If that customer had purchased these from different bartenders, could this have occurred?

3 What are the implications of a serve/no serve decision (due to overindulgence) from the customer viewpoint and The Nook?

3.4 Data warehouses and data marts

Today, the most successful companies are those that can respond quickly and flexibly to market changes and opportunities. A key to this response is the effective and efficient use of data and information by analysts and managers. The problem is providing users with access to corporate data so that they can analyse it to make better decisions. Let's look at an example. If the manager of a local bookstore wanted to know the profit margin on used books at her store, she could find out from her database, using SQL or QBE. However, if she needed to know the trend in the profit margins on used books over the last ten years, she would have a very difficult query to construct in SQL or QBE.

This example illustrates several reasons why organisations are building data warehouses and/or data marts. First, the bookstore's databases have the necessary information to answer the manager's query, but this information is not organised in a way that makes it easy for her to find what she needs. Second, the organisation's databases are designed to process millions of transactions per day. Therefore, complicated queries might take a long time to answer and might degrade the performance of the databases. Third, transactional databases are designed to be updated. This update process requires extra processing. Data warehouses and data marts are read-only and the extra processing is eliminated because data already in the data warehouse are not updated. Fourth, transactional databases are designed to access a single record at a time. Data warehouses are designed to access large groups of related records.

As a result of these problems, companies are using a variety of tools with data warehouses and data marts to make it easier and faster for users to access, analyse and query data. You will learn about these tools in chapter 5, 'Business intelligence'.

Describing data warehouses and data marts

In general, data warehouses and data marts support business intelligence (BI) applications. As you will see in chapter 5, business intelligence is a broad category of applications, technologies and processes for gathering, storing, accessing and analysing data to help business users make better decisions. A **data warehouse** is a repository of historical data that are organised by subject to support decision makers in the organisation.

Because data warehouses are so expensive, they are used primarily by large companies. A **data mart** is a low-cost, scaled-down version of a data warehouse that is designed for the end-user needs in a strategic business unit (SBU) or a department. Data marts can be implemented more quickly than data warehouses, often in less than 90 days. Further, they support local rather than central control by conferring power on the using group. Typically, groups that need a single or a few BI applications require only a data mart, rather than a data warehouse.

The basic characteristics of data warehouses and data marts include the following.

- *Organised by business dimension or subject.* Data are organised by subject (for example, by customer, vendor, product, price level and region). This arrangement is different from transactional systems where data are organised by business process, such as order entry, inventory control, or accounts receivable.
- *Use online analytical processing*. Typically, organisational databases are oriented towards handling transactions. That is, databases use **online transaction processing** (OLTP), where business transactions are processed online as soon as they occur. The objectives are speed and efficiency, which are critical to a successful internet-based business operation. Data warehouses and data marts, which are not designed to support OLTP but to support decision makers, use online analytical processing. *Online analytical processing (OLAP)* involves the analysis of accumulated data by end users.
- *Integrated.* Data are collected from multiple systems and are integrated around subjects. For example, customer data may be extracted from internal (and external) systems and integrated around a customer identifier so that a comprehensive view of the customer is created.
- *Time variant.* Data warehouses and data marts maintain historical data (i.e. it includes time as a variable). Unlike transactional systems, where only recent data (such as for the

last day, week, or month) are maintained, a warehouse or mart may store years of data. Historical data are needed to detect deviations, trends and long-term relationships.

- *Non-volatile*. Data warehouses and data marts are non-volatile — no one can change or update the data. Non-volatility means that the warehouse or mart reflects history, which is critical for trend analysis. Warehouses and marts are updated, but through IT-controlled load processes rather than by users.
- *Multidimensional*. Typically the data warehouse or mart uses a multidimensional data structure. Recall that relational databases store data in two-dimensional tables. In contrast, data warehouses and marts store data in more than two dimensions. For this reason, the data are said to be stored in a **multidimensional structure**. A common representation for this multidimensional structure is the *data cube*.

The data in data warehouses and marts are organised by *business dimensions*, which are the edges of the data cube and are subjects such as product, geographic area and time period. If you look ahead briefly to figure 3.11 (overleaf) for an example of a data cube, you see that the product dimension is comprised of nuts, screws, bolts and washers; the geographic area dimension is comprised of east, west and central; and the time period dimension is comprised of 2013, 2014 and 2015. Users can view and analyse data from the perspective of these business dimensions. This analysis is intuitive because the dimensions are in business terms, easily understood by users.

A generic data warehouse environment

The environment for data warehouses and marts includes the following:

- source systems that provide data to the warehouse or mart
- data integration technology and processes that are needed to prepare the data for use
- different architectures for storing data in an organisation's data warehouse or data marts
- different tools and applications for the variety of users (you will learn about these tools and applications in chapter 5)
- metadata, data quality and governance processes that are in place to ensure that the warehouse or mart meets its purposes.

Figure 3.9 shows a generic data warehouse/data mart environment. Let's drill down into the component parts.

FIGURE 3.9 Data warehouse framework and views.

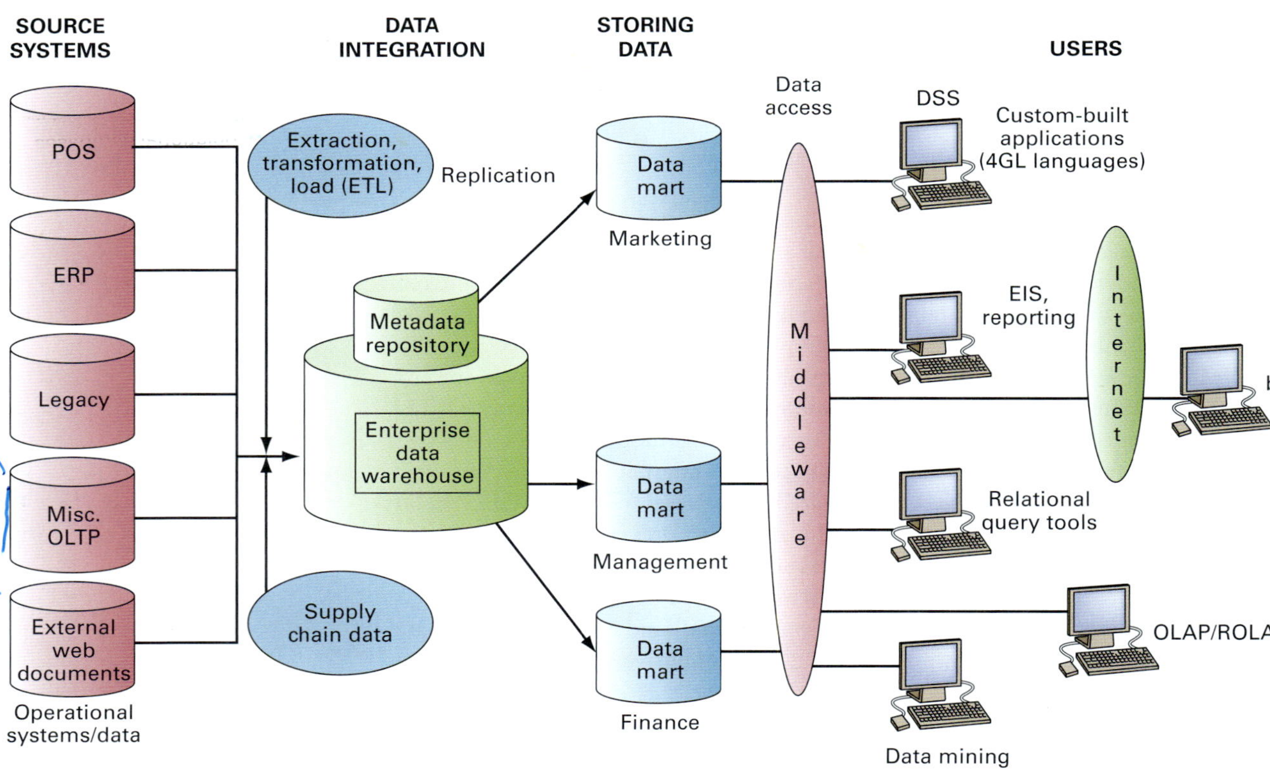

Source systems

There is typically some 'organisational pain' (i.e. business need) that motivates the development of BI capabilities in a firm. Working backward, this pain leads to information requirements, BI applications and source system data requirements. The data requirements can require only a single source system, as in the case of a data mart, or hundreds of source systems, as in the case of an enterprise-wide data warehouse.

A variety of source systems can be used. Possibilities include operational/transactional systems, enterprise resource planning (ERP) systems, website data, third-party data (e.g. customer demographic data) and more. The trend is to include more types of data (e.g. sensing data from RFID tags). These source systems often use different software packages (e.g. IBM, Oracle) and store data in different formats (e.g. relational, hierarchical).

A common source for the data in data warehouses is the company's operational databases, which can be relational databases. To differentiate between relational databases and multidimensional data warehouses and marts, suppose your company has four products — nuts, screws, bolts and washers — that have been sold in three territories — East, West and Central — for the previous three years — 2013, 2014 and 2015. In a relational database, these sales data would look like figures 3.10 (a), (b) and (c). In a multidimensional database, these data would be represented by a three-dimensional matrix (or data cube), as shown in figure 3.10. You would say that this matrix represents sales *dimensioned by* products and regions and year. Notice that in figure 3.10 (a) you can see only sales for 2013. Therefore, sales for 2014 and 2015 are presented in figures 3.10 (b) and 3.10 (c), respectively. Figures 3.12 (a), (b) and (c) (overleaf) show the equivalence between these relational and multidimensional databases.

Many source systems have been in use for years and contain 'bad data' (e.g. missing or incorrect data) and are poorly documented. As a result, data profiling software should be used at the beginning of a data warehousing project to better understand the data. For example, data profiling software can provide statistics on missing data, identify possible primary and foreign keys, and reveal how derived values (e.g. column 3 = column 1 + column 2) are calculated. Subject area database specialists (e.g. marketing, human resources) can also help in understanding and accessing the data in source systems.

Other source systems issues must be addressed. Often there are multiple systems that contain some of the same data and the best system must be selected as the source. Organisations must also decide how granular (i.e. detailed) the data should be. For example, are daily sales figures needed or are data at the individual transaction level needed? The conventional wisdom is that it is best to store data at a highly granular level because the data are likely to be requested at some point.

FIGURE 3.10 Relational databases.

(**a**) 2013

Product	Region	Sales
Nuts	East	50
Nuts	West	60
Nuts	Central	100
Screws	East	40
Screws	West	70
Screws	Central	80
Bolts	East	90
Bolts	West	120
Bolts	Central	140
Washers	East	20
Washers	West	10
Washers	Central	30

(**b**) 2014

Product	Region	Sales
Nuts	East	60
Nuts	West	70
Nuts	Central	110
Screws	East	50
Screws	West	80
Screws	Central	90
Bolts	East	100
Bolts	West	130
Bolts	Central	150
Washers	East	30
Washers	West	20
Washers	Central	40

(**c**) 2015

Product	Region	Sales
Nuts	East	70
Nuts	West	80
Nuts	Central	120
Screws	East	60
Screws	West	90
Screws	Central	100
Bolts	East	110
Bolts	West	140
Bolts	Central	160
Washers	East	40
Washers	West	30
Washers	Central	50

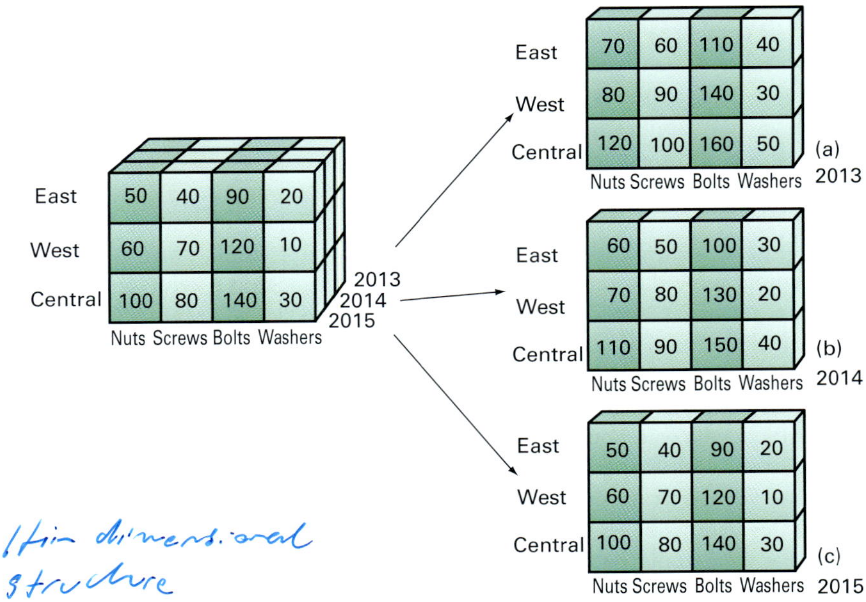

FIGURE 3.11 Data cube.

Data integration

It is necessary to extract data from source systems, transform it and load it into a data mart or warehouse. This is often called ETL, but the term *data integration* is increasingly used because of the growing number of ways that source system data can be handled. For example, in some cases, data are extracted, loaded into a mart or warehouse and then transformed (i.e. ELT rather than ETL).

Data extraction can be performed by handwritten code (e.g. SQL queries) or by commercial data integration software. Most companies ultimately use commercial software. It makes it relatively easy to specify the tables and attributes in the source systems that are to be used, map and schedule the movement of the data to the target (e.g. a data mart or warehouse), make the required transformations and ultimately load the data.

The data are transformed to make them more useful. For example, data from different systems may be integrated around a common key, such as a customer identification number. This is the approach taken with customer data in order to have a 360-degree view of all interactions with customers (discussed in chapter 12). For example, think of a bank. Customers may go to a branch, bank online, use an ATM, have a car loan and more. The systems for these touchpoints (the numerous ways that organisations interact with customers, such as email, the web, direct contact, the telephone, etc.) are typically separate. To analyse and fully understand how customers are using the bank, it is necessary to integrate the data from the various source systems in a data mart or warehouse.

Other kinds of transformations are also made. For example, format changes to the data may be required, such as using *male* and *female* to denote gender, as opposed to 0 and 1 or M and F. Aggregations may be performed, say on sales figures, so that queries can use the summaries rather than recalculating them each time. Data cleansing software may be used to 'clean up' the data, such as eliminating duplicate records (e.g. for the same customer).

Data are loaded into the warehouse or mart during a 'load window'. This window (i.e. the period for loading new data) is getting smaller as companies seek to have ever-fresher data in their warehouses. Many companies have moved to real-time data warehousing where data are moved (using data integration processes) from source systems to the data warehouse or mart almost immediately. For example, within 15 minutes of a purchase at Target, the details of the sale are in a warehouse and available for analysis.

Storing the data

A variety of possible architectures can store decision support data. The most common architecture is *one central enterprise data warehouse*, without data marts. Most organisations use this approach, as the data in the warehouse is accessed by all users and is the *single version of the truth*.

Product	Region	Sales
Nuts	East	50
Nuts	West	60
Nuts	Central	100
Screws	East	40
Screws	West	70
Screws	Central	80
Bolts	East	90
Bolts	West	120
Bolts	Central	140
Washers	East	20
Washers	West	10
Washers	Central	30

2013

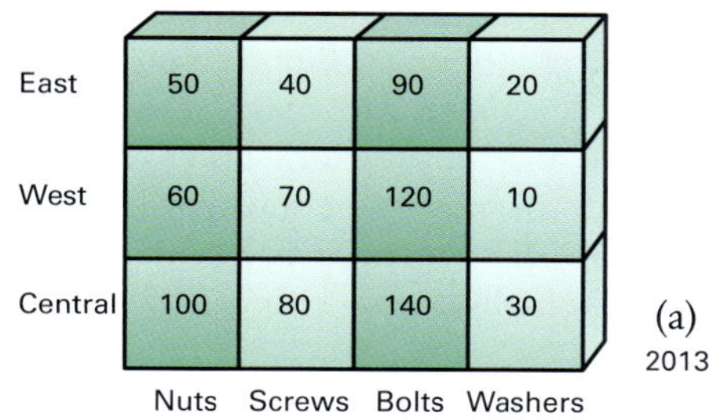

Product	Region	Sales
Nuts	East	60
Nuts	West	70
Nuts	Central	110
Screws	East	50
Screws	West	80
Screws	Central	90
Bolts	East	100
Bolts	West	130
Bolts	Central	150
Washers	East	30
Washers	West	20
Washers	Central	40

2014

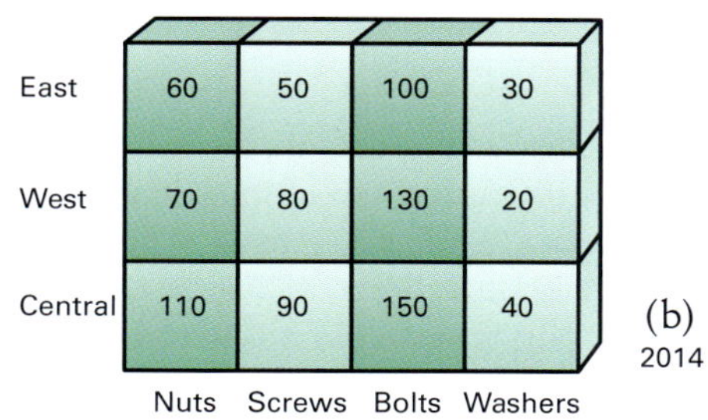

Product	Region	Sales
Nuts	East	70
Nuts	West	80
Nuts	Central	120
Screws	East	60
Screws	West	90
Screws	Central	100
Bolts	East	110
Bolts	West	140
Bolts	Central	160
Washers	East	40
Washers	West	30
Washers	Central	50

2015

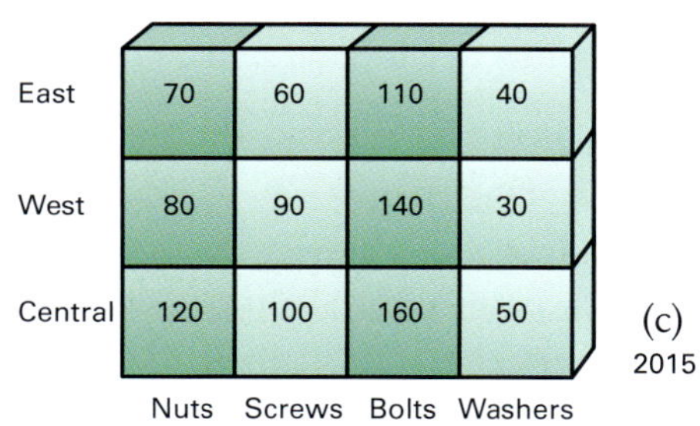

FIGURE 3.12 Equivalence between relational and multidimensional databases.

Another architecture is *independent data marts*. With this architecture, data are stored for a single or a few applications, such as in marketing or finance. Limited thought is given to how the data might be used for other applications and throughout the organisation. This is a very application-centric approach to storing data.

This approach is not very good. Although it may meet a specific organisational need, it does not take an enterprise-wide approach to data management. What happens is that independent data marts are created throughout the organisation by various organisational units. Not only are the marts expensive to build and maintain, but they often contain inconsistent data. For example, they may have inconsistent data definitions (such as, What is a customer? Is one a potential or current customer?) or use different source systems (which may have different data for what should be the same, such as for a customer address). Although independent data marts are an organisational reality, larger companies have increasingly moved to data warehouses.

Still another data warehouse architecture is the *hub and spoke*. With this architecture, data are stored in a central data warehouse with dependent data marts that source their data from the central repository. Because the dependent data marts get their data from the central repository, the data in the dependent data marts still comprise the *single version of the truth* for decision support purposes.

The dependent data marts store the data in a format appropriate for how the data will be used and for providing faster response times to queries and applications. As you have learned, users can view and analyse data from the perspective of business dimensions and measures. This analysis is intuitive because the dimensions are in business terms, easily understood by users.

Metadata

It is important to maintain data about the data (i.e. metadata) in the data warehouse. Both the IT personnel who operate and manage the data warehouse and the users who access the warehouse's data need metadata. IT personnel need information about data sources; database, table and column names; refresh schedules; and data usage measures. Users' needs include data definitions; the report/query tools that are available; report distribution information; and help desk contact information.

Data quality

The quality of the data in the warehouse must meet users' needs. If it does not, the data will not be trusted and ultimately will not be used. Most organisations find that the quality of the data in source systems is poor and must be improved before it can be used in the data warehouse. Some of the data can be improved with data-cleansing software, but the better, long-term solution is to improve the quality at the source system level. This requires that the business owners of the data take responsibility for making the changes necessary to improve the quality of the data.

To illustrate a need to improve data quality, a large hotel chain wanted to conduct targeted marketing promotions using postcode data collected during the check-in process. When the postcode data were profiled, many of the postcodes were found to be 5000. Obviously, the check-in operators were not asking customers for their postcodes but needed to enter something to complete the registration process. A short-term solution was to conduct the marketing campaign using city and state data. The long-term solution was to get the check-in operators to enter the actual postcodes. The latter required the hotel managers to take the responsibility for getting their check-in operators to enter better data.

Governance

To ensure that BI is meeting organisational needs, it is necessary to have governance to plan and control BI activities. This requires that people, committees and processes be in place. Companies that are effective in BI governance often have a senior-level committee made up of vice-presidents and directors who ensure that the business and BI strategies are in alignment, prioritise projects and allocate resources. Then there is a middle management–level committee that oversees the various projects in the BI portfolio and sees that the projects are being completed effectively and efficiently. Lower level operational committees perform tasks such as creating data definitions and identifying and solving data problems. All these committees require the collaboration and contributions of business and IT personnel.

Users

Once the data are in a data mart or warehouse, access is possible. This access begins the process of receiving business value from BI; everything else constitutes creating BI infrastructure.

Potential BI users are many, including IT developers; frontline workers; analysts; information workers; managers and executives; and suppliers, customers and regulators. Some of these users are *information producers* in that they primarily create information for others. IT developers and analysts typically are in this category. On the other hand, some users are *information consumers*, including managers and executives, because they consume information created by others.

Companies have reported hundreds of successful data-warehousing applications. For example, you can read client success stories and case studies at the websites of vendors such as Oracle (**www.oracle.com**) and Mark Gurry and Associates (**www.mga.com.au**). For a more detailed discussion, visit the Data Warehouse Institute Australia (tdwi.org/australia). The benefits of data warehousing include the following.

- End users can access needed data quickly and easily via web browsers because these data are located in one place.
- End users can conduct extensive analysis with data in ways that may not have been possible before.
- End users can obtain a consolidated view of organisational data.

These benefits can improve business knowledge, provide competitive advantage, enhance customer service and satisfaction, facilitate decision making and streamline business processes. IT's About Business demonstrates the benefits of data warehousing to the Australian tourism business.

IT'S ABOUT BUSINESS

How data warehousing is supporting tourism business in Australia

The Australian Tourism Data Warehouse (ATDW) is Australia's national distribution platform for tourism information[16] that supports the growth of the tourism industry in Australia.[17] ATDW was originally developed in 2001 as a joint effort of Tourism Australia and other state and territory tourism organisations. It is a centralised storage and distribution facility for tourism products and information. Data stored in the ATDW include tourist attractions and destinations, events and guided tours, accommodation and transportation[18] using nationally agreed data formatting standards. Tourism business owners and operators, wholesalers, retailers and distributors can access ATDW and use it for their booking systems and websites. In 2013 the Australian Tourism Booking Widget (ATBW)[19] was launched by ATDW. It was developed specifically for SMEs operating in the tourism industry that do not have online booking capabilities in order to enable them to enter the online tourism market supporting real-time online bookings and online payments from consumers and customer support services. Together, the ATDW and the ATBW offer a cost-effective solution for tourism business owners and operators, enhancing the dissemination of tourism information electronically and online exposure by way of a rich and flexible content in a central data warehouse that can be easily used to populate their websites. Presently, the ATDW includes over 33 000 tourism product listings that can be published across ATDW's multi-channel partner distribution network. Tourism business owners can experience a number of benefits when they join the ATDW, including:[20]

- enhanced cost-effective online marketing including content dissemination through state, territory and Tourism Australia sponsored websites
- efficient content distribution as business information is supplied once to the ATDW and distributed to multiple partners
- the ATDW offers tourism business owners opportunities for information quality control
- increased exposure of tourism business through licensed tourism distributors and through inclusion in the most comprehensive tourism data warehouse in Australia
- effective and efficient participation in state and federal sponsored tourism campaign initiatives.

In October 2013, ATDW also offered the Tourism e-Kit,[21] which offers an online training course and educational resource for Australian tourism businesses focusing on the benefits of joining the ATDW and being online.

QUESTIONS

1. Why is it so important for tourism businesses to integrate data in the ATDW?
2. What are some potential disadvantages of consolidating tourism data into one data warehouse?

BEFORE YOU GO ON . . .

1. Differentiate between data warehouses and data marts.
2. Describe the characteristics of a data warehouse.
3. What are three possible architectures for data warehouses and data marts in an organisation?

Despite their many benefits, data warehouses do have problems. First, they can be very expensive to build and to maintain. Second, incorporating data from obsolete mainframe systems can be difficult and expensive. Finally, people in one department might be reluctant to share data with other departments.

3.5 Knowledge management

As noted throughout this text, data and information are critically important organisational assets. Knowledge is a vital asset as well. Successful managers have always used intellectual assets and recognised their value. But these efforts were not systematic and they did not ensure that knowledge was shared and dispersed in a way that benefited the overall organisation. Moreover, industry analysts estimate that most of a company's knowledge assets are not housed in relational databases. Instead, they are dispersed in email, word processing documents, spreadsheets and presentations on individual computers. This arrangement makes it extremely difficult for companies to access and integrate this knowledge. The result frequently is less-effective decision making.

Concepts and definitions

Knowledge management (KM) is a process that helps organisations manipulate important knowledge that is part of the organisation's memory, usually in an unstructured format. For an organisation to be successful, knowledge, as a form of capital, must exist in a format that can be exchanged among persons. In addition, it must be able to grow.

Knowledge

In the information technology context, knowledge is distinct from data and information. As you learned in chapter 1, data are a collection of facts, measurements and statistics; information is organised or processed data that are timely and accurate. Knowledge is information that is *contextual*, *relevant* and *useful*. Simply put, knowledge is *information in action*. **Intellectual capital** (or **intellectual assets**) is another term for knowledge.

To illustrate with an example, a program listing all the courses offered by your university during one semester would be considered data. When you register, you process the data from the program to create your schedule for the semester. Your schedule would be considered information. Awareness of your work schedule, your major, your desired social schedule and characteristics of different faculty members could be construed as knowledge, because it can affect the way you build your schedule. You see that this awareness is contextual and relevant (to developing an optimal schedule of classes) as well as useful (it can lead to changes in your schedule). The implication is that knowledge has strong experiential and reflective elements that distinguish it from information in a given context. Unlike information, knowledge can be exercised to solve a problem.

Numerous theories and models classify different types of knowledge. Here you will focus on the distinction between explicit knowledge and tacit knowledge.

Explicit and tacit knowledge

Explicit knowledge deals with more objective, rational and technical knowledge. In an organisation, explicit knowledge consists of the policies, procedural guides, reports, products, strategies, goals, core competencies and IT infrastructure of the enterprise. In other words, explicit knowledge is the knowledge that has been codified (documented) in a form that can be distributed to others or transformed into a process or a strategy. A description of how to process a job application that is documented in a firm's human resources policy manual is an example of explicit knowledge.

In contrast, **tacit knowledge** is the cumulative store of subjective or experiential learning. In an organisation, tacit knowledge consists of an organisation's experiences, insights, expertise, know-how, trade secrets, skill sets, understanding and learning. It also includes the organisational culture, which reflects the past and present experiences of the organisation's people and processes, as well as the organisation's prevailing values. Tacit knowledge is generally imprecise and costly to transfer. It is also highly personal.

Finally, because it is unstructured, it is difficult to formalise or codify, in contrast to explicit knowledge. A salesperson who has worked with particular customers over time and has come to know their needs quite well would possess extensive tacit knowledge. This knowledge is typically not recorded. In fact, it might be difficult for the salesperson to put into writing.

Knowledge management systems

The goal of knowledge management is to help an organisation make the most effective use of the knowledge it has. Historically, management information systems have focused on capturing, storing, managing and reporting explicit knowledge. Organisations now realise they need to integrate explicit and tacit knowledge in formal information systems. **Knowledge management systems (KMSs)** refer to the use of modern information technologies — the internet, intranets, extranets, databases — to systematise, enhance and expedite intrafirm and interfirm knowledge management. KMSs are intended to help an organisation cope with turnover, rapid change and downsizing by making the expertise of the organisation's human capital widely accessible. IT's About Business describes a new type of knowledge management at Quora.

IT'S ABOUT BUSINESS

A website for gathering subjective knowledge

Two decades after the invention of the world wide web, vast areas of knowledge and experience are still not online, let alone searchable. 'Ninety per cent of the information people have is still in their heads and not on the web', says one of Quora's cofounders. Quora's other cofounder calls it 'experiential knowledge'. Wikipedia (www.wikipedia.org) has amazing breadth and scope, but there is only so much that any encyclopedia, limited to verifiable facts about discrete nouns, can capture within the entire database of human knowledge. On the other end of the 'knowledge' spectrum, websites such as Facebook and Twitter allow people to describe their lives and to make personal observations. However, it is very difficult on such networks to separate informed opinions from speculation.

Quora (www.quora.com), a question-and-answer (Q&A) website, straddles the space between the two approaches — the objective (Wikipedia) and the subjective (social networks). Other Q&A sites include Yahoo! Answers (answers.yahoo.com) and WikiAnswers (wiki.answers.com). Yahoo! Answers is the leading Q&A site, with approximately 85 800 unique visitors daily and approximately 354 354 daily page views in March 2013.[22] But few searches can be satisfied with Yahoo! Answers, where the questions are often silly and the replies are often conflicting or flat-out inaccurate. Many replies tend to be guesswork offered by people with little or no knowledge of the subject at hand.

On Quora's website, you can get started with the page — framed as a question — about getting started on Quora. Or you can begin by sifting through random questions that are displayed in the centre of the screen. On the top of the Quora homepage is a large search bar. Using key words, you can find questions that others have already posed or choose topics to follow so that the website can begin serving up queries more suited to your interests. You can also start following people. That way, the questions that people you are following ask, the answers they get and the questions they follow will show up in your feed. You can also vote 'up' answers that you think are helpful and vote 'down' those that are not. All of your activity shows up in your feed. Quora offers several advantages over other Q&A sites, including the following.

- Real names are mandatory, so there is a heavy social cost to acting the fool. Real names increase the quality of answers and reduce bad behaviour and flaming. Quora does allow anonymous posts, however, which helps when asking about a personal health issue, for example, or responding about your own experience as a fellow sufferer.
- Many websites provide only one viewpoint at a time on a particular issue, meaning that the user has to search for referencing articles or scan through many comments to find a counterpoint. Quora allows both point and counterpoint to coexist at an equal level in a discussion.
- Quora encourages answers that are thorough and in-depth. In Quora's community, the most valued responses reflect honest intelligence and wisdom.
- Users can vote an answer up or down, the better to push quality to the top and frivolous or poorly conceived answers to the bottom (if not off the page entirely). Users can also deem an answer 'not helpful' — a signal →

to the Quora team or one of the site's hundred-plus volunteers that perhaps they should consider deleting it.

- Unlike on Facebook, everything users write can be trimmed, corrected, or otherwise edited by one of the rigorous volunteers. Volunteers often send answers back to their authors marked up with suggested edits. Questions, too, can get extensively reworded.

Quora's goal is to capture as much subjective knowledge as possible. By creating an environment for members to post questions, answer questions and rate the quality of others' answers, Quora is building a searchable repository of information while it also builds a community. Quora hopes to attract so many users that its subjective, experiential, inherent knowledge will construct a comprehensive picture of the world.[23] In 2013 Quora also launched a blogging service.[24]

Despite these admirable goals, one major complaint about Quora has emerged. Veteran members have noted a declining quality associated with the rapid growth in Quora membership. Both founders acknowledge that the average quality of answers on Quora has declined significantly. Another problem with Quora is the large gaps in its knowledge areas, which is only to be expected as the website is relatively young, having emerged in 2009. One example of a knowledge gap is that Quora has brilliant entries for high-tech startups but almost no entries for Hollywood.

Despite these shortcomings, according to recent statistics, monthly visitors grew to over 700 000 during the first quarter of 2013.[25] According to AppData that measures the proportion of Quora's audience that log in via Facebook, the site has around 520 000 monthly active users and around 60 000 daily active users.[26]

Quora has not yet earned any revenue. But, if Quora can fulfil its vision of getting experts to engage in conversation and thus generate searchable and authoritative answers to many thousands of questions, then it may someday grab more page views than Wikipedia by filling in gaps that no encyclopedia could ever address. For marketers Quora can be an effective means of finding out about the types of issues that are perceived or considered to be interesting and even identify a potential user base that can ultimately help determine the direction of future content.[27]

Sources: Compiled from N Robertson (2011), 'Five reasons why Quora matters to marketers', *Marketingprofs.com*, 14 June; G Rivlin (2011), 'Does Quora really have all the answers?', *Wired*, 26 April; M Lowman (2011), 'The mystery behind Quora', *BostInnovation*, 1 February; S Goodson (2011), 'Why is Quora exploding?', *Forbes*, 11 January; M Ingram (2011), 'Can Quora survive its growing popularity?', *GigaOm*, 9 January; C Arthur and J Kiss (2011), 'Quora: the hottest question-and-answer website you've probably never heard of', *The Guardian*, 5 January; M Siegler (2011), 'Quora signups exploded in late December', *TechCrunch*, 5 January; Q Hardy (2010), 'What does Quora know?', *Forbes*, 18 November; www.quora.com.

QUESTIONS

1. Compare and contrast Quora to knowledge management systems in individual organisations. Could a Quora-type knowledge management system be used inside an organisation? Why or why not? Support your answer.
2. Provide examples of how Quora can fill in the gaps in its searchable knowledge base.

Organisations can realise many benefits with KMSs. Most importantly, they make **best practices**, the most effective and efficient ways of doing things, readily available to a wide range of employees. Enhanced access to best practice knowledge improves overall organisational performance. For example, account managers can now make available their tacit knowledge about how best to handle large accounts. The organisation can then use this knowledge to train new account managers. Other benefits include improved customer service, more efficient product development, and improved employee morale and retention.

At the same time, however, implementing effective KMSs presents some challenges. First, employees must be willing to share their personal tacit knowledge. To encourage this behaviour, organisations must create a knowledge management culture that rewards employees who add their expertise to the knowledge base. Second, the knowledge base must be continually maintained and updated. New knowledge must be added, and old, outdated knowledge must be deleted. Finally, companies must be willing to invest in the resources needed to carry out these operations.

The KMS cycle

A functioning KMS follows a cycle that consists of six steps (see figure 3.13). The reason the system is cyclical is that knowledge is dynamically refined over time. The knowledge in an effective KMS is never finalised because the environment changes over time and knowledge must be updated to reflect these changes. The cycle works as follows.

1. *Create knowledge*. Knowledge is created as people determine new ways of doing things or develop know-how. Sometimes external knowledge is brought in.

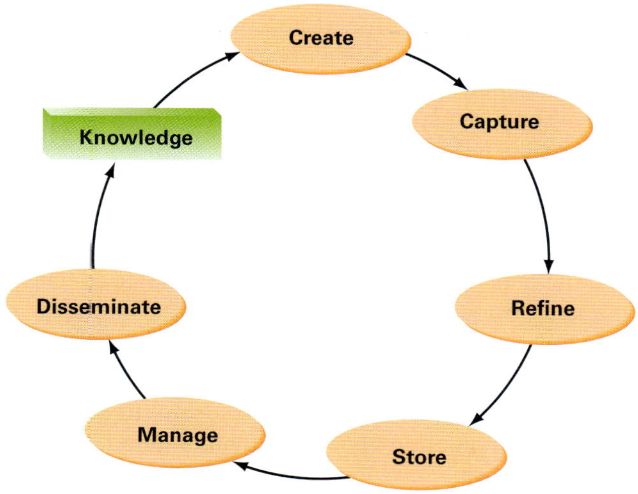

FIGURE 3.13 The knowledge management system cycle.

2 *Capture knowledge*. New knowledge must be identified as valuable and be represented in a reasonable way.
3 *Refine knowledge*. New knowledge must be placed in context so that it is actionable. This is where tacit qualities (human insights) must be captured along with explicit facts.
4 *Store knowledge*. Useful knowledge must then be stored in a reasonable format in a knowledge repository so that others in the organisation can access it.
5 *Manage knowledge*. Like a library, the knowledge must be kept current. It must be reviewed regularly to verify that it is relevant and accurate.
6 *Disseminate knowledge*. Knowledge must be made available in a useful format to anyone in the organisation who needs it, anywhere and anytime.

BEFORE YOU GO ON . . .

1. What is knowledge management?
2. What is the difference between tacit knowledge and explicit knowledge?
3. Describe the knowledge management system cycle.

THE NOOK

QUESTIONS

1. Explicit and tacit knowledge are two very different animals. Explicit knowledge is defined as knowledge that is easily captured. Tacit knowledge is more difficult to manage. Think of the bartender who works for Malakai and Abbie. What are some examples of explicit and tacit knowledge he/she may acquire over time?
2. Can you think of any ways to capture the tacit knowledge from a bartender and pass it on to another new employee?

WHAT'S IN IT FOR ME?

FOR THE ACCOUNTING MAJOR

The accounting function is intimately concerned with keeping track of the transactions and internal controls of an organisation. Modern databases enable accountants to perform these functions more effectively. Databases help accountants manage the flood of data in today's organisations so that they can keep their firms in compliance with the standards imposed by regulators and industry associations (e.g. Australian Auditing and Assurance Standards Board (AAASB)).

Accountants also play a role in cost, justifying the creation of a knowledge base and then auditing its cost-effectiveness. In addition, if you work for a large CPA company that provides management services or sells knowledge, you will most likely use some of your company's best practices that are stored in a knowledge base.

FOR THE FINANCE MAJOR

Financial managers make extensive use of computerised databases that are external to the organisation, such as CompuStat, to obtain financial data on organisations in their industry. They can use these data to determine if their organisation meets industry benchmarks in return on investment, cash management and other financial ratios.

Financial managers, who produce the organisation's financial status reports, need to understand relevant rules and regulations issued by industry bodies and regulators (e.g. Australian Stock Exchange (ASX)). Databases help these managers comply with the law's standards.

FOR THE MARKETING MAJOR

Databases help marketing managers access data from the organisation's marketing transactions, such as customer purchases, to plan targeted marketing campaigns and to evaluate the success of previous campaigns. Knowledge about customers can make the difference between success and failure. In many databases and knowledge bases, the vast majority of information and knowledge concerns customers, products, sales and marketing. Marketing managers regularly use an organisation's knowledge base and they often participate in its creation.

FOR THE PRODUCTION/OPERATIONS MANAGEMENT MAJOR

Production/operations personnel access organisational data to determine optimum inventory levels for parts in a production process. Past production data enable production/operations management (POM) personnel to determine the optimum configuration for assembly lines. Firms also collect quality data that inform them not only about the quality of finished products but also about quality issues with incoming raw materials, production irregularities, shipping and logistics, and after-sale use and maintenance of the product.

Knowledge management is extremely important for running complex operations. The accumulated knowledge regarding scheduling, logistics, maintenance and other functions is very valuable. Innovative ideas are necessary for improving operations and can be supported by knowledge management.

FOR THE HUMAN RESOURCES MANAGEMENT MAJOR

Organisations keep extensive data on employees, including gender, age, race, current and past job descriptions, and performance evaluations. HR personnel access these data to provide reports to government agencies regarding compliance with federal equal opportunity guidelines. HR managers also use these data to evaluate hiring practices, evaluate salary structures and manage any discrimination grievances or lawsuits brought against the firm.

Databases help HR managers provide assistance to all employees as companies turn over more and more decisions about health care and retirement planning to the employees themselves. The employees can use the databases for help in selecting the optimal mix among these critical choices.

HR managers also need to use a knowledge base frequently to find out how past cases were handled. Consistency in how employees are treated is not only important, but it also protects the company against legal actions. In addition, training for building, maintaining and using the knowledge system is sometimes the responsibility of the HR department. Finally, the HR department might be responsible for compensating employees who contribute their knowledge to the knowledge base.

FOR THE MIS MAJOR

The MIS function manages the organisation's data as well as the databases. MIS database administrators standardise data names by using the data dictionary. This process ensures that all users understand which data are in the database. Database personnel also help users access needed data and generate reports with query tools.

SUMMARY

1 Discuss ways that common challenges in managing data can be addressed using data governance.

The following are three common challenges in managing data.

> Data are scattered throughout organisations and are collected by many individuals using various methods and devices. These data are frequently stored in numerous servers and locations and in different computing systems, databases, formats, and human and computer languages.
> Data come from multiple sources.
> Information systems that support particular business processes impose unique requirements on data, which results in repetition and conflicts across an organisation.

One strategy for implementing data governance is master data management. Master data management provides companies with the ability to store, maintain, exchange and synchronise a consistent, accurate and timely 'single version of the truth' for the company's core master data. Master data management consistently manages data gathered from across an organisation, consistently manages data from multiple sources and consistently manages data across business processes in an organisation.

2 Explain how to interpret relationships depicted in an entity–relationship diagram.

See figure 3.4 and its accompanying explanation for a demonstration of interpreting relationships in an ER diagram.

3 Discuss the advantages and disadvantages of relational databases.

Relational databases allow people to compare information quickly by row or column. In addition, items are easy to retrieve by finding the point of intersection of a particular row and column. On the other hand, large-scale relational databases can be composed of many interrelated tables, making the overall design complex with slow search and access times.

4 Explain the elements necessary to successfully implement and maintain data warehouses.

To successfully implement and maintain a data warehouse, an organisation must:

> link source systems that provide data to the warehouse or mart
> prepare the necessary data for the data warehouse using data integration technology and processes
> decide on an appropriate architecture for storing data in the data warehouse or data mart
> select the tools and applications for the variety of organisational users
> ensure that metadata, data quality and governance processes are in place to ensure that the data warehouse or mart meets its purposes.

5 Describe the benefits and challenges of implementing knowledge management systems in organisations.

Organisations can realise many benefits with KMSs:

> best practices are readily available to a wide range of employees
> improved customer service
> more efficient product development
> improved employee morale and retention.

Challenges to implementing KMSs include the following.

> Employees must be willing to share their personal tacit knowledge.
> Organisations must create a knowledge management culture that rewards employees who add their expertise to the knowledge base.
> The knowledge base must be continually maintained and updated.
> Companies must be willing to invest in the resources needed to carry out these operations.

Organisations can use knowledge management to develop best practices, to establish the most effective and efficient ways of doing things and to make these practices readily available to a wide range of employees. Other benefits of knowledge management include improved customer service, more efficient product development and improved employee morale and retention.

A functioning KMS follows a cycle that consists of six steps: create knowledge, capture knowledge, refine knowledge, store knowledge, manage knowledge and disseminate knowledge.

>>> CHAPTER GLOSSARY

attribute Each characteristic or quality describing a particular entity.

best practices The most effective and efficient ways to do things.

bit A binary digit; that is, a 0 or a 1.

byte A group of eight bits that represents a single character.

clickstream data Data collected about user behaviour and browsing patterns by monitoring users' activities when they visit a website.

data dictionary Collection of definitions of data elements; data characteristics that use the data elements; and the individuals, business functions, applications and reports that use this data element.

data governance An approach to managing information across an entire organisation.

data mart A low-cost, scaled-down version of a data warehouse that is designed for the end-user needs in a strategic business unit (SBU) or a department.

data model Definition of the way data in a DBMS are conceptually structured.

data rot Physical problems with the media on which data are stored due to temperature, humidity and exposure to light. Data rot can make it difficult to access data.

data warehouse A repository of historical data that are organised by subject to support decision makers in the organisation.

database A group of logically related files that stores data and the associations among them.

database management system (DBMS) The software program (or group of programs) that provides access to a database.

entity A person, place, thing, or event about which information is maintained in a record.

entity classes Groupings of entities of a given type.

entity–relationship (ER) diagram Document that shows data entities and attributes and relationships among them.

entity–relationship (ER) modelling The process of designing a database by organising data entities to be used and identifying the relationships among them.

explicit knowledge The more objective, rational and technical types of knowledge.

field A grouping of logically related characters into a word, a small group of words, or a complete number.

file A grouping of logically related records.

identifiers Attributes that are unique to an entity instance.

instance A particular entity within an entity class.

intellectual capital (or intellectual assets) Other terms for knowledge.

knowledge management (KM) A process that helps organisations identify, select, organise, disseminate, transfer and apply information and expertise that are part of the organisation's memory and that typically reside within the organisation in an unstructured manner.

knowledge management systems (KMSs) Information technologies used to systematise, enhance and expedite intrafirm and interfirm knowledge management.

master data A set of core data, such as customer, product, employee, vendor, geographic location and so on, that spans an enterprise's information systems.

master data management A process that provides companies with the ability to store, maintain, exchange and synchronise a consistent, accurate and timely 'single version of the truth' for the company's core master data.

multidimensional structure Storage of data in more than two dimensions; a common representation is the data cube.

normalisation A method for analysing and reducing a relational database to its most streamlined form for minimum redundancy, maximum data integrity and best processing performance.

online transaction processing (OLTP) Processing of business transactions online as soon as they occur.

primary key The identifier field or attribute that uniquely identifies a record.

query by example (QBE) Database language that enables the user to fill out a grid (form) to construct a sample or description of the data wanted.

record A grouping of logically related fields.

relational database model Data model based on the simple concept of tables in order to capitalise on characteristics of rows and columns of data.

secondary key An identifier field or attribute that has some identifying information but typically does not identify the file with complete accuracy.

structured query language (SQL) Popular relational database language that enables users to perform complicated searches with relatively simple instructions.

table A grouping of logically related records.

tacit knowledge The cumulative store of subjective or experiential learning, which is highly personal and hard to formalise.

>>> DISCUSSION QUESTIONS

1 Explain the difficulties involved in managing data.
2 What are the problems associated with poor quality data?
3 What is master data management? What does it have to do with high quality data?
4 Explain why master data management is so important in companies that have multiple data sources.
5 Describe the advantages of relational databases.
6 Explain why it is important to capture and manage knowledge.
7 Compare and contrast tacit knowledge and explicit knowledge.

>>> PROBLEM-SOLVING ACTIVITIES

1 Access various employment websites (e.g. www.seek.com.au and www.mycareer.com.au) and find several job descriptions for a database administrator. Are the job descriptions similar? What are the salaries offered in these positions?

2 Access the websites of several real estate companies. Find the sites that take you through a step-by-step process for buying a home, that provide virtual reality tours of homes in your price range and location, that provide mortgage and interest rate calculators, and that offer financing for your home. Do the sites require that you register to access their services? Can you request that an email be sent to you when properties in which you might be interested become available?

3 It is possible to find many websites that provide demographic information. Access several of these sites and see what they offer. Do the sites differ in the types of demographic information they offer? If so, how? Do the sites require a fee for the information they offer? Would demographic information be useful to you if you wanted to start a new business? If so, how and why?

4 The internet contains many websites that provide information on financial aid resources for students. Access several of these sites. Do you have to register to access the information? Can you apply for financial aid on the sites, or do you have to request paper applications that you must complete and return?

5 Draw an entity–relationship diagram for a small retail store. You wish to keep track of the product name, description, unit price and number of items of that product sold to each customer. You also wish to record customer name, mailing address and billing address. You must track each transaction (sale) as to date, product purchased, unit price, number of units, tax and total amount of the sale.

6 Draw the entity–relationship diagram for the following patient appointment system. The business rules of this system are the following:

A doctor can be scheduled for many appointments but might not have any scheduled at all. Each appointment is scheduled with exactly one doctor. A patient can schedule one or more appointments. One appointment is scheduled with exactly one patient. An appointment must generate exactly one invoice and an invoice is generated by only one appointment. One payment is applied to exactly one invoice, and one invoice can be paid off over time by several payments. An invoice can be outstanding, having nothing yet paid on it at all. One patient can make many payments, but a single payment is made by only one patient. Some patients are insured by an insurance company. If they are insured, they can only carry insurance with one insurance company. An insurance company can have many patients carry their policies. For patients who carry insurance, the insurance company will make payments, with each single payment made by exactly one insurance company.

7 Access the websites of IBM (www.ibm.com.au), Sybase (www.sybase.com.au) and Oracle (www.oracle.com.au), and trace the capabilities of their latest data management products, including web connections.

8 Enter the website of the Gartner Group (www.gartner.com). Examine the company's research studies pertaining to data management. Prepare a report on the state of the art.

9 Calculate your personal digital footprint at www.johnwiley.com.au/highered/rainer/ausnz/studentresources.

10 Diagram a knowledge management system cycle for a fictional company that sells customised T-shirts to students.

>>> COLLABORATION EXERCISE

Background

Imagine that you and a few colleagues are given the job of designing a database for a pet store. The manager has asked that the following data be collected. Of course, there are multiple attributes for each of these entities. Your team has been tasked with outlining the specific data required to make this database a reality:

- customer data
- product data
- employee data
- financial data
- vendor data
- sales data
- inventory data
- building data
- other data (specify).

Recall from the chapter that an entity–relationship diagram (ER diagram) displays the data that would be contained within multiple tables as well as the relationships between those tables.

Activity

Divide into teams as instructed by your lecturer. Then equally divide the team by functional area. You will need some operations, marketing, accounting, human resources, management, etc., representatives on your team. Decide which functional area should work with the entities listed above.

Independently define the attributes for each entity. Once you complete this individual task, work with your group to find relationships among the attributes. You may have to add or remove or change some to reconcile the data you would collect in the individual tables.

Build your ER diagram using Google Docs. If you are not familiar with Google Drawings, visit www.johnwiley.com.au/highered/rainer/ausnz/studentresources and click on the link for chapter 3 collaboration exercise. It will take you to a YouTube and search for 'Introduction to Google Drawing' by 'logontolearn'.

Deliverable

Submit your group's ER diagram to your instructor to review.

CLOSING CASE **1 >**

Big data

Organisations and individuals need to process an unimaginably vast amount of data that is growing ever more rapidly. Research at the University of California at Berkeley has found that currently, approximately five quintillion (5 000 000 000 000 000 000) bytes of data are generated every two days, which equates to all of the information ever produced by all conversations that have ever taken place worldwide. Furthermore, the McKinsey Global Institute estimates that data volumes are growing at the rate of 40 per cent annually. According to Gartner, the world's leading ICT research company, 2013 is considered to be the year of big data experimentation and early deployment. While big data adoption is still considered to be in the early stages, in a recent survey Gartner found that approximately 20 per cent of the respondents are developing big data pilots and experimenting with them, 18 per cent are developing a big data strategy, 19 per cent are gathering knowledge concerning big data, whereas the rest have no plans or do not know. The industries that use big data include media communications, finance and banking, and services. Almost half of the respondents using big data are doing so in order to both improve their customer experience and enhance business process efficiencies.

Analysts have coined the term *big data* for the superabundance of data available today. Big data generally consists of the following.

- Traditional enterprise data — examples include customer information from customer relationship management systems, transactional enterprise resource planning data, web store transactions and general ledger data.
- Machine-generated/sensor data — examples include smart meters, manufacturing sensors, equipment logs and trading systems data.
- Social data — examples include customer feedback comments, microblogging sites such as Twitter and social media sites such as Facebook.

THE PROBLEM

Big data makes it possible to do many things that were previously impossible (e.g. spot business trends more rapidly and accurately, prevent disease, track crime, etc.). Big data, properly analysed, can reveal valuable patterns and information that were previously hidden because of the amount of work required to discover them. Leading corporations, such as Google, have been able to process big data for years, but they have had to do so at great expense. Today's commodity hardware, cloud computing (see Plug IT In #3) and open source software bring big data processing within budget for most organisations.

The problems with big data fall into three general categories: volume, velocity and variety.

- *Volume:* Irrespective of the source, structure, format and frequency of data, data is always valuable. If a certain kind of data seems to have no value today, it is because we have not yet been able to analyse it effectively. For example, several years ago when Google began harnessing satellite imagery, capturing street views and then sharing this geographical data for free, few people understood its value at that time. Today, we recognise that such data is incredibly valuable. Consider machine-generated data, which is produced in much larger quantities than non-traditional data. For instance, sensors in a single jet engine can generate 10 terabytes of data in 30 minutes. With more than 25 000 airline flights per day, the daily volume of data from just this single source is incredible. Other machine-generated data includes log files of smart electrical meters, sensor networks in heavy industrial equipment and machine-to-machine data which includes device status reporting data concerning the maintenance planning for fleets of vehicles or aircraft or general telemetry monitoring. Taken together, these add to the volume problem.
- *Velocity:* The rate at which data flows into an organisation is rapidly increasing. Velocity is critically important because it increases the speed of the feedback loop between a company and its customers. For example, the internet and mobile technology mean that online retailers are able to compile histories not just on final sales, but on their customers' every click and interaction. Companies that are able to quickly utilise that information — for

example, by recommending additional purchases — gain competitive advantage.

- *Variety:* Traditional data formats tend to be relatively well described and change slowly. Examples of traditional data include financial market data, point-of-sale transactions and many others. In contrast, non-traditional data formats change rapidly. Non-traditional data formats include satellite imagery, broadcast audio streams, digital music files, web page content, scans of government documents and comments on social networks.

THE IT SOLUTION

The first step for many organisations toward managing big data was to integrate information silos into a database environment and then to develop data warehouses for decision making. After completing this step, many organisations turned their attention to the business of information management — helping to make sense of their proliferating data. In recent years, Oracle, IBM, Microsoft and SAP have spent billions of dollars all together buying software firms that specialise in data management and business intelligence. (You will learn about business intelligence in chapter 5.)

Many organisations are turning to NoSQL databases (think of them as 'not only SQL' databases) to process big data. These databases provide an alternative when a firm does not have traditional, structured data that fits neatly into the rows and columns of relational databases.

NoSQL databases can handle unstructured data and inconsistent or missing data. Many products utilise NoSQL databases, including Cassandra (cassandra.apache.org), CouchDB (couchdb.apache.org), MongoDB (www.mongodb.org) and Hadoop (hadoop.apache.org). As of mid-2012, Hadoop was receiving the most attention.

Hadoop is a software platform that stores and manages large volumes of structured and unstructured data. Clickstream and social media applications are driving much of the demand for Hadoop, with particular emphasis on MapReduce. MapReduce is a dataprocessing approach supported on Hadoop (and other software packages) that is ideal for processing big volumes of these new data types. MapReduce breaks a big data problem into subproblems, distributes those onto hundreds or thousands of servers, then combines the results to come up with an answer to the overarching data problem.

THE RESULTS

At the turn of the twentieth century, new flows of information through channels such as the telegraph and telephone supported mass production. Today, the availability of abundant data from a myriad of sources enables companies to cater to small niche markets (and even individual customers) anywhere in the world.

Some industries have led the way in their ability to gather and exploit data. Consider these industry examples.

- Credit card companies monitor every purchase and can accurately identify fraudulent ones, using rules derived from analysing billions of transactions.
- Insurance companies can analyse data in such a way as to spot suspicious claims.
- Mobile phone companies analyse subscribers' calling patterns to determine whether most of their frequent contacts are on a rival network. If that rival network is offering an attractive promotion that might cause that subscriber to defect, he or she can be offered an incentive to stay.
- Retailers effectively analyse customer transactions to tailor promotions. Retailers also watch online sales and marketing trends, and closely monitor and analyse social media comments about their products, brands and the companies themselves.
- The oil industry examines seismic data before drilling new wells in order to increase the likelihood that oil companies will find oil and not a 'dry hole'.

Unfortunately, despite years of effort, law enforcement and intelligence agencies' databases are not particularly well integrated with each other. For instance, in the healthcare industry, large-scale efforts to computerise health records have hit bureaucratic, technological and ethical roadblocks.

Despite these difficulties, stories of effective data management in organisations are emerging. As just one example, let's look at the Australian Customs and Border Protection Service (ACBPS). Since June 2013 the ACBPS has introduced an advanced passenger analysis solution that uses an IBM application big data solution to help ACBPS identify suspicious visitors. The IBM solution uses passenger name record (PNR) data which is shared between airlines and the ACBPS. PNR data is assessed in relation to other relevant information — including existing government risk assessment tools and criteria — to identify with greater precision, potentially high-risk passengers to protect Australia's borders more effectively. With the IBM solution, the ACBPS now have access to real-time data for all departures and arrivals and can eliminate the traditional onerous and tedious processes of manually extracting data from multiple systems. This solution is particularly important given massive amounts of data that the ACBPS typically relies on to fulfil its objectives. For example, almost 30 million airline passengers crossed Australia's borders in the last 12 months, generating an enormous amount of data. The effectiveness and efficiency of solutions such as the one used by the ACBPS will continue to become the norm for companies around the world, leading to improved decision making and competitive success.

Sources: Compiled from S Lohr (2012), 'The age of big data', *The New York Times*, 11 February; 'Volume, velocity, variety: what you need to know about big data' (2012), *O'Reilly Media*, 19 January; E Dumbill (2011), 'Five big data predictions for 2012', *O'Reilly Media*, 14 December; 'IDC Digital University Study 2011' (2011), www.emc.com/collateral/demos/microsites/emc-digital-universe-2011/index.htm; J Enriquez (2011), 'The glory of big data', *Popular Science*, November; R Pacella (2011), 'Where data lives', *Popular Science*, November; D McCafferty (2010), 'The big data conundrum', *CIO Insight*, 9 November; D Henschen (2011), 'Big data', *InformationWeek*, 10 October; M Korn and S Tibken (2011), 'Fumbling over data', *The Wall Street Journal*, 3 October; R King (2011), 'Getting a handle on big data with Hadoop', *Bloomberg BusinessWeek*, 7 September; D Henschen (2010), 'What's at stake in the big data revolution?', *InformationWeek*, 18 August; S Nunziata (2010), 'Business analytics: turning IP into opportunity', *CIO Insight*, 17 August; D Henschen (2010), 'The big data era: how data strategy will change', *InformationWeek*, 7 August; M Loukides (2010), 'What is data science?', *O'Reilly Media*, 2 June; 'Data, data everywhere' (2010), *The Economist*, 25 February; D Bollier (2010), 'The promise and peril of big data', *The Aspen Institute*, 1 January; T Davenport, J Harris and R Morison (2010), 'Analytics at work: smarter decisions, better results', *Harvard Business Press*; 'Big data — it's not just for Google anymore' (2010), *AMD White Paper*; Nestlé website, www.nestle.com; IBM website, www.ibm.com; A Romanov (2013), 'Putting a dollar value on big data insights', *Wired*, www.wired.com/2013/07/putting-a-dollar-value-on-big-data-insights; Oracle (2013), *Oracle: Big data for the enterprise: an Oracle white paper*, June, www.oracle.com/us/products/database/big-data-for-enterprise-519135.pdf; K Mackie (2013), 'Big data generating interest but few deployments', *Redmond Magazine*, 24 September, redmondmag.com/articles/2013/09/24/big-data-generating-interest.aspx; 'Gartner survey reveals that 64 percent of organizations have invested or plan to invest in big data in 2013', Gartner website, www.gartner.com/newsroom/id/2593815; S Siewert (2013), 'Big data in the cloud: Data velocity, volume, variety, veracity', *IBM developerWorks*, 9 July, www.ibm.com/developerworks/library/bd-bigdatacloud/bd-bigdatacloud-pdf.pdf; H Barwick (2013), 'Australian Customs uses big data to assess visitors', *CIO*, 27 August, www.cio.com.au/article/524794/australian_customs_uses_big_data_assess_visitors/; D Braue (2013), 'Customs' big data passenger analysis respects Australian, EU privacy controls', *CSO*, 27 August, www.cso.com.au/article/524806/customs_big_data_passenger_analysis_respects_australian_eu_privacy_controls; B Karlovsky (2013), 'Big Data deployed to protect our borders', *ARN*, 28 August, www.arnnet.com.au/article/524933/big_data_deployed_protect_our_borders; S Sweeney (2013), 'Australia secures borders with big data tools', *futureGOV Asia Pacific*, 2 September, www.futuregov.asia/articles/2013/sep/02/australia-secures-borders-big-data-tools.

QUESTIONS

1. Is big data really a problem on its own, or are the use, control and security of the data the true problem? Provide specific examples to support your answer.
2. What are the implications of having incorrect data points in your big data? What are the implications of incorrect or duplicated customer information? How valuable are decisions that were made based on faulty information derived from incorrect data?

CLOSING CASE **2 >**

How Nimble is affecting the short-term micro lending industry in Australia

THE PROBLEM

The short-term lending services industry in Australia is characterised by a general lack of customer-focus which is inconsistent with customer expectations. Today customers expect individualised and quick service. However, according to the findings of a recent Gallup survey 66 per cent of retail banking customers indicate that their banks sent to them offers that were 'too generic' and over half were receiving offers for products which they already had. Additionally, the current business model of most lending service providers including credit card companies appears to be based on profit generation when borrowers are unable to repay their loans.

THE IT SOLUTION

Queensland-based short-term lender Nimble (www.nimble.com.au) is addressing these problems in the short-term micro lending industry using big data. Originally, known as Cash Doctors, Nimble was established in 2005 by Sean Teahan and Greg Ellis. The big data-based Nimble system analyses both credit history and behavioural data to assess an applicant's capacity to repay a loan. Specifically, the Nimble system is a self-learning profiling technology that streamlines and strengthens loan application processes by evaluating credit profiles objectively by way of automatically triangulating multiple sources of data and online behaviour. That is, the Nimble system computes a score for each submitted application by analysing Dun & Bradstreet credit histories, reported income data and behavioural data as the application form is filled in. Behavioural data includes data concerning how fast applicants type information in their application, how they move through the form, how they use the mouse, whether they delete characters, use of capital letters and how they arrive at the Nimble website. Taken together, this data is processed using complex mathematical algorithms to evaluate whether applicants are likely to repay or default on their loans, or even if they are defrauding, thereby informing Nimble's loan approval decisions. In the process, Nimble is impacting the industry by promoting a business model that focuses on responsible lending.

THE RESULTS

Nimble operates completely online, with the entire application taking approximately 5 minutes. With the big data technology used, Nimble can approve a loan in as little as 11 seconds with current default rates being approximately 4.5 per cent. By October 2013, Nimble had approved over 400 000 loans of up to $1200.

Nimble's results have been recognised by many industry awards. For example, Nimble is one of the winners of the SmartCompany — Crowe Horwath Smart50 Awards which recognise the fastest growing SMEs in Australia in 2012–13. In 2013, Nimble also won the Australian Customer Service Platinum Award. Fuelled by recent investments, Nimble's new membership base has grown approximately 300 per cent in the last six months.

Sources: M Hammond (2013), 'Tech start-up stays Nimble with $1.5 million cash boost', *Startup Smart*, 5 February, www.startupsmart.com.au/financing-a-business/tech-start-up-stays-nimble-with-15-million-cash-boost/201302058824.html; A Rosenfeld (2013), 'Big data, small brokerage: Is it worth it?', *MPA Magazine*, 17 June, www.mpamagazine.com.au/sections/businessstrategy/big-data-small-brokerage-is-it-worth-it-176370.aspx; 'About Nimble', Nimble website, nimble.com.au/about-us; J Gardner (2013), 'Nimble start-up takes on short-term loans sector', *The Australian Financial Review Smart Investor*, 5 February, www.afrsmartinvestor.com.au/p/technology/nimble_start_up_takes_on_short_term_4Xfz7DCJLKaiRnPuaa8lVI; 'Nimble's world-leading technology transforms online lending experience', Nimble website, nimblemoney.pressdoc.com/33631-nimble-s-world-leading-technology-transforms-online-lendingexperience; B Howarth (2013), 'Big data: Knowledge might be power, but data is money', *BRW.*, 10 April, brw.com.au/p/tech-gadgets/big_data_knowledge_might_be_power_n9agOMt0jTtVpRUN01ySeK; 'How Nimble loans work', Nimble website, www.nimble.com.au/faq/how-it-works; S Foster (2013), 'Gold Coast start-up Nimble set to disrupt online loan market', *The Courier-Mail*, 11 October, www.couriermail.com.au/business/gold-coast-startup-nimble-set-to-disrupt-online-loan-market/story-fnihsps3-1226738651462; 'Meet the smart50 of 2013', Smart Company website, www.smartcompany.com.au/smart50-2013.html; 'With Nimble world class service is cash in the bank' (2013), *Service Excellence*, 18 May, www.serviceexcellence.com.au/content_common/ns-with-nimble-world-class-service-is-cash-in-the-bank.seo; A Knight (2013), 'Nimble is a new way to access credit', *The Sydney Morning Herald*, April 3, www.smh.com.au/smallbusiness/nimble-is-a-new-way-to-access-credit-20130402-2h4b0.html.

QUESTIONS

1. Explain the ways that Nimble uses big data in achieving its business objectives.
2. How else could big data be used to enhance existing services in the financial services industry?

THE NOOK

It is important for Malakai and Abbie (on the front end) to determine the structure of their database. As you have learned in the chapter, this structure is called an entity–relationship (ER) model and is illustrated by an ER diagram. They would like to collect customer name, drinks and/or food purchased by customer, sale amount, payment method, date and time of transaction, drinks sold by time, food sold by time, time from entrance or last purchase (i.e. how long it took a customer to buy the first drink), drink ingredients used, food ingredients used, band playing and genre for starters.

Ultimately, Malakai and Abbie want a system to capture data on the way out the door for an exit survey. It would be simple and only include a couple of items, but a quick rating of the overall experience by users would be worth a lot for the club's planning process. They really feel these data items could be combined in various ways to give them very useful information. For now, these two business owners just need help getting the structure right. Take these items and create an appropriate ER diagram and submit it to Malakai and Abbie (your lecturer).

SPREADSHEET ACTIVITY

OBJECTIVE

Normalisation is taught in this chapter. Often, normalisation begins when organisations are ready to transition from a large spreadsheet to a multidimensional database. This exercise will have you work your way through this transition.

Chapter connection

Primary key, secondary key, and attributes: These terms are a bit abstract until you have to make these determinations yourself. The process of normalisation is best when it is practiced. Spreadsheets provide the perfect opportunity.

ACTIVITY

When schools first began keeping digital records of students, they used a spreadsheet to manage the data. It did not take long before it was obvious that the spreadsheet alone was not sufficient to manage this information. The problem was that the spreadsheet recorded each student as a single event. Every time someone accessed the page to update a grade, contact information, receipt of payment, or class enrolment, that person had to access the main page to make changes. This meant that everyone had access to everything. The registrar could see financial information and the bursar could see academic information.

A database, no doubt, is more suited for this type of application and the normalisation process will prepare the spreadsheet for conversion. Visit www.johnwiley.com.au/highered/rainer/ausnz/studentresources and download the spreadsheet for this exercise (MIS — chapter 3.xlsx). Carefully choose a primary key according to the definitions provided in this chapter. Look for data that will uniquely identify each student. Perhaps this will be a student number or a combination of the student's last and first name. Whatever you decide, normalise the data and allow the primary key to tie the information together from one sheet to another. Your normalised spreadsheet will have multiple sheets rather than one single sheet. Perhaps you will have student information, financial information, academic enrolment, major, grades, etc. Take the single sheet and move the data into multiple sheets. Be sure to copy your primary keys onto each page so that the data can be reconciled.

DELIVERABLE

The final product will be a normalised spreadsheet that is much easier to understand and update and that is ready to be converted to a database.

DISCUSSION QUESTIONS

1. Even though this exercise is about normalisation for a database, is it also helpful to have data normalised in a spreadsheet? Why or why not?
2. What are the differences in spreadsheets and databases when it comes to data manipulation?

DATABASE ACTIVITY **ENTITY-RELATIONSHIP DIAGRAMS (ERDS)**

OBJECTIVE

Just as every house begins with an architectural drawing, every database must begin with a data model. In this activity, you will develop the most common type of data model: an *entity–relationship diagram* (ERD).

Chapter connection

Section 2 of this chapter introduces you to data modelling, specifically entity–relationship diagramming, as part of learning about database management. This activity applies those concepts.

Understanding the structure of a database is a good guide to developing it. It reduces the chances of errors that will be difficult to correct later on. In addition, professional database developers communicate with ERDs when they design a database for business needs. The ERD defines what the database will be. Knowing their language will improve your chances of getting a database that meets your needs.

Prerequisites

Read the following material before proceeding on to the activity. Reading this chapter will also put the activity in perspective.

ERD styles

The ERD style that the book uses is one of many. They are similar but differ in details. If you learn one, you will be able to understand an ERD in another, much as an English speaker from Sydney can converse with someone from Wellington. Some differences among versions follow.

- The name of an entity may be shown outside its box (usually just above it, as in part b of the figure in the book) or inside it (as in part a of the figure).
- The attributes of an entity may be shown in a separate box (as in the figure in the book), within its box, or in ovals surrounding the box and connected to it.
- An entity's primary key may be in bold type; starred; underlined; or if the name of the entity is outside the box, in a separate part of the box.
- Foreign keys can be shown in italics or set off in any other way that is not the same as the one used for primary keys, not identified at all, or not shown at all. In this last case, the lines connecting entities convey the relationship information.
- Relationships can be described in diamonds on the lines (as in part a of the figure in the book), in text next to the lines, or not described in the ERD.

  When relationships are described once, the direction of the description is not always clear. In the figure, does 'Can have' between Class and Lecturer mean 'a class can have a lecturer' or 'a lecturer can have a class?' It does not say. That is why some diagramming methods describe each relationship twice, once for each direction.
- When a relationship has 'one' at one end, there may be a short line across the relationship line or no symbol at all. In that case, the information is conveyed by the absence of crows' feet.

ERD symbols

An ERD shows the kind of relationship two entities have by symbols at the ends of the line that connects the entities. Each end of each line has two symbols.

The symbol all the way at the end of the line defines the *maximum cardinality* of the relationship: how many of that entity can there be? Rather than an exact count, the options are simply *1* or *many*, because that is all that matters in most database designs. A maximum of 1 is indicated by a short line across the line that connects the entities. A maximum of more than 1 is indicated by 'crows' feet': three lines spreading out like the toes on a bird's foot.

Further away from that symbol is a symbol for minimum cardinality: what is the smallest valid number of this entity that there can be? Here, the choices are 0 (there does not have to be one) and 1 (there must be at least one). Zero is shown by a circle. You can think of it as representing the digit 0 or the first letter of the word *optional*. A short line across the line that connects the entities means a minimum of 1. This is the same symbol as is used to indicate a maximum of 1, but there is no possible confusion because they are in different places.

The four possible combinations of these two pairs of symbols are illustrated below.

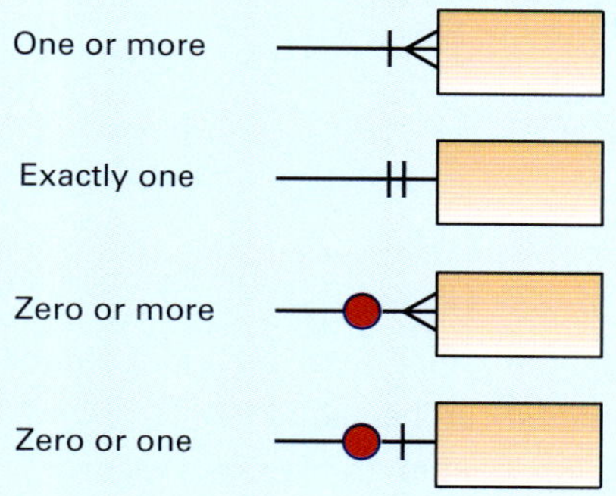

Suppose you have a database with information about students and their computers. Each computer belongs to exactly one student. A student, however, may have more than one computer — or may not have any. That *one-to-many relationship* would be shown this way:

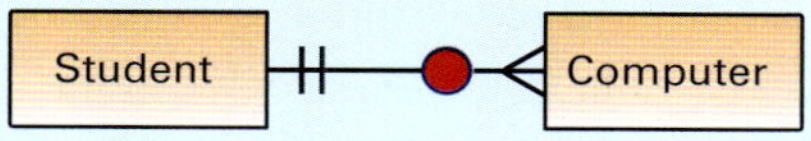

A relationship in which both entities have a maximum cardinality of *one* is called a *one-to-one* relationship. If one of the entities has a maximum cardinality of *many*, it is called a *one-to-many* (or *many-to-one*) relationship. If they both do, it is called a *many-to-many* relationship.

Associative entities

Because foreign keys only work in one direction at a time, a many-to-many relationship requires a new table between the two entities. For example, consider a school database. There is a many-to-many relationship between students and courses: each student can take more than one course and each course can have more than one student. A database cannot show that directly. A row of the course table cannot have a foreign key for students, because there can be more than one. A row of the student table cannot have a foreign key for courses either, because there can also be more than one. The solution is to put a third entity between them. Each row in it reflects one student taking one course. Its ERD would look like this:

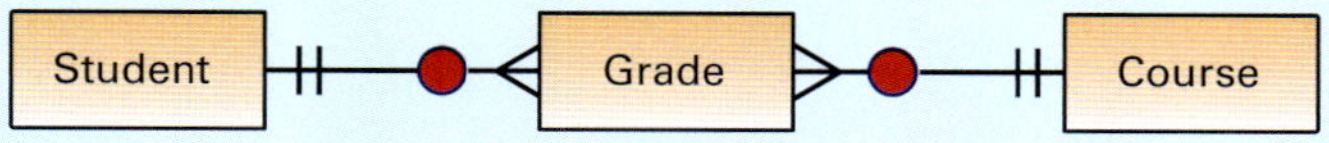

In this example, that entity also stores each student's grade in that course and takes its name from this. The grade cannot be in the student table, because students may earn different grades in different courses. It cannot be in the course table, because different students in the same course may earn different grades. It has to go in a table that describes that unique combination of student and course.

The circle symbols in this ERD fragment show that a student might not be in any courses and that a course might not have any students. This would be the situation before students register for courses. It also shows that, if there is a record in the Grade table, it goes with exactly one student, no more and no less, and with exactly one course, also no more and no less. Finally, it shows that a student may be in more than one course and that a course may have more than one student. Be sure you understand how the ERD shows these things.

Sales databases usually have a Line Item table that works this way. (The ORDERED-PARTS table in section 3.16 is an example of this.) Each order can be for many products. Each product can appear in many orders. Each row of this table is for one product in one order. In this case, the additional data in that entity is the quantity of the item in the order.

An entity that goes in the middle of a many-to-many relationship is called an *associative entity*. As a minimum, it contains two foreign keys: one for each connection. Often, as in these two examples, it also carries data. When an associative entity carries data, an ERD must show it. If it exists only to make the many-to-many relationship work and has no data of its own, some ER diagramming approaches show it but others do not.

An associative entity, like any other entity, needs a primary key. Neither foreign key is unique, so they will not work. Suppose Susan is registered for English 307. The foreign key that identifies Susan is not unique in the Grades table, because she has other courses. The one that identifies English 307 is not unique either, because other students also take it. However, Susan is only registered for it once, so the combination of Susan and English 307 *is* unique. Such a primary key, a unique combination of columns that are not unique individually, is called a *composite* key. To avoid dealing with composite keys, associative entities can be given separate primary keys such as sequence numbers. They do not mean anything, but they satisfy the requirement that every table must have a primary key.

ACTIVITY

1 Read the following description of a business situation.

   A university needs a database to record student information. You know the following.

   - The database will store information on departments, courses, sections and students.
   - Each department can teach many courses.
   - Each course is taught by one department.
   - Each course can have many sections.
   - Each section belongs to one course.
   - Each section has many students.
   - Each student enrols in many sections.

2 Draw an ERD for a database that will convey the information in the above description. Use the graphics program of your choice, or paper and pencil. (People

who draw ERDs for a living use specialised graphics programs that have the required shapes built in and that can enforce the rules of entity–relationship diagramming.)

- Show all relationships among entities. For each end of each relationship, use ERD symbols to show both the minimum cardinality (0 or 1; that is, can it be absent or must there be one?) and the maximum cardinality (1 or many). Use a short line across the relationship line to show a maximum cardinality of 1, as in the book.
- Show the primary key of each entity in a separate area at the top of the entity box, as in the figure in the book.
- Show all the foreign keys in each entity. Underline them.
- Show at least three attributes of each entity, based on your understanding of the situation described. If you cannot think of three, show all you have.

DELIVERABLE

Your completed ER diagram.

QUIZ QUESTIONS

1 Which of the following is *not* a possible type of relationship between database entities as shown in an ERD?

   a One to one

   b Many to many

   c Two to one

   d Many to one

2 True or false: A many-to-one relationship requires an associative entity.

3 An associative entity has a primary key and at least this many foreign keys:

   a 0

   b 1

   c 2

   d 3

4 The *attributes* of an entity are

   a The data items that describe it in a database

   b The names it can be called by

   c The foreign keys in its database record

   d The date and time it was entered into the database, and the user ID of the person who entered it

DISCUSSION QUESTIONS

1 Why is it important for people who are not database specialists to be familiar with ER concepts and diagramming?

2 Where does an ERD show the attributes of an entity?

3 What ERD symbols indicate a many-to-one relationship?

4 Telecommunications and networking

CHAPTER OUTLINE

LEARNING OBJECTIVES

1. Compare and contrast the two major types of networks.
2. Describe the wireline communications media and transmission technologies.
3. Describe the most common methods for accessing the internet.
4. Explain the impact that networks have had on business and everyday life for each of the six major categories of network applications.

OPENING CASE >

Studio G

Using the right network to expand the reach to potential new customers can make all the difference. What is the right network? Well, it depends. As a business organisation grows, its network and telecommunication needs will change and evolve to meet new business demands and adopt new technologies to meet customer expectations. This is exactly the case with Studio G, an architecture firm based in Melbourne, Victoria. Originally when the business started, it had only two employees and they needed only two telephone lines to communicate with their customers. However, as the business grew, Studio G began to realise they needed a better telecommunication solution.

Initially, Studio G solved this problem by installing a private branch exchange (PBX) in the office to route calls and help customers reach the appropriate person without the need of a receptionist to manage incoming calls. A PBX is a telephone exchange that serves a particular business or office, as opposed to a telephone exchange operated by a telephone company for several businesses or for the public. A PBX makes connections among the internal telephones of a private organisation and connects them to the public switched telephone network.

While this was an acceptable communication solution that served the business well, Studio G began to see that the internet offered wider network capabilities, new opportunities and technologies to engage directly with customers via online communication (email) and through a business website. However, there were limitations related to Australia's ageing copper telecommunications network and with seemingly ever increasing data demands. Studio G recognised the need to incorporate access to the National Broadband Network (NBN) infrastructure into the business. The NBN represents a significant increase in broadband performance, quality and speed that can support a wide range of high bandwidth applications that is very scalable to meet increasing bandwidth needs for future growth.

What was the result? Studio G was now able to keep pace with their larger competitors because of their ability to communicate with their customers at a fraction of the cost spent by other organisations. Kelly Simcox, owner of Studio G Architects, Inc. said, 'We have grown substantially . . . [and] are competing for projects against firms that are substantially larger than ours'.

As we can see, in this situation, the right telecommunication solution was not the age-old telephone line. In fact, it was the fibre optic networking solution that utilises the internet technology and high-speed broadband access and capabilities of the NBN. Many similar solutions are available today for small businesses to help them communicate with their customers in more efficient ways. As you have seen in this case, networking solutions will continue to allow small businesses to compete on a more level playing field with their larger competitors, which may have significant ramifications for the customer in terms of pricing and available options.

Source: www.studio-g.net.au

Introduction

You need to know three fundamental points about network computing. First, computers do not work in isolation in modern organisations. Rather, they constantly exchange data with one another. Second, this exchange of data — facilitated by telecommunications technologies — provides companies with a number of very significant advantages. Third, this exchange can take place over any distance and over networks of any size.

Without networks, the computer on your desk would be merely another productivity-enhancement tool, just as the typewriter once was. The power of networks, however, turns your computer into an amazingly effective tool for accessing information from thousands of sources, thereby making both you and your organisation more productive. Regardless of the type of organisation (profit/not-for-profit, large/small, global/local) or industry (manufacturing, financial services, healthcare), networks in general, and the internet in particular, have transformed — and will continue to transform — the way we do business.

Networks support new ways of doing business, from marketing to supply chain management to customer service to human resources management. In particular, the internet and private intranets — networks located within a single organisation — have an enormous impact on our lives, both professionally and personally. In fact, for all organisations, having an internet strategy is no longer just a source of competitive advantage. Rather, it is necessary for survival.

THE NOOK

The network at The Nook has consisted of digital subscriber line (DSL) and a computer. This is not much of a local area network (LAN) at all. To accomplish their desire to collect data from different customer contact points (such as cover charge, food and/or drink purchases, exit questionnaire), they will need multiple computers or devices connected to their network. Additionally, to create the community atmosphere they desire, they want to offer wireless internet access to their customers so they never feel out of touch.

This will require lots of networking hardware on both the internal wired LAN and the public wireless LAN. To make matters more difficult, Malakai and Abbie know nothing about establishing a network. They did not even install their own DSL line — it was connected by Telstra several years ago. All they know is how to turn it on and the right phone number to call when they have a problem. Establishing and maintaining a LAN that connects employees and customers, while providing adequate security for all parties, will be quite an undertaking. However, they believe the benefits of establishing this network will far outweigh the costs.

Because you are learning about telecommunication and networks, it will be very helpful for you to share this information with them with a recommendation on how to build their network.

Computer networks are essential to modern organisations, for many reasons. First, networked computer systems enable organisations to be more flexible so they can adapt to rapidly changing business conditions. Second, networks enable companies to share hardware, computer applications and data across the organisation and among different organisations. Third, networks make it possible for geographically dispersed employees and work groups to share documents, ideas and creative insights. This sharing encourages teamwork, innovation and more efficient and effective interactions. In addition, networks are a critical link between businesses, their business partners and their customers.

Clearly, networks are essential tools for modern businesses. But, why do *you* need to be familiar with networks? The simple fact is that if you operate your own business or work in a business, you cannot function without networks. You will need to communicate rapidly with your customers, business partners, suppliers, employees and colleagues. Until about 1990, you would have used the postal service or telephone system with voice or fax capabilities for business communication. Today, however, the pace of business is much faster — almost real time. To keep up with this incredibly fast pace, you will need to use computers, email, the internet, mobile phones and other mobile devices. Further, all of these technologies will be connected via networks to enable you to communicate, collaborate and compete on a global scale.

Networking and the internet are the foundation for commerce in the twenty-first century. Recall that one important objective of this book is to help you become an informed user of information systems. Therefore, a knowledge of networking is an essential component of modern business literacy.

You begin this chapter by learning what a computer network is and identifying the various types of networks. You then study network fundamentals and follow by turning your attention to the basics of the internet and the world wide web. You conclude the chapter by seeing the many network applications available to individuals and organisations — that is, what networks help you do.

4.1 What is a computer network?

A **computer network** is a system that connects computers and other devices (e.g. printers) via communications media so that data and information can be transmitted among them. Voice and data communication networks are continually becoming faster — that is, their bandwidth is increasing — and cheaper. **Bandwidth** refers to the transmission capacity of a network; it is stated in bits per second. **Broadband** refers to network transmission capacities ranging from approximately 1 million bits per second (megabits/sec) to as much as 20 megabits/sec with fibre-to-the-home (discussed later in this chapter). You are familiar with certain types of broadband connections, such as **digital subscriber line (DSL)** and cable to your homes and student residences. DSL and cable fall within the range of transmission capacity mentioned here and so are defined as broadband connections.

The various types of computer networks range from small to worldwide. They include (from smallest to largest) personal area networks (PANs), local area networks (LANs), metropolitan area networks (MANs), wide area networks (WANs) and the internet. PANs are short-range networks — typically a few metres — used for communication among devices close to one person. PANs can be wired or wireless. MANs are relatively large computer networks that cover a metropolitan area. MANs fall between LANs and WANs in size. WANs typically cover large areas and can span the entire planet.

Local area networks

Regardless of their size, networks represent a compromise among three objectives: speed, distance and cost. Organisations can generally have any two of the three. To cover long distances, organisations can have fast communication if they are willing to pay for it, or cheap communication if they are willing to accept slower speeds. A third possible combination of the three trade-offs is fast, cheap communication with distance limitations. This is the idea behind local area networks.

A **local area network (LAN)** connects two or more devices in a limited geographical region, usually within the same building, so that every device on the network can communicate with every other device. Most LANs today use ethernet (discussed later in this chapter). Figure 4.1 illustrates an ethernet LAN that consists of four computers, a server and a printer, all of which connect via a shared cable. Every device in the LAN has a *network interface card* (NIC) that allows the device to physically connect to the LAN's communications medium. This medium is typically unshielded twisted-pair wire (UTP).

Although it is not required, many LANs have a **file server** or **network server**. The server typically contains various software and data for the network. It also houses the LAN's network operating system, which manages the server and routes and manages communications on the network.

Wide area networks

When businesses have to transmit and receive data beyond the confines of the LAN, they use wide area networks. Interestingly, the term *wide area network* did not even exist until local area networks appeared. Before that time, what we call a wide area network today was simply called a 'network.'

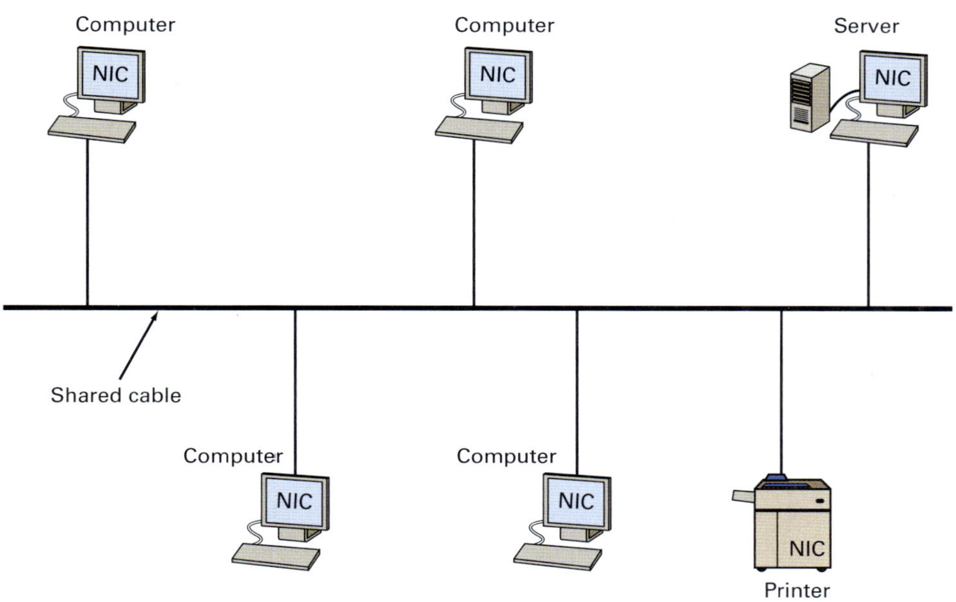

FIGURE 4.1 An ethernet LAN.

A **wide area network (WAN)** is a network that covers a large geographic area. WANs typically connect multiple LANs. WANs generally are provided by common carriers such as telephone companies and the international networks of global communications services providers. WANs have large capacity and they typically combine multiple channels (for example, fibre-optic cables, microwave and satellite). The internet is an example of a WAN.

WANs also contain routers. A **router** is a communications processor that routes messages from a LAN to the internet, across several connected LANs, or across a wide area network such as the internet.

Enterprise networks

Organisations today have multiple LANs and may have multiple WANs, which are interconnected to form an **enterprise network**. Figure 4.2 (overleaf) displays a model of enterprise computing. Note that the enterprise network in the figure has a **backbone network**. Corporate backbone networks are high-speed central networks to which multiple smaller networks (such as LANs and smaller WANs) connect. The LANs are called *embedded LANs* because they connect to the backbone WAN.

> **BEFORE YOU GO ON . . .**
>
> 1. What are the primary business reasons for using networks?
> 2. What is the difference between LANs and WANs?
> 3. Describe an enterprise network.

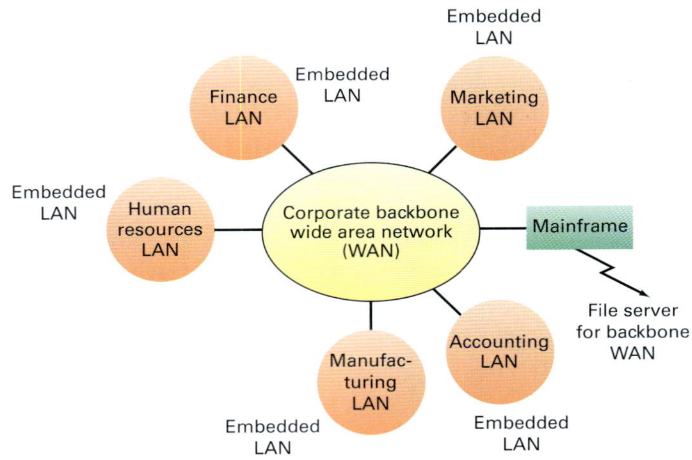

FIGURE 4.2 An enterprise network.

Apply the Concept

Background

This section has introduced you to the different types of networks that connect businesses around the world. Because of this, today's organisations are spread out over many locations. Often headquarters are in one city and various branches are in other cities. Many times, employees even work from home and do not have a physical office to go to. The computer network is the technology that allows all of this to happen. For a network to function, a few components are required. In this activity, you will place these components in the appropriate places to create a computer network.

Activity

Consider the following company called Redware Technologies and potential network components.

Redware Technologies locations

1. *Headquarters:* This international company manufactures and sells computer equipment; the firm also services equipment it has sold. The company's headquarters are in Perth, Australia, and offices there include marketing, accounting, HR and manufacturing. Each office has a number of PCs that connect with a main server in an IS. All offices are closely located and share data and printers.
2. *Offshore manufacturing:* A new manufacturing facility is opening in New Zealand and needs to be connected 24/7 to company headquarters. There are 30 terminals at this plant. Inventory, orders and schedules are shared during the workday at both locations.
3. *Sales force:* Redware Technologies has about 15 technicians who service equipment sold within Australia. Each technician has a laptop that needs to connect off and on to the database (at headquarters) about 3 hours each day for checking inventory and entering repairs and orders. Technicians are constantly on the road to small, rural and regional cities and need to be able to check inventory whether in a hotel or at a customer site. Each evening technicians must log on for updates and to post daily activity. You may want to include multiple options so they can always connect!
4. *Employees from home:* Redware Technologies has a number of employees that work from home part-time on flexitime. These employees need a fast, secure connection because some are dealing with financial data and the main computer and its databases at headquarters. They all live within 50 kilometres of their workplace.

Components

1 *Network:* LAN, MAN, WAN
2 *Connection:* direct connection (in-house), dial-up, internet
3 *Interface devices:* network interface card (ethernet or wireless), server, routers, DSL/cable
4 *Channel:* twisted pair (UTP-Cat3 or 5), fibre, wireless, satellite, or tower)

Deliverable

From the lists above, indicate which components are needed to connect Redware Technologies employees to a database that is located at the company's headquarters. Without this, they will not be able to do their jobs and answer customer-related questions. (You may need multiple components for each group.) If you are not familiar with any of the terms, review the text for more information.

QUESTIONS

THE NOOK

1 Which type of network would best suit the needs of The Nook? A LAN, a MAN, or a WAN? Why?
2 What type of wired connections would you recommend to Malakai and Abbie within their club? Be sure to pick something that is widely used so it will be easy to find support.

4.2 Network fundamentals

In this section, you will learn the basics of how networks actually operate. You will then distinguish between analogue and digital signals and explain how modems enable computer networks to 'translate' among them. You follow by studying cable communications media, which enable computers in a network to transmit and receive data. You conclude this section by looking at network protocols and types of network processing.

Analogue and digital signals

Networks transmit information with two basic types of signals, analogue and digital. **Analogue signals** are continuous waves that transmit information by altering the characteristics of the waves. Analogue signals have two parameters, *amplitude* and *frequency*. For example, all sounds — including the human voice — are analogue, travelling to human ears in the form of waves. The higher the waves (or amplitude), the louder the sound; the more closely packed the waves, the higher the frequency or pitch. In contrast, **digital signals** are discrete pulses that are either on or off, representing a series of *bits* (1s and 0s). This quality allows digital signals to convey information in a binary form that can be interpreted by computers. Figure 4.3 (overleaf) illustrates both analogue and digital signals.

The function of a **modem** is to convert digital signals to analogue signals — a process called *modulation* — and analogue signals to digital signals — a process called *demodulation*. (The name *modem* is a contraction of *mo*dulator-*dem*odulator.) Modems are used in pairs. The modem at the sending end converts a computer's digital information into analogue signals for transmission over analogue lines, such as telephone lines. At the receiving end, another modem converts the analogue signal back into digital signals for the receiving computer. There are three types of modems: dial-up modems, cable modems and DSL modems.

The Australian public telephone system was originally designed as an analogue network to carry voice signals or sounds in an analogue wave format. In order for this type of circuit to carry digital information, that information must be converted into an analogue wave pattern by a *dial-up modem*. Dial-up modems have transmission speeds of up to 56 kilobytes per second (Kbps).

Cable modems are modems that operate over coaxial cable — for example, cable TV. They offer broadband access to the internet or corporate intranets. Cable modem speeds

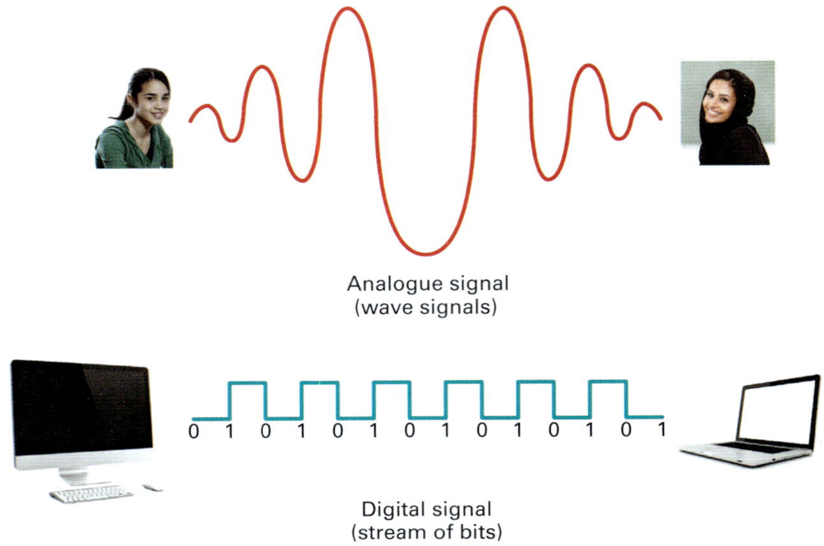

FIGURE 4.3 Analogue and digital signals.

vary widely. Most providers offer bandwidth between 1 and 6 million bits per second (Mbps) for downloads (from the internet to a computer) and between 128 and 768 thousand bits per second (Kbps) for uploads. Cable modem services share bandwidth among subscribers in a locality. That is, the same cable line connects to many households. Therefore, when large numbers of neighbours access the internet at the same time, cable speeds can decrease significantly during those times.

DSL (discussed later in this chapter) *modems* operate on the same lines as voice telephones and dial-up modems. DSL modems always maintain a connection, so an internet connection is immediately available.

Communications media and channels

Communicating data from one location to another requires some form of pathway or medium. A **communications channel** is such a pathway and is comprised of two types of media: cable (twisted-pair wire, cable, or fibre-optic cable) and broadcast (microwave, satellite, radio or infrared).

Cable media or **wireline media** use physical wires or cables to transmit data and information. Twisted-pair wire and coaxial cables are made of copper and fibre-optic cable is made of glass. The alternative is communication over **broadcast media** or **wireless media**. The key to mobile communications in today's rapidly moving society is data transmissions over electromagnetic media — the 'airwaves.' In this section you will study the three wireline channels. Table 4.1 summarises the advantages and disadvantages of each of these channels.

TABLE 4.1 Advantages and disadvantages of wireline communications channels

Channel	Advantages	Disadvantages
Twisted-pair wire	Inexpensive Widely available Easy to work with	Slow (low bandwidth) Subject to interference Easily tapped (low security)
Coaxial cable	Higher bandwidth than twisted-pair Less susceptible to electromagnetic interference	Relatively expensive and inflexible Easily tapped (low to medium security) Somewhat difficult to work with
Fibre-optic cable	Very high bandwidth Relatively inexpensive Difficult to tap (good security)	Difficult to work with (difficult to splice)

Twisted-pair wire

Twisted-pair wire is the most prevalent form of communications wiring; it is used for almost all business telephone wiring. **Twisted-pair wire** consists of strands of copper wire twisted into pairs (see figure 4.4). It is relatively inexpensive to purchase, widely available and easy to work with. However, it also has some significant disadvantages. Specifically, it is relatively slow for transmitting data, it is subject to interference from other electrical sources and it can be easily tapped by unintended receivers for gaining unauthorised access to data.

FIGURE 4.4 Two views of twisted-pair wire: cross-section view (left) and how twisted pair looks to us (right).

Coaxial cable

Coaxial cable (figure 4.5) consists of insulated copper wire. It is much less susceptible to electrical interference than is twisted-pair wire and it can carry much more data. For these reasons, it is commonly used to carry high-speed data traffic as well as television signals (thus the term *cable TV*). However, coaxial cable is more expensive and more difficult to work with than twisted-pair wire. It is also somewhat inflexible.

FIGURE 4.5 Two views of coaxial cables: cross-section (left) and how coaxial cables look to us (right).

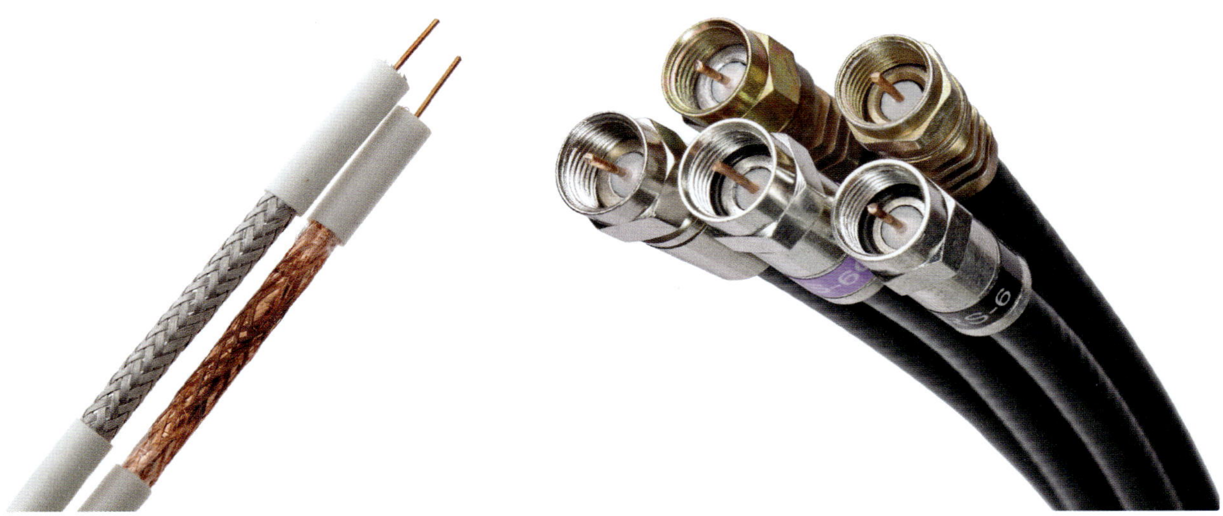

Fibre optics

Fibre-optic cable (figure 4.6) consists of thousands of very thin filaments of glass fibres that transmit information via light pulses generated by lasers. The fibre-optic cable is surrounded by cladding, a coating that prevents the light from leaking out of the fibre.

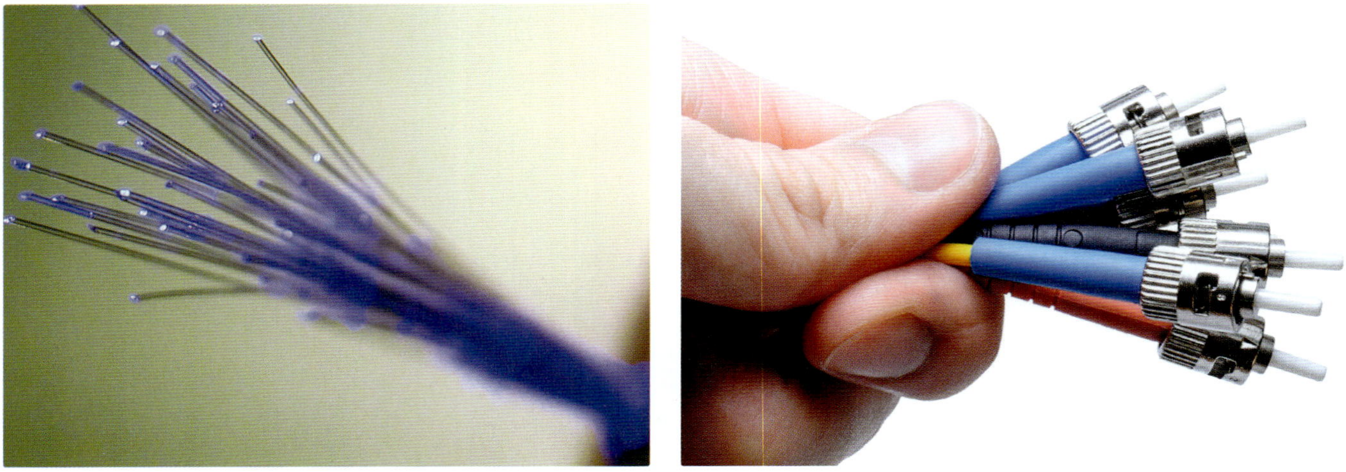

FIGURE 4.6 Two views of fibre-optic cables: cross-section (left) and how it looks to us (right).

Fibre-optic cables are significantly smaller and lighter than traditional cable media. They can also transmit far more data, and they provide greater security from interference and tapping. As of 2011, optical fibre had reached data transmission rates of more than 50 trillion bits (terabits) per second in laboratory experiments. Fibre-optic cable is typically used as the backbone for a network, whereas twisted-pair wire and coaxial cable connect the backbone to individual devices on the network.

Network protocols

Computing devices that are connected to the network must access and share the network to transmit and receive data. These devices are often referred to as *nodes* of the network. They work together by adhering to a common set of rules and procedures — known as a **protocol** — that enable them to communicate with one another. The two major protocols are the ethernet and transmission control protocol/internet protocol.

Ethernet

A common LAN protocol is **ethernet**. Most large corporations use 10-gigabit ethernet, where the network provides data transmission speeds of 10 gigabits (10 billion bits) per second. However, 100-gigabit ethernet is becoming the standard.

Transmission control protocol/internet protocol

The **transmission control protocol/internet protocol (TCP/IP)** is the protocol of the internet. TCP/IP uses a suite of protocols, the main ones being the transmission control protocol (TCP) and the internet protocol (IP). The TCP performs three basic functions. (1) It manages the movement of data via packets between computers by establishing a connection between the computers, (2) it sequences the transfer of packets, and (3) it acknowledges the packets that have been transmitted. The **internet protocol (IP)** is responsible for disassembling, delivering and reassembling the data during transmission.

Before data are transmitted over the internet, they are divided into small, fixed bundles of data called *packets*. The transmission technology that breaks up blocks of text into packets is called **packet switching**. Each packet carries the information that will help it reach its destination — the sender's IP address, the intended receiver's IP address, the number of packets in the message and the number of the particular packet within the message. Each packet travels independently across the network and can be routed through different paths in the network. When the packets reach their destination, they are reassembled into the original message.

It is important to note that packet-switching networks are reliable and fault tolerant. For example, if a path in the network is very busy or is broken, packets can be dynamically ('on the fly') rerouted around that path. Also, if one or more packets do not get to the receiving computer, then only those packets need to be resent.

Why do organisations use packet switching? The main reason is to achieve reliable end-to-end message transmission over sometimes unreliable networks that may have transient (short-acting) or persistent (long-acting) faults.

The packets use the TCP/IP protocol to carry their data. TCP/IP functions in four layers (see figure 4.7). The *application layer* enables client application programs to access the other layers and it defines the protocols that applications use to exchange data. One of these application protocols is the **hypertext transfer protocol (HTTP)**, which defines how messages are formulated and how they are interpreted by their receivers. The *transport layer* provides the application layer with communication and packet services. This layer includes TCP and other protocols. The *internet layer* is responsible for addressing, routing and packaging data packets. The IP is one of the protocols in this layer. Finally, the *network interface layer* places packets on, and receives them from, the network medium, which can be any networking technology.

Email: sending a message via SMPT (simple mail transfer protocol)	Application	Email: message received
Break message into packets and determine order	Transport	Packets reordered and replaced (if lost)
Assign sending and receiving IP addresses and apply to each packet	Internet	Packets routed through internal network to desired IP address
Determine path across network/ internet to intended destination	Network interface	Receipt of packets

FIGURE 4.7 The four layers of the TCP/IP.

Two computers using TCP/IP can communicate even if they use different hardware and software. Data sent from one computer to another proceed downward through all four layers, beginning with the sending computer's application layer and going through its network interface layer. After the data reach the receiving computer, they travel up the layers.

TCP/IP enables users to send data across sometimes unreliable networks with the assurance that the data will arrive in uncorrupted form. TCP/IP is very popular with business organisations because of its reliability and the ease with which it can support intranets and related functions.

Let's look at an example of packet-switching across the internet. Figure 4.8 (overleaf) illustrates a message being sent from Brisbane to Perth over a packet-switching network. Note that the different coloured packets travel by different routes to reach their destination in Perth, where they are reassembled into the complete message.

FIGURE 4.8 Packet switching.

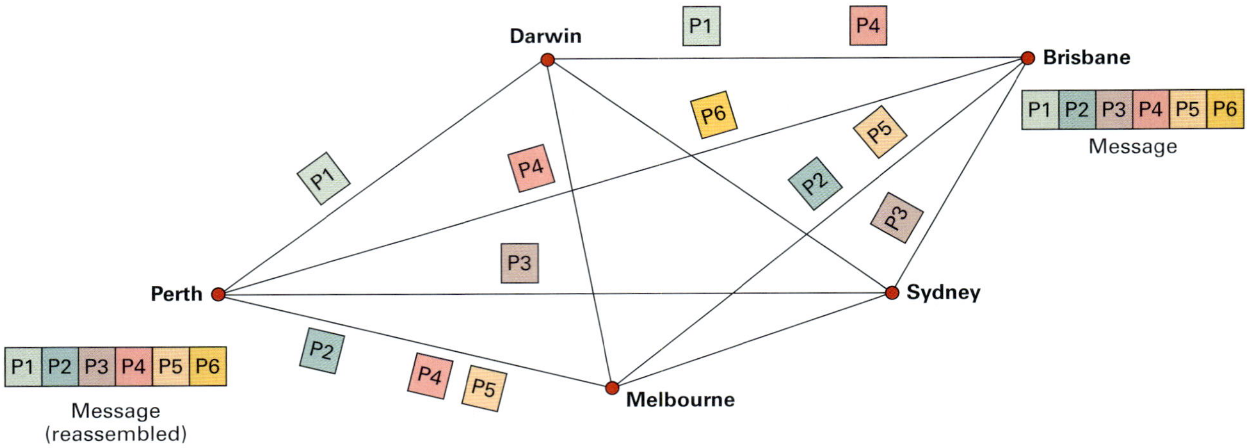

Types of network processing

Organisations typically use multiple computer systems across the business. **Distributed processing** divides processing work among two or more computers. This process enables computers in different locations to communicate with one another via telecommunications links. A common type of distributed processing is client/server processing. A special type of client/server processing is peer-to-peer processing.

Client/server computing

Client/server computing links two or more computers in an arrangement in which some machines, called **servers**, provide computing services for user PCs, called **clients**. Usually, an organisation performs the bulk of its processing or application/data storage on suitably powerful servers that can be accessed by less powerful client machines. The client requests applications, data, or processing from the server, which acts on these requests by 'serving' the desired commodity.

Client/server computing leads to the ideas of 'fat' clients and 'thin' clients. As discussed in Plug IT In 2, *fat clients* have large storage and processing power and therefore can run local programs (such as Microsoft Office), if the network is down. In contrast, *thin clients* may have no local storage and limited processing power. Thus, they must depend on the network to run applications. For this reason, they are of little value when the network is not functioning.

Peer-to-peer processing

Peer-to-peer (P2P) processing is a type of client/server distributed processing where each computer acts as *both* a client and a server. Each computer can access (as assigned for security or integrity purposes) all files on all other computers.

There are three basic types of peer-to-peer processing. The first accesses unused CPU power among networked computers. A well-known application of this type is SETI@home. These applications are from open-source projects and can be downloaded at no cost.

The second form of peer-to-peer is real-time, person-to-person collaboration, such as Microsoft SharePoint Workspace. This product provides P2P collaborative applications that use buddy lists to establish a connection and allow real-time collaboration within the application.

The third peer-to-peer category is advanced search and file sharing. This category is characterised by natural-language searches of millions of peer systems. It enables users to discover other users, not just data and web pages. One example of this category is BitTorrent.

BitTorrent is an open-source, free, peer-to-peer file-sharing application that is able to simplify the problem of sharing large files by dividing them into tiny pieces, or 'torrents.' BitTorrent addresses two of the biggest problems of file sharing: (1) downloading bogs down when many people access a file at once, and (2) some people leech, meaning they

BEFORE YOU GO ON . . .

1. Compare and contrast the three wireline communications channels.
2. Describe the various technologies that enable users to send high-volume data over any network.
3. Describe the ethernet and TCP/IP protocols.
4. Differentiate between client/server computing and peer-to-peer processing.

download content but refuse to share. BitTorrent eliminates the bottleneck by enabling all users to share little pieces of a file at the same time — a process called *swarming*. The program prevents leeching because users must upload a file while they download it. This means that the more popular the content, the more efficiently it zips over a network.

QUESTIONS

1. What networking model should work best for the employees of The Nook? A client/server or peer-to-peer network? What aspects cause you to make this choice?
2. If the client/server method is chosen, do you think the data should be stored on the client or the server? Defend your view.

4.3 The internet and the world wide web

The **internet ('the net')** is a global WAN that connects approximately 1 million organisational computer networks in more than 200 countries on all continents, including Antarctica, and features in the daily routine of almost 2 billion people. Participating computer systems include smart phones, PCs, LANs, databases and mainframes.

The computers and organisational nodes on the internet can be of different types and makes. They are connected to one another by data communications lines of different speeds. The primary network connections and telecommunications lines that link the nodes are referred to as the backbone. For the internet, the backbone is a fibre-optic network that is operated primarily by large telecommunications companies.

As a network of networks, the internet enables people to access data in other organisations and to communicate, collaborate and exchange information seamlessly around the world, quickly and inexpensively. Thus, the internet has become a necessity for modern businesses.

The internet grew out of an experimental project of the Advanced Research Project Agency (ARPA) of the US Department of Defense. The project began in 1969 as the *ARPAnet*. Its purpose was to test the feasibility of a WAN over which researchers, educators, military personnel and government agencies could share data, exchange messages and transfer files.

Today, internet technologies are being used both within and among organisations. An **intranet** is a network that uses internet protocols so that users can take advantage of familiar applications and work habits. Intranets support discovery (easy and inexpensive browsing and search), communication and collaboration inside an organisation.

In contrast, an extranet connects parts of the intranets of different organisations. In addition, it enables business partners to communicate securely over the internet using virtual private networks. **Extranets** offer limited accessibility to the intranets of participating companies, as well as necessary interorganisational communications. They are widely used in the areas of business-to-business (B2B) electronic commerce and supply chain management.

No central agency manages the internet. Instead, the cost of its operation is shared among hundreds of thousands of nodes. Thus, the cost for any one organisation is small. Organisations must pay a small fee if they wish to register their names, and they need to have their own hardware and software to operate their internal networks. The organisations are obliged to move any data or information that enters their organisational network, regardless of the source, to their destination, at no charge to the senders. The senders, of course, pay the telephone bills for using either the backbone or regular telephone lines.

Accessing the internet

The internet may be accessed in several ways. From your place of work or your university, you can access the internet via your organisation's LAN. A campus or company backbone connects all of the various LANs and servers in the organisation to the internet. You can also log onto the internet from your home or on the road, using either wireline or wireless connections.

Connecting via an online service

You can also access the internet by opening an account with an internet service provider. An **internet service provider (ISP)** is a company that provides internet connections for a fee. Large ISPs include Telstra BigPond, iiNet, iPrimus and Internode. In addition, many telephone providers and cable companies sell internet access, as do computer companies such as Microsoft. To use this service you need a modem and standard communication software. To find a local ISP, access the internet, where you can search for an ISP that services your area.

ISPs connect to one another through **network access points (NAPs)**. NAPs are exchange points for internet traffic. They determine how traffic is routed. NAPs are key components of the internet backbone.

Connecting via other means

There have been several attempts to make access to the internet cheaper, faster and easier. For example, terminals known as internet kiosks have been located in such public places as libraries and airports (and even in convenience stores in some countries) for use by people who do not have their own computers. Accessing the internet from smart phones and iPads is common, and fibre-to-the-home (FTTH) is growing rapidly. FTTH involves connecting fibre-optic cable directly to individual homes. This system was initially restricted to new residential developments, but it is rapidly spreading. Table 4.2 summarises the various means that you can use to connect to the internet.

TABLE 4.2 Internet connection methods

Service	Description
Dial-up	Still used where broadband is not available
DSL	Broadband access via telephone companies
Cable modem	Access over your cable TV coaxial cable. Can have degraded performance if many of your neighbours are accessing the internet at the same time.
Satellite	Access where cable and ADSL are not available
Wireless	Very convenient and increases the use of broadband wireless
Fibre-to-the-premises	Expensive and usually only placed in new housing developments

Addresses on the internet

Each computer on the internet has an assigned address, called the **internet protocol (IP) address**, that distinguishes it from all other computers. The IP address consists of numbers, in four parts, separated by dots. For example, the IP address of one computer might be 135.62.128.91. You can access a website by typing this number in the address bar of your browser.

Currently, there are two IP addressing schemes. The first scheme, IPv4, is the most widely used. IP addresses using IPv4 consist of 32 bits, meaning that there are 2^{32} possibilities for IP addresses, or 4 294 967 295 distinct addresses. Note that the IP address in the preceding paragraph (135.62.128.91) is an IPv4 address. At the time that IPv4 was developed, there were not as many computers needing addresses as there are today. Therefore, a new IP addressing scheme has been developed, called IPv6.

IP addresses using IPv6 consist of 128 bits, meaning that there are 2^{128} possibilities for distinct IP addresses, which is an unimaginably large number. IPv6, which is replacing IPv4, will accommodate the rapidly increasing number of devices that need IP addresses, such as smart phones.

IP addresses must be unique so computers on the internet know where to find one another. The Internet Corporation for Assigned Names (ICANN) (**www.icann.org**) coordinates these unique addresses throughout the world. Without that coordination, we would not have one global internet.

Because the numeric IP addresses are difficult to remember, most computers have names as well. ICANN accredits certain companies called *registrars* to register these names, which are derived from a system called the **domain name system (DNS)**. **Domain names** consist of multiple parts, separated by dots, that are read from right to left. For example, consider the domain name *business.auburn.edu*. The rightmost part of an internet name is its *top-level domain (TLD)*. The letters *edu* in business.auburn.edu indicate that this is an educational site. The following are popular Australian TLDs:

com	commercial sites
net	commercial sites
edu	educational sites
asn	association sites
gov	exclusively Australian government sites
org	non-commercial organisations.

To finish our domain name example, *auburn* is the name of the organisation (Auburn University) and *business* is the name of the particular machine (server) within the organisation to which the message is being sent.

In other countries, the country name or designator is the TLD. For example, *de* stands for Germany, *nz* for New Zealand, *uk* for the United Kingdom and *ru* for Russia. In essence, every country decides for itself whether to use TLDs. Moreover, those countries that use TLDs do not necessarily follow the US system. For example, the United Kingdom uses *.co* where Australia uses *.com.au*, and *.ac* (for academic) where Australia uses *.edu*. However, many other countries use US TLDs, especially *.com*, as the basis of their domain name system.

The future of the internet

Research undertaken by the University of Adelaide estimates that Australian internet traffic will increase by more than five times by 2016.[1] The analysis was based on Australian Bureau of Statistics data and indicates internet traffic has been doubling every 465 days since 2004 and is likely to exceed one exabyte of data per month by 2016.

Many experts are now concerned that internet users will experience reduced internet speeds from three factors:

(1) the increasing number of people who work online,

(2) the soaring popularity of websites such as YouTube that require large amounts of bandwidth, and

(3) the tremendous demand for high-definition television delivered over the internet.

This means that network providers will have to incorporate designs to enable more efficient network communications to cope with the increased traffic and new technological innovations. This will also require additional physical infrastructure investment to support this growth; otherwise the Australian internet will begin to function at a much reduced speed.

Even today, the internet is sometimes too slow for data-intensive applications such as full-motion video files (movies) or large medical files (X-rays). In addition, the internet is unreliable and not secure, and the broadband capability of Australia's ageing copper telecommunications network is reaching its performance limitations. Through Australian Government investment, the national broadband network (NBN) will deliver high-speed broadband access to all Australian homes and businesses via a mix of three technologies: fibre-optic cable, fixed wireless networks and next generation satellite coverage. Ninety-three per cent of Australian homes and businesses will have access via fibre to the premises (one gigabit per second) technology and the remaining 7 per cent of homes and businesses will have NBN access via fixed wireless and satellite technologies (12 megabits per second). With technology advancing faster than ever and telecommunication access occupying a major part of our daily lives — from education and communication to healthcare and business — the NBN infrastructure delivers a significant improvement to telecommunication quality, speed and data volume. The NBN is a major part of securing Australia's telecommunication infrastructure capabilities and performance for the future.[2]

The world wide web

Many people equate the internet with the world wide web. However, they are not the same thing. The internet functions as a transport mechanism, whereas the world wide web is an application that uses those transport functions. Other applications, such as email, also run on the internet.

The **world wide web (the web, WWW, or W3)** is a system of universally accepted standards for storing, retrieving, formatting and displaying information via a client/server architecture. The web handles all types of digital information, including text, hypermedia, graphics and sound. It uses graphical user interfaces (GUIs), so it is very easy to navigate.

Organisations that wish to offer information through the web must establish a *home page*, which is a text and graphical screen display that usually welcomes the user and provides basic information on the organisation that has established the page. In most cases, the home page will lead users to other pages. All the pages of a particular company or individual are collectively known as a **website**. Most web pages provide a way to contact the organisation or the individual. The person in charge of an organisation's website is its *webmaster*. (*Note: webmaster* is a gender-neutral title.)

To access a website, the user must specify a **uniform resource locator (URL)**, which points to the address of a specific resource on the web. For instance, the URL for Microsoft is **http://www.microsoft.com**. Recall that HTTP stands for hypertext transport protocol. The remaining letters in this URL — **www.microsoft.com** — indicate the domain name that identifies the web server that stores the website.

Users access the web primarily through software applications called **browsers**. Browsers provide a graphical front end that enables users to point-and-click their way across the web, a process called *surfing*. Web browsers became a means of universal access because they deliver the same interface on any operating system under which they run. As you see in IT's About Business, companies are pouring resources into improving their browsers.

BEFORE YOU GO ON . . .

1. Describe the various ways that you can connect to the internet.
2. Identify the parts of an internet address.
3. What are the functions of browsers?
4. Describe the difference between the internet and the world wide web.

IT'S ABOUT BUSINESS

Browser competition heats up

Businesses are investing increasingly large amounts of time and effort in maintaining compatibility specifications for their business websites to cater for the different types and versions of web browser software. However, in June 2012 in an effort to encourage customers to upgrade their web browser software, Australian online electronics retailer Kogan.com proposed to tax those customers using Internet Explorer 7.0 (IE7) web browser for online purchases, an extra 6.8 per cent surcharge on their purchase if they insisted on not upgrading. CEO and founder Ruslan Kogan stated that 'the business had been spending too much time and money making the site compatible with IE7.' The entrepreneur believed that those wishing to avoid the surcharge would simply switch browsers or update to a more recent version.

Companies are investing increasing amounts of resources in browsers, which are the programs through which users access content on the web. The credit for this trend of increased investments (which is highly beneficial to the consumer) goes to two parties. The first party is Google, whose big plans for its Chrome browser (www.google.com/chrome) have forced Microsoft to pay fresh attention to its own browser, Internet Explorer (IE). Previously, Microsoft had all but stopped efforts to enhance IE after the company won the last browser war by defeating Netscape.

The European Union (EU) is the second party responsible for increased investments in web browsers. Starting in March 2010, the EU required personal computer manufacturers to offer their Europe-based customers more freedom to choose. This requirement originated as part of an antitrust settlement with Microsoft. Under the new regime, when European purchasers boot up their computers for the first time, they will be presented with a screen that lists a dozen browsers (all free) in random order. Users can then download any of these browsers and start surfing the web.

When considering the subject of web browsers, users should bear in mind the business reasons for companies to provide free web browsers. Chrome, for instance, is a key part of Google's strategy to make computer users comfortable with cloud computing (discussed in Plug IT In 3). The objective of Chrome is to convince users to spend less money and time on programs that they have to license from software companies (e.g. from Microsoft) and to instead use free data and services such as Google Docs, which resides on servers and storage systems on the internet. In this way, Chrome — which is available in versions for Windows, Mac and Linux — is designed to drive user dependency on Google's own ad-driven services.

In order for this strategy to work, the browser (in this case, Chrome) has to be good. It turns out that Chrome *is* good — Chrome is fast, takes up little space on users' hard drives and offers advanced support for HTML5. Chrome Instant even has your web page ready to read before you finish typing in the web address!

Other good browsers are out there, however. Mac users, for instance, can use Apple's own browser, Safari (www.apple.com/safari), which is excellent. Safari is also available in a Windows version. Safari mostly adds support for OS X Lion (Apple's latest version of its OS X operating system). Both Mac and Windows users of Safari get the added bonus of a Reading List panel, which provides a personal to-do list that you can edit.

Another excellent browser is Mozilla Firefox (www.mozilla.com/en-US/firefox/fx/), a next-generation descendant of Netscape. Maintained by an open-source community, Firefox is not affiliated with any one corporation and is noted for its constant creative innovation. It is available for Windows, Macs and Linux systems. Firefox benefits from a well-developed application base that includes thousands of add-ons for everything from speeding up YouTube downloads to StumbleUpon, which helps users discover and share websites that match their interests.

Another good browser choice is Opera (www.opera.com), created by the Norwegian company Opera Software. Like Firefox, Opera is available in Windows, Mac and Linux versions. Opera is fast, HTML5 compliant and provides features such as Opera Turbo, which speeds up weak internet connections. Users occasionally encounter a website that does not cooperate with Opera, but that situation is becoming quite rare.

Finally, there is Microsoft Internet Explorer (www.microsoft.com/IE9). IE 10 contains many enhancements, including additional security features and HTML5 compliance. Microsoft has promised that IE 9 will run faster than the previous IE version.

Regardless of which browser users select, they should take into consideration issues of security and privacy. Every company brags about its web browser's security features, but there is truly no such thing as a 'secure browser', because that would imply 100 per cent security (100 per cent security is impossible). Furthermore, browsing privacy can never be truly guaranteed. All browsers offer 'private' or 'incognito' modes, but for the most part such settings only prevent people looking at your computer from seeing the websites you have browsed. They do not stop those sites from keeping records of your visits. In light of these issues, different browsers have taken different approaches to security and privacy. IE10, Chrome and Firefox do offer Tracking Protection, which allows users to subscribe to block lists, so that advertising networks do not have access to your data (and therefore cannot exchange data) about your browsing habits.

Usage statistics in June 2013 for the major desktop browsers were as follows[3]:

Microsoft IE	25.44 per cent
Google Chrome	42.68 per cent
Mozilla Firefox	20.01 per cent
Apple Safari	8.39 per cent
Opera	1.03 per cent.

Sources: Compiled from M Muchmore (2012), 'Browser wars', *PC Magazine*, 14 March; '*Internet browser software review*' (2011), TopTenReviews, May; R Jaroslovsky (2010), 'Browser wars: the sequel', *Bloomberg BusinessWeek*, 8 March; Kogan website, www.kogan.com; C Connelly (2012), 'Kogan wages war on Internet Explorer: Users taxed', *News.com.au*, 14 June, www.news.com.au/technology/kogan-wageswar-on-internet-explorer-users-taxed/story-e6frfro0-1226395298505.

QUESTIONS

1 Given that all browsers are free, what features do the major browser companies focus on to gain competitive advantage?

2 Which browser do you use? Why? Provide examples of why you use this particular browser.

3 Do you believe that online retailers can dictate that customers use the latest versions of web browser software? What might be some of the potential issues for customers and the business, if a surcharge applied to purchases?

Apply the Concept

Background

This section has introduced you to the difference in the internet and the world wide web. Additionally, it has shown that the internet is the largest network in the world and it would not function without domain names and IP addresses. Domain names work much like the address book on your phone. It is much easier to remember the name of the person you want to call than to remember that person's specific number. You typically open your address book and click a name and it calls the related number.

Domain names are similar to this in that the internet actually runs on IP addresses (strings of numbers) and we use domain names to point to them. When you type a domain name, there is an 'address book' (technically called a domain name server) on the web that finds the right string of numbers to which to direct your request.

Activity

HowStuffWorks.com includes a clear explanation of how this domain-naming system works. Visit the site and search 'How domain name servers work'. Read this section of content as well as the content in the chapter that explains domain name servers.

Deliverable

Write an email to your best friend explaining how excited you are (and if you are not excited, just fake it) that you have learned how a domain name server works. Consider the following questions as you prepare your email:

1. What is the function of a domain name server?
2. What are three top-level domains?
3. What is the country code for Germany?
4. How many bits are in IPv4? Give an example of IPv4.
5. How many bits are in IPv6? Give an example of IPv6.

THE NOOK

QUESTIONS

1. What is the difference between the internet and an intranet? How can The Nook use the strengths of each to better serve its customers and make its vision a reality?
2. Malakai and Abbie want to build a new website. Do you think they should host it locally or use a web hosting service? What hardware and connectivity would they need to support a locally run website?

4.4 Network applications

Now that you have a working knowledge of what networks are and how you can access them, the key question is, how do businesses use networks to improve their operations? This section addresses that question. Stated in general terms, networks support businesses and other organisations in all types of functions.

This section will explore numerous network applications, including discovery, communication, collaboration, e-learning and distance learning, open universities and telecommuting. These applications, however, are merely a sampling of the many network applications currently available to users. Even if these applications formed an exhaustive list today, they would not do so tomorrow when something new will be developed. Further, placing network applications in categories is difficult because there will always be borderline cases. For example, the difference between chat rooms (in the communications category) and teleconference (in the collaboration category) is only one of degree.

Discovery

The internet enables users to access or discover information located in databases all over the world. By browsing and searching data sources on the web, users can apply the internet's discovery capability to areas ranging from education to government services to entertainment to commerce. Although having access to all this information is a great benefit, it is critically important to realise that there is no quality assurance for information on the web. The web is truly democratic in that *anyone* can post information to it. Therefore, the fundamental rule about information on the web is 'User beware!'

In addition, the web's major strength — the vast stores of information it contains — also presents a major challenge. The amount of information on the web can be overwhelming and it doubles approximately each year. As a result, navigating through the web and gaining access to necessary information are becoming more and more difficult. To accomplish these tasks, people are increasingly using search engines, directories and portals.

Search engines and metasearch engines

A **search engine** is a computer program that searches for specific information by key words and then reports the results. A search engine maintains an index of billions of web pages. It uses that index to find pages that match a set of user-specified keywords. Such indexes are created and updated by *webcrawlers*, which are computer programs that browse the web and create a copy of all visited pages. Search engines then index these pages to provide fast searches.

In November 2012 three search engines accounted for almost all searches in Australia: Google (**www.google.com**, 70.23 per cent), Yahoo (**www.yahoo.com**, 15.2 per cent) and Microsoft Network (now called Bing, **www.msn.com**, 12.67 per cent).[4] The global market share of search engines in July 2013 saw Google (88.8 per cent), Bing (4.2 per cent), Baidu (3.5 per cent as China's leading search engine) and Yahoo (2.4 per cent) as the market leaders.[5]

For an even more thorough search, you can use a metasearch engine. **Metasearch engines** search several engines at once and then integrate the findings to answer users' queries. Examples are Surf-wax (**www.surfwax.com**), Metacrawler (**www.metacrawler.com**), Mamma (**www.mamma.com**), KartOO (**www.kartoo.com**) and Dogpile (**www.dogpile.com**). Figure 4.9 illustrates the KartOO home page.

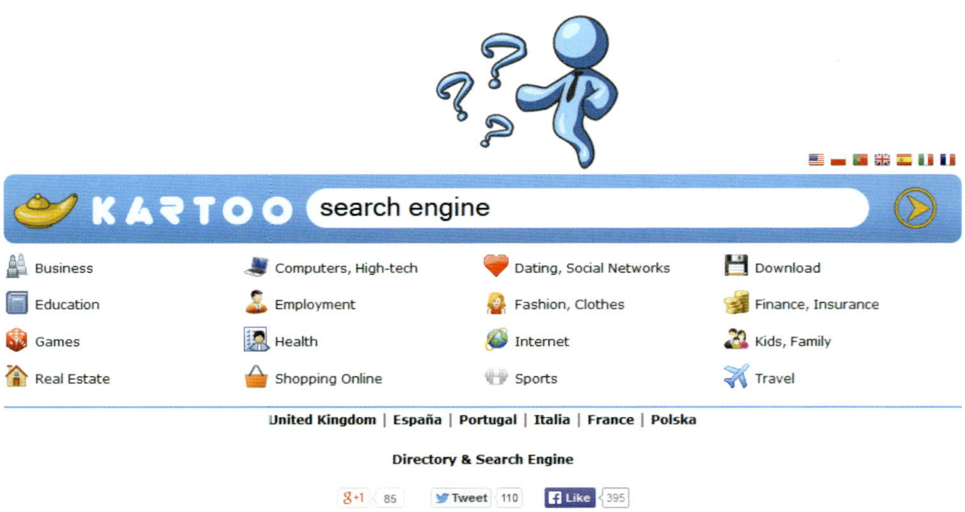

FIGURE 4.9 The Kartoo home page (www.kartoo.com).

Publication of material in foreign languages

Not only is there a huge amount of information on the internet, but it is written in many different languages. How, then, do you access this information? The answer is that you use an *automatic translation* of web pages. Such translation is available to and from all major languages, and its quality is improving with time. Some major translation products are Microsoft's Bing translator (**www.microsofttranslator.com**) and Google (**www.google.com/language_tools**) (see figure 4.10, overleaf), as well as products and services available at Trados (**www.trados.com**).

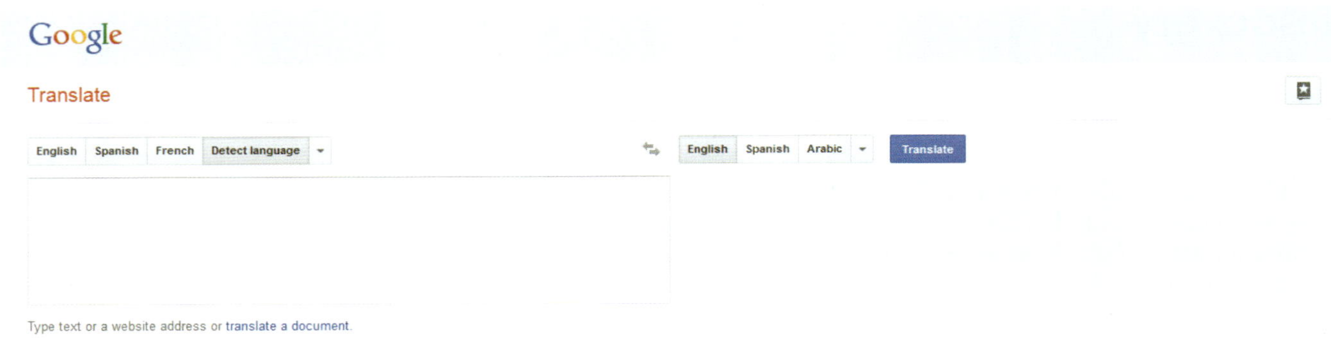

FIGURE 4.10 Google Translate.

IT'S ABOUT BUSINESS

All hail Taxi Pro?

Numerous mobile applications are appearing with the aim of making taxi booking easier via mobile phones. One such example is Taxi Pro, developed by 19-year-old Sydney-based entrepreneur Zac Altman. Taxi Pro is a free online and mobile service application for taxi users that operates in direct competition with the established taxi system Cabcharge, which is the charge account system for taxis across Australia and in various other countries like Singapore.

Altman initially developed the Taxi Pro application during his final year at high school after learning iPhone development in his free time at school. Taxi Pro was conceived and developed by Altman alone and he was subsequently awarded a scholarship to the University of Technology Sydney. The initial consequence was that his iPhone application attracted over 40 000 users even before it was formally advertised, which was achieved predominantly by word of mouth.

Altman's aim was to allow users to book a taxi simply. His approach was to have the Taxi Pro application directly connect with the authorised taxi networks to enable bookings to be made, while the taxi network still maintained full control over fulfilling the bookings accordingly. This provided the users with the best taxi booking experience because according to Altman, users did not want or need extra features such as a taxi whistle or data-heavy maps. What users really cared about was simply booking a taxi with the minimum of fuss.

Taxi Pro allows users to book taxis in cities all over Australia, including Sydney, Cairns and the Gold Coast with more to come. It features the following:

- simple and easy to use interface
- cancel bookings with the touch of a button
- check the status of your bookings
- multi-city support — you don't need multiple taxi booking apps!
- selecting your pickup address is easy. Use a map, search or select a past location
- extremely fast bookings over wi-fi and 3G
- saves your information for future bookings
- keeps track of your bookings
- book a taxi now, or in the future.

In New South Wales, Taxi Pro follows other earlier taxi booking apps like Ingogo and GoCatch, although GoCatch had been accused of compromising passenger safety. Earlier in 2011, the NSW Taxi Council noted that the GoCatch app's ability to track (via GPS) and book nearby taxis directly from a user's mobile phone was creating a potential hazard because it was bypassing the traditional call dispatch process. The result is that if unauthorised networks are dispatching taxis, then passengers cannot be guaranteed that the driver has been authorised by NSW Transport. GoCatch was working to improve the safety aspects of its service, however.

Other proposed features for Taxi Pro would enable both drivers and passengers to rate each other, which would help build a driver's professional reputation and provide an insight into the passenger's reliability without imposing too many limitations. This industry is likely to remain both competitive and challenging, however, since the taxi industry is somewhat conservative and resistant to changing its already established systems.

In December 2011, Taxi Pro released its Android application version. This won Altman the second place in the Optus Unleash Your App competition that invited entries from all over the country. Furthermore, Apple has featured the application a number of times and it is very popular because of its simplicity. Users in Sydney can book a taxi within 5 seconds, making Taxi Pro one of Sydney's fastest and simplest taxi booking services.

Many other booking networks keep appearing and attempting to make taxi booking simple and reliable. According to Altman, it is not as easy as it sounds, requiring a perfect balance in the complicated two-way relationship between the taxi driver and the application itself. Altman's approach towards taxi booking is to connect directly with the existing networks, which he says provides Taxi Pro users with the best booking experience.

Sources: 'Taxi Pro', Google play website, play.google.com/store/apps/details?id=com.basind.taxipro&hl=en; M Hammond (2012), 'Taxi Pro drives into taxi app traffic jam', *Startup Smart*, 30 January, www.startupsmart.com.au/young-entrepreneurs/taxi-pro-drives-into-taxi-app-traffic-jam/201201305218.html; '19-year-old Aussie pumps taxi booking app' (2012), *Delimiter*, 28 January, delimiter.com.au/2012/01/28/19-year-old-aussie-pumps-taxi-booking-app.

QUESTIONS

1. What are the advantages of the Taxi Pro app? Do you see any disadvantages with using the product?
2. Has Altman actually created a new kind of taxi booking application? Why do you say that? Support your answer.
3. What other challenges do you think Taxi Pro will have to contend with in the future? Can you identify additional app features that could be incorporated?
4. What other industries could an app of this nature be applied to? Would you use the same approach with existing systems and networks? Support your answer.

Should companies invest their time and resources to make their websites accessible in multiple languages? The answer is, absolutely. In fact, multilingual websites are now a competitive necessity because of the global nature of the business environment. Companies are increasingly looking outside their home markets to grow revenues and attract new customers. When companies are disseminating information around the world, getting that information correct is essential. It is not enough for companies to translate web content. They must also localise that content and be sensitive to the needs of the people in local markets.

To reach 80 per cent of the world's internet users, a website needs to support a minimum of ten languages: English, Chinese, Spanish, Japanese, German, Korean, French, Italian, Russian and Portuguese. At 20 cents and more per word, translation services are expensive. Companies supporting ten languages can spend \$200 000 annually to localise information and another \$50 000 to maintain the websites. Translation budgets for major multinational companies can run in the millions of dollars. Many large companies use Systran S.A. (**www.systransoft.com**) for high-quality machine translation services.

Portals

Most organisations and their managers encounter information overload. Information is scattered across numerous documents, email messages and databases at different locations and systems. Finding relevant and accurate information is often time-consuming and may require users to access multiple systems.

One solution to this problem is to use portals. A **portal** is a web-based, personalised gateway to information and knowledge that provides relevant information from different IT systems and the internet using advanced search and indexing techniques. After reading the next section, you will be able to distinguish among four types of portals: commercial, affinity, corporate and industry-wide.

A **commercial (public) portal** is the most popular type of portal on the internet. It is intended for broad and diverse audiences and offers routine content, some of it in real time (for example, a stock ticker). Examples are Lycos (**www.lycos.com**) and Microsoft Network (**www.msn.com**).

In contrast, an **affinity portal** offers a single point of entry to an entire community of affiliated interests, such as a hobby group or a political party. Your own university most likely has an affinity portal for its alumni (see the Australian Alumni Association website, **www.australianalumniassociation.org**). Figure 4.11 displays the affinity portal for the Australian Alumni Association. Other examples of affinity portals are **www.techweb.com** and **www.zdnet.com.**

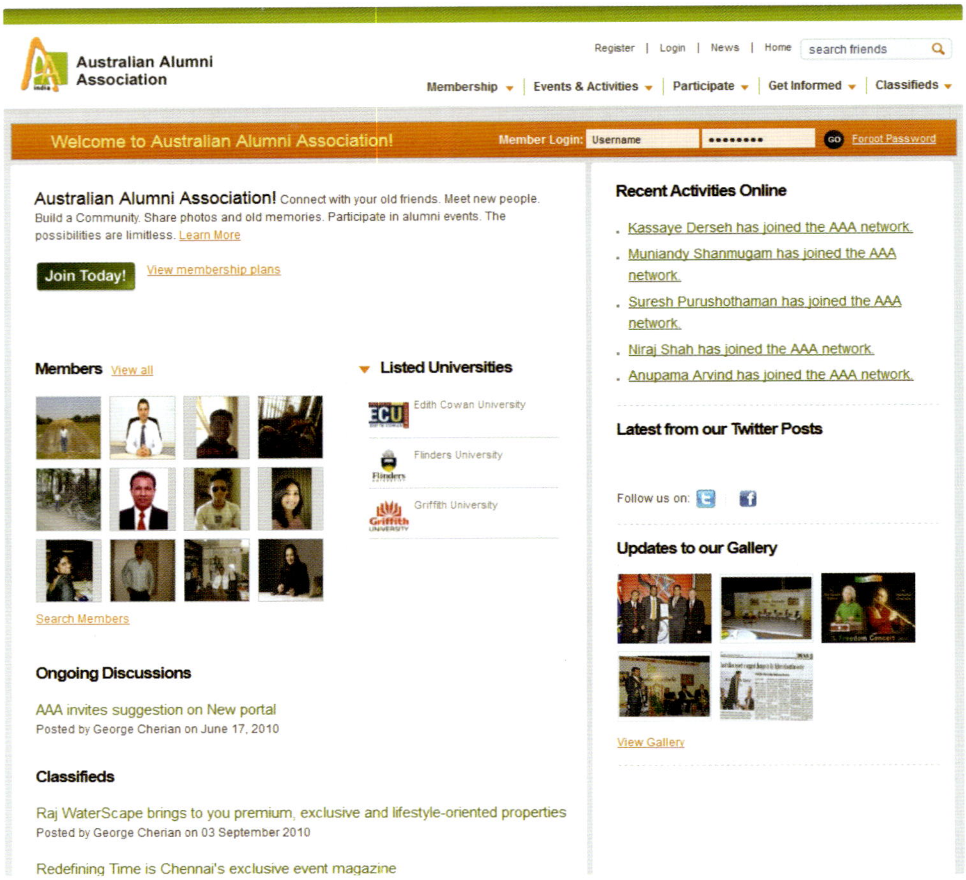

FIGURE 4.11 Australian Alumni Association affinity portal.

As the name suggests, a **corporate portal** offers a personalised, single point of access through a web browser to critical business information located inside and outside an organisation. These portals are also known as *enterprise portals*, *information portals* and *enterprise information portals*. In addition to making it easier to find needed information, corporate portals offer customers and employees self-service opportunities.

Whereas corporate portals are associated with a single company, an **industry-wide portal** serves entire industries. An example is the Industry Capability Network (ICN) (**www.icn.org.au**), an Australian and New Zealand, state and territory government funded, independent organisation established in 1984. The ICN portal is a powerful online tool that acts as an industry-wide information resource to introduce Australian and New Zealand companies and suppliers to projects and new business opportunities.[6] The principal role of the ICN is to locate suppliers and service providers who are best equipped to meet the needs and requirements of hundreds of projects in both Australia and New Zealand. The ICN does this through working with local suppliers and project managers as an industry 'matchmaker', to secure billions of dollars in contracts and jobs that may otherwise have sourced suppliers from abroad rather than locally.

These four types of portals are differentiated by the audiences they serve. Another type, the mobile portal, is distinguished by its technology. A **mobile portal** is accessible from mobile devices, although any of the four portals just discussed can be typically accessed by wireless capable mobile devices.

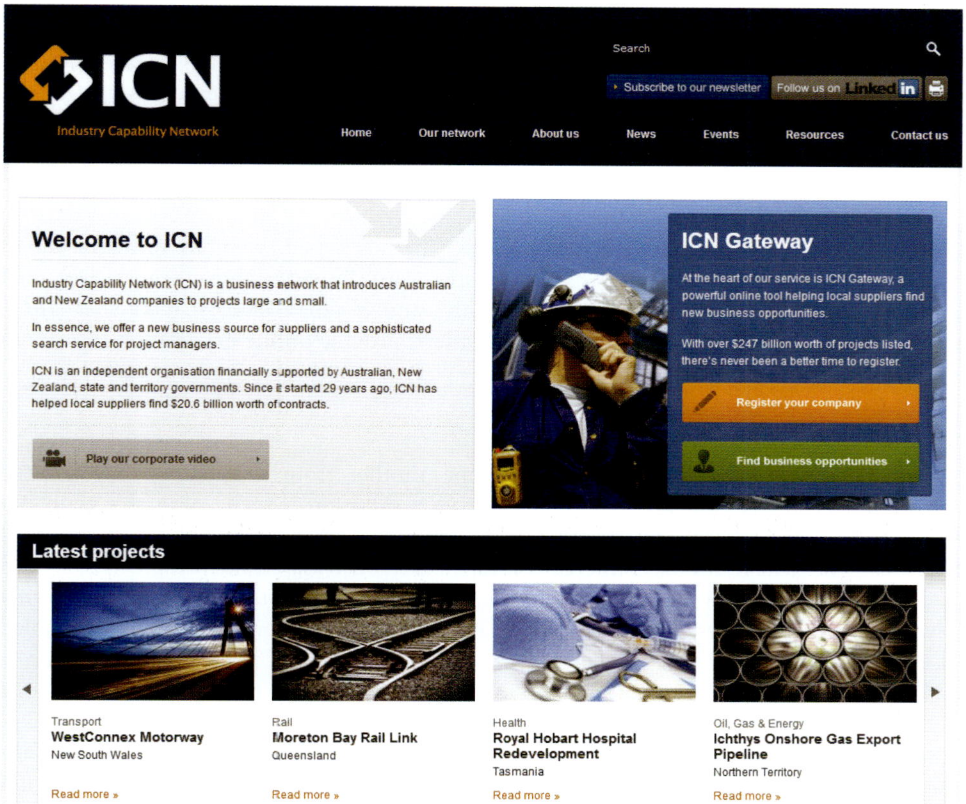

FIGURE 4.12 The Industry Capability Network (ICN) portal.

Communication

The second major category of network applications is communication. There are many types of communication technologies, including email, call centres, chat rooms and voice. You learn about each one in this section.

Electronic mail

Electronic mail (email) is the largest-volume application running over the internet. Studies have found that almost all companies conduct business transactions via email and the vast majority confirm that email is tied to their means of generating revenue. In fact, for many users, email has all but replaced the telephone.

Web-based call centres

Effective personalised customer contact is becoming an important aspect of web-based customer support. Such service is provided through *web-based call centres*, also known as *customer care centres*. For example, if you need to contact a software vendor for technical support, you will usually be communicating with the vendor's web-based call centre, using email, a telephone conversation, or a simultaneous voice/web session. Web-based call centres are sometimes located in foreign countries such as India. Such *offshoring* is an important issue for Australian companies.

For several reasons, some Australian companies are moving their call centre operations back to Australia. First, they feel that they have less control of their overseas call centre operations. They must depend on the vendor company, ensuring that it can uphold their standards, such as quality of service. Second, language difficulties can occur. Third, companies that manage sensitive information can run the risk of breaching customer confidentiality. Finally, the vendor company's call centre representatives typically work with many companies. As a result, they may not deliver the same level of customer services that is required.

Electronic chat rooms

Electronic chat refers to an arrangement whereby participants exchange conversational messages in real time. A **chat room** is a virtual meeting place where many people (in fact, anyone) come to chat. Chat programs allow you to send messages to people who are connected to the same channel of communication at the same time. Anyone can join in the conversation. Messages are displayed on your screen as they arrive, even if you are in the middle of typing a message.

There are two major types of chat programs. The first type is web based, which allows you to send messages to internet users by using a web browser and visiting a web chat site. The second type is email based (text only) and is called *internet relay chat (IRC)*. A business can use IRC to interact with customers, provide online experts for answers to questions and so on.

Voice communication

When people need to communicate with one another from a distance, they use the telephone more frequently than any other communication device. With the plain old telephone service (POTS), every call opened up a dedicated circuit for the duration of the call. A dedicated circuit connects you to the person with whom you are talking and is devoted only to your call. In contrast, as you saw earlier in this chapter, the internet divides data into packets, which traverse the internet in random order and are reassembled at their destination.

With **internet telephony**, also known as **voice-over internet protocol** or **VoIP**, phone calls are treated as just another kind of data. That is, your analogue voice signals are digitised, sectioned into packets and then sent over the internet. In the past, to utilise VoIP you needed a computer with a sound card and a microphone. Today, however, you do not need special phones or headsets for your computer.

VoIP can reduce your monthly phone bills. However, packet switching can cause garbled communications. For example, if the packets of a message arrive out of order, that is not a problem when you are sending an email or transmitting a photo. Correctly reassembling the packets of a voice message, however, can garble the message. Fortunately, this is less of a problem than in the past, because VoIP software continues to improve and typical communications links are much faster. So, although VoIP is not perfect, it is ready for prime time.

Skype (**www.skype.com**) provides several VoIP services for free: voice and video calls to users who also have Skype, instant messaging, short message service, voice mail, one-to-one and group chats, and conference calls with up to nine people. As of

mid-2013 the most current version of Skype for Windows was version 6.6. Skype 6.6 offers full-screen, high-definition video calling using P2P (peer-to-peer) technology to connect with others and greater integration with Facebook and Microsoft (Hotmail) accounts,[7] Skype Access (to access WiFi hotspots), call transfer to a Skype contact on a mobile or landline, improved quality of calls and ease of use. In addition, it offers other functions for which users pay. For example, SkypeOut allows you to make calls to landline phones and mobile phones. SkypeIn provides a number that your friends can call from any phone and you pick up the call in Skype.

Vonage (**www.vonage.com**) also provides VoIP services, but for a fee (approximately $25 per month). With Vonage you make and receive calls with your existing home phone through your broadband internet connection. Your phone connects to Vonage instead of an actual phone company. The person whom you are calling does not need to have Vonage or even an internet connection.

Unified communications

In the past, organisational networks for wired and wireless data, voice communications and videoconferencing operated independently, and the IT department managed each network separately. This arrangement increased costs and reduced productivity.

Unified communications (UC) simplifies and integrates all forms of communications — voice, voice mail, fax, chat, email, instant messaging, short message service, presence (location) services and videoconferencing — on a common hardware and software platform. *Presence services* enable users to know where their intended recipients are and if they are available, in real time.

UC unifies all forms of human and computer communications into a common user experience. For example, UC allows an individual to receive a voice mail message and then read it in his or her email inbox. In another example, UC enables users to seamlessly collaborate with another person on a project, regardless of where the users are located. One user could quickly locate the other user by accessing an interactive directory, determine if that user were available, engage in a text messaging session and then escalate the session to a voice call, or even a video call, all in real time.

Collaboration

The third major category of network applications is collaboration. An important feature of modern organisations is that people collaborate to perform work. **Collaboration** refers to efforts by two or more entities — that is, individuals, teams, groups, or organisations — who work together to accomplish certain tasks. The term **work group** refers specifically to two or more individuals who act together to perform some task.

Workflow is the movement of information as it flows through the sequence of steps that make up an organisation's work procedures. Workflow management makes it possible to pass documents, information and tasks from one participant to another in a way that is governed by the organisation's rules or procedures. Workflow systems are tools for automating business processes.

If group members are in different locations, they constitute a **virtual group (team)**. Virtual groups conduct *virtual meetings* — that is, they 'meet' electronically. **Virtual collaboration** (or *e-collaboration*) refers to the use of digital technologies that enable organisations or individuals to collaboratively plan, design, develop, manage and research products, services and innovative applications. Organisational employees frequently collaborate virtually with one another. In addition, organisations collaborate virtually with customers, suppliers and other business partners to improve productivity and competitiveness.

One type of collaboration is *crowdsourcing*, which refers to outsourcing a task to an undefined, generally large group of people in the form of an open call. Let's look at some examples of crowdsourcing at university campuses.

- *University of South Australia's Unijam*: In 2013 UniSA utilised IBM's Collaborative Innovation platform to host an online conversation to help inform its long-term strategic direction. Consisting of almost 17 000 posts and approximately 8000 participants over 38 hours, the crowdsourcing event comprised a series of forums, drawing together a diverse mix of business, industry and community voices, including students and UniSA staff and alumni, to propose fresh ideas for the future.[8]

- *Scitable* combines social networking and academic collaboration. Through crowdsourcing, students, professors and scientists discuss problems, find solutions and swap resources and journals. It is a free site that lets each individual user turn to crowdsourcing for answers even while helping others.
- *The Great Sunflower Project:* Gretchen LeBuhn, an associate biology professor at San Francisco State University, needed help with her studies of honeybees, but she had limited grant money, so she contacted gardening groups around the country. Through this crowdsourcing strategy, LeBuhn ultimately created a network of more than 25 000 gardeners and schools to assist with her research. She then sent these participants seeds for plants that attract bees. In return, the participants recorded honeybee visits and activity for her on her website.

Collaboration can be *synchronous*, meaning that all team members meet at the same time. Teams may also collaborate *asynchronously* when team members cannot meet at the same time. Virtual teams, whose members are located throughout the world, typically must collaborate asynchronously.

A variety of software products are available to support all types of collaboration. Among the most prominent are Microsoft SharePoint Workspace, Google Docs, IBM Lotus Quickr and Jive. In general, these products provide online collaboration capabilities, workgroup email, distributed databases, bulletin whiteboards, electronic text editing, document management, workflow capabilities, instant virtual meetings, application sharing, instant messaging, consensus building, voting, ranking and various application development tools.

These products also provide varying degrees of content control. Wikis, Google Docs, Microsoft SharePoint Workspace and Jive provide for shared content with *version management*, whereas Microsoft SharePoint Workspace and IBM Lotus Quickr offer *version control*. Products that provide version management track changes to documents and provide features to accommodate multiple people working on the same document at the same time. In contrast, version-control systems provide each team member with an account that includes a set of permissions. Shared documents are located in shared directories. Document directories are often set up so that users must check out documents before they can edit them. When one team member checks out a document, no other member can access it. Once the document has been checked in, it becomes available to other members.

In this section, we review the major collaboration software products. We then shift our attention to two tools that support collaboration — electronic teleconferencing and videoconferencing.

Microsoft SharePoint

Microsoft's SharePoint product (**www.microsoft.com/Sharepoint/default.mspx**) provides shared content with version control. SharePoint supports document directories and has features that enable users to create and manage surveys, discussion forums, wikis, member blogs, member websites and workflow. It also has a rigorous permissions structure, which allows organisations to control users' access based on their organisational role, team membership, interest, security level, or other criteria.

One company that has used SharePoint effectively is Continental Airlines. When new federal regulations regarding long runway delays went into effect, Continental responded by implementing a SharePoint system that puts various aspects of flight operations aircraft status, pilots, crews and customer care — on the same page. Using the system, the 135 general managers at the airline's domestic airports fill out a 16-page form online. The form includes the names and numbers of airport workers, from the airport authority to the person who drives the stairs to planes waiting on the runway. The general managers have to specify how they would manage delays of an hour, two hours and two-and-one-half hours. The Sharepoint system includes a dashboard for Continental's centralised system operations centre. People in the centre can use the dashboard to find information about delays quickly and to communicate with pilots, crews and dispatchers to decide what to do to mitigate any delays.

Google Docs

Google Docs (docs.google.com) is a free web-based word processor, spreadsheet and presentation application. It enables users to create and edit documents online while collaborating with other users. In contrast to Microsoft SharePoint Workspace, Google Docs allows multiple users to open, share and edit documents at the same time.

IBM Lotus Quickr

IBM's Lotus Quickr (**www.ibm.com/lotus/quickr**) product provides shared content with version control in the form of document directories with check-in and check-out features based on user privileges. Quickr provides online team spaces where members can share and collaborate by utilising team calendars, discussion forums, blogs, wikis and other collaboration tools for managing projects and other content.

Compagnie d'Enterprises (CFE), one of Belgium's largest construction companies, has put the collaboration tools of Quickr to good use. Construction projects require many parties to collaborate effectively. When these projects are conducted on a global scale and the parties are scattered throughout the world, the projects become incredibly complex. CFE needed to tap its best resources for its projects, regardless of where those resources were located. The company was using email to share documents with suppliers and clients, but this process resulted in version-control errors and security vulnerabilities. To eliminate these problems, CFE deployed Quickr with its centralised document libraries and version control. The software reduced both the volume of large attachments sent through email and the impact of those emails on the system. As a result, project teams were able to work more efficiently.

Jive Clearspace

Jive's (**www.jivesoftware.com**) newest product, Clearspace, uses web collaboration and communication tools such as forums, wikis and blogs to allow people to share content with version management, via discussion rooms, calendars and commotion lists. For example, Nike originally used Clearspace Community to run a technical support forum on Nike Plus (**nikerunning.nike.com**), a website where runners track their kilometres and kilojoules burned using a sensor in their shoes. The company soon noticed that runners were also using the forum to meet other athletes. In response, Nike expanded its forum to include a section where runners could meet and challenge one another to races. Since that time, 40 per cent of visitors to the site who did not own the Nike Plus sensor ended up buying the product.

Electronic teleconferencing

Teleconferencing is the use of electronic communication technology that enables two or more people at different locations to hold a simultaneous conference. There are several types of teleconferencing. The oldest and simplest is a telephone conference call, where several people talk to one another from multiple locations. The biggest disadvantage of conference calls is that they do not allow the participants to communicate face to face. In addition, participants in one location cannot see graphs, charts and pictures at other locations.

To overcome these shortcomings, organisations are increasingly turning to video teleconferencing, or videoconferencing. In a **videoconference**, participants in one location can see participants, documents and presentations at other locations. The latest version of videoconferencing, called *telepresence*, enables participants to seamlessly share data, voice, pictures, graphics and animation by electronic means. Conferees can also transmit data along with voice and video, which allows them to work together on documents and to exchange computer files.

Several companies are offering high-end telepresence systems. For example, Hewlett-Packard's Halo system (**www.hp.com**), Cisco's TelePresence 3000 (**www.cisco.com**) and Polycom's HDX (**www.polycom.com**) use massive high-definition screens up to 2.4 metres wide to show people sitting around conference tables (see figure 4.13, overleaf). Telepresence systems also have advanced audio capabilities that let everyone talk at once

FIGURE 4.13 Telepresence system.

without cancelling out any voices. Telepresence systems can cost up to $400 000 for a room, with network management fees ranging up to $18 000 per month. Financial and consulting firms are quickly adopting telepresence systems. For example, the Blackstone Group (**www.blackstone.com**), a private equity firm, has 40 telepresence rooms around the world and Deloitte & Touche has 12.

Let's look at two other organisations that use telepresence systems.

The telepresence system of international law firm DLA Piper (**www.dlapiper.com**) saves the company approximately $1 million per year in travel costs and lost productivity. The firm realises these savings by rescheduling half of its in-person board meetings as telepresence conferences and relying on at least two lawyers per week to use telepresence rather than travel. Making it possible for globally based attorneys to work closely together via telepresence helps drive home the reality that the firm has offices all over the world and therefore should have an international focus. This benefit of telepresence cannot be quantified in terms of dollars and cents.

The insurance giant MetLife (**www.metlife.com**) is using telepresence in three dedicated conference rooms in Chicago, New York and New Jersey and is expanding the system to other offices nationally and internationally. MetLife has experienced a direct cost savings as well as better employee time efficiency. Further, telepresence is helping the company meet its 'green initiative' goal of reducing its carbon emissions by 20 per cent. Interestingly, one MetLife executive noted that when the company uses telepresence for meetings, employees who would not normally be asked to travel to headquarters now have the opportunity to make presentations and get valuable exposure to company executives.

E-Learning and distance learning

E-learning and distance learning are not the same thing, but they do overlap. **E-learning** refers to learning supported by the web. It can take place inside classrooms as a support to conventional teaching, such as when students work on the web during class. It also can take place in virtual classrooms, in which all coursework is done online and classes do not meet face-to-face. In these cases, e-learning is a part of distance learning. **Distance learning (DL)** refers to any learning situation in which teachers and students do not meet face-to-face.

Today, the web provides a multimedia interactive environment for self-study. Web-enabled systems make knowledge accessible to those who need it, when they need it, anytime, anywhere. For this reason, e-learning and DL can be useful both for formal education and for corporate training. IT's About Business (opposite) illustrates how high school students are using e-learning and distance learning to take advanced placement (AP) classes online.

IT'S ABOUT BUSINESS

Massive open online courses

Technology enabling online mass delivery is fostering the development of hybrid degrees combining massive open online content with traditional learning. Massive open online courses — known as MOOCs — offer a myriad of possibilities for the Australian higher education sector. Hundreds of thousands of students around the world who lack access to elite universities have been embracing MOOCs as a way to acquire sophisticated skills and high-paying jobs without having to attend or secure a university place.

MOOCs offer visions of economies of scale and discrete courses offered by well-known institutions that boast thousands of students, but critics point to very low completion rates, often weak pedagogy and a questionable business model. However, MOOCs have the potential to bring down the cost of higher education.

Most early MOOC course providers were based in the United States. Consider Stanford University's experience.

In autumn 2011, 160 000 students in 190 countries enrolled in a single artificial intelligence (AI) course offered by Stanford. An additional 200 registered for the course on campus. A few weeks into the semester, attendance for the on-campus course decreased to about 30, as students decided to watch online videos instead of physically attending the class. The course gave rise to its own community, including a Facebook group, online discussions among participants and volunteer translators who made the course available in 44 languages.

The 23 000 students who completed the course received a PDF file (suitable for framing) by email showing their percentile score. However, the file did not contain the name 'Stanford University'. A total of 248 students, none from Stanford, earned grades of 100 per cent.

Besides the AI course, Stanford offered two other MOOCs in autumn 2011 — Machine Learning (104 000 registered, 13 000 completed the course) and Introduction to Databases (92 000 registered, 7000 completed the course). In spring 2012, Stanford offered 13 MOOCs, including Anatomy, Cryptography, Game Theory and Natural Language Processing.

On 13 February 2012, the Massachusetts Institute of Technology, which had been posting course materials online for 10 years, opened registration for its first MOOC, a circuits and electronics course. The course served as a prototype for the university's MITx project, which will eventually offer a wide range of courses and some sort of credential for those who complete them.

Several factors enabled the creation of MOOCs, including improved technology and the rapidly increasing costs of traditional universities. MOOCs are highly automated, with computer graded assignments and exams. Nonetheless, MOOCs offer many opportunities for social interaction. The Stanford MOOCs, for example, offered virtual office hours and online discussion forums where students could ask and answer questions — and vote on which questions were important enough to filter up to the professors.

One Stanford professor noted that in a classroom, when a professor asks a question to the class, one student answers and the others do not get a chance to participate. On the other hand, in an online environment with embedded quizzes, *everyone* has to try to answer the questions. If they do not know the answer to the questions, they can go back and listen to the lecture over and over until they do. The professor noted that MOOCs allow students to work at their own pace and keep practising until they master the content.

A student in one of Stanford's autumn 2011 MOOCs had not been a technology major, nor did she follow a technological career path. She studied psychology at the University of Pittsburgh and was a physician's assistant in charge of the presurgical ward at New York Downtown Hospital. She took the Stanford MOOC on technology in order to better understand her husband's career (he was a developer at Foursquare). Despite the fact that she did not initially take the class to affect her own job, she has since used her new software skills to automate some of the routine tasks she performs at work, such as keeping track of which patients require follow-up before surgery. Her skills also help her communicate with the information technology specialists installing electronic medical records systems at the hospital.

In what some academicians see as a threat to higher education, some MOOCs now offer an informal credential (although such a credential, in most cases, is not free). The provost at Stanford notes that there are many issues to consider with MOOCs, from questions of copyright of course materials to implications for Stanford's accreditation if the university provides an official credential for these courses.

One of the professors who taught Stanford's first MOOC co-founded Udacity (www.udacity.com), a for-profit startup that offers a variety of MOOCs. Udacity is not the only such startup — Udemy (www.udemy.com), ➜

founded in 2010, is a similar startup with backing from the founders of Groupon (www.groupon.com). Both sites plan to monetise their students' skills and obtain their permission to sell leads to recruiters, thereby helping them to find jobs. Both companies will have detailed records on thousands of students who have learned new skills and many of those students will want to make those skills known to potential employers. For example, if a recruiter were searching for the top 100 people in a certain geographic area who have knowledge about machine learning, Udacity and Udemy would be able to provide that information for a fee.

Some of the world's best known higher education institutional brands are lending their names, though not their degrees, to online ventures. The University of Melbourne recently signed up to Coursera. Its media release stressed that Coursera was a 'prestigious online course provider', indicating that it considers its image can be enhanced by association with an online provider. With its combination of student selectivity and research strength, the University of Melbourne is probably the leading higher education institution in Australia.

With a number of other universities including Deakin, University of Queensland, University of Western Australia, La Trobe and University of NSW embracing open online courses and international partnerships with MOOC providers and institutions, Australian universities will need a very clear sense of their own mission and purpose, a focus on their unique aspects and a relentless effort to ensure that the technology underpinning their educational mission is of a quality and capacity to meet the expectations of an increasingly demanding student audience. However, in Australia existing regulations regarding accreditation are barriers to local universities giving students credit for completing MOOCs.

Yet campus-based education will remain. There is still the practical training and laboratory aspect that cannot be moved online, and the university student on-campus lifestyle and experience will still remain attractive to undergraduate students, even for subjects that can be undertaken wholly online.

Sources: Compiled from T Lewin (2012), 'Instruction for masses knocks down campus walls', *The New York Times*, 4 March; B Sheridan and B Greeley (2012), 'Computer coding: not for geeks only', *Bloomberg BusinessWeek*, 26 January; L Chamberlin and T Parish (2011), 'MOOCs: massive open online courses or massive and often obtuse courses?', *eLearn Magazine*, August; I de Waard (2011), 'Explore a new learning frontier: MOOCs', *Learning Solutions Magazine*, 25 July; R Kop (2011), 'The challenges to connectivist learning on open online networks: learning experiences during a massive open online course', *International Review of Research in Open and Distance Learning*, v. 12, no. 3; K Masters (2011), 'A brief guide to understanding MOOCs', *The Internet Journal of Medical Education*, v. 1, no. 2; E Fuller (2010), 'Top 10 benefits of a college degree', *Christian Science Monitor*, October; UDACITY website, www.udacity.com; Stanford University website, www.stanford.edu; Massachusetts Institute of Technology website, www.mit.edu; J Ross (2013), 'Internals "primary" winners from MOOCs revolution', *The Australian*, 26 February, www.theaustralian.com.au/higher-education/internals-primary-winners-frommoocs-revolution/story-e6frgcjx-1226585199258; A Norton (2012), 'MOOCs offer options as quest for knowledge evolves', *The Age*, 2 October, www.theage.com.au/national/education/moocs-offer-options-as-quest-for-knowledge-evolves-20121001-26vdt.html; C Palmer (2012), 'Credit for MOOCs presents challenges in Australia', *The Conversation*, 7 November, theconversation.edu.au/credit-for-moocs-presentschallenges-in-australia-10585; J Rowbotham (2013), 'Do the maths — MOOCs break the mould', *The Australian*, 20 February, www.theaustralian.com.au/higher-education/do-the-maths-moocs-break-the-mould/story-e6frgcjx-1226581417851.

QUESTIONS

1 Discuss possible quality control issues with MOOCs. For each issue that you list, please also describe how you would go about solving the problem.

2 What are some specific examples of the impact that MOOCs could have on traditional higher education? Please explain your answer.

3 Would you be willing to enrol in a MOOC as a full-time student at your university? Would you be willing to enrol in a MOOC after you graduate? Why or why not?

There are many benefits to e-learning. For example, online materials can deliver very current content that is of high quality (created by content experts) and consistent (presented the same way every time). It also gives students the flexibility to learn at any place, at any time and at their own pace. In corporate training centres that use e-learning, learning time is generally shorter, which means that more people can be trained within a given timeframe. This system reduces training costs as well as the expense of renting facility space.

Despite these benefits, e-learning has some drawbacks. For one, students must be computer literate. Also, they may miss the face-to-face interaction with instructors. In addition, accurately assessing students' work can be problematic because instructors really do not know who completed the assignments.

E-learning does not usually replace the classroom setting. Rather, it enhances it by taking advantage of new content and delivery technologies. Advanced e-learning support environments, such as Blackboard (**www.blackboard.com**), add value to traditional learning in higher education.

Open University

Open Universities Australia is a national leader in the provision and delivery of online higher education. For more than 17 years Open Universities Australia has been offering students online higher education or professional development. Courses and units are provided by a number of established partner universities around Australia offering Open University students a flexible way to access higher education and professional development via distance education. Open Universities Australia offers a wide range of undergraduate and postgraduate degrees across arts and humanities, business, education, health, information technology, law, science and engineering, as well as selected TAFE courses.[9]

Telecommuting

Knowledge workers are being called the distributed workforce, or digital nomads. This group of highly prized workers is now able to work anywhere and anytime, a process called **telecommuting**. Distributed workers are those who have no permanent office at their companies, preferring to work at home offices, in airport lounges or client conference rooms. The growth of the distributed workforce is driven by globalisation, extremely long commutes to work, rising petrol prices, ubiquitous broadband communications links (wireline and wireless), and powerful laptop computers and computing devices.

Telecommuting has a number of potential advantages for employees, employers and society. For employees, the benefits include reduced stress and improved family life. In addition, telecommuting offers employment opportunities for housebound people such as single parents and persons with disabilities. Employer benefits include increased productivity, the ability to retain skilled employees and the ability to attract employees who do not live within commuting distance.

However, telecommuting also has some potential disadvantages. For employees, the major disadvantages are increased feelings of isolation, possible loss of fringe benefits, lower pay (in some cases), no workplace visibility, the potential for slower promotions and lack of socialisation. In addition, telecommuting employees often have difficulties 'training' their families to understand that they are at work even though they are physically at home. Families have to understand that they should not disturb the telecommuter for anything that they would not have disturbed him or her about in a 'real' office. The major disadvantages to employers are difficulties in supervising work and potential data security problems.

BEFORE YOU GO ON . . .

1. Discuss the network applications that you studied in this section and the tools and technologies that support each one.
2. Identify the business conditions that have made videoconferencing more important.
3. Differentiate between e-learning and distance learning.
4. Describe virtual universities.
5. What is telecommuting? Do you think you would like to telecommute? Why or why not?

THE NOOK

QUESTIONS

1. How can The Nook capitalise on network tools such as email, chat or instant messaging?
2. What type of workflow projects could help streamline the operations for The Nook?

WHAT'S IN IT FOR ME?

FOR THE ACCOUNTING MAJOR

Accounting personnel use corporate intranets and portals to consolidate transaction data from legacy systems to provide an overall view of internal projects. This view contains the current costs charged to each project, the number of hours spent on each project by individual employees and an analysis of how actual costs compare to projected costs. Finally, accounting personnel use internet access to government and professional websites to stay informed on legal and other changes affecting their profession.

FOR THE FINANCE MAJOR

Corporate intranets and portals can provide a model to evaluate the risks of a project or an investment. Financial analysts use two types of data in the model: historical transaction data from corporate databases via the intranet and industry data obtained via the internet. In addition, financial services organisations can use the web for marketing and to provide services.

FOR THE MARKETING MAJOR

Marketing managers use corporate intranets and portals to coordinate the activities of the sales force. Sales personnel access corporate portals via the intranet to discover updates on pricing, promotion, rebates, customer information and information about competitors. Sales staff can also download and customise presentations for their customers. The internet, particularly the web, opens a completely new marketing channel for many industries. Just how advertising, purchasing and information dispensation should occur appears to vary from industry to industry, product to product and service to service.

FOR THE MANAGEMENT MAJOR

Companies are using intranets and portals to speed product development by providing the development team with three-dimensional models and animation. All team members can access the models for faster exploration of ideas and enhanced feedback and collaboration. Corporate portals, accessed via intranets, enable managers to supervise their inventories carefully as well as real-time production on assembly lines. Extranets are also proving valuable as communication formats for joint research and design efforts among companies. The internet is also a great source of cutting-edge information for production and operational managers.

FOR THE HUMAN RESOURCES MANAGEMENT MAJOR

Human resources personnel use portals and intranets to publish corporate-policy manuals, job postings, company telephone directories and training classes. Many companies deliver online training obtained from the internet to employees through their intranets. Human resources departments use intranets to advertise jobs internally and provide access to job descriptions, enterprise agreements, pay rates, staff development programs/workshops and HR adviser contact details. The internet supports worldwide recruiting efforts; it can also be the communications platform for supporting geographically dispersed work teams.

FOR THE MIS MAJOR

As important as the networking technology infrastructure is, it is invisible to users (unless something goes wrong). The MIS function is responsible for keeping all organisational networks up and running all the time. MIS personnel, therefore, provide all users with an 'eye to the world' and the ability to compute, communicate and collaborate anytime, anywhere. For example, organisations have access to experts at remote locations without having to duplicate that expertise in multiple areas of the firm. Virtual teaming allows experts physically located in different cities to work on projects as though they were in the same office.

SUMMARY

1 Compare and contrast the two major types of networks.

The two major types of networks are local area networks (LANs) and wide area networks (WANs). LANs encompass a limited geographic area and are usually composed of one communications medium. In contrast, WANs encompass a broad geographical area and are usually composed of multiple communications media.

2 Describe the wireline communications media and channels.

Twisted-pair wire, the most prevalent form of communications wiring, consists of strands of copper wire twisted in pairs. It is relatively inexpensive to purchase, widely available and easy to work with. However, it is relatively slow for transmitting data, it is subject to interference from other electrical sources and it can be easily tapped by unintended receivers.

Coaxial cable consists of insulated copper wire. It is much less susceptible to electrical interference than is twisted-pair wire and it can carry much more data. However, coaxial cable is more expensive and more difficult to work with than twisted-pair wire. It is also somewhat inflexible.

Fibre-optic cables consist of thousands of very thin filaments of glass fibres that transmit information via light pulses generated by lasers. Fibre-optic cables are significantly smaller and lighter than traditional cable media. They also can transmit far more data, and they provide greater security from interference and tapping. Fibre-optic cable is often used as the backbone for a network, whereas twisted-pair wire and coaxial cable connect the backbone to individual devices on the network.

3 Describe the most common methods for accessing the internet.

Common methods for connecting to the internet include dial-up, DSL, cable modem, satellite, wireless and fibre to the premises.

4 Explain the impact that networks have had on business and everyday life for each of the six major categories of network applications.

> *Discovery* involves browsing and information retrieval, and provides users the ability to view information in databases, download it and/or process it. Discovery tools include search engines, directories and portals. Discovery tools enable business users to efficiently find needed information.

> *Networks* provide fast, inexpensive communications, via email, call centres, chat rooms, voice communications and blogs. Communications tools provide business users with a seamless interface among team members, colleagues, business partners and customers.

> *Collaboration* refers to mutual efforts by two or more entities (individuals, groups, or companies) who work together to accomplish tasks. Collaboration is enabled by workflow systems. Collaboration tools enable business users to collaborate with colleagues, business partners and customers.

> *E-learning* refers to learning supported by the web. Distance learning refers to any learning situation in which teachers and students do not meet face-to-face. E-learning provides tools for business users to enable their lifelong learning.

> *Online universities* offer online courses in which students take classes via the internet at home or an off-site location. Online universities make it possible for students to obtain degrees while working full time, thus increasing their value to their organisations.

> *Telecommuting* is the process whereby knowledge workers are able to work anywhere and anytime. Telecommuting provides flexibility for employees, with many benefits and some drawbacks.

>>> CHAPTER GLOSSARY

affinity portal A website that offers a single point of entry to an entire community of affiliated interests.

analogue signals Continuous waves that transmit information by altering the amplitude and frequency of the waves.

backbone networks High-speed central networks to which multiple smaller networks (such as LANs and smaller WANs) connect.

bandwidth The transmission capacity of a network, stated in bits per second.

broadband A transmission speed ranging from approximately one megabit per second up to several terabits per second.

broadcast media (also called wireless media) Communications channels that use electromagnetic media (the 'airwaves') to transmit data.

browsers Software applications through which users primarily access the web.

cable media (also called wireline media) Communications channels that use physical wires or cables to transmit data and information.

chat room A virtual meeting place where groups of regulars come to 'gab' electronically.

client/server computing Form of distributed processing in which some machines (servers) perform computing functions for end-user PCs (clients).

clients Computers, such as users' personal computers, that use any of the services provided by servers.

coaxial cable Insulated copper wire; used to carry high-speed data traffic and television signals.

collaboration Mutual efforts by two or more individuals who perform activities in order to accomplish certain tasks.

commercial (public) portal A website that offers fairly routine content for diverse audiences; offers customisation only at the user interface.

communications channel Pathway for communicating data from one location to another.

computer network A system that connects computers and other devices via communications media so that data and information can be transmitted among them.

corporate portal A website that provides a single point of access to critical business information located inside and outside of an organisation.

digital signals A discrete pulse, either on or off, that conveys information in a binary form.

digital subscriber line (DSL) A high-speed, digital data-transmission technology using existing analogue telephone lines.

distance learning (DL) Learning situations in which teachers and students do not meet face-to-face.

distributed processing Network architecture that divides processing work between two or more computers, linked together in a network.

domain name system (DNS) The system administered by the Internet Corporation for Assigned Names (ICANN) that assigns names to each site on the internet.

domain names The name assigned to an internet site, consisting of multiple parts, separated by dots, which are translated from right to left.

e-learning Learning supported by the web; can be done inside traditional classrooms or in virtual classrooms.

enterprise network An organisation's network composed of interconnected multiple LANs and WANs.

ethernet A common local area network protocol.

extranet A network that connects parts of the intranets of different organisations.

fibre-optic cable A communications medium consisting of thousands of very thin filaments of glass fibres, surrounded by cladding, that transmit information via light pulses generated by lasers.

file server (also called network server) A computer that contains various software and data files for a local area network and contains the network operating system.

hypertext transport protocol (HTTP) The communications standard used to transfer pages across the WWW portion of the internet; defines how messages are formulated and transmitted.

industrywide portal A web-based gateway to information and knowledge for an entire industry.

internet (the net) A massive global WAN that connects approximately 1 million organisational computer networks in more than 200 countries on all continents, including Antarctica, and features in the daily routine of almost 2 billion people. Participating computer systems include smart phones, PCs, LANs, databases and mainframes.

internet protocol (IP) A set of rules responsible for disassembling, delivering and reassembling packets over the internet.

internet protocol (IP) address An assigned address that uniquely identifies a computer on the internet.

internet service provider (ISP) A company that provides internet connections for a fee.

internet telephony (voice-over internet protocol or VoIP) The use of the internet as the transmission medium for telephone calls.

intranet A private network that uses internet software and TCP/IP protocols.

local area network (LAN) A network that connects communications devices in a limited geographical region, such as a building, so that every user device on the network can communicate with every other device.

metasearch engine A computer program that searches several engines at once and integrates the findings of the various search engines to answer queries posted by users.

mobile portal A website that is accessible from mobile devices.

modem Device that converts signals from analogue to digital and vice versa.

network access points (NAPs) Computers that act as exchange points for internet traffic and determine how traffic is routed.

network server (see file server)

online universities Online universities deliver university courses in which students take classes via the internet at home or an off-site location.

packet switching The transmission technology that divides blocks of text into packets.

peer-to-peer (P2P) processing A type of client/server distributed processing that allows two or more computers to pool their resources, making each computer both a client and a server.

portal A web-based personalised gateway to information and knowledge that provides information from disparate information systems and the internet, using advanced search and indexing techniques.

protocol The set of rules and procedures governing transmission across a network.

router A communications processor that routes messages from a LAN to the internet, across several connected LANs, or across a wide area network such as the internet.

search engine A computer program that searches for specific information by key words and reports the results.

servers Computers that provide access to various network services, such as printing, data and communications.

telecommuting A work arrangement whereby employees work at home, at the customer's premises, in special workplaces, or while traveling, usually using a computer linked to their place of employment.

teleconferencing The use of electronic communication that allows two or more people at different locations to have a simultaneous conference.

transmission control protocol/internet protocol (TCP/IP) A file transfer protocol that can send large files of information across sometimes unreliable networks with assurance that the data will arrive uncorrupted.

twisted-pair wire A communications medium consisting of strands of copper wire twisted together in pairs.

unified communications Common hardware and software platform that simplifies and integrates all forms of communications — voice, email, instant messaging, location and videoconferencing — across an organisation.

uniform resource locator (URL) The set of letters that identifies the address of a specific resource on the web.

videoconference A virtual meeting in which participants in one location can see and hear participants at other locations and can share data and graphics by electronic means.

virtual collaboration The use of digital technologies that enable organisations or individuals to collaboratively plan, design, develop, manage and research products, services and innovative information systems and electronic commerce applications.

virtual group (team) A work group whose members are in different locations and who meet electronically.

voice-over internet protocol (VOIP; see internet telephony)

website Collectively, all of the web pages of a particular company or individual.

wide area network (WAN) A network, generally provided by common carriers, that covers a wide geographic area.

wireless media (see broadcast media)

wireline media (see cable media)

work group Two or more individuals who act together to perform some task, on either a permanent or temporary basis.

workflow The movement of information as it flows through the sequence of steps that make up an organisation's work procedures.

world wide web (the web, WWW, or W3) A system of universally accepted standards for storing, retrieving, formatting and displaying information via a client/server architecture; it uses the transport functions of the internet.

>>> DISCUSSION QUESTIONS

1 What are the implications of having fibre-optic cable to everyone's home?
2 What are the implications of BitTorrent for the music industry? For the motion picture industry?
3 Discuss the pros and cons of P2P networks.
4 Should the internet be regulated? If so, by whom?
5 Discuss the pros and cons of delivering this book over the internet.
6 Explain how the internet works. Assume you are talking with someone who has no knowledge of information technology (in other words, keep it very simple).
7 How are the network applications of communication and collaboration related? Do communication tools also support collaboration? Give examples.
8 Search Google Australia using the term 'medical self-diagnosis Australia'. View the results. Is this unwise or is it a prudent approach to assessing your medical condition? If so, why and if not, support your answer.
9 Search online for the article from *The Atlantic:* 'Is Google Making Us Stupid?' *Is* Google making us stupid? Support your answer.

>>> PROBLEM-SOLVING ACTIVITIES

1 Calculate how much bandwidth you consume when using the internet every day. How many emails do you send daily and what is the size of each? (Your email program may have email file size information.) How many music and video clips do you download (or upload) daily and what is the size of each? If you view YouTube often, surf the web to find out the size of a typical YouTube file. Add up the

number of email, audio and video files you transmit or receive on a typical day. When you have calculated your daily internet usage, determine if you are a 'normal' internet user or a 'power' internet user. What impact does network neutrality have on you as a 'normal' user? As a 'power' user?

2 Access several P2P applications, such as SETI@home. Describe the purpose of each application and indicate which ones you would like to join.

3 Access ipv6.com and www.ipv6news.info and learn about more advantages of IPv6.

4 Access www.icann.org and learn more about this important organisation.

5 Set up your own website using your name for the domain name (for example, KellyRainer).
   - Explain the process for registering a domain.
   - Which top-level domain will you use and why?

6 Access www.icann.org and obtain the name of an agency or company that can register a domain for the TLD that you selected. What is the name of that agency or company?

7 Access the website for the agency or company in question 6 to learn the process that you must use. How much will it initially cost to register your domain name? How much will it cost to maintain that name in the future?

8 You plan to take a two-week holiday in New Zealand this year. Using the internet, find information that will help you plan the trip. Such information includes, *but is not limited to*, the following.
   a Geographical location and weather conditions at the time of your trip
   b Major tourist attractions and recreational facilities
   c Travel arrangements (airlines, approximate fares)
   d Car rental; local tours
   e Alternatives for accommodation (within a moderate budget) and food
   f Estimated cost of the holiday (travel, lodging, food, recreation, shopping, etc.)
   g Regulations regarding the entrance of your dog
   h Shopping
   i Passport information (either to obtain one or to renew one)
   j Information on the country's language and culture
   k What else do you think you should research before going to New Zealand?

9 From your own experience or from the vendor's information, list the major capabilities of Lotus Notes/Domino. Do the same for Microsoft Exchange. Compare and contrast the products. Explain how the products can be used to support knowledge workers and managers.

10 Visit websites of companies that manufacture telepresence products for the internet. Prepare a report. Differentiate between telepresence products and videoconferencing products.

11 Access Google (or YouTube) videos and search for 'Cisco Magic'. This video shows Cisco's next-generation telepresence system. Compare and contrast it with current telepresence systems.

12 Access the website of your university. Does the website provide high-quality information (right amount, clear, accurate, etc.)? Do you think a high-school student who is thinking of attending your university would feel the same way?

13 Compare and contrast Google Sites (www.google.com/sites) and Microsoft Office Live (www.liveoffice.com). Which site would you use to create your own website? Explain your choice.

14 Access the website of the Australian Recording Industry Association (ARIA) (www.aria.com.au). Discuss what you find there regarding what sort of sound recordings reproductions ARIA is able to license. Debate this issue from your point of view and from the ARIA point of view.

15 Research the companies involved in internet telephony (Voice-over IP). Compare their offerings as to price, necessary technologies, ease of installation and so on. Which company is the most attractive to you? Which company might be the most attractive for a large company?

16 Access some of the alternative search engines at www.johnwiley.com.au/highered/rainer/ausnz/studentresources. Search for the same terms on several of the alternative search engines and on Google. Compare the results on breadth (number of results found) and precision (results are what you were looking for).

17 Second Life (www.secondlife.com) is a three-dimensional, online world built and owned by its residents. Residents of Second Life are avatars who have been created by real people. Access Second Life, learn about it and create your own avatar to explore this world. Learn about the thousands of people who are making 'real-world' money from operations in Second Life.

18 Access Microsoft's Bing translator (www.microsofttranslator.com) or Google (www.google.com/language_tools) translation pages. Type in a paragraph in English and select, for example, English-to-French. When you see the translated paragraph in French, copy it into the text box and select French-to-English. Is the paragraph that you first entered the same as the one you are looking at now? Why or why not? Support your answer.

>>> COLLABORATION EXERCISE

Background

Napster was initially created as a music-sharing site where users would copy songs from CDs they had purchased and then share them with other users. It was wildly popular in spite of the fact that the majority of users at the time were connected via dial-up networks. It could take up to an hour to download a 3 MB music file over an old 56K modem! Eventually it became so big that it caught the eye of the music industry, which began a series of lawsuits against the heaviest users. Today, the music industry operates off multiple 'subscription'-type sites that have legalised digital music.

Activity

Work with a group to imagine the type of data sharing you may experience on the job. Divide your group into functional areas. What kind of files would benefit from a centralised file sharing site? This would not necessarily be a database, but large files that are easier stored and shared through file sharing services — things like handbooks, catalogues, manuals, etc., that are often too large to email. For the functional area you are assigned, search the web for different files that are too large for email and download them. Once everyone in your group has his or her files (make sure they are all public files), upload them into a single group file sharing service. You can use Dropbox, LimeWire, or whatever you want. Most will offer a free trial account you can use.

Deliverable

Share your folder with your instructor with an accompanying document explaining what documents have been placed there from each department. Include an explanation of your experience as a group of using the web for discovery, communication and collaboration.

CLOSING CASE **1** >

Managing information flow

The goal of the National Broadband Network (NBN) roll-out across Australia is to deliver the capability of high-speed broadband internet network access to Australian homes, schools and businesses using a mix of three technologies — fibre-optic cable, fixed wireless and next generation satellite — at speeds of up to one gigabit per second.

In late 2012 the Australian Federal Government abandoned a plan for introducing a mandatory internet filter policy that would require internet service providers (ISPs) to block inappropriate websites as listed on Interpol's 'worst of' database. Furthermore, at a conference gathering of United Nations (UNs) International Telecommunications Union, an attempt by member state governments to establish a worldwide oversight policy for the internet collapsed after several Western countries could not reach a consensus agreement regarding suitable text for the International Telecommunications Regulations. Technologists were alarmed that an agreement would essentially legitimise more governments to impose censorship and surveillance.

From this perspective, the technology capability currently exists for ISPs to control the speed and flow of information to the consumer from the internet and under these circumstances represents an ethical issue regarding the freedom of choice and legitimate use of network access within Australia for business and consumers alike.

Telstra and other internet service providers could be investigated if they slow down file-sharing programs like BitTorrent in favour of providing their own video content to customers, the Australian Competition and Consumer Commission (ACCC) says.

Telstra recently revealed plans to test new ways of managing its broadband network with some Victorian customers, which would lead to some high-bandwidth internet content being slowed down.

The trial sparked panic among some users who threatened to leave the telco. Industry rivals have called the move the 'first shot in a battle on net neutrality', a debate over whether ISPs should treat all online content the same.

The chairman of the ACCC, Rod Sims, told *The Australian Financial Review* that he would look to investigate any attempts to advantage some content over others.

'Clearly there is a vertical integration issue where internet service providers can control what comes down their pipe and obviously if, unrelated to the reports about Telstra, we see that ISPs were using that technology to influence their own content over other content then that would be of concern to us,' he said.

The issue is becoming particularly pertinent in Australia as telecommunications players continue a transition from being dumb pipe providers to small media empires, delivering television and online content alongside internet and telephone access.

At the same time, the prevalence of file-sharing programs like BitTorrent continues to take up valuable network space, accounting for 35 per cent of all internet traffic in the Asia–Pacific region, according to United States company Sandvine.

The programs, though available for legitimate uses, are often linked to the illegal downloading of movies, music and television shows.

Industry sources say the vast majority of providers in Australia throttle some types of traffic to ensure that uses like file sharing do not impede on programs that require no disruptions, like Skype or online gaming.

Telstra sought to downplay the trials as an attempt to better manage its network traffic, which it says has doubled on average every 12 months for the past four years.

It said the trial would not prioritise its own content and that combating illegal downloading was not a part of the trial, despite mentioning online piracy in its first response.

Telstra chief executive David Thodey also stepped in to defend the trial, calling news reports 'a little over-hyped'.

'It's absolutely standard for most ISPs, we want to be absolutely transparent on it, there's nothing to hide', he told media at the company's first-half financial results briefing on Thursday.

'I think most operators around the world do a degree of shaping anyway, it's always been the case.'

But it has been met with hesitation from the wider industry. John Lindsay, the chief technology officer of second-tier service provider iiNet, said that while the trial is initially limited to some of Telstra's 2.7 million broadband customers, it could have reverberations throughout the industry.

'It feels like you've paid your fee to go to an all-you-can-eat buffet and the restaurant owners have put a fence up in front of it and will only let one person in at a time,' he said.

'That one person can cram all the food they want onto a plate, but if you make the plate smaller, you limit the access to the buffet.'

Mr Lindsay acknowledged iiNet used the same type of technology Telstra will use to slow web content, but said the company did not actively throttle a specific program or content type.

iiNet, along with other ISPs, also 'unmeters' some content, not counting downloads over those services to the user's monthly quota.

Mr Lindsay compared the issue to the 'net-neutrality' or 'open-internet' debate in the US, which has seen most internet giants battle over whether to prioritise cable television content over others.

The US equivalent of the ACCC implemented measures in 2010 prohibiting the blocking of lawful content and 'unreasonable discrimination' on broadband networks.

An agreement struck between Google and US carrier Verizon that same year was seen as backtracking for the search giant, traditionally a bastion of internet values. Online streaming and DVD rental video provider Netflix has since surpassed BitTorrent as the single biggest source of internet traffic in the US.

Stephen Langsford, the chairman of Netflix's Australian equivalent Quickflix, said he was opposed to any form of discrimination online.

'Starting to impose restrictions prematurely ahead of fully developing the opportunity would seem to be an unfortunate consequence', he said.

'The world is moving to choice and there's an expectation ultimately from customers that they're able to have choice in the way that they access content without restrictions.

'Particularly with the NBN in the background. I think those sorts of restrictions seem to smack of short-termism, well and truly.'

One senior telco industry executive said the rollout of the national broadband network would require video providers like Quickflix to align themselves with ISPs in order to efficiently and cost-effectively distribute video.

However, Mr Langsford said Quickflix was 'not banking on special favour from any particular player'.

Sources: J Hutchinson (2013), 'ACCC takes aim at ISPs' BitTorrent slowdowns', *BRW.*, 12 February, www.brw.com.au/p/technology/accc_takes_aim_at_isps_bittorrent_3J0NWdGgtnlm15clkwgABJ; 'National Broadband Network', Australian Government Department of Communications website, www.communications.gov.au/broadband/national_broadband_network; S Cullen (2012), 'Government abandons plans for internet filter', *ABC News*, 9 November, www.abc.net.au/news/2012-11-09/government-abandons-plans-for-internet-filter/4362354; M Smith & J Menn (2012), 'Australia, US refuse to sign internet treaty', *The Age*, 14 December, www.theage.com.au/technology/technology-news/australia-us-refuse-tosign-internet-treaty-20121214-2bdsf.html; J Hutchinson (2013), 'ACCC takes aim at internet slowdowns', *The Australian Financial Review*, 12 February, www.afr.com/p/technology/accc_takes_aim_at_internet_slowdowns_DNxYfamGg7IZdqO1IcZC1L.

QUESTIONS

1 How do you feel about the ethics of ISPs controlling the 'freedom of choice and speed of access' to the internet? Is it appropriate for the government to compel ISPs to use the network technologies to effectively censor the internet? Do you think it is ethical for ISPs to be deliberately influencing the content available to consumers and business?

2 Is it appropriate to enforce a digital divide between those with largely unbiased access and those ISPs

using technology to promote their own content over other content? Would consumers know or even care?

3 Should business monitor its employees' internet usage? Do you see a problem with employees using company owned computing equipment and broadband network access for personal use? Explain how you would develop and manage an internet usage policy for a business.

4 How do you feel about the neutrality ideal of the internet? Do you believe that ISPs or national governments have the right to impose restrictions or should there be unbiased access to internet content? What do you consider to be the ramifications if network neutrality was eliminated? Explain your response.

CLOSING CASE **2 >**

Marriott's corporate portal

Marriott International operates more than 3500 hotel properties worldwide under its portfolio of brands, including Marriott Hotels & Resorts, JW Marriott, Renaissance, Edition, Autograph Collection and Courtyard by Marriott. The properties fall into the following categories: luxury, collections, lifestyle and boutique, signature, select service and extended stay.

Until 2011, Marriott used a 'one size fits all' approach for its advertising, marketing and branding efforts in different locations, despite the fact that independent franchisers own most of its properties. For years, regardless of location or brand, each property was offered the exact same (low) level of marketing support.

As a result of this policy, each Marriott property was largely responsible for its own marketing efforts, meaning that there was little consistency from location to location, or brand to brand. Furthermore, many properties did not have the funds to support their own marketing efforts. Finally, to compound the problem even further, Marriott had no easy method set up for sharing of marketing materials between corporate headquarters and the various properties.

As customer attitudes and preferences changed, Marriott realised that its corporate marketing practices needed to evolve as well. Consequently, the company launched a rebranding effort to tailor its marketing and branding decisions to each unique brand and target market. To fully implement this shift in strategy, the company needed a better way to share and leverage its marketing assets. Therefore, it created a user-friendly online corporate portal to manage the creation, distribution and review of marketing practices and material, as well as to support its new brand standards.

To help address its marketing concerns, Marriott International deployed BrandWorks, an automated online marketing portal, in all of its locations. BrandWorks makes it quick, easy and cost-effective for each of the company's properties to create their own customised marketing materials. Marriot hotels, advertising agencies and marketing managers use the portal to share and/or download stock photography, view brand standards and guidelines, download marketing templates and use document wizards to create customised marketing material.

With BrandWorks, Marriott is able to offer different programs and strategies to each of its distinct brands to better appeal to their respective target audiences (for instance, leisure travellers and business travellers use very different criteria when deciding which hotel to stay in). Using BrandWorks, Marriott compiled a comprehensive catalogue of updated brand guidelines, templates, strategies and materials so that its promotions and marketing activities could be implemented properly and cost-effectively across all of its markets and in multiple languages.

Marriott also deployed a centralised offer-management system in BrandWorks. This system allows its properties worldwide to create Marriott rewards offers and deals, and then promote them on the Marriott website and in other marketing channels.

BrandWorks also has built-in tracking capabilities to report on promotional programs, as well as automated analyses to identify which offers, programs and marketing campaigns are most successful. In 2012, Marriott integrated social media strategies for all its brands and properties into the portal.

BrandWorks enabled Marriott to improve information sharing and collaboration among its global locations and corporate teams. Internal users can report on total log-ins, the number of documents currently in the system based on brand and category, and the number of offers created and disseminated through each marketing channel. This data enables the company to determine what marketing information to activate for each brand and for each audience, and thereby deliver a better customer experience, educate global properties on brand, ensure consistency across locations and languages, and enable executives to make better decisions.

The offer management system within BrandWorks enables Marriott users to deliver revenue-generating offers to customers more rapidly. Because BrandWorks has built-in capabilities to tailor its offers to distinct audiences, demographics and marketing channels, more than three times as many offers have been submitted through the portal than were submitted without it.

Other Marriott departments have started to use BrandWorks as well. For example, the HR department has begun posting its presentations on the portal. The food and beverage department also posts its menus to the portal, as well as information on group sales and event management.

From 2009 to 2011, user log-ins to Marriott's website increased by 186 per cent, while the amount of marketing material distributed through the portal more than doubled. In 2011 alone, more than 6000 users from Marriott properties, corporate headquarters and regional departments logged in to BrandWorks. The users came from 70 countries and territories, and represented 16 different brands. They accessed BrandWorks remotely through any internet browser using desktops, laptops, tablets and smart phones.

Sources: Compiled from S Brier (2012), 'How Marriott got marketing right', *Baseline Magazine*, 17 January; S Brier (2011), 'Marriott saves estimated $9.2 million in marketing costs with online portal', *Hospitality Technology*, 19 December; T McQuilken (2011), 'Marriott brings marketing to next level with BrandWorks', *Hotel Business*, 21 September; 'Case study: Marriott International' (2012), *Excella Consulting*, accessed 28 February; www.marriott.com.

QUESTIONS

1 Provide examples of the advantages BrandWorks brought to Marriott's franchisees.
2 Provide examples of how BrandWorks could be used for functional areas of Marriott other than marketing.

SPREADSHEET ACTIVITY **BUILDING CHARTS AND TABLES**

OBJECTIVE

Creating charts and graphs is a really nice skill for you to develop. Visual data can be shared more quickly, comprehended more easily and displayed much more cleanly than simply numbers in a spreadsheet. This activity requires you to build both charts and tables to present data surrounding network speeds.

Chapter connection

As you learn about network connections and speeds, this exercise will show you how to do an analysis on your own. It is possible that your internet connection is not providing the speeds you are paying for! This tool is also useful when your internet does not seem to be running as quickly as it should. Knowing how to test the speed will help you determine where the possible problem could be.

Prerequisites

There are no prerequisites for this activity.

Activity

Calculating return on investment (ROI) is extremely difficult when it comes to ROI for information systems. For example, when network administrators sense a strain on their network (from network diagnostics or user complaints), they may look into upgrading their network.

To get a feel for the type of information someone might see, create your own spreadsheet of data while watching your internet connection at home. If you are not at home regularly, choose a computer in a convenient location and test the speed there. Go to www.johnwiley.com.au/highered/rainer/ausnz/studentresources and look for the link provided for chapter 4. This link will take you to 'speedtest.net' and the network test will be on the home page asking you to 'Begin Test.' The test will take only a few minutes. In a new spreadsheet, create columns for the following:

- date
- time
- ping speed
- upload speed
- download speed
- test location (not your location, but the host of the test).

Collect this data for a week, preferably three times a day (i.e. morning, afternoon and evening). Once you have your 15 data points, create a chart that shows the change in bandwidth available over time. This is exactly what a network administrator might see when trying to determine if it is necessary to upgrade the system. Additionally, calculate the average, minimum and maximum for each day and for the entire week. Place this data in a chart for quick reference.

Back at www.johnwiley.com.au/highered/rainer/ausnz/studentresources you will also find a short video on creating charts and graphs to help you create your final product.

Deliverable

The deliverable will be a line chart that shows data speeds over time.

Note: There is no correct answer, but there are wrong answers if you do not collect enough data or do not create the chart appropriately.

DISCUSSION QUESTIONS

1 What is it about a chart that makes it easier to comprehend than raw numbers?
2 Is it possible for charges and graphs to depict real data in a way that misleads the viewer?

DATABASE ACTIVITY **REPORTS I**

OBJECTIVE

In this activity, you will learn how to create an Access report, with grouping and summaries. A database is not useful if you can't get information out of it. Reports are one way users get information from a database. Reports can connect data from several tables, organise it, sort it, group it, summarise it and more. Once designed, a report can be run as needed, reflecting the database content as of that instant.

Chapter connection

Companies must monitor their network performance to make sure it's reliable, secure and free of performance bottlenecks. Reports such as those in this activity help them do this.

The database in this activity tracks network problems. Users who notice problems submit 'trouble tickets'. These describe the problem and, later, its resolution. They identify the user who submitted it, the equipment involved and the technician who fixed it.

Management can use reports derived from this database to identify problem devices and vendors, to evaluate technician performance, to identify users who are helpful in finding problems or who report non-existent ones and more.

Prerequisites

None.

ACTIVITY

In this activity, which you will find online at www.johnwiley.com.au/highered/rainer/ausnz/studentresources, you'll take a database and create multi-level reports from it. You will add summary fields to this report and reformat it to improve its appearance.

1. Download the **Ch 04 NeTrouble** database from www.johnwiley.com.au/highered/rainer/ausnz/studentresources and open it. (You saw this database earlier if you did the chapter 1 activity. This version does not include the report, query or form you used there. Here, you'll create other reports from the same underlying data.)
2. To create a new report, click the Create tab over the ribbon.
3. The section labelled 'Reports' offers several reporting tools. We'll use the Report Wizard, a compromise between the Report button (which doesn't offer much control) and Report Design (which forces us to do all the 'heavy lifting' ourselves, without the head start that the Wizard can provide). Click on it.
4. The first screen lets us choose which tables we'll base our report on and which fields from those tables we want to use. (It also lets us base the report on queries. A query creates a temporary table, so for this purpose they're the same. You'll create reports based on queries in later activities.) Our report will list trouble tickets by user, so start by selecting the UserTbl table. from the pull-down list under the Tables/Queries heading.
5. The left box shows all fields in the selected table. To move a field into the report, select it and click '>.' It moves into the right box. If you move a field you don't want, '<' moves it back. '>>'moves all the fields of that table into the report. This is useful when you want most of them, since '>>' followed by one or two '<' can be faster than moving all those you want individually. Finally, '<<' moves everything in this table out of the report and back to the table so you can start over.

   Here, move the user's name into the report.
6. Next, select DeptTbl, move DeptName into the report.
7. Finally, select the TicketTbl table. Move TicketSubmitted, TicketResolved and TicketStatus into the report. Click Next.
8. This is the panel where you structure your report. Choose each of the three tables, one after another, and see how the report organisation changes. For this report, select 'by DeptTbl' and click Next.
9. We don't need any more grouping levels. Click Next.
10. Within each category, choose to sort the tickets by when they were submitted. Pull down the first sorting menu and select TicketSubmitted. Click Next.
11. Leave the layout unchanged here. Click Next.
12. Change the title of the report to DeptRpt. Then click Finish and see the result.

    Usage hint: If you see '###' in any of the fields, the reason is almost certainly that the standard field width isn't wide enough to show the data. Switch to Layout view by clicking the second icon from the right in the lower right corner of the window, click in each field that has this problem to select it and make it wide enough to see the data. You may have to move column headers to keep them aligned with the data. Or, click on the data and shift-click on the heading to select them both, then make them wider together.
13. Our second report will add summary fields to this report. First, make a copy of the report so your instructor can see the version without summary fields. Right-click on the report in the navigation panel at the left of the Access window and select Copy. Then click Paste in the ribbon. (It's under the Home tab, so click that tab if it's not already selected.) Name the new report SumDeptRpt and confirm.
14. Open SumDeptRpt and select Layout view. Make sure the Design tab is selected, and click Group & Sort from the Grouping & Totals section.

    Usage hint: Access calls any kind of summary a 'total'. If you want an arithmetic total, you must ask for a sum. We'll use the term 'summary' rather than 'total' here to avoid this common source of confusion, but you'll see 'total' on Access screens.

15 A new panel will open up at the bottom of the window. Its top row starts 'Group on DeptID' and ends with 'More' and a triangle pointing to the right. That word 'more' hides many options. Click the triangle to see them.

16 We want to count the number of tickets each department submits. Pull down the triangle next to 'with no totals'. The first option lets us summarise TicketSubmitted, TicketStatus or TicketResolved. We should count TicketSubmitted since every trouble ticket has a value in this field. Next, select either count. (They would be different if we counted a field that is blank for some tickets. Therefore, if we had selected TicketResolved or TicketStatus, we would use Count Records so that records that are blank in this field would be counted.) Check boxes to show the grand total and department totals in the group footer. When you click the triangle again to release the dialogue box, you'll see department totals after each department with the grand total at the bottom.

If we had wanted to total by user, we would have clicked on the 'More' triangle at that level in the panel at the bottom of the window.

Close your report, saving your changes.

17 Now we'll improve the appearance of this report. Make a copy of SumDeptRpt. Call it FmtDeptRpt, open it and go to Layout view. (Layout changes can also be made in Design view. Design view gives more control over some aspects of the layout, but Layout view can often suffice and gives immediate visual feedback when you make a change. It's preferable when it will do the job.)

18 First, change the column headings. Access sets them to the names of the database fields. However, database field names are for developers. Report headings should be for people who will read the report. Select each, just as in a word processor, and change them to read 'Department', 'User', 'Date Submitted', 'Date Resolved' and 'Status'. Change the main report heading to 'Trouble Tickets by Department and User'. Shrink the width of the User column to bring the data elements closer together. Click 'Logo' in the ribbon (Design tab, Header/Footer section), find a suitable picture and insert. (By default, Access puts logos in the main heading area.) Switch to Report view. Your report should now start like this:

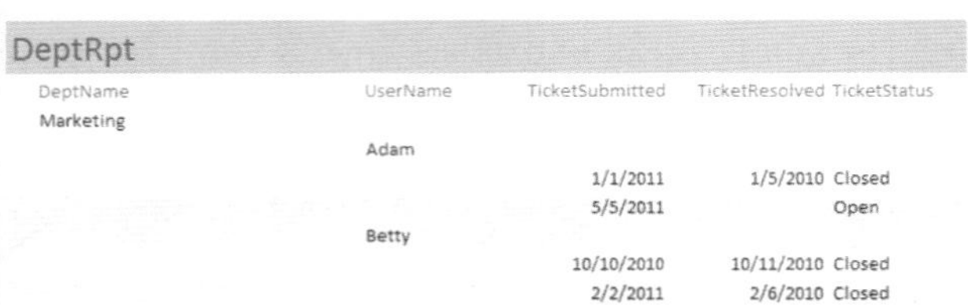

19 Now it's your turn. Develop a report that shows trouble tickets by device ID. Group devices by name (category). Within a name, group by ticket status: Closed, Open or Cancelled. Provide counts for each category and for the entire report. Edit column headings and report title to be meaningful to business-oriented readers of the report. Name your report 'DeviceRpt' and be sure to save it when you're done.

As with other aspects of Access, many videos on creating reports are available on the web. You can find them by searching for 'Access report', 'Access report tutorial', or any similar string on a video hosting site such as YouTube, or using the general search engine of your choice while restricting its answers to videos.

DELIVERABLES

Your database with the four reports as specified above. Your instructor may add additional requirements.

QUIZ QUESTIONS

1. A report shows the content of the database as of:
   - a the time the report is run (opened)
   - b the time the report was designed
   - c the time the user looks at the report
   - d the time the user keys into the Report Effective Time field.
2. True or false: A report can contain information from no more than two tables.
3. True or false: Report design can only be changed in Design mode.

DISCUSSION QUESTIONS

1. Suppose you own or manage a restaurant. You have a typical restaurant computer system in which servers enter orders, which the kitchen uses to prepare orders, and which later creates bills and processes payments. Describe three reports that this system could prepare for your use. Draw, using paper and pencil, the top of each: header, column headings, a few lines of sample data and the first summary field.
2. Your instructor may have received a report with a class roster soon after the term started. It is based on two tables: a class table that lists the student IDs of everyone in the class, and a student table that gives the name, major, GPA and so on for each student. Students are normally listed alphabetically by family name. (It's also based on a query, which finds only students in this class, but that's a separate topic.)
   - a Discuss two ways this list could be organised, besides the usual order by name.
   - b Discuss two summaries that this report, organised either in its usual way or in one of the above two ways (your choice), could have.
3. Your email program has an address list. Each entry in it includes an email address. Some entries also include the sender's real name. A few may have other information. Describe a report that could be produced from this list and other information that your email program stores. Give it at least one summary field. Draw its first few rows.

5 Business intelligence

CHAPTER OUTLINE

5.1 Managers and decision making

5.2 What is business intelligence?

5.3 Business intelligence applications for data analysis

5.4 Business intelligence applications for presenting results

5.5 Business intelligence in action: corporate performance management

LEARNING OBJECTIVES

1 Explain different ways in which IT supports managerial decision making.

2 Provide examples of different ways that organisations make use of BI.

3 Explain the value that different BI applications provide to large and small businesses.

4 Offer examples of how businesses and government agencies can use different BI applications to analyse data.

5 Explain how your university could use CPM to effect solutions to two campus problems.

OPENING CASE >

Farmer wants an app

Information and communications technology (ICT) has become a significant decision-making instrument for stakeholders globally, and Australian farmers are embracing a transformational period of technological innovation. From the implementation of efficient data management systems to taking the guesswork out of weather forecasting, an explosion of iPhone, iPad and iCloud apps are empowering agriculture businesses who cannot afford their workers spending long stretches of time in front of a computer.

One such example is the Agworld app which helps farmers control accurate farm management data all from one location. When farmers plug data into their iPhone or iPad it automatically synchronises with their home computer, meaning they never have to double up on data entry. The app enables farmers to communicate easily with business contacts, engage with farm planning information and access other tools assisting business decision making. For instance, farmers could switch their tractors to auto steer while they take care of a contractor invoice on their iPhone.

Other prominent agriculture apps include the following.

- CropMate™ Variety Chooser: Developed by the NSW Department of Primary Industries, this app helps farmers choose varieties of barley, canola, chickpeas, fava beans, field peas, lupins, oats, triticale and wheat by filtering under parameters like region and characteristics such as quality and disease resistance.
- Weeds: the Ute Guide: Created by the Grains Research and Development Organisation, this app identifies the most common weeds in southern Australia.
- My Environment: This app uses GPS to show heritage places, wetlands, protected species, weeds and invasive species around your area.
- Harvest Time and Expense Tracker: This app tracks billable hours as farmers work and log expenses, including photos of receipts.
- CalcSpray: This app calculates the right chemical mixes including total chemical required per tank, per area and water per area.

CliMate, a new app which was developed for managing the climate variability programs (MCVP), has vastly improved the accuracy of weather forecasting. Created by RPS Australia East Pty Ltd — with the program written by DHM Environmental Software Engineering Pty Ltd — CliMate aims to support farmers and natural resource managers to minimise the risks and exploit the opportunities afforded by Australia's variable and changing climate by:

- improving forecasting accuracy, lead-time and ease of use
- providing tools and services for managing climate risk
- getting more farmers managing their climate risk.

These apps have unobtrusively enhanced day-to-day farm operations across Australia. Armed with around-the-clock, accurate data relating to varietal and seasonal information, farmers no longer have to fully rely on their hunches alone to make business decisions.

Sources: 'Agworld iPad app offline capability an agribusiness world 1st' (2011), *Agworld Blog*, 2 November, www.agworld.com.au/2011/11/agworld-app-world-first-and-record-review; 'Features for farmers', Agworld website, www.agworld.com.au/who-is-agworld-for/features-for-farmers/; 'Australian CliMate', Apple iTunes Preview website, https://itunes.apple.com/au/app/australian-climate/id582572607?mt=8/;T Cattle (2012), 'Agworld app opens up whole new world ', *Farm Weekly*, 19 March, www.farmweekly.com.au/news/agriculture/agribusiness/general-news/agworld-app-opens-up-whole-new-world/2488540.aspx; C Collisae (2012), 'Smart phones dial up variety options', *Australian Government Grains Research and Development Corporation*, 2 March, www.grdc.com.au/Media-Centre/Ground-Cover/Ground-Cover-Issue-97-March-April-2012/Smart-phones-dial-up-variety-options; 'New free CliMate app for farmers' (2013), Managing Climate Variability website, 7 January, www.managingclimate.gov.au/news/new-free-climate-app-for-farmers/; Department of Primary Industries (2012), *Useful apps for Australian agriculture — iPhone and iPad*, NSW Government, 16 July, http://n.b5z.net/i/u/10169267/f/Useful_apps_for_Australian_agriculture-_iPhone_and_iPad.pdf; C Pearce (2012), ' Smartphone apps aiding farmers', *WeeklyTimes Now*, 17 January, www.weeklytimesnow.com.au/article/2012/01/18/431921_business-news.html.

QUESTIONS

1. From your perspective, will CliMate really assist Australian farmers to increase opportunities and decrease risks in their work? Provide a rationale for your answer.
2. Are there any improvements that could be made to the CliMate app? Please list them and explain why.
3. In your opinion, are there any other industries that might benefit from phone application technology? Please list the industries and the types of apps that would be useful.

Introduction

Business intelligence (BI) is a broad category of applications, technologies and processes for gathering, storing, accessing and analysing data to help business users make better decisions. BI applications enable decision makers to quickly ascertain the status of a business enterprise by examining key information. Managers need current, timely and accurate information that their current systems often cannot provide. Implementing BI applications can generate significant benefits throughout a company, supporting important decisions about the firm's overall business goals.

Consider these examples that illustrate how Australian organisations adopted BI tools to increase opportunities, reduce risk and enhance their decision making.

- The Water Corporation upgraded to Business Intelligence version 7.0 to reduce costs and enhance business functionality.
- St Vincent's Hospital Sydney used business intelligence tools to diminish error reduction, as well as improved compliance, safety and efficiency.

THE NOOK

As Malakai and Abbie prepare to reopen The Nook for business, they need to establish some measurements to help them stay on track. They have a goal of a $300 000 net profit for their first year after their grand reopening. This is an increase from $150 000 the previous year. To achieve this, they have to deal with one of the biggest problems they face — shrinkage.

Shrinkage occurs when a bartender pours someone a little more alcohol than the drink recipe calls for, gives someone a free drink, or accidentally spills alcohol on the floor. The result is that a bottle of alcohol that (for example) should provide enough alcohol to make 40 drinks only actually brings in money for 30 drinks. This shrinkage may not seem like much, but on a large scale (including food items) it can make a huge difference.

What Malakai and Abbie need is data and decision support. This chapter refers to this as business intelligence. They need to know how to set and measure monthly and weekly goals to know whether or not they are on track to make their overall goal of $300 000 net profit when they reopen.

- CSC Cybersecurity adopted the business intelligence tool eGRC to ensure faster return on investment and provide better security solutions across the whole organisation. This tool assisted CSC Cybersecurity to meet their requirements as well their customers'.

Currently, organisations and markets are handling enormous volumes of big data for their stakeholders. Therefore, to have fast storage, new decision making, reliable data access and intelligence information retrieval, organisations must employ an intelligence system to serve this purpose.[1] Business intelligence can analyse data via query tools to produce reports that assist organisations to arrive at their decisions.

Furthermore, BI is used by organisations to improve performance, reduce costs and identify new business opportunities. BI can analyse customers' behaviour, track and measure sales, assist forecasting and budgeting, as well as improve delivery customer relationships and prevent risk. Furthermore, organisations can improve business decision making by using Agile BI method. Agile BI allows developer and the end user working together to create a report, graph or chart in series of discussions or within a short period of time. Adopting this method will improve business decision making as well business needs. Finally, technology has become a significant instrument for communication, collaboration, cooperation, connection, commerce, business, research and entertainment. The use of technology in organisations enhances business performance by increasing efficiency and effectiveness. However, this technology can cause huge challenges as it consumes many natural resources, such as raw materials and power. Recycling these devices poses another challenge to users globally and locally. To tackle this problem, sustainable computing should be introduced to delay obsolescence and improve utilisation. **Cloud BI** and **mobile BI** are examples of sustainable computing.

This chapter describes information systems that support *decision making*. We begin by reviewing the manager's job and the nature of modern managerial decisions. This discussion will help you to understand why managers need computerised support. You then learn about the concepts of business intelligence for supporting individuals, groups and entire organisations.

It is impossible to overstate the importance of BI to you. Recall from chapter 1 that the essential goal of information systems is to provide the right information to the right person in the right amount at the right time in the right format. In essence, BI achieves this goal. BI systems provide business intelligence that you can act on in a timely fashion.

It is also impossible to overstate the importance of your input into the BI process within an organisation, for several reasons. First, you (the user community) will decide what data should be stored in your organisation's data warehouse. You will then work closely with the MIS department to obtain these data.

Going further, you will use your organisation's BI applications, probably from your first day on the job. With some BI applications, such as data mining and decision support systems, you will decide how you want to analyse the data (user-driven analysis). With other BI applications such as dashboards, you will decide which data you want to see and in which format. Again, you will work closely with your MIS department to ensure that the dashboard meets your needs.

Much of this chapter is concerned with large-scale BI applications. However, you should keep in mind that smaller organisations, and even individual users, can implement small-scale BI applications as well. For example, Excel spreadsheets provide some BI functions, as do SQL queries of a database.

The most popular BI tool by far is Excel. For years, BI vendors 'fought' against the use of Excel. Eventually, however, they decided to 'join it' by designing their software so that it interfaces with Excel. How does this process work? Essentially, users download plug-ins that add functionality (e.g. the ability to list the top 10 per cent of customers, based on sales) to Excel (or any of the Microsoft Office products). This process can be thought of as creating 'Excel on steroids'. Excel then connects to the vendor's application server — which provides additional data-analysis capabilities — which in turn connects to a back-end database, such as a data mart or warehouse. This arrangement gives Excel users the functionality and access to data that are typical of sophisticated BI products, while allowing users to work with a familiar client: Excel.

Microsoft has made similar changes to its product line. In particular, Excel can now be used with MS SQL Server (a database product), and it can be utilised in advanced BI applications, such as dashboards and data mining/predictive analysis.

After you finish this chapter, you will have a basic understanding of decision making, the business intelligence process and BI applications in organisations today. This knowledge will enable you to immediately and confidently provide input into your organisation's BI processes and applications. Further, the hands-on exercises in this chapter will familiarise you with the actual use of BI software. These exercises will enable you to use your organisation's BI applications to effectively analyse data and thus make better decisions. Enjoy!

5.1 Managers and decision making

Management is a process by which an organisation achieves its goals through the use of resources (people, money, materials and information). These resources are considered to be *inputs*. Achieving the organisation's goals is the *output* of the process. Managers oversee this process in an attempt to optimise it. A manager's success is often measured by the ratio between inputs and outputs for which he or she is responsible. This ratio is an indication of the organisation's productivity.

The manager's job and decision making

To appreciate how information systems support managers, you must first understand the manager's job. Managers do many things, depending on their position in the organisation, the type and size of the organisation, the organisation's policies and culture, and the personalities of the managers themselves. Despite these variations, however, all managers perform three basic roles:

1. *interpersonal roles:* figurehead, leader, liaison
2. *informational roles:* monitor, disseminator, spokesperson, analyser
3. *decisional roles:* entrepreneur, disturbance handler, resource allocator, negotiator.[2]

Early information systems primarily supported the informational roles. In recent years, information systems have been developed that support all three roles. In this chapter, you will focus on the support that IT can provide for decisional roles.

A **decision** refers to a choice among two or more alternatives that individuals and groups make. Decisions are diverse and are made continuously. Decision making is a systematic process. Economist Herbert Simon described decision making as composed of three major phases: intelligence, design and choice.[3] Once the choice is made, the decision

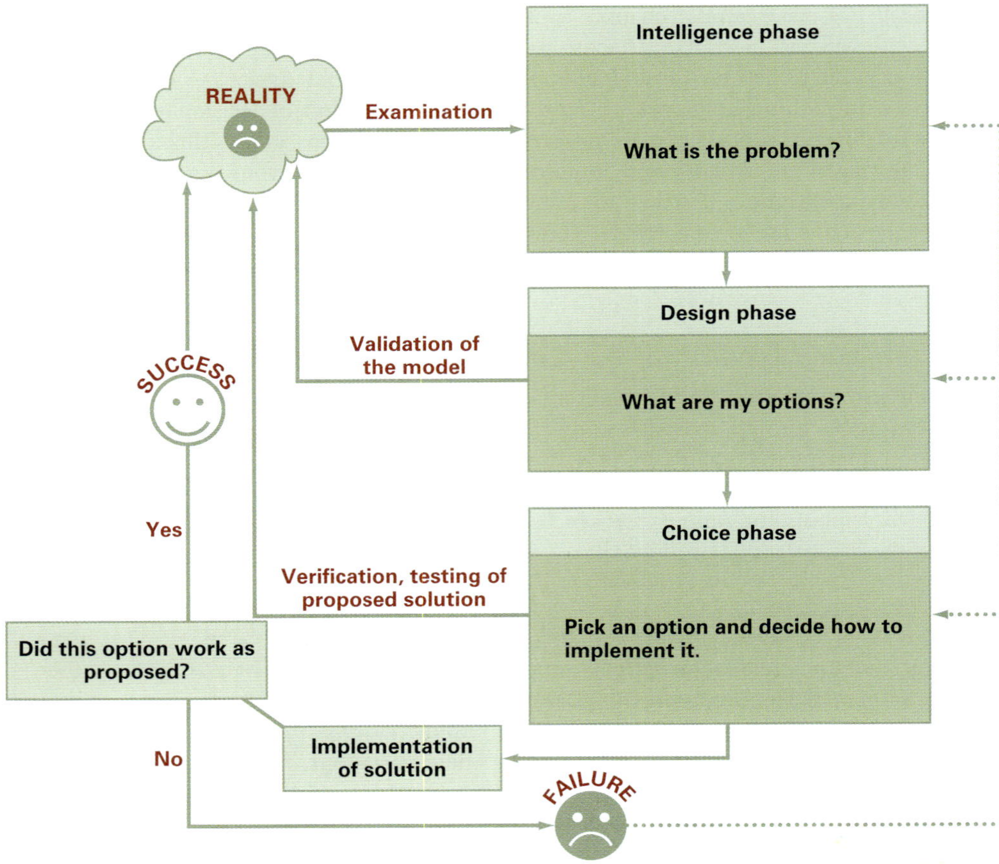

FIGURE 5.1 The process and phases of decision making.

is implemented. Figure 5.1 illustrates this process, indicating which tasks are included in each phase. Note that there is a continuous flow of information from intelligence to design to choice (bold lines), but at any phase there may be a return to a previous phase (broken lines).

This model of decision making is quite general. Undoubtedly, you have made decisions where you did not construct a model of the situation, validate your model with test data, or conduct a sensitivity analysis. The model we present here is intended to encompass all of the conditions that might occur when making a decision. For some decisions, some steps or phrases may be minimal, implicit (understood), or absent.

The decision-making process starts with the *intelligence phase*, in which managers examine a situation and identify and define the problem or opportunity. In the *design phase*, decision makers construct a model for the situation. They do this by making assumptions that simplify reality and by expressing the relationships among all the relevant variables. Managers then validate the model by using test data. Finally, decision makers set criteria for evaluating all of the potential solutions that are proposed. The *choice phase* involves selecting a solution or course of action that seems best suited to resolve the problem. This solution (the decision) is then implemented. Implementation is successful if the proposed solution solves the problem or seizes the opportunity. If the solution fails, then the process returns to the previous phases. Computer-based decision support assists managers in the decision-making process.

Why managers need IT support

Making good decisions is very difficult without solid information. Information is vital for each phase and activity in the decision-making process. Even when information is available, however, decision making is difficult because of the following trends.

- The *number of alternatives* is constantly *increasing* from innovations in technology, improved communications, the development of global markets, and the use of the internet and e-business. A key to good decision making is to explore and compare many relevant alternatives. The more alternatives that exist, the more a decision maker needs computer-assisted searches and comparisons.

- Most decisions must be made *under time pressure*. It is often not possible to process information manually fast enough to be effective.
- Because of increased uncertainty in the decision environment, decisions are becoming more complex. It is usually necessary to *conduct a sophisticated analysis* in order to make a good decision.
- It is often necessary to rapidly access remote information, consult with experts, or conduct a group decision-making session, all without incurring large expenses. Decision makers can be situated in different locations, as can the information. Bringing them all together quickly and inexpensively can be a major challenge.

These trends create major difficulties for decision makers. Fortunately, as you will see throughout this chapter, a computerised analysis can be of enormous help.

What information technologies are available to support managers?

In addition to discovery, communication and collaboration tools (chapter 4) that provide indirect support to decision making, several other information technologies have been successfully used to support managers. As noted, these technologies are collectively referred to as business intelligence (BI). BI is closely linked to data warehousing, which provides the data needed for BI. You will now learn about additional aspects of decision making to place our discussion of BI in context. You will first look at the different types of decisions that managers face.

A framework for computerised decision analysis

To better understand BI, you will note that various types of decisions can be placed along two major dimensions: problem structure and the nature of the decision.[4] Figure 5.2 provides an overview of decision making along these two dimensions.

Problem structure

The first dimension of decision making is *problem structure*, where decision-making processes fall along a continuum ranging from highly structured to highly unstructured (see the left column in figure 5.2). *Structured decisions* refer to routine and repetitive problems for which standard solutions exist, such as inventory control. In a structured problem,

FIGURE 5.2 Decision support framework. Technology is used to support the decisions shown in the column at the far right.

	Operational control	Management control	Strategic planning	IS support
Structured	Accounts receivable, order entry 1	Budget analysis, short-term forecasting, personnel reports, make-or-buy analysis 2	3	MIS, statistical models (management science, financial, etc.)
Semistructured	Production scheduling, inventory control 4	Credit evaluation, budget preparation, plant layout, project scheduling, reward systems design 5	Building a new plant, mergers and acquisitions, planning (product, quality assurance, compensation, etc.) 6	Decision support systems, business intelligence
Unstructured	7	Negotiating, recruiting an executive, buying hardware, lobbying 8	New technology development, product R&D, social responsibility planning 9	Decision support systems, expert systems, enterprise resource planning, neural networks, business intelligence, big data

the first three phases of the decision process — intelligence, design and choice — are laid out in a particular sequence and the procedures for obtaining the best (or at least a good enough) solution are known. Two basic criteria that are used to evaluate proposed solutions are minimising costs and maximising profits. These types of decisions are candidates for decision automation.

At the other extreme of problem complexity are *unstructured decisions*. These are 'fuzzy', complex problems for which there are no cut-and-dried solutions. An unstructured problem is one in which there is no standardised procedure for carrying out any of the three phases. In such a problem, human intuition and judgement often play an important role in making the decision. Typical unstructured problems include planning new service offerings, hiring an executive, and choosing a set of research and development (R&D) projects for the coming year. Although BI cannot make unstructured decisions, it can provide information that assists decision makers.

Located between structured and unstructured problems are *semistructured* problems, in which only some of the decision process phases are structured. Semistructured problems require a combination of standard solution procedures and individual judgement. Examples of semistructured problems are evaluating employees, setting marketing budgets for consumer products, performing capital acquisition analysis and trading bonds.

The nature of decisions

The second dimension of decision support deals with the *nature of decisions*. All managerial decisions fall into one of three broad categories:

1 *operational control:* executing specific tasks efficiently and effectively
2 *management control:* acquiring and using resources efficiently in accomplishing organisational goals
3 *strategic planning:* the long-range goals and policies for growth and resource allocation.

These categories are displayed along the top row of figure 5.2.

Note: strategic decisions define the context in which management control decisions are made. In turn, management control decisions define the context in which operational control decisions are made.

BEFORE YOU GO ON . . .

1 Describe the decision-making process proposed by Simon.
2 You are registering for classes next semester. Apply the decision-making process to your decision about how many and which courses to take. Is your decision structured, semistructured, or unstructured?
3 Consider your decision-making process when registering for classes next semester. Explain how information technology supports (or does not support) each phase of this process.

The decision matrix

The decision matrix. The three primary classes of decision types and the three broad categories of the nature of decisions can be combined in a decision-support matrix that consists of nine cells, as shown in figure 5.2. Lower level managers perform tasks in cells 1 and 4, but not 7 because operational managers are not expected to make strategic decisions. The tasks in cells 2, 5 and 8 are usually the responsibility of middle-managers and professional staff. Finally, the tasks in cells 6 and 9 are generally carried out by senior executives while cell 3 is empty because senior executives are not involved in day-to-day operational tasks.

Computer support for structured decisions

Examples of computer support that might be used for the nine cells in the matrix are displayed in the right-hand column of figure 5.2. Structured and some semistructured decisions, especially of the operational and management control type, have been supported by computers since the 1950s. Decisions of this type are made in all functional areas, but particularly in finance and operations management.

Problems that lower-level managers encounter on a regular basis typically have a high level of structure. Examples are capital budgeting (for example, replacement of equipment), allocating resources, distributing merchandise and controlling inventory. For each type of structured decision, prescribed solutions have been developed, which often include mathematical formulas that can often be used. This approach is called *management science* or *operations research* and it is executed with the aid of computers.

QUESTIONS

1. Discuss how the three roles of a manager (interpersonal, informational and decisional) might play out as Malakai and Abbie tackle shrinkage. Will bartenders become defensive? Should they share financial information? How much should they monitor the bartenders?
2. Which of the four reasons why a manager needs IT support do you feel is most applicable in this situation? Is it that the number of alternatives is increasing? Time pressure? Uncertainty? Or the need to bring remote individuals and data into the picture?
3. Is the shrinkage problem a structured, semistructured, or unstructured situation? If it is structured, what controls may be put in place to handle it? If it is unstructured, what policies might be instituted to help reign in the problem?
4. Does this situation fall into operational control, management control, or strategic planning? Or does it fall into all three?
5. In what ways could IT provide help to Malakai and Abbie as they try to make their $300 000 net profit and control shrinkage?

THE NOOK

5.2 What is business intelligence?

To provide users with access to corporate data, many organisations are implementing data warehouses and data marts, which you learned about in chapter 3. Users analyse the data in warehouses and marts using a wide variety of BI tools. Many vendors offer integrated packages of these tools under the overall label of 'business intelligence (BI)' software. Major BI vendors include:

- SAS (**www.sas.com**)
- Hyperion (**www.hyperion.com**, now owned by Oracle)
- Business Objects (**www.businessobjects.com**, now owned by SAP)
- Information Builders (**www.informationbuilders.com**)
- SPSS (**www.spss.com**, now owned by IBM)
- Cognos (**www.ibm.com/cognos**).

In Australia and New Zealand the major BI vendors include:

- YellowFin (**www.yellowfinbi.com**)
- JetReports (**www.jetreports.com/aunz**)
- Phocas (**www.phocassoftware.com/contact/australianz-office**)
- Montage (**www.montage.co.nz**).

As has been shown, BI is vital to modern decision making and organisational performance. Let's now consider in greater detail the technical foundation for BI and the wide variety of ways that BI can be used.

The term *business intelligence* is relatively new. Business and IT analyst Howard Dresner coined the term in 1989 while he was an analyst at Gartner, a market research firm. The term is especially popular in industry, where it is used as an umbrella term that encompasses all decision support applications.

BI encompasses not only applications but also technologies and processes. It includes both 'getting data in' (to a data mart or warehouse) and 'getting data out' (through BI applications).

In addition, a significant change is taking place within the BI environment. In the past, organisations used BI only to support management. Today, however, BI applications are increasingly available to front-line personnel (e.g. call centre operators), suppliers, customers and even regulators. These groups rely on BI to provide them with the most current information.

The scope of business intelligence

The use of BI in organisations varies considerably. In smaller organisations, BI may be limited to Excel spreadsheets. In larger ones, BI is often enterprise wide, and it includes

IT'S ABOUT BUSINESS

Virgin Australia's BI performance

Virgin Australia (formerly known as Virgin Blue) places high value on customer satisfaction, having received numerous industry awards in this area over recent years. Virgin holds 31 per cent of the Australian domestic market, operating 3000 flights per week to 28 Australian cities for 18 million travellers annually. Sir Richard Branson's audacious personal brand is well known to Australian consumers, but lesser known is the extent to which Virgin's BI performance contributes to their ongoing success.

Business problem

Virgin Australia operated a number of IT systems in various departments. The reporting systems were not integrated to distribute useful business intelligence reports on the budget, forecasting and financial information to assist the top management and other Virgin stakeholders in decision making. Virgin staff were required to:

- generate base information from each system
- re-enter information into spreadsheets, and
- generate and format information into the spreadsheet.

Once the information was consolidated, it then needed to be distributed to a geographically scattered team. This set of processes was impracticable, unrealistic, time consuming and disposed to errors. To solve the problem, Virgin required a central data warehouse in conjunction with a BI solution to improve the reporting systems and to support the job performance and growth within Virgin Australia.

Solution

In order to solve the reporting system problem, IBM Business Partner, Catapult BI and Cognos 8 BI were selected to provide a quick solution for the Virgin Australia reporting system. The solution provided rapid, easy, 24-hour online access to the reports, in turn enabling Virgin to focus more on their business instead of the legitimacy of reporting data.

Benefits

Working with BI gave Virgin managers and employees the freedom to spend more time on winning new business opportunities and servicing existing customers to the highest possible standards, thereby maintaining growth both locally and globally.

BI enables Virgin Australia to:

- track customer's behaviour
- develop meaningful reports
- create easy financial, operations, customer and vendor reports
- easily analyse, evaluate and distribute reports among Virgin Australia top management, employees and stakeholders
- consolidate data from various departments and databases, and
- minimise manual work and monotonous work.

QUESTIONS

1. Do the advantages outweigh the disadvantages of BI usage at Virgin? Provide a rationale for your response.
2. At an operational level, list the risks that face an organisation with non-integrated systems.

Sources: Catapult BI (n.d.), *Virgin Blue cabin crew dashboard*, www.catapultbi.com/workspace/uploads/pdf/catapult_bi_virgin_blue_case_study.pdf; Catapult BI (nd), '*Virgin Blue uses automated business intelligence reporting to support growth during economic downturn*', www.catapultbi.com/workspace/uploads/pdf/catapult_bi_virgin_flyer.pdf; IBM (2010), 'Virgin Blue uses automated business intelligence reporting to support growth during economic downturn', www-01.ibm.com/software/success/cssdb.nsf/CS/SANS-8A8QRZ?OpenDocument&Site=default&cty=en_us; Virgin Australia (2013), '*Virgin Australia history*', www.virginaustralia.com/au/en/about-us/company-overview/virgin-australia-history.

applications such as data mining/predictive analytics, dashboards and data visualisation. It is important to recognise that the importance of BI to organisations continues to grow. It is not an exaggeration to say that for many firms, BI is now a requirement for competing in the marketplace, as illustrated in IT's About Business (above).

Not all organisations use BI in the same way. For example, some organisations employ a single or a few applications, while others utilise enterprise wide BI. The following subsections examine three specific BI targets that represent different levels of change:

- the development of a single or a few related BI applications
- the development of infrastructure to support enterprise wide BI
- support for organisational transformation.

These targets differ in terms of their focus; scope; level of sponsorship, commitment and required resources; technical architecture; impact on personnel and business processes; and benefits.

The development of a single or a few related BI applications

This BI target is often a point solution for a departmental need, such as campaign management in marketing. Sponsorship, approval, funding, impacts and benefits typically occur at the departmental level. For this target, organisations usually create a data mart to store the necessary data. Organisations must be careful that the mart — an 'independent' application — does not become a 'data silo' that stores data that are inconsistent with and cannot be integrated with data used elsewhere in the organisation.

The development of infrastructure to support enterprise wide BI

This BI target supports current and future BI needs. A crucial component of BI at this level is an enterprise data warehouse. Because it is an enterprise wide initiative, senior management often provides sponsorship, approval and funding. In addition, the impacts and benefits are felt throughout the organisation.

An example of this target is the 3M Corporation. Traditionally 3M's various divisions had operated independently and had utilised separate decision support platforms. Not only was this arrangement costly, but it also prevented 3M from integrating the data and presenting a 'single face' to its customers. Thus, for example, sales representatives did not know whether or how business customers were interacting with other 3M divisions. The solution was to develop an enterprise data warehouse that enabled 3M to operate as an integrated company. As an added benefit, the cost of implementing this system was covered by savings resulting from the consolidation of the various platforms.

Support for organisational transformation

With this target, BI is used to transform fundamentally the ways in which a company competes in the marketplace. BI supports a new business model and it enables the business strategy. Because of the scope and importance of these changes, critical elements such as sponsorship, approval and funding originate at the highest organisational levels. The impact on personnel and processes can be significant, and the benefits are organisation wide.

Pepper Australia, the market-leading 'non-bank' lender in Australia, provides a good example of this BI target. Prior to 2013, Pepper acquired several new portfolios and hosted seven separate data warehouses across the country. This meant that whenever internal business reports were required by different departments, the IT staff had to manually create them in each location. Pepper chose IBM to migrate a 75GB data warehouse made up of 57 000 loans for 250 000 customers on their new system, described as a 'fully integrated data warehouse-in-a-box' that automates business reporting and does not need IT support. Pepper offers home, car and small business loans as well as equipment leases for businesses. The new streamlined system enables the company opportunities for additional diversification in the future, and more consistent customer engagement across locations.

Nonprofit organisations also use BI to transform the way they operate. As you see in IT's About Business (overleaf), Marwell Wildlife uses BI to transform the organisation's conservation efforts.

In chapter 3, you studied the basics of data warehouses and data marts. In this section, you have seen how important data warehouses and marts are to the different ways that organisations use BI. In the next section, you will learn how the user community can analyse the data in warehouses and marts, how the results of these analyses are presented to users and how organisations can use the results of these analyses.

BEFORE YOU GO ON . . .

1. Define BI.
2. Discuss the breadth of support provided by BI applications to organisational employees.
3. Identify and discuss the three basic targets of BI.

IT'S ABOUT BUSINESS

Using analytics to save Grevy's zebra

Marwell Wildlife (www.marwell.org.uk) is an international conservation charity and zoo based in Hampshire, England, that works to preserve the wild population of Grevy's zebra. This species of zebra is on the endangered species list, with a wild population of only 2500. Marwell relies heavily on analytics software from IBM to aid in its conservation efforts. The software allows Marwell to analyse information from the field, including data from aerial surveys, camera traps and radio collars. This analysis gives the conservation group a crucial understanding of both the threats facing the zebras and the policies that could help the zebra population to recover organically.

Some of the most important data available to Marwell comes from a survey of nomadic herdsmen in northern Kenya, the area where most of the remaining Grevy's zebras live. People in the local pastoral communities are able to provide valuable information to Marwell because they have such an in-depth knowledge about the landscape and its wildlife.

To extract information from the local communities, field researchers from Marwell and other organisations partnering in the survey spent a month in remote areas of Kenya, conducting a questionnaire-based survey. These field researchers gathered information about the distribution of the zebra population and threats to zebras, and learned about the attitudes of the people of the region toward the zebra.

The survey confirmed what conservationists have long recognised — that the needs of the local human population can conflict with those of an endangered species. An obvious example of this conflict is the fact that local herdsmen were hunting the zebras, but there were also more subtle manifestations of this conflict. The zebras live in dry areas near herdsmen who raise livestock, so the zebras often compete with livestock for water and pasture space.

The researchers also analysed their data for insights into human practices and attitudes that may have an impact on the zebra population. The IBM analytics software enabled them to examine multiple variables affecting attitudes, such as education level and whether or not people had been previously exposed to conservation efforts, to better understand the reasons behind people's various attitudes and beliefs.

Some of the patterns the researchers uncovered did not relate to the zebras, but rather to the humans sharing their habitat. Marwell researchers discovered that herdsmen saw benefits from living close to the zebras. For example, zebras can point the way to pastures in dry years and they attract tourists, which boosts the economy. The researchers further found that zebras are hunted not just for their meat, but also for medicine. Zebra fat is highly valued by the pastoral communities as a treatment for illnesses ranging from headaches to tuberculosis. Most of the survey respondents said that they would be glad to switch to conventional medicines if they were available. These findings show promising opportunities to make changes that have the potential to benefit people and zebras.

Sources: Compiled from M Behan (2011), 'Analytics helps save an endangered species', *Baseline Magazine*, 28 July; 'Marwell Wildlife uses analytics in the conservation of endangered species' (2011), *IBM Case Study*, 5 April; A Bridgwater (2010), 'IBM predictive analytics software helps save Grevy's zebra', *ComputerWeekly.com*, 15 September; www.marwell.org.uk.

QUESTIONS

1 What other types of data could Marwell analyse to better understand the problem of the Grevy's zebra?

2 What advantages does the IBM software provide to Marwell in its goal to save endangered species? Are there other advantages not mentioned in this case? Provide specific examples.

THE NOOK

QUESTIONS

1 BI tools allow better decisions to be made by presenting information to the right person at the right time. Imagine a scenario where the bartender has a computer screen that monitors the club's collections vs its sales. What would keep this system from working properly?

2 How would you collect information to make this a reality?

5.3 Business intelligence applications for data analysis

A good strategy to study the ways in which organisations use BI applications is to consider how the users analyse data, how the results of their analyses are presented to them, and how managers and executives implement these results. Recall from chapter 3 that the data are stored in a data warehouse or data mart. The user community analyses these data using a variety of BI applications. The results of these analyses can be presented to users via other BI applications. Finally, managers and executives put the overall results to good use. You will become familiar with data analysis and presentation, and use them in depth in the next three sections.

A variety of BI applications for analysing data are available. They include multidimensional analysis (also called online analytical processing, or OLAP), data mining and decision support systems.

Multidimensional analysis or online analytical processing

Some BI applications include **online analytical processing (OLAP)** capabilities, also referred to as **multidimensional data analysis**. OLAP involves 'slicing and dicing' data stored in a dimensional format, drilling down the data to greater detail and aggregating the data.

Consider our example from chapter 3. Recall figure 3.11 showing the data cube. The product is on the x-axis, geography is on the y-axis and time is on the z-axis. Now, suppose you want to know how many nuts the company sold in the West region in 2009. You would slice and dice the cube using nuts as the specific measure for product, West as the measure for geography and 2009 as the measure for time. The value(s) in the cell(s) that remain after our slicing and dicing is (are) the answer to our question. You might also want to know how many nuts were sold in January 2009; this is an example of drilling down. Alternatively, you might want to know how many nuts were sold during 2008–2010, which is an example of aggregation, also called 'rollup.'

Data mining

Data mining refers to the process of searching for valuable business information in a large database, data warehouse, or data mart. Data mining can perform two basic operations: (1) predicting trends and behaviours and (2) identifying previously unknown patterns. BI applications typically provide users with a view of what has happened. Data mining helps to explain why it is happening and it predicts what will happen in the future.

Regarding the first operation, data mining automates the process of finding predictive information in large databases. Questions that traditionally required extensive hands-on analysis can now be answered directly and quickly from the data. A typical example of a predictive problem is *targeted marketing*. Data mining can use data from past promotional mailings to identify those people who are most likely to respond favourably to future mailings. Another example of a predictive problem is forecasting bankruptcy and other forms of default.

Data mining can also identify previously hidden patterns in a single step. For example, it can analyse retail sales data to discover seemingly unrelated products that people often purchase together. One such example is Barbie dolls and confectionery. Data mining found that consumers tend to buy Barbie dolls and confectionery at the same time when they shop in department stores. This is known as affinity analysis, or more commonly 'market basket analysis'.

One significant pattern-discovery operation is detecting fraudulent credit card transactions. After you use your credit card for a time, a pattern emerges of the typical ways you use your card — the places you use your card, the amount you spend and so on. If your card is stolen and used fraudulently, this usage is often different from your pattern. Data mining tools can discern this difference and bring this issue to your attention.

Numerous data mining applications are used in business and in other fields. According to a Gartner report (**www.gartner.com**), most of the Fortune 1000 companies worldwide currently use data mining, as the following representative examples illustrate. Note that in most cases the intent of data mining is to identify a business opportunity in order to create a sustainable competitive advantage.

- *Retailing and sales:* predicting sales, preventing theft and fraud, and determining correct inventory levels and distribution schedules among outlets. For example, retailers such as AAFES (stores on military bases) use Fraud Watch from SAP (**www.sap.com**) to combat fraud by employees in their 1400 stores.
- *Banking:* forecasting levels of bad loans and fraudulent credit card use, predicting credit card spending by new customers, and determining which kinds of customers will best respond to (and qualify for) new loan offers.
- *Manufacturing and production:* predicting machinery failures and finding key factors that help optimise manufacturing capacity.
- *Insurance:* forecasting claim amounts and medical coverage costs, classifying the most important elements that affect medical coverage and predicting which customers will buy new insurance policies.
- *Policework:* tracking crime patterns, locations and criminal behaviour; identifying attributes to assist in solving criminal cases.
- *Health care:* correlating demographics of patients with critical illnesses, and developing better insights on how to identify and treat symptoms and their causes.
- *Marketing:* classifying customer demographics that can be used to predict which customers will respond to a mailing or buy a particular product.

Decision support systems

Decision support systems (DSS) combine models and data in an attempt to analyse semistructured and some unstructured problems with extensive user involvement. **Models** are simplified representations, or abstractions, of reality. DSS enable business managers and analysts to access data interactively, to manipulate these data and to conduct appropriate analyses.

Decision support systems can enhance learning and contribute to all levels of decision making. DSS also employ mathematical models. In addition, they have the related capabilities of sensitivity analysis, what-if analysis and goal-seeking analysis, which you will learn about next. You should keep in mind that these three types of analysis are useful for any type of decision support application. For example, Excel supports them.

Sensitivity analysis

Sensitivity analysis is the study of the impact that changes in one or more parts of a decision-making model have on other parts. Most sensitivity analyses examine the impact that changes in input variables have on output variables.

Most models include two types of input variables: decision variables and environmental variables. 'What is our reorder point for these raw materials?' is a decision variable (internal to the organisation). 'What will the rate of inflation be?' is an environmental variable (external to the organisation). The output in this example would be the total cost of raw materials. The point of a sensitivity analysis is usually to determine the impact of environmental variables on the result of the analysis.

Sensitivity analysis is extremely valuable because it enables the system to adapt to changing conditions and to the varying requirements of different decision-making situations. It provides a better understanding of the model and the problem that the model purports to describe.

What-if analysis

A model builder must make predictions and assumptions regarding the input data, many of which are based on the assessment of uncertain futures. The results depend on the accuracy of these assumptions, which can be highly subjective. *What-if analysis* attempts to predict the impact of a change in the assumptions (input data) on the proposed solution. For example, what will happen to the total inventory cost *if* the originally assumed cost of carrying inventories is not 10 per cent but 12 per cent? In a well-designed BI system, managers themselves can interactively ask the computer these types of questions as many times as needed.

Goal-seeking analysis

Goal-seeking analysis represents a 'backward' solution approach. It attempts to find the value of the inputs necessary to achieve a desired level of output. For example, let's say that an initial BI analysis predicted a profit of $2 million. Management might want to know what sales volume would be necessary to generate a profit of $3 million. To find out, the company would perform a goal-seeking analysis.

However, managers cannot simply press a button that says 'increase sales'. Some action(s) will be necessary to make the sales increase possible. The action(s) could be to lower prices, to increase research and development, to provide a higher commission rate for the sales force, to increase advertising, to take some other action, or to implement some combination of these actions. Whatever the action is, it will cost money and the goal-seeking analysis must take this into account.

BEFORE YOU GO ON . . .

1 Describe multidimensional analysis and construct a data cube with information from IT's About Business (p. 162). (*Hint:* You must decide which three business dimensions you would like to analyse in your data cube.)
2 What are the two basic operations of data mining?
3 What is the purpose of decision support systems?

THE NOOK

QUESTIONS

1 Malakai and Abbie hope to use Excel as their decision support tool. Which analysis would be best suited for their goal and shrinkage problem? The what-if analysis? The goal-seeking analysis? Or the sensitivity analysis? Or, do you think it would be a combination of all three?
2 What tools can you find in Excel that would support these analyses? (*Hint:* Google 'sensitivity analysis Excel'.)

5.4 Business intelligence applications for presenting results

The results of the types of data analyses you just learned about can be presented with dashboards and data visualisation technologies. Today, users increasingly rely on data that are real time or almost real time. Therefore, you will note a discussion of real-time BI in this section.

Dashboards

Dashboards evolved from executive information systems, which were information systems designed specifically for the information needs of top executives. However, as you saw in this chapter's opening case, today all employees, business partners and customers can use digital dashboards.

A **dashboard** provides easy access to timely information and direct access to management reports. It is very user friendly and is supported by graphics. Of special importance, it enables managers to examine exception reports and drill down into detailed data. Table 5.1 (overleaf) summarises the various capabilities that are common to many dashboards. In addition, some of the capabilities discussed in this section are now part of many BI products, as illustrated in figure 5.3 (overleaf).

One outstanding example of a dashboard is the 'Bloomberg'. Bloomberg LLP (**www.bloomberg.com**), a privately held company, provides a subscription service that sells financial data, software to analyse these data, trading tools and news (electronic, print,

TABLE 5.1 The capabilities of dashboards

Capability	Description
Drill down	The ability to go to details, at several levels. Can be done through a series of menus or by clicking on a drillable portion of the screen.
Critical success factors (CSFs)	The factors most critical for the success of business. Can be organisational, industry, departmental, or for individual workers.
Key performance indicators (KPIs)	The specific measures of CSFs.
Status access	The latest data available on KPIs or some other metric, often in real time.
Trend analysis	Short-term, medium-term and long-term trend of KPIs or metrics, which are projected using forecasting methods.
Exception reporting	Reports that highlight deviations larger than certain thresholds. Reports may include only deviations.

FIGURE 5.3 Sample performance dashboard.

TV and radio). All of this information is accessible through a colour-coded Bloomberg keyboard that displays the desired information on a computer screen, either the user's or one that Bloomberg provides. Users can also set up their own computers to access the service without a Bloomberg keyboard. The subscription service plus the keyboard is called the 'Bloomberg'. It literally represents a do-it-yourself dashboard, because users can customise their information feeds as well as the look and feel of those feeds (see figure 5.4).

In another example, figure 5.5 shows a human resources dashboard/scorecard developed by iDashboards, one of the leading BI software vendors. At a glance, users can see employee productivity, hours, team, department and division performance in graphical, tabular, summary and detailed form. The selector box to the left enables the user to easily change between specific analysts to compare their performance.

A unique and interesting application of dashboards to support the informational needs of executives is the Management Cockpit. Essentially, a Management Cockpit is a strategic management room containing an elaborate set of dashboards that enable top-level decision makers to pilot their businesses better. The goal is to create an environment that encourages more efficient management meetings and boosts team performance via effective communication. To help achieve this goal, the dashboard graphically displays key performance indicators and information relating to critical success factors on the walls of a

FIGURE 5.4 The Bloomberg Terminal is a specific set of hardware and software used by financial professionals on trading floors around the world.

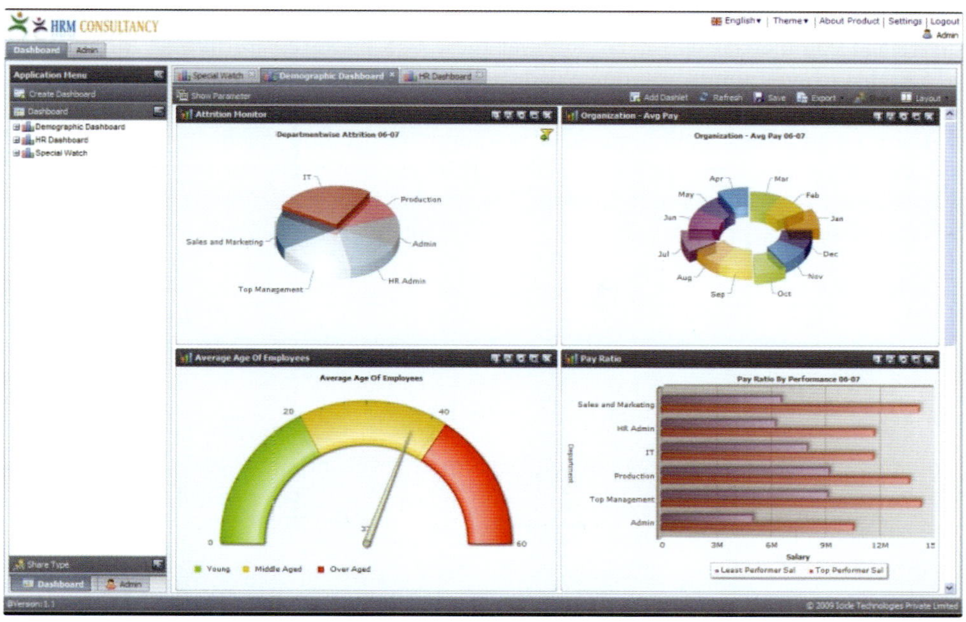

FIGURE 5.5 A human resource dashboard/scorecard.

meeting room, called the Management Cockpit Room. The cockpit-like arrangement of instrument panels and displays helps managers visualise how all the different factors in the business interrelate.

Within the room, the four walls are designated by colour: Black, Red, Blue and White. The Black Wall displays the principal success factors and financial indicators. The Red Wall measures market performance. The Blue Wall projects the performance of internal processes and employees. The White Wall indicates the status of strategic projects. The Flight Deck, a six-screen, high-end PC, enables executives to drill down to detailed information. External information needed for competitive analyses can easily be imported into the room.

Board members and other executives hold meetings in the Cockpit Room. Managers also meet there with the comptroller to discuss current business issues. For this purpose, the Management Cockpit can implement various what-if scenarios. It also provides a common basis for information and communication. Finally, it supports efforts to translate a corporate strategy into concrete activities by identifying performance indicators.

Data visualisation technologies

After data have been processed, they can be presented to users in visual formats such as text, graphics and tables. This process, known as *data visualisation*, makes IT applications more attractive and understandable to users. Data visualisation is becoming more and more popular on the web for decision support. A variety of visualisation methods and software packages that support decision making are available. Two particularly valuable applications are geographic information systems and reality mining.

Geographic information systems

A **geographic information system (GIS)** is a computer-based system for capturing, integrating, manipulating and displaying data using digitised maps. Its most distinguishing characteristic is that every record or digital object has an identified geographical location. This process, called *geocoding*, enables users to generate information for planning, problem solving and decision making. In addition, the graphical format makes it easy for managers to visualise the data.

Today, relatively inexpensive, fully functional PC-based GIS packages are readily available. Representative GIS software vendors are ESRI (**www.esri.com**), Intergraph (**www.intergraph.com**) and Pitney Bowes Mapinfo (**www.pbinsight.com/welcome/mapinfo**). In addition, both government sources and private vendors provide diversified commercial GIS data. Some of these GIS packages are free — for example, CD-ROMs from Mapinfo and downloadable material from **www.esri.com** and **data.geocomm.com**.

There are countless applications of GISs to improve decision making in both the public and private sectors. For example, IT's About Business shows how Australian cardiologists are using the latest mapping technology, Geographic Information Systems (GIS), to prevent heart disease.

IT'S ABOUT BUSINESS

Australian cardiologists using GIS technology

Currently in Australia, leading cardiologists are using the latest mapping technology to prevent Australia's biggest killer — heart disease. This technology is called the Geographic Information System (GIS).

GIS is a system designed to seize, store, analyse, manage and present geographical data. The technology allows users to view, understand, question, interpret and visualise data based on their requirements. Furthermore, this technology will assist users to solve problems and make decisions. GIS can be integrated into any enterprise information system framework.

According to Esri, a global supplier of GIS software, GIS provides several benefits to users including increased efficiency, cost savings, enhanced decision making and more accurate recordkeeping.

Based on the above benefits, Australian cardiologists are using GIS technology to study and access cardiac services before and after cardiac events.

Queensland University of Technology Associate Professor Robyn Clark said measuring access to cardiac care through a 'geographic lens' helped identify a significant gap between regional and metropolitan access to cardiac care.

'We looked at the distance to cardiac treatment centre locations in all of Australia's 20 000 population centres', Associate Professor Clark said.

'By mapping the huge amounts of statistical data we collected with GIS technology we could identify critical patterns and relationships that would not have been so apparent in table form. More specifically, we could identify locations and groups of people with limited access to cardiac services. For example, we found that only 40 per cent of indigenous people reside within an hour of appropriate cardiac medical facilities and cardiac rehabilitation services, while 12 per cent of indigenous Australians live three or more hours from any kind of hospital.'

According to David Purkiss from Esri Australia, GIS is widely used in the health sector, such as in mental health, midwifery, cancer treatment and burns services.

Finally, using GIS technology will create a cardiac health index, which ranks geographic areas according to fatal heart-attack risk.

'The Cardiac Accessibility and Remoteness Index of Australia is a simple ranking system that helps governments and local communities prioritise locations in terms of risk', Associate Professor Clark said.

'Because the index is backed by reputable research, community members and medical bodies have greater leverage to lobby governments for improved cardiac care where it is needed most.'

'It is also a valuable tool for governments when deciding how best to distribute health care infrastructure efficiently and cost-effectively.'

Sources: Esri (2013), 'Top five benefits of GIS', www.esri.com/what-is-gis/overview#top_five_panel; Esri (2013), 'What is GIS?', www.esri.com/what-is-gis/overview#overview_panel; A. Kouparitsas (2012), 'GIS technology at the heart of new medical study', esriaustralia.com.au/p/news/gis-technology-at-the-heart-of-new-medical-study-nar-104#sthash.RJt99KyR.dpuf.

QUESTIONS

1 List and discuss the benefits behind using GIS in business.
2 Is GIS an effective solution for Australian cardiologists? If so, why? If not, why not? Can you anticipate another health application for the technology?

Reality mining

One important emerging trend is the integration of GISs and global positioning systems (GPSs, discussed in chapter 10). Using GISs and GPSs together can produce an interesting new type of technology, called **reality mining**. Reality mining allows analysts to extract information from the usage patterns of mobile phones and other wireless devices.

Real-time business intelligence

Until recently, BI has focused on the use of historical data. This focus has changed with the emergence of technology for capturing, storing and using real-time data. Real-time BI enables users to employ multidimensional analysis, data mining and decision support systems to analyse data in real time. In addition, it helps organisations to make decisions and to interact with customers in new ways.

THE NOOK

QUESTIONS

1 Dashboards are very nice, but seem very complex to create. Do you think graphs and charts in Excel could be as effective as the elaborate dashboard examples provided in the chapter?
2 What type of chart do you think would be beneficial in tackling the problem of shrinkage? Would it be a bar chart? Pie chart? Line chart? How could this be developed in Excel?

5.5 Business intelligence in action: corporate performance management

Corporate performance management (CPM) is involved with monitoring and managing an organisation's performance according to *key performance indicators* (KPIs) such as revenue, return on investment (ROI), overhead and operational costs. For online businesses, CPM includes additional factors such as the number of page views, server load, network traffic and transactions per second. BI applications allow managers and analysts to analyse data to obtain valuable information and insights concerning the organisation's KPIs.

BEFORE YOU GO ON . . .

1 What is corporate performance management?
2 How do BI applications contribute to corporate performance management?

WHAT'S IN IT FOR ME?

FOR THE ACCOUNTING MAJOR

BI is used widely in accounting study as well as the workforce, because this technology is designed to analyse accounting and financial data from specific systems; for example, ERP to assist top management in making decisions. Additionally, BI will assist accountants and CPAs to develop easier solutions and explanations in real time. Finally, BI is used extensively in auditing to uncover irregularities. It is also used to uncover and prevent fraud. CPAs use BI for many of their duties, ranging from risk analysis to cost control.

FOR THE FINANCE MAJOR

Using BI in the finance sector will allow users to manage risk, especially in projects, reduce ongoing costs, and maximise existing resources and expertise by analysing the current operational processes and activities. Integrating these applications in the finance and banking sectors will meet user satisfaction and fulfilment and reduce the churn rate. Finally, people have been using computers for decades to solve financial problems. Innovative BI applications have been created for activities such as making stock market decisions, refinancing bonds, assessing debt risks, analysing financial conditions, predicting business failures, forecasting financial trends and investing in global markets.

FOR THE MARKETING MAJOR

Using BI in the marketing sector will allow users to collect, analyse, manage and transform data and statistics by using statistical methods and financial analysis and marketing. Using these applications in study as well as business will allow users to have the fundamental and foundation skills in database systems, data visualisation, business modelling and managerial leadership. Finally, marketing personnel utilise BI in many applications, from planning and executing marketing campaigns to allocating advertising budgets to evaluating alternative routings of salespeople. New marketing approaches such as targeted marketing and database marketing are heavily dependent on IT in general, and on data warehouses and BI applications in particular.

FOR THE HUMAN RESOURCES MANAGEMENT (HRM) MAJOR

BI is used in HRM to analyse and transmute information in HRM and other departments. This information will assist in solving problems and providing an effective and efficient decision to managers as well as employees. Using these applications and tools in HRM will assist organisations to develop, manage change and make organisations more unique and exceptional in the market. Finally, human resources personnel use BI for many of their activities. For example, BI applications can find résumés of applicants posted on the web and sort them to match needed skills and to support management succession planning.

FOR THE MIS MAJOR

BI is used widely in the MIS major, as BI is a set of theories, methodologies and technologies, and MIS provides the data infrastructure used in BI.
MIS personnel are also involved in building, deploying and supporting BI applications. Using BI in any sector, including information systems, will bring new opportunities and apply a successful strategy in a competitive and economic market advantage.

SUMMARY

1 Explain different ways in which IT supports managerial decision making.

When making a decision, either organisational or personal, the decision maker goes through a three-step process: intelligence, design and choice. When the choice is made, the decision is implemented.

Several information technologies have been successfully used to directly support managers. Collectively, they are referred to as business intelligence information systems. Figure 5.2 provides a matrix that shows how technology supports the various types of decisions that managers must make.

2 Provide examples of different ways that organisations make use of BI.

> *The development of a single or a few related BI applications.* This BI target is often a point solution for a departmental need, such as campaign management in marketing. A data mart is usually created to store necessary data.

> *The development of infrastructure to support enterprise wide BI.* This target supports current and future BI needs. A critical component is an enterprise data warehouse.

> *Support for organisational transformation.* With this target, BI is used to fundamentally change how a company competes in the marketplace. BI supports a new business model and enables the business strategy.

3 Explain the value that different BI applications provide to large and small businesses.

Users have a variety of BI applications available to help them analyse data. These applications include multidimensional analysis, data mining and decision support systems.

Multidimensional analysis, also called online analytical processing (OLAP), involves 'slicing and dicing' data stored in a dimensional format, drilling down to greater data detail and aggregating data. Data mining refers to the process of searching for valuable business information in a large database, data warehouse, or data mart. Decision support systems (DSS) combine models and data in an attempt to analyse semistructured and some unstructured problems with extensive user involvement. (The examples of using each application at your university, we leave to you.)

4 Offer examples of how businesses and government agencies can use different BI applications to analyse data.

A dashboard provides easy access to timely information and direct access to management reports. A geographic information system (GIS) is a computer-based system for capturing, integrating, manipulating and displaying data using digitised maps. Reality mining analyses information extracted from the usage patterns of mobile phones and other wireless devices. (Examples of how these technologies might be used by businesses and government agencies, we leave to you.)

5 Explain how your university could use CPM to provide solutions to two campus problems.

CPM is involved with monitoring and managing an organisation's performance according to key performance indicators (KPIs) such as revenue, return on investment (ROI), overhead and operational costs. (An example of how your university might use CPM, we leave to you.)

>>> CHAPTER GLOSSARY

business intelligence A broad category of applications, technologies and processes for gathering, storing, accessing and analysing data to help business users make better decisions.

cloud BI An internet application used by organisations to improve work performance. An example is a dashboard.

corporate performance management The area of business intelligence involved with monitoring and managing an organisation's performance, according to key performance indicators (KPIs) such as revenue, return on investment (ROI), overhead and operational costs.

dashboard A BI application that provides rapid access to timely information and direct access to management reports.

data mining The process of searching for valuable business information in a large database, data warehouse, or data mart.

decision A choice among two or more alternatives that individuals and groups make.

decision support systems (DSS) Business intelligence systems that combine models and data in an attempt to solve semistructured and some unstructured problems with extensive user involvement.

geographic information system A computer-based system for capturing, integrating, manipulating and displaying data using digitised maps.

management A process by which organisational goals are achieved through the use of resources.

mobile BI Ability to access business critical information via mobile facility to handheld and remote users.

models (in decision making) Simplified representations, or abstractions, of reality.

online analytical processing (OLAP) (or multidimensional data analysis) A set of capabilities for 'slicing and dicing' data using dimensions and measures associated with the data.

reality mining Extraction by analysts of information from the usage patterns of mobile phones and other wireless devices.

>>> DISCUSSION QUESTIONS

1 Your company is considering opening a new factory in China. List several typical activities involved in each phase of the decision (intelligence, design and choice).

2 Recall that data mining found that consumers tend to buy Barbie dolls and confectionery at the same time when they shop in department stores. Now that you know this relationship exists, can you provide a rationale for it?

3 American Can Company announced that it was interested in acquiring a company in the health maintenance organisation (HMO) field. Two decisions were involved in this act: (1) the decision to acquire an HMO and (2) the decision of which HMO to acquire. How can the company use BI to assist it in this endeavour?

4 Discuss the strategic benefits of BI systems.

5 Will BI replace business analysts?
(*Hint:* See E Israeli (2013), 'BI and analytics — with or without a data warehouse', www.sys-con.com/node/2749805.)

6 Can BI be easily integrated with the system infrastructure most companies have?

>>> PROBLEM-SOLVING ACTIVITIES

1 The city of London (United Kingdom) charges an entrance fee for cars and trucks into the central city district. About 1000 digital cameras photograph the licence plate of every vehicle passing by. Computers read the plate numbers and match them against records in a database of cars for which the fee has been paid for that day. If the computer does not find a match, the car owner receives a citation by mail. Examine the issues pertaining to how this process is accomplished, the mistakes it can make and the consequences of those mistakes. Also examine how well the system is working by checking media reports. Finally, relate the process to business intelligence.

2 Enter www.cognos.com and visit the demos on the right side of the page. Prepare a report on the various features shown in each demo.

3 Enter www.fico.com and find products for fraud detection and risk analysis. Prepare a report.

4 Enter www.teradatastudentnetwork.com (TSN) (you will need a password) and find the paper titled 'Data warehousing supports corporate strategy at First American Corporation' (by Watson, Wixom and Goodhue). Read the paper and answer the following questions:
   a What were the drivers for the data warehouse/business intelligence project in the company?
   b What strategic advantages were realised?
   c What were the critical success factors for the project?

5 Access www.johnwiley.com.au/highered/rainer/ausnz/studentresources to find the video of Hans Rosling's presentation. Comment on his data visualisation techniques.

6 Enter www.visualmining.com. Explore the relationship between visualisation and business intelligence. See how business intelligence is related to dashboards.

7 Access www.johnwiley.com.au/highered/rainer/ausnz/studentresources. Identify all types of business intelligence software. Join a discussion group about topics discussed in this chapter. Prepare a report.

8 Visit the sites of some GIS vendors (such as www.mapinfo.com, www.esri.com, or www.autodesk.com). Download a demo. What are some of the most important capabilities and applications?

9 Analyse Microsoft Virtual Earth (www.microsoft.com/virtualearth) as a business intelligence tool.
(*Hint:* Access www.johnwiley.com.au/highered/rainer/ausnz/studentresources.) What are the business intelligence features of this product?

10 Enter itunes.apple.com/au/app/reportplus-mobile-business/id556853421?mt=8, and explore the advantages and disadvantages of mobile business intelligence dashboards.

>>> COLLABORATION EXERCISE

Background

The company MicroStrategy offers many products for business use that are intended to help companies manage and interpret their data. One of these products is a free tool called 'MicroStrategy Cloud Personal' where you can upload your own data and let MicroStrategy software create reports for you. Go to www.johnwiley.com.au/highered/rainer/ausnz/

studentresources and click the link provided. It will take you to Microstrategy's website explaining some 'cloud' tools available for personal data analysis.

Activity

Work with a team to create data on the money you spend on food for a week. Have each team member create 10 rows of data in a spreadsheet. You will first have to agree on the type of data you will create and the column titles so everyone's data will match up. Once you all create your data points, combine them into one spreadsheet and upload it into the MicroStrategy Personal Cloud.

Deliverable

Share your work with your teammates. Let everyone on the team have some time to look through the data and then compile a report for your lecturer based on the data your team put together. Be sure to include images of your graphs and reports. Is there anything in this analysis that surprises you? Did you determine if you should change any habits based on this work?

CLOSING CASE **1** >

Procter & Gamble uses analytics in novel ways

THE PROBLEM

Procter & Gamble (www.pg.com), the world's largest consumer products company with $79 billion in sales and 127 000 employees, manages massive streams of data in order to effectively operate its global business. The company has been forecasting its profits on a monthly basis for about 40 years, trying to predict components such as sales, commodity prices and exchange rates. Before P&G deployed new information technologies, decisions took weeks or months, because data had to be manually gathered, collated and channelled through various committees before reaching high-level company executives.

THE IT SOLUTION

Today, P&G uses high-speed networks, data visualisation and high-speed analysis on multiple streams of data and information. More efficient software and increased computing power has vastly increased the amount of real-time data that P&G can process compared to what IT could do previously. In order to make better, faster decisions, P&G implemented the information technologies Business Sphere, the Immersion Lab, and the Handshake Room.

P&G implemented Business Sphere early in 2011. Business Sphere is an umbrella technology that integrates 14 different technologies from multiple vendors. The room contains two huge monitors, which give the executives a visual of the 4 billion times each day that P&G products are used in more than 80 countries.

In the Immersion Lab, another information technology employed by P&G, managers work in a mock hotel room where they try out many different mobile devices, building confidence that their employees can work anywhere on any type of phone or tablet.

In the Handshake Room, P&G solves customers' business problems and makes sales. The Handshake Room provides virtual store simulations with two screens along one wall. One of the screens, about 2.4 metres square, shows blank store shelves onto which can be projected three-dimensional images of any P&G product that a manager might want to stock in any size or label configuration. Another monitor shows store interiors of big retailers such as Walmart and Safeway. P&G can insert any new store display into these views so buyers can observe the display's look and its effect on store flow.

THE RESULTS

P&G's executives hold their meetings in the Business Sphere at the company's headquarters. In four clicks on a tablet computer, they can change the image on a screen from a view of a world map to a graph of toothpaste prices in India with a sales comparison that shows local brands are gaining market share. A few clicks on another computer can bring up a view of shampoo sales in Australia, which renders it immediately apparent that P&G will need to sell 585 000 more cases of shampoo for sales just to break even. Yet another view might indicate big opportunities for hair care in Germany and pet food in the United States.

One of the great advantages of the Business Sphere is that from day 1, it enabled managers in some 40 locations worldwide to see the exact same data. This data consistency meant that everyone can recognise and agree upon target countries, regions, or products for particular attention. Everyone can also easily judge the company's progress against its strategic plan and inroads made against the competition, in some cases even down to individual retailers.

The Business Sphere also enables P&G executives and managers to make decisions in minutes based on data provided. All information about sales is now decided at the executive level each week and production is viewed in near real time worldwide. The company is also increasing the amount of data collected by a factor of seven.

The Immersion Lab allows P&G managers to test various information technologies to ensure that they will work on whatever device an employee prefers. P&G analysts are also testing various tools that could allow employees to collaborate more effectively, such as wikis (discussed in detail in Chapter 8) for project management.

In the Handshake Room, P&G analysts ask customers to present a business problem. The analysts use the technology in the room to present a solution to the problem, and often make a sale on the spot.

Sources: Compiled from C Murphy (2011), 'How to get one version of the truth', *InformationWeek*, 7 November; D Henschen (2011), 'P&G turns analysis into action', *InformationWeek*, 14 September; Q Hardy (2011), 'The matrix of soap', *Forbes*, 22 August; Q Hardy (2011), 'At Procter & Gamble toothpaste is data', *Forbes*, 3 August; www.pg.com.

QUESTIONS

1 Why is the Business Sphere so important to P&G executives? Provide examples to support your answer.

2 Why is the Handshake Room so important in gaining new business for P&G? Provide examples to support your answer.

CLOSING CASE 2 >

North East Water

THE BACKGROUND AND PROBLEM

North East Water (NEW) provides water and sewerage services to more than 39 towns in North East Victoria. The NEW service covers 20 000 square kilometres and 113 000 people, and provides new developers' plumbing and trade waste services. It aims to provide high-quality water services to the Victorian community, which should be aligned with NEW objectives and aims.

NEW has several operators and team leaders who are located in nine dispersed depots, so receiving accurate financial reports about all towns under its jurisdiction was a challenge. Therefore, to improve the NEW job performance and reduce inaccurate information, it was recommended to centralise budget reporting using a BI application known as Technology One. According to the Finance Manager for NEW, Nicholas Moore, it is currently very difficult for NEW stakeholders to analyse and dissect financial information and discover what is happening across individual towns, or to drill down across depots or facilities.

THE IT SOLUTION

To solve the financial reporting among NEW's stakeholders, the BI Technology One Financial Solution was successfully implemented. This system aimed to interpret accounting and financial information in an effective and efficient way. Technology One budgeting and forecasting provided an outstanding budgeting process based on accurate, real-time information.

THE RESULTS

After implementing Technology One in NEW, the top management as well as employees were very pleased with the outcomes, as reports and budgets were produced quickly, which assisted NEW stakeholders to improve their decision making. Technology One demonstrated the flexibility to tailor reporting for different audiences. Finally, NEW's experience with BI Technology One was unique and exceptional as the system minimises the complexity and timeframe in delivering budgets for approval.

Source: Technologyone (2013), *Case study: North East Water*, retrieved from www.technologyonecorp.com.

QUESTIONS

1 What are the benefits of implementing BI Technology One in North East Water?

2 What are the main challenges facing service providers in preparing consolidated financial reporting?

SPREADSHEET ACTIVITY **LINKING SHEETS WITH FORMULAE**

OBJECTIVE

The objective of this activity is to help you understand that while spreadsheets are powerful, an interconnected workbook is even more so. You will learn how to write formulae that use information contained in different pages to help tie the workbook together.

Chapter connection

Even though the opening case makes the point that spreadsheets are antiquated and often not able to keep up with the vast amounts of data needed to run an organisation, spreadsheets still occupy an important place in smaller organisations. This activity brings business intelligence to the smaller mum-and-dad organisations.

ACTIVITY

As you have seen, business intelligence is a huge concept. It can, however, also apply in much smaller ways to everyday business. Business intelligence can help small mum-and-dad organisations in tremendous ways. Consider the following example.

Ted is a 45-year-old full-time accountant. He loves his job and has had quite a successful career. He also takes great pride in working with his hands. Specifically, he has always enjoyed working with wood and making small rocking horses for children. For years he just made these for family and friends, but lately he has decided to start selling his work. The accountant side of him has kept detailed records of his inventory, costs, sales, hours, profits, losses and so on. Now it is time to take his workbook and create business intelligence out of it.

Ted's spreadsheet contains some basic information but no formulae. Notes describe what he has done and the decisions he wants to make. You can download the spreadsheet from www.johnwiley.com.au/highered/rainer/ausnz/studentresources (look for chapter 5 links). Specifically, Ted wants to know how much he has invested in each rocking horse. His time, materials, advertising and other costs will definitely make a difference in his final price. Keep in mind that the point of this spreadsheet is to provide business intelligence. Although spreadsheet skills are required, they are the means to the end of helping Ted set appropriate prices.

DELIVERABLE

The final product will be a spreadsheet with Ted's data calculated to provide business intelligence in a small business scenario.

DISCUSSION QUESTIONS

1 How does algebra play a role in writing formulae?
2 What happens to your data if you build a formula off a previously incorrect formula?
3 If formulae are set up to predict or forecast (such as in regression), how many scenarios could be calculated?

DATABASE ACTIVITY **USING PIVOT TABLES**

OBJECTIVE

To learn how to turn a database into a *pivot table*, which is a structured representation of the database content that lets you observe the relationships of any data field, or group of data fields, to others.

Chapter connection

In this chapter, you read how information systems can be used for better decisions. Most of what you read discussed specialised tools for organising and presenting data. These are found mostly in medium–large organisations and up. What's a small business to do?

Even a small business can use a database management system (DBMS) to organise and store information. In this module, we will see one way to use an Access database to support decision making: the pivot table.

This is a small-scale example of business intelligence (section 5.2) and a BI application (section 5.3).

Prerequisites

None.

Activity

In this activity, which you will find online at www.johnwiley.com.au/highered/rainer/ausnz/studentresources, you will use a sales database for a group of computer stores. You will analyse it for differences among stores, for trends, and to see how the group could improve sales.

1 Download the **Ch 05 CarlaComputerStores** database from www.johnwiley.com.au/highered/rainer/ausnz/studentresources and open it.
2 Open the OrderQry query by clicking on it in the Navigation Pane at the left of the Access window.

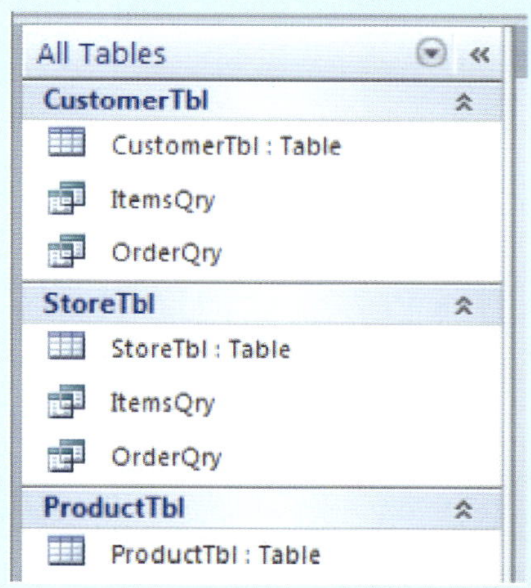

Usage hint: If you do not see the navigation pane, but the words 'Navigation Pane' run vertically at the far left of the window, click on those words or on the » above them to expand it.

Usage hint: Depending on how your copy of Access is set up, navigation pane items may open with a single or double click. If a single click does not work, double-click. If you are using your own copy, you can set this preference in Options under the File tab. In the Current Database section, click 'Navigation Options....'

You will see what looks like a table with sales information in this database. (Its first few rows are shown below.) As you will learn in the chapter 10 activity, this 'table' is not stored in the database. It is created as needed by combining data from other tables in a *query*. Those other tables are listed under Tables in the navigation pane. You can see how they are related to each other by clicking 'Relationships' in the Database Tools ribbon.

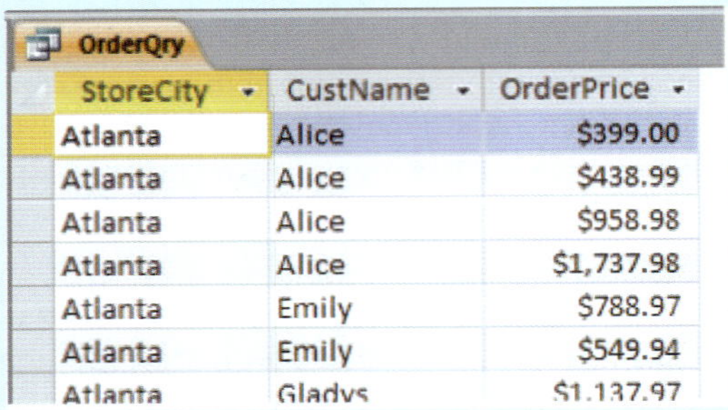

OrderQry

StoreCity	CustName	OrderPrice
Atlanta	Alice	$399.00
Atlanta	Alice	$438.99
Atlanta	Alice	$958.98
Atlanta	Alice	$1,737.98
Atlanta	Emily	$788.97
Atlanta	Emily	$549.94
Atlanta	Gladys	$1,137.97

These tables are a simplified version of what a real store would use. For example, a real database would include order date and method of payment. However, this database has purchase history: what each customer bought, when, at what store and with what other items. That is what we will use here.

3 To analyse customer spending, look at this query in PivotTable view. Select that view from the drop-down View menu at the left of the Home ribbon, or click the second icon from the left at the bottom right of the window.

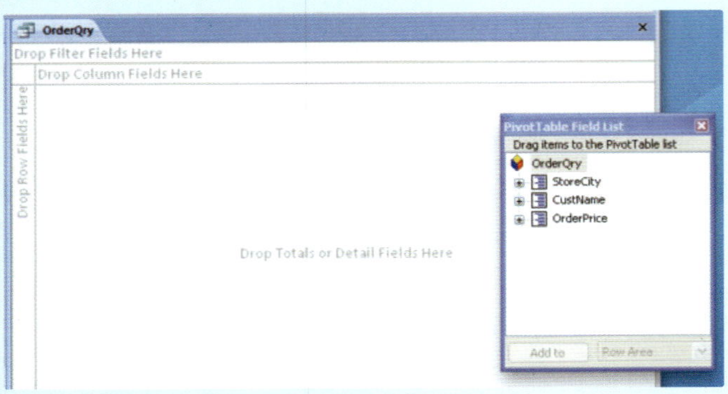

Usage hint: Access often provides multiple ways to do something. It usually does not matter which you choose. As you use Access more, you will develop preferences. They do not have to be the same as anyone else's.

4 A windoid labelled 'PivotTable Field List' floats above the main Access window. It lists all the fields in the query, plus other items that can be derived from them. You will drag these into sections of the pivot table pane to analyse the data.

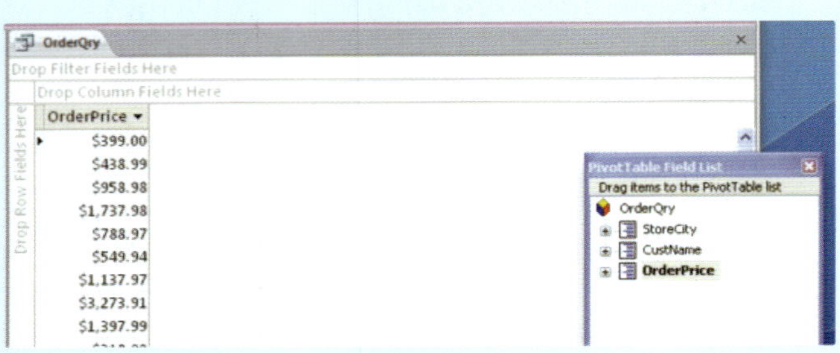

Usage hint: If you do not see the Field List windoid, click the Field List icon in the Show/Hide section toward the left end of the ribbon, under the Design tab.

Let's see if there are differences in order size among stores. Drag OrderPrice into the main area of the pane, labelled 'Drop Totals or Detail Fields Here.'

5 You will see all the order amounts in the central section of the pivot table. It is useless by itself. In terms of chapter 1 concepts, it is data, not information. To organise them by store, drag StoreCity into the 'Drop Row Fields Here' area at the left of the pane.

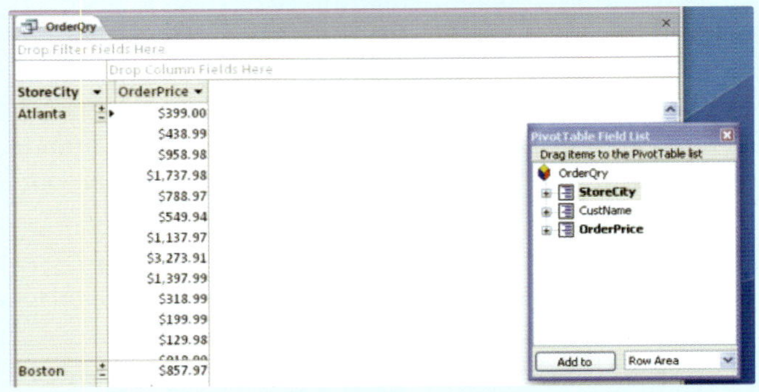

6 We want to see the average order size for each store. Select the OrderPrice column by clicking on its header. Then click the AutoCalc icon on the Design ribbon (S, the uppercase Greek letter sigma, a common mathematical symbol for summation). From the drop-down menu, select Average. You will see each store's average order size below the list of orders.

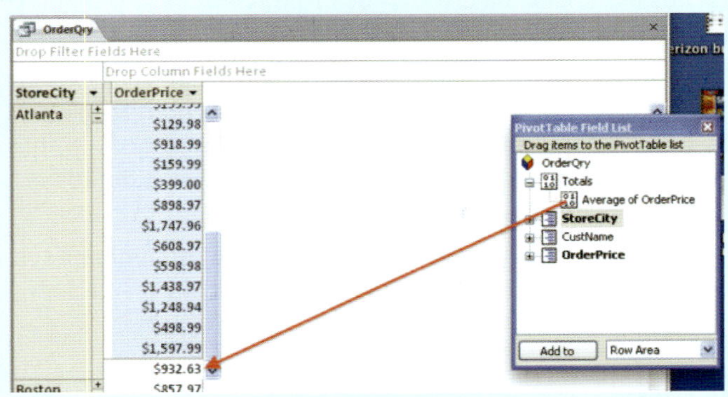

Usage hint: The overall average is labelled 'Grand Total.' In everyday language, a 'total' is what you get when you add several numbers. Access refers to that concept as a *sum*. To Access, a 'total' is any summary calculation: sum, average, count, or any of the others listed under the AutoCalc icon.

Which city has the highest average sales? The lowest?

7 Suppose we only care about averages, not individual sales. To hide the details, select that column again and click 'Hide Details' in the Show/Hide area at the left of the Design ribbon. 'Show Details' in the same

section will toggle them back on. You can hide or show details for one store by clicking '–' (hide) or '+' (show) under the store's city.

8 This is called a 'pivot table' because you can *pivot* data

OrderQry

Drop Filter Fields Here

	Drop Column Fields Here
StoreCity	**Average of OrderPrice**
Atlanta	$932.63
Boston	$832.86
Chicago	$871.29
Denver	$989.55
Grand Total	$898.81

from the top to the left and vice versa to make it easier to analyse. Drag the StoreCity label from its current position, above the city names, to the 'Drop Column Fields Here' area at the top of the table. Hide and show details. See how the display changes.

Usage hint: If you get an error message when you move the label, delete one of the totals and re-create it. To delete a total, right-click it in the field list and select Delete, the only item in the drop-down menu that appears.

9 Select Show Details, if they are not already showing, to display order prices. Select it by clicking OrderPrice near the top of any city column. Under AutoCalc, display the sum and the count. One store has the highest total sales but the smallest average sale. Why?

10 Close the query, saving changes when prompted.

11 We want to analyse our sales by city. Open ItemsQry. The TotPrice column in this table is not in the database. It is a calculated field: it is derived on the fly by multiplying the price of the product (in ProductTbl, for consistency across all orders) and the quantity in a given order. Switch to PivotTable view.

Usage hint: If you are curious about how calculated fields work, switch to Design View of the query and look at the rightmost column in the lower pane. You will have to make the column wider to see the entire formula, but it is not complicated.

Now, move TotPrice into the main section of the pivot table pane and StoreCity into the Row Fields section. Select TotPrice in the pivot table, add its sum, and click Hide Details in the Show/Hide section of the ribbon.

12 It seems that Boston sold more during the period than any of the other stores. To find out why, we must *drill down* into the data. (Drilling down is central to most data analysis.) Add ProdCategory to the pivot table as a column field. What you get should look like this:

ItemsQry

Drop Filter Fields Here

		Drop Column Fields Here
StoreCity	**ProdCategory**	**Sum of TotPrice**
⊟ Atlanta	CPU	$7,889.00
	Display	$2,851.00
	Memory	$959.87
	Portable	$4,891.00
	Printer	$2,419.89
	Storage	$2,439.68
	Total	$21,450.44
⊟ Boston	CPU	$10,085.00

Usage hint: If your product categories ended up to the left of the city names, just select its name at the top of the column and drag it to the right until a thick blue line shows up to the right of the StoreCity column. Then release your mouse button.

13 You realise that this table is not easy to interpret. A chart would be better. Choose Pivot Chart view from the drop-down menu at the left end of the ribbon, or click the Pivot Chart icon at the bottom right of the Access window. Add a legend with the tool in the Show/Hide section of the Design ribbon.

14 You now realise that this is not the ideal chart design. It tells us that Atlanta, for example, got more revenue from CPUs than from memory, but anyone who knows computers would expect that. We would like to know how Atlanta compares with other stores in terms of memory revenue. Click Switch Row/Column in the Active Field section of the Design ribbon. You should get a chart whose lower left corner looks like this:

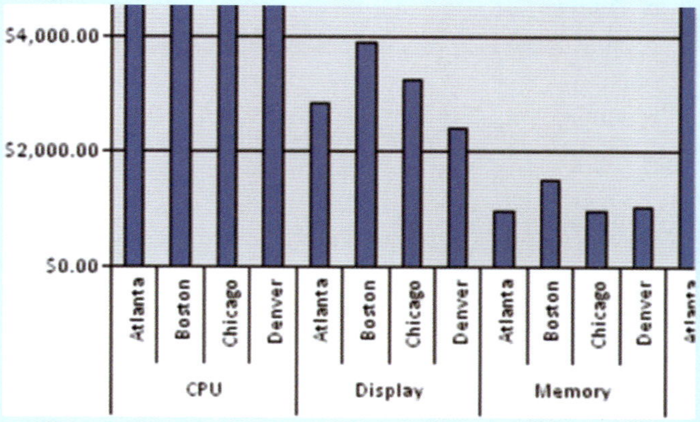

Usage hint: If your chart does not look like this, try returning to PivotTable view, swapping categories and cities by dragging one column past the other and returning to the chart. You may have to switch chart row and columns again.

15 From the part of this chart above the screen shot, we see that Chicago's CPU sales are a concern. Before calling the Chicago store manager, however, we need to do more research. Go back to PivotTable view and drag ProdDescrip into the row field area. Each category will be broken down by product. To see only products in the CPU category, click the down arrow next to ProdCategory to get a list of categories to filter. Uncheck everything except CPU and confirm.

Usage hint: Rather than unchecking all the categories except the one we care about, it is easier to uncheck everything by clicking 'All', then check 'CPU'.

16 Now look at the chart again. The Chicago store did not sell any SuperCPUs! Its sales of the three slower models are more or less in line with expectations. We do not know the reason for this, of course. Maybe there are few gamers and graphic artists in the store's sales area. (These are two major markets for top-of-the-line systems.) Maybe the Chicago store ran a promotion for these during an earlier period and most of its potential customers bought one then. Maybe a competitor is running such a promo now. We do know, however, what we want to ask when we call the Chicago store manager.

17 Close your database, saving changes when prompted.

DELIVERABLE

1 Your database, with the most recent pivot table and chart.

2 Answers to the questions in items 6 and 9 on the previous pages, in the form specified by your instructor.

QUIZ QUESTIONS

1 In step 6, which store had the highest average order amount?
   - a Atlanta
   - b Boston
   - c Chicago
   - d Denver

2 A pivot table is a way of looking at this type of Access object:
   - a Query
   - b Table
   - c Form
   - d Either A or B
   - e Either B or C

3 The central section of the pivot table pane contains this type of information:
   - a Names of pivot table categories
   - b Summary data for pivot table cells
   - c Individual data elements from the database, but not totals
   - d Links to the underlying Access tables

4 If a pivot table has only one column (that is, it has categories down the left but none across the top), then:
   - a You can create categories across the top by dragging categories from the side.
   - b You can create categories across the top by dragging new table fields into the 'Drag Column Fields Here' area.
   - c You can analyse data in that column without having fields across the top.
   - d All of the above are correct.

DISCUSSION QUESTIONS

1 How could pivot tables be useful for someone in the kind of job you hope to have after you graduate? (Say what that job is.)

2 Describe a business decision for which pivot tables would *not* be helpful. Explain why you don't think they would help with it.

3 Suppose you worked for a large chain of photo stores. Your database has millions of rows with a few dozen columns in each, but its structure is much like this one. Would that change your approach to using pivot tables? If so, how? (Assume your computer is fast enough that the database size does not cause slow response times. In practice, that might not be true.)

6
Ethics and privacy

CHAPTER OUTLINE

LEARNING OBJECTIVES

1. Describe the four categories of ethical issues related to information technology.
2. Discuss potential threats to the privacy of personal data stored in different locations.

OPENING CASE >

Big brother watching you work

You probably consider yourself an honest person who would never deliberately break the law, correct? You certainly would not go into a retail store and steal a DVD, or go to a bookshop and take a book without paying. However, do you download or share music and films that you did not pay for? Would you copy an image from someone else's blog and claim it as your own? Would you download an obscure article or essay, customise it and claim it as your own original work?

What about at work? Would you read a colleague's printouts or personal emails without their knowledge? What if you were an employer? Would you monitor your employees' internet usage and track their history? Would you install key logging software on work-issued devices without their knowledge? With many mobile devices incorporating GPS (global positioning system) capabilities, would you monitor the movements of your mobile fleet?

Your immediate response may be that you would not engage in these activities because it is mistrustful, deceitful, dishonest or potentially illegal. However, these issues are very important considerations as the capabilities and innovations of modern technologies continue to diffuse throughout our daily lives as we become ever more interconnected both at home and at work. This is more apparent when we consider the profound impact that social networks now play in most of our lives, enabling us to easily share and re-share information to the extent of blurring the actual ownership of information posted on the internet.

Applications that track the location of employees are transforming the day-to-day operation of workforces. The costs of installing GPS tracking devices have significantly decreased in recent years, enabling large multinationals right down to small business and local government to monitor their mobile fleets. Putting aside the technological capabilities, is it ethical — or indeed legal — to use GPS software to trace employees' whereabouts?

Consider the recent case of a New Zealand maintenance worker being dismissed as a result of information garnered through GPS technology. The Nelson City Council worker submitted false timesheets, claiming overtime pay when in fact the GPS device fitted to his truck revealed he was at home, not work during that period. The New Zealand Employee Relations Authority upheld the dismissal, stating the behaviour of the worker constituted 'serious misconduct'.

However, GPS surveillance in the workplace can also pose significant risks for employers. New South Wales and Victoria are the only states that have legislation specifically addressing workplace surveillance. Both states demand strict procedures for employers to comply in obtaining permission to perform covert surveillance on their employees. In New South Wales, surveillance by GPS tracking must not commence without prior written notice to each of the employees in question, and notice has to be given two weeks before the actual surveillance begins.

Some Australian fleet tracking programs have tried to allay employers' fears of breaching their workers' privacy by enabling a 'register as invisible' function, so that employees are not able to be tracked during lunch breaks or when they are off duty.

Sources: M Backhouse (2012), 'Worker sacked for overstating work hours', *The New Zealand Herald*, www.nzherald.co.nz/nz/news/article.cfm_worker_sacked_for_overstating_work_hours.html; G Hanrahan (2012), *GPS tracking in work vehicles: Make sure it's legal!*, Turnbull Hill Lawyers, www.turnbullhill.com.au/articles/gps-tracking-in-work-vehicles-make-sure-it-s-legal.html; M Papadakis (2013), 'New ways to watch your workers', *BRW*, www.brw.com.au/p/new_ways_to_watch_your_workers.html; WorkplaceInfo (2013), *Surveillance in the workplace*, www.workplaceinfo.com.au/resources/employment-topics-a-z/surveillance-in-the-workplace.html.

QUESTIONS

1. From an employer's perspective, does the benefit of ongoing surveillance of workers outweigh the presumption of privacy? Please provide a rationale for your response.
2. When is it appropriate to be tracking employees' assets and by association their representatives outside business hours?
3. If a company owns a device, such as a company-issued iPad, should employees expect any data they communicate through that device to be tracked?

Introduction

You will study two major issues in this chapter: ethics and privacy.

You will encounter numerous ethical and privacy issues in your career, many of which will involve IT in some manner. This chapter will give you insights into how to respond to these issues. Further, it will help you to make immediate contributions to your company's code of ethics and its privacy policies. You will also be able to provide meaningful input concerning the potential ethical and privacy impacts of your organisation's information systems on people inside and outside the organisation.

THE NOOK

Malakai and Abbie have never developed an ethics and privacy statement for their club. They never thought they would need one. But with the new information systems that will collect customer data and establish memberships, they realise it is now imperative that they develop a statement of this type.

Malakai and Abbie have both seen privacy statements. They get them in the mail from their credit card companies and agree to them any time they create their own memberships online. However, they have never really paid attention to them and now have a lot of questions about their own statements.

Obviously, they know they need to deal with how they will handle the privacy of online information. But they are unsure of how to deal with ethical issues in their club. Should they use their information systems to track the number of alcoholic beverages their customers purchase? If they do, is it ethical to limit a customer? Should they request a release form to continue to sell drinks after a certain point?

Use the information in this chapter to help them make these decisions.

For example, suppose your organisation decides to adopt web 2.0 technologies to include business partners and customers in new product development. You will be able to analyse the potential privacy and ethical implications of implementing these technologies.

6.1 Ethical issues

Ethics refers to the principles of right and wrong that individuals use to make choices that guide their behaviours. Deciding what is right or wrong is not always easy or clear-cut. Fortunately, many frameworks are available to help us make ethical decisions.

Ethical frameworks

There are many sources for ethical standards. Here we consider four widely used standards: the utilitarian approach, the rights approach, the fairness approach and the common good approach. There are many other sources, but these four are representative.

The *utilitarian approach* states that an ethical action is the one that provides the most good or does the least harm. The ethical corporate action would be the one that produces the greatest good and does the least harm for all affected parties — customers, employees, shareholders, the community and the environment.

The *rights approach* maintains that an ethical action is the one that best protects and respects the moral rights of the affected parties. Moral rights can include the rights to make one's own choices about what kind of life to lead, to be told the truth, not to be injured and to a degree of privacy. Which of these rights people are actually entitled to — and under what circumstances — is widely debated. Nevertheless, most people acknowledge that individuals are entitled to some moral rights. An ethical organisational action would be one that protects and respects the moral rights of customers, employees, shareholders, business partners and even competitors.

The *fairness approach* posits that ethical actions treat all human beings equally, or, if unequally, then fairly, based on some defensible standard. For example, most people might

All ethical frameworks attempt to balance good for all.

believe it is fair to pay people higher salaries if they work harder or if they contribute a greater amount to the firm. However, there is less certainty regarding CEO salaries that are hundreds or thousands of times larger than those of other employees. Many people question whether this huge disparity is based on a defensible standard or whether it is the result of an imbalance of power and hence is unfair.

The *common good approach* highlights the interlocking relationships that underlie all societies. This approach argues that respect and compassion for all others is the basis for ethical actions. It emphasises the common conditions that are important to the welfare of everyone. These conditions can include a system of laws, effective police and fire departments, health care, a public educational system and even public recreation areas.

If we combine these four standards, we can develop a general framework for ethics or ethical decision making (figure 6.1). This framework consists of five steps.

- Recognise an ethical issue.
  - Could this decision or situation damage someone or some group?
  - Does this decision involve a choice between a good and bad alternative?
  - Is this issue about more than what is legal? If so, how?
- Get the facts.
  - What are the relevant facts of the situation?
  - Do I know enough to make a decision?
  - Which individuals and/or groups have an important stake in the outcome?
  - Have I consulted all relevant persons and groups?
- Evaluate alternative actions.
  - Which option will produce the most good and do the least harm? (the utilitarian approach)
  - Which option best respects the rights of all stakeholders? (the rights approach)
  - Which option treats people equally or proportionately? (the fairness approach)
  - Which option best serves the community as a whole, and not just some members? (the common good approach)
- Make a decision and test it.
  - Considering all the approaches, which option best addresses the situation?
- Act and reflect on the outcome of your decision.
  - How can I implement my decision with the greatest care and attention to the concerns of all stakeholders?
  - How did my decision turn out and what did I learn from this specific situation?

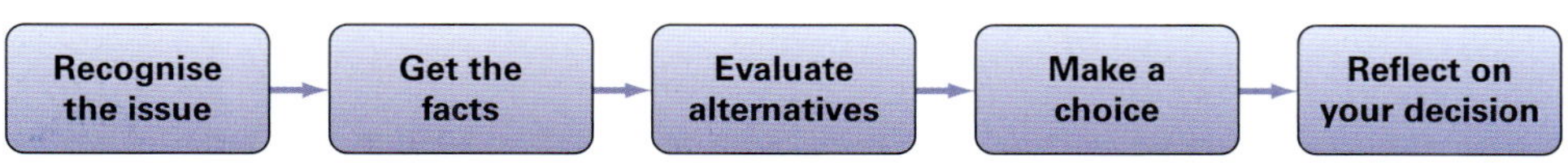

FIGURE 6.1 General framework for ethical decision making.

Now that we have created a general ethical framework, we will focus specifically on ethics in a corporate environment.

Ethics in the corporate environment

Many companies and professional organisations develop their own codes of ethics. A **code of ethics** is a collection of principles that are intended to guide decision making by members of the organisation. For example, the Australian Computer Society (ACS), an organisation of computing professionals, has a thoughtful code of ethics for its members.[1]

Keep in mind that different codes of ethics are not always consistent with one another. Therefore, an individual might be expected to conform to multiple codes. For example, a person who is a member of two large professional computing-related organisations may be required by one organisation to comply with all applicable laws and at the same time be required by the other organisation to refuse to obey unjust laws.

Fundamental tenets of ethics include responsibility, accountability and liability. **Responsibility** means that you accept the consequences of your decisions and actions. **Accountability** refers to determining who is responsible for actions that were taken. **Liability** is a legal concept that gives individuals the right to recover the damages done to them by other individuals, organisations, or systems.

Before you go any further, it is very important that you realise that what is *unethical* is not necessarily *illegal*. For example, a bank's decision to foreclose on a home can be technically legal, but it can raise many ethical questions. In many instances, then, an individual or organisation faced with an ethical decision is not considering whether to break the law. As the foreclosure example illustrates, however, ethical decisions can have serious consequences for individuals, organisations and society at large.

In recent years we have witnessed a large number of extremely poor ethical decisions, not to mention outright criminal behaviour. At the beginning of 2001 One.Tel was the fourth largest telecommunications company in Australia but it collapsed in May 2001 with more than two million customers and operations in eight countries. It is suggested that One.Tel's rapid rise and sudden collapse was associated with poor corporate governance practices relating to internal systems control, financial reporting, audit quality, failed expectations, poor strategic decisions, poor pricing policy and unchecked growth. This and other corporate collapses at the time were the catalyst for the development of an Australian Standard, *AS/NZS ISO/IEC 38500:2010: Corporate Governance of Information Technology*, for the governance of and effective, efficient and acceptable use of information technology in all organisations.[2]

More recently, the subprime mortgage crisis exposed unethical lending practices throughout the mortgage industry. The crisis also highlighted pervasive weaknesses in the regulation of the US financial industry as well as the global financial system. It ultimately contributed to a deep recession in the global economy.

Improvements in information technologies have generated a new set of ethical problems. Computing processing power doubles about every two years according to Moore's Law, meaning that organisations are more dependent than ever before on their information systems. Organisations can store increasing amounts of data at decreasing cost, enabling them to store more data on individuals for longer periods of time. Computer networks, particularly the internet, enable organisations to collect, integrate and distribute enormous amounts of information on individuals, groups and institutions. As a result, ethical problems are arising concerning the appropriate collection and use of customer information, personal **privacy** and the protection of intellectual property, as IT's About Business illustrates.

IT'S ABOUT BUSINESS

Know thy customer

Recent studies show that Australians are sharing more information about themselves than ever before, and yet they continue to be concerned about their privacy being compromised, especially since marketers are increasingly collecting online information about their spending practices. Add to this the popular growth and use of Facebook among Australian users, and it soon becomes apparent how much information customers are providing through social network engagement with business organisations.

As a consequence, Facebook is able to track where its users shop, how much they spend, how often they purchase and the actual items purchased. This is enabling Facebook to develop consumer profiles utilising its marketing tool Custom Audience that allows advertisers to identify individual users via their Facebook ID, email or phone number. Facebook can now directly target users with specific advertisements based on their shopping habits. Coupled with deals with large data collection organisations running retailer loyalty programs that collect data relating to customer offline purchases, this represents a powerful marketing capability that can be directed at the individual user level.

Access to this data and information empowers marketers with the capability to customise Facebook advertisements specifically to users through enabling a business to integrate information they have already collected about the customer with information received from third parties to create customer campaigns on Facebook, or even create customer-specific programs. This level of refined marketing capability enables businesses of any size to target specific categories of customers based on their online and offline shopping history and preferences.

The principal fear with this direct individual marketing approach is privacy, with the concern being that Facebook is effectively providing marketers with very valuable personal information about its users' shopping habits, although Facebook denies that any personal information is exchanged between Facebook, marketers and third party organisations. Instead they use de-identified or 'hashes' of customer information to create audience groups, ensuring that when marketers advertise to these audiences they only get back anonymous aggregated advertisement reporting data.

What organisations have realised is that vast amounts of data is easily accessible through customer use of technology, and marketing and sales are driving the analysis of this data to personalise, proactively engage and target their marketing at the individual level. The primary goal is to develop a '360 degree' view of customer activity. Organisations are continuing to invest significant time and money to analyse the unstructured data from Twitter and Facebook using advanced analytics tools to derive insights.

Facebook is one example that exemplifies the push to combine or blend together all structured, unstructured, internal and external data sources to develop an insightful and unified view of the customer, based on their online activities. The intention is to create a better and intuitive customer experience through leveraging the advantages that technology provides. Other industries, such as banking and insurance, are also well advanced in plotting their marketing strategies accordingly.

Business organisations see a lot of benefit in making their interactions with customers more personalised and relevant to their needs, which is progressing towards a more 'sense and respond' customer relationship. However, the main barrier remains the consideration of privacy and this approach exemplifies where technology and audience sentiment have outpaced legislation.

Furthermore, unstructured social data and consumer activity data are not the only types of data being used to deliver better outcomes for customers. For example, the (not-for-profit) health insurer HCF utilises health statistics provided by the federal government. Their analysis of this data is used to generate a greater understanding of their customer needs, for improved product development and to better understand what their clients want to claim for and how much.

From the health statistics, HCF can generate a view of how many members in a particular postcode have suffered a disease, or the age demographic, which is then used to inform the overall claiming process and the calculation of benefits and likely claims. However, with the unstructured nature of social media data it is much harder to integrate with specific customer records and therefore, many organisations only monitor social media for sentiment analysis and ad hoc responses to questions or complaints, rather than for customer acquisition or proactive marketing purposes.

Another example is the National Australia Bank (NAB) which is an extensive user of social media. In 2012 NAB established a specific centre to monitor different social media channels and to analyse and provide feedback to the bank about social media activities and conversations. The proposition is to create business benefits, valuable products and service propositions for NAB customers, although the challenge remains to turn these propositions into valuable products that customers appreciate and are willing to pay a premium for.

The difficult issue surrounds the association and level of certainty of integrating social media data with a specific customer's need. It is almost impossible to be confident with such propositions and yet even allowing for errors of assumption, the potential for targeted marketing remains very attractive, particularly when you consider that a person who indicates that they have booked a holiday may be interested in travel insurance, or another discussing a wedding with friends may be a candidate for a personal loan.

Sources: B Howarth (2013), 'The new faces of customer management', *CIO*, 15 July, www.cio.com.au; N Khadem (2013), '"Creepy" targeted ads spooking Australians worried about loss of privacy', *Business Review Weekly*, 13 June, www.brw.com.au; J Linde (2013), 'Facebook knows where you shop, even offline', *Business Review Weekly*, 1 March, www.brw.com.au.

QUESTIONS

1. Describe the ethical implications of data collection, blending and analysis as discussed.
2. Is it ethical to utilise customer data in this manner for targeted marketing purposes?
3. What are the potential ethical implications for any incorrect assumptions drawn from data analysis and individual marketing?
4. Describe the potential privacy implications. Is it unethical to utilise customer data as discussed?

Should organisations audit employees' computers for unauthorised software or illegally downloaded music or video files?

The diversity and ever-expanding use of IT applications have created a variety of ethical issues. These issues fall into four general categories: privacy, accuracy, property and accessibility.

1 *Privacy issues* involve collecting, storing and disseminating information about individuals.
2 *Accuracy issues* involve the authenticity, fidelity and accuracy of information that is collected and processed.
3 *Property issues* involve the ownership and value of information.
4 *Accessibility issues* revolve around who should have access to information and whether they should have to pay for this access.

Figure 6.2 lists representative questions and issues for each of these categories. Many of the issues and scenarios we have examined, such as photo tagging and geotagging, involve privacy as well as ethics. In the next section, you will learn about privacy issues in more detail.

BEFORE YOU GO ON . . .

1 What does a code of ethics contain?
2 Describe the fundamental tenets of ethics.

- **Privacy issues**
  - What information about oneself should an individual be required to reveal to others?
  - What kind of surveillance can an employer use on its employees?
  - What types of personal information can people keep to themselves and not be forced to reveal to others?
  - What information about individuals should be kept in databases and how secure is the information there?
- **Accuracy issues**
  - Who is responsible for the authenticity, fidelity and accuracy of the information collected?
  - How can we ensure that the information will be processed properly and presented accurately to users?
  - How can we ensure that errors in databases, data transmissions and data processing are accidental and not intentional?
  - Who is to be held accountable for errors in information and how should the injured parties be compensated?
- **Property issues**
  - Who owns the information?
  - What are the just and fair prices for its exchange?
  - How should we handle software piracy (copying copyrighted software)?
  - Under what circumstances can one use proprietary databases?
  - Can corporate computers be used for private purposes?
  - How should experts who contribute their knowledge to create expert systems be compensated?
  - How should access to information channels be allocated?
- **Accessibility issues**
  - Who is allowed to access information?
  - How much should companies charge for permitting accessibility to information?
  - How can accessibility to computers be provided for employees with disabilities?
  - Who will be provided with equipment needed for accessing information?
  - What information does a person or an organisation have a right to obtain, under what conditions and with what safeguards?

FIGURE 6.2 A framework for ethical issues.

Apply the Concept

Background

As you move into the business world, you need to be aware of the current trends and happenings dealing with the four areas of concern presented in figure 6.2 (privacy, property, accuracy and accessibility). It is important that you are aware of these issues as you move into the business world because these are the exact issues you will have to deal with.

Activity

Review various articles in mainstream, business and IS/IT-related sources and identify articles with an IT ethical issue in the article. Mainstream sources might include *The Age, Sydney Morning Herald* and *The Australian*. Business sources might include the *Australian Financial Review* and *Business Review Weekly*. IS/IT-related sources might include *PC World Australia, Australian Personal Computer (APC), PC & Tech Authority and Macworld Australia*.

Review (scan for the main topic) at least two articles from a mainstream source, a business source and an IS/IT-related source, then classify the articles based upon the four categories of ethical issues (privacy, property, accuracy and accessibility) found in Section 6.1. Note that more than one category may apply to the same article.

Deliverable

Create a table to submit to your lecturer that identifies the following:

- article's title
- source of the article (mainstream, business, or IS/IT-related)
- ethical category or categories in the article (they may fall into multiple areas)
- summary of the article's main points.

THE NOOK

QUESTIONS

1. Which framework do you think is the best for The Nook: utilitarian, rights, fairness, or the common good? Why do you feel this way?
2. How do the concepts of responsibility, accountability and liability play into the number of drinks an individual has consumed? At what point does The Nook become responsible for the condition in which a customer leaves the club?
3. Because purchase does not necessarily equal consumption (perhaps the person is buying drinks for a friend), should The Nook limit the number of drinks a customer can purchase?

6.2 Privacy

In Australia, privacy law relates to the protection of an individual's personal information which could identify you or could be used to reasonably identify you.[3]

The *Privacy Act 1988* regulates how personal information is handled and includes information such as:

- your name or address
- bank account details and credit card information
- photos
- information about your opinions and what you like.

As an individual the Privacy Act gives you greater control over the way your personal information is handled. The Privacy Act allows you to:

- know why your personal information is being collected, how it will be used and who it will be disclosed to
- ask for access to your records (including your health information)
- stop receiving unwanted direct marketing material
- correct inaccurate information about you
- make a complaint about an agency or organisation, if you think that they have mishandled your personal information.[4]

The Privacy Act is not prescriptive about the way in which personal information is handled by individuals and business. Additionally, there are differing privacy regimes in some states and territories that regulate the way state and territory government agencies handle information.

The Privacy Act includes 10 national privacy principles (NPPs) that apply to certain public sector organisations and 11 information privacy principles (IPPs) that apply to Australian, ACT and Norfolk Island agencies.

The IPPs and NPPs require that each agency or organisation apply these principles according to their own circumstance. The principles cover:

- how personal information is collected
- how it is used and disclosed
- maintaining the quality of the information
- keeping it secure
- general rights for individuals to access and correct their information.

The Privacy Act also covers more specific matters, such as:

- the use of tax file numbers
- how credit worthiness information is handled by credit reporting agencies and credit providers
- the handling of health or medical information.

The Privacy Act places obligations on agencies and organisations with regard to handling 'sensitive information' with particular care. Sensitive information includes:

- an individual's racial or ethnic origin
- health and medical information
- political opinion
- membership of a political association, professional or trade association or trade union
- religious beliefs or affiliations
- philosophical beliefs
- sexual preferences or practices
- criminal record
- genetic information.

Some other concepts that can be related to privacy are as follows.

- Confidentiality: this refers to communication between individuals with an inherently private relationship; for example, the medical practitioner and patient, lawyer and client, source and journalist, or individual and their spiritual adviser.
- Secrecy: this generally refers to laws that impose an obligation of confidentiality in relation to handling government information.
- Freedom of information: this refers to the public's right to access government information.

Although these matters are not regulated directly by the Privacy Act, in most cases there are other Australian laws that regulate these matters.[5]

Rapid advances in information technologies have made it much easier to collect, store and integrate data on individuals in large databases. On an average day, you generate data about yourself in many ways: surveillance cameras on toll roads, in public places and at work; credit card transactions; telephone calls (landline and mobile); banking transactions; queries to search engines; and government records.

Electronic surveillance

The *Surveillance Devices Bill 2004* regulates the use of surveillance devices (data, optical, listening and tracking devices) by law enforcement agencies and significantly widens the circumstances in which they can be used and the types that can be used.

The Bill seeks to regulate the use of data surveillance, optical surveillance, listening and tracking devices by the Australian Federal Police, the Australian Crime Commission and State/Territory police investigating Commonwealth offences. It significantly widens the existing range of offences for which surveillance devices can be used as part of an investigation and the type of devices that can be used.[6]

This complex and lengthy Bill raises a number of serious issues in relation to the appropriate balance between individuals' privacy and freedom from surveillance and the legitimate needs of law enforcement agencies. Among other things, it enables Federal Police to obtain *data surveillance* warrants permitting them to covertly install key logging devices in computers.[7]

In general, employees have very limited legal protection against surveillance by employers. The law supports the right of employers to read their employees' email and other electronic documents and to monitor their employees' internet use. Today, more than three-quarters of organisations are monitoring employees' internet usage. In addition, two-thirds use software to block connections to inappropriate websites, a practice called *URL filtering*. Further, organisations are installing, monitoring and filtering software to enhance security by stopping malicious software and to increase productivity by discouraging employees from wasting time.

In one organisation, the chief information officer (CIO) monitored about 13 000 employees for three months to determine the type of traffic they engaged in on the network. He then forwarded the data to the chief executive officer (CEO) and the heads of the human resources and legal departments. These executives were shocked at the questionable websites the employees were visiting, as well as the amount of time they were spending on those sites. The executives quickly made the decision to implement a URL filtering product.

Surveillance is also a concern for private individuals regardless of whether it is conducted by corporations, government bodies, or criminals and finding the appropriate balance between personal privacy and **electronic surveillance** is especially difficult where threats to national security are concerned.

Electronic surveillance of employees is legal, but not of customers. But would you do it if you could make money from the information?

Personal information in databases

Modern institutions store information about individuals in many databases. Perhaps the most visible locations of such records are credit-reporting agencies. Other institutions that store personal information include:

- banks and financial institutions
- cable TV, telephone and utilities companies
- employers
- mortgage companies
- hospitals
- schools and universities
- retail establishments
- government agencies (such as the Australian Taxation Office, your state, your town council or shire).

There are several concerns about the information you provide to these record keepers. Some of the major concerns are these:

- Do you know where the records are?
- Are the records accurate?
- Can you change inaccurate data?
- How long will it take to make a change?

- Under what circumstances will personal data be released?
- How are the data used?
- To whom are the data given or sold?
- How secure are the data against access by unauthorised people?

Information on internet bulletin boards, newsgroups and social networking sites

Every day you see more and more *electronic bulletin boards*, *newsgroups*, *electronic discussions* such as chat rooms and *social networking sites*. These sites appear on the internet, within corporate intranets and on blogs. A *blog*, short for *weblog*, is an informal, personal journal that is frequently updated and intended for general public reading. How does society keep owners of bulletin boards from disseminating information that may be offensive to readers or simply untrue? This is a difficult problem because it involves the conflict between freedom of speech on one hand and privacy on the other. This conflict is a fundamental and continuing ethical issue in Australian society.

There is no better illustration of the conflict between free speech and privacy than the internet. Many websites contain anonymous, derogatory information on individuals, who typically have little recourse in the matter. Many organisations now use the internet in examining job applications, including searching for individuals on Google and on social networking sites. Consequently, derogatory information that can be found on the internet can harm your chances of being hired. This problem has become serious enough that specialised businesses will search for damaging content online and destroy it on behalf of clients.

Social networking sites can also present serious privacy concerns. IT's About Business takes a look at privacy problems arising as the government mines publicly available data on the internet.

Privacy codes and policies

Privacy policies or **privacy codes** are an organisation's guidelines for protecting the privacy of its customers, clients and employees. In many corporations, senior management has begun to understand that when an organisation collects vast amounts of personal information, it must be protected. In addition, many organisations give their customers some voice in how their information is used by providing them with opt-out choices. The **opt-out model** of informed consent permits an entity to collect personal information until the individual specifically requests that the data not be collected. Privacy advocates prefer the **opt-in model** of informed consent, which prohibits an entity from collecting any personal information unless the individual specifically authorises it.

IT'S ABOUT BUSINESS

AFP and Australians' private data

Revelations emerged from a 2013 Senate estimates hearing that the Australian Federal Police (AFP) were trying to access Facebook and Google data similar to that gathered by the US National Security Agency's (NSA) controversial PRISM program. This draws Australia into the fierce global debate about secret surveillance, after US whistleblower Edward Snowden leaked sensitive details of the NSA's surveillance program.

Privacy advocates and experts believe that Australians' data would undoubtedly be included in the data collected and gathered by the PRISM program, which taps directly into the world's largest technology organisations including Facebook, Google and Apple. This raises questions about whether the AFP, law enforcement and Australian intelligence organisations were receiving any data directly from the NSA's PRISM program activities.

The AFP deputy commissioner told the Senate hearing that for the last financial year the AFP made 43 362 internal requests relating to Australians' telephone and internet records. Such information requests require no application for a warrant prior, with the AFP able to request the telephone number called, the duration and time of day of the call. In 2010–11 the AFP made 50 841 requests.

A spokesperson for the online lobby group Electronic Frontier Australia stated that it was highly likely that

Australians' private data was gathered and collected by the NSA surveillance program, because many Australians had created online accounts and profiles that existed on US servers. Furthermore, given the close working relationship between US and Australian intelligence agencies, it is not impossible to suspect that the NSA may have been sharing information collected on Australians with Australian intelligence agencies.

In broader terms, the US government implemented the NSA's PRISM program in 2007 under the guise of the 'war on terror' and proceeded with collecting data from Microsoft, Apple, Facebook, Google, Skype and so on, which were not allowed to reveal that they were passing data to the US government. The program secretly trawled the telecommunications networks of the world for information on not only potential terrorism activity, but any other subject pertaining to US interests.

Foreign governments were very angry that the NSA had been targeting them. Countries targeted included not only the obvious candidates of China and Russia, but also US allies such as France, Italy, Greece, Japan and South Korea. However, foreign protests will not force the closure of the PRISM program as it would in all likelihood be renamed and re-hidden as the US government seeks an advantage by knowing everyone else's secrets.

Sources: G Dyer (2013), 'Making examples of whistle-blowers', *Otago Daily Times*, 16 July, www.odt.co.nz/opinion; D Wroe (2013), 'Federal police spying on phone and internet records', *The Age*, 11 June, www.theage.com.au/it-pro.

QUESTIONS

1 Discuss the ethical and privacy implications of data collection on this scale.

2 Would data collection on this scale change the way you use the internet and online organisations like Google and Facebook? Explain how.

One privacy tool currently available to consumers is the Platform for Privacy Preferences (P3P), a protocol that automatically communicates privacy policies between an electronic commerce website and visitors to that site. P3P enables visitors to determine the types of personal data that can be extracted by the websites they visit. It also allows visitors to compare a website's privacy policy to the visitors' preferences or to other standards, such as the Federal Trade Commission's (FTC) Fair Information Practices Standard or the European Directive on Data Protection. Therefore, P3P can help to inform users about website privacy practices and more importantly, develop predictable behaviour when blocking user data collecting content like cookies and is a real incentive for e-commerce websites to behave in a privacy friendly manner.[8]

Figure 6.3 provides a sampling of privacy policy guidelines. It is important to note that all the good privacy intentions in the world are useless unless they are supported and enforced by effective security measures.

- **Data collection**
  - Data should be collected on individuals only for the purpose of accomplishing a legitimate business objective.
  - Data should be adequate, relevant and not excessive in relation to the business objective.
  - Individuals must give their consent before data pertaining to them can be gathered. Such consent may be implied from the individual's actions (e.g. applications for credit, insurance, or employment).
- **Data accuracy**
  - Sensitive data gathered on individuals should be verified before they are entered into the database.
  - Data should, where and when necessary, be kept current.
  - The file should be made available so the individual can ensure that the data are correct.
  - If there is disagreement about the accuracy of the data, the individual's version should be noted and included with any disclosure of the file.
- **Data confidentiality**
  - Computer security procedures should be implemented to ensure against unauthorised disclosure of data. These procedures should include physical, technical, and administrative security measures.
  - Third parties should not be given access to data without the individual's knowledge or permission, except as required by law.
  - Disclosures of data, other than the most routine, should be noted and maintained for as long as the data are maintained.
  - Data should not be disclosed for reasons incompatible with the business objective for which they are collected.

FIGURE 6.3 Privacy policy guidelines: a sampler.

International aspects of privacy

As the number of online users has increased globally, governments throughout the world have enacted a large number of inconsistent privacy and security laws. This highly complex global legal framework is creating regulatory problems for companies. Approximately 50 countries have some form of data-protection laws. Many of these laws conflict with those of other countries, or they require specific security measures. Other countries have no privacy laws at all.

The absence of consistent or uniform standards for privacy and security obstructs the flow of information among countries, which is called *transborder data flows*. The European Union (EU), for one, has taken steps to overcome this problem. In 1998 the European Community Commission (ECC) issued guidelines to all its member countries regarding the rights of individuals to access information about themselves. The EU data-protection laws are stricter than US laws and thus could create problems for multinational corporations, which could face lawsuits for privacy violation.

The transfer of data in and out of a nation without the knowledge of either the authorities or the individuals involved raises a number of privacy issues. Whose laws have jurisdiction when records are stored in a different country for reprocessing or retransmission purposes? For example, if data are transmitted by a Polish company through a US satellite to a British corporation, which country's privacy laws control the data and when? Questions like these will become more complicated and frequent as time passes. Governments must make an effort to develop laws and standards to cope with rapidly changing information technologies in order to solve some of these privacy issues.

The United States and the EU share the goal of privacy protection for their citizens, but the United States takes a different approach. To bridge the different privacy approaches, the US Department of Commerce, in consultation with the EU, developed a 'safe harbour' framework to regulate the way that US companies export and handle the personal data (such as names and addresses) of European citizens.

BEFORE YOU GO ON . . .

1 Describe the issue of privacy as it is affected by IT.
2 Discuss how privacy issues can affect transborder data flows.

Apply the Concept

Background

Privacy is the right to be left alone and to be free of unreasonable personal intrusions. **Information privacy** is the right to determine when, and to what extent, information about you can be gathered and/or communicated to others. And we are in control, right?

If so, then why do people seem to always fear big government? Now that the entire world is connected by the internet, it seems inevitable that people will fear the 'big brother' of the government spying on us and invading our privacy. However, as this section points out, the law usually allows the right of society to have information over an individual's right to privacy.

In 2002 the movie *Minority Report* presented a future time where a special police group was able to predict when and where crimes were going to happen. This group could arrest criminals before they committed the crime. In 2008 the movie *Eagle Eye* showed a computer system becoming so smart that it chose to abide by the US Constitution even if it meant having the president of the United States killed.

Activity

Movie night! If you have not seen the movies mentioned above, have a movie night and watch them from the perspective of privacy and information security. Talk to your friends about the movies and get their thoughts on these issues.

Deliverable

Summarise the movies and illustrate the privacy concerns they present. In your summary, attempt to answer the following question: At what point has data collection gone too far? When will consumers wake up and realise what is being stored? Will the government ever go as far as the movies present?

QUESTIONS

1. If privacy needs must be balanced against society's need to know information, at what point should The Nook inform a customer's friends (on Facebook or Twitter) that the customer is about to leave the club a little too intoxicated?
2. With their new network, Malakai and Abbie hope to offer wireless internet access. However, they are concerned about whether or not they should block certain websites. In particular, they want to be sure their customers are not using their network to download offensive material. Although it may not be illegal content, it may not be appropriate or representative of the atmosphere they want to present in their club. What are your thoughts?

WHAT'S IN IT FOR ME?

FOR THE ACCOUNTING MAJOR

Public companies, their accountants and auditors have significant information security responsibilities. Accountants are now being held professionally and personally responsible for reducing risk, eliminating fraud, increasing the transparency of transactions and ensuring compliance with generally accepted accounting principles (GAAP). Australian professional and legally recognised accounting bodies, including the Institute of Chartered Accountants (CA), Institute of Public Accountants (IPA), Certified Practising Accountants (CPA) and the Association of Chartered Certified Accountants (ACCA) require members to act ethically and monitor information security, fraud prevention and detection, and internal controls over financial reporting.[9] Forensic accounting, a combination of accounting and information security, is one of the most rapidly expanding areas in accounting today.

FOR THE FINANCE MAJOR

Because information security is essential to the success of modern organisations, it is no longer just the concern of the CIO. In the US context, as a result of global regulatory requirements and the passage of Sarbanes-Oxley, responsibility for information security lies with the CEO and the chief financial officer (CFO). In Australia compliance with the Corporate Law Economic Reform Program (Audit Reform and Corporate Disclosure) Act 2004 (CLERP 9) stipulates the obligations, measures, processes and procedures necessary to meet the Act relating particularly to those involved in auditing and company financial reporting. All aspects of the security audit, including the security of information and information systems, are key concerns for financial managers.[10]

FOR THE MARKETING MAJOR

Marketing professionals have new opportunities to collect data about their customers — for example, through business-to-consumer electronic commerce. Business ethics clearly mandate that these data should be used only within the company and should not be sold to anyone else. Marketers do not want to be sued for invasion of privacy over data collected for the marketing database.

Customers expect their data to be properly secured. However, profit-motivated criminals want that data. Therefore, marketing managers must analyse the risks of their operations. Failure to protect corporate and customer data will cause significant public relations problems and outrage customers. Customer relationship management operations and tracking customers' online buying habits can expose unencrypted data to misuse or result in privacy violations.

FOR THE PRODUCTION/OPERATIONS MANAGEMENT MAJOR

POM professionals decide whether to outsource (or offshore) manufacturing operations. In some cases, these operations are sent overseas to countries that do not have strict labour laws. This situation raises serious ethical questions. For example, is it ethical to hire employees in countries with poor working conditions in order to reduce labour costs?

FOR THE HUMAN RESOURCES MANAGEMENT MAJOR

Ethics are critically important to HR managers. HR policies explain the appropriate use of information technologies in the workplace. Questions such as these arise: Can employees use the internet, email or chat systems for personal purposes while at work? Is it ethical to monitor employees? If so, how? How much? How often? HR managers must formulate and enforce such policies while at the same time maintaining trusting relationships between employees and management.

FOR THE MIS MAJOR

Ethics might be more important for MIS personnel than for anyone else in the organisation, because these individuals have control of the information assets. They also have control over a huge amount of personal information on all employees. As a result, the MIS function must be held to the highest ethical standards. The chapter-closing case about Dunedin City Council considers the implications of internet usage for non-work related activities and the potential issues that can ensue.

SUMMARY

1 Describe the four categories of ethical issues related to information technology.

The major ethical issues related to IT are privacy, accuracy, property (including intellectual property) and accessibility to information. Privacy may be violated when data are held in databases or transmitted over networks. Privacy policies that address issues of data collection, data accuracy and data confidentiality can help organisations avoid legal problems.

2 Discuss potential threats to the privacy of personal data stored in different locations.

Threats to privacy include advances in information technologies, electronic surveillance and personal information in databases, internet bulletin boards, newsgroups and social networking sites. The personal threat in internet bulletin boards, newsgroups and social networking sites is that you might post too much information about yourself that many unknown people can see.

>>> CHAPTER GLOSSARY

accountability A tenet of ethics that refers to determining who is responsible for actions that were taken.

code of ethics A collection of principles that are intended to guide decision making by members of the organisation.

electronic surveillance Tracking people's activities with the aid of computers.

ethics The principles of right and wrong that individuals use to make choices to guide their behaviours.

information privacy The right to determine when, and to what extent, information about you can be gathered and/or communicated to others.

liability A legal concept that gives individuals the right to recover the damages done to them by other individuals, organisations, or systems.

opt-in model A model of informed consent that prohibits an entity from collecting any personal information unless the individual specifically authorises it.

opt-out model A model of informed consent that permits an entity to collect personal information unless the individual specifically requests that the data not be collected.

privacy The right to be left alone and to be free of unreasonable personal intrusions.

privacy codes (see privacy policies)

privacy policies (also known as privacy codes) An organisation's guidelines for protecting the privacy of customers, clients and employees.

responsibility A tenet of ethics whereby you accept the consequences of your decisions and actions.

>>> DISCUSSION QUESTIONS

1 Consider that you are a consultant that has been engaged to undertake the task of preparing a report for the board of management of an insurance company that is currently considering the implementation of electronic monitoring throughout its business process operations. Your task is to investigate and prepare an accurate report that considers the issues related to electronic monitoring of all business process operations, including staff actions, and make suitable recommendations. Your report should include a discussion of the current trend to use electronic monitoring to measure employee productivity and business process operations.
   a You are to make a recommendation to the board of management about what it should do. Include the principal ethical issues and the stakeholders involved.
   b Justify your ideas and recommendations relating to your analysis of how the impacts of electronic monitoring are likely to affect you personally, as an employee.

2 Frank Abagnale, the criminal played by Leonardo DiCaprio in the motion picture *Catch Me If You Can*, ended up in prison. However, when he left prison, he worked as a consultant to many companies on matters of fraud.
   a Why do companies hire perpetrators (if caught) as consultants? Is this a good idea?
   b You are the CEO of a company. Discuss the ethical implications of hiring Frank Abagnale as a consultant.

>>> PROBLEM-SOLVING ACTIVITIES

1 An information security manager routinely monitored the web surfing done by her company's employees. She discovered that many employees were visiting the 'sinful six' websites. (*Note:* The sinful six are websites with material related to pornography, gambling, hate, illegal activities, tastelessness and violence.) She then prepared a list of the employees and their surfing histories and gave the list to management. Some managers punished their employees. Some employees, in turn, objected to the monitoring, claiming that they should have a right to privacy.
   a Is monitoring of web surfing by managers ethical? (It is legal.) Support your answer.
   b Is employee web surfing on the 'sinful six' ethical? Support your answer.
   c Is the security manager's submission of the list of abusers to management ethical? Why or why not?
   d Is punishing the abusers ethical? Why or why not? If yes, then what types of punishment are acceptable?
   e What should the company do in this situation? (*Note:* There is a variety of possibilities here.)

2 The Electronic Frontier Foundation (www.eff.org) has a mission of protecting rights and promoting freedom in the 'electronic frontier'. Review the organisation's suggestions about how to protect your online privacy and summarise what you can do to protect yourself.

3 Access your university's guidelines for ethical computer and internet use. Are there limitations as to the types of websites that you can visit and the types of material you can view? Are you allowed to change the programs on the lab computers? Are you allowed to download software from the lab computers for your personal use? Are there rules governing the personal use of computers and email?

4 Access www.cookiecentral.com. Does this site provide information that helps you protect your privacy? If so, then explain how.

5 Do you believe that your university should be allowed to monitor email sent and received on university computers? Why or why not? Support your answer.

>>> COLLABORATION EXERCISE

Background

We all receive privacy statements each day. But how many of us read them? Do you actually read every statement you agree to when you click the 'I Agree' button? Periodically it is a good idea to skim over these to know exactly what you agree with when you check the box. It is even more important to study revisions to see what has changed when the company sends out a new and updated version.

Activity

Work with your team to research various privacy statements. Use popular sites like Facebook, Google, Twitter, LinkedIn, YouTube, Flickr and so on as your main sources of information.

For example, in 2012 Google updated its privacy and information sharing policy and would not allow anyone to opt out of it. You either agreed to Google's policy or you stopped using Google. What about Facebook and its privacy statements? Have each team member analyse a company and report back to the team. In most cases, you will be able to find websites that have already analysed and put together histories of privacy issues.

Deliverable

Work with your team to prepare a short paper that highlights the major issues and trends you have found. Do you think companies are moving toward protecting customers' data? Do you think customers are becoming smarter about what they share? Do social media have the best interest of their users in mind? Put some thought into these issues, prepare your paper and submit it to your tutorial group.

CLOSING CASE **1** >

Dunedin City Council blocks hate site

The Dunedin City Council internal network web content filter has deemed that the Family First New Zealand Christian lobby group's 'Protect Marriage' website, advocating traditional marriage values, is a 'hate' site and blocked access for all council staff. The website promotes marriage between a man and a woman. The council's action has raised the ire of the Family First director, who claimed that the action was discriminatory and the result of an alternative agenda being pushed by someone at the council or the content filter company.

This action occurred during the sometimes heated public debate surrounding legislation to legalise 'gay' marriage being introduced to the New Zealand parliament. The Family First NZ group, who opposes the legislation, claimed that this incident further demonstrated the extent that activists were willing to go to eliminate all opposing debate about this important family issue. Family First NZ believes that this is part of the 'culture wars' surrounding this issue and went on to claim that they had experienced unprecedented hacking of their website since they first launched their campaign against this legislative bill.

In response the Dunedin City Council said that they were not aware of any decision to intentionally block the website. The Family First lobby group was contacted by a Dunedin City Council staff member who indicated that they were surprised when they tried to access the group's petition against the Labor Party Bill to gay marriage, and that the site was deemed a 'hate' website and therefore contravened the Dunedin City Council's acceptable usage policy.

The council's communications and marketing manager later explained that the council did not control the filtering process, which was done by a United States-based company. When the company was employed, the council outlined the broad categories of offensive content that it wanted limited. Based on these categories the company's web filter automatically scanned sites for words or phrases and placed those that were deemed offensive into those categories. These sites were then blocked from access.

The council's spokesperson further stated that they could not say why the Protect Marriage site was blocked, except that the action may have been the result of someone leaving a comment on the site, or using language in a manner determined by the filter to be offensive, resulting in the site being added to the banned list. However, he was confident that none of the administrators or owners of the website had previously done anything that could be construed as offensive or 'hate' related, but Family First should provide the evidence to support their claim.

Council staff were still able to access gay marriage websites and at least two other websites 'blacklisted' by web filters at other companies. Family First went on to claim that it was inconsistent and highly hypocritical that one side to the gay marriage debate was blocked, but not the other. It was apparent that this was discrimination at its worst and the council seemed to be initiating and imposing its own version of the hate speech laws.

In response the council spokesperson outlined that if sites promoting gay marriage had not been blocked or picked up by the same filter, it was because no offending words or phrases were used that placed them in the same category and therefore they were not blocked. If council staff members wanted to fill out the Family First petition then they could do so at home, but they would not unblock the site from the council network as it was not a work-related website anyway.

Following on from this incident, the Dunedin City Council chief executive ordered a review of the organisation's policy on non-work related internet usage during work hours after discovering that staff were also accessing online auctions sites and other non-work related sites. After having studied the council's policy on acceptable internet usage, the chief executive thought that there was a lack of sufficiently clear guidelines for managers and staff in a public organisation with regard to non-work related internet usage.

Sources: Dunedin City Council, *Dunedin City Council — latest news*, www.dunedin.govt.nz/your-council/latest-news/august-2012; D Porteus (2012), 'Council web filter blocks marriage site as "hate"', *Otago Daily Times*, 23 August, www.odt.co.nz/news; D Porteus (2012), 'DCC revisits staff internet use figures', *Otago Daily Times*, 24 August, www.odt.co.nz/news; D Porteous (2012), 'Review of internet use "a priority"', *Otago Daily Times*, 25 August, www.odt.co.nz/news.

QUESTIONS

1 Discuss the ethical dilemma of internet usage at work. Is it ethical for an employer to monitor their staff's usage of the internet while at work?

2 Discuss whether these actions constitute an invasion of privacy. What guidelines would you implement to manage employee internet usage at work?

3 Discuss the ethical implications for the organisation with regard to the claims and accusations outlined. Were they founded or unfounded? Explain.

CLOSING CASE **2** >

Google and China

THE PROBLEM

Google wished to open a search page in China, but in order to do so, it looked like the company would need to accept censorship by the Chinese government. Google wanted to comply with government regulations so that it could expand its business to China, but Google did not wish to compromise the usefulness or appeal of its website's search function.

ATTEMPTS AT A SOLUTION

On 27 January 2006, Google launched its China-based search page (www.google.cn). Google hoped that its decision to create a search engine in the .cn domain — one that followed the Chinese government's rules of censorship — would lead to a level playing field with Baidu, the leading Chinese search engine. Baidu was launched in 2000 and therefore would compete directly with google.cn.

Unfortunately, even as Google rolled out its google.cn web address, there were indications that its compromise on censorship would not satisfy the Chinese government. For example, unexplained outages of its website occurred, but Baidu did not experience any outages.

Not long after Google received its operating license in December 2005, the Chinese government declared that the license was no longer valid. They stated that it was not clear whether Google's activities made it an internet service or a news portal. (Foreigners are forbidden by the Chinese government from operating news portals in China.) Google then began an 18-month long negotiation to restore its license, which it finally received in June 2007. The negotiation was resolved in secret.

In 2007, Google was granted a valuable concession. Chinese users had only to type 'g.cn' and they would go to the google.cn site. By then, however, many Chinese web users had written off Google as an unwelcome outsider with less than reliable service.

Google had a firm policy against storing personal data inside China in order to avoid a situation in which the government could demand that Google turn over that data. Therefore, the company did not offer a number of its key services for local Chinese users — no Gmail, no Blogger, no Picasa, no YouTube.

As Chinese employees were hired, it took some time for some of them to adjust to the Google style. For instance, many were uncomfortable with Google's worldwide policy that employees initiate and pursue independent projects during 20 per cent of their work time. Engineers had to be told by a visiting Google executive that they did not need permission to do a 20 per cent project.

However, the most pressing concern of Google's Chinese engineers was their lack of access to Google's production code. Google was a collaborative company that wanted its engineers around the world to innovate on its existing products and create exciting new ones. The company empowered them to do so by giving them access to its production code base. Without this access, Chinese engineers were limited in what they could do and felt that their lack of access sent a message that they were second-class employees. Suspicion lingered that the Google executives behind this no-access policy had intentionally placed rigid restrictions on Google's employees in China as a form of corporate civil disobedience against Google's cooperation with Chinese government censors.

Google's success in China depended in part on having a government relations point person who could navigate the problems associated with preserving Google's values without offending Chinese officials. Google's first such point person was experienced in the ways of Chinese bureaucracies, but did not speak English and seemed to fail to appreciate issues from Google's perspective.

Her tenure at Google ended when she took it upon herself to give iPods to Chinese officials. She charged the iPods to Google and another executive approved the charge. In Chinese business culture, such gifts are routine, but the act unambiguously violated Google policy, not least because it was an explicit violation of the US Foreign Corrupt Practices Act.

To replace their first (unsuccessful) government liaison, Google chose a three-person, all-female government relations team. However, as it turned out, they had their hands full fending off Chinese government directives. For example, a demand might come from a government ministry to take down 10 items. Google would typically take down seven and hope that the compromise resolved the matter. Then, after a few days or weeks, Google would quietly restore links it had censored. Every 5 months, Google's policy review committee in China would meet to make sure it was filtering the minimum it could possibly get away with.

Google executives began to think that the company's great China compromise was not working because of the heavy censorship. A turning point came in 2008, the year China hosted the summer Olympics. In the months before the Games, China apparently decided to increase its restrictions on web content. It demanded that, in addition to censoring google.cn search results, Google also purge objectionable links from the Chinese-language version of Google.com. That was unacceptable to Google. Complying with these demands would mean that Google was acting as an agent of repression to Chinese-speaking people all over the world, including in the United States. Other search engines, including Microsoft, agreed to such demands. But Google stalled, hoping that after the Olympics the Chinese would back off their demands. However, they did not and the demands for more censorship became both broader in scope and more frequent.

Then, a new problem arose involving Google Suggest, a Google search feature that instantly offers fully developed search queries when users type just a few characters or words into the search box. This innovation was first offered in China after Google's search team realised that, because of difficulties associated with typing Chinese characters, Chinese users generally entered shorter queries into the search box. But, Chinese officials discovered that in many instances, the suggestions offered by Google were related to sexual matters. Google China executives tried to explain that apparently someone had spammed keywords to artificially boost the popularity of sex sites in Google Suggest. The officials were not impressed and told Google that the company 'would be punished'.

At the end of 2009, Google was hacked and some of the company's more closely guarded intellectual property was stolen. The hack was geographically tied to China and both the sophistication of the attack and the nature of its targets pointed to the Chinese government itself as an instigator of, or a party to, the attack. Even worse, the attackers had penetrated the Gmail accounts of Chinese dissidents and human rights activists. All their contacts, their plans and their most private information had fallen into the hands of the intruders.

THE RESULTS

On 10 January 2010, Google's top executives decided to shut down google.cn. The company decided that it would no longer carry out censorship on behalf of the Chinese government. Google subsequently stopped offering web search on google.cn, and instead directed web goers to a search site based in Hong Kong that is not subject to government censorship requirements. For users in mainland China, the Hong Kong search site, along with other Google services such as Gmail, suffers frequent service disruptions.

In 2012, Google acknowledged that it could not afford to miss out on the world's biggest internet market and renewed its push to expand in China. One goal is to introduce its Android Market to China. The Android Market offers thousands of mobile applications to users of Android-powered smartphones and tablets, but is not available in China despite the fact that it powers some 60 per cent of all Chinese smartphones. Google is trying to win over Chinese consumers with services that do not require official censorship, such as Shihui. Shihui helps people search Chinese sites that offer discounts at local stores.

Google's move comes at a pivotal time for China's internet industry. Despite the prevalence of government censorship, the web is increasingly an outlet for Chinese citizens to share information and express discontent, even about the government. Twitter-like microblogging services such as Sina Corporation's Weibo have become popular platforms for sharing opinions and information about controversial topics, even as Google has been on the sidelines.

Perhaps the most telling change is that in 2011, China renewed Google's license to operate a website in the country.

Sources: Compiled from S Li and B Womack (2012), 'Google China business grows, "continues to thrive", Alegre says', *Bloomberg BusinessWeek*, 24 January; J Maragioglio (2012), 'Google renews expansion efforts in China', *Mobiledia*, 13 January; A Efrati and L Chao (2012), 'Google softens tone on China', *The Wall Street Journal*, 12 January; M Brian (2011), 'Google gains China internet license renewal, still avoids search censorship', *TheNextweb*, 7 September; S Levy (2011), 'Inside Google's China misfortune', *CNN*, 15 April; S LaFraniere and D Barboza (2011), 'China tightens censorship of electronic communications', *The New York Times*, 21 March; D MacMillan (2010), 'Google's Quixotic China challenge', *Bloomberg BusinessWeek*, 25 March.

QUESTIONS

1 Google's informal corporate motto is 'Don't be evil'. Discuss this motto in light of Google's decision to stop censoring its search results on behalf of the Chinese government.

2 Discuss Google's decision to stop censoring its search results in China in terms of the ethical framework at the beginning of this chapter.

SPREADSHEET ACTIVITY **PROTECTING INFORMATION IN A SPREADSHEET**

OBJECTIVE

You will learn how to lock and protect spreadsheets to keep private information protected. You will also learn the difference between a 'protected' spreadsheet and a secure database.

Chapter connection

Ethics are a difficult subject in information systems. The tighter you keep a system, the less useful it is. However, the more freely you allow people to access data, the more privacy issues you have on your hands. The object of this exercise is to help establish the necessary balance between ethics, privacy and data usefulness.

ACTIVITY

Recently, a student union group made plans to host a party and took reservations for T-shirt orders. One of the members was an MIS student who had set up a Google Survey for the orders and had exported all of the data into a spreadsheet. The data included name, address, shirt size, address, phone number and so on. The university has asked the union to keep this data confidential due to problems in the past.

Specifically, a year earlier, the same data were stored in an unsecured spreadsheet that was emailed around the union. One of the members took some of the information and used it to exploit and make fun of a physically larger member. To ensure that this does not happen again, the university is asking the group to show evidence that the spreadsheet is locked and will only be seen by those approved to deliver the T-shirts within the union group.

As a member of those approved by the university to manage this information, your job is to take the data collected by the Google Survey and move private information to the private page and lock it so that it cannot be used to exploit students. You will need to use your own judgement to determine which information needs to be moved to the private, locked page of the spreadsheet.

Go to www.johnwiley.com.au/highered/rainer/ausnz/studentresources to download the Excel file you will need. Then watch the accompanying video to learn how to make a spreadsheet secure.

DELIVERABLE

The final product will be a spreadsheet with the survey data in a spreadsheet with the single page of data divided between a secure page and an 'open' page.

DISCUSSION QUESTIONS

1 How can a spreadsheet be helpful if it is so easy to secure and hack?
2 Are Google spreadsheets more secure than Excel spreadsheets?
3 If a sheet needs to be 'very hidden', then why not go ahead and delete it?

DATABASE ACTIVITY **FILTERING AND SORTING**

OBJECTIVE

In this activity, you will learn how to select only the useful rows of a table, hiding the others and sort a table on any column in it. A database is useless if you cannot get information out of it. Access offers many ways to do that. Some are simple but limited. Others are more capable but require more work. Filtering and sorting a table are at the low end but are still often useful. We will start with them here and go on to more complex (but more capable) methods in later activities.

Chapter connection

All organisations keep critical information in databases. Security and privacy considerations govern who can access that database and what they are allowed to see there. This means being able to see some parts of a database but not others. Hence, the way people select parts of a database to see is closely connected to privacy and security considerations. Discussion questions 1 and 2 at the end of this activity go into this connection more deeply.

Prerequisites

None.

ACTIVITY

In this activity, which you will find online, you will learn how to filter and sort an Access table to zero in on exactly the rows you want. The techniques are simple, but will be useful often.

The database you may have used with the chapter 4 activity has information a company might use to track problems with network equipment. Its central element is the *trouble ticket*. A ticket is submitted by a user, who works in a department, and refers to a device (item of network equipment). A ticket is initially open. It is assigned to a technician, may go to 'in process' or 'on hold' (if there is any delay in resolving it), and is eventually closed or cancelled. That database has five tables: users, departments, technicians, devices and trouble tickets. You can see how they are connected in the NeTrouble database on the website. Choose the Database Tools tab above the ribbon and click on the relationship map.

1 Download and open the **Ch 06 NetSimple** database from www.johnwiley.com.au/highered/rainer/ausnz/studentresources. It has one table with the same information as in NeTrouble, minus some columns (such as employee date of birth and date of hire) to save screen space.

   This is usually a poor way to organise a database. It violates the normalisation rules you learned in Chapter 3. However, this 'flat file' data structure is common; it is not always bad and it is where filtering works best.

2 Suppose you want to see the trouble tickets for all your routers. Open TroubleTbl in NetSimple. Make sure it is in Datasheet view. (It should open that way.) The second column of the table, DeviceName, gives the type of device.

3 Pull down the triangle to the right of the column name by clicking on it. You will see a list of all the different devices in the table, sorted alphabetically.

(You will see entries for both 'Router', which is correct, and 'Rooter', a misspelling. The chance of this sort of error is one reason that a flat file database is not a good idea for anything but the simplest data storage requirements.)

4 You will also see two entries in the table above the list of types: one that reads 'Select All' and one that refers to blank (empty) cells in the datasheet. At this point all the boxes are checked. Click Select All to uncheck all the boxes. Then click 'Bridge' and OK.

5 All the rows have gone away except for those with Bridge in the DevName column — that is, except for all the trouble tickets that refer to bridges. You will see a small funnel next to the triangle in that column. It means the data you see are filtered on the content of that column.

6 Click the Home tab above the ribbon. In the Sort & Filter section toward the right side of the ribbon, Toggle Filter (a funnel icon) will be highlighted. Click it a few times to see what it does.

7 You can filter for more than one column at a time. Pull down the filtering menu for the Department column. It shows only the departments that are now visible — that is, those that reported a problem with a bridge. Since HR did not report any problems with bridges, HR is not in the list.

Now, click Marketing. The Marketing box will be unchecked. So will the Select All box because all the choices are no longer selected. Click OK. Trouble tickets from Marketing are now hidden, leaving those from all other departments. Both columns show funnels next to their triangles. The Toggle Filter button in the ribbon alternates between both filters on and both off. If you want to turn one of them off while leaving the other on, you must clear it individually in its column.

8 To sort the visible trouble tickets by the date they were submitted, pull down the sorting and filtering menu of the TicketSubmitted column. Choose Sort Newest to Oldest and click OK. The table now shows the trouble tickets with the newest at the top. This is useful if you need to find out about the latest problems.

Usage hint: You can also sort by selecting a column and clicking one of the icons on the left side of the Sort & Filter section of the Home ribbon. The top icon sorts in ascending order; the middle one sorts in descending order; and the last one clears any existing sorts on that column. This may be faster if the Home ribbon is already selected, but probably is not if you are working with a different ribbon.

9 Select the TicketSubmitted column of the table by clicking on its heading. Pull down its Sort & Filter menu and move your mouse pointer to Date Filters. (The type of filters you get here depends on the data type of the column you are working with.) Another menu will come out from the side of the main menu. Select After ..., the fourth entry. In the dialogue box that appears, enter 3/1/2011.

10 Close this database, being sure to save your work.

Usage hint: If you open your database again at this point, it may seem that your sort and filters disappeared. They did not. They were saved with the database. They are just not applied. Clicking Toggle Filters will reactivate them.

11 Now, download and open the **Ch 06 NeTrouble** database from the website. It is a better way to structure the trouble reporting data. However, as you will see, it is more awkward to filter on a multiple-table database. That is why we will learn about other query techniques for such databases later, in the chapter 10 activity. To get the same result that was so easy to get above, proceed as follows.

12 Open DeviceTbl. Find the Bridge row or rows. Because this table is short, you can scan it by eye in a couple of seconds. Record its primary key (DeviceID, its first column) and close it.

13 Open the TicketTbl. Find its Device column. Filter that column for the device key or keys you just recorded. This will select the trouble tickets for all bridges.

This is a lot of work to get a result that you obtained more easily the first time — and you only needed to use two tables, not seven or eight. That is one downside of multiple-table databases versus flat files. Their business advantages still outweigh their drawbacks. You will see how to get around those difficulties by using other query tools in future activities.

14 Close this database, being sure to save your work.

DELIVERABLES

1 Your Ch 06 NetSimple database, with the filters you applied.

2 Your Ch 06 NeTrouble database, with the filters you applied.

QUIZ QUESTIONS

1 True or false: Clicking on a Sort icon, with a table column selected, does exactly the same as selecting the corresponding Sort option from that column's pull-down filtering menu.

2 Consider the filter you applied to the single-table database in activity steps 3 to 5 above. Could you

have used the same basic method, but checking different boxes, to select

- a all devices other than bridges?
- b all devices that are either bridges or switches?
- c all devices that are routers or rooters, to include misspellings?
- d any of the above?

3 True or false: You apply a filter to a database table, close the database, then reopen it. When you look at that table in Datasheet view, its rows will still be filtered as they were.

4 The Sort & Filter section of the ribbon is found under which ribbon tab?

- a Home
- b Create
- c Database Tools
- d Datasheet

DISCUSSION QUESTIONS

1 Suppose you have the five-table version of this database (NeTrouble) and have been asked to analyse the distribution of trouble tickets by department. You understand the difficulty of doing this, as you did it for a different problem in activity steps 8 to 10, and are willing to put up with that. However, for privacy reasons, you are not allowed to access the user table. Would this be a problem? Why or why not? If it would, suggest a solution.

2 Sometimes a person should see only certain rows of a table. Student access to grades is one example: you may see your own rows, but not those of other students. One way to make this happen is to create a copy of the table, filter for rows this person should *not* see, select them all, delete them, and then clear the filter to show the remaining rows. (This would have to be done automatically, or by someone who is allowed to see the entire table.) The result can then be emailed to the student, plugged into a web page template and so on.

Think of two other situations where access to a table must be controlled on a row basis. Would this solution work for each of them? Why or why not?

The filtering menu of a column shows all data values in that column with check boxes. Rows containing checked values will remain visible when the filter is applied. Other rows will be hidden, but can be shown by clearing the filter or toggling it off. More complex criteria can be applied by selecting [] Filters, where the blank specifies the data type of the column (e.g. text) and providing any parameters as in activity step 6 opposite.

Choose any column of any table that contains text data. Select Text Filters from the drop-down menu. Consider the eight types of filters in the submenu that appears. Think of two situations in which those eight types do not meet the filtering needs. Be specific in explaining what these situations call for that they cannot handle.

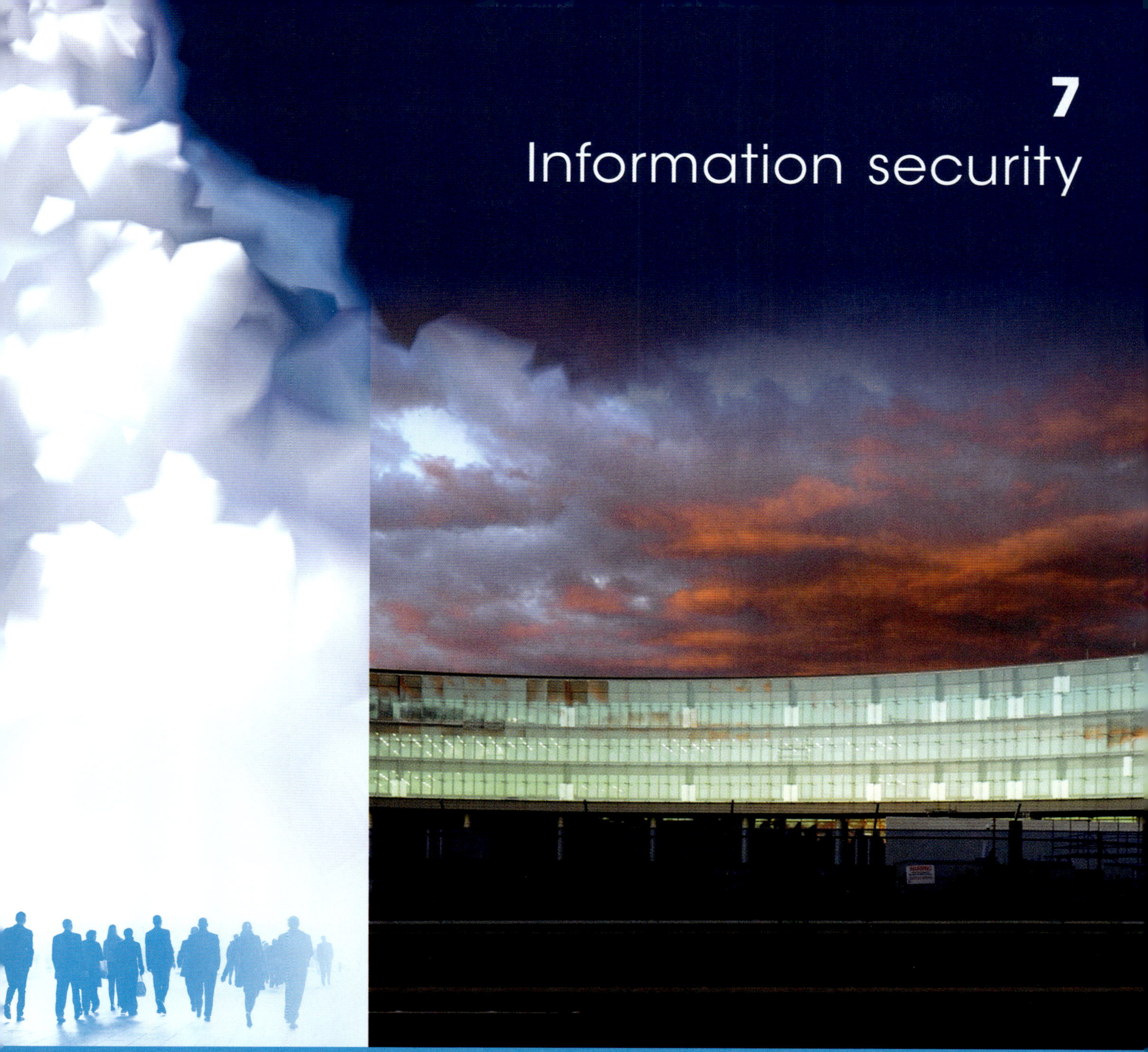

7 Information security

CHAPTER OUTLINE

LEARNING OBJECTIVES

1. Give one specific example of each of the five factors that are contributing to the increasing vulnerability of information resources.
2. Compare and contrast human mistakes and social engineering by way of specific examples.
3. Describe negative consequences that might result from at least three different kinds of deliberate attacks on information systems.
4. Assess how you might employ each of the three risk mitigation strategies in the context of your owning a home.
5. Identify the three major types of controls that organisations can use to protect their information resources.

OPENING CASE >

Small businesses in danger

Picture your graduation day. You have finally completed your undergraduate degree. You initially looked for a job, but you have since decided that you want to start your own business. You pitch your idea to your best friend and ask him/her to join you in a new business venture. Because your degree is in marketing, you would like to start a small promotions business. You and your new business partner develop a solid business strategy, get a small business loan from the bank to purchase your computer equipment, and then head over to the courthouse to set up your new Limited Liability Corporation.

Two years later, things could not have turned out better! Hard work, late nights and social media exposure have landed your business quite a few clients. The two computers you purchased with your small business loan (one for you and one for your business partner) have turned out to be invaluable. In fact, you now realise more than ever how much you depend on your computers and how lost your business would be without them. You wonder if your antivirus software is up-to-date and if there is anything else you should be doing to protect your critical business data, especially your clients' data. But you are too busy to research these issues and you just trust that everything will run smoothly.

You and your partner have never had computers this nice. Fast processors, big monitors, and plenty of memory (all purchased with business intent of course) make for much better computers than either of you have at home. Naturally you both use your computers for personal work as well. Why not, right?

But then, suddenly, your business partner's computer starts to slow down dramatically. Your machine is identical to his, but yours runs much faster. Your partner takes his computer back to Harvey Norman to have it looked over. The technician determines that malware has infected his computer so thoroughly that the hard drive must be replaced. Additionally, the data on his hard drive cannot be recovered and he has not backed up any of his files (not even the business data).

Now, you have problems. Lost data may result in lost (certainly irritated) customers. In addition, you will have to spend time and money re-creating that data.

How could your partner's unprotected web surfing have resulted in so much lost data? The fact is that even though you both consider yourselves somewhat tech savvy, neither of you ever took steps to protect your computers. You just assumed that a malware infection would never happen to you.

Now, what would you say if you knew that you are not alone? A recent report by GFI Software showed that over 40 per cent of small to medium enterprises (SMEs) reported a security breach that resulted from an employee visiting a website that hosted malware. Amazingly, even though 40 per cent of SMBs have experienced this problem, 55 per cent reported that preventing this from happening again was not a priority! Furthermore, 70 per cent of the respondents do not have any policy about web use at work and say that web use is not a problem!

As you can see from this case, security on computers and information systems is vital to avoid losing business relationships and significant amounts of time and money. Many third-party companies provide security solutions (see for example, GFI Software at www.gfi.com), but you are responsible for seeking out their services and implementing security controls on your own systems and customer data. If you do not prioritise security measures, you expose your computer and your files to potentially irrevocable damage from thousands of malware systems and viruses.

As you saw in this case, information security controls are essential to all businesses, regardless of size. In addition, a solid backup plan is critical to information security. As you consider this case, think about the devastating impact that a security breach would have on a small business. The loss of important data about the business, coupled with the loss of customer data, could shut down the business.

Sources: Compiled from 'GFI software survey: 40% of SMBs have suffered a security breach due to unsafe web surfing' (2011), *Enhanced Online News*, 12 October; 'Small businesses hacked but still not taking precautions: survey says' (2011), *The Huffington Post*, 7 November; www.gfi.com.

QUESTIONS

1 What security controls should you and your business partner have adopted *at a minimum*?
2 How important are backup plans and file backup procedures to small businesses?
3 Why is it important to protect customer information in businesses of any size?

THE NOOK

Malakai and Abbie are very excited about their new website and the opportunity to sell merchandise online. However, it seems that every day they hear of an attack where credit card information has been stolen; disgruntled employees have shared passwords and made customer data vulnerable; computers physically stolen from behind locked doors; fire creating loss of data; and other situations where customer information has been compromised. They really feel stuck between a 'rock and a hard place' because they are experiencing immense pressure to move into the e-commerce realm, yet they are very concerned about information security by doing so! They want to know what kind of threats are really out there and which ones are legitimate for them as a nightclub? In what ways would The Nook make itself vulnerable to cybercrime by adding e-commerce to its website? How many of these threats can be avoided by having a third party (such as Amazon, Yahoo, Google, or PayPal) provide e-commerce tools that provide some level of security and confidence, but how much does The Nook need? How much training do employees need to truly create a secure environment for their customers and their private information?

Introduction

Information security is closely related to IT and raises significant questions. These questions include the following.

- How do organisations show due diligence in protecting sensitive, classified information?
- Is the cause of security breaches in organisations managerial, technological, or some combination of both?
- How should organisations protect their information more effectively?

The most important question raised in this chapter, however, is whether it is possible to secure the internet. The answer to this question affects every one of us.

The answers to these and other questions are not clear. As you learn about information security in the context of information technology, you will acquire a better understanding of these issues, their importance, their relationships, and their trade-offs.

Information technologies, properly used, can have enormous benefits for individuals, organisations and entire societies. So far, you have learned about diverse ways in which IT has made businesses more productive, efficient and responsive to consumers. You have explored areas such as medicine and philanthropy in which IT has improved people's health and wellbeing. Unfortunately, information technologies can also be misused, often with devastating consequences. Consider the following.

- Individuals can have their identities stolen.
- Organisations' customer information can be stolen, leading to financial losses, erosion of customer confidence and legal action.
- Countries face the threat of cyberterrorism and cyberwarfare. The Australian Government recognises that cyber security is a challenging and critical aspect of national security and defence. As part of Australia's national security strategy, the Cyber Security Operations Centre (CSOC) within the Australian Signals Directory (ASD) agency is charged with providing the government with a better understanding of sophisticated cyber threats against Australian cyber accessible assets, and to assist and coordinate operational responses that inform and mitigate against a conflation of cyber-based threats.[1]

In fact, the misuse of information technologies has come to the forefront of any discussion of IT. For example, the Ponemon Institute (**www.ponemon.org**), a research firm, found that organisations spent an average of $7.20 million for each security breach in 2011.

The study measured the direct costs of a data breach, such as hiring forensic experts, notifying customers, setting up telephone hotlines to field queries from concerned or affected customers, offering free credit monitoring subscriptions, and discounts for future products and services. The study also measured more intangible costs of a breach, such as the loss of business from increased customer turnover (known as *customer churn*) and decreases in customer trust.

According to the study, employee negligence caused many of the data breaches. This finding confirms that organisational employees are a weak link in information security. As a result, it is very important for you to learn about information security so that you will be better prepared when you enter the workforce.

7.1 Introduction to information security

Security can be defined as the degree of protection against criminal activity, danger, damage and/or loss. Following this broad definition, **information security** means protecting an organisation's information and information systems (known as an organisation's *information assets*) from unauthorised access, use, disclosure, disruption, modification or destruction. Clearly, information and information systems can be compromised by deliberate criminal actions and by anything that can impair the proper functioning of an organisation's information systems.

Before you continue, let's look at these key terms. Organisations have huge amounts of information and numerous information systems that are subject to many threats.

A **threat** to an information resource is any danger to which a system may be exposed. The **exposure** of an information resource is the harm, loss, or damage that can result if a threat compromises that resource. An information resource's **vulnerability** is the possibility that the system will suffer harm by a threat.

Human mistakes such as unattended equipment often leave resources vulnerable to theft.

A number of factors are contributing to the increasing vulnerability of organisational information resources, making it much more difficult to secure them, including:

- today's interconnected, interdependent, wirelessly networked business environment
- smaller, faster, cheaper computers and storage devices
- decreasing skills necessary to be a computer hacker
- international organised crime taking over cybercrime
- lack of management support.

The first factor is the evolution of the information technology resource from mainframe only to today's highly complex, interconnected, interdependent, wirelessly networked business environment. The internet now enables millions of computers and computer networks to freely and seamlessly communicate with one another. Organisations and individuals are exposed to a world of untrusted networks and potential attackers. A trusted network, in general, is any network within your organisation. An *untrusted network*, in general, is any network external to your organisation. In addition, wireless technologies enable employees to compute, communicate and access the internet anywhere and anytime. Significantly, wireless is an inherently insecure broadcast communications medium.

The second factor reflects the fact that modern computers and storage devices (e.g. USB drives, USB sticks or flash drives) continue to become smaller, faster, cheaper and more portable, with greater storage capacity. These characteristics make it much easier to steal or lose a computer or storage device that contains huge amounts of sensitive information. Also, many more people are able to afford powerful computers and connect inexpensively to the internet, thus increasing the target size of an attack on information assets.

The third factor is that the computing skills necessary to be a hacker are *decreasing*. The reason is that the internet contains information and computer programs (called *scripts*) that users with few skills can download and use to attack any information system connected to the internet. (Security experts can also use these scripts for legitimate purposes, such as testing the security of various systems.)

The fourth factor is that international organised crime is taking over cybercrime. **Cybercrime** refers to illegal activities taking place over computer networks, particularly the internet. VeriSign's iDefense Security Intelligence Services (idefense.com) provides security information to governments and Fortune 500 companies. VeriSign states that groups of well-organised criminals have taken control of a global billion-dollar crime network.

The network, powered by skilful hackers, targets known software security weaknesses. These crimes are typically nonviolent but quite lucrative. For example, the losses from armed robberies average hundreds of dollars and those from white-collar crimes average tens of thousands of dollars. In contrast, losses from computer crimes average hundreds of thousands of dollars. In fact, the 2011 Norton Cybercrime Report estimates the total cost of cybercrime at $388 billion per year. Also, these crimes can be committed from anywhere in the world, at any time, effectively providing an international safe haven for cybercriminals. Computer-based crimes cause billions of dollars in damages to businesses each year, including the costs to repair information systems and the costs of lost business.

The fifth and final factor is lack of management support. For the entire organisation to take security policies and procedures seriously, senior managers must set the tone. Ultimately, however, lower-level managers may be even more important. These managers are in close contact with employees every day and thus are in a better position to determine whether employees are following security procedures.

BEFORE YOU GO ON . . .

1. Define information security.
2. Define a threat, an exposure and a vulnerability.
3. Why are the skills needed to be a hacker decreasing?

Apply the Concept

Background

This section has taught you about the importance of information security when doing business over the web. It is important to note that the chain is only as strong as its weakest link. Therefore, while you may have been careful to maintain security across your network, if your business partners do not, then as your information passes over their networks it will be at risk.

Activity

Visit VeriSign's website. As you read over this page, keep in mind that VeriSign is a company that is in the business of protecting websites and web users and that is something that we all appreciate. In fact, it is likely that you feel some level of comfort when you see the VeriSign symbol on an e-commerce site.

Deliverable

After reading the article, write a paragraph from VeriSign to a potential business that explains the following questions:

1. What are the five steps that occur when a browser connects to a secure website?
2. What is an SSL certificate and how does it fit in the five steps mentioned in question 1?
3. What are the normal visual cues that a connection is secure and what is the extended verification that is seen on some sites?
4. What are the benefits of using VeriSign to both the merchant and the customer?

THE NOOK

QUESTIONS

1. Describe the ways The Nook is vulnerable to security threats based on the nature of its business.
2. Based on the current operating environment, do you think it is acceptable for Malakai and Abbie to continue to operate without upgrading their IS because they are afraid of security issues? If they are too afraid, where will their business be in another 5 years with no information system?

7.2 Unintentional threats to information systems

Information systems are vulnerable to many potential hazards and threats, as you see in figure 7.1 (overleaf). The two major categories of threats are unintentional threats and deliberate threats. In this section you will learn about unintentional threats. The next section addresses deliberate threats.

Unintentional threats are those acts with no malicious intent. Human errors are unintentional and represent a serious threat to information security.

Human errors

Organisational employees span the breadth and depth of the organisation, from mail administrators to the CEO and across all functional areas. There are two important points to be made about employees. First, the higher the level of employee, the greater the threat the employee poses to information security. This situation exists because higher level employees typically have greater access to corporate data and enjoy greater privileges on organisational information systems. Second, employees in two areas of the organisation pose significant threats to information security: human resources and information systems. Human resources employees generally have access to sensitive personal information about all employees. Likewise, information systems employees not only have access to sensitive organisational data, but they also often control the means to create, store, transmit and modify that data.

Other employees include contract labour, consultants, cleaners and security personnel. Contract labour, such as temporary hires, may be overlooked in information security. However, these employees often have access to the company's network, information systems and information assets. Consultants, while technically not employees, do work for the company. Depending on the nature of their work, these people may also have access to the company's network, information systems and information assets.

Cleaners and security personnel are the most frequently ignored people in information security. Companies might outsource their security and cleaning services, meaning that, although these individuals technically are not employees, they nevertheless do work for the company. Moreover, they are usually present when most — if not all — other employees have gone home. They typically have keys to every office and nobody questions their presence in even the most sensitive parts of the building. In fact, an article from the Winter 1994 edition of *2600: The Hacker Quarterly* described how to get a job as a cleaner for the purpose of gaining physical access to an organisation.

Human errors or mistakes by employees pose a large problem as the result of laziness, carelessness, or a lack of awareness concerning information security. This lack of awareness comes from poor education and training efforts by the organisation. Human mistakes manifest themselves in many different ways, as you see in table 7.1 (overleaf).

The human errors that you have just studied are unintentional on the part of the employee. However, employees can also make unintentional mistakes as a result of actions by an attacker. Attackers often employ social engineering to induce individuals to make unintentional mistakes and disclose sensitive information.

Social engineering

In a **social engineering** attack, the perpetrator uses social skills to trick or manipulate a legitimate employee into providing confidential company information such as passwords. The most common example of social engineering occurs when the attacker impersonates someone else on the telephone, such as a company manager or information systems employee. The attacker claims to have forgotten the password and asks the legitimate employee to provide a password to use. Other common exploits include posing as an exterminator, an air conditioning technician, or a fireman. Examples of social engineering abound.

In one company, a perpetrator entered a company building wearing a company ID card that looked legitimate. He walked around and put up signs on bulletin boards saying, 'The help desk telephone number has been changed. The new number is 2555 1234.' He then

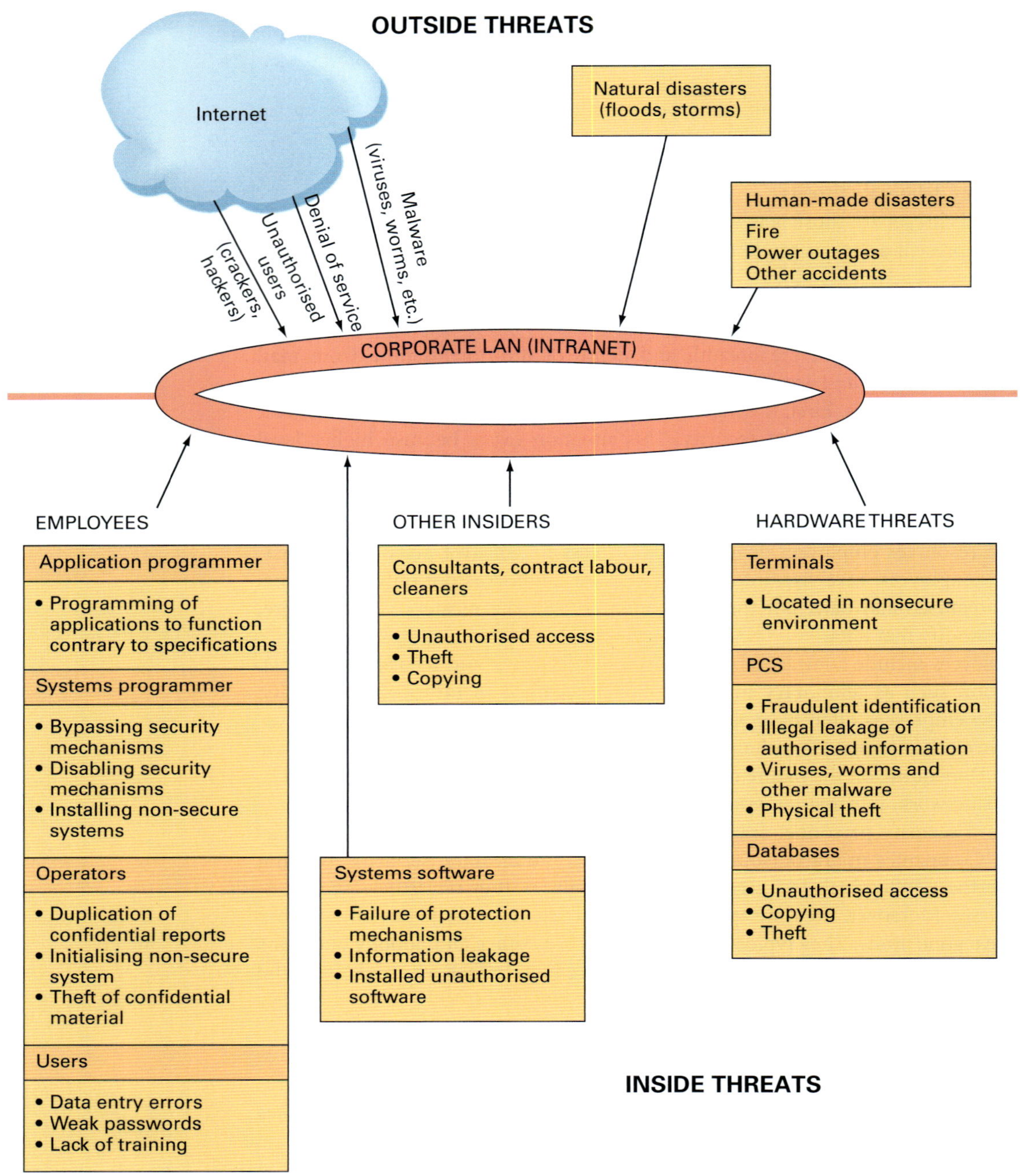

FIGURE 7.1 Security threats.

exited the building and began receiving calls from legitimate employees thinking they were calling the company help desk. Naturally, the first thing the perpetrator asked for was user name and password. He now had the information necessary to access the company's information systems.

Two other social engineering techniques include tailgating and shoulder surfing. *Tailgating* is a technique designed to allow the perpetrator to enter restricted areas that are controlled with locks or card entry. The perpetrator follows closely behind a legitimate employee and, when the employee gains entry, asks the person to 'hold the door'. *Shoulder surfing* occurs when a perpetrator watches the employee's computer screen over that person's shoulder. This technique is particularly successful in public areas such as airports, trains and on aeroplanes.

BEFORE YOU GO ON . . .

1. What is an unintentional threat to an information system?
2. Provide other examples of social engineering attacks.

TABLE 7.1 Human mistakes

Mistake	Description and examples
Carelessness with laptops	Losing laptops, misplacing laptops, leaving them in taxis and so on.
Carelessness with computing devices	Losing or misplacing these devices, or using them carelessly so that malware is introduced into an organisation's network.
Opening questionable emails	Opening emails from someone unknown, or clicking on links embedded in emails (see table 7.2 for more about phishing attacks).
Careless internet surfing	Accessing questionable websites; can result in malware and/or alien software being introduced into the organisation's network.
Poor password selection and use	Choosing and using weak passwords (read more about strong passwords later in this chapter).
Carelessness with one's office	Unlocked desks and filing cabinets when employees go home at night; not logging off the company network when gone from the office for any extended period of time.
Carelessness using unmanaged devices	Unmanaged devices are those outside the control of an organisation's IT department and company security procedures. These devices include computers belonging to customers and business partners, computers in the business centres of hotels and computers in Starbucks, McDonalds, Westfield shopping centres and so on.
Carelessness with discarded equipment	Discarding old computer hardware and devices without completely wiping the memory; includes computers, mobile phones, Blackberries, and digital copiers and printers.
Careless monitoring of environment	These hazards, which include dirt, dust, humidity and static electricity, are harmful to the safe operation of computing equipment.

Shoulder surfing is particularly successful in public areas.

THE NOOK

QUESTIONS

1. To which of the social engineering methods do you think The Nook is most vulnerable?
2. Given the threat that small USB-powered storage devices make it easy to store information, what type of policy could The Nook implement to avoid information being stolen?

7.3 Deliberate threats to information systems

There are so many types of deliberate acts that a brief list is provided here for your convenience:

- espionage or trespass
- information extortion
- sabotage or vandalism
- theft of equipment or information
- identity theft
- compromises to intellectual property
- software attacks
- alien software
- supervisory control and data acquisition (SCADA) attacks
- cyberterrorism and cyberwarfare.

Espionage or trespass

Espionage or trespass occurs when an unauthorised individual attempts to gain illegal access to organisational information. It is important to distinguish between competitive intelligence and industrial espionage. Competitive intelligence consists of legal information gathering techniques, such as studying a company's website and press releases and attending trade shows. In contrast, industrial espionage crosses the legal boundary.

Information extortion

Information extortion occurs when an attacker either threatens to steal, or actually steals, information from a company. The perpetrator demands payment for not stealing the information, for returning stolen information, or for agreeing not to disclose the information.

Sabotage or vandalism

Sabotage and vandalism are deliberate acts that involve defacing an organisation's website, possibly causing the organisation to lose its image and its customers to experience a loss of confidence. One form of online vandalism is a hacktivist or cyberactivist operation. These are cases of high-tech civil disobedience to protest the operations, policies, or actions of an organisation or government agency.

Theft of equipment and information

Computing devices and storage devices are becoming smaller yet more powerful with vastly increased storage (e.g. laptops, Blackberries, personal digital assistants, smart phones, digital cameras, thumb drives and iPads). As a result, these devices are becoming easier to steal and easier for attackers to use to steal information.

Table 7.1 points out that one type of human mistake is carelessness with laptops. In fact, such carelessness often leads to laptops being stolen. The cost of a stolen laptop includes the loss of data, the loss of intellectual property, laptop replacement, legal and regulatory costs, investigation fees and lost productivity.

One form of theft, colloquially known as *skip dipping*, involves the practice of rummaging through commercial or residential rubbish to find information that has been discarded. Paper files, letters, memos, photographs, IDs, passwords, credit cards and other forms of information can be found in rubbish. Unfortunately, many people never consider that the sensitive items they throw in the garbage may be recovered. Such information, when recovered, can be used for fraudulent purposes.

Identity theft

Identity theft is the deliberate assumption of another person's identity, usually to gain access to his or her financial information or to frame him or her for a crime. Techniques for obtaining information include the following:

- stealing mail or dumpster diving
- stealing personal information in computer databases
- infiltrating organisations that store large amounts of personal information (e.g. data aggregators such as Acxiom, **www.acxiom.com**)
- impersonating a trusted organisation in an electronic communication (**phishing**).

Recovering from identity theft is costly, time-consuming and difficult. Victims also report problems in obtaining credit and obtaining or holding a job, as well as adverse effects on insurance or credit rates. In addition, victims state that it is often difficult to remove negative information from their records, such as their credit reports.

Anyone's personal information can be compromised in other ways. For example, an identity can be uncovered just from examining searches in a search engine. The ability to analyse all searches by a single user can enable a criminal to identify who the user is and what he or she is doing. As just one example, the *New York Times* tracked down a particular person based solely on her AOL searches.

Compromises to intellectual property

Intellectual property is an overarching term used to describe a group of laws covering **copyright**, **patents**, trademarks, designs, circuit layouts and plant breeder's rights. Each type of intellectual property is protected by a specific Act of the Australian Commonwealth Parliament, which are further based on Australia's obligations under international treaties.

Copyright is free and automatically granted in Australia with no registration required. It is regarded as a type of property that is based on a person's creative ability and labour. Copyright protects the form or way an idea or information is expressed and is extended to works and other subject matter covered under the *Copyright Act 1968*. This affords the owner exclusive economic rights to undertake certain activities with the original work, which include the right to copy, publish, communicate (broadcast or make available online) and perform the copyrighted material publicly.

However, there is a clear distinction between the copyright of the created work and ownership of the physical form in which the work exists. For example, an author may own the copyright of the text expressed in a book even though the physical book can be purchased and owned by another person. Similarly, the buyer of an original artwork does not have the right to reproduce the artwork without first gaining the artist's express permission.

Likewise the *Patent Act 1990* applies where an inventor has created new or improved products or devices, substances and methods or industrial processes; this applies where the mode of manufacture is new, is not obvious and is useful. A registered patent document grants the inventor exclusive rights to exploit and develop the invention for the life of the patent document, which is 20 years. This also provides protection for incremental or lower level inventions for eight years.

The intellectual property of trademarks is covered by the *Trade Marks Act 1995*. The initial registration is for 10 years with further renewals possible while the trademark remains in use. This affords protection relating to a letter, word, phrase, sound, smell, shape, logo, picture, aspect of packaging or combination of these used by traders as a means of distinguishing the origin of their specific products or goods from other traders.

The *Design Act 2003* grants protection of the visual appearance or design of a new or original manufactured item. The protection is based on a registration system that can last up to 10 years and relates to the features of shape, pattern or ornamentation as applied to the item.

The most common intellectual property related to IT deals with software. In Australia, software is regarded as a 'literary work' and therefore protected by copyright. This applies to all types of software including desktop applications, mobile apps and web-based applications. The *Copyright Act 1968* uses the term 'computer program' to refer to software and defines it as 'a set of statements or instructions to be used directly or indirectly in a computer in order to bring about a certain result'. The owners of software are granted exclusive rights to:

- reproduce the software in a material form
- publish the software
- make an adaptation of the software
- communicate the software to the public.

Generally, most software is accompanied by a licensing agreement that outlines the terms and conditions of use, which can vary considerably between products. If anyone other than the copyright owner wants to undertake any of the protected rights, then they can only do so with the owner's express permission. For software, this includes making copies, porting software across different platforms, and making software available for download. To do otherwise without the owner's permission is deemed to have infringed copyright.

For example, copying a software program without making payment to the owner or obtaining permission — including giving a disc to a friend to install on his or her computer — is a copyright violation. Not surprisingly, this practice, called **piracy**, is a major problem for software vendors. The global trade in pirated software amounts to billions of dollars.[2]

Computer software is copyright. Giving a disc to a friend to install on his or her computer is a copyright violation.

Software attacks

Software attacks have evolved from the outbreak era — during which malicious software (**malware**) tried to infect as many computers worldwide as possible — to the profit-driven, web-based attacks of today. Cybercriminals are heavily involved with malware attacks to make money and they use sophisticated, blended attacks typically via the web. Table 7.2 shows a variety of software attacks. You will see that software attacks are grouped into three categories: remote attacks needing user action; remote attacks needing no user action; and software attacks by programmers during the development of a system. IT's About Business (overleaf) provides an example of a software attack.

TABLE 7.2 Types of software attacks

Type	Description
1. *Remote attacks needing user action*	
Virus	Segment of computer code that performs malicious actions by attaching to another computer program.
Worm	Segment of computer code that performs malicious actions and will replicate or spread by itself (without requiring another computer program).
Phishing attack	Phishing attacks use deception to acquire sensitive personal information by masquerading as official-looking emails or instant messages.
Spear phishing attack	Phishing attacks target large groups of people. In spear phishing attacks, the perpetrators find out as much information about an individual as possible to improve their chances that phishing techniques will be able to obtain sensitive, personal information.
2. *Remote attacks needing no user action*	
Denial-of-service attack	Attacker sends so many information requests to a target computer system that the target cannot handle them successfully and typically crashes (ceases to function).
Distributed denial-of-service attack	An attacker first takes over many computers, typically by using malicious software. These computers are called *zombies*, or *bots*. The attacker uses these bots (which form a *botnet*) to deliver a coordinated stream of information requests to a target computer, causing it to crash.
3. *Attacks by programmer developing a system*	
Trojan horse	Software programs that hide in other computer programs and reveal their designed behaviour only when they are activated.
Back door	Typically, a password, known only to the attacker, that allows him or her to access a computer system at will, without having to go through any security procedures (also called a *trap door*).
Logic bomb	Segment of computer code that is embedded within an organisation's existing computer programs and is designed to activate and perform a destructive action at a certain time or date.

IT'S ABOUT BUSINESS

Hacktivists 'Anonymous' attack Australian government websites

Anonymous is a loosely associated international group of hackers and activists that is well known for a number of widely publicised hacks and distributed denial-of-service (DDoS) attacks perpetrated on government, religious and corporate websites. The Anonymous group has become increasingly renowned for these acts of collaborative, international hacktivism.

Hacktivism is a combination of political activism and computer hacking. Like normal activism except that it takes place online rather than in a physical sit-in, a DDoS attack is usually executed against the targeted website. Instead of using graffiti, hacktivists have defaced websites. Generally, Anonymous uses individual or group computer hacking skills, the internet and technology to try to effect social change, protest or spread a message of awareness or ideas relating to a particular cause. It communicates its activities more broadly using social media tools like Twitter.

In August 2012, two Twitter accounts claiming to represent the Anonymous group had been boasting that it would attack both the Australian Secret Intelligence Organisation (ASIO) and Australian Signals Directorate (ASD) websites. Then Anonymous Australia announced via Twitter that Operation Australia hackers were busy attacking the ASD and ASIO spy agency's government website which had been down or loading slowly for some time. ASIO later described this as their website suffering some technical issues and that the disruptions did not represent a risk to ASIO's business.

This attack was only part of a number of DDoS attacks and website defacement campaigns levelled against 10 Australian government agencies. Furthermore, Anonymous activists had also taken customer records and data belonging to business telco AAPT and posted the information on a public website. This action was undertaken to highlight the concerns regarding the then Federal Government's draft internet surveillance and security legislative proposal to force Australian telco companies to store and retain every Australian's web history data for two years. This exemplifies a hacktivism protest action.

However, after some high-profile arrests, hacker groups similar to Anonymous are changing the way they operate. For instance, on 5 November 2012 hackers under the name of Anonymous wanting to highlight Guy Fawkes Day undertook a hacking operation to deface a number of Australian websites, including the Fremantle Arts Centre, the Clinical Practice Guidelines Portal for medical professionals and the Quality of Life disability support network. Previously, hackers claiming to be aligned to Anonymous had only undertaken their acts of hacktivism based on the values of *social justice* and *freedom of information*. However, public recriminations and loss of support for the cause can be swift once hackers begin attacking art, medical and disability websites.

Once public sympathy is lost, like any activism or protest it loses impetus and tends to be consigned to just another event in history. Yet the potential remains for hacktivism to continue when passionate causes arise in terms of social justice, freedom of information, awareness or communicating a message or alternate point of view. However, rather than using the largely illegal actions of hacking websites, stealing, or damaging or publishing sensitive data, activists are now turning to social media as a responsible means of communication and as a legitimate avenue for garnering support and spreading their message.

Sources: ABC News Online (2012), 'Anonymous Australia claims ASIO attack', www.abc.net.au/news/2012-08-10/anonymous-claims-asio-attack/4190874.html; L Battersby, B Grubb (2012), 'Hackers cripple ASIO site to protest web spy plan', *Sydney Morning Herald*, www.smh.com.au/it-pro/security-it/hackers-cripple-asio-site-to-protest-web-spy-plan-20120810.html; P Dorling (2012), 'Roxon puts web surveillance plans on ice', *Sydney Morning Herald*, www.smh.com.au/technology/technology-news/roxon-puts-web-surveillance-plans-on-ice-20120809-23x9l.html; T McCormick (2013), 'A short history of hacktivism', *Canberra Times*, www.canberratimes.com.au/it-pro/security-it/a-short-history-of-hacktivism-20130510.html; A Wolf (2012), 'The future of hacktivism', *New Matilda*, www.newmatilda.com/2012/11/13/future-hacktivism.

QUESTIONS

1 What implications could these attacks have for the organisations targeted? What concerns might there be for organisations if customers' personal information is released publicly?

2 Do hactivism actions and campaigns have the power to change community values and attitudes? Is it a sustainable method of political or social activism or just a public nuisance?

3 Identify the primary goals that hacktivism actions are trying to achieve. Is this a sustainable approach, or would public opinion view these actions differently? Describe each of the differing perspectives.

IT'S ABOUT BUSINESS

Melbourne IT: an Australian internet success

Melbourne IT supports organisations of all sizes to successfully do business online. Melbourne IT provides a range of internet-based technology services to more than 400 000 customers. These services range from helping small businesses to build an online presence through to the design and management of sophisticated web environments for corporate businesses and governments. The company employs approximately 400 staff and currently operates four main offices in Australia (Sydney, Melbourne, Brisbane and Perth) and two offshore offices (Wellington, New Zealand and Phoenix, United States). Melbourne IT was formed in 1996 and listed on the ASX in December 1999. For the financial year 2012, Melbourne IT reported both revenue and profit drops of 5 and 16 per cent respectively. In the 2012 financial year, the company recorded a net profit of $11.4 million, down from $11.5 million the previous year, and revenue of $170.6 million, down from the previous year's figure of $179.8 million.

While the company has diversified since its formation, the history of Melbourne IT is very much linked with domain name registration. In 1999, Melbourne IT was selected by ICANN as one of the first five registrars to register *.com*, *.net*, and *.org* names in competition with the incumbent Network Solutions. Melbourne IT immediately established itself as a significant player within the overall domain name registrar space, introducing such innovations as trademark checking and differentiated pricing models for different levels of turnaround time.

A hacking attack

The *New York Times* website was unavailable to readers on Tuesday afternoon, 13 August 2013 following an attack on the company's domain name registrar. In addition, the attack temporarily caused a number of emails that had been sent to the company to be returned to senders as undeliverable. Management at the *New York Times* issued a statement that afternoon that the disruption was the result of a malicious external attack carried out by a group known as the Syrian Electronic Army (SEA).

The subsequent investigation of this incident pinpointed Melbourne IT as the focus for the security attack. Melbourne IT is the registrar for the *New York Times*. This means that Melbourne IT manages the Domain Name Service (DNS) entries for the *New York Times*. DNS entries are like a phone book for the internet and map a logical URL (used by people) to an IP address (used by web browsers). The SEA had used phishing tactics to obtain an appropriate username and password from a Melbourne IT affiliate company — and subsequently used these credentials to enter the Melbourne IT system. Once inside the Melbourne IT system, the SEA had proceeded to change the DNS records of several domain names, as later acknowledged by Melbourne IT. By changing these DNS records, the SEA was able to reroute traffic for the *New York Times* to another address, and consequently take the media company offline. Melbourne IT subsequently announced that it had initiated correction and recovery action the moment it was aware of the breach.

Source: Peter Clutterbuck, The University of Queensland.

QUESTIONS

1 The initial security breach in this chain of events was a phishing attack. Explain what this term means and describe the major type of control for countering phishing.

2 Melbourne IT is clearly a successful technology company. What do you assess to be its level of sophistication in terms of using log-in/password authentication credentials?

Alien software

Many personal computers have alien software (also called *pestware*) running on them that the owners do not know about. Alien software is clandestine software that is installed on a computer through duplicitous methods. **Alien software** is typically not as malicious as viruses, worms, or Trojan horses, but it does use up valuable system resources. In addition, it can report on your web surfing habits and other personal behaviour.

The vast majority of pestware is **adware** — software designed to help pop-up advertisements appear on your screen. Adware is so common because it works. According to advertising agencies, for every 100 people who ignore such an ad, three click on it. This hit rate is extremely high for internet advertising.

Spyware is software that collects personal information about users without their consent. Two types of spyware are addressed here: keystroke loggers and screen scrapers.

Keystroke loggers (also called *keyloggers*) record keystrokes and internet web browsing history. The purposes range from criminal (e.g. theft of passwords and sensitive personal information such as credit card numbers) to annoying (e.g. recording internet search history for targeted advertising).

Companies have attempted to counter key loggers by switching to other forms of input for authentication. For example, all of us have been forced to look at wavy, distorted letters and type them correctly into a box. That string of letters is called a CAPTCHA and it is a test. The point of CAPTCHA is that reading those distorted letters is something that computers cannot do accurately (yet). The fact that you can transcribe them means that you are probably not a software program run by an unauthorised person, such as a spammer. As a result, attackers have turned to *screen scrapers* (or *screen grabbers*), software that records a continuous 'movie' of a screen's contents rather than simply recording keystrokes.

Spamware is pestware that is designed to use your computer as a launch pad for spammers. **Spam** is unsolicited email, usually for the purpose of advertising for products and services. When your computer is used this way, emails from spammers appear to come from you. Even worse, spam will be sent to everyone in your email address book.

Not only is spam a nuisance, but it wastes time and money. Spam costs companies billions of dollars per year. These costs come from productivity losses, clogged email systems, additional storage, user support and antispam software. Spam can also carry viruses and worms, making it even more dangerous.

Cookies are small amounts of information that websites store on your computer, temporarily or more or less permanently. In many cases, cookies are useful and innocuous. For example, some cookies store passwords and user IDs that you do not have to retype every time you load a new page at the website that issued the cookie. Cookies are also necessary if you want to shop online, because they are used for your shopping carts at various online merchants.

Tracking cookies, however, can be used to track your path through a website, the time you spend there, what links you click on and other details that the company wants to record, usually for marketing purposes. Tracking cookies can also combine this information with your name, purchases, credit card information and other personal data, to develop an intrusive profile of your spending habits.

Most cookies can be read only by the party that created them. However, some companies that manage online banner advertising are, in essence, cookie-sharing rings. These companies can track information such as which pages you load and which ads you click on. They then share this information with their client websites (which may number in the thousands). For a cookie demonstration, see **cookiedemo.com**.

Supervisory control and data acquisition (SCADA attacks)

SCADA refers to a large-scale, distributed, measurement and control system. SCADA systems are used to monitor or to control chemical, physical, or transport processes such as oil refineries, water and sewage treatment plants, electrical generators and nuclear power plants. Essentially, SCADA systems provide the link between the physical world and the electronic world.

SCADA systems consist of multiple sensors, a master computer and communications infrastructure. The sensors connect to physical equipment and read status data such as the open/closed status of a switch or a valve, as well as measurements such as pressure, flow, voltage and current. By sending signals to equipment, sensors control that equipment, such as opening or closing a switch or valve or setting the speed of a pump.

The sensors are connected in a network and each sensor typically has an internet (internet protocol, or IP) address. (See chapter 4 for more about IP addresses.) If an attacker can gain access to the network, he or she can disrupt the power grid over a large area or disrupt the operations of a large chemical plant. Such actions could have catastrophic results.

Cyberterrorism and cyberwarfare

With both **cyberterrorism** and **cyberwarfare**, attackers use a target's computer systems, particularly via the internet, to cause physical, real-world harm or severe disruption, usually to carry out a political agenda. Cyberterrorism and cyberwarfare range from gathering data to attacking critical infrastructure (via SCADA systems). The two types of attacks are discussed synonymously here, even though cyberterrorism typically is carried out by individuals or groups, whereas cyberwarfare involves nations.

BEFORE YOU GO ON . . .

1. Why has the theft of computing devices become more serious over time?
2. What are the three types of software attacks?
3. Define *alien software*.
4. What is a SCADA system?

EXAMPLE Plotting likely plan of cyberattack at QUT

The systems that run large, critical infrastructure such as electricity, water treatment and traffic control are high-risk targets for cyberattack in Australia, according to industry expert Ernest Foo. The Queensland University of Technology cybersecurity expert said existing industrial control systems were not designed to protect against cyberattacks.

Dr Foo's team is investigating what attackers are capable of undertaking, to provide feedback to industry. 'We need to understand what kind of possible attacks can take place and how easy or how difficult it is for them to actually do it', he said. The team is also looking at more sophisticated attacks that operators may not be able to detect by sitting at their computer screens.

'These involve things like man-in-the-middle-type attacks where the attacker gets in between the human interface and the actual control system itself', Dr Foo said. The group is also developing intrusion detection technology to better warn operators of a cyberattack. 'As corporations and management want to be able to see what is happening themselves, and they don't want to have to go out to the plant site, with ICT technology we can connect them up to the internet and that is where the danger is', Dr Foo said.

He said there was greater probability of an attack coming from another country or state. 'If they were able to get into a system, they would make the processes do different things than they are expected to do and maybe cause an accident or cause those plants or electricity substations to break down. A hacker could do whatever they wanted once they gained access to the control system network', he said. 'The caveat is that not all of them (control systems) are on the internet directly, but some might be', Dr Foo said.

'I would imagine that there certainly have been attacks that have happened, but they haven't been disclosed publicly.' The team is looking at signature-based intrusion detection systems and anomaly-based intrusion detection systems, and aims to develop new protocols and device designs to mitigate and prevent such attacks. Dr Foo's team has received $350 000 under an Australian Research Council Linkage grant with electricity transmission authority Powerlink in Queensland to study the security of substation automation.

Source: J Foreshew (2013), *The Australian* (Technology section), 25 June.

Apply the Concept

Background

It is sad that there are many people out there who are proud of the fact that they can take advantage of others. Fraud, espionage, information extortion, identity theft, cyberterrorism, spamming, phishing and many other deliberate acts have created a world where we must always confirm the identity and validity of those we share information with.

Activity

Go to the Australian Competition and Consumer Commission website, SCAMwatch, and read about lottery and sweepstake scams. This scam has taken advantage of many elderly people simply because they are not aware that scams exist. Search the web for other scams that involve Gumtree, eBay and any other site you may find.

Deliverable

Imagine that you are the owner of a site such as Gumtree. Write a memo to your users (both buyers and sellers) explaining your intention to run a 'clean' site where all parties are safe. In your memo, give your own definition of fraud for your users' information. Include expectations of ethical behaviour and legal transactions.

THE NOOK

QUESTIONS

1. Given the stories in the chapter, what are some scenarios where someone might use USB drives to access The Nook's private customer data?
2. Because The Nook is being redesigned, where should 'back office' operations be housed to help deter theft of equipment?

7.4 What organisations are doing to protect information resources

Why is it so difficult to stop cybercriminals? Figure 7.2 lists the major difficulties involved in protecting information. Because organising an appropriate defence system is so important to the entire enterprise, it is one of the major responsibilities of any prudent CIO as well as the functional managers who control information resources. In fact, IT security is the business of *everyone* in an organisation.

Hundreds of potential threats exist.
Computing resources may be situated in many locations.
Many individuals control information assets.
Computer networks can be located outside the organisation and are thus difficult to protect.
Rapid technological changes make some controls obsolete as soon as they are installed.
Many computer crimes are undetected for a long period of time, so it is difficult to learn from experience.
People tend to violate security procedures because the procedures are inconvenient.
The amount of computer knowledge necessary to commit computer crimes is usually minimal. As a matter of fact, one can learn hacking, for free, on the internet.
The cost of preventing hazards can be very high. Therefore, most organisations simply cannot afford to protect against all possible hazards.
It is difficult to conduct a cost–benefit justification for controls before an attack occurs because it is difficult to assess the value of a hypothetical attack.

FIGURE 7.2 The difficulties in protecting information resources.

Another reason why it is difficult to protect information resources is that the online commerce industry is not particularly willing to install safeguards that would make it harder to complete transactions. It would be possible, for example, to demand passwords or personal identification numbers for all credit card transactions. However, these requirements might discourage people from shopping online. Also, there is little incentive for companies like AOL to share leads on criminal activity either with one another or with the FBI. For credit card companies, it is cheaper to block a stolen credit card and move on than to invest time and money on a prosecution.

Despite these difficulties, the information security industry is battling back. Companies are developing software and services that deliver early warnings of trouble on the internet. Unlike traditional antivirus software, which is reactive, early warning systems are proactive, scanning the web for new viruses and alerting companies to dangers.

Organisations spend a great deal of time and money protecting their information resources. Before doing so, they perform risk management.

Risk is the probability that a threat will impact an information resource. The goal of **risk management** is to identify, control and minimise the impact of threats. In other words, risk management seeks to reduce risk to acceptable levels. Risk management encompasses three processes: risk analysis, risk mitigation and controls evaluation.

Risk analysis is the process by which an organisation assesses the value of each asset being protected, estimates the probability that each asset will be compromised, and compares the probable costs of the asset being compromised with the costs of protecting that asset. Organisations perform risk analysis to ensure that their information systems' security programs are cost effective. The risk analysis process prioritises the assets to be protected based on each asset's value, its probability of being compromised and the estimated cost of its protection. The organisation then considers how to mitigate the risk.

In **risk mitigation**, the organisation takes concrete actions against risks. Risk mitigation has two functions: (1) implementing controls to prevent identified threats from occurring and (2) developing a means of recovery should the threat become a reality. Several risk mitigation strategies may be adopted by organisations. The three most common are risk acceptance, risk limitation and risk transference.

- **Risk acceptance**: accept the potential risk, continue operating with no controls and absorb any damages that occur.
- **Risk limitation**: limit the risk by implementing controls that minimise the impact of the threat.
- **Risk transference**: transfer the risk by using other means to compensate for the loss, such as by purchasing insurance.

BEFORE YOU GO ON . . .

1. Describe several reasons why it is difficult to protect information resources.
2. Compare and contrast risk management and risk analysis.

In controls evaluation, the organisation examines the costs of implementing adequate control measures against the value of those control measures. If the costs of implementing a control are greater than the value of the asset being protected, then control is not cost effective. In the next section, you will study the various controls that organisations use to protect their information resources.

THE NOOK

QUESTIONS

1 A risk analysis is crucial for The Nook. Is the e-commerce part of the club's site crucial to its business plan? If not, should the club accept the risk and go with its e-commerce plans? Should Malakai and Abbie limit the risk by simply displaying products but only selling them at their club? Or should they transfer the risk and use a third-party company to run the e-commerce of the site?

2 Malakai and Abbie should be familiar with the 'penetration attack' given that they sell alcohol and are often tested by the NSW Government Licensing Service to see if they will sell alcohol to underage patrons. How could they use this same concept and test their own security against intentional and unintentional threats?

7.5 Information security controls

To protect their information assets, organisations implement **controls**, or defence mechanisms (also called *countermeasures*). **Information security controls** are designed to protect all of the components of an information system, including data, software, hardware and networks. Because there are so many diverse threats, organisations utilise layers of controls, or defence-in-depth.

Controls are intended to prevent accidental hazards, deter intentional acts, detect problems as early as possible, enhance damage recovery and correct problems. Before you study controls in more detail, it is important to emphasise that the single most effective control is user education and training, leading to increased awareness of the vital importance of information security on the part of every organisational employee. As you have learned in this chapter, an organisation's employees are its greatest information security risk. In fact, the fastest way to build a botnet is to attack individual employees. Once a botnet has been established, it is difficult to combat. However, IT's About Business shows a company that has been successful in thwarting botnets.

IT'S ABOUT BUSINESS

SaaS and Cancer Council SA

Software-as-a-service (SaaS) is an attractive option for IT departments as it has some upfront capital expenditure and operational cost benefits by reducing software support costs and can be deployed quickly to meet business needs. However, there are risks involved when moving from the traditional application software to the SaaS model.

The Cancer Council SA (South Australia) has core programs of cancer research, prevention and support. These services are delivered by 145 staff members, 249 regular volunteers and thousands of occasional volunteers involved with events. This not-for-profit organisation requires an annual revenue of around $20 million per annum and directs expenditure to administration including IT, cancer research and prevention programs, as well as supporting people affected by cancer.

Prior to the implementation of a centralised customer relationship management (CRM) system, the Cancer Council SA had been operating on a legacy system consisting of 17 separate databases. The data contained within these databases represented a range of information including the personal details of people within the organisation (volunteers and donors) and those using the organisation's services. Within the organisation, four business units were administering the databases and there were multiple records of interactions that were being maintained redundantly in various databases and spreadsheets. This situation was preventing the organisation from having a single, streamlined view of its data and information, which also prevented effective information and knowledge sharing within the organisation.

Consultants brought in to analyse the situation recommended that the organisation needed a common platform to consolidate their systems and provide a 360° view of the people interacting with the organisation. The cloud-based solution proposed would reduce the internal management of the technology infrastructure and system maintenance, while delivering the benefits of scalability, flexibility and reliability. After consultation and legal advice regarding whether a cloud-based system was suitable for storing personal data for the Cancer Council SA, the core components of the Salesforce CRM were gradually implemented across the organisation as the databases from each of the business units and their software programs were brought into the new system.

The priority issues leading to the change were a lack of a clear vision of all the key operating aspects and relationships of people to the organisation. The knowledge required to maintain and report from multiple databases was problematic and the move to a single system was expected to resolve this issue and improve efficiency. Overall the organisation's primary need was for a centralised, consolidated system to improve the efficiency and effectiveness of their fundraising and to better understand their relationships with people involved with the organisation.

The expectations were that this would lead to improvements in the efficiency and effectiveness of fundraising campaigns through a better utilisation of people's capabilities and contributions to the organisation as volunteers. While staff were accustomed to working with locally located databases and spreadsheets, it was hoped that the new system would significantly improve their level of responsiveness and efficiency. Furthermore, it was expected that the centralised system would provide improved disaster recovery capabilities and that the cloud-based system would deliver significant adaptability benefits such as scalability, flexibility and reliability.

The objective was to implement the CRM system as a SaaS, thereby consolidating all databases into the system, creating a single source of truth and 360° view of the organisation. This required the data from all the disparate systems to be cleansed, ensuring that the new system provided accurate and consistent information across the organisation.

Some of the challenges for the new system have been that some of the response times have been slower than the locally stored databases previously used. The per-user licensing model of Salesforce was an impediment to the broad use of the system. While not-for-profit organisations could have 10 free licences, the Cancer Council SA required over 100 licences. Therefore the broad distribution of system access represented a significant cost burden.

Uptake and acceptance of the new system by existing staff has been challenging, particularly with the issue of sensitive personal information residing in the cloud being accessible to other areas of the organisation, such as marketing and fundraising. However, these concerns have been resolved with security measures implemented to effectively quarantine sensitive data, ensuring that only those staff members with approved access can view the sensitive data and information.

Salesforce is not integrated with the Cancer Council SA online fundraising tool, so donor information has to be manually entered into the Salesforce CRM with the associated data integrity implications and requiring an interface capability as a priority for the organisation.

Risk management considerations of cloud-based computing systems like Salesforce are increasingly becoming the focus of businesses as larger amounts of personal and customer data are being held by these cloud services. This makes them an enticing target for hackers. However, Salesforce is well regarded and has a good track record relating to security. Salesforce adheres to best practices and holds certifications relating to security standards.

Hosting the Cancer Council SA core system in the cloud represents other unique risks too. If Salesforce suffers an outage then the Cancer Council SA will be likewise affected, causing the entire organisation to become unavailable too. There were two major outages of Salesforce in 2012 that impacted customers in North America and these issues were attributed to storage problems and infrastructure power issues.

Salesforce offers a data recovery service that can recover data up to 3 months back from the current date. However, this process must be completed manually, usually taking a minimum of 15 working days and the minimum price is US$10 000. As a result the Cancer Council SA performs its own database backups to remove the need for this service.

The resulting outcomes of the implementation of the new system has opened access to previously unavailable data and information residing within the organisation's old disparate databases, enabling greater functionality. Process and planning efficiencies have been gained through a greater understanding of the resources needed and the scheduling of support programs. For example, marketing and fundraising can now plan and execute specially targeted campaigns that have improved effectiveness and levels of incoming funds. Gradual consolidation and cleansing of data is delivering benefits in error identification and correction. →

For example, errors in postal addresses have been significantly reduced with the number of incorrect addresses now at a more manageable level. The time spent entering data into multiple locations has been reduced and the implementation of the Salesforce system has been the catalyst for reviewing and redesigning business processes to better take advantage of the organisation-wide information sharing capabilities. Lastly, the Salesforce system is now integrated with the telephone system, enabling information about the caller to be immediately displayed to the staff member taking the call, providing an understanding of the person's involvement and relationship with the Cancer Council SA that has led to improving the quality and effectiveness of telephone conversations.

Since its initial implementation in April 2009, the system has continued to gradually evolve as staff come to appreciate the advantages, possibilities and functionality of the system. Salesforce have been able to further customise system modules and workflows to better meet the requirements of the Cancer Council SA. The organisation is very satisfied with the resulting outcomes of implementing the Salesforce cloud-based solution.

Sources: Weiser Solutions (2013), 'Case study — software as a service', Cancer Council SA, www.weisersolutions.com.au/wp-content/uploads/2013/08/2013-07-Weiser-Solutions-Case-Study-Cancer-Council-SAAS-final.pdf; S Santhosh (2008), 'Benefits and risks of the SaaS model — a case study', *The Sterling Report*, December, www.sterlinghoffman.com/newsletter/articles/article485.html; 'Business needs to balance SaaS benefit and risk' (2009), *Computer Weekly*, 17 March, www.computerweekly.com/news/2240088762/Business-needs-to-balance-SaaS-benefit-and-risk.

QUESTIONS

1. Describe why it is important to fully understand the security requirements of the organisation before implementing any cloud-based services.
2. What other concerns might arise as a consequence of poor security implementation or lack of proper system access and data management policies and processes?
3. What are the potential impacts for the organisation if the cloud-based solution became unavailable for an extended period? Suggest some contingency plans or processes that might address these impacts and keep the organisation functioning in a secure manner.
4. Suggest a process suitable for managing staff that leave the organisation. What actions and steps do you suggest for managing staff members that no longer work for the organisation? Outline a simple step-by-step process to manage this security situation.

Physical controls

Physical controls prevent unauthorised individuals from gaining access to a company's facilities. Common physical controls include walls, doors, fencing, gates, locks, badges, guards and alarm systems. More sophisticated physical controls include pressure sensors, temperature sensors and motion detectors. One weakness of physical controls is that they can be inconvenient to employees (see figure 7.3).

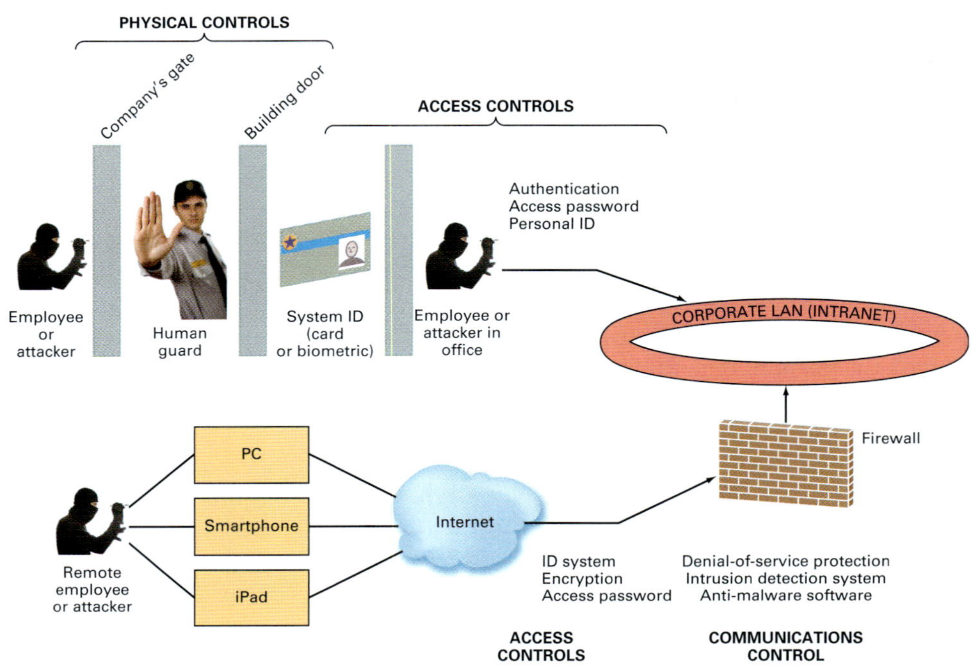

FIGURE 7.3 The location of defence mechanisms.

Guards deserve special mention because they have very difficult jobs for at least two reasons. First, their jobs are boring and repetitive and generally do not pay well. Second, if they do their jobs thoroughly, other employees harass them, particularly if their being conscientious slows up the process of entering a facility.

Organisations also put other physical security considerations in place. Such controls limit users to acceptable log-in times and locations. These controls also limit the number of unsuccessful log-in attempts and they require all employees to log off their computers when they leave for the day. In addition, computers are set to automatically log off the user after a certain period of disuse.

Access controls

Access controls restrict unauthorised individuals from using information resources. These controls involve two major functions: authentication and authorisation. **Authentication** determines the identity of the person requiring access. After the person is authenticated (identified), authorisation is applied. **Authorisation** determines which actions, rights, or privileges the person has, based on verified identity.

Authentication

To authenticate (identify) authorised personnel, an organisation can use one or more of the following methods: something the user is, something the user has, something the user does, and/or something the user knows.

Something the user is (also known as **biometrics**), is an authentication method that examines a person's innate physical characteristics. Common biometric applications are fingerprint scans, palm scans, retina scans, iris recognition, and facial recognition. Of these, fingerprints, retina scans and iris recognition provide the most definitive identification. The following example shows how powerful biometrics can be for identification purposes.

EXAMPLE The biometric identification project of India

India has vast numbers of anonymous poor citizens. As a result, the nation is deploying its Unique Identification Project, also known as Aadhaar, which means 'the foundation' in several Indian languages. The goal of the Unique Identification Project is to issue identification numbers linked to the fingerprints and iris scans of every single person in India. This process will ultimately encompass some 1.2 billion people who speak more than 300 languages and dialects. The biometrics and the Aadhaar identification number will serve as a verifiable, portable and unique national ID.

This project seeks to remedy a key problem with the poor. The existence of many poor Indian citizens is not officially acknowledged by the government because they lack birth certificates and other official documentation. Therefore, these citizens are not able to access government services to which they are entitled. For example, in 2012, less than half of Indian households had an associated bank account. The rest of households are 'unbanked' and must stash their savings in cash around their homes.

Aadhaar kicked off the ground in September 2010, when officials armed with iris scanners, fingerprint scanners, digital cameras and laptops began registering the first few villagers and Delhi slum dwellers. By 2014, the government had 600 million people entered into its biometric database.

Each individual record is between 4 and 8 megabytes, meaning that the database will ultimately hold some 20 petabytes. The unprecedented scale of the Aadhaar database will make managing it extraordinarily difficult. Therefore, one of the most important tasks is to ensure that each record in the database is matched to one and only one person. For this process, Aadhaar must check all 10 fingerprints and both irises of each person against those of everyone else. Using 10 prints and both irises boosts the accuracy rate to 99 per cent. However, in a country the size of India, 99 per cent accuracy means that 12 million people could end up with faulty records.

Additionally, Aadhaar faces enormous physical and technical challenges: reaching millions of illiterate Indians who have never seen a computer, persuading them to have their irises scanned, ensuring that their scanned information is accurate and safeguarding the resulting massive amounts of data. Another problem is that civil libertarians object to the project on privacy grounds.

As an example of the impact of this project, consider Kiran, a poor citizen of India. She thinks she is 32, but she is not sure. She has no birth certificate or ID of any kind — no driver's licence, no voting card, nothing at all to document her existence. When she was 24, she left her home in a destitute farming village and ended up in a Delhi slum. She and her children were among the first to have their personal information entered into the Aadhaar system.

The first thing Kiran plans to use her Aadhaar number for, she says, is to obtain a city government card that will entitle her to subsidised groceries. 'I've tried very hard to get one before but they wouldn't give it to me because I couldn't prove I live in Delhi.' In sum, the Aadhar project should allow millions of poor Indian citizens to access government services that previously were out of reach to them.

Sources: Compiled from 'World's biggest biometric ID scheme forges ahead' (2012), *BBC News India*, 12 February; M Magnier (2012), 'India's biometric ID number plan divided by bureaucracy', *Los Angeles Times*, 28 January; B Turbeville (2012), 'Cashless society: India implements first biometric ID program for all of its 1.2 billion residents', *Infowars.com*, 12 January; V Beiser (2011), 'Identified', *Wired*, September; www.iaadhaar.com.

QUESTIONS

1. Describe the problems that India is facing in implementing this biometric identification system.
2. Describe the benefits that India hopes to gain in implementing the biometric identification system.
3. Describe the benefits that the biometric identification system should provide to India's impoverished citizens.

Something the user has is an authentication mechanism that includes regular identification (ID) cards, smart ID cards and tokens. *Regular ID cards*, or *dumb cards*, typically have the person's picture and often his or her signature. *Smart ID cards* have a chip embedded in them with pertinent information about the user. (Smart ID cards used for identification differ from smart cards used in electronic commerce [see chapter 9]. Both types of card have embedded chips, but they are used for different purposes.) *Tokens* have embedded chips and a digital display that presents a log-in number that the employees use to access the organisation's network. The number changes with each log-in.

Something the user does is an authentication mechanism that includes voice and signature recognition. In **voice recognition**, the user speaks a phrase (e.g. his or her name and department) that has been previously recorded under controlled, monitored conditions. The voice recognition system matches the two voice signals. In **signature recognition**, the user signs his or her name, and the system matches this signature with one previously recorded under controlled, monitored conditions. Signature recognition systems also match the speed of the signature and the pressure of the signature.

Something the user knows is an authentication mechanism that includes **passwords** and passphrases. Passwords present a huge information security problem in all organisations. All users should use strong passwords so that the password cannot easily be discovered. **Strong passwords** have the following characteristics.

- They should be difficult to guess.
- They should be longer rather than shorter.
- They should contain uppercase letters, lowercase letters, numbers and special characters.
- They should not be a recognisable word.
- They should not be the name of anything or anyone familiar, such as family names or names of pets.
- They should not be a recognisable string of numbers, such as a pin number or birthday.

Unfortunately, strong passwords are irritating. If the organisation mandates longer (stronger) passwords and/or frequent password changes, they become more difficult to remember, causing employees to write them down. What is needed is a way for a user to create a strong password that is easy to remember. A passphrase can help, either by being a password itself or by helping you create a strong password.

A **passphrase** is a series of characters that is longer than a password but can be memorised easily. Examples of passphrases are 'may the force be with you always', 'go ahead make my day', 'live long and prosper' and 'a man's got to know his limitations'. A user can turn a passphrase into a strong password in this manner. Start with the last passphrase above and use the first letter of each word. You will have amgtkhl. Then capitalise every other letter, to have AmGtKhL. Then add special characters and numbers, to have 9AmGtKhL//*. Now you have a strong password that you can remember.

Many organisations are using *multifactor authentication* (more than one type of authentication) to more efficiently and effectively identify authorised users. This type of authentication is particularly important when users are logging in from remote locations.

Single-factor authentication, which is notoriously weak, commonly consists of simply a password. Two-factor authentication consists of a password plus one type of biometric identification (e.g. a fingerprint). Three-factor authentication is any combination of three authentication methods. You should keep in mind that stronger authentication is more expensive and can be irritating to users as well.

Authorisation

Once users have been properly authenticated, the rights and privileges that they have on the organisation's systems are established, a process called *authorisation*. Companies use the principle of least privilege for authorisation purposes. A **privilege** is a collection of related computer system operations that can be performed by users of the system. **Least privilege** is a principle that users be granted the privilege for some activity only if there is a justifiable need to grant this authorisation.

Communications controls

Communications (network) controls secure the movement of data across networks. Communications controls consist of firewalls, anti-malware systems, whitelisting and blacklisting, encryption, virtual private networking (VPN), secure socket layer (SSL) and employee monitoring systems.

Firewalls

A **firewall** is a system that prevents a specific type of information from moving between untrusted networks, such as the internet, and private networks, such as your company's network. Put simply, firewalls prevent unauthorised internet users from accessing private networks. All messages entering or leaving your company's network pass through a firewall. The firewall examines each message and blocks those that do not meet specified security rules. Firewalls filter network traffic according to categories of activities likely to cause problems, whereas anti-malware systems filter traffic according to a database of specific problems.

Firewalls range from simple for home use, to very complex for organisational use. Figure 7.4(a) (overleaf) shows a basic firewall for a home computer. In this case, the firewall is implemented as software on the home computer. Figure 7.4(b) shows an organisation that has implemented an external firewall, which faces the internet and an internal firewall, which faces the company network. Corporate firewalls typically consist of software running on a computer dedicated to the task. A **demilitarised zone (DMZ)** is located between the two firewalls. Messages from the internet must first pass through the external firewall. If they conform to the defined security rules, then they are sent to company servers located in the DMZ. These servers typically handle web page requests and email. Any messages designated for the company's internal network (e.g. its intranet) must pass through the internal firewall, again with its own defined security rules, to gain access to the company's private network.

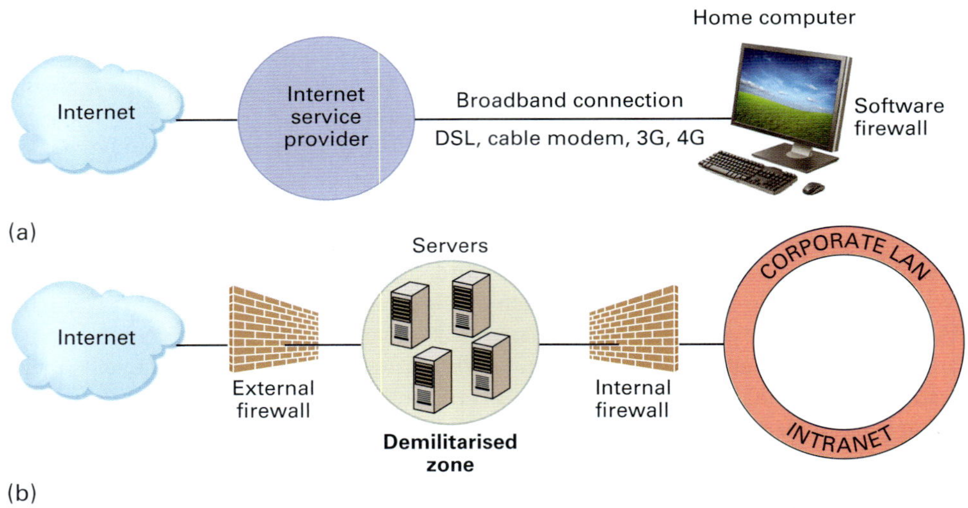

FIGURE 7.4 (a) Basic firewall for home computer (b) Organisation with two firewalls and demilitarised zone.

The danger from viruses and worms is so severe that many organisations are placing firewalls at strategic points *inside* their private networks. In this way, if a virus or worm does get through both the external and internal firewalls, then the internal damage may be contained.

Anti-malware systems

Anti-malware systems (antivirus software), also called AV, are software packages that attempt to identify and eliminate viruses, worms and other malicious software. This software is implemented at the organisational level by the information systems department. Hundreds of AV software packages are currently available. Among the best known are Norton Antivirus (**www.symantec.com**), McAfee Virusscan (**www.mcafee.com**) and Trend Micro PC-cillin (**www.trendmicro.com**).

Anti-malware systems are generally reactive. They work by creating definitions, or signatures, of various types of malware and then updating these signatures in their products. The anti-malware software then examines suspicious computer code to see if it matches a known signature. If it does, then the anti-malware software will remove it. This is the reason why organisations update their malware definitions so often. (See Chapter Closing Case 2.)

Because malware is such a serious problem, the leading vendors are rapidly developing anti-malware systems that function proactively as well as reactively. These systems evaluate behaviour rather than relying on signature matching. In theory, therefore, it is possible to catch malware before it can infect systems.

Whitelisting and blacklisting

A report by the Yankee Group (**www.yankeegroup.com**), a technology research and consulting firm, stated that 99 per cent of organisations had anti-malware systems installed, but 62 per cent of companies still suffered successful malware attacks. Anti-malware systems are usually reactive and malware continues to infect information systems.

One solution to this problem is whitelisting. **Whitelisting** is a process in which a company identifies the software that it will allow to run and does not try to recognise malware. Whitelisting permits acceptable software to run and either prevents anything else from running or lets new software run in a quarantined environment until the company can verify its validity.

Whereas whitelisting allows nothing to run unless it is on the whitelist, **blacklisting** allows everything to run unless it is on the blacklist. A blacklist, then, includes certain types of software that are not allowed to run in the company environment. For example, a company might blacklist peer-to-peer file sharing on its systems. In addition to software, people, devices and websites can also be whitelisted and blacklisted.

Encryption

When organisations do not have a secure channel for sending information, they use encryption to stop unauthorised eavesdroppers. **Encryption** is the process of converting an original message into a form that cannot be read by anyone except the intended receiver.

All encryption systems use a key, which is the code that scrambles, and then decodes, the messages. The majority of encryption systems use public-key encryption. **Public-key encryption** — also known as *asymmetric encryption* — uses two different keys: a public key and a private key (see figure 7.5). The public key (locking key) and the private key (unlocking key) are created simultaneously using the same mathematical formula or algorithm. Because the two keys are mathematically related, the data encrypted with one key can be decrypted by using the other key. The public key is publicly available in a directory that all parties can access. The private key is kept secret, never shared with anyone and never sent across the internet. In this system, if Malala wants to send a message to Radek, she first obtains Radek's public key (locking key), which she uses to encrypt her message (put the message in the 'two-lock box'). When Radek receives Malala's message, he uses his private key to decrypt it (open the box).

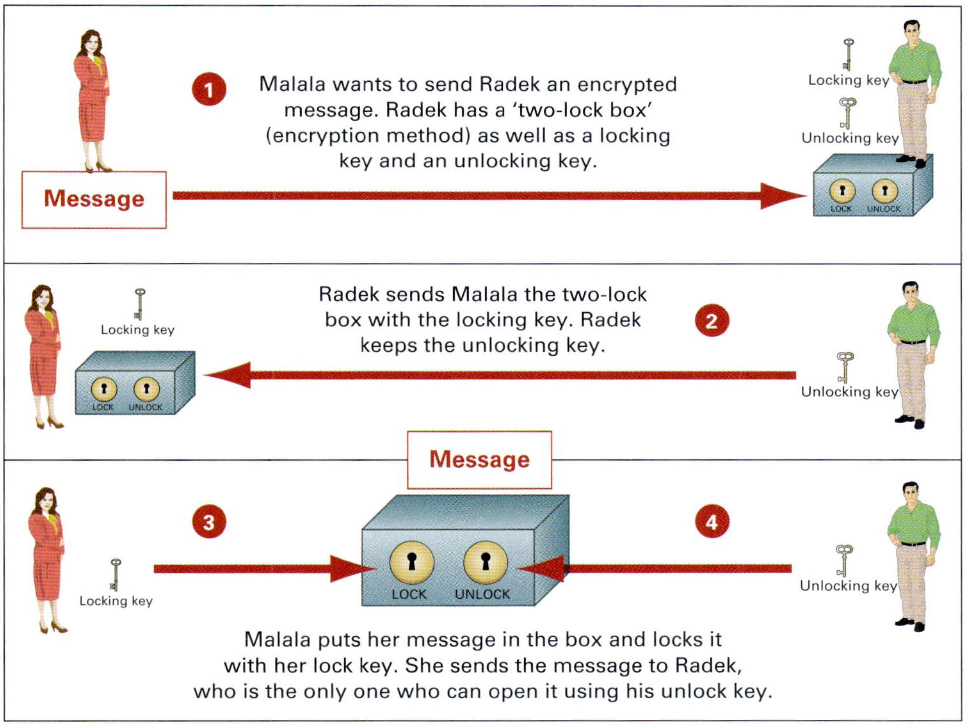

FIGURE 7.5 How public key encryption works.

Although this system is adequate for personal information, organisations doing business over the internet require a more complex system. In such cases, a third party, called a **certificate authority**, acts as a trusted intermediary between companies. As such, the certificate authority issues digital certificates and verifies the worth and integrity of the certificates. A **digital certificate** is an electronic document attached to a file certifying that the file is from the organisation it claims to be from and has not been modified from its original format. As you can see in figure 7.6 (overleaf), Sony requests a digital certificate from VeriSign, a certificate authority, and uses this certificate when doing business with Dell. Note that the digital certificate contains an identification number, the issuer, validity dates and the requester's public key. For examples of certificate authorities, see **www.entrust.com**, **www.verisign.com**, **www.cybertrust.com**, **www.secude.com** and **www.thawte.com**.

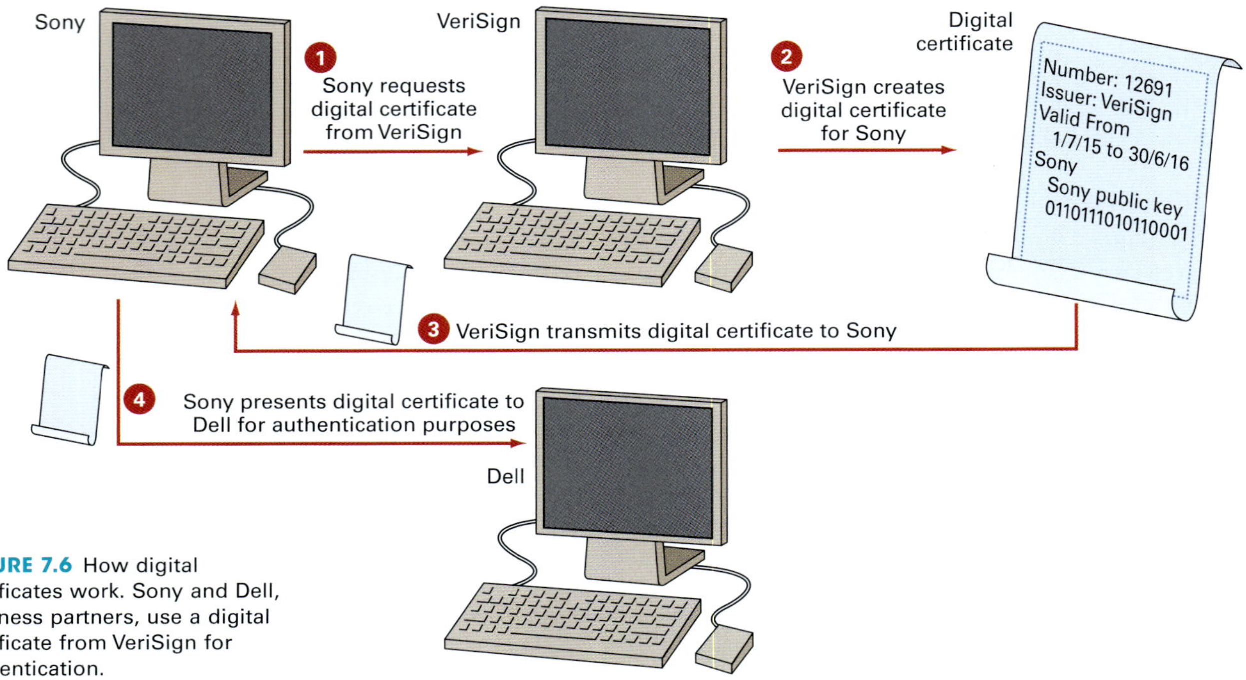

FIGURE 7.6 How digital certificates work. Sony and Dell, business partners, use a digital certificate from VeriSign for authentication.

Virtual private networking

A **virtual private network (VPN)** is a private network that uses a public network (usually the internet) to connect users. As such, VPNs integrate the global connectivity of the internet with the security of a private network and thereby extend the reach of the organisation's networks. VPNs are called 'virtual' because they have no separate physical existence. They use the public internet as their infrastructure. They create a *virtual private* network by using log-ins, encryption and other techniques to enhance privacy.

VPNs have several advantages.

- First, they allow remote users to access the company network.
- Second, they allow flexibility. That is, mobile users can access the organisation's network from properly configured remote devices.
- Third, organisations can impose their security policies through VPNs. For example, an organisation may dictate that only corporate email applications are available to users when they connect from unmanaged devices.

To provide secure transmissions, VPNs use a process called tunnelling. **Tunnelling** encrypts each data packet to be sent and places each encrypted packet inside another packet. In this manner, the packet can travel across the internet with confidentiality, authentication and integrity. Figure 7.7 illustrates a VPN and tunnelling.

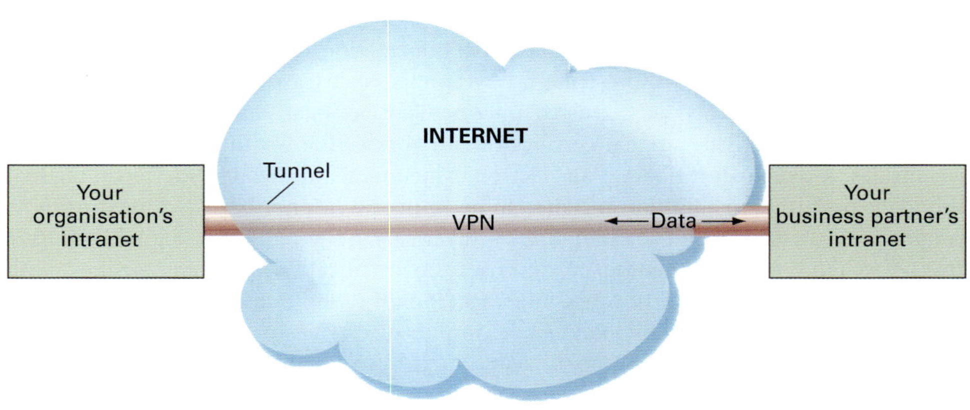

FIGURE 7.7 Virtual private network and tunnelling.

Transport layer security (TLS)

Transport layer security (TLS) (formerly called secure socket layer), is an encryption standard used for secure transactions such as credit card purchases and online banking. TLS encrypts and decrypts data between a web server and a browser end to end.

TLS is indicated by a URL that begins with https rather than http and it often includes a small padlock icon in the browser's status bar. Using a padlock icon to indicate a secure connection and placing this icon in a browser's status bar are artefacts of specific browsers. Other browsers use other icons (e.g. a key that is either broken or whole). The important thing to remember here is that browsers usually provide visual confirmation of a secure connection.

Employee monitoring systems

Many companies are taking a proactive approach to protecting their networks from what they view as one of their major security threats, namely employee mistakes. These companies are implementing **employee monitoring systems**, which monitor their employees' computers, email activities and internet surfing activities. These products are useful to identify employees who spend too much time surfing on the internet for personal reasons, who visit questionable websites, or who download music illegally. Vendors that provide monitoring software include SpectorSoft (www.spectorsoft.com) and Websense (www.websense.com).

Business continuity planning

An important strategy for organisations is to be prepared for any eventuality. A critical element in any security system is a business continuity plan, also known as a disaster recovery plan. Large businesses have these plans. For you as an individual, or for a small business, a plan for backing up your important data will suffice. For example, Enterprise Data Corporation (EDC) (www.enterprisedata.com.au) will build, design and manage IT systems, data centre infrastructure and cloud computing environments for Australian and international clients.[3]

Business continuity is the chain of events linking planning to protection and to recovery. The purpose of the business continuity plan is to provide guidance to people who keep the business operating after a disaster occurs. Using this plan, employees prepare for, react to and recover from events that affect the security of information assets and the subsequent restoration to normal business operations. The plan helps to ensure that critical business functions continue.

In the event of a major disaster, organisations can employ several strategies for business continuity. These strategies include hot sites, warm sites and cold sites.

A **hot site** is a fully configured computer facility, with all services, communications links and physical plant operations. A hot site duplicates computing resources, peripherals, telephone systems, applications and workstations.

A **warm site** provides many of the same services and options of the hot site. However, a warm site typically does not include the actual applications the company needs. A warm site does include computing equipment such as servers, but it often does not include user workstations.

A **cold site** provides only rudimentary services and facilities, such as a building or room with heating, air conditioning and humidity control. This type of site provides no computer hardware or user workstations. The point of a cold site is that it takes care of long lead-time issues. Building or even renting space takes a long time. Installing high-speed communication lines, often from two or more carriers, takes a long time. Installing high-capacity power lines takes a long time. By comparison, buying and installing servers should not take a particularly long time.

Hot sites reduce risk to the greatest extent, but they are the most expensive option. Conversely, cold sites reduce risk the least, but they are the least expensive option.

Information systems auditing

Companies implement security controls to ensure that information systems work properly. These controls can be installed in the original system or they can be added after a system is in operation. Installing controls is necessary but not sufficient to provide adequate security. In addition, people responsible for security need to answer questions such as: Are all controls installed as intended? Are they effective? Has any breach of security occurred? If so, what actions are required to prevent future breaches?

These questions must be answered by independent and unbiased observers. Such observers perform the task of *information systems auditing*. In an IS environment, an **audit** is an examination of information systems, their inputs, outputs and processing.

Types of auditors and audits

The two types of auditors and audits are internal and external. IS auditing is usually a part of accounting *internal auditing* and it is frequently performed by corporate internal auditors. An *external auditor* reviews the findings of the internal audit as well as the inputs, processing and outputs of information systems. The external audit of information systems is frequently a part of the overall external auditing performed by a certified public accounting (CPA) firm.

IS auditing considers all potential hazards and controls in information systems. It focuses on topics such as operations, data integrity, software applications, security and privacy, budgets and expenditures, cost control and productivity. Guidelines are available to assist auditors in their jobs, such as those from ISACA (formerly the Information Systems Audit and Control Association, **www.isaca.org**).

How is auditing executed?

IS auditing procedures fall into three categories: (1) auditing around the computer, (2) auditing through the computer and (3) auditing with the computer.

Auditing around the computer means verifying processing by checking for known outputs using specific inputs. This approach is best used in systems with limited outputs. In *auditing through the computer*, inputs, outputs and processing are checked. Auditors review program logic and test data. *Auditing with the computer* means using a combination of client data, auditor software, and client and auditor hardware. This approach allows the auditor to perform tasks such as simulating payroll program logic using live data.

BEFORE YOU GO ON . . .

1. What is the single most important information security control for organisations?
2. Differentiate between authentication and authorisation. Which one of these always comes first?
3. Compare and contrast whitelisting and blacklisting.
4. What is the purpose of a disaster recovery plan?
5. What is information system auditing?

Apply the Concept

Background

Security controls are designed to protect all components of an information system, including data, software, hardware and networks. Because there are so many diverse threats, organisations utilise layers of controls. One area discussed in the book is public key encryption. This method of encryption requires a public key and a private key. The public key is shared and used to encrypt a message that only the individual's private key can decrypt.

Activity

Go to the YouTube clip titled 'SSL explained'. This video introduces you to the inventors of public key encryption as well as the method that it uses to work. After watching this video, visit HowStuffWorks.com and read the article titled 'How encryption works'.

Deliverable

Write an email to an elderly person (or just anyone who may be hesitant to share his or her credit card online) that explains how the public key encryption works. Discuss the benefits of public key encryption (two keys) over private key encryption (one key).

QUESTIONS

1. What security controls should Malakai and Abbie put in place to help ensure the safety of sensitive customer information?
2. Should Malakai and Abbie put these controls in place, or should they hire a third-party vendor to put them in place?

THE NOOK

WHAT'S IN IT FOR ME?

FOR THE ACCOUNTING MAJOR

Public companies, their accountants and their auditors have significant information security responsibilities. Accountants are now being held professionally responsible for reducing risk, ensuring compliance, eliminating fraud, and increasing the transparency of transactions according to generally accepted accounting principles (GAAP). The Institute of Chartered Accountants Australia[4] and the Certified Practicing Accountant (CPA) accountancy associations,[5] among other regulatory agencies, require information security, fraud prevention and detection, and internal controls over financial reporting. Forensic accounting, a combination of accounting and information security, is one of the most rapidly growing areas in accounting today.

FOR THE FINANCE MAJOR

Because information security is essential to the success of organisations today, it is no longer just the concern of the chief information officer (CIO). As a result of global regulatory requirements and the passage of Sarbanes-Oxley, responsibility for information security lies with the chief executive officer (CEO) and chief financial officer (CFO). Consequently, all aspects of the security audit, including the security of information and information systems, are a key concern for financial managers.

In addition, CFOs and treasurers are increasingly involved with investments in information technology. They know that a security breach of any kind can have devastating financial effects on a company. Banking and financial institutions are prime targets for computer criminals. A related problem is fraud involving stocks and bonds that are sold over the internet. Finance personnel must be aware of both the hazards and the available controls associated with these activities.

FOR THE MARKETING MAJOR

Marketing professionals have new opportunities to collect data on their customers (e.g. through business-to-consumer electronic commerce). Customers expect their data to be properly secured. However, profit-motivated criminals want that data. Therefore, marketing managers must analyse the risk of their operations. Failure to protect corporate and customer data will cause significant public relations problems and make customers very angry. Customer relationship management (CRM) operations and tracking customers' online buying habits can expose data to misuse (if they are not encrypted) or result in privacy violations.

FOR THE PRODUCTION/OPERATIONS MANAGEMENT MAJOR

Every process in a company's operations — inventory purchasing, receiving, quality control, production and shipping — can be disrupted by an information technology security breach or an IT security breach at a business partner. Any weak link in supply chain management or enterprise resource management systems puts the entire chain at risk. Companies may be held liable for IT security failures that affect other companies.

FOR THE HUMAN RESOURCES MANAGEMENT MAJOR

HR managers have responsibilities to secure confidential employee data. In addition, they must ensure that all employees explicitly verify that they understand the company's information security policies and procedures.

FOR THE MIS MAJOR

The MIS function provides the security infrastructure that protects the organisation's information assets. This function is critical to the success of the organisation, even though it is almost invisible until an attack succeeds. All application development, network deployment and introduction of new information technologies have to be guided by IT security considerations. MIS personnel must customise the risk-exposure security model to help the company identify security risks and prepare responses to security incidents and disasters.

Senior executives of publicly held companies look to the MIS function for help in meeting corporate governance of information technology requirements, particularly in detecting 'significant deficiencies' or 'material weaknesses' in internal controls and remediating them. Other functional areas also look to the MIS function to help them meet their security responsibilities.

SUMMARY

1 Give one specific example of each of the five factors that are contributing to the increasing vulnerability of information resources.

The five factors are as follows.

> Today's interconnected, interdependent, wirelessly networked business environment

>> Example: the internet

> Smaller, faster, cheaper computers and storage devices

>> Examples: netbooks, thumb drives, tablets

> Decreasing skills necessary to be a computer hacker

>> Example: information system hacking programs circulating on the internet

> International organised crime taking over cybercrime

>> Example: Organised crime has formed transnational cybercrime cartels. Because it is difficult to know exactly where cyberattacks originate, these cartels are extremely hard to bring to justice.

> Lack of management support

>> Example: Suppose that your company spent $10 million on information security countermeasures last year and experienced no successful attacks on information resources. Shortsighted management might conclude that the company could spend less during the next year and obtain the same results. Bad idea.

2 Compare and contrast human mistakes and social engineering by way of specific examples.

Human mistakes are unintentional errors. However, employees can also make unintentional mistakes because of actions by an attacker, such as social engineering. *Social engineering* is an attack in which the perpetrator uses social skills to trick or manipulate a legitimate employee into providing confidential company information.

An example of a human mistake is tailgating. An example of social engineering is when an attacker calls an employee on the phone and impersonates a superior in the company.

3 Describe negative consequences that might result from at least three different kinds of deliberate attacks on information systems.

The types of deliberate attacks are as follows.

> *Espionage or trespass* occurs when an unauthorised individual attempts to gain illegal access to organisational information.

> *Information extortion* occurs when an attacker either threatens to steal, or actually steals, information from a company. The perpetrator demands payment for not stealing the information, for returning stolen information, or for agreeing not to disclose the information.

> *Sabotage and vandalism* are deliberate acts that involve defacing an organisation's website, possibly causing the organisation to lose its image and experience a loss of confidence by its customers because of sabotage or vandalism.

- Computing devices and storage devices are becoming smaller yet more powerful with vastly increased storage, making these devices easier and more valuable to *steal*.
- *Identity theft* is the deliberate assumption of another person's identity, usually to gain access to his or her financial information or to frame him or her for a crime.
- *Protecting intellectual property* is a vital issue for people who make their livelihood in knowledge fields. Protecting intellectual property is particularly difficult when that property is in digital form.
- *Software attacks* occur when malicious software penetrates a computer system. Today, these attacks are typically profit driven and web based.
- *Alien software* is clandestine software installed on a computer through duplicitous methods. Alien software uses valuable system resources and can report on your web surfing habits and other personal behaviour.
- Supervisory control and data acquisition (SCADA) refers to a large-scale, distributed measurement and control system. SCADA systems are used to monitor or to control chemical, physical, or transport processes. A *SCADA attack* attempts to compromise such a system in order to cause damage to the real-world processes that the system controls.
- With both *cyberterrorism* and *cyberwarfare*, attackers use a target's computer systems, particularly via the internet, to cause physical, real-world harm or severe disruption, usually to carry out a political agenda.

4 **Assess how you might employ each of the three risk mitigation strategies in the context of your owning a home.**

The three risk mitigation strategies are the following.

- With *risk acceptance*, the organisation accepts the potential risk, continues operating with no controls and absorbs any damages that occur. If you own a home, you may decide not to insure it. Thus, you are practising risk acceptance. Clearly, this is a bad idea.
- With *risk limitation*, the organisation limits the risk by implementing controls that minimise the impact of threats. As a homeowner, you practise risk limitation by putting in an alarm system or by cutting down weak trees near your house.
- With *risk transference*, the organisation transfers the risk by using other means to compensate for the loss, such as by purchasing insurance. The vast majority of homeowners practise risk transference by purchasing insurance on their houses and contents.

5 **Identify the three major types of controls that organisations can use to protect their information resources.**

Physical controls prevent unauthorised individuals from gaining access to a company's facilities. Common physical controls include walls, doors, fencing, gates, locks, badges, guards and alarm systems. More sophisticated physical controls include pressure sensors, temperature sensors and motion detectors.

Access controls restrict unauthorised individuals from using information resources. These controls involve two major functions: authentication and authorisation. Authentication determines the identity of the person requiring access. As an example, authentication can be established with biometrics. After the person is authenticated (identified), authorisation is applied. Authorisation determines which actions, rights, or privileges the person has, based on verified identity. As an example, authorisation is based on least privilege.

Communications (network) controls secure the movement of data across networks. Communications controls consist of firewalls, anti-malware systems, whitelisting and blacklisting, encryption, virtual private networking (VPN), transport layer security (TLS) and vulnerability management systems.

>>> CHAPTER GLOSSARY

access controls Controls that restrict unauthorised individuals from using information resources and are concerned with user identification.

adware Alien software designed to help pop-up advertisements appear on your screen.

alien software Clandestine software that is installed on a computer through duplicitous methods.

anti-malware systems (antivirus software) Software packages that attempt to identify and eliminate viruses, worms and other malicious software.

audit An examination of information systems, their inputs, outputs and processing.

authentication A process that determines the identity of the person requiring access.

authorisation A process that determines which actions, rights, or privileges the person has, based on verified identity.

back door (also known as *trap door*) Typically a password, known only to the attacker, that allows the attacker to access the system without having to go through any security procedures.

biometrics The science and technology of authentication (i.e. establishing the identity of an individual) by measuring the subject's physiological or behavioural characteristics.

blacklisting A process in which a company identifies certain types of software that are not allowed to run in the company environment.

certificate authority A third party that acts as a trusted intermediary between computers (and companies) by issuing digital certificates and verifying the worth and integrity of the certificates.

cold site A backup location that provides only rudimentary services and facilities.

communications (network) controls Controls that deal with the movement of data across networks.

controls Defence mechanisms (also called *countermeasures*).

cookies Small amounts of information that websites store on your computer, temporarily or more or less permanently.

copyright A grant that provides the creator of intellectual property with ownership of it for the life of the creator plus 70 years.

cybercrime Illegal activities executed on the internet.

cyberterrorism Can be defined as a premeditated, politically motivated attack against information, computer systems, computer programs and data that results in violence against noncombatant targets by subnational groups or clandestine agents.

cyberwarfare War in which a country's information systems could be paralysed from a massive attack by destructive software.

demilitarised zone (DMZ) A separate organisational local area network that is located between an organisation's internal network and an external network, usually the internet.

denial-of-service attack A cyberattack in which an attacker sends a flood of data packets to the target computer, with the aim of overloading its resources.

digital certificate An electronic document attached to a file certifying that this file is from the organisation it claims to be from and has not been modified from its original format or content.

distributed denial-of-service (DDoS) A denial-of-service attack that sends a flood of data packets from many compromised computers simultaneously.

employee monitoring systems Systems that monitor employees' computers, email activities and internet surfing activities.

encryption The process of converting an original message into a form that cannot be read by anyone except the intended receiver.

exposure The harm, loss, or damage that can result if a threat compromises an information resource.

firewall A system (either hardware, software, or a combination of both) that prevents a specific type of information from moving between untrusted networks, such as the internet, and private networks, such as your company's network.

hot site A fully configured computer facility, with all information resources and services, communications links and physical plant operations, that duplicates a company's computing resources and provide near real-time recovery of IT operations.

identity theft Crime in which someone uses the personal information of others to create a false identity and then uses it for fraudulent purposes.

information security Protecting an organisation's information and information systems from unauthorised access, use, disclosure, disruption, modification, or destruction.

information security controls The procedures, devices, or software aimed at preventing a compromise to a system.

intellectual property The intangible property created by individuals or corporations that is protected under trade secret, patent and copyright laws.

keystroke loggers (keyloggers) Hardware or software that can detect all keystrokes made on a compromised computer.

least privilege A principle that users be granted the privilege for some activity only if there is a justifiable need to grant this authorisation.

logic bomb Segments of computer code embedded within an organisation's existing computer programs.

malware Malicious software such as viruses and worms.

network controls (see communications controls)

passphrase A series of characters that is longer than a password but that can be memorised easily.

passwords Private combinations of characters that only the user should know.

patent A document that grants the holder exclusive rights on an invention or process for 20 years.

phishing attack An attack that uses deception to fraudulently acquire sensitive personal information by masquerading as an official-looking email.

physical controls Controls that restrict unauthorised individuals from gaining access to a company's computer facilities.

piracy Copying a software program (other than freeware, demo software, etc.) without making payment to the owner.

privilege A collection of related computer system operations that can be performed by users of the system.

public-key encryption (also called *asymmetric encryption*) A type of encryption that uses two different keys: a public key and a private key.

risk The likelihood that a threat will occur.

risk acceptance A strategy in which the organisation accepts the potential risk, continues to operate with no controls and absorbs any damages that occur.

risk analysis The process by which an organisation assesses the value of each asset being protected, estimates the probability that each asset might be compromised and compares the probable costs of each being compromised with the costs of protecting it.

risk limitation A strategy in which the organisation limits its risk by implementing controls that minimise the impact of a threat.

risk management A process that identifies, controls and minimises the impact of threats, in an effort to reduce risk to manageable levels.

risk mitigation A process whereby the organisation takes concrete actions against risks, such as implementing controls and developing a disaster recovery plan.

risk transference A process in which the organisation transfers the risk by using other means to compensate for a loss, such as by purchasing insurance.

SCADA (Supervisory Control and Data Acquisition) Large-scale, distributed, measurement and control systems used to monitor or to control chemical, physical, or transport processes.

security The degree of protection against criminal activity, danger, damage and/or loss.

signature recognition The user signs his or her name and the system matches this signature with one previously recorded under controlled, monitored conditions.

social engineering Getting around security systems by tricking computer users inside a company into revealing sensitive information or gaining unauthorised access privileges.

spam Unsolicited email.

spamware Alien software that uses your computer as a launch platform for spammers.

spyware Alien software that can record keystrokes and/or capture passwords.

strong passwords Passwords that are difficult to guess; longer rather than shorter; contain uppercase and lowercase letters, numbers, and special characters; and are not a recognisable word or string of numbers.

threat Any danger to which an information resource may be exposed.

transport layer security (TLS) An encryption standard used for secure transactions such as credit card purchases and online banking.

trap doors (see back door)

Trojan horse A software program containing a hidden function that presents a security risk.

tunnelling A process that encrypts each data packet to be sent and places each encrypted packet inside another packet.

virtual private network (VPN) A private network that uses a public network (usually the internet) to securely connect users by using encryption.

virus Malicious computer code that can attach itself to (or 'infect') other computer programs without the owner of the program being aware of the infection.

voice recognition The user speaks a phrase that has been previously recorded under controlled, monitored conditions and the voice recognition system matches the two voice signals.

vulnerability The possibility that an information resource will suffer harm by a threat.

warm site A site that provides many of the same services and options of a hot site but does not include the company's applications.

whitelisting A process in which a company identifies acceptable software and permits it to run, and either prevents anything else from running or lets new software run in a quarantined environment until the company can verify its validity.

worm Destructive computer code that replicates itself without requiring another program to provide a safe environment for replication.

>>> DISCUSSION QUESTIONS

1 Why are computer systems so vulnerable?

2 Why should information security be of prime concern to management?

3 Is security a technical issue? A business issue? Both? Provide a rationale for your answer.

4 Compare information security in an organisation with insuring a house.

5 Why are authentication and authorisation important to e-commerce?

6 Why is cross-border cybercrime expanding rapidly? Discuss possible solutions.

7 Discuss why the corporate governance of IT is having an impact on information security.

8 What types of user authentication are used at your university and/or place of work? Do these authentication measures seem to be effective? What if a higher level of authentication were implemented? Would it be worth it, or would it decrease productivity?

9 Why are federal government authorities so worried about SCADA attacks?

>>> PROBLEM-SOLVING ACTIVITIES

1 A critical problem is assessing how far a company is legally obligated to go in order to secure personal data. Because there is no such thing as perfect security (i.e., there is always more that can be done), resolving this question can significantly affect cost.
   a When are security measures that a company implements sufficient to comply with its obligations?
   b Is there any way for a company to know if its security measures are sufficient? Can you devise a method for any organisation to determine if its security measures are sufficient?
2 Assume that the daily probability of a major earthquake in Brisbane is .07 per cent. The chance of your computer centre being damaged during such a quake is 5 per cent. If the centre is damaged, the average estimated damage will be $4 million.
   a Calculate the expected loss in dollars.
   b An insurance agent is willing to insure your facility for an annual fee of $25 000. Analyse the offer and discuss whether to accept it.
3 Enter www.scamwatch.gov.au. Find out what the organisation does. Learn about email frauds and website scams. Report your findings.
4 Enter www.biometricsinstitute.org/ or www.alltrustnetworks.com and other vendors of biometrics. Find the devices they make that can be used to control access into information systems. Prepare a list of products and major capabilities of each.
5 Software piracy is a global problem. Access the following websites: ww2.bsa.org and www.microsoft.com/piracy. What can organisations do to mitigate this problem? Are some organisations dealing with the problem better than others?
6 Investigate the Sony Playstation Network hack that occurred in April 2011.
   a What type of attack was it?
   b Was the success of the attack because of technology problems at Sony, management problems at Sony, or a combination of both? Provide specific examples to support your answer.
   c Which Sony controls failed?
   d Could Sony have prevented the hack? If so, how?
   e Discuss Sony's response to the hack.
   f Describe the damages that Sony incurred from the successful hack.

>>> COLLABORATION EXERCISE

Background

This chapter has shown the importance of information security. The 'What's In IT For Me?' section illustrated the different ways each business area needs to be aware of security. In some cases there are government regulations, in others there are strategic, logistical, or technical reasons for needing security.

Activity

Divide your team into functional areas. Assign one person to each of the following: vice-president of accounting, vice-president of finance, vice-president of human resources and vice-president of production. Imagine that your chief executive officer (CEO) is really having a hard time understanding why you need to invest in a chief information officer (CIO) to oversee your information systems. Right now each department is doing its own thing and managing its own systems. Everyone needs help and direction from an expert and the group of vice presidents has agreed that you need a CIO.

Deliverable

Write an executive summary that accompanies an imaginary full report. The imaginary report would include a full description of how the CIO would help each functional area, so the executive summary will include the highlights of what this position would mean to you. Have each team member research from his or her respective position why you need a CIO to help maintain information security. Finally, submit your executive summary to your tutorial group. For help formatting your executive summary, search Google for 'executive summary template'. You will find many examples there to help you.

CLOSING CASE **1 >**

An inside look at the Australian government's cyber security plans

It is no longer an option to be complacent about securing computer networks. There is growing evidence that groups such as Anonymous, state-based actors and individuals are intent on stealing valuable data or causing disruption to computer-based services. From governments to religious organisations, global enterprises to small business owners, everyone has been a victim of these types of attacks. The motives of attackers range from a self-deluded intention of doing good for society, to monetary or political gain or for no other reason than to demonstrate the ability to affect such an attack.

Our world economy, governments, industry and citizens rely heavily on the capabilities that the internet provides, attacks to these fundamental infrastructures and the devices connected to it are frequent, visible and damaging. Disruptions to internet services can have a catastrophic effect on our banking systems, utilities and the way we communicate across the globe.

The new Australian Cyber Security Centre, announced by former prime minister Julia Gillard in early 2013, recognises this growing threat. It became operational towards the end of 2013 and will act as a hub for security professionals from the Defence Signals Directorate, Defence Intelligence Organisation, Australian Security Intelligence Organisation, the Attorney-General's Department's Computer Emergency Response Team Australia, Australian Federal Police and the Australian Crime Commission.

Its aim is to protect Australia's most valuable networks and systems and provide advice and support to develop preventative strategies to counter cyber threats.

According to the Australian government, there were more than 400 cyber incidents against government systems requiring a significant response by the Cyber Security Operations Centre (CSOC) during 2011–12.

The establishment of the new Australian Cyber Security Centre will help the government devise a comprehensive cyber security strategy, but there are also other initiatives that are already underway within federal government to tackle this growing problem.

The Australian Signals Directorate (ASD) advocates implementing a Defence-in-Depth strategy and Australian government agencies are now required to implement certain ICT protective security controls. Each layer of the defence-in-depth strategy should provide either a form of protection to thwart or slow the pace of attack, or provide intelligence that can be used to adapt to and remediate the situation. The end game is to secure the organisation's assets including its data confidentiality, integrity and availability.

ASD understands the increased need to protect federal government computer networks and the threat to Australia. Utilising a defence-in-depth security methodology, ASD has developed a series of documents entitled 'Top 35 Mitigation Strategies'. The list is informed by ASD's experience in operational cyber security, including responding to serious cyber incidents and performing vulnerability assessments and penetration testing for Australian government agencies. These strategies can be divided into categories including patching/hardening, monitoring/inspection, white/black listing, blocking/filtering and governance/security policy.

In April 2013, on recommendation of the Attorney-General, the Australian government Protective Security Policy Framework (PSPF) was updated and the changes now mandate Australian government agencies to implement ICT protective security controls to meet the ASD's top four out of the total 35 mitigation strategies for cyber intrusions, which are:

1 use application whitelisting to help prevent malicious software and other unapproved programs from running
2 patch applications such as PDF readers, Microsoft Office, Java, Flash Player and web browsers
3 patch operating system vulnerabilities
4 minimise the number of users with administrative privileges.

ASD findings show that no single strategy can prevent malicious activity, but the effectiveness of implementing the top four strategies is very high. When ASD analysed intrusions they responded to in 2011, they found that the defence-in-depth strategy as a whole would have prevented at least 85 per cent of these intrusions. They also found that most of the attacks involved adversaries using unsophisticated techniques that would have been mitigated by implementing the top four mitigation strategies as a package.

Sourcefire is working alongside ASD to provide Australian government agencies with the security solutions they need to comply with the top 35 mitigation strategies. While recognising that there is no silver bullet to address security challenges, Sourcefire's Agile Security approach and network and endpoint device security solutions support defence-in-depth and assist organisations in complying with ASD's top 35 mitigations.

As the de facto standard in NGIPS (Next-Generation Intrusion Prevention Systems), we can support government agencies in detecting and blocking malware and intrusion events, providing application control and security compliance enforcement.

Organisations are continually asked to provide more services and a higher level of security with reduced budgets and fewer personnel. CTOs and ITSAs are constantly challenged to meet these conflicting requirements. Through informed architectures, products and supplementary security controls, solutions can be implemented to meet both of these elements and more compliance requirements in a true defence-in-depth strategy.

Source: C Wood (2013), *Business Spectator*, Technology Spectator, 10 June.

QUESTIONS

1 If cyberattacks are inevitable, what contingency strategies can be put in place to enable these critical computer networks and infrastructures to withstand and be more resilient to attack? Outline some disaster recovery strategies for recovery after an incident.

2 Describe some useful mitigation strategies for responding to serious cyber incidents and performing vulnerability assessments. Suggest some immediate incident response actions that may lessen an incident's impact.

3 Suggest ways in which government departments and organisations can continue to meet their own security obligations amid reducing budgets with less personnel. What risk management strategies can be implemented to meet this challenge?

CLOSING CASE 2 >

Compliance

THE PROBLEM

Modern businesses face an incredible array of regulatory and compliance requirements. Various problems and scandals have forced political leaders and entire industries to introduce new laws, regulations and industry standards (for example, Sarbanes-Oxley [SOX], the Health Insurance Portability and Accountability Act [HIPAA], the Payment Card Industry Data Security Standard [PCI DSS], the European Union Privacy Directive and many others). Therefore, governance, risk management and compliance (GRC) solutions have become increasingly important to all organisations.

GRC involves almost every part of any organisation, including business operations, security and IT assets. Moreover, new information technologies — including mobile computing, cloud computing and social media — have made it more difficult than ever to keep data secure and comply with government and industry requirements. To make matters even more difficult, as systems and organisations become more interconnected, firms need to be able to track where data originates, where it travels, where it is stored and who has access to it. Enterprises must therefore be able to provide constant real-time protection for applications, files and data.

In addition, organisations must often deal with the foreign corrupt practices, differing business practices of contractors and third-party providers, obtaining background checks in other countries and many other issues. The ability to track internal transactions and processes is only one part of the problem. GRC typically spans an entire supply chain.

SOLUTIONS

Although many organisations have constructed GRC frameworks — with applications designed to monitor, report and provide alerts about compliance activities — gaps and potential hazards still exist. Many organisations deal with potential problems by writing a policy, procedure, or prohibition. Unfortunately, employees often violate policies and undermine procedures. As a result, GRC must focus on many key areas: information security, privacy, threat and risk analysis, compliance with government regulations and industry requirements, enforcement strategies, internal audits and others.

Let's look at some examples of organisations that are making progress with their GRC obligations:

- The business regulatory environment continues to evolve meaning that there is an ongoing tension between pursuing corporate goals and maintaining compliance with regulatory requirements. KPMG offers their clients GRC services to assist clients with meeting the challenges and maintaining a balance between governance, risk management, regulatory compliance and business performance.

  KPMG's GRC services assist their clients to develop a vision and approach to their organisation's GRC processes through alignment with the organisation's business goals, taking a holistic approach to ensure that the management of GRC is also linked to the corporate culture. This provides an integrated approach to developing a sustainable GRC framework within the organisation.

  For example, KPMG's holistic model consists of four components:

  - risk profile — understanding the risks that face the organisation and quantifying their management at the lowest cost
  - culture and behaviour — establishing a culture and behaviour towards risk management that permeates throughout the everyday activities of the organisation
  - governance, organisation and infrastructure — enabling an oversight of the business processes and decision making to ensure compliance and regulatory requirements are addressed in a cost-effective manner
  - enterprise assurance — the ongoing evaluation, monitoring and reporting of the effectiveness of controls and benchmarking responses to regulatory change.

  This approach can assist in developing and fostering a risk-aware culture that informs decision-making and addresses assurance and compliance obligations. It improves operational efficiency through clever use of IT and data management processes that enable the organisation to quickly respond to challenges of evolving risk profiles and regulatory requirements.[41]

- CardSmith (www.card-smith.com) provides electronic payment and transaction processing systems used primarily by colleges and universities. The firm manages cashless payment cards for nearly 150 universities. Students rely on the cards to purchase meals, supplies and other campus goods. Parents transfer money into the accounts as necessary, making it essential that they have the highest level of trust in the system.

  The payment cards — in many cases multiuse smartcards that also provide access control for dorms and other areas — require tight oversight and adherence to a number of regulatory and compliance issues, including PCI DSS, GLBA, the Patriot Act, and the Credit Card Accountability, Responsibility, and Disclosure (CARD) Act of 2009 (all North American legislation).

  As a result, CardSmith turned to Hosting.com (www.hosting.com), a hosted security solution that provides a variety of protection and reporting tools that meet the PCI Council's Data Security Standard. The system handles host intrusion detection, vulnerability management, monitoring and testing, and PCI DSS security scanning.

  CardSmith has to secure computers, point-of-sale terminals and mobile payment terminals; use encryption, and protect logs from tampering. For example, the Hosting system maintains snapshots of logs, which are written and recorded in real time.

  CardSmith controls and manages data flowing to and from smartphones, tablet devices and other mobile tools. As a result, students can securely check their account balances using these devices, as data travels across wireless networks in an encrypted state.

  CardSmith is also pushing for tamper-proof terminals at universities and health care provider locations, and the use of tokens as a substitute for sending actual card numbers. The result is that the company sees very little fraud and has achieved very high levels of compliance.

- The Northern Ireland Civil Service (NICS) takes a broad approach to GRC. The government organisation has more than 25 000 civil servants delivering key services and economic and social policy data to government ministers and citizens throughout the country. Protecting sensitive data and records while adhering to regulatory requirements, including the United Kingdom's Data Protection and Freedom of Information Acts, is vital for NICS.

  NICS data resides in documents and systems that span 11 government departments in more than 250 locations. Using Hewlett-Packard (www.hp.com) TRIM records management software, NICS has built a single virtual data repository known as Records Northern Ireland. The system contains both structured and unstructured data, including more than 9 million documents and information about email accounts, network devices and hard disks. It allows the agency to control who may access the information; the system also tracks documents and how they are used and shared.

  The Records NI system makes it easier to find needed information. The system has helped NICS achieve a much higher level of compliance while improving workflows.

RESULTS

Companies and application vendors are increasingly focusing on merging the information technology and business aspects of GRC. Although authentication, passwords, robust reporting, monitoring and other controls are an important part of GRC, systems must integrate technology, process controls and risk management. These are the three cornerstones of effective GRC.

An effective GRC framework finds ways to capture and establish ownership of information. GRC also cuts across multiple entities, including shareholders, stakeholders, investors and insurers. Balancing productivity with protection is essential. Ultimately, effective GRC revolves around well-defined processes, the right tools and technologies; it also ensures that employees and partners are trustworthy and educated about the risks inherent in today's business environment.

Unfortunately, technology, by its nature, advances faster than the ability to provide an appropriate framework. As a result, organisations today face enormous, continuing GRC challenges as firms try to keep abreast of advances in technology.

Sources: Compiled from J Goodchild (2012), '12 tips for implementing GRC', *CIO*, 23 February; E Savitz (2011), 'Managing cloud risks', *Forbes*, 25 October; S Greengard (2011), 'Navigating the GRC maze', *Baseline Magazine*, 30 September; J Buchanan (2011), 'Cloud computing: 4 tips for regulatory compliance', *CIO*, 8 August; D Woods (2010), 'Compliance in the best-of-breed cloud', *Forbes*, 20 July; C Dunlap (2010), 'Trends in identity and access management', *Forbes*, 27 April; www.card-smith.com; KPMG (2012), *A good offense is the best defense: managing regulatory compliance with GRC*, www.kpmg.com/US/en/IssuesAndInsights/ArticlesPublications/Documents/managing-regulatory-compliance-grc.pdf; KPMG (2013), *Governance, risk and compliance*, www.kpmg.com/us/en/services/advisory/risk-and-compliance/internal-audit-risk-and-regulatory-compliance/pages/governance-risk-and-compliance.aspx; KPMG (2013), *Internal audit, risk and compliance services*, www.kpmg.com/US/en/services/Advisory/risk-and-compliance/internal-audit-risk-and-regulatory-compliance/Pages/default.aspx; KPMG (2013), *Risk consulting*, www.kpmg.com/au/en/services/advisory/risk-compliance/pages/default.aspx.

QUESTIONS

1. Describe the GRC problem that all organisations face. What is the relationship between information technology and the GRC problem? Provide specific examples of this relationship.
2. In the examples in this case, all the organisations used external vendors to help them achieve GRC compliance. Why did these organisations use external vendors? Why didn't they manage the GRC problem inhouse? Support your answer with examples.

SPREADSHEET ACTIVITY **RISK ANALYSIS WITH A SPREADSHEET**

OBJECTIVE

This activity will bring together the ideas of security and formula writing in a spreadsheet. Upon completion, you will be able to take data presented in written form, translate it into numbers, create formulas and then rank security issues based on the spreadsheet you create.

Chapter connection

Security issues are not all created equal. Some are frequent and inexpensive to overcome; others are rare and costly. Intentional and unintentional threats must be dealt with. But as a network manager, how do you know what deserves the most resources? Given that you never know where the next threat will come from, how will you allocate resources? This activity will bring this discussion to a spreadsheet and help you apply your maths and spreadsheet skills to this very 'real world' situation.

Activity

Consider the following situation. You are the network manager at a local bank. A number of security issues must be dealt with. However, like everyone else, you have limited resources. You only have $10 000 in your budget to allocate to security. This money can be spent on hardware, software, training, or anything else you deem worthy of this money. Here is a list of potential threats.

- *Malware:* If malware ends up installed on a computer in the system, it could easily spread to the other machines without anyone knowing it is there. The expense of repairing the machines and restoring data are minimal when compared to the cost of rebuilding trust in the consumer. Estimated total cost of marketing and repairing customer trust: $25 000. Probability of occurring: 35 per cent. Cost of preventative maintenance and training: $3 500.
- *Careless employees:* Judy has to run to the toilet. Because she trusts everyone she works with, she walks away from her computer without locking it. When she is away from her desk and her computer is unlocked, Johnny walks in. No one thinks anything about Johnny on Judy's computer because he is the local 'computer guru' even though he is a cleaner. While Judy is away and Johnny is on her computer, he transfers a total of $7500 from over 150 total accounts by running a script in the computer system. When Judy returns, she sees Johnny on the computer and thanks him for watching it, laughing about how she accidentally left it unlocked. Probability of occurring: 5 per cent. Cost of preventative maintenance and training: $2000.
- *Cloud computing:* Banks rely on many software packages to accomplish their goals. Not the least of these are the many packages run by the home office. These are accessed over the internet and private data are transferred back and forth. A hacker who is able to hack into the local system would by default have access to the cloud. The cost of this is monumental. Customer data from across the nation would be compromised. Having a backup of all data is imperative. Keeping employees trained on using the system, avoiding social engineering, changing passwords and other issues are paramount to help protect the home office and the local office. Total potential loss: $2.5 million. Probability of occurrence: 2.5 per cent. Cost of preventative maintenance and training: $7000.
- *Fire:* This is always a threat. If a fire breaks out, it could be devastating. Loss of technology equipment alone would run close to $20 000. Loss of records would be almost unrecoverable. However, the chance of fire is relatively low. At a 2 per cent chance of fire, this is a minimal concern. The cost of preventative maintenance is not cheap. Sprinklers have to be inspected, fire-retardant material must be tested and fire extinguishers must be replaced. Total preventative maintenance cost is $1500. However, the total potential loss is a devastating $250 000.

Given that most people agree that risk (R) is equal to the consequence (C) multiplied by the probability of occurrence (P):

$$R = C * P$$

Create a spreadsheet that calculates this formula. Then use your estimated risk to figure the return on security investment (ROSI) that most consider to be equal to risk avoided (R; hopefully it will be avoided by the investment) divided by the cost of preventative maintenance (PM).

$$ROSI = R/PM$$

This number represents the 'impact' of an investment and can be used to help determine how to create a budget so that the return is maximised. The higher the number, the more of the risk is covered by the investment. Use this number to prioritise where to make security investments.

Because your budget is only $10 000, you will need to determine where to spend your money. According to this scenario, total coverage would cost $14 000. Use the ROSI to recommend a budget. Also provide your spreadsheet for justification of the budget.

Deliverable

The final product will be a spreadsheet formula, ranking and presentation of a suggested budget.

DISCUSSION QUESTIONS

1 Discuss the advantages and disadvantages of building a formula once and copying it to multiple rows or columns.

2 Discuss the importance of taking verbal or written clues and being able to build a spreadsheet. Is a

spreadsheet the ultimate combination of math and business?

3 Given that no one has unlimited resources, is it ever possible to cover all the bases and ensure security?

What type of agreement must there be between the business and the consumer for this situation to exist and be acceptable?

DATABASE ACTIVITY **TABLES II**

OBJECTIVE

Information systems need checks to catch errors in the entry of data. Errors can lead to bad decisions, producing the wrong products, ordering too much or too little, sending one group messages meant for another and more. If you develop a database for yourself or your team, you should check for as many errors as you can. When you use a database, you can form an opinion of its reliability by seeing how it checks its inputs.

Not all errors can be caught, of course. If a street address is entered as 63 instead of 36 Elm, a database cannot tell it is wrong. Many errors can be caught, however. You will learn a few of the methods here using the following features of Microsoft Access:

- default values
- range checks
- value checks against a list.

Chapter connection

Security includes keeping bad data out of databases. Checking data as entered can prevent many errors and some mischief. Here, you will see how Access checks data as it is entered. Other database management systems work in much the same way.

Prerequisites

Before you begin this activity, you will need to familiarise yourself with and practice three concepts in this activity: default values, validation checks based on a range of valid data and validation checks against a list. The following sections introduce these concepts and provide practice in dealing with them. Read these sections and complete the brief practice items before moving to the larger activity.

Default values

A *default value* is the value of a data item if no other value is entered. Say a Queensland university attracts students primarily from the Brisbane area. Most of its applicants have home phones in area code 07. A database could pre-enter 07 as the area code of new applicants. The administrative assistant who enters applicant information into a database can change it for those with different home phone area codes, but having it saves time and reduces errors.

To enter a default value for a field in an Access table:

1 Open the table in Design view.

2 Select the field for which you want to specify a default value.

3 Find the Default Value row in the Field Properties pane, under the General tab.

4 Click on the right side of this row and key in the desired value, as shown below.

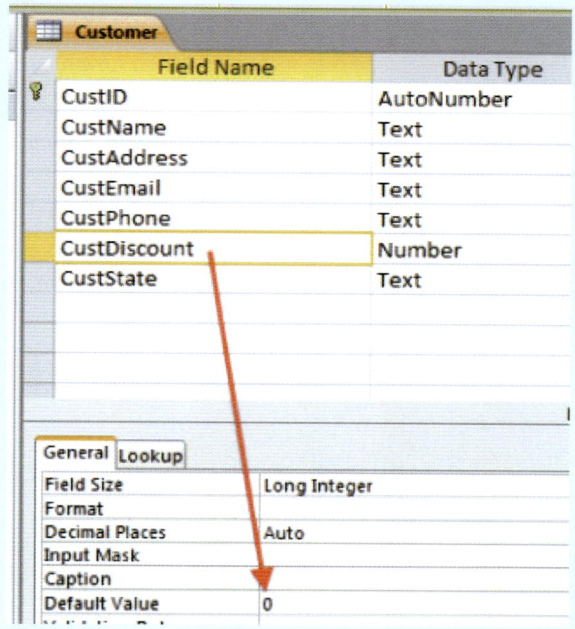

AU: Kindly provide caption for this figure.

Usage hint: You can also assign default values and perform validation checks on fields in forms instead of in tables. In the form's Layout or Design view, open its Property Sheet, select a field, select the Data or All tab on the Property Sheet, and continue as above. The check will be applied only to data entered via that form. Checks entered in table definitions are applied to all data entered in any way.

5 Go to Datasheet view to confirm that the default value was entered correctly. You should see the value in the bottom (New) row of the table. If you enter a default value in a form, you will not see it in the table's Datasheet view, but you will see it if you enter a new record via the form.

Range checks

Database designers often need to make sure data are in an allowable range. For example, the quantity of something in an order must be greater than zero, or the year of birth of a pupil entering kindergarten in September 2012 might have to be 2007.

This, by the way, shows one reason for putting checking in a form rather than in the table on which the form is based. Suppose an occasional student born outside the usual year enters kindergarten. The school principal might have a different form, in which a new student's year of birth can be 2006, 2007 or 2008. Supervisors can often override data checks that apply to the workers they supervise.

To enter a range check for a field in an Access table.

1 Open the table in Design view.
2 Select the field for which you want to enter a range check.
3 In the Field Properties pane below the list of fields, under the General tab, find the Validation Rule row.
4 In the right side of this row, enter an expression that will evaluate to True or False, and is True for valid data. For example, the expression '>5' (without quotation marks) means the value entered in the field must be greater than 5. The data the user enters is implied to the left of the '>'.

These comparison operators are used in validation expressions:

= (equal to) Seldom useful by itself. If a database designer knows what a value must be, why require a user to enter it?

> (greater than)

< (less than)

>= (greater than or equal to)

<= (less than or equal to)

<> (less than or greater than; that is, *not* equal to).

In addition, these are often useful in validation and other expressions:

AND requires *both* the condition on its left and the condition on its right to be met. '>= 0 AND <=10' requires a value of at least zero but not over ten.

OR requires *either* the condition on its left or the one on its right, possibly both, to be met. '<5 OR >50' excludes numbers from 5 to 50 but allows all others. (Be sure you understand why the expression means this.)

BETWEEN ... AND ... means just what you would think. 'BETWEEN 0 AND 10' is another way to write the condition that was used as an example for AND.

IS NULL lets you leave a field blank. Some versions of Access will not let you leave one blank if it has a validation rule, because blank data does not satisfy the rule. If you want to allow the field to be left empty, write 'IS NULL OR ...' where the rest of the rule is whatever you want as validation if anything at all is entered.

If you want to use a date in a condition, enclose it between #s. '>=#1/1/2010#' (without quotation marks) will accept any date in 2010 or later.

Instead of an actual date, you can write 'DATE()' to mean today's date. '>DATE()' will accept any date in the future. This can be useful, for example, for delivery date estimates. It does not guarantee that the order will arrive then, but it prevents a company from promising to deliver something last week.

There is more. For example, you could make sure an account number consists of a letter followed by five digits, the last of which is even. Once you understand how validation rules work, you can read up on the rest if you need to.

5 Optionally, but a good practice, enter an error message in the right side of the Validation Text row. Access will display it to the user if the test fails. A few suggestions are as follows.
   - Make messages informative. Say 'Quantity must be greater than zero', not 'Quantity error'.
   - Do not try to be funny. It is nearly impossible to do this well. Even a genuinely funny message loses its humour after someone has seen it five (or 50) times.
   - Do not insult the user. (The user might be your boss.)
   - Do not end the message with an exclamation point. 'Must be from 1 to 5' is fine. 'Must be from 1 to 5!' is scolding. Nobody likes to be scolded.

If you do not provide a message, Access will display the rule that the data did not satisfy in a standard message format. Some users will be able to figure out the problem from this, but many nontechnical people will find it confusing.

6 Test your work by going to Datasheet view, entering sample data values and confirming that valid ones are accepted but invalid ones are not. Pick values that provide good tests. Try values at the limits: if a number is supposed to be *less than* 10, not *less than or equal to* 10, make sure 10 is rejected.

   Usage hint: Access does not apply validation checks to default values. This can lead to problems when a user changes a default, realises that the change was in error and tries to change it back. If there are both a default and a validation rule for the same field, be sure the validation rule allows the default value. That way, users can restore the default value if they change it by mistake.

Checking values against a list

Sometimes there is no simple formula to define valid data, but there is a list of valid values. For example, you might require a state code in an Australian postal address to be one of the four-letter codes that Australia Post recognises or you might require a department name to match one of the departments in your company.

The simplest way to handle this is to list them in the rule. The expression 'IN (a, b, c, ...)' does this. This evaluates as True if the entered value is a, b, c, up to as many as you have. (Replace a, b, c and so on with the valid values.) If items are text, put them in quotation marks. A rule to see if a location is one of your firm's offices might look like this:

```
IN('Boston', 'Paris', 'Sydney', 'Santiago')
```

Longer lists should be in tables. (This is a flexible concept that can do more than reduce data entry errors.) To get a pull-down list with all valid values:

1. Create a new table with one field. Give it the same data type as the field whose data you want to validate. Enter all valid data values into this column. Save the table, giving it a suitable name, and close it. You can change it whenever the list of valid data values changes.
2. Open the table that contains the field you want to check against this list. In Design view, select that field. Select its Data Type column and change its data type to 'Lookup Wizard ...'
3. On the first page of the wizard, tell it you want to look up values in a table or query.
4. On the next page, select the table you just created.
5. On the next page, select the only column this table has and move it to the right-hand pane by clicking the '>' symbol. Click 'Next' a few times until the wizard exits figure 7A.1.
6. A value list created this way lets the user select values from a pull-down list. It also lets the user enter a value that is not in the list. If you want to prevent that, while this field is still selected, click the Lookup tab in the Field Properties pane. Change 'Limit to list' to Yes via the down arrow at the right of the row. (If you do not do this now, you can do it later.)

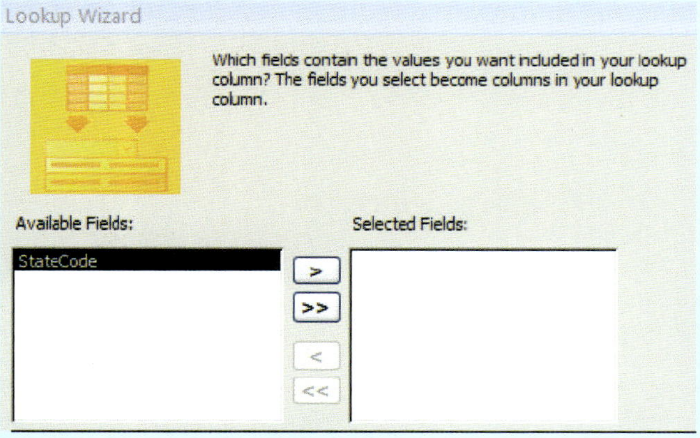

FIGURE 7A.2

Usage hint: If you do this with a table that already contains data, you may have to re-enter the data in the column you were working with. In that case, make sure to keep a record of it, or have some other way to re-create it, before you confirm all the steps in closing the wizard.

7. Switch to Datasheet view to confirm that the field behaves correctly.
8. You can click the Database Tools ribbon tab and look at the relationship map. If it does not show the new table, click Show Table and add it to the map. You will see a link between the new table and the table that contains the data to be validated against it.

ACTIVITY

1. Download the **Ch 07 CustOrder** database from www.johnwiley.com.au/highered/rainer/ausnz/studentresources and open it. It has tables for customers, orders, line items and products. Its structure resembles the example in section 3.3 of the book. The Ordered Parts table there corresponds to the line item table here.
2. Open the Line Item table and specify a default value of 1 for Quantity.
3. Open the Customer table and enter a default value of 0 for customer discount. Also, for the same field, add a rule to limit the discount to a range of 0 to 25. (If this column was formatted as a percentage, you would have to enter the upper limit as 0.25, not 25. Access can display fractions as percentages, but that is just for display. It treats them as fractions internally and validates them that way. Here, however, because the column is not formatted as a percentage, use 25.) Enter an error message to display if a user tries to enter a value outside this range.
4. In the Order table, add a validation rule to the order date: it must be no later than today. (The limiting value, today, is allowable.)
5. Create a table CountryList with one column: countries from which you expect orders. Enter ten countries into it, including your home country, the other countries in the sample data, and enough others of your choice to make ten. Link the table to the Country field in the Customer table. The user should be allowed to enter a new country in the Customer table if a customer's country is not in the list. (Because you are doing this to a table that already has data in it, you will have to re-enter the country names when you are done. If you cannot figure them out from the city names, write them down first.)

DELIVERABLE

Your completed database, with the above changes.

QUIZ QUESTIONS

1. True or false: A person entering data into an Access database can change a field from its default value to a different value.
2. In which of the following places can you specify a default value for a data element?
   a. In a table, in Datasheet view
   b. In a table, in Design view
   c. In a report
   d. In a form

   Choose one of the following four answers, (a) through (d):
   a. 2.2
   b. 2.2 and 2.4
   c. 2.1 and 2.4
   d. 2.2 and 2.3

3 Which of the following validation rules will allow only dates between 13 July and 16 December 2011 (including both endpoints)?
   a >#7/12/2011# AND <#12/17/2011#
   b BETWEEN #7/13/2011 AND #12/16/2011#
   c >=5#7/13/2011# AND <=5#12/16/2011#
   d All of the above
4 If a validation rule has no validation text, which of the following will happen?
   a The rule will not be applied. Any data can be entered without checking.
   b The rule will be applied to Number and Date data, but not to Text data.
   c The rule will be applied, but the error message may not be informative.
   d The rule will be applied to new data, but not to data that someone changes later.

DISCUSSION QUESTIONS

1 How would you write a validation rule to permit a data value to be either 0 or any number from 5 through 10?
2 What is the purpose of Validation Text in an Access table definition?
3 How would you write a validation rule that requires a data value to be one of the six letters A, B, C, D, F or I?

8
Social computing

CHAPTER OUTLINE

LEARNING OBJECTIVES

1. Describe six web 2.0 tools and the two major types of web 2.0 sites.
2. Describe the benefits and risks of social commerce to companies.
3. Identify the methods used for shopping socially.
4. Discuss innovative ways to use social networking sites for advertising and market research.
5. Describe how social computing improves customer service.
6. Discuss different ways in which human resource managers make use of social computing.
7. Discuss the advantages and disadvantages of crowdsourcing to organisations.

OPENING CASE >

La Casa Ristorante's Twitter dream

Carmel Ruggeri had a dream. She wanted to open a Sicilian restaurant, so she tweeted about it. People tweeted back, providing advice, locations, contacts and all manner of support. With every tweet she responded and/or retweeted. 'The most important thing to remember about Twitter', she recalls, 'if someone tweets you, respond and retweet them.' With the support and encouragement of friends and contacts on Twitter her dream turned into a reality. Twitter friend and Capital Wines owner Jennifer Mooney recalls, 'My friend Carmel (who I met on Twitter @carmR) has built her entire restaurant business from Twitter. Via Twitter, we watched as she searched for a restaurant site, through to employing the chef and then opening her gorgeous Italian restaurant' (blog.capitalwines.com.au, 2011). Due to Carmel's tweets the restaurant was an instant success. Bridget Davis, The Internet Chef, writes on her blog, 'Thanks to the tweeting by part owner Carmel Ruggeri aka @carmr who also tweets under the guise @lacasa, La Casa Ristorante has the food media world at her feet. Within weeks of opening all the top food writers in the city in both traditional and new media had been in to sample and then write about Carmel, Tony and the La Casa Ristorante team, which has been driving hoards of new traffic their way. Carmel's online personality is so infectious that you can't help but fall in love with her wit and good humour.'

The Daily Telegraph named La Casa as the Best Suburban Eatery in their 2010 Insider Awards, the year that the restaurant opened, stating that 'Brother and sister team Carmel and Tony Ruggeri have made their inner-west Italian restaurant an instant classic'. Bridget Davis wrote, 'The official unofficial Queen of Twitter has a great looking bottom line ... among her other wonderful asset and is a living, breathing, operating example of how social media can positively influence bums on seats and dollars in the till. As her following increases so shall her customer base, because if you're lucky enough to secure a table, you're a guaranteed customer for life because Carmel and the team know how to deliver the goods.' Bridget also pointed to La Casa Ristorante's marketing success using social computing by stating, 'Restauranteurs take note, this will be the single most important thing that you will read since they announced the allowance for 7-day trading. La Casa Ristorante has social media'.

But this is not the end of Carmel's social media and restaurant dream. Carmel wanted to share her passion for Sicilian food. She wanted to take her customers to her birth place, a fishing village called Scoglitti on the South Coast of Sicily, to experience not just the food but the culture that has inspired her. After tweeting with Brisbane-based Taste Trekkers (@tastetrekker) she launched Sicilian Food Tours in May 2012, where else but on Facebook and Twitter. The tour was planned for May 2013. By June the itinerary was officially launched on the new Sicilian Food Tours website (**www.sicilianfoodtours.com**). But this wasn't any old food tour. Carmel asked Gina Milicia (@GinaMilicia), another Twitter friend, to provide photographic support, as well as lessons for the tour group. The enthusiasm of both women had people excited about the trip from day one of planning. Sicilian Food Tours (@sicilyFoodTours) started tweeting in November 2012, five months before the tour was to begin. Carmel counted down the weeks, tweeting mouthwatering photos of Sicilian food and sites the tour guests could expect to see.

On 3 May 2013, Sicilian Food Tours began with a tweet from Carmel: '#SicilianFoodTours kicked off with Aperol Spritz and lunch by the sea in #Scoglitti and so the eating began'. Carmel understood the importance of maintaining her tweets throughout the 7 day tour. Not only was she able to share the tour with her many customers and followers through Twitter, but the success of the first tour and limited numbers of people and tours available (one annually) has the "Twitter queen" just as busy as ever.'

Sources: Compiled from authors' interviews with Carmel Ruggeri, blogs by Jennifer Mooney and Bridget Davis and *The Daily Telegraph*; www.theinternetchef.biz, 2011.

Introduction

Humans are social individuals and thus human behaviour is innately social. Humans, therefore, typically orient their behaviour around other members of their community. As a result, people are sensitive to the behaviour of those around them and many of their decisions are influenced by their social context.

Social computing is a type of IT that combines social behaviour and information systems to create a digital social context that has value. Social computing therefore, concentrates on improving collaboration and interaction among people through user-generated content. In social computing, social information is not anonymous, but is significant precisely because it is linked to particular individuals, who are in turn linked to their own networks of individuals.

Social computing makes socially produced information available to all. This information may be provided directly, as when users rate a movie (for example, Rotten Tomatoes

THE NOOK

The Nook introduced their website only five years ago. Since then, it has been a very basic web 1.0 site, containing static information that has changed very little over the course of the years. Now, with the rise of web 2.0 technology and the growing skills of internet users, it seems natural that Malakai and Abbie use this technology to reach their customers.

Although they are aware of this technology, neither of them is very experienced with it. Malakai only joined Facebook last year because he was trying to learn more about a DJ that was going to perform at the club. He has not explored it much from a business standpoint and really does not know what is possible. And Twitter is not even on their radar yet.

In addition, they want to explore options such as blogs, wikis and other web 2.0 material. But where do they go? What should they hope to accomplish?

by Flixter), or provided indirectly, as with Google's PageRank algorithm, which sequences search results.

In social computing, users, rather than organisations, produce, control, use and manage content via interactive communications and collaboration. As a result, social computing is transforming power relationships in organisations. Employees and customers are empowered by their ability to use social computing to organise themselves. Thus, social computing can influence those in power to listen to the concerns and issues of ordinary people. Organisational customers and employees are joining this social computing phenomenon, with serious consequences for most organisations.

Most governments and companies in modern developed societies are not prepared for the new social power of the masses. Today, managers, executives and government officials can no longer control the conversation around policies, products and other issues, let alone the various social media used to share these opinions.

In the new world of business and government, organisational leaders will have to demonstrate authenticity, even-handedness, transparency, good faith and humility. If they do not, customers and employees may distrust them, to potentially disastrous effect. For example, customers who do not like a product or service can quickly broadcast their disapproval. Another example is that prospective employees do not have to take their employers at their word for what life is like at their companies — they can find out from people who already work there. A final example is that employees now have many more options to start their own companies, which could compete with their former employers. However, social media use in the business world is not one sided, empowering the employee. It is also being used by employers seeking out potential employees in professional social media sites such as LinkedIn. They also use social media for searching information about applicants via social media sites to gain a broader understanding of the type of person they are considering and how they would fit within the existing work group environment.

As you see from these examples, the world is becoming more democratic and reflective of the will of ordinary people, enabled by the power of social computing. On the one hand, social power can help keep a company vital and can enable customers and employee activists to become a source of creativity, innovation and new ideas that will move a company forward. On the other hand, companies that show insensitivity towards customers or employees quickly find themselves on a downward slide. Consider the following examples.

- In May 2013, MYER boss Bernie Brookes apologised for comments he made about the government's proposed National Disability Insurance Scheme. The Myer chief executive warned that the proposed increase to the Medicare levy would hurt sales at its stores. Fairfax reported, Mr Brookes told a Macquarie Investment seminar the estimated $350 a year increase to the levy 'is something they would have spent with us'. He was quoted as saying the proposed levy increase was 'not good for our customers and may have an impact'. The hashtag #Myer became a trending topic on Twitter overnight as outraged comments from Myer customers rolled in. Mr Brookes apologised in a statement 'to those who may have been offended or hurt' by the comments he made. However, customers weren't satisfied with the apology, which was also posted on Myer's Facebook page, and have dubbed it a 'non-apology apology'. One Twitter user @samedog wrote: 'Good to see that @Myer_MyStore have been to the Alan Jones Academy of Non-Apology. #NDIS'. Another Twitter user @admpstr wrote: 'Read closely, Myer's statement today contains no additional context, no clarification and neither regret nor apology. Just 122 empty words.'[1]
- Adidas came under attack in New Zealand when fans of the country's hugely popular national rugby team were outraged to learn that Adidas team jerseys were being sold for significantly more at home than in other countries. Fans found this information by researching product prices in New Zealand and the United States online. Armed with this information, fans organised protests. Soon, national news programs picked up coverage of the protest and of Adidas's slow response to the consumer outrage. Customers started returning Adidas clothing to stores in disgust, and employees felt so threatened by the populace that they removed Adidas's logos from their company vehicles.
- In the Netherlands in 2011, a social media campaign against bankers' bonuses focused on the Amsterdam-based company ING. Bank customers began threatening en masse

to withdraw deposits. In response, CEO Jan Hommen voluntarily waived his own upcoming $1.8 million bonus and then ordered all company directors to do the same.

Organisations today are using social computing in a variety of innovative ways, including marketing, customer relationship management and human resource management. In fact, so many organisations are competing to use social computing in as many new ways as possible that an inclusive term for the use of social computing in business has emerged: *social commerce*.

Because social computing is facilitated by web 2.0 tools and sites, you begin this chapter by examining these technologies. You then turn your attention to a diverse number of social commerce activities, including shopping, advertising, market research, customer relationship management, human resource management and crowdsourcing. You conclude the chapter by studying the risks and concerns associated with social computing.

When you complete this chapter, you will have a thorough understanding of social computing and the ways in which modern organisations use it. You will be familiar with the advantages and disadvantages of social computing, and the risks and rewards it can bring to your organisation. For example, most of you already have pages on social networking sites, so you are familiar with the benefits and drawbacks of such sites. This chapter will enable you to apply this knowledge to your organisation's efforts in the social computing arena. You will be in a position to contribute to your organisation's policies on social computing. You will also be able to help your organisation design its own strategy for social computing.

Significantly, social computing can help you start your own business. For example, many entrepreneurs have developed successful businesses using Twitter and Facebook (see this chapter's opening case).

As we noted earlier, social computing is facilitated by web 2.0 tools and sites. In the next section, you will learn about web 2.0 tools such as AJAX, tagging, really simple syndication, blogs, microblogs and wikis. You will also learn about two major types of web 2.0 sites, social networking sites and mashups.

8.1 Web 2.0

The world wide web, which you learned about in chapter 4, first appeared in 1990. Web 1.0 was the first generation of the web. We did not use this term in chapter 4 because there was no need to say 'web 1.0' until web 2.0 emerged.

The key developments of web 1.0 were the creation of websites and the commercialisation of the web. Users typically had minimal interaction with web 1.0 sites. Rather, they passively received information from those sites.

Web 2.0 is a popular term that has proved difficult to define. According to Tim O'Reilly, a noted blogger, **web 2.0** is a loose collection of information technologies and applications, plus the websites that use them. These websites enrich the user experience by encouraging user participation, social interaction and collaboration. Unlike web 1.0 sites, web 2.0 sites are not so much online places to visit as web locations that facilitate information sharing, user-centred design and collaboration. Web 2.0 sites often harness collective intelligence (for example, wikis); deliver functionality as services, rather than packaged software (for example, web services); and feature remixable applications and data (for example, mashups). Web 2.0 has also been defined as a new digital ecosystem, with characteristics of creativity, connectivity, collaboration, convergence and community.

AJAX

Most web 2.0 applications have rich, user-friendly interfaces based on AJAX. **AJAX** is a web development technique that enables portions of web pages to reload with fresh data instead of requiring the entire web page to reload. This process speeds up response time and increases user satisfaction.

Tagging

A **tag** is a keyword or term that describes a piece of information — for example, a blog, a picture, an article, or a video clip. Users typically choose tags that are meaningful to them. Tagging allows users to place information in multiple, overlapping associations rather than in rigid categories. For example, a photo of a car might be tagged with 'Holden', 'V8' and 'SUV'. Tagging is the basis of *folksonomies*, which are user-generated classifications that use tags to categorise and retrieve web pages, photos, videos and other web content.

One specific form of tagging, known as *geo-tagging*, refers to tagging information on maps. For example, Google Maps allows users to add pictures and information, such as restaurant or hotel ratings, to maps. Therefore, when users access Google Maps, their experience is enriched because they can see pictures of attractions, reviews and things to do, all related to the map location they are viewing.

Really Simple Syndication (RSS)

Really Simple Syndication (RSS) allows you to receive the information you want (customised information), when you want it, without having to surf thousands of websites. RSS allows anyone to syndicate (publish) his or her blog, or any other content, to anyone who has an interest in subscribing. When changes to the content are made, subscribers receive a notification of the changes and an idea of what the new content contains. Subscribers can then click on a link that will take them to the full text of the new content.

For example, theaustralian.com.au provides RSS feeds for each of its main topic areas, such as news, business, sports, technology and entertainment. ABC uses RSS feeds and Podcasts to allow viewers to download the most current version of shows such as *ABC News 24* and *The Drum*.

You can find thousands of websites that offer RSS feeds at Syndic8 (**www.syndic8.com**) and NewsIsFree (**www.newsisfree.com**). Figure 8.1 shows a website's RSS feed subscription link.

There are two types of RSS readers, cloud or desktop. Examples of cloud readers are NewsBlur, Feedly and Pulse. For example Pulse is supported on Android, iOS and in browsers (Lifehacker, 2013).[2]

To use RSS, you can utilise a special news reader that displays RSS content feeds from websites you select. Many such readers are available, several of them for free, such as AmphetaDesk (**www.disobey.com/amphetadesk**) and Pluck (**www.pluck.com**). In addition, most browsers have built-in RSS readers or have extensions such as Pulse's Chrome extension that enable feeds from web pages, RSS Feeds and other posts. To view an excellent RSS tutorial visit **www.mnot.net/rss/tutorial**.

FIGURE 8.1 RSS feed subscription link.

Blogs

A **weblog** (**blog** for short) is a personal website, open to the public, in which the site creator expresses his or her feelings or opinions via a series of chronological entries. *Bloggers* — people who create and maintain blogs — write stories, convey news and provide links to other articles and websites that are of interest to them. The simplest method of creating a blog is to sign up with a blogging service provider (see figure 8.2), such as **www.blogger.com** (now owned by Google), **www.xanga.com**, and **www.sixapart.com**. The **blogosphere** is the term for the millions of blogs on the web.

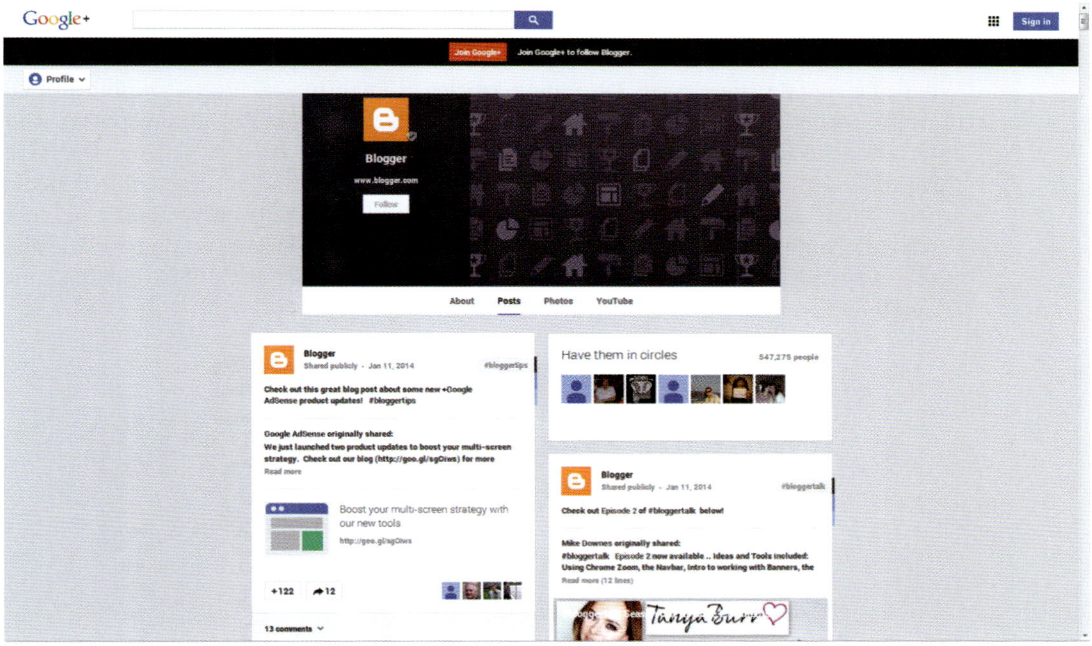

FIGURE 8.2 Blogger is one of the world's most popular blogging service providers.

Many companies listen to consumers in the blogosphere who express their views on the companies' products. In marketing, these views are called *consumer-generated media*. For example, Nielsen (**www.nielsen-online.com**) 'mines' the blogosphere to provide information for its clients in several areas. Nielsen helps clients find ways to serve potential markets, ranging from broad-based to niche markets. The company also helps clients detect false rumours before these rumours appear in the mainstream press and gauges the potency of a marketing push or the popularity of a new product.

Although blogs can be very useful, they also have shortcomings. Perhaps the primary value of blogs is their ability to bring current, breaking news to the public in the fastest time possible. Unfortunately, in doing so, bloggers sometimes cut corners and their blogs can be inaccurate. Regardless of their various problems, blogs have transformed the ways in which people gather and consume information.

Microblogging

Microblogging is a form of blogging that allows users to write short messages (or capture an image or embedded video) and publish them. These messages can be submitted via text messaging from mobile phones, instant messaging, email, or just over the web. The content of a microblog differs from that of a blog because of the limited space per message (usually up to 140 characters). The most popular microblogging service is Twitter.

Twitter is a free microblogging service that allows its users to send messages and read other users' messages and updates, known as **tweets**. Tweets are displayed on the user's profile page and delivered to other users who have signed up to receive them.

Twitter is becoming a very useful business tool. It allows companies to quickly share information with people interested in their products, thereby creating deeper relationships with their customers. Businesses also use Twitter to gather real-time market intelligence and customer feedback. As an individual user, you can use Twitter to tell companies about your experience with their business, offer product ideas and learn about great offers.

The case study at the beginning of this chapter is a great example of a company using Twitter to get closer to customers.

Wikis

A **wiki** is a website made up entirely of content posted by users. Wikis have an 'edit' link on each page that allows any user to add, change, or delete material, fostering easy collaboration.

Wikis take advantage of the combined input of many individuals. Consider Wikipedia (**www.wikipedia.org**), an online encyclopedia which is the largest wiki in existence. Wikipedia contains more than 3.4 million articles in English, which get a combined total of nearly 500 million views every day. Wikipedia relies on volunteer administrators who enforce a neutral point of view and encourage users to delete copy displaying clear bias. Nevertheless, there are still major debates over the reliability and accuracy of Wikipedia articles. Many educators will not allow students to cite references from Wikipedia because Wikipedia content is of uncertain origin. Moreover, as Wikipedia does not provide any quality assessment or fact checking by experts, academics and others still have major concerns about the accuracy of user-provided content.

A wiki allows open contribution to a document.

Organisations use wikis in several ways. In project management, for example, wikis provide a central repository for capturing constantly updated product features and specifications, tracking issues, resolving problems and maintaining project histories. In addition, wikis enable companies to collaborate with customers, suppliers and other business partners on projects. Wikis are also valuable in knowledge management. For example, companies use wikis to keep enterprise wide documents, such as guidelines and frequently asked questions, accurate and current.

Social networking websites

A **social network** is a social structure composed of individuals, groups, or organisations linked by values, visions, ideas, financial exchange, friendship, kinship, conflict, or trade. **Social networking** refers to activities performed using social software tools (e.g. blogging) or social networking features (e.g. media sharing).

A social network can be described as a map of all relevant links or connections among the network's members. Such a map of all relevant links or connections for one member is that person's **social graph**. Mark Zuckerberg of Facebook originally coined this term to refer to the social network of relationships among users of Facebook. The idea was that Facebook would take advantage of relationships among individuals to offer a richer online experience.

Social networks can also be used to determine the social capital of individual participants. **Social capital** refers to the number of connections a person has within and between social networks.

Social networking allows convenient connections to those of similar interest.

Participants congregate on *social networking websites* where they can create their own profile page for free and on which they can write blogs and wikis; post pictures, videos, or music; share ideas; and link to other web locations they find interesting. Social networkers chat using instant messaging and Twitter, and tag posted content with their own key words, making content searchable and facilitating interactions and transactions. Social networkers converse, collaborate and share opinions, experiences, knowledge, insights and perceptions with each other. Through these sites, users are able to find like-minded people online, either to pursue an interest or a goal or just to establish a sense of community among people who may never meet in the real world.

Figure 8.3 shows the variety of online social networking platforms. Social networking websites allow users to upload their content to the web in the form of text, voice, images and videos. This is not an exhaustive list as sites are developed, updated or removed depending on popularity and the organisation's business decisions regarding their ability to support these sites. For example, Google's RSS Feed Reader was removed in July 2013, which prompted a number of other RSS Feed sites to promote how to transition to their RSS Feed reader from Google Reader.[3]

Enterprise social networks

Business-oriented social networks can be public, such as LinkedIn.com, in that they are owned and managed by an independent company. However, an increasing number of companies have created their own inhouse, private social networks for their employees, former employees, business partners and/or customers. Such networks are considered to be 'behind the firewall' and are often referred to as *corporate social networks*. By establishing these networks, companies enable connections among employees that allow them to establish virtual teams, bring new employees up to speed, improve collaboration and increase employee retention by creating a sense of community. Employees are able to interact with their coworkers on a level that is typically absent in large organisations or when people work remotely.

Corporate social networks are used for many processes, including:

- networking and community building, both inside and outside an organisation
- crowdsourcing: gathering ideas, insights and feedback from crowds
- social collaboration: collaborative work and problem solving using wikis, blogs, instant messaging, collaborative office and other special-purpose web-based collaboration platforms; for example, see Laboranova (**www.laboranova.com**)
- social publishing: employees and others creating either individually or collaboratively and posting contents — photos, videos, presentation slides and documents — into a member's or a community's accessible-content repository such as YouTube, Flickr, SlideShare, and DocStoc
- social views and feedback
- social intelligence and social analytics: monitoring, analysing and interpreting conversations, interactions and associations among people, topics and ideas to gain insights. Social intelligence is useful for examining relationships and work patterns of individuals and groups, and for discovering people and expertise.

Think about IBM. With more than 426 000 employees across 170 countries, more than 100 000 contractors, and a broad range of business partners and customers, IBM has no choice but to be a social business. In fact, IBM has become the largest corporate consumer of social technologies. On any given day, 50 per cent of IBMers regularly work away from traditional IBM offices. About 12 per cent work at home and another 20 per cent are mobile workers.

IBM Australia is so committed to social business for the future that they suggest 'a Social Business isn't just a company that has a Facebook page and a Twitter account. A Social Business is one that embraces and cultivates a spirit of collaboration and community throughout its organisation — both internally and externally.'[4]

To enable its social networking, IBM has deployed Social Blue (formerly Beehive), an internal social networking site that gives IBM employees a rich connection to the people they work with on both a personal and a professional level. Social Blue helps employees make new connections, track current friends and co-workers, and renew contacts with people they have worked with in the past. When employees join Social Blue, they get a profile page. They can use the status message field and the free-form 'About Me' section of their profile page to let other people at IBM know where they are and what they are doing.

Employees can also use Social Blue to post photos, create lists and organise events. If users are hosting an event, they can create an event page in Social Blue and invite people to attend.

Users can create top-five lists, called 'hive fives', to share their thoughts on any topic they are passionate about. Social Blue also comes in handy when preparing for conference calls. If users do not know the other people on the call, they can check out the participants'

Socially oriented
Socially focused public sites, open to anyone
- Facebook (www.facebook.com)
- Google Orkut (www.orkut.com)
- Google+ (plus.google.com)
- Hi5 (www.hi5.com)

Professional networking
Focused on networking for business professionals
- LinkedIn (www.linkedin.com)

Media sharing
- *Netcasting* includes podcasting (audio) and videocasting (audio and video). For example, educational institutions use netcasts to provide students with access to lectures, lab demonstrations and sports events.
- *Web 2.0 media* sites allow people to come together and share user-generated digital media, such as pictures, audio and video.
  - Video (Amazon Video on Demand, YouTube, Hulu, Facebook)
  - Music (Amazon MP3, Last.fm, Rhapsody, Pandora, Facebook, iTunes)
  - Photographs (Photobucket, Flickr, Shutterfly, Picasa, Facebook)

Communication
- *Blogs*: Blogger, LiveJournal, Open Diary, TypePad, WordPress, Vox, Expression Engine, Xanga
- *Microblogging/Presence applications*: Twitter, Plurk, Tumblr, Yammer, Qaiku

Collaboration
Wikis (Wikimedia, PBworks, Wetpaint)

Social bookmarking (or ***social tagging***)
Focused on helping users store, organise, search and manage bookmarks of webpages on the internet
  - Delicious (www.delicious.com)
  - StumbleUpon (www.stumbleupon.com)
  - CiteULike (www.citeulike.com)

Social news
Focused on user-posted news stories that are ranked by popularity based on user voting
- Digg (www.digg.com)
- Chime.in (chime.in)
- Reddit (www.reddit.com)

Events
Focused on alerts for relevant events, people you know nearby, etc.
- Eventful (www.eventful.com)
- Meetup (www.meetup.com)
- Foursquare (www.foursquare.com)
- Google Hangouts (www.google.com/+/learnmore/hangouts/)

Virtual meeting place
Sites that are essentially three-dimensional worlds, built and owned by the residents (the users)
- Second Life (www.secondlife.com)

Interesting new social networks
- Empire Avenue (www.empireavenue.com) is a social exchange network where members invest virtual currency in people and brands that interest them.
- Color (www.color.com) is a free mobile app that creates an instant social network based on users' locations and proximity to others. Users can instantly share images, videos and text conversations with others nearby.
- Foursquare (foursquare.com) is a location-based mobile service that enables participants to share their location with friends by checking in via a smartphone app.
- Hunch (www.hunch.com) maps people's interests by asking them a series of questions. The site creates a 'taste graph' which tracks everything that a user likes and dislikes.

Online marketplaces for microjobs
TaskRabbit (www.taskrabbit.com) and Zaarly (www.zaarly.com) enable people to farm out tasks to a growing number of temporary personal assistants. Thousands of unemployed or under-employed workers use these sites. The part-time or full-time tasks are especially popular with stay-at-home parents, retirees and students. Workers choose their jobs and negotiate their own rates.

FIGURE 8.3 Categories of social networking websites.

Social Blue profiles before the call and find out if they have current interests, either work related or recreational, or if they have colleagues in common.

In addition to social goals, the Social Blue team created the site to help IBM employees meet the challenge of building relationships that are vital to working in large, distributed enterprises. Social Blue helps project leaders find people with the right skills for their project.

BEFORE YOU GO ON . . .

1. Differentiate among blogs, microblogs and wikis.
2. What are the differences between public and private social networking sites?

Mashups

A **mashup** is a website that takes different content from a number of other websites and mixes them together to create a new kind of content. The launch of Google Maps is credited with providing the start for mashups. A user can take a map from Google, add his or her own data, then display a map mashup on his or her website that plots crime scenes, cars for sale, or anything else.

There are many examples of mashups (for a complete list of mashups, see **www.programmableweb.com**):

- Figure 8.4 shows TransLink.com.au, which is a mashup of travel services across the southeast Queensland region that integrates timetables with time and fare calculators from services including rail, ferry, Citycat® and buses with Google Maps©.

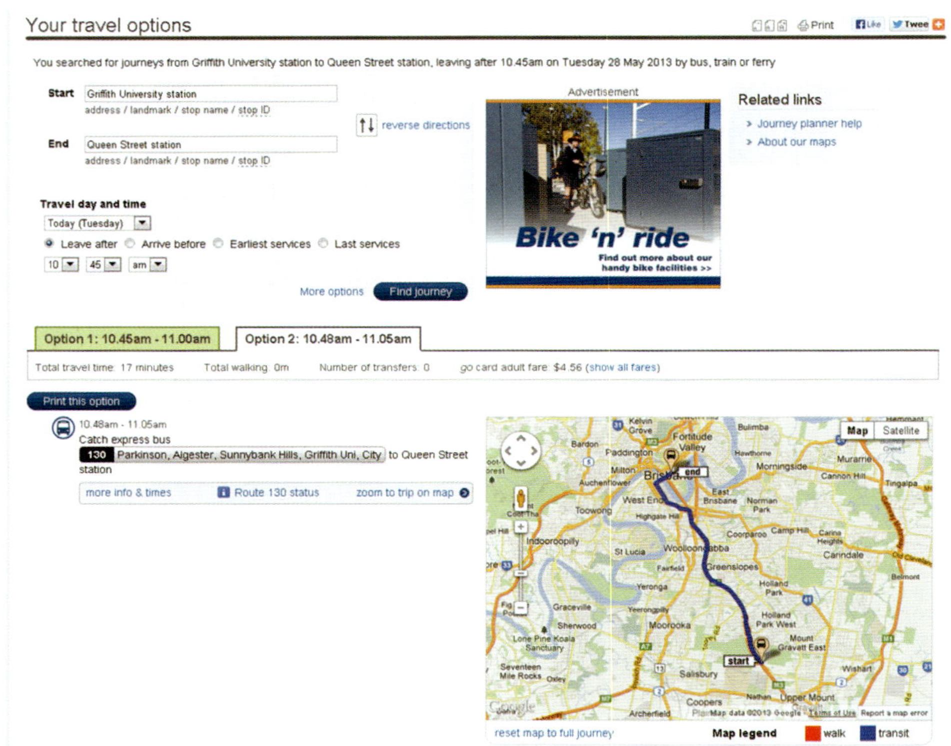

FIGURE 8.4 TransLink.com.au is an example of a mashup using Google Maps.

THE NOOK

QUESTIONS

1. Search for RSS feeds and see how most people use them. Are they for advertising? newsletters? articles? new products? promotions?
2. Are there any bars or clubs in your area that use RSS feeds? What seems to be their purpose?
3. Blogs allow for posts and comments. Although it creates a space for interaction, comments and praise, it also allows for negative comments. Is a blog something The Nook could benefit from? Can you find other bars/clubs that use blogs? How do they seem to be incorporated into their strategy?

8.2 Fundamentals of social computing in business

Social computing in business, or **social commerce**, refers to the delivery of electronic commerce activities and transactions through social computing. Social commerce also supports social interactions and user contributions, allowing customers to participate actively in the marketing and selling of products and services in online marketplaces and communities. With social commerce, individuals can collaborate online, get advice from trusted individuals, find goods and services, and then purchase them. Here are a few examples of social commerce.

- Australia's Darren Rowse's ProBlogger site **www.problogger.net** is listed as the 10th top blogging site in the world and number one in Australia. ProBlogger provides and sells information and resources to other bloggers wanting to make money blogging. ProBlogger also enables the over 320 000 readers to comment on his various posts.
- Nutrition Complete's website provides tools to enable health and fitness professionals to expand their client support business to online support, enabling social interaction among their members.
- In 2012 Queensland's Griffith University moved 'from an on-premise Lotus Notes environment to Google Apps. Main benefits include an increase in mailbox capacity to 25GB through Gmail and access to a suite of other web-based tools like Google docs, Google spreadsheets, Google Calendar and Google Talk.[5] These tools enable real time collaboration, enhanced sharing and access to information through a variety of mobile devices.'[6]
- Retailer David Jones maintains communication with their customers through Facebook and Twitter, but are yet to take the step to selling through social computing.
- One company, Aradium, have made social business computing for small to medium Australian businesses possible with their new shopping cart app for Facebook. A few examples of these social commerce pages include:
  - Little Miss Quilty in Townsville, supplying handmade handbags across Australia and potentially the globe
  - Groovy Little Guys, specialising in boyswear and accessories
  - Tea Drops, specialising in a variety of teas.

There are many potential benefits of social commerce. Figure 8.5 shows potential benefits to customers and to vendors.

Using social computing does have risks. It is risky to allow a product, brand, or company to appear on social computing websites where content is user generated and not edited or filtered. In this process, companies must be willing to accept negative reviews and feedback. In fact, negative reviews and feedback can be some of the most valuable information that a company receives.

Companies using social computing are always concerned with negative posts. For example, when a company creates a Facebook business page, by default the site allows

Benefits to customers

- Better and faster vendor responses to complaints, because customers can air their complaints in public (on Twitter, Facebook, and YouTube) and because of crowdsourcing complaints
- Customers can assist other customers (e.g. in online forums)
- Customers' expectations can be met more fully and quickly
- Customers can easily search, link, chat and buy while staying on a social network's page

Benefits to businesses

- Can test new products and ideas quickly and inexpensively
- Learn a lot about their customers
- Identify problems quickly and alleviate customer anger
- Learn about customers' experiences via rapid feedback
- Increase sales when customers discuss products positively on a social network site
- Create better marketing campaigns and brand awareness
- Use low-cost user-generated content, for example, in marketing campaigns
- Get free advertising through viral marketing
- Identify influential brand advocates and reward them

FIGURE 8.5 Potential benefits of social commerce.

other members of the website — potentially including disgruntled customers or unethical competitors — to post notes on the firm's Facebook wall or comment on what the firm has posted.

But, if the company turns off the feature that lets others write on its wall, people may wonder what the company is afraid of. The company will also be eliminating its opportunity to have great customer conversations take place, perhaps marketing the firm's products and services better than it could do. Further, the company could delete posts, but that only encourages the post author to scream louder about being censored.

Another risk is the 20–80 rule of thumb, which posits that a minority of individuals (20 per cent) contribute most of the content (80 per cent) to blogs, wikis, social computing websites and so on. For example, in an analysis of thousands of submissions over a three-week time frame to news voting site Digg, the *Wall Street Journal* reported that one-third of the stories that made it to Digg's homepage were submitted by 30 contributors (out of 900 000 registered members). Other risks of social computing include:

- information security concerns
- invasion of privacy
- violation of intellectual property and copyright
- employees' reluctance to participate
- data leakage of personal information or corporate strategic information
- poor or biased quality of users' generated content
- cyberbullying/cyberstalking and employee harassment.

Consider Rosetta Stone (**www.rosettastone.com**), which produces software for language translation. To get the most mileage possible out of social computing, Rosetta Stone has a strategy to control its customer interaction on Facebook. The strategy involves both human intervention and software to help monitor the firm's Facebook presence. Specifically, the software helps to monitor wall posts and respond to them constructively.

Fans of facebook.com/RosettaStone who post questions on its wall are likely to get a prompt answer because the Facebook page is integrated with customer service software from Parature (**www.parature.com**). The software scans wall posts and flags those that require a company response, as opposed to those that represent fans of the company talking among themselves. Rosetta Stone customer service representatives are also able to post responses to the wall that are logged in the Parature issue tracking database.

Companies are engaged in many types of social commerce activities, which include shopping, advertising, market research, customer relationship management, human resource management and crowdsourcing. In the next sections of this chapter, you will learn about each social commerce activity.

Other software such as HootSuite enables managing all your social networking from a single web location.

BEFORE YOU GO ON . . .

1. Differentiate between electronic commerce and social commerce.
2. Describe the potential benefits of social commerce to customers and vendors.
3. Why are companies so worried about negative posts on social networking sites? Link your answer to the capabilities of social computing.
4. Describe several risks associated with social computing.

THE NOOK

QUESTIONS

1. Would it be reasonable for The Nook to allow their patrons to easily post comments about bands, drinks, food and so on their website? What if someone said something negative?
2. Social computing comes with many risks as noted here in the text. What additional risks would be associated with alcohol sales and social media?
3. What if one of The Nook's customers tagged a photo (on The Nook's social media page) of someone else who appeared extremely intoxicated? On the drive home, the intoxicated customer was in an accident but the breath test indicated a blood alcohol level within the legal limit. Should the content on The Nook's social site be available for use in court against the consumer who caused the accident? The business didn't tag the photo or authorise the tag. Is The Nook liable?

8.3 Social computing in business: shopping

Social shopping is a method of electronic commerce that takes all of the key aspects of social networks — friends, groups, voting, comments, discussions, reviews and so on — and focuses them on shopping. Social shopping helps shoppers connect with each other based on an individual's information tastes, location, age and gender.

The nature of shopping is changing, especially for brand-name clothes and related items. For example, popular brands such as Tony Bianco, RMK and Sass & Bide as well as more than 500 other brands are joining communities on The Iconic (**www.theiconic.com.au**) to help promote the season's latest fashion collections. Boston Babe (**www.bostonbabe.com.au**), an Australian online shoe store, brings together a variety of shoe brands for the SME shoe business. While their shoes, service and accessories are discussed on Facebook and Twitter, they are yet to embrace the social computing store in their Facebook page.

BuyFruit.com.au, founded in 2011, provides a unique service by selling fruit and vegetables online, then providing customer support and recipes on their Facebook page, which is linked to their website. Customers are able to ask about exotic fruits or delivery locations and are answered within 24 hours (often within minutes). These responses and feedback times provide other online shoppers with confidence in this new online firm. Shoppers are using sites like ThisNext (**www.thisnext.com**) to create profiles and blog about their favourite products in social communities. By tagging each item, everything becomes searchable. This process means that your search within these websites can yield results targeted to you.

There are several methods to shop socially. You will learn about each of them in the next section.

Ratings, reviews and recommendations

Prior to a purchase, customers typically collect information such as what brand to buy, from which vendor and at what price. Online customers do this by using shopping aids such as comparison agents and looking at websites such as Epinions (**www.epinions.com**). Today, customers also use social networking to guide them in purchase decisions. They resort to ratings, reviews and recommendations from friends, fans, followers and experienced customers.

Ratings, reviews and recommendations are usually available in social shopping. In addition to seeing what is already posted, shoppers also have an opportunity to contribute their own ratings and reviews and discuss those from others (see figure 8.6, overleaf). The ratings and reviews come from the following:

- customer ratings and reviews: integrated into the vendor's webpage, a social network page, a customer review site, or in customer feeds (e.g. Amazon, iTunes, Buzzillions, Epinions)
- expert ratings and reviews: views from an independent authority (e.g. see Metacritic)
- sponsored reviews: paid-for reviews (e.g. SponsoredReviews, PayPerPost)
- conversational marketing: individuals converse via email, blog, live chat, discussion groups, and tweets. Monitoring these conversations yields rich data for market research and customer service.

For example, Maui Jim (**www.mauijim.com**), the sunglass company, used favourable word-of-mouth marketing as a key driver of sales for the company. Recently, the company used Bazaarvoice's Ratings & Reviews to allow customers to contribute 5-point ratings and authentic product reviews on the company's entire line of sunglasses and accessories. In effect, Maui Jim wanted to extend customers' word-of-mouth reviews across the web.

Maui Jim wants its customers to share their candid opinions on the style, fit and performance of all sunglass models. The reviews are integrated into its website search function to ensure that customers searching for a particular product will see that product's rating in the search results. The company has seen a huge positive response to its ratings efforts.

Social recommendation websites such as ShopSocially (**www.shopsocially.com**), Blippy (**www.blippy.com**) and Swipely (**www.swipely.com**) encourage conversations

FIGURE 8.6 Amazon allows customers to rate and review all items on its site.

about purchases. The product recommendations come from users' friends and acquaintances and arguably are more trustworthy than reviews by strangers.

ThisNext (**www.thisnext.com**) is a website where people recommend their favourite products to others. The site blends two powerful elements of real-world shopping: word-of-mouth recommendations from trusted sources and the ability to browse products in a way that naturally leads to discovery. IT's About Business discusses another website of this type, Pinterest (**www.pinterest.com**) in detail.

IT'S ABOUT BUSINESS

Pinterest

Social networks originated with blogging tools such as Blogger and WordPress, where users had to write an entire blog post to express themselves. Then Twitter and Facebook emerged and a simple status update was all that was required to share a thought on the web. These websites then discovered even simpler ways to share — for example, retweeting the updates of others and 'liking' web pages on Facebook. Tumblr, now one of the largest blogging platforms, also fits the trend. Not only is the site largely used to share images, but realigning the posts of others is a primary activity on the site.

Social sharing itself now involves less effort and is more visual; 'people-centric' recommendations are being augmented by 'topic-centric' networks. This means that while Facebook lets you explore the web through information shared by friends, newer social networks organise content by topics of interest.

Pinterest (www.pinterest.com) is a visual social network that organises images by topic and lets you reshare with just one click. Pinterest lets users create online scrapbooks to share images of projects or coveted products. The site is a kind of visual bulletin — or inspiration — board. Users, who currently must request an invitation to join Pinterest, create boards with categories like 'Books I love' or 'Beautiful places' or 'Products that save me time'. Users can then link images from websites (using a Pinterest browser bookmark) or upload images from their computers and 'pin' the images to the boards. As with Twitter, users can follow other users, and Pinterest images can be repinned and shared.

Pinterest has a devoted base of users — most of them female — who enjoy 'pinning' items they find around the web. Although clothing, home décor and recipes dominate the site, inspirational quotes and humour are also popular topics for users to add to their pinboards.

Generating revenue from social networking sites, which are usually free to users, has historically been a challenge. Options for Pinterest include selling targeted advertising and data on users' interests. Unfortunately, neither option is original and both run the risk of alienating Pinterest users.

In order to address these issues, Pinterest added a service called 'product pins' that introduced 'products price' to their 'product pins' service in August 2013. This sends a notification when the listed price of a product you've pinned drops, opening up another marketing tool for the social networking shopper.

Retailers are looking to piggyback off the popularity of Pinterest. Bergdorf Goodman, a unit of the Neiman Marcus Group, has begun actively trying to develop a following for its high-end clothing and accessories on Pinterest. Lands' End Canvas added a widget to its product pages, making it easier for users to immediately pin or repost images to their Pinterest profiles.

Etsy.com, an online crafts marketplace with over 50 000 Pinterest followers, is using Pinterest's price display feature. This means that when Pinterest users 'pin', for example, an Etsy chair on a board for their followers to see, the image of the chair will automatically include the chair's title and a banner showing the price.

Pinterest has also been helpful to small businesses. Consider The Wedding Chicks (www.weddingchicks.com). The four-year-old online retailer of wedding-party gifts said Pinterest brings its website more than double the traffic that Facebook and Twitter do. In addition, Warby-Parker (www.warbyparker.com), an eyewear brand sold online, saw a 400 per cent increase from October 2011 to February 2012 in the number of visitors to its website that came directly from Pinterest. Finally in October 2011, UncommonGoods (www.uncommongoods.com), an online gift retailer, began noticing traffic coming to its website from Pinterest. In March 2012, traffic from Pinterest to the UncommonGoods website rivalled traffic from Facebook.

Sources: Compiled from K Bischoff (2012), 'Winning the mommy market — our StumbleUpon vs Pinterest vs Facebook experiment', *Forbes*, 8 March; D Donston-Miller (2012), 'Pinterest: why your company should take an interest', *InformationWeek*, 6 March; T Watson (2012), 'Pinterest and the hype factor', *Forbes*, 24 February; S Needleman (2012), 'Start-ups follow Pinterest's lead', *The Wall Street Journal*, 23 February; S Needleman and P Tam (2012), 'The rite of web passage — huge traffic, no revenue', *The Wall Street Journal*, 16 February; P Cashmore (2012), 'Why Pinterest is 2012's hottest website', CNN Tech, 6 February 2012; www.pinterest.com; abcnews.go.com/Technology/pinterest-now-sends-alerts-price-drops-pinned-items/story?id=19831392.

QUESTIONS

1. Describe two other ways in which Pinterest could generate revenue without alienating its users.
2. Are Facebook and Pinterest competitors? Why or why not? Support your answer.

Group shopping

Group-shopping websites such as Groupon (www.groupon.com.au), Our Deal (www.ourdeal.com.au) and Prplness (www.prplness.com, launched in 2013), offer major discounts or special deals during a short time frame. Group buying is closely associated with special deals (flash sales).

For example, Our Deal offers discounts and special deals on goods and services for a limited time. Deals may be for items that can be delivered Australia-wide, or for products in a specified area, such as gym membership or dinner at a restaurant.

Prplness has taken the group shopping concept a step further by offering cash back on purchases. As a social shopping site they promote products from a variety of retailers and share 'their' commissions with the Prplness members. For instance, a member purchasing from Apple iTunes Australia–New Zealand can receive 4 per cent cash back just for shopping through the Prplness site. As members shop they are encouraged to 'Like' and leave feedback on social media sites Facebook, Twitter, Digg and LinkedIn.

FIGURE 8.7 Groupon (www.groupon.com.au) is a popular example of a group shopping website.

Prplness founder, Lucas McEntee, was frustrated at the number of Google searches required to get 'really good deals'. His frustrations led to the development of Prplness. Mr McEntee said, 'Prplness is a social shopping site I believe to be an Australian first, offering cash back, coupons, comparison as well as offering over 10 million products all on the one platform unlike other cash back sites that only feature one of these features'.[7]

Shopping communities and clubs

Shopping clubs host sales for their members that last just a few days and usually feature luxury brands at heavily discounted prices. Club organisers host three to seven sales per day, usually via email messages that entice club members to shop at more than 70 per cent off retail — but quickly, before the product runs out.

Luxury brands effectively partner with online shopping clubs, as they offer a means to dispose of special-run, sample, overstock, or liquidation goods, while the relative exclusivity of the clubs avoids diminishing a brand's image. Examples include Beyond the Rack (**www.beyondtherack.com**), Gilt Groupe (**www.gilt.com**), Rue La La (**www.ruelala.com**) and One King's Lane (**www.onekingslane.com**).

Kaboodle (**www.kaboodle.com**) is another example of a shopping community. Kaboodle is a free service that lets users collect information from the web and store it on a Kaboodle list that can be shared with others. Kaboodle simplifies shopping by making it easier for people to find items they want in a catalogue and by allowing users to share recommendations with one another using Kaboodle lists and groups. Kaboodle lists can also be used for planning holidays, sharing research for work and school, sharing your favourite bands with friends, and basically everything else you might want to collect and share information about.

The 'Our Add' Kaboodle button simplifies the online shopping experience because once you have it, you simply click on it whenever you see a product anywhere online and you will automatically upload a snapshot of the item, its price and other product information, and a link that sends you to where to buy it to one of your Kaboodle lists. Then, you can find it again any time you want.

Social marketplaces and direct sales

Social marketplaces act as online intermediaries that harness the power of social networks for introducing, buying and selling products and services. A social marketplace should enable the marketing of members' own creations (see Etsy in figure 8.8). Other examples include the following.

- Craigslist (**www.craigslist.com.au**) provides online classifieds in addition to supporting social activities such as meetings and events.
- Fotolia (**www.fotolia.com**) is a social marketplace for the community of creative people who enjoy sharing, learning, and expressing themselves through images, forums, and blogs. Members provide royalty-free stock images that other individuals and professionals can legally buy and share.
- Flipsy (**www.flipsy.com**) can be used by anyone to list, buy, and sell books, music, movies and games.

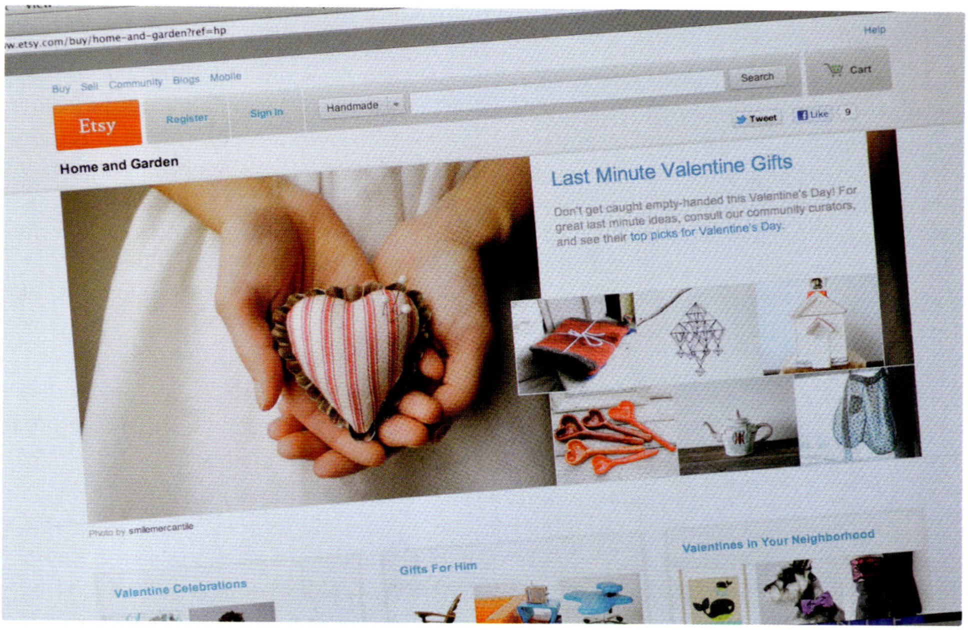

FIGURE 8.8 Etsy (www.etsy.com) is a social marketplace for handmade or vintage items.

Peer-to-peer shopping models

Peer-to-peer shopping models are the high-tech version of old-fashioned bazaars and bartering systems. Individuals use these models to sell, buy, rent, or barter online. For example, many websites have emerged to facilitate online sharing. SnapGoods created a community of people who rent goods to people in need, usually for the short term. SnapGoods helps these people connect over the internet.

All of the sites encourage **collaborative consumption** — that is, peer-to-peer sharing or renting. This trend is the result of the recession, but it has a green aspect as well. One of collaborative consumption's most surprising benefits, however, turns out to be social. In an era when we may not know our neighbours that well, sharing things — even with strangers we have just met online — allows us to make meaningful connections. Some people share cars and others invite travellers to stay in their homes for free. The following example shows the benefits of collaborative consumption.

BEFORE YOU GO ON . . .

1. Why are ratings, reviews and recommendations so important in social shopping?
2. Why do companies selling on shopping clubs have to pay attention to protecting their brands?
3. How is peer-to-peer shopping related to sustainability (i.e. the green movement)?

EXAMPLE Collaborative consumption

An entirely new generation of businesses is emerging, created by the intersection of the economic crisis, environmental concerns and the maturation of social computing. These firms facilitate the sharing of cars, clothing, couches, apartments, tools, meals and even skills. The basic characteristic of these sharing marketplaces is that they extract value out of the 'stuff' we already have.

The premise of collaborative consumption is simple: access to goods and skills is more important than ownership of them. There are three types of collaborative consumption:

- product–service systems that facilitate the sharing or renting of a product (e.g. car sharing)
- redistribution markets, which enable the reownership of a product (e.g. Craigslist)
- collaborative lifestyles in which assets and skills can be shared (e.g. co-working spaces).

Consider our second most expensive asset, our cars. Cars are the ultimate expensive, under-utilised commodity. In 2012 GoGet (**www.goget.com.au**) launched a new approach to car use. No longer do you need to own a car to travel, whether that be for short or long trips, and for multiple purposes. If you need a people mover or a van, GoGet the van. You choose the right car for the right job. For people living in cities and walking to work, this is an eco and economically friendly alternative to owning a car. For Brisbane users GoGet has now been integrated with the public transport system, so users can rent a GoGet car with their Translink Go Card.

There are environmental benefits to car sharing as well. When people's mobility costs shift from being fixed (ownership) to variable (renting), they make more efficient decisions about when they actually need to drive. Research has shown that the average car sharer drives 40 per cent less than the average owner.

German car manufacturer Daimler is taking car sharing seriously. Its Car2Go (**www.car2go.com**) service is similar to GoGet, except that it does not require a reservation or a two-way trip. Car2Go's mobile app allows a person walking down the street in a city to locate a Smart car on that block, access it immediately via a windshield card reader and PIN number, drive it anywhere locally and leave it there for someone else to use. The fuel-efficient Smart car has a 100-watt solar roof, which powers the car's telematics and its battery.

Daimler is also developing an app called Car2Gether (**www.car2gether.com**), which matches local drivers with people looking for a ride. Riders submit a request to a driver of any type of car, and both profiles are linked to their Facebook pages and Twitter feeds. After the ride, both driver and rider rate each other.

The challenge that worries everyone in the sharing space is trust. Sharing only really works when there is reputation involved. Most sharing platforms try to combat this issue by building a self-policing community. Almost all platforms require profiles for both parties and feature community rating systems.

Startups like TrustCloud (**trustcloud.com**) would like to become the portable reputation system for the web. The company has built an algorithm to collect (if you choose to opt in) your online 'data exhaust' — the trail you leave as you engage with others on Facebook, LinkedIn, Twitter, commentary-filled sites like TripAdvisor and others — and calculate your reliability, consistency and responsiveness. The result is a contextual badge that you carry to any website, a trust rating similar to the credit rating you have in the 'offline' world.

Of course, Facebook is already collecting a huge amount of your data exhaust on its own site. As a result, Facebook has the potential to become the arbiter of online trust.

Collaborative consumption has the potential to be extremely disruptive to existing organisations. For example, if the people formerly known as 'consumers' began consuming 10 per cent less and sharing 10 per cent more, the effect on the margins of traditional corporations is going to be disproportionately greater.

Sources: Compiled from D Sacks (2011), 'The sharing economy', *Fast Company*, May; www.car2go.com, trustcloud.com; CNET Australia (2013), 'GoGet expands into Brisbane, integrates with public transport', www.cnet.com.au/goget-expands-into-brisbane-integrates-with-public-transport-339340576.htm; www.goget.com.au/how-it-works/faqs.

QUESTIONS

1 What are some potential disadvantages of car sharing?

2 Describe how collaborative consumption can be disruptive to traditional organisations.

Apply the Concept

Background

Social shopping is nothing new. This section defines it as taking the key aspects of social networks (groups, reviews, discussions, etc.) and focusing these aspects on shopping. People have done this for years offline just through general conversation.

Today, most consumers do a lot of research before they make a purchase by reading the reviews other customers have made. Take for example the travel website TripAdvisor. Recently, the validity of some reviews have been questioned. While you learn about social shopping, you should also be aware of the potential misrepresentation that takes place online.

Activity

Go to TripAdvisor.com.au and reflect on a review of a venue that you have recently visited in your local area.

Talk to five of your friends about this and get their feedback. How did they respond to the fact that some reviews are anonymous or unsubstantiated? Ask them the following questions.

- What star rating do you require to consider a product?
- Do you read reviews or just look at stars?
- If you read reviews, do you read only the good, only the bad, or a mixture?

Deliverable

Summarise your conversations in a couple of paragraphs and present it to your tutorial group. Keep these thoughts in mind as you progress through the rest of this chapter.

8.4 Social computing in business: marketing

Marketing may be defined as the process of building profitable customer relationships by creating value for customers and capturing value in return. Advertising and market research are two marketing processes where social computing is particularly useful. In this section, you learn about social computing in advertising and market research.

Advertising

Social advertising represents advertising formats that make use of the social context of the user viewing the ad. Social advertising is the first form of advertising to leverage user dynamics such as peer pressure, friend recommendations and likes, and other forms of social influence.

Advertising is considered by many to be the answer to the challenge of making money off social networking sites and social commerce sites. Advertisers have long noted the large number of visitors on social networks and the amount of time they spend there.

As a result, they are willing to pay to place ads and run promotions on social networks. Advertisers now place ads on all major social networking websites.

Most ads in social commerce are branded content paid by advertisers. These ads come in two major categories: social ads and social apps. Social advertisements are ads placed in paid-for media space on social media networks.

Social apps are branded online applications that support social interactions and user contributions (e.g. Nike+).

Viral marketing (word of mouth) is especially effective with social networking. For example, Jennifer Mooney, director of Capital Wines (**www.capitalwines.com.au**), started tweeting about Capital Wines after reading an article about 'anti-social' media by Larry Lockshin. In her tweets she asked those who had never heard of Capital Wines before Twitter to retweet. Soon @capitalwines began trending. Capital Wines has over 7600 followers, but as Jennifer put it 'you don't actually sell on Twitter, you just tweet and talk to people and build relationships — sometimes I just tweet a lot of rubbish — but it's fun and the relationships build'.[8]

Other innovative ways to advertise in social media include the following.

- Use a company Facebook page, including a store that attracts fans and lets them 'meet' other customers. Then advertise in your Facebook store.
- Tweet business success stories to your customers.
- Integrate ads into YouTube videos.
- Add a Facebook 'Like' button with its sponsored story to your product (e.g. Gatorade brand scored 1.2 million conversations in six months using their 'Mission Control' campaign).
- Facebook has a feature called the 'sponsored story'. When a member chats with friends and one of them indicates that he or she 'checked into' a place or 'like it', say at Starbucks, a boxed 'sponsored story' will appear with the logo of Starbucks (fee paid to Facebook). Furthermore, the name Starbucks will also appear in the user's news feed (another fee paid to Facebook). The users have the option to delete the boxed advertisement.
- Customers are using Google maps to 'check in' to places they visit, adding comments, photos, feedback and reviews. This is then used by potential customers searching Google maps to locate places of interest close to their GPS location on their mobile devices.

IT's About Business illustrates how Twitter helped grow a wine business.

IT'S ABOUT BUSINESS

How tweeting has grown our wine business

Capital Wines is a small winery — tiny actually, but it moved production from 2000 cases to 5000 in 2011. Part of the reason for the increase is because it opened its cellar door in 2011 and the other reason is because of Twitter.

Capital Wines was formed in August 2008 when Mark and Jennie Mooney purchased Kyeema Wines, one of the more established Canberra District wineries, and became custodians of the renowned Kyeema Vineyard. They knew they had a great product, but weren't sure how to cut through in a marketplace flooded with good product. A friend told Jennie about Twitter so she thought she would log in and have a look. Within a few seconds of sending her first tweet someone tweeted her back. Soon Jennie had a few followers and found a few new friends. Now Capital Wines is the second most followed Australian winery with more than 7600 followers. Some of these followers are people who don't buy wine, but there are many interesting followers too. Many prominent wine and food journalists are on Twitter and Jennie chats with them regularly. She has exchanged tweets with Jancis Robinson, Oz Clarke, Gary Vaynerchuk and celebrity chefs such as Jamie Oliver. In 2011, Neil Perry re-tweeted a video Jennie made of the Capital Wines vineyard, restaurant and kitchen gardens. Normally, she would be watching Perry on television, but on Twitter the boundaries change.

In October 2010 Professor Larry Lockshin, the Head of Marketing at the University of South Australia, published an article in the Wine Business Magazine (WBN) that social media was useful between businesses, but wasn't useful for marketing a business. This was not Capital Wines' experience.

Jennie has been on Twitter since 15 May 2009 and has tweeted more than 34692 times, an average of 23.52 times per day. Jennie can't remember her first tweet and had no idea where the journey would take her, but thought she should explore Twitter as a way to promote Capital Wines. She spends approximately 28.75 minutes per day on Twitter, so it is really not that much extra effort to flick in and out of Twitter. How many sales calls could you realistically make in that time and at what expense? Bringing the brand to the consumer's notice can be done through other means, but at a cost. Twitter has a reach beyond traditional channels of selling, at a cost of less than 30 minutes a day in the case of Capital Wines.

Jennie has made a lot of friends on Twitter — wineries, restaurants and others across Australia and the world. By getting to know restaurateurs via Twitter, Capital Wines is not just another winery making cold calls to their restaurant. Most of their stockists came from Twitter — certainly all of their interstate restaurants, east coast distributors and Western Australian distributors are all new buyers due to Twitter. As well as trade, Capital Wines has lots of consumers buying their wine and new members in their cellar club, all due to Twitter. Jennie has sent their wine to people around the world and discussed export potential to distributors. October 2010 sales from Twitter were just over three pallets, which is significant for a small winery like Capital Wines.

Reminding consumers of the Capital Wine brand is why Twitter is so powerful, because it is in real time. When it comes to brand, Twitter has put Capital Wines' name out among the big players. Jennie has had large South Australian wineries contact her to buy Kyeema shiraz for benchmarking.

Many people get Twitter wrong — they just blast advertising or spam at people with little interaction or interest in other tweeters. Cordie from @ryn_and_cordie is a consumer on Twitter. She had this to say: 'Some people will do Twitter well and some will not. Those that don't are unfortunately likely to blame the tool. People like us represent the consumer part of the puzzle, and through Twitter and Facebook, consumers now have a much louder voice, so rock on! Clearly it works!'

So Capital Wines will continue to build their business through Twitter. Jennie will keep tweeting and the interest in Capital Wines' product will keep growing.

Source: Adapted from blog.capitalwines.com.au/read/371/how-29-tweets-per-day-has.html.

QUESTIONS

1. Jennie used videos on Twitter to promote her business. Describe how she could use YouTube's basic model for revenue generation as another marketing strategy.
2. What other social computing tools could Capital Wines use to promote and/or sell their wines?

Market research

Traditionally, marketing professionals used demographics compiled by market research firms as one of their main tools to identify and target potential customers. Obtaining this information was time-consuming and costly, as marketing professionals had to ask potential customers to provide it. Today, however, members of social networks provide this information voluntarily on their pages! (Think about all the information that you provide on your favourite social networking websites.) Because of the open nature of social networking, merchants can easily find their customers, see what they do online and see who their friends are.

This information provides a new opportunity to assess markets in near real time. Word of mouth has always been one of the most powerful marketing methods — more often than not, people use products that their friends like and recommend. Social media sites can provide this type of data on numerous products and services.

Companies are utilising social computing tools to get feedback from customers. This trend is referred to as *conversational marketing*. These tools enable customers to supply feedback via blogs, wikis, online forums and social networking sites. Again, customers are providing much of this feedback to companies voluntarily and for free.

Social computing not only generates faster and cheaper results than traditional focus groups, but also fosters closer customer relationships. For example, Dell Computer operates a feedback website called IdeaStorm, where it allows customers to suggest and vote on improvements in its offerings.

Retailers know that customers, especially the younger ones, want to be heard and they also want to know whether others agree with them. Retailers are opening up their websites to customers, letting them post product reviews, ratings, and in some cases photos and videos.

The result is that customer reviews are emerging as a prime place for online shoppers to visit. Approximately one-half of consumers consult reviews before making an online purchase, and almost two-thirds of consumers are more likely to purchase from a site if it has ratings and reviews.

For example, oo.com.au, through its online shopping website, gathers data from its customers through email newsletter memberships. It also provides customers with the opportunity to provide written reviews of products purchased as well as rating the products on their site. Its approach to social computing helps oo.com.au make decisions about products, and understand buying preferences to inform their decisions on new items and product changes.

Using social computing for market research is not only a tool for businesses. Customers enjoy the capabilities that social computing offers when they are shopping as well. In IT's About Business, you see how social computing helps shoppers perform market research to find the car they want on Carsales.com.au.

IT'S ABOUT BUSINESS

Buying a vehicle takes work!

Carsales.com.au commands 80 per cent of the time Australians spend looking at online motor vehicle classifieds, but until December 2012 it had not raised its listing prices for four years. That's how seriously it took the threat from carsguide.com.au, a joint venture between News Ltd and some big car dealerships, whose 'free listings' strategy had encouraged hedge funds to make Carsales one of the most shorted stocks on the ASX. With car listings of almost 250 000, Carsales is a formidable online car sales site across Australia. Their smaller cousin, Carsguide.com.au, has approximately 5 per cent of the online sales market and is constantly looking for opportunities to improve customers' (buyers and sellers) experience on their website.

Carsguide.com.au, a business unit of News Limited, advertises more than 10 000 new and used cars each month. The company knows that comparing features on vehicles can be confusing to buyers. To make a wise buying decision, customers must compare many different types of information, including performance specifications, a variety of high-tech systems and numerous safety features. As a result, the website of Carsguide provides a buying guide that simplifies searching and reviewing different types of data from different sources and presents it in a way that customers can use to shop for vehicles, compare features, read reviews and obtain price quotes directly from dealerships or private sales.

The company provides sophisticated web capabilities and mobile tools that make it easier for customers to find, view and extract the information they need to make a buying decision. Carsguide recognises that a seamless experience on its website equals clicks, which equals revenue. The company earns revenue from online classified ads place by automakers, dealers and private-party sellers, as well as offering finance to potential purchasers. It also sells banner advertisements and provides lead-generation services.

Carsguide offers comprehensive pricing information, photo galleries, buying guides, original editorial content, expert car reviews, and other relevant content from vehicle manufacturers and others. The company's website contains online portals for dealers, employees and customers.

The company's website contains many useful tools. A few examples include the following:

- a tool focused on helping dealers list used vehicles at an optimal price when they place a classified ad
- a tool that helps dealers manage their advertising
- tools that help value a car, investigate car finance, another for car insurance and a Q&A section if a buyer or seller have a problem.

Carsguide is also using social media such as Facebook, Twitter, Google+ and RSS Feeds to further integrate content and offerings. The company wants to increase its visibility, while making information more accessible and useful to a larger audience.

Sources: www.carsales.com.au; www.carsguide.com.au; www.brw.com.au/p/investing/australia_online_monopolies_are_np2sLreue05CSgDcpsDx4N.

QUESTIONS

1 Is it possible for the Carsguide website to provide too much information to its customers? If so, how could providing too much information hurt the company?

2 What other web 2.0 functionality could Carsguide include on its website to provide additional information for visitors to the company's website?

Conducting market research using social networks

Customer sentiment expressed on Twitter, Facebook and other such sites represents an incredibly valuable source of information for companies. Customer activities on social networking sites generate huge amounts of data that must be analysed, so that management can conduct better marketing campaigns, product design and service offerings. The monitoring, collection and analysis of socially generated data, and the resultant strategic decisions are combined in a process known as **social intelligence**.

For example, Wendy's International (**www.wendys.com**) uses software to sift through over 500 000 customer messages the fast-food chain collects each year. Using Clarabridge (**www.clarabridge.com**) text analytics software, Wendy's analyses comments from its online notes, emails, receipt-based surveys and social media. Before, the company used a combination of spreadsheets and keyword searches to review comments in what it describes as a slow and expensive manual approach. The new software enables Wendy's to track customer experiences at the store level within minutes.

Social networks provide excellent sources of valuable information for market research. Here you see illustrative examples of how to use Facebook, Twitter and LinkedIn for market research.

Using Facebook for market research

There are several ways to use Facebook for market research.

- Get feedback from your Facebook followers (and their friends if possible) on advertising campaigns, market research and so on. It is like having a free focus group.
- Test market your messages. Provide two or three options and ask fans which one they prefer and why.
- Use Facebook for survey invitations (i.e. to recruit participants). Essentially, turn Facebook into a giant panel and ask Facebook users to participate in a survey. Facebook offers a self-service model for displaying ads and ads can be invitations to take a survey. Facebook also allows you to target your audience very specifically based on traditional demographic models (age, gender, etc.).

Using Twitter for market research

Your customers, your prospects, and industry thought leaders all use Twitter, making it a rich source of instantly updated information.

- Visit Twitter Search (**www.Twitter.com/search**). Enter a company's Twitter name. Not only can you follow what companies are saying, you can also follow what everyone is saying to them. Monitoring replies to your competitors and their employees will help you develop your own Twitter strategy by allowing you to see (a) what they are doing and more importantly (b) what people think about it. You can also see the company's response.
- Take advantage of the tools that enable you to find people in the industries they operate in. Use search. Twitter.com to monitor industry-specific keywords. Check out Twellow (**www.twellow.com**). This site automatically categorises a Twitter user into one to three industries based on that person's bio and tweets.
- Want to see what topic is on most people's minds today? Look at the chart on TweetStats (**www.tweetstats.com**). It will show you the most frequently used words so you can be a part of those conversations.
- An increasing number of companies are utilising Twitter to solicit information from customers and interact with them. Examples include Dell (connecting with customers), JetBlue (learning about customers), Teusner Wines (gathering feedback, sharing information) and Pepsi (fast response time in dealing with complaints).

Using LinkedIn for market research

Post a question (e.g. solicit advice) regarding the topic or issue you are interested in. You may get a better result if you go to a specific LinkedIn group.

BEFORE YOU GO ON . . .

1. What is social advertising?
2. Describe several ways to advertise in social media.
3. Why are the social aspects of market research so valuable to market researchers?
4. Define *social intelligence*.
5. Describe several ways to conduct market research on social networking sites.

Apply the Concept

Background

This section focused on the ways that some businesses use social advertising to create a competitive advantage. They allow customers to share product information and make purchases right in the social network. You have probably received some note on a social network that asked you to share with five of your friends. This type of social commerce is here to stay, but just how many people can you really reach with this type of virtual word-of-mouth marketing?

For example, imagine you want to know how many users could be reached at the third level of friends away from the initial group, when the initial group consists of 100 people and each person shares the message with three people. For this example, assume that each person shares with another unique individual. Level 1 is the initial 300 people. Level 2 is the initial 300 multiplied by three people each. This equals 900 customers. This group of 900 customers shares with three more people each. So at the third level, there is the potential to reach 2700 customers. The table below demonstrates this concept.

Level	100 Share with 2	100 Share with 3	200 Share with 4	200 Share with 5
1	200	300	800	
2	400	900		
3	800	2700		

Activity

Build and complete your own table just to see how quickly social commerce can help sell products. Label your columns as shown in the table above. Finally, use the table you build to determine how many initial contacts a company has to make to reach over 12 000 people at the third level assuming that each user shares with four people.

Deliverable

Complete your table down to the fifth level for all four columns and submit this to your instructor. Include a paragraph answering the question above about determining how many initial contacts are needed to reach the 12 000 mark at the third level.

THE NOOK

QUESTIONS

1. Social advertising would be easy to get going. Are there any pubs or clubs in your area that engage in social advertising? How do they do it? Does it work?
2. If Malakai and Abbie post a survey after a big night to learn more about who was there and what they thought about it, how could they ensure that they only received comments from people who were actually there?
3. Should survey results be posted for the public to see or kept private?

8.5 Social computing in business: customer relationship management

The customer service profession has undergone a significant transformation, both in the way that customer service professionals do business and the way that customers adapt to interacting with companies in a newly connected environment. Social computing has vastly altered both the expectations of customers and the capabilities of corporations in the area of customer relationship management.

How social computing improves customer service

Customers are now incredibly empowered. Companies are closely monitoring social computing because they are mindful of the negative comments posted by social network members, but also because they see an opportunity to involve customers proactively to reduce problems by improved customer service.

Empowered customers know how to use the wisdom and power of crowds and communities to their benefit. These customers choose how they interact with companies and brands, and they have elevated expectations. These customers are participatory and have active involvement with businesses, not just as purchasers, but also as advocates and influencers as well. As a result, businesses must respond to customers quickly and accurately. Fortunately, social computing provides many opportunities for businesses to do just that, thereby giving businesses the opportunity to turn disgruntled customers into champions for the firm. Consider the following examples.

- Qantas airlines (**www.qantas.com.au**) had a policy that required large musical instruments to be stored in the cargo hold, sometimes causing damage to the instruments. After suffering $1200 in damage to his saxophone, Jamie Oehlers of Australia organised a Facebook campaign to persuade the airline to reverse the policy. When one person complains, he or she typically gets a nice letter, but company policy will most likely not change. But when more than 8700 people joined forces on Facebook (including members of national symphony orchestras), posting stories and pictures of instruments that had been damaged in the cargo hold and saying they would boycott the airline, Qantas had to listen carefully. The airline announced that they had listened to their customers and changed the policy. The new policy allows small musical instruments as carry-on baggage.

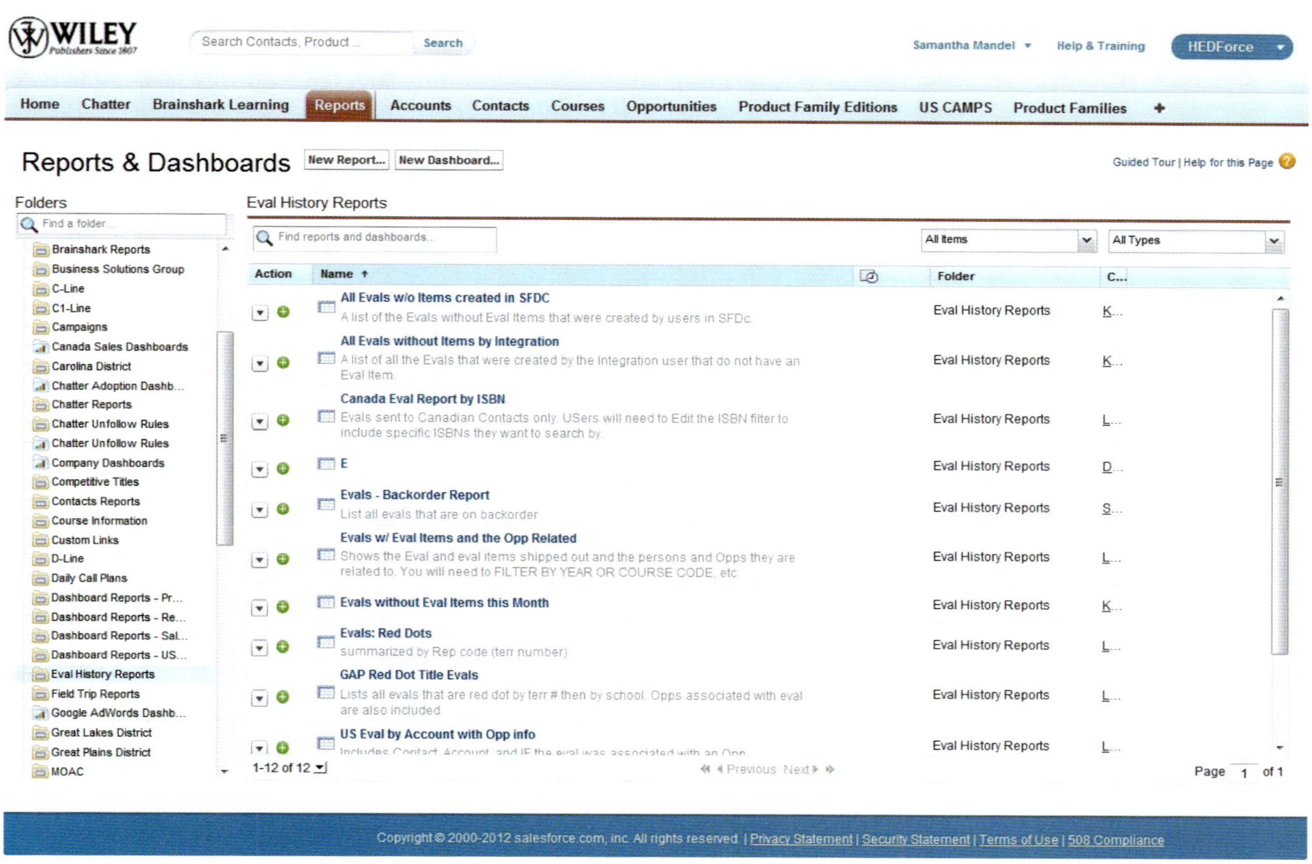

FIGURE 8.9 Salesforce.com is a powerful customer relationship management tool that allows companies to track business opportunities. This is an example of different customer reports that can be pulled from Salesforce in the version used by John Wiley & Sons.

- Coles offers online shopping facilities as well as linking to their social network sites, but they are managing feedback by allowing only Likes to their Facebook page or follows to their Twitter. Although there are 410 000 followers of their Facebook page, locating the link to go to the Facebook page is difficult, limiting the 'social networking' capacity for customers to easily provide feedback. Coles' YouTube channel provides added value for their customers in the form of cooking instruction videos recorded by Curtis Stone, their celebrity chef. Additionally, Coles uses Google+ for community updates and dinner ideas, while also promoting current specials to their 23 000 followers.
- In December 2010, Groupon featured a discount to a restaurant delivery service in Tokyo for the New Year. The promotion was wildly successful as more than 500 'Groupons' were sold. Unfortunately, the restaurant was not prepared for the success and was unable to accommodate all the orders. Deliveries were late and many of them were in terrible condition.

  Andrew Mason, the CEO of Groupon, took on the responsibility. He acknowledged that he contracted to an organisation that was not prepared to deal with the volume of the Groupon promotion. Groupon refunded money to the customers who bought the coupons and gave away vouchers for future business. Groupon also created a video that featured a public apology about the incident. It was sincere and informative, explaining exactly what happened and holding nothing back.

BEFORE YOU GO ON . . .

1. Describe how social computing has changed customer service.
2. How do empowered customers change the power relationships in an organisation?

   Hint: refer to the introduction.

Apply the Concept

Background

Social customer relationship management is about using social networks to maintain loyal relationships. One company that is very good at doing that is ZAGG (Zealous About Great Gadgets). ZAGG makes and sells accessories for mobile devices such as smartphones and tablets. To help sell its products, the company has developed one of the best social customer relationship management plans around.

When ZAGG develops a new product, the company not only posts notes about this product on its social networking page, but also involves customers. For example, when ZAGG was releasing its ZAGGFolio for the iPad, the company allowed fans to vote on the colours of the new product.

ZAGG is also good at monitoring the social network to watch for product issues. It is not uncommon for someone to complain and then receive feedback from a ZAGG employee regarding this issue. Not only does the company maintain that customer, but it also develops a sense of trust with all its customers who feel they would be given the same treatment.

Activity

Visit ZAGG's website (www.zagg.com). Near the top of the page, you see a link to their Facebook page. Visit this and review their timeline. Look for customer complaints and see how the company deals with them. Do you find a customer representative present on the social networking site? Are there any competitions? Surveys? Giveaways? Can you reverse engineer the company's social customer relationship management methodology?

Now imagine that you are a marketing manager and have been asked to help develop a strategy for using Facebook to help manage customer relationships. Is there anything you can use from the text and what you have seen here?

Deliverable

Create a list of the top ten ideas you have for ways to engage in social customer relationship management. If they are not your own ideas, reference the source. However, it will be better for you to synthesise both the chapter material and what you have seen at ZAGG's website and to develop your own ideas.

QUESTIONS

1 Malakai and Abbie feel a deep sense of responsibility in taking care of their customers even if their customers do not take care of themselves. A dead customer is not profitable! How might they employ tools in social networks to help their customers make good decisions regarding alcohol consumption, driving and so on?
2 How might customers feel about a club recommending that they not drive home based on comments their friends made on a social network?

THE NOOK

8.6 Social computing in business: human resource management

Human resources (HR) departments in many organisations use social computing applications mainly in the areas of recruiting and training. For example, Deloite Touche Tohmatsu set up a social network to assist its HR managers in downsizing and regrouping teams.

Recruiting

Both recruiters and job seekers are moving to online social networks as new recruiting platforms. Enterprise recruiters are scanning online social networks, blogs and other social resources to identify and find information about potential employees. If job seekers are online and active, there is a good chance that they will be seen by recruiters. In addition, on social networks there are many passive job seekers — people who are employed but would take a better job if it appeared. So, it is important that both active and passive job seekers maintain profiles online that truly reflect them. IT's About Business takes a look at the difficulties of the online recruiting process and provides some tips when you are looking for a job yourself.

BEFORE YOU GO ON . . .

1 Describe the impact of social computing on the recruitment process. (*Note:* There are pros and cons in this process.)
2 Describe the impact of social computing on looking for a job. Again, there are pros and cons in this process.

IT'S ABOUT BUSINESS

So you want to find a job

The problem

Let's say you want to find a job. Like the majority of job hunters, you will probably conduct your search almost exclusively online. Together, the most popular employment websites, such as Seek (www.seek.com.au) and Careerone (www.careerone.com.au), now list some 126 000 plus openings in Australia and New Zealand.

Using a job site has clear advantages for you: It is the cheapest, fastest and most efficient way to connect employers and potential employees. Unfortunately, the clear advantages of these sites have led to a runaway success that the sites are sometimes not equipped to handle. Luckily for you, there are new competitors poised to fix those problems.

The key issue for the companies that own the job sites is that the sites are neither as cheap nor as efficient as they once were. Job hunters such as yourself send these companies too many résumés for them to process effectively. Combined with the economic downturn, this inundation of résumés may lead you to feel that your applications are ending up in a 'black hole'.

To add to your difficulty in finding a job, many employers have downsized their recruiting staff in recent years, so they cannot keep up with the flood of applications produced by the job sites' sorting applications. Even if they try to replace human recruiters with software to sift applications, that has serious downsides as well. If their sorting algorithm is too rigid, it can yield irrelevant results that waste time and money. →

Not only that, but less-qualified candidates can play the system by loading their résumés with the correct keywords. Finally, sorting applications removes any human interaction (e.g. actual human job interviews) that can signal a good fit between candidate and position.

A variety of solutions

In response to these problems, a number of new job-search startups are moving beyond traditional job sites. These companies are trying to create better-targeted matching systems that reduce the possibility of gaming the system and that leverage social networking trends.

Gumtree (www.gumtree.com.au) offers both listings for jobs available and résumés of current job seekers. In 2013, during the financial downturn in Australia, Gumtree listed in excess of 44000 résumés, more than 20 per cent more jobs than were listed at the time. While not currently tapping into social networks, the searching and look and feel of the Gumtree site has the potential to use the ratings and communications tools from their sister auction site to enable a level of social computing.

In perhaps the most dramatic shift in the online employment business, job searchers are turning away from traditional sites and turning towards social networks such as LinkedIn and Facebook, where many feel more comfortable and in control. Applicants have helped LinkedIn raise its market share in job search from 4.7 per cent in 2010 to a projected 12.2 per cent by 2013. LinkedIn have added a skills ranking facility for their clients, where people within your social networking group endorse your individual skills, providing a quick reference for potential employers to your skill strengths as your social network describes you. Employers are also recognising the benefits of LinkedIn by requesting either a résumé or access to your LinkedIn profile when advertising jobs.

That shift is why Careerone (www.careerone.com.au) integrated social networking into its search process to allow job seekers to integrate their networks with Careerone's job listings, making contacts and referrals to target companies easier.

Fortune 500 companies are also using social networking in their hiring. Forty-two per cent of them now have a Facebook or LinkedIn page. Further, Jobvite's (www.jobvite.com) annual survey found that the percentage of recruiters who plan to hire through social media increased to 89 per cent in 2011.

So, how are job sites responding? They are trying to imitate and surpass their competitors. They offer an array of products, some with social networking features.

The job search industry is extremely competitive, with the lines between company offerings blurring. For example, in September 2011 Taleo announced a linkage with LinkedIn, allowing LinkedIn users to fill out online applications with their LinkedIn data and giving recruiters access to LinkedIn profiles, all with a single click of a mouse. In another example, CareerBuilder is offering new software and products, including one that looks much like Jobvite.

The results

The bottom line for all job sites is that they do not want to produce 2000 candidates, but rather 20 great candidates. However, there is enormous overlap in what different sites offer, with each borrowing from the others. In mid-2012, innovative technologies had increased job sites' revenues. Questions remain as to whether or not the job sites are making the process more effective for job seekers. However, career coaches offer valuable tips to help you find a job.

The most important secret to making online job search sites work for you: use them sparingly. When looking for a job, it is too easy to spend all day on your keyboard, combing through listings, trying endless search filters and sending your résumé into black holes. Job coaches say to spend your time this way: 80 per cent of your day networking and directly contacting the people in charge of jobs you want, 10 per cent of your time should go to headhunters and spend only the remaining 10 per cent of your time online.

Here is how to make your time online count. To start with, you should be on LinkedIn. LinkedIn is an incredibly powerful job search tool.

Next, access the Google-like job aggregators such as SimplyHired (www.simplyhired.com.au), which make it easy to narrow your search using filters. These filters include title, company name, location and many others.

Spend a little time playing with search commands. Try plugging in the name of a company you might want to work for or an advanced degree that qualifies you for specialised work. For example, you could enter 'CFA' if you are a certified financial analyst or 'LEED' if you are a building engineer with expertise in environmental efficiency.

Careerone has two useful tools called 'Find your inside connections' and 'Find jobs in your networks'. By using their BeKnown tool you allow Careerone to access your public Facebook profile for potential employers to view. What do you put on your Facebook page that you don't want a potential employer to see?

One more trick to using the aggregators: have them deliver listings to your inbox. Set up an email alert that delivers new job postings to you via email each day. Also look for niche sites that are specific to your field.

Beyond locating listings for specific jobs, career coaches say job sites can be a resource for key words and phrases that you can pull from job descriptions and include in your résumé, letters, and emails. Use the language from a job description in your cover letter.

The bottom line: it is critically important to extend most of your efforts *beyond* online search. There is just too much competition online.

Sources: Compiled from T Team (2012), 'LinkedIn looks to hitch ride from mobile ads', *Forbes*, 14 February; R Silverman (2012), 'No more resumes, say some firms', *The Wall Street Journal*, 24 January; L Weber (2012), 'Your resume vs oblivion', *The Wall Street Journal*, 24 January; S Adams (2012), 'Secrets of making the most of job search websites', *Forbes*, 18 January; G Anders (2011), 'The rare find', *Bloomberg BusinessWeek*, 17–23 October; J Francis (2011), 'Facebook joins Labor Department in online job-search project', *Bloomberg BusinessWeek*, 20 October; F Russo (2011), 'The new online job hunt', *Time*, 3 October; S Adams (2011), 'Unemployment: the good news, the bad news, and what to do about it', *Forbes*, 1 April; K Jones (2009), 'Online job searches rise as economy slices', *InformationWeek*, 26 January; www.monster.com, www.careerbuilder.com, www.jobvite.com, www.simplyhired.com, www.beyondcredentials.com.

QUESTIONS

1. What are the advantages of using social networking when searching online job sites, when you look for your first job?
2. What are the disadvantages of only using online job sites when you look for your first job?

Training

Several companies use virtual worlds for training purposes. For example, Cisco uses its virtual campus in Second Life for product training and executive briefings. IBM runs management and customer interaction training sessions in Second Life as well.

Apply the Concept

Background

Social human resource management is changing the way we search and apply for jobs and make hiring decisions. Going digital was a natural step but it was an awkward step. When position announcements went from the bulletin board and local newspaper to SEEK.com.au, the result was overwhelming. However, we are too connected today to go back. We live in a connected world and you will no doubt use social networks to find and apply for jobs.

This section has already given a good description of how to get connected to professional sites. Many of you are already on the personal social networks, but are unaware of how to use these to get a job.

Activity

Visit the professional social network, LinkedIn. Create a profile there that includes the university you currently attend. Connect to your classmates as they also complete this activity. You never know when you will need to call on one of these relationships.

Next, visit the other links provided (**SEEK.com.au**, **Gumtree.com.au** and **Careerone.com.au**) and see which ones will allow you to connect your LinkedIn or Facebook profile. As you connect to these professional sites, think of the differences in a professional social network (LinkedIn) and a personal social network (Facebook).

Deliverable

Write a journal entry for today, the day you established yourself online in professional, social HR networks. In your journal entry, give yourself advice on the types of connections you should look for, whether or not you want personal friends connected to your professional network, and how to keep your personal network separate.

THE NOOK

QUESTIONS

1. Malakai will need some help with all of his new IT. Where should he look to post a job?
2. What tools are available to help sort through applicants? Malakai received over 300 applications and does not have time to go through all of them to find the top 20 people.

8.7 Crowdsourcing

Suppose an organisation has a problem it needs to solve. Why not offer the problem to a crowd to determine whether their collective knowledge and wisdom can come up with a solution? This process, called **crowdsourcing**, involves taking a job traditionally performed by an employee or a consultant and outsourcing it to an undefined group of people in the form of an open call. Crowdsourcing harnesses crowds to solve problems, innovate and get work done. Crowdsourcing embraces freelancers, volunteers, customers and low-paid amateurs to create content, solve problems, and perform research and development. Crowdsourcing presumes that a large number of enthusiasts can outperform a small group of experienced professionals.

Crowdsourcing provides many potential benefits to organisations.

- First, problems can be explored at relatively low cost, and often very quickly.
- Second, many times crowds solve problems for free.
- Third, the organisation can tap a wider range of talent than might be present in its own organisation.
- Fourth, by listening to the crowd, organisations gain firsthand insight into their customers' desires.
- Finally, crowdsourcing taps into the global world of ideas, helping companies work through a rapid design process.

Can crowds really outperform experts employed by a company? Let's look at some examples where they have done so.

- Procter & Gamble (P&G) uses InnoCentive (**www.innocentive.com**), where company researchers post their problems. P&G offers cash rewards to problem solvers.
- At defence contractor HCL Technologies (**www.hcltech.com**), crowdsourcing provides the foundation for strategic business planning. More than 8000 employees review internal business plans to create transparency across business units and open up the strategic planning process across the company. The process has provided more honest assessments and better overall business analysis. As a result, HCL has changed its strategic focus from providing application support to providing strategic services to its clients.
- Retailbiz.com.au provides daily updates on domestic and international news, and conference and employment information impacting the retail sector in Australia. By providing current research and retail trend information they support innovative thinking in the retail sector enabling timely decision making that can impact a retailer's bottom line. Retail CEOs can receive RSS feeds from the site, enabling up-to-date information as it's released.
- Empowered Communications (**www.empoweredcomms.com.au**), offer e-marketing solutions for organisations to use crowdsourcing to test advertising, products and service client knowledge through social marketing via email, SMS and online surveys and competitions. This approach to crowdsourcing gives organisations access to over 500 000 email members, 140 000 plus SMS members with additional databases of 150 000 plus individuals to source retail and marketing information from for large and small retailers. The groups that Empowered Communications manage include WDYT.com.au, SMSPup, iDonate and BigGiveAway.com.au, which offer incentives such as cash, rewards and giveaways (competition prizes) to the individuals that complete

surveys and research studies issued to them. Empowered Communications databases can be filtered into 19 demographic profiles and 53 special interest areas. These are not limited as the group is constantly updating these filters. This service enables trend or product specific research to be collected and analysed at affordable costs to the organisations, with reports from the target demographic.

- Until a few years ago, book publishers had to rely on stock photography for many of the images used in their books. These photos were taken by professional photographers and were quite expensive. Today, high-quality digital cameras cost less than $1000 and, with available photo-editing software, amateur photographers can create images that almost match those of the professionals. The amateurs can upload their pictures to image-sharing websites such as Shutterstock (**www.shutterstock.com**), where interested parties can license and download the images for $1 to $5 per image, which is a fraction of the price of a regular stock photo. Because overhead costs are extremely low, Shutterstock can make a profit while still sharing part of the revenue with the pictures' creators.

There are many questions and concerns about crowdsourcing. Here are some of these concerns.

- How accurate is the content created by non-experts in the crowd? How is accuracy maintained?
- How is crowd-created content being updated? How can companies be sure the content is relevant?
- Should the crowd be limited to only experts? How would a company go about doing that?
- The crowd may submit too many ideas, with most being worthless. If this happens, it can cost too much money to evaluate all of the ideas. For example, during the BP oil spill in 2010, more than 20 000 suggestions were submitted on how to stem the flow of oil. The problem was very technical, so there were many poor suggestions. Despite the fact that BP was under severe time constraints, it had to evaluate all of the ideas.
- Content contributors may violate copyrights, intentionally or unintentionally.
- The quality of decisions depends on the composition of the crowd. The best decisions may come if the crowd is made up of diverse opinions and ideas. But, in many cases, companies do not know the makeup of the crowd in advance.

Despite the many questions and concerns about crowdsourcing, the process does have great value. IT's About Business shows an innovative use of crowdsourcing with online gamers.

When you work in a team on a class project, are you crowdsourcing? Why or why not?

BEFORE YOU GO ON . . .

1. Define crowdsourcing.
2. Describe the potential benefits of crowdsourcing.
3. Describe the concerns with crowdsourcing.

IT'S ABOUT BUSINESS

Scientific discoveries via crowdsourcing and online gamers

Players of the online game, Foldit (fold.it/portal), helped to discover an enzyme involved in the reproduction of AIDS in rhesus monkeys. In just three weeks, the gamers deciphered the structure of a retrovirus protein that has stumped scientists for over a decade. The discovery added to the understanding of the disease and raised hope that games could help in other research.

Scientists had been trying to understand the structure of this enzyme for years, but had previously been unable to find the right protein structure through other techniques, such as computer simulations. Proteins can be folded into many different shapes and the Foldit game encourages players to try various combinations, guided by the kind of human intuition and reasoning that computers cannot yet match.

Foldit was developed by the Center for Game Science at the University of Washington. In addition to trying to solve problems directly, university researchers are collecting data on people's pattern-recognition and puzzle-solving techniques, which the researchers will try to re-create in computer models. Other folding games under way include one to explore the H2N2 flu virus.

Others have tried applying the game approach to scientific or business problems. InnoCentive (**www.innocentive.com**) organises contests that it bills as 'challenges', usually with a corporate sponsor that puts up prize money. The hard part is formulating the problem in a specific form with very clear rules. Players have to know what the rules are and what they are going to get if they succeed with the challenge. →

InnoCentive runs a number of scientifically oriented challenges. For example, Life Technologies (www.lifetechnologies.com), the manufacturer of a DNA sequencing machine that has been miniaturised to the size of a laser printer, has been working with InnoCentive on a series of seven $1 million challenges for improvements in the device's speed and accuracy.

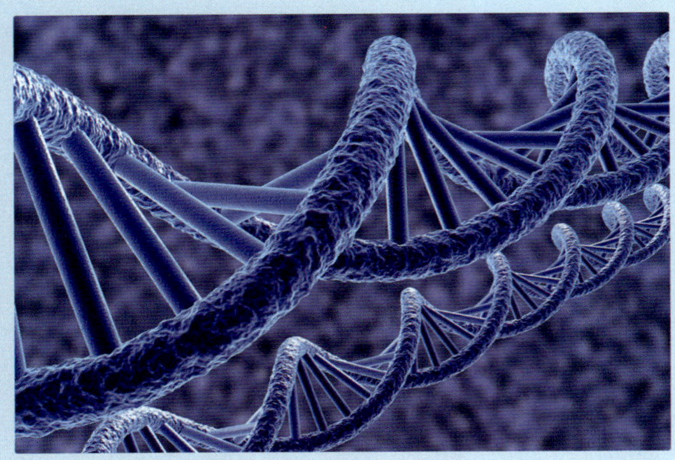

InnoCentive also hosts more business-oriented challenges. One example is a $5000 prize for suggesting a 'unique way to package and differentiate a new microbrew beer'. Other InnoCentive challenges have included helping NASA gather ideas related to astronaut health and performance, and soliciting ideas for the response to the 2010 BP oil spill in the Gulf of Mexico.

Sources: Compiled from D Mukherjee (2011), 'Could collaboration cure cancer?', *Forbes*, 16 December; D Carr (2011), 'Online gamers crack AIDS mystery', *InformationWeek*, 10 October; 'US gamers crack puzzle in AIDS research that stumped scientists for years' (2011), *Fox News*, 19 September; F Khatib et al. (2011), 'Crystal structure of a monomeric retroviral protease solved by protein folding game players', *Nature Structural and Molecular Biology*; www.innocentive.com.

QUESTIONS

1. Why is crowdsourcing so valuable in solving difficult problems?
2. What are the disadvantages of crowdsourcing?

Apply the Concept

Background

Crowdsourcing is sort of like taking your problems, throwing them onto the mosh pit at a concert and hoping they will stay on top for a perfect body surf. The issue is that sometimes they get dropped and stomped on. While crowdsourcing at times can be very profitable, the text brings up many excellent concerns about this method of problem solving.

These concerns are very much like the issues presented by open source software. Open source systems are just that — open. You can modify, customise, change, improve, or do anything to the software you want as long as you share it with the general community for someone else to build on. Closed systems, on the other hand (such as Microsoft), are editable. You must wait on the developer to offer upgrades, patches, or fixes.

Activity

Visit the Wikipedia article that discusses open versus closed source system development. Read this article as a close comparison to crowdsourcing. Many of the concerns will be the same.

Now imagine that you are the mayor of a large city that is going to make drastic changes to its public transportation. Bus routes will be redrawn, technology will be upgraded, payment methodologies will be changed, policies rewritten and so on. Given the governmental nature of this project, it may seem best to handle it completely 'inhouse' and not allow the public to play any role in the decision making. But as it is a public transportation system, perhaps the 'crowd' could make some good decisions.

Deliverable

Imagine the topics that would need to be addressed for this type of project and build a list of things you feel would be better crowdsourced and the ones you feel would be better kept inhouse. Give a short explanation with each item on your list.

WHAT'S IN IT FOR ME?

FOR THE ACCOUNTING MAJOR

Audit teams use social networking technologies internally to stay in touch with team members who are working on multiple projects. These technologies serve as a common channel of communications. For example, an audit team manager can create a group, include his or her team members as subscribers and then push information regarding projects to all members at once. Externally, these technologies are useful in interfacing with clients and other third parties for whom the firm and its staff provide services.

FOR THE FINANCE MAJOR

Many of the popular social networking sites have users who subscribe to finance-oriented subgroups. Among these groups are finance professionals who collaborate and share knowledge as well as non-financial professionals who are potential clients.

FOR THE MARKETING MAJOR

Social computing tools and applications enable marketing professionals to become closer to their customers in a variety of ways, including blogs, wikis, ratings and recommendations. Marketing professionals now receive almost real-time feedback on products.

FOR THE MANAGEMENT MAJOR

Social computing tools and applications allow management personnel to build interorganisational relationships forging better relationships between organisations, while also supporting management skills and development.

FOR THE HUMAN RESOURCES MANAGEMENT MAJOR

Social networks offer tremendous benefits to human resources professionals. HR personnel can perform a great deal of their recruiting activities by accessing such sites as LinkedIn. They can also check out potential new hires by accessing a large number of social networking sites. Internally, HR personnel can utilise private, internal social networks for employee expertise and experience in order to find the best person for a position or project team.

FOR THE MIS MAJOR

The MIS department is responsible for two aspects of social computing usage: (1) monitoring employee usage of social computing applications while at work, both time and content, and (2) developing private, internal social networks for company employees and then monitoring the content of these networks.

SUMMARY

1 Describe six web 2.0 tools and two major types of web 2.0 sites.

AJAX is a web development technique that enables portions of web pages to reload with fresh data instead of requiring the entire web page to reload.

A *tag* is a key word or term that describes a piece of information (for example, a blog, a picture, an article, or a video clip).

Really Simple Syndication (RSS) allows you to receive the information you want (customised information), when you want it, without having to surf thousands of websites.

A *weblog* (*blog* for short) is a personal website, open to the public, in which the site creator expresses his or her feelings or opinions with a series of chronological entries. Companies are using blogs in different ways. Some companies listen to the blogosphere for marketing purposes. Others open themselves up to the public for input into their processes and products.

A *wiki* is a website on which anyone can post material and make changes to already posted material. Wikis foster easy collaboration and they harness the collective intelligence of internet users.

Social networking websites allow users to upload their content to the web in the form of text (for example, blogs), voice (for example, podcasts), images and videos (for example, videocasts).

A *mashup* is a website that takes different content from a number of other websites and mixes them together to create a new kind of content.

2 Describe the benefits and risks of social commerce to companies.

Social commerce refers to the delivery of electronic commerce activities and transactions through social computing.

Benefits of social commerce to customers include the following: better and faster vendors' response to complaints; customers can assist other customers; customers' expectations can be met more fully and quickly; customers can easily search, link, chat and buy while staying in the social network's page.

Benefits of social commerce to vendors include the following: can test new products and ideas quickly and inexpensively; learn much about their customers; identify problems quickly and alleviate anger; learn from customers' experiences with rapid feedback; increase sales when customers discuss products positively on social network site; create better marketing campaigns and brand awareness; use low-cost user-generated content, for example in marketing campaigns; get free advertising through viral marketing; identify influential brand advocates and reward them.

Risks of social computing include information security concerns; invasion of privacy; violation of intellectual property and copyright; employees' reluctance to participate; data leakage of personal information or corporate strategic information; poor or biased quality of users' generated content; cyberbullying/cyberstalking and employee harassment.

3 Identify the methods used for shopping socially.

Social shopping is a method of electronic commerce that takes all of the key aspects of social networks — friends, groups, voting, comments, discussions, reviews and so on — and focuses them on shopping.

Methods for shopping socially include what other shoppers say; group shopping; shopping communities and clubs; social marketplaces and direct sales; and peer-to-peer shopping.

4 Discuss innovative ways to use social networking sites for advertising and market research.

Social advertising represents advertising formats that employ the social context of the user viewing the ad.

Innovative ways to advertise in social media include the following: create a company Facebook page; tweet business success stories to your customers; integrate ads into YouTube videos; add a Facebook 'Like' button with its sponsored story to your product; use sponsored stories.

Using Facebook for market research: get feedback from your Facebook followers (and their friends if possible) on advertising campaigns, market research and so on; test market your messages; use Facebook for survey invitations.

Using Twitter for market research: use Twitter Search; use Twellow; look at the chart on TweetStats.

Using LinkedIn for market research: post a question (e.g. solicit advice) regarding the topic or issue you are interested in.

5 Describe how social computing improves customer service.

Customers are now incredibly empowered. Companies are closely monitoring social computing because they are mindful of the negative comments posted by social network members, but also because they see an opportunity to involve customers proactively to reduce problems by improved customer service.

Empowered customers know how to use the wisdom and power of crowds and communities to their benefit. These customers choose how they interact with companies and brands, and they have elevated expectations. These customers are participatory and have active involvement with businesses, not just as purchasers, but also as advocates and influencers. As a result, businesses must respond to customers quickly and accurately. Fortunately, social computing provides many opportunities for businesses to do just that, thereby giving businesses the opportunity to turn disgruntled customers into champions for the firm.

6 Discuss different ways in which human resource managers make use of social computing.

Recruiting: Both recruiters and job seekers are moving to online social networks as new recruiting platforms. Enterprise recruiters are scanning online social networks, blogs and other social resources to identify and find information about potential employees. If job seekers are online and active, there is a good chance that they will be seen by recruiters. In addition, on social networks there are many passive job seekers — people who are employed but would take a better job if it appeared. So, it is important that both active and passive job seekers maintain profiles online that truly reflect them.

Training: Several companies use virtual worlds for training purposes. For example, Cisco uses its virtual campus in Second Life for product training and executive briefings. IBM runs management and customer interaction training sessions in Second Life as well.

7 **Discuss the advantages and disadvantages of crowdsourcing to organisations.**

Crowdsourcing is the process of taking a job traditionally performed by an employee or a consultant and outsourcing it to an undefined group of people in the form of an open call.

Crowdsourcing potential benefits to organisations: problems can be explored at relatively low cost and often very quickly; many times crowds solve problems for free; the organisation can tap a wider range of talent than it has in its own organisation; organisations gain firsthand insight on their customers' desires; crowdsourcing taps into the global world of ideas, helping companies work through a rapid design process.

Concerns with crowdsourcing include the following: the accuracy of the results; the relevance of the results; the quality of the results; whether the crowd should be limited to only experts and how a company does that; crowd may submit too many ideas, and it costs too much money to evaluate all of the ideas; content contributors may violate copyrights, intentionally or unintentionally.

>>> CHAPTER GLOSSARY

AJAX A web development technique that allows portions of web pages to reload with fresh data rather than requiring the entire web page to reload.

blog (weblog) A personal website, open to the public, in which the site creator expresses his or her feelings or opinions with a series of chronological entries.

blogosphere The term for the millions of blogs on the web.

collaborative consumption Peer-to-peer sharing or renting.

crowdsourcing The process of taking a job traditionally performed by an employee or consultant and outsourcing it to an undefined group of people in the form of an open call.

mashup Website that takes different content from a number of other websites and mixes them together to create a new kind of content.

microblogging A form of blogging that allows users to write short messages (or capture an image or embedded video) and publish them.

Really Simple Syndication (RSS) A technology that allows users to receive the information they want, when they want it, without having to surf thousands of websites.

social advertising Advertising formats that make use of the social context of the user viewing the ad.

social capital The number of connections a person has within and between social networks.

social commerce The delivery of electronic commerce activities and transactions through social computing.

social computing A type of information technology that combines social behaviour and information systems to create value.

social graph A map of all relevant links or connections for one member of a social network.

social intelligence The monitoring, collection and analysis of socially generated data and the resultant strategic decisions.

social marketplaces These act as online intermediaries that harness the power of social networks for introducing, buying and selling products and services.

social network A social structure composed of individuals, groups, or organisations linked by values, visions, ideas, financial exchange, friendship, kinship, conflict, or trade.

social networking Activities performed using social software tools (e.g. blogging) or social networking features (e.g. media sharing).

social shopping A method of electronic commerce that takes all of the key aspects of social networks — friends, groups, voting, comments, discussions, reviews, etc. — and focuses them on shopping.

tag A keyword or term that describes a piece of information.

tweet Messages and updates posted by users on Twitter.

Twitter A free microblogging service that allows its users to send messages and read other users' messages and updates.

web 2.0 A loose collection of information technologies and applications, plus the websites that use them.

weblog (see blog)

wiki A website on which anyone can post material and make changes to other material.

>>> DISCUSSION QUESTIONS

1 How would you describe web 2.0 to someone who has not taken a course in information systems?

2 If you were the CEO of a company, would you pay attention to blogs about your company? Why or why not? If yes, would you consider some blogs to be more important or more reliable than are others? If so, which ones? How would you find blogs relating to your company?

3 Do you have a page on a social networking website? Is there any content that you definitely would *not* post on such a page? If yes, why? If no, what is keeping you from creating one?

4 How can an organisation best employ social computing technologies and applications to benefit its business processes?
5 What factors might cause an individual, an employee, or a company to be cautious in the use of social networks?
6 Why are advertisers so interested in social networks?
7 What sorts of restrictions or guidelines should firms place on the use of social networks by employees? Are social computing sites a threat to security? Can they tarnish a firm's reputation? If so, how? Can they enhance a firm's reputation? If so, how?
8 Why are marketers so interested in social networks?
9 Why are human resource managers so interested in social networks?
10 List three web 2.0 social networking tools and describe how you would use each for marketing your products.

>>> PROBLEM-SOLVING ACTIVITIES

1 Enter www.programmableweb.com and study the various services that the website offers. Learn how to create mashups and then propose a mashup of your own. Present your mashup to the class.
2 Go to Amazon's Mechanical Turk website (www.mturk.com). View the available Human Intelligence Tasks (HITs). Are there any HITs that you would be interested in to make some extra money? Why or why not?
3 Access Pandora (www.pandora.com). Why is Pandora a social networking site?
4 Access ChatRoulette (www.chatroulette.com). What is interesting about this social networking site?
5 Using a search engine, look up the following.
   - *Most popular or most visited blogs.* Pick two and follow some of the posts. Why do you think these blogs are popular?
   - *Best blogs* (try www.bloggerschoiceawards.com). Pick two and consider why they might be the 'best blogs'.
6 Research how to be a successful blogger. What does it take to be a successful blogger? What time commitment might be needed? How frequently do successful bloggers post?
7 Design a mashup for your university. Include the purpose of the mashup, sources of data and intended audience.

>>> COLLABORATION EXERCISE

Background
This chapter has shown that there are many positives associated with social computing as well as many negatives. However, in spite of the negatives, it is something that you will have to deal with as a job applicant, employee, or business manager.

In some cases, you will need to develop your own social tools. To give you some experience with this, this collaboration exercise will have you create a social network for a small business venture.

Activity
You are cofounder of a local bicycle shop and need some publicity. To help with this, you have decided to sponsor an annual bike race in your local area. There is already a runner's club and you hope to draw some athletes to the bike race from that group.

You have a support team from all departments working with you. Your team (classmates) should consist of someone from marketing, logistics, finance and legal.

Visit www.johnwiley.com.au/highered/rainer/ausnz/studentresources and click on the link provided. It will take you to the home page for Ning, a company that allows you to create your own social network. Using the trial period, build a social community to promote your bike race. Be sure to mark your calendar and cancel your subscription if you want to before you are charged!

Invite your friends to join the network and give you feedback on what your team has created. Have them ask questions about the plan, legal issues, pricing, organisation and so on.

Deliverable
Send an invitation to your instructor to join your social community. With the invitation, send an explanation of what your team has accomplished and how the different areas have contributed.

CLOSING CASE 1 >
Facebook commerce

THE PROBLEM

With almost 1 billion members, Facebook is a very desirable website on which to advertise, sell and conduct other social commerce activities. Facebook's size alone is enough to attract the attention of all companies. Clearly, Facebook offers opportunities for companies to reach out to customers and conduct business transactions. However, what is the best way to take advantage of Facebook's size (customers are already there) to do business?

A VARIETY OF SOLUTIONS

Facebook commerce (or F-commerce) refers to commerce executed on, or influenced by, the Facebook platform. Two major types of F-commerce are emerging, commerce-on Facebook and commerce-off Facebook. *Commerce-on Facebook* is a type of electronic commerce in which the transaction occurs inside Facebook, specifically the purchase of goods and/or services inside Facebook with a credit card or other valid monetary system. *Commerce-off Facebook* (which occurs on other websites) is a type of electronic commerce that takes advantage of Facebook's Open Graph, allowing shoppers to sign in to Facebook from any online website with any computing device (e.g. laptop, netbook, phone).

COMMERCE-ON FACEBOOK

Facebook Stores, Facebook Credits, and Complete Selling Through Facebook are three types of commerce-on Facebook.

FACEBOOK STORES

Facebook Stores occur in a variety of formats and are not limited to traditional retailers. There are many examples. Oxfam Australia offer a cookbook that lists ingredients indicating you should use 'Fair Trade' where possible to also help people in the developing world help themselves. ASOS became Europe's first fully integrated F-store allowing consumers to complete purchases without ever leaving Facebook. Delta Airlines launched Delta Ticket Counter, allowing consumers to book and pay for flights inside Facebook. Other examples of Australian Facebook Stores are discussed in Chapter 10.

FACEBOOK CREDITS

Facebook Credits are just like tokens at an arcade or amusement park. Credits are a secure way to play games and buy virtual and digital goods on Facebook. You can buy credits using your credit card, PayPal, mobile phone, or other payment methods. Warner Brothers allows consumers to use Facebook credits to stream movies in Facebook for 30 Facebook credits ($3).

COMPLETE SELLING THROUGH FACEBOOK

1-800-Flowers has pioneered a selling process that never takes the user away from Facebook. Shoppers can select products, options, see delivery dates and even include a personal message without interrupting their Facebook experience. However, 1-800-Flowers does not take full advantage of the social environment. It does not, for example, provide an easy way to ask a relative what Mum's favourite flowers are or what her postcode is.

Delta Airlines has built a complete ticketing system into its Facebook page, and while the airline allows the user to promote Delta by posting a general message on his or her Wall, it does not do much to help the user share details with friends involved in the trip, something that a Send Button could do nicely.

1-800-Flowers and Delta do their selling via *Facebook apps*. The primary advantage of using an app is screen real estate. iFrame content is restricted to the 520 pixel-wide middle page column, while an app can control the left most 760 pixels, a 46 per cent increase in visible selling space. The disadvantage of apps is that they are more difficult to maintain and they may stress smaller budgets within businesses lacking Facebook development expertise.

To solve the dilemma of technical skills requirement for *Facebook apps* development, an Australian organisation, ThinkTankSocial.com.au, creates Facebook apps for promotional, marketing and competitions as an outsourced option for businesses. These are time limited apps that also work on mobile devises including Android, Apple and Windows operating systems. For example, Gecko's Adventure game 'Finders Keepers' was one of three games that ran over a period of 12 months. It received over 7000 unique visits and more than 2800 YouTube views.

COMMERCE-OFF FACEBOOK

There are several examples of Commerce-off Facebook. Merchant integration with Facebook works in four ways: Facebook-enabled websites, Facebook in-store retail, Facebook-initiated selling and Facebook check-in deals.

FACEBOOK-ENABLED WEBSITES

These are traditional websites and e-commerce sites that integrate with Facebook to offer customers a Facebook experience while shopping or researching purchases. Brands can bring the Facebook experience to their websites, tapping users' connections and interests to support the purchasing process. The simplest examples involve using social plugins, which are short code snippets that ping Facebook's network for information about the user visiting the brand's site. Social plugins include the Like Button, Send Button, Subscribe Button, Recommendations, Login Button and many others.

The Like Button is the most common plugin and is usually regarded as a content-sharing device. However, when it is used in conjunction with a product page, it can provide peer support by displaying the names and profile images of people who have Liked the product. Most appealing for brands is the fact that it also highlights any of the user's Facebook friends who have Liked the product.

A more sophisticated approach uses Facebook's Open Graph application programmer interface to retrieve the Likes and interests of the user, as well as those of his or her friends. There is a permission screen involved and every friend's privacy settings are individually respected.

Amazon offers a 'Tap into Your Friends' option. After the permission screen, the user is taken to an Amazon page showing the upcoming birthdays of Facebook friends and their Amazon Wish List if they have one. Amazon uses a user's friends' profile data, which often includes favourite books and music, to make gift suggestions.

Log in to www.TripAdvisor.com with Facebook Connect and users have a personalised experience that allows them to see their friends' travel recommendations, thereby socialising their travel planning and purchases. The Levi's Friend Store allows shoppers to browse their friends' 'likes' by product category.

FACEBOOK IN-STORE RETAIL

In this program, brick-and-mortar retailers integrate with Facebook to offer customers a Facebook experience while shopping in their stores. Macy's Magic Fitting Room is a Facebook-connected fitting room equipped with a camera-enhanced 72-inch mirror and an iPad that allows customers to try on clothes and then share the experience with their Facebook friends.

FACEBOOK-INITIATED SELLING

Businesses can set up a storefront for free on their Facebook pages. They start the shopping process on Facebook and then have the customer jump to their e-commerce pages at some point in the process to complete the purchase process.

For example, Lady Gaga's Facebook store takes users on a rather abrupt transition. Users can browse products on her Facebook page, but any click takes them to the product page at www.bravadousa.com, a licensed merchandise marketer and fulfilment service. The Facebook branding is gone, and the look and feel changes completely. A new window opens that makes any Facebook multitasking (e.g. chat) cumbersome. Apparently, a page with over 30 million Likes can get away with this. Justin Bieber has the same arrangement.

Best Buy keeps shoppers in the Facebook environment a bit longer and takes advantage of its social features while they are there. Best Buy's store app is labelled 'Shop 1 Share'. Users can search or browse for products. When they find something that interests them, they have two options: Ask Friends or Shop Now. Ask Friends leads to a wall post asking about the product. Interestingly, Best Buy makes Ask Friends much more noticeable than Shop Now, which takes the user to the product page at www.bestbuy.com for the shopping cart and checkout process.

FACEBOOK 'CHECK-IN DEALS'

This program allows local retailers to drive traffic to their stores by offering special discounts to consumers who check in to their location with Facebook Places on their mobile phones. In a promotion, The Gap leveraged check-in deals by offering a free pair of blue jeans to the first 10 000 consumers who checked in at Gap stores. Mazda UK offered a 20 per cent discount off the Mazda X5 for Check-in Deals when Facebook Places launched in the United Kingdom.

THE RESULTS

F-commerce is still in its infancy and barely survived its birth. In 2007, Facebook tried Project Beacon, which collected e-commerce activity on third-party sites and announced a user's purchases on his or her friends' news feed. Facebook quickly withdrew from that privacy nightmare but its poor reputation for freely dispersing user data still deters F-commerce. Many Facebook users have become so accustomed to Facebook's aggressive data-sharing policies that they automatically assume the worst. A JWT study (www.jwt.com) found that some 75 per cent of people have concerns about Facebook privacy and security.

Experienced e-commerce managers also see problems with Facebook itself. Facebook does have relatively slow page loads and smaller page size because of Facebook's advertising and navigation. Analysts wonder why customers would bother shopping through Facebook when a faster and better experience is only a browser tab away, at the e-commerce website of a vendor. Facebook advertising is also an issue. No matter how you structure your F-commerce store, the user will still be served targeted Facebook ads during the buying process.

Many web marketers question the social nature of shopping itself, and there is considerable opinion that people visit Facebook to catch up with their friends and not to be sold products. After all, the average Facebook user is connected to 130 friends and 80 interest groups and makes his or her preferences known through rich profiles and by posting 90 pieces of content per month. Facebook users spend 700 billion minutes per month in an active, relaxed environment where word of mouth is built into every click. However, the good news for businesses on that front, from the JWT study, is that 48 per cent of millennials (aged 20 to 33) would like to see the places where they shop give them the ability to buy directly on Facebook.

In January 2012, P&G announced that the company was scaling back its $10 billion annual ad budget (mostly in traditional media) to take advantage of free impressions offered by Facebook in the form of Likes and status updates. Then in May 2012, General Motors cancelled its entire $10 million Facebook ad budget. The two decisions were made for different reasons: GM was not convinced that Facebook ads are effective and P&G was looking for free media advertising efficiencies.

Some industry analysts are pointing out that advertising on Facebook is not as effective for some advertisers as advertising on search engine websites. The reason is that people searching for information on purchase decisions are better targets for ads than people checking out messages from friends. Further, these analysts have fundamental doubts about whether advertising on Facebook is a good idea because the process interrupts personal conversations with impersonal branding.

WordStream (www.wordstream.com), a search marketing management company, compared advertising on Google with advertising on Facebook. WordStream's findings suggest that Facebook is a much less effective ad medium than Google. Let's take a look at the findings.

Total reach

Facebook: 51 per cent of all internet users

Google: 90 per cent of all internet users

First quarter revenues, 2012

Facebook: $1.06 billion, down 6.5 per cent (compared with first quarter, 2011)

Google: $2.9 billion, up one per cent (compared with first quarter, 2011)

Click-through rates

Facebook: 0.051 per cent

Google: 0.4 per cent

Average: 0.1 per cent

The click-through rate of an advertisement is the number of clicks on an ad divided by the number of times the ad is shown, expressed as a percentage. The average click through rate for an ad on the internet in general is 0.1 per cent. That is, an ad that is shown 10 000 times on the internet in general would be clicked on 10 times. If an ad is shown 10 000 times on Facebook, it would be clicked on 5 times. Correspondingly, an ad shown 10 000 times on Google would be clicked on 40 times. Google ads receive 8 times as many clicks as ads on Facebook, a definite competitive advantage.

Regardless of the pros and cons of F-commerce, there is one overwhelming fact. Facebook is where the customers are, and they should be able to buy wherever and whenever they like. Today, over two-thirds of companies use Facebook to drive customers to their e-commerce sites, 44 per cent use Facebook apps for product launches and promotions, and 26 per cent build e-commerce applications (e.g. a web store) on Facebook itself.

Sources: H Elliott (2012), 'GM retools: goodbye Facebook, hello Manchester United', *Forbes*, 31 May; J Edwards (2012), 'Here's the real reason GM pulled $10 million in ads from Facebook', *Business Insider*, 29 May; J Edward (2012), 'Facebook's worst nightmare: after GM, here's how the other dominoes could fall', *Business Insider*, 15 May; J Edwards (2012), 'Data: Google totally blows away Facebook on ad performance', *Business Insider*, 15 May; J Corpus (2011), 'F-Commerce for Hollywood: turning fans into customers', *Forbes*, 19 September; J Ente (2011), 'The beginner's guide to Facebook commerce', *Mashable*, 14 July; E Savitz (2011), 'Attention Facebook shoppers: get ready for F-commerce', *Forbes*, 27 June; T McMullen (2011), 'Attention Facebook shoppers: get ready for F-Commerce', *Forbes*, 27 June; J Hird (2011), '101 examples of F-Commerce', *EConsultancy*, 19 May; J Diner (2011), 'F-Commerce, the arrival of the Facebook consumer', *ClickZ.com*, 10 May; M Lazerow (2011), 'Facebook takes people-centric ads to the next level', *Ad Age Digital*, 27 January; www.facebook.com.

QUESTIONS

1 What are the advantages for a business conducting commerce on Facebook? The disadvantages?

2 What are the advantages for customers conducting commerce on Facebook? The disadvantages?

CLOSING CASE **2 >**

Tourism Australia's social strategy

THE PROBLEM

The global financial crisis and the increase in the value of the Australian dollar saw the tourism industry face a severe slump. Much of tourism's pain was caused by the high dollar, which made Australia more expensive for foreigners, while also tempting Australians to head overseas instead of holidaying at home.

In January 2012 the *Sydney Morning Herald* reported that 'Australia's high dollar is battering the nation's tourism industry, with figures showing monthly income from foreign visitors has dropped by almost $450 million from a year earlier. The Australian Bureau of Statistics confirmed Australia's international tourism earnings slumped to $2.43 billion in November 2011, the lowest monthly result in almost five years. While spending by overseas tourists is difficult to measure, figures from November 2010 suggest foreigners spent about $2.86 billion — almost $450 million more than the November 2011 monthly figure.'

THE SOLUTION

To increase the number of tourists choosing to come to Australia and Australians choosing to holiday locally, in early 2010 the then new managing director of Tourism Australia, Andrew McEvoy, decided to prioritise social media.

Experimentation began to be encouraged from the top down. A key moment came on 22 May 2010, when Tourism Australia invited fans to submit their snapshots informally for its first Friday Fan Photos album. It wasn't a formalised concept. Instead, it was an organic, viral hit. Fans responded eagerly when they saw other fans' images being showcased, and then they shared their own photos via the site's wall. Asking followers to share their photos may have been a commonplace tactic at the time, but Tourism Australia looked at the concept's popularity and drew unique conclusions from it.

In early 2012, the organisation doubled down on social by bringing on a second full-time staffer for social media. It also began enlisting contributions from its entire staff, including digital and PR managers in its regional offices. It hired a third full-timer for social in January 2013. It's notable that all of this investment has been in people, not equipment. While some organisations outsource their social media operations to third parties, Tourism Australia keeps its inhouse. While other groups rely on expensive enterprise software solutions for running social, Tourism Australia gets things done on the Facebook and Instagram platforms themselves, without shortcuts.

FACEBOOK

Over 4 million people like Australia on Facebook. The page includes photos of current tourism interests, including Friday Fan Photos each week.

Tourism Australia's 'Best Jobs in the World' is promoted on the site, with finalists and shortlists enabling both fans' comments and keeping informed. Other state competitions are also promoted on the site.

INSTAGRAM

Tourism Australia's Instagram site @SeeAustralia has over 110 000 followers, which encourages followers to give Tourism Australia permission to use their images on Instagram (#SeeAustralia) and Facebook (on.fb.me/SeeAustralia) and Twitter (@Australia).

GOOGLE+

Tourism Australia's Google+ site (plus.google.com/+Australia/posts) has over 780 000 followers, which encourages followers to give feedback on images and videos that promote tourism in Australia.

TWITTER

On 13 December 2012, Tourism Australia entered the Twitter world by announcing their award for winning the 2012 World Leading Tourism Authority Website.

YOUTUBE

Tourism Australia YouTube channel is interactive, enabling viewers to select videos from locations across Australia before creating a 'holiday playlist' from the chosen videos. The YouTube channel also promotes and links to their Facebook page, encouraging traffic across the social networking sites.

TOURISM AUSTRALIA WEBSITE

While providing news and market statistics for tourists and the tourism industry in Australia, the site also encourages engagement with their social networking sites, Facebook, Twitter, Google+, Instagram and YouTube.

THE RESULTS

Tourism Australia has the most popular destination page in the world. In 2012 alone, it grew its fan base from 1.2 million to 4.1 million and launched social media campaigns that elicited 1 million views a day. Australia does well on other social media platforms, too, but Facebook still delivers 'the best reach, engagement, and conversion', says the country's tourism agency. Aussie dominance on Facebook is all the more impressive given that the travel sector as a whole is behind other sectors when it comes to social marketing. Today, 95 per cent of Tourism Australia's social media content is user-generated.

Sources: Compiled from S O'Neill (2013), 'In a Q&A, Tourism Australia reveals the secrets of its Facebook dominance', *TTNooz, Talking Travel Tech*, 27 February, www.tnooz.com/2013/02/27/news/in-a-qa-tourism-australia-reveals-the-secrets-of-its-facebook-dominance; C Yeates (2012), 'Dollar's rise leaves tourism "doing it tough"', *Sydney Morning Herald*, 6 January; T Reid (2011), 'Price cuts not the answer to tourism slump', *Gold Coast Business News*, April, www.smh.com.au/travel/travel-news/dollars-rise-leaves-tourism-doing-it-tough-20120105-1pmwe.html.

QUESTIONS

1 Compare and contrast Tourism Australia's marketing strategies across the various social networking sites.

2 How can Tourism Australia measure the impact of this social networking strategy in monetary terms (ROI)?

SPREADSHEET ACTIVITY

OBJECTIVE

When someone uses the phrase 'social network', we generally think of Facebook or Twitter. However, many online tools allow people to collaborate and work together on projects. Google Docs is one of these. This activity will introduce the Google Spreadsheet Survey tool.

Chapter connection

Although Google Spreadsheets are not social networks like Facebook and Twitter, they are definitely examples of web 2.0. They allow multiple people to work together and collaborate on many projects. The Google Spreadsheet Survey tool is no exception. It allows for the easy collection and sharing of data.

Activity

Consider the following scenario. You are the marketing officer for 'Students for Better Campus Lunches' and have been charged with a campuswide survey to find out how people feel about the current food offerings and their desires for future possibilities. You decide to use a Google Form because the data are automatically saved in a Google Spreadsheet and will be easy for you to analyse. The following questions have been recommended. You will likely need to reword some of these so they will fit a multiple-choice question format. You also may want to have a couple of open-ended questions to allow for comments.

1 How often do you eat on campus?
2 Which meals do you eat?
3 Are you satisfied with the current choices?
4 What cuisines would you like to see more of?
5 What do you think we could do without?
6 Is eating on campus too expensive?
7 Do you have any general recommendations for food on campus?

To complete this exercise, you will need to create a Google account if you do not already have one. Then log in to docs.google.com and create a new form. Go to the Google Docs website and watch the tutorials on how to create Google Forms. Or simply search Google for 'Google Form Videos' and have a look at the tutorials.

Once you have created your form, have some friends complete your survey and have a look at the data in your spreadsheet. Export this spreadsheet as a Microsoft Excel file and submit it to your tutorial group.

Deliverables

The final product will be a workable survey/form built in Google Docs and the spreadsheet that it creates.

DISCUSSION QUESTIONS

1 Discuss the advantages and disadvantages of using this type of tool. For example, how do you know how many times someone completes the survey? Given this lack of control, in how many situations would this truly be useful?
2 If you were to embed a Google Form into another web page, do you think you should tell people that your form was created on a Google site? Should you explain the security levels available? How much do you want them to know about how easily they could take and retake the survey?

DATABASE ACTIVITY: **FORMS I**

OBJECTIVE

In this activity, you will learn how to use forms that select columns of interest from one or more related tables, to view or to enter new data. So far we have entered all our data directly into our tables and looked at them that way too (or in reports). We opened tables in Datasheet view, selected a row and keyed in the data or examined it. In this activity, you will learn a better way to enter or view data.

Working with one table at a time is not ideal for two main reasons:

1 Understanding information in a meaningful way often means looking at more than one table. Registering for a new course may involve a registration table, a student table, a course table and perhaps others.
2 Looking at a table shows all its columns. A real table may have hundreds of columns. Most database users do not need all, or even most, of them. Grouping those needed for one purpose will not be ideal for a different one.

Using forms solves both of these problems. In this activity, you will see how.

Chapter connection

The unifying characteristic of social network applications is that users, not site owners, provide the content. For this to work, the interfaces they use must hide the underlying complexity of the database. Forms can do this.

Prerequisites

None.

ACTIVITY

In this activity, which you will find online, you will learn about creating forms with the Form tool and the Form Wizard. You will create complex forms, using up to three tables.

1 Download and open the Ch 08 PhotoNet database from www.johnwiley.com.au/highered/rainer/ausnz/studentresources. It contains three tables: members, photos and comments. Each comment is by a member, about a photo posted by a member. (They may be the same — that is, a member may comment on his or her own photo.) Open the relationship map, under the Database Tools ribbon tab, to see how they are related.
2 We will start with a one-table form to provide a user-friendly data entry environment. To create a form based on the Member table, open it and make sure it is in front so Access will know which table to base the form on. Then click the 'Create' ribbon tab, find the Forms section and click 'Form'. A simple form based on MemberTbl will show up.
3 The form will be in Layout view. In the chapter 9 activity you will learn to modify a form in this view. Here, just close the form. When prompted, name it NewMemberFrm.
4 Open it again. It will be in Form view, showing data for Member 1. Use the navigation tools at the bottom to move through the rows of MemberTbl. Tool tips on each symbol tell what it does. You can also enter a record number in the field that says '*n* of *m*,' where *n* is the number of the current record (table row) and *m* is the number of records in the table.

5 Enter a new record by first clicking the far right icon in the navigation area at the bottom of the form. Enter yourself as a new member, with today's date as your joining date. Fill the other fields with data of your choice.

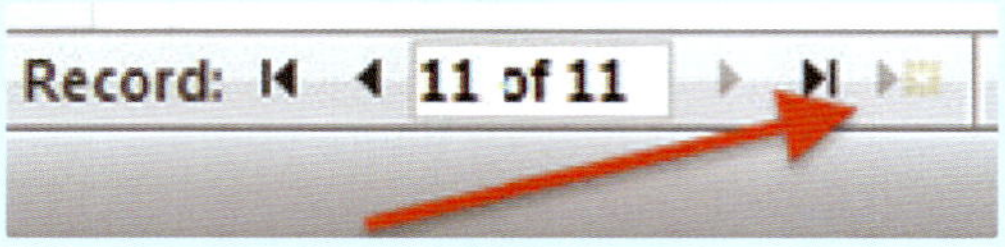

6 Suppose we want to see all of a member's photos. PhotoTbl lists them by MemberID. People do not know members by their IDs. We use names in the real world, handles on most websites. These are in MemberTbl. So, a form to show a member's handle and photos must use two tables. To create this form, again click the 'Create' ribbon tab. This time, select the Form Wizard. If your window is not wide enough for Access to display its label, it is the icon in that section with the wizard's wand sprinkling magic dust.

7 The Wizard asks you to select tables and columns for this form. First, select MemberTbl from the Tables/ Queries pull-down list. When its fields are showing, move MemberHandle to the right panel ('Selected Fields') by selecting it and clicking '>'. Then select PhotoTbl from the pull-down list, and move PhotoTitle and PhotoLink into the form. Then click 'Next'.

8 Because we want to list each member with his or her photos, view it by MemberTbl. (If we view by photo, the form will treat member data as an extension of photo data.) Click 'Next'.

9 A Datasheet view of the subform means that, within each member form, the member's photos will be listed in an embedded datasheet. Select this option and click 'Next'.

10 Title the main form 'Photos by Member' and the subform 'Photo List'. Select 'Open the form to view or enter information' and click 'Finish' to see the form you created.

11 You will see a form with Member 1's photos. The navigation tools at the bottom of the subform go through them. Those at the bottom of the entire window go through members. As you change members, the subform changes to show each one's photos. To enter a new photo, find the desired member and add it to the subform. Access will enter the correct MemberID in PhotoTbl. Confirm this: Enter a new photo for the first user, then open PhotoTbl. Your new item will be at the end, with that user's MemberID.

12 If a member forgets to add a photo link, the post should display a photo of the founder's dog. To make this happen, do either (a) or (b) in the following list. Method a, using the table, will enter this link whenever a new member is added in any way. Method b, using the form, will enter it only when a new member is added via this form.

a Open PhotoTbl in Design view. Select the PhotoLink row. Enter 'www.johnwiley.com.au/ highered/rainer/ausnz/studentresources' (*with* the quotation marks) in the Default Value row as shown in the following screen shot. Close the table.

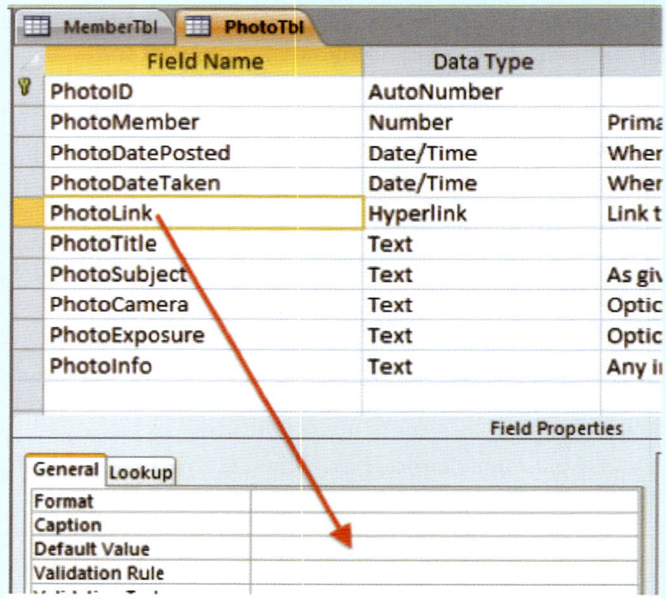

b Open the Photos by Member form in either Design or Layout view. (Layout view is shown in the following screen shot, but either one works as well as the other.) In either view, click the 'Design' tab. Then click the 'Property Sheet' icon at the far right. On that sheet, select its 'Data' tab. Enter 'www.johnwiley.com.au/highered/rainer/ausnz/ studentresources' (*with* the quotation marks) in the Default Value row. Then return to Form view. The property sheet will vanish, because it is not usable in Form view. This URL will be in the 'New' row of the table. Because it is a default, not a fixed value, a user can replace it with a real link.

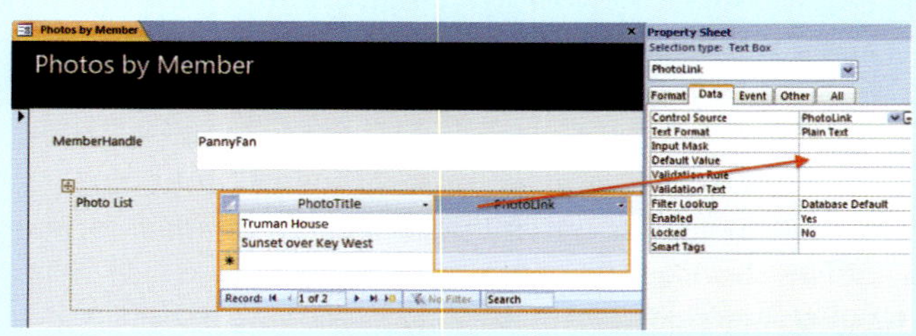

Usage hint: An Access object's property sheet describes it in full. It is the 'go-to place' for when all other attempts to change something about an object fail, to set precise dimensions that cannot be set as accurately by dragging on the screen, or to change some object characteristics that are not visible anywhere else.

13 The third form, to show members, photos and comments, is more complex. Because both PhotoTbl and CommentTbl link to MemberTbl (the first for who posted a photo, the second for who commented on it) and to each other (as each comment is about a photo), the Form Wizard cannot figure out their connections. We must do this form in stages. First, we will create a *subform* to show photos and their comments. Then, we will put it into a form with member information. For the subform, use the Form Wizard as before using all three tables, organising it by PhotoTbl. You will see member data treated as part of the comment data. This time, in what was step 9 (opposite), choose the 'Tabular' format. Save this as PhotoSubform.

14 Again using Form Wizard, create a form from only MemberTbl, with MemberName and MemberHandle. Go to Design view. With the mouse, grab the Form Footer (bottom of the form) by its top edge and drag it down to make as much space as possible for the subform.

15 Select the Design ribbon, and click 'Subform' in the Controls section. (It is probably at the bottom of the left column of three small icons, but Access will sometimes rearrange ribbons to fit the window. Mouse around until you get a Subform/Subreport tool tip.) The mouse pointer will become a 1 when you move it to the form design area. Drag it over the space you created when you expanded the form to create a rectangle where the subform will go.

16 Click the 'Property Sheet' icon at the right of the ribbon, or double-click the edge of the rectangle you just drew. (Hitting the edge takes precise positioning.) The first row under the Data tab reads 'Source Object'. Pull down the menu of possible source objects via the down arrow at the right of that row, and select 'PhotoSubform'. It will appear in the rectangle.

17 Switch to Form view and see what you created. You probably feel that you can improve its layout. In a real situation, you would. In the chapter 9 activity, you will learn how. For now, close your database, saving it if prompted.

DELIVERABLES

Your three forms, as described in the problem.

QUIZ QUESTIONS

1 Consider the following four statements:

- i You can edit the relationships among database tables.
- ii You can see the contents of more than one table at a time.
- iii You can set a default value for a data field.
- iv You are not distracted by data fields you do not need for what you are doing.

Which of the preceding statements describe(s) the advantages of using Access forms over using a table directly?

- a Only (ii)
- b Both (ii) and (iv)
- c Both (ii) and (iii)
- d All of the listed items are advantages of Access forms over using a table directly.

2 True or false? When table relationships are simple, the Form Wizard can figure out which rows of one table are associated with a row in another table.

3 True or false? The Form button in the Access Create ribbon can create a form that uses data from more than one table.

4 Which of the following *cannot* be done in the Form Wizard?

- a Selecting tables on which to base the form being designed
- b Selecting a design theme/colour scheme for the form being designed
- c Selecting totals to be placed in the form being designed
- d None of the above (All three can be done in the Form Wizard.)

DISCUSSION QUESTIONS

1 Consider the onscreen grade report you get at the end of each semester. It is a form, although your institution's course information system probably does not use Access. It is based on tables that contain student information such as your name, course information such as full course titles, and a table with grades that connects your record in the student table to the records of your courses in the course table.

Suppose you were designing this form in the Form Wizard. Describe, in words, the steps you would go through. Invent table names and column names as necessary.

2 Go to www.johnwiley.com.au/highered/rainer/ausnz/studentresources (Digital Photography Review). At the top, click 'Forums.' Select any camera type forum from the menu that drops down. In the list of threads for that forum, select any thread with at least ten messages (in the rightmost column of the thread listing). You will see that replies to other messages are listed, indented, under the message to which they reply. A long thread can have many levels of indentation.

What additional information must be added to the CommentTbl of this activity's database to make this possible? (Ignore the complexities of actually displaying things this way, whether in an Access form or anywhere else. It takes a lot of programming to make it work. Just discuss the information a program would need in order to do this at all.)

3 A city tax department has a table of real estate properties and a table of property owners. A property belongs to only one owner. An owner may own more than one property. Using paper and pencil (or other tools that your instructor may specify), draw a form it could use to show all of one owner's properties. Make reasonable assumptions about the columns in both tables.

9
E-business and e-commerce

CHAPTER OUTLINE

9.1 Overview of e-business and e-commerce

9.2 Business-to-consumer (B2C) electronic commerce

9.3 Business-to-business (B2B) electronic commerce

9.4 Ethical and legal issues in e-business

LEARNING OBJECTIVES

1 Describe the six common types of electronic commerce.

2 Describe the various online services of business-to-consumer (B2C) commerce, providing specific examples of each.

3 Describe the three business models for business-to-business electronic commerce.

4 Identify the ethical and legal issues related to electronic commerce, providing examples.

OPENING CASE >

Matt Barrie's Freelancer.com

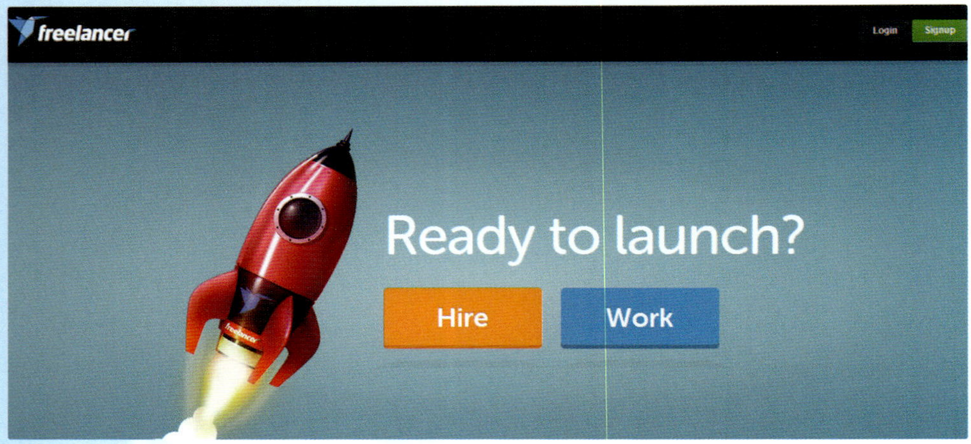

As Chief Executive of Freelancer.com, the world's largest outsourcing marketplace, Matt Barrie empowers entrepreneurs and connects seven million professionals from around the globe. Freelancer.com is a global marketplace for online and freelance jobs where businesses connect with independent service providers and freelancers to outsource their work. Through the website, employers can hire freelancers to do work in areas such as software, writing, data entry and design right through to engineering and the sciences, sales and marketing, and accounting and legal services. The average job is around US$200, making it extremely cost effective for small businesses. Freelancer.com allows small business owners to get jobs done by outsourcing to entrepreneurs in the developing world.

'It's about using technology to connect people who are looking to provide a service with those who need it, at a reasonable price and in an innovative way', Barrie says. Over 4 million projects have been outsourced through Freelancer.com, providing livelihoods for hundreds of thousands of entrepreneurs in economies where work is desperately needed. Freelancer.com started in 2009 when Barrie bought GetAFreelancer.com, a Swedish marketplace with 500 000 users that was ranked as the 5000th largest website in the world. Improving the business model and using the cash flow to buy a number of regional marketplaces in the United Kingdom, Germany, Australia, Hong Kong and the United States, Barrie has grown Freelancer.com into a household name in the developing world. It now ranks among the top 250 websites globally.

Barrie's goal for Freelancer.com is for it to be the next eBay, but for services. The company achieved 82 per cent compound revenue growth for the last four years. This success has attracted numerous acquisition offers for Freelancer, with latest offer by Japanese recruitment site Recruit Co worth a reputed $430 million in 2013. Freelancer now claims to be the world's largest marketplace for outsourcing freelance work that enables freelancers to bid for individual projects posted online.

It is from this base that Barrie is currently working towards floating the company publicly on the Australian Stock Exchange. Although in recent years public listings of other technology companies have had mixed results, notably iSelect, others like Seek, Xero and Carsales have been a success. More broadly, Barrie hopes that this will help boost Australia's technology sector, and encourage others to build up their businesses, follow suit and grow Australia's small technology sector.

For 12 years Barrie has lectured on entrepreneurship to engineering students and says he became an entrepreneur by default. 'I often joke that I'm fundamentally unemployable', he says. 'I like to do things differently and question authority. I figured out that I would have to create a job for myself if I was going to get anywhere.'

Sources: Ernst & Young (2012), 'Matt Barrie', *Exceptional*, p. 12; B Grubb (2013), 'Freelancer.com founder Matt Barrie rejects $430 million buy-out to list on Australian stock exchange', *The Sydney Morning Herald, Technology*, 18 September, www.smh.com.au/technology/technology-news/freelancercom-founder-matt-barrie-rejects-430-million-buyout-to-list-on-australian-stock-exchange.html; C Palmer (2013), 'Matt Barrie to float Freelancer.com in Aussie tech sector push', *IT News for Australian Business*, 18 September, www.itnews.com.au/News/matt-barrie-to-float-freelancercom-in-aussie-tech-sector-push.aspx.

Introduction

One of the most profound changes in the modern world of business is the emergence of electronic commerce, also known as e-commerce (EC). E-commerce is transforming all business functional areas and their fundamental tasks, from advertising to paying bills. Its impact is so widespread that it is affecting almost every organisation. This means that, regardless of where you land a job, your organisation likely will be practicing electronic commerce.

Electronic commerce influences organisations in many significant ways. First, it increases an organisation's reach, defined as the number of potential customers to whom the company can market its products. In fact, e-commerce provides unparalleled opportunities for companies to expand worldwide at a small cost, to increase market share and to reduce costs. By utilising electronic commerce, many small businesses can now operate and compete in market spaces once dominated by larger companies.

Another major impact of electronic commerce has been to remove many of the barriers that previously impeded entrepreneurs seeking to start their own businesses. E-commerce offers amazing opportunities for you to open your own business by developing an e-commerce website. IT's About Business (overleaf) shows you how smartphone technology used e-commerce to start an extremely successful business.

Electronic commerce is also drastically changing the nature of competition, because of the development of new online companies, new business models, and the diversity of EC-related products and services. Recall your study of competitive strategies in chapter 2, particularly the impact of the internet on Porter's five forces. You learned that the internet can both endanger and enhance a company's position in a given industry.

It is important for you to have a working knowledge of electronic commerce because your organisation almost certainly will be employing e-commerce applications that affect

THE NOOK

Malakai and Abbie are ready to implement e-business on their website. They intend to sell The Nook branded T-shirts, bracelets, necklaces, soundtracks and other paraphernalia. They do not need a complicated site because they will sell only around 20 items.

They have decided to use PayPal as the payment mechanism. It appears that PayPal provides a nice set of e-commerce tools that they can integrate into their site. Additionally, many people already have a PayPal account. This will allow them to tap into an existing set of customers without having to develop their own platform. It will also give them instant credibility in the online marketplace.

Given their decision, they want you to learn about the e-commerce market. Use this chapter's material to help them understand how they can use these tools to create an online retail store. By the end, they hope you can give them an idea of the concerns they may face as they move to this system. Also, they want some specific directions on implementing PayPal on their site.

IT'S ABOUT BUSINESS

Need a taxi? Ingogo is a mobile app that utilises smartphone technology to enable taxi passengers to place a request with nearby taxis during peak periods or late at night. Ingogo is an easy to use app for requesting a taxi, predominantly in the Sydney market. It is also moving into the Melbourne market as a pilot study, but the goal is to go nationwide once they are well established in the Sydney market.

Ingogo puts the passenger in direct contact with a nearby fully licensed taxi driver. The taxi can also be seen approaching the passenger 'live', on a GPS (global positioning system) enabled map on their mobile device. The Ingogo app is safe and works because all taxi drivers must be trained and validated to ensure that they meet security and transport legislative requirements. The drivers are tracked via GPS for driver and passenger personal safety, and as a tracking mechanism for any lost property.

Furthermore, if the passenger is out of money or has lost their wallet or purse, Ingogo has a safe payment function that enables passengers to securely authorise payments from their own mobile phone. It keeps the card details private with a 4 digit Ingogo payment code. Taxi users can preload personal and business debit and credit card details, then choose the appropriate payment on completion of the trip, with receipts conveniently emailed directly to the passenger.

The Ingogo app was initially launched in Sydney at the beginning of 2012. In late 2013, Ingogo joined forces with the ANZ bank to directly equip taxi industry drivers with mobile phones that can accept all forms of payments, including corporate accounts. Previously, taxis were compelled to use existing proprietary terminals to process credit and debit card payments, as well as using the magnetic strip dockets from the likes of the Cabcharge system.

These dedicated mobile phones are equipped with a payment 'sleeve' from US supplier Ingenico, which wraps around the phone, enabling the mobile device to accept card payments such as Visa payWave, MasterCard Tap & Go, magstrip and EFTPOS chip and PIN. The mobile package for drivers complements Ingogo's existing free taxi booking app for consumers on Apple's iOS and Android platforms, while still enabling cash payments for those passengers who did not book via the Ingogo app.

Ingogo is just one example of a number of taxi booking companies looking to disrupt the dominance of taxi industry incumbent payment systems and the Cabcharge system by facilitating direct bookings and payment, bypassing the current monopolised taxi industry systems and using smartphone technology to facilitate e-commerce transactions.

Sources: H Aston and M Russell (2012), 'Click for a cab: ride home goes to the highest bidder', *The Age*, 26 February, www.theage.com.au/digital-life/smartphone-apps/click-for-a-cab-ride-home-goes-to-the-highest-bidder.html; F Foo (2013), 'Ingogo first cab off the smartphone rank', *The Australian*, 15 October, www.theaustralian.com.au/technology/ingogo-first-cab-off-the-smartphone-rank/story.html; Google Play, 'Ingogo the free taxi app', www.play.google.com/store/apps/ingogo.passenger; M Hammond (2013), 'Ingogo on the go after securing fresh funds', *Startup Smart*, 13 February, www.startupsmart.com.au/financing-a-business/ingogo-on-the-go-after-securing-fresh-funds.html; B Hurley (2013), 'Taxi app Ingogo snares extra $1.5m funding', *BRW*, 5 April, www.brw.com.au/entrepreneurs/taxi_app_ingogo_snares_extra_funding.html; Ingogo (2013), *Ingogo Press*, www.ingogo.mobi/press; *Newcastle Herald* (2013), 'Top apps for digital wallet', 28 April, www.theherald.com.au/story/top-apps-for-digital-wallets.

QUESTIONS

1. Describe the business model applied here. Where else could a similar approach to e-commerce be taken and applied?
2. What are the advantages and disadvantages for customers using smartphone technology to facilitate e-commerce transactions?

the firm's strategy and business model. This knowledge will make you more valuable to your organisation and will enable you to quickly contribute to e-commerce applications in your functional area. As you read What's In IT For Me? at the end of the chapter, envision yourself performing the activities discussed in your functional area.

Going further, you may decide to become an entrepreneur and start your own business. In this case, it is even more essential for you to understand electronic commerce, because e-commerce, with its broad reach, will probably be critical for your business to survive and thrive.

In this chapter, you will discover the major applications of e-business and will be able to identify the services necessary for its support. You then study the major types of electronic commerce: business-to-consumer (B2C), business-to-business (B2B), consumer-to-consumer (C2C), business-to employee (B2E) and government-to-citizen (G2C). You conclude by examining several legal and ethical issues that have arisen as a result of the rapid growth of e-commerce.

9.1 Overview of e-business and e-commerce

Any entrepreneur or company that decides to practice electronic commerce must develop a strategy to do so effectively. The first step is to determine exactly *why* you want to do business over the internet using a website. There are several reasons for employing websites:

- to sell goods and services
- to induce people to visit a physical location
- to reduce operational and transaction costs
- to enhance your reputation.

A website can accomplish many of these goals. Unless a company (or you) has substantial resources, however, it is difficult to accomplish all of them at the same time. The appropriate website for achieving each goal will be somewhat different. As you set up your website, you must consider how the site will generate and retain traffic, as well as a host of other issues. The point here is that, when you are studying the various aspects of electronic commerce, keep the strategy of the organisation or entrepreneur in mind and you will have a good idea as to the type of website to use.

This section examines the basics of e-business and e-commerce. First, you define these two concepts and then become familiar with pure and partial electronic commerce. You then take a look at the various types of electronic commerce. Next, you focus on e-commerce mechanisms, which are the ways that businesses and people buy and sell over the internet. You conclude this section by considering the benefits and limitations of e-commerce.

Definitions and concepts

Electronic commerce (**EC** or **e-commerce**) describes the process of buying, selling, transferring, or exchanging products, services, or information via computer networks, including the internet. **Electronic business** (e-business) is a somewhat broader concept. In addition to the buying and selling of goods and services, **e-business** refers to servicing customers, collaborating with business partners and performing electronic transactions within an organisation.

Electronic commerce can take several forms depending on the degree of digitisation involved. The *degree of digitisation* is the extent to which the commerce has been transformed from physical to digital. This concept can relate to both the product or service being sold and the delivery agent or intermediary. In other words, the product can be either physical or digital, and the delivery agent can be either physical or digital.

In traditional commerce, both dimensions are physical. Purely physical organisations are referred to as **brick-and-mortar organisations**. (You may also see the term *bricks-and-mortar.*) In contrast, in *pure EC* all dimensions are digital. Companies engaged only in EC are considered **virtual** (or **pure-play**) **organisations**. All other combinations that include a mix of digital and physical dimensions are considered *partial* EC (but not pure EC). **Clicks-and-mortar organisations** conduct some e-commerce activities, yet their primary business is carried out in the physical world. A common alternative to the term *clicks-and-mortar* is *clicks-and-bricks*. You will encounter both terms. Therefore, clicks-and-mortar organisations are examples of partial EC. E-commerce is now so well established that people generally expect companies to offer this service in some form.

Purchasing a shirt at Big W online or a book from Amazon.com is partial EC because the merchandise, although bought and paid for digitally, is physically delivered by Australia Post, FedEx or DHL. In contrast, buying an e-book from Amazon.com or a software product from Buy.com is pure EC because the product itself as well as its delivery, payment and transfer are digital. To avoid confusion, we use the term *electronic commerce* to denote both pure and partial EC.

Types of e-commerce

E-commerce can be conducted between and among various parties. In this section, you will identify the six common types of e-commerce and learn about three of them — C2C, B2E and e-government — in detail. You then consider B2C and B2B in separate sections because they are very complex.

- **Business-to-consumer electronic commerce (B2C)**. In B2C, the sellers are organisations and the buyers are individuals. You learn about B2C electronic commerce in section 9.2.
- **Business-to-business electronic commerce (B2B)**. In B2B transactions, both the sellers and the buyers are business organisations. The vast majority of EC volume is of this type. You will learn more about B2B electronic commerce in section 9.3. Figure 1.8 also illustrates B2B electronic commerce.
- **Consumer-to-consumer electronic commerce (C2C)**. In C2C (also called customer-to-customer), an individual sells products or services to other individuals. The major strategies for conducting C2C on the internet are auctions and classified ads.
  In dozens of countries, C2C selling and buying on auction sites are exploding. Most auctions are conducted by intermediaries such as eBay (**www.ebay.com**). Consumers can also select general sites such as Gumtree Australia (**www.gumtree.com.au**), a community website that is an easy to use search tool of people advertising and listing items for sale, which people can use to locate items they need at a bargain price, or to swap and trade close to where they live.
  The major categories of online classified ads are similar to those found in print ads: vehicles, real estate, employment, pets, tickets and travel. Classified ads are available through most internet search and social network sites (Google, Facebook, Twitter, etc.), at some portals (Yahoo!, YouTube etc.), and from internet directories and online newspapers. Many of these sites contain search engines that help shoppers narrow their searches.
  Internet-based classified ads have one big advantage over traditional types of classified ads: they provide access to an international, rather than a local, audience. This wider audience greatly increases both the supply of goods and services and the number of potential buyers. It is important to note that the value of expanded geographic reach depends greatly on what is being bought or sold. For example, you might buy software from a company located 1000 kilometres away from you, but you would not buy firewood from someone at such a distance.
- **Business-to-employee (B2E)**. In B2E, an organisation uses EC internally to provide information and services to its employees. For example, companies allow employees to manage their benefits and to take training classes electronically. In addition, employees can buy discounted insurance, travel packages, and tickets to events on the corporate intranet. They also can order supplies and materials electronically. Finally, many companies have electronic corporate stores that sell the company's products to its employees, usually at a discount.
- **E-government**. E-government is the use of internet technology in general and e-commerce in particular to deliver information and public services to citizens (called government-to-citizen or G2C EC) and to business partners and suppliers (called government-to-business or G2B EC). G2B EC is much like B2B EC, usually with an overlay of government procurement regulations. That is, G2B EC and B2B EC are similar conceptually. However, the functions of G2C EC are conceptually different from anything that exists in the private sector (e.g. B2C EC).
- E-government is also an efficient way of conducting business transactions with citizens and businesses and within the governments themselves. E-government makes government more efficient and effective, especially in the delivery of public services. An example of G2C electronic commerce is electronic benefits transfer, in which governments transfer benefits, such as social security and pension payments, directly to recipients' bank accounts.
- **Mobile commerce (m-commerce)**. The term *m-commerce* refers to e-commerce that is conducted entirely in a wireless environment. An example is using mobile phones to shop over the internet. You will learn about m-commerce in chapter 10.

Each type of EC is executed in one or more business models. A **business model** is the method by which a company generates revenue to sustain itself. Table 9.1 summarises the major EC business models.

TABLE 9.1 E-commerce business models

Online direct marketing	Manufacturers or retailers sell directly to customers. Very efficient for digital products and services. Can allow for product or service customisation. (www.dell.com.au)
Electronic tendering system	Businesses request quotes from suppliers. Uses B2B with a reverse auction mechanism.
Name-your-own-price	Customers decide how much they are willing to pay. An intermediary tries to match a provider. (www.priceline.com)
Find-the-best-price	Customers specify a need; an intermediary compares providers and shows the lowest price. Customers must accept the offer in a short time or may lose the deal. (www.hotwire.com/au or www.webjet.com.au)
Affiliate marketing	Vendors ask partners to place logos (or banners) on partner's site. If customers click on logo, go to vendor's site, and buy, then vendor pays commissions to partners.
Viral marketing	Receivers send information about your product to their friends.
Group purchasing (e-coops)	Small buyers aggregate demand to get a large volume; then the group conducts tendering or negotiates a low price.
Online auctions	Companies run auctions of various types on the internet. Very popular in C2C, but gaining ground in other types of EC. (www.ebay.com.au)
Product customisation	Customers use the internet to self-configure products or services. Sellers then price them and fulfil them quickly (*build-to-order*). (www.jaguar.com/au/en)
Electronic marketplaces and exchanges	Transactions are conducted efficiently (more information to buyers and sellers, lower transaction costs) in electronic marketplaces (private or public).
Bartering online	Intermediary administers online exchange of surplus products and/or company receives 'points' for its contribution and the points can be used to purchase other needed items. (www.smartbarter.com.au)
Deep discounters	Company offers deep price discounts. Appeals to customers who consider only price in their purchasing decisions.(www.yelp.com.au)
Membership	Only members can use the services provided, including access to certain information, member benefits, etc. (www.catchoftheday.com.au or www.qantas.com.au/travel/airlines/qantas-club/global/en)

Major e-commerce mechanisms

Businesses and customers can buy and sell on the internet through a number of mechanisms. The most widely used are electronic catalogues, electronic auctions, e-storefronts, e-malls and e-marketplaces.

Catalogues have been printed on paper for generations. Today, however, they are available on CD-ROM and the internet. Electronic catalogues consist of a product database, directory and search capabilities, and a presentation function. They are the backbone of most e-commerce sites.

An **auction** is a competitive process in which either a seller solicits consecutive bids from buyers or a buyer solicits bids from sellers. The primary characteristic of auctions is that prices are determined dynamically by competitive bidding. Electronic auctions (e-auctions) generally increase revenues for sellers by broadening the customer base and shortening the cycle time of the auction. Buyers generally benefit from e-auctions because they can bargain for lower prices. In addition, they do not have to travel to an auction at a physical location.

The internet provides an efficient infrastructure for conducting auctions at lower administrative costs and with many more involved sellers and buyers. Individual consumers and corporations alike can participate in auctions. The two major types of auctions are forward and reverse.

Forward auctions are auctions that sellers use as a channel to many potential buyers. Usually, sellers place items at sites for auction and buyers bid continuously for them. The highest bidder wins the items. Both sellers and buyers can be individuals or businesses. The popular auction site eBay.com is a forward auction.

In **reverse auctions**, one buyer, usually an organisation, wants to buy a product or a service. The buyer posts a request for quotation (RFQ) on its website or on a third-party site. The RFQ provides detailed information on the desired purchase. The suppliers study the RFQ and then submit bids electronically. Everything else being equal, the lowest-price bidder wins the auction. The reverse auction is the most common auction model for large purchases (in terms of either quantities or price). Governments and large corporations frequently use this approach, which may provide considerable savings for the buyer.

Auctions can be conducted from the seller's site, the buyer's site, or a third party's site. For example, eBay, the best-known third-party site, offers hundreds of thousands of different items in several types of auctions. Overall, more than 300 major companies, including Amazon.com and Dellauction.com, offer online auctions.

An *electronic storefront* is a website that represents a single store. An *electronic mall*, also known as a *cybermall* or *e-mall*, is a collection of individual shops under one internet address. Electronic storefronts and electronic malls are closely associated with B2C electronic commerce. You study each one in more detail in section 9.2.

An **electronic marketplace** (e-marketplace) is a central, virtual market space on the web where many buyers and many sellers can conduct e-commerce and e-business activities. Electronic marketplaces are associated with B2B electronic commerce. You learn about electronic marketplaces in section 9.3.

Electronic payment mechanisms

Implementing EC typically requires electronic payments. **Electronic payment systems** enable buyers to pay for goods and services electronically, rather than writing a cheque or using cash. Payments are an integral part of doing business, whether in the traditional manner or online. Traditional payment systems have typically involved cash and/or cheques.

In most cases, traditional payment systems are not effective for EC, especially for B2B. Cash cannot be used because there is no face-to-face contact between buyer and seller. Not everyone accepts credit cards or cheques, and some buyers do not have credit cards or chequing accounts. Finally, contrary to what many people believe, it may be *less* secure for the buyer to use the telephone or mail to arrange or send payments, especially from another country, than to complete a secured transaction on a computer. For all of these reasons, a better way is needed to pay for goods and services in cyberspace. This better method is electronic payment systems. Let's now take a closer look at four types of electronic payment: electronic cheques, electronic credit cards, purchasing cards and electronic cash.

Electronic cheques

Electronic cheques (*e-cheques*) are similar to regular paper cheques. They are used primarily in B2B. A customer who wishes to use e-cheques must first establish a cheque account with a bank. Then, when the customer buys a product or a service, he or she emails an encrypted electronic cheque to the seller. The seller deposits the cheque in a bank account and funds are transferred from the buyer's account into the seller's account.

Like regular cheques, e-cheques carry a signature (in digital form) that can be verified (see **www.authorize.net**). Properly signed and endorsed e-cheques are exchanged between financial institutions through electronic clearinghouses. (See **www.eccho.org** and **www.troygroup.com** for details.)

Electronic cards

There are a variety of electronic cards. These cards are used for different purposes and include electronic credit cards, virtual credit cards, purchasing cards, stored-value money cards and smart cards.

Electronic credit cards allow customers to charge online payments to their credit card account. These cards are used primarily in B2C and in shopping by small-to-medium enterprises (SMEs). Here is how e-credit cards work (see figure 9.1).

- Step 1: When you buy a book from Amazon, for example, your credit card information and purchase amount are encrypted in your browser. This way the information is safe while it is 'travelling' on the internet to Amazon.
- Step 2: When your information arrives at Amazon, it is not opened. Rather, it is transferred automatically (in encrypted form) to a *clearinghouse*, where it is decrypted for verification and authorisation.
- Step 3: The clearinghouse asks the bank that issued you your credit card (the card issuer bank) to verify your credit card information.
- Step 4: Your card issuer bank verifies your credit card information and reports this to the clearinghouse.
- Step 5: The clearinghouse reports the result of the verification of your credit card to Amazon.
- Step 6: Amazon reports a successful purchase and amount to you.
- Step 7: Your card issuer bank sends funds in the amount of the purchase to Amazon's bank.
- Step 8: Your card issuer bank notifies you (either electronically or in your monthly statement) of the debit on your credit card.
- Step 9: Amazon's bank notifies Amazon of the funds credited to its account.

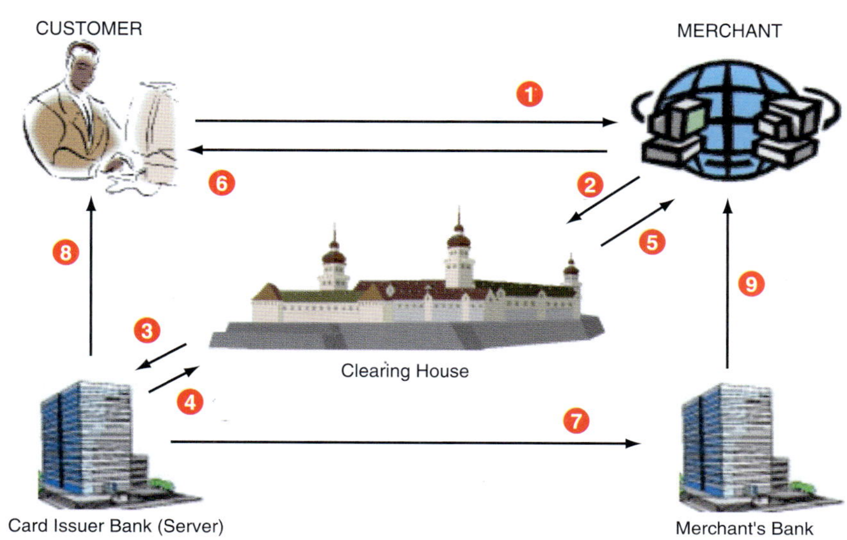

FIGURE 9.1 How e-credit cards work. (The numbers 1–9 indicate the sequence of activities.)

Virtual credit cards allow customers to shop online (see figure 9.2 overleaf). These cards are for a single use. The goal is to thwart criminals by using a different, random card number every time you shop online. A virtual number is good only on the website where you make

FIGURE 9.2 Example of virtual credit card.

your purchase. An online purchase made with a virtual card number shows up on your bill just like any other purchase.

Purchasing cards are the B2B equivalent of electronic credit cards (see figure 9.3). In some countries, purchasing cards are the primary form of payment between companies. Unlike credit cards, where credit is provided for 30 to 60 days (for free) before payment is made to the merchant, payments made with purchasing cards are settled within a week.

Stored-value money cards allow you to store a fixed amount of prepaid money and then spend it as necessary. One example is public transport cards like Myki (figure 9.4), which is a reusable smart card for Melbourne's trains, trams and buses. Public transport users preload their Myki card with money before travelling. They then simply touch-on via the Myki Reader with their card when boarding and touch-off again when exiting. The fare is automatically deducted at the completion of each trip.[1]

FIGURE 9.3 Example of purchasing card.

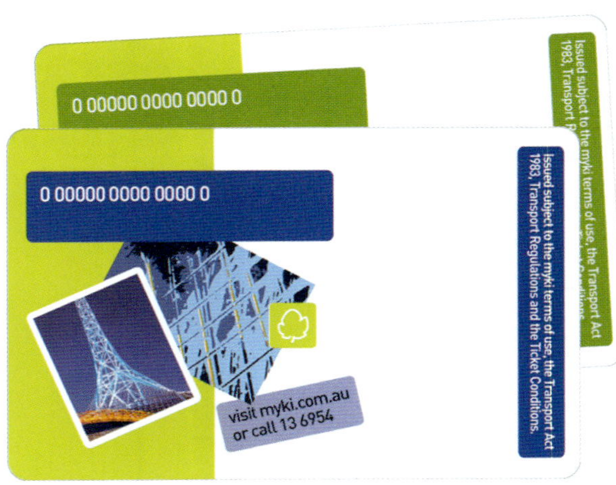

FIGURE 9.4 The Melbourne Myki card.

Smart cards contain a chip that can store a considerable amount of information — more than 100 times that of a stored-value money card (see figure 9.5). Smart cards are frequently multipurpose — that is, you can use them as a credit card, a debit card, a stored-value money card, or a loyalty card. Smart cards are ideal for *micropayments*, which are small payments of a few dollars or less.

FIGURE 9.5 Smart cards are frequently multipurpose.

Person-to-person payments

Person-to-person payments enable two individuals, or an individual and a business, to transfer funds without using a credit card. One of the first companies to offer this service was PayPal (an eBay company). An attractive security feature of PayPal is that you have to put only enough money in the account to cover any upcoming transactions. Therefore, if anyone should gain access to your account, that person will not have access to all of your money.

Person-to-person payment services work this way. First, you select a service and open up an account. Basically, this process entails creating a user name, selecting a password and providing the service with a credit card or bank account number. Next, you transfer funds from your credit card or bank account to your new account. Now you are ready to send money to someone over the internet. You access the service — for example, PayPal — with your user name and password, and you specify the email address of the person to receive the money, along with the dollar amount that you want to send. The service then sends an email to the payee's email address. The email contains a link back to the service's website. When the recipient clicks on the link, he or she is taken to the service. There, the recipient is asked to set up an account to which the money that you sent will be credited. The recipient can then credit the money from this account to either a credit card or a bank account. The service charges the payer a small amount, roughly $1 per transaction.

Benefits and limitations of e-commerce

Few innovations in human history have provided as many benefits to organisations, individuals and society as e-commerce has. E-commerce benefits organisations by making national and international markets more accessible and by lowering the costs of processing, distributing and retrieving information. Customers benefit by being able to access a vast number of products and services, around the clock. The major benefit to society is the ability to easily and conveniently deliver information, services and products to people in cities, rural areas and developing countries.

Despite all these benefits, EC has some limitations, both technological and non-technological, that have restricted its growth and acceptance. One major technological limitation is the lack of universally accepted security standards. Also, in less-developed countries, telecommunications bandwidth often is insufficient and accessing the web is expensive. Non-technological limitations include the perceptions that EC is insecure, has

BEFORE YOU GO ON . . .

1. Define e-commerce and distinguish it from e-business.
2. Differentiate among B2C, B2B, C2C and B2E electronic commerce.
3. Define *e-government*.
4. Discuss forward and reverse auctions.
5. Identify some benefits and limitations of e-commerce.

unresolved legal issues, and lacks a critical mass of sellers and buyers. As time passes, the limitations, especially the technological ones, will diminish or be overcome.

Apply the Concept

Background

Today there are many companies who specialise in making e-commerce a reality for small businesses. Amazon, Yahoo, PayPal and others offer services that provide all a small business needs to sell product and accept payment over the internet. In fact, it seems that many consumers prefer for their transactions to go through these larger global companies because they trust these companies' security.

Activity

Go to PayPal's website. Click on the business tab at the top of the page. At the time of this writing there were lots of links at the bottom of that page that described the services they offered. Review the payment options described in the text and see how many of them PayPal offers to its customers.

Deliverable

Build a table that lists in one column the payment mechanism discussed in this section, the PayPal equivalent in a second column and a discussion of how it is similar or why PayPal does not offer this type of payment in a third. Your table will look something like this:

Payment types	PayPal equivalent	Description

THE NOOK

QUESTIONS

1 The Nook is definitely not a pure e-commerce business. Its main product is entertainment and the owners simply want to sell their brand via t-shirts and other paraphernalia. To what degree can they digitise the entertainment aspect of their product?

2 In what ways might The Nook utilise B2B or B2C E-commerce?

9.2 Business-to-consumer (B2C) electronic commerce

B2B EC is much larger than B2C EC by volume, but B2C EC is more complex. The reason is that B2C involves a large number of buyers making millions of diverse transactions per day with a relatively small number of sellers. As an illustration, consider Amazon, an online retailer that offers thousands of products to its customers. Each customer purchase is relatively small, but Amazon must manage that transaction as if that customer were its most important one. Each order must be processed quickly and efficiently, and the products must be shipped to the customer in a timely manner. In addition, returns must be managed. Multiply this simple example by millions, and you get an idea of the complexity of B2C EC. Overall, B2B complexities tend to be more business related, whereas B2C complexities tend to be more technical and volume related.

This section addresses the primary issues in B2C EC. We begin by studying the two basic mechanisms that customers utilise to access companies on the web: electronic storefronts and electronic malls. In addition to purchasing products over the web, customers also access online services. Therefore, the next section covers several online services, such as banking, securities trading, job searching and travel. The complexity of B2C EC creates two major challenges for sellers: channel conflict and order fulfilment. We examine these two topics in detail. Finally, companies engaged in B2C EC must 'get the word out' to prospective customers. This section concludes with a look at online advertising.

Electronic storefronts and malls

For several generations, home shopping from catalogues, and later from television shopping channels, has attracted millions of customers. Today, shopping online offers an alternative to catalogue and television shopping. **Electronic retailing (e-tailing)** is the direct sale of products and services through electronic storefronts or electronic malls, usually designed around an electronic catalogue format and/or auctions.

Like any mail-order shopping experience, e-commerce enables you to buy from home and to do so 24 hours a day, 7 days a week. However, EC offers a wider variety of products and services, including the most unique items, often at lower prices. Furthermore, within seconds, shoppers can access very detailed supplementary product information. In addition, they can easily locate and compare competitors' products and prices. Finally, buyers can find hundreds of thousands of sellers. Two popular online shopping mechanisms are electronic storefronts and electronic malls.

Electronic storefronts

As noted earlier, an **electronic storefront** is a website that represents a single store. Hundreds of thousands of electronic storefronts can be found on the internet. Each one has its own uniform resource locator (URL), or internet address, at which buyers can place orders. Some electronic storefronts are extensions of physical stores such as Rodd and Gunn, Myer, Harvey Norman and Big W. Others are new businesses started by entrepreneurs who discovered a niche on the web (e.g. **theiconic.com.au**). Manufacturers (e.g. **www.dell.com.au**) and retailers (e.g. **www.officeworks.com.au** or **www.kogan.com/au**) also use storefronts. IT's About Business illustrates how David Jones is expanding its online presence.

IT'S ABOUT BUSINESS

David Jones building an online shopping presence

When he opened his first store in 1838 in Sydney, Welsh-born immigrant and merchant David Jones's mission was to sell 'the best and most exclusive goods', and now David Jones is the oldest department store in the world still trading under its original name. In that time, David Jones has grown to 35 stores, 2 warehouse outlets and David Jones Online, offering consumers quality brand products across men's and women's fashion, beauty, homewares, books and small appliances.

However, it was not until well after the dotcom crash of the early 2000s that David Jones launched a serious revamp of its initial online store (**www.davidjones.com.au**) in 2010 to meet customer and the marketplace's changing shopping expectations. However, initially this website offering seemed to lack some attention to detail, particularly with fundamental site search functionality problems and restricted search filtering options.

However, since then David Jones have been steadily improving their online shopping experience for consumers and in early 2012 engaged IBM to build a better web presence and integrate social networking sites for the company. The aim is to revitalise lacklustre online sales and build upon the 10 per cent of their sales revenue from their online business. The focus is on improving customer service and passing on price cuts from major brands, enabling the online business to compete more effectively with other online competitors and to tap into the growing popularity of online shopping among Australian consumers.

In late 2013 David Jones launched its 'click and collect' strategy, enabling customers to order their product online and collect it in person from dedicated pick-up areas in David Jones stores. This approach is part of the retailer's wider Horizon 2 Omni Channel Retailing Strategy, which is designed to enable the purchase of products physically in store or via computer, mobile phone or iPad devices.

Social commerce is also a key aspect of Horizon 2 strategy, with the retailer establishing a new →

Facebook store to further facilitate sales. In addition, other initiatives include incremental delivery, where the customer can choose same-day or standard delivery services. 'Store Check' via the website enables customers to check whether a particular product is available at their chosen David Jones store location. Furthermore, 'Drop-ship' capabilities were introduced so suppliers can send goods directly to customers, after they complete their sale transaction on the David Jones e-tail site.

Another element is 'shopable videos' that allows the customer to shop from videos posted on the retailer's website, such as seasonal fashion shows for example. Earlier in 2013, David Jones had over 20 000 views of its summer/autumn 2013 collections live-stream video.

The 'click and collect' is a classic cross-channel retailing strategy to engage customers in both the online and in-store shopping experience by bringing online customers into stores to collect goods. It is attractive to customers looking for big-ticket items too. The basis of the 'click and collect' strategy is that it is fundamentally an education process for customers. It enables David Jones to inform customers of the options available to them and to encourage the customer to become more accustomed to browsing and ordering goods online.

Sources: G Arnott (2012), *David Jones' new online store a let-down, Power Retail*, www.powerretail.com.au/news/david-jones-launches-new-online-store; David Jones (2013), *About David Jones — the story of David Jones*, www.davidjones.com.au/About-David-Jones/The-Story-of-David-Jones; C Kruger (2012), 'Widespread price cuts as David Jones races to catch up with online competition', *Sydney Morning Herald, Business Day*, 22 March, www.smh.com.au/business/widespread-price-cuts-as-david-jones-races-to-catch-up-with-online-competition.html; M Oliver (2013), 'David Jones strives to boost online revenue and in-store traffic with new "click and collect" service', 26 August, *Smart Company*, www.smartcompany.com.au/growth/economy/33325-david-jones-strives-to-boost-online-revenue-and-in-store-traffic-with-new--click-and-collect--service.html; *Sydney Morning Herald* (2012), 'David Jones aims for 10% of sales online', *Business Day*, 24 February, www.smh.com.au/business/david-jones-aims-for-10-of-sales-online.html.

QUESTIONS

1. Why is it important for David Jones to have an online presence? What factors are they using to engage and build their customer base?
2. What is the relationship between David Jones online and physical department stores with regard to increasing customer traffic and retail sales? Explain.
3. Discuss the strategic Omni Channel retail approach taken by David Jones. Is this strategy transferrable to other established retail businesses? If so how? If not, why not?

Electronic malls

Whereas an electronic storefront represents a single store, an **electronic mall**, also known as a *cybermall* or an *e-mall*, is a collection of individual shops grouped under a single internet address. The basic idea of an electronic mall is the same as that of a regular shopping mall: to provide a one-stop shopping place that offers a wide range of products and services. A cybermall may include thousands of vendors. For example, the Westfield (**www.westfield.com.au**) website is an example of a cybermall that includes tens of thousands of products from many different vendors.

There are two types of cybermalls. In the first type, known as *referral malls* (for example, **www.hawaii.com**), you cannot buy anything. Instead, you are transferred from the mall to a participating storefront. In the second type of mall (for example, **www.westfield.com.au**), you can actually make a purchase. At this type of mall, you might shop from several stores, but you make only one purchase transaction at the end. You use an *electronic shopping cart* to gather items from various vendors and then pay for them all together in a single transaction. The mall organiser, such as Google, takes a commission from the sellers for this service.

Online service industries

In addition to purchasing products, customers can also access needed services via the web. Selling books, toys, computers and most other products on the internet can reduce vendors' selling costs by 20 to 40 per cent. Further reduction is difficult to achieve because the products must be delivered physically. Only a few products, such as software or music, can be digitised and then delivered online for additional savings. In contrast, services, such as buying an airline ticket and purchasing stocks or insurance, can be delivered entirely through e-commerce, often with considerable cost reduction. Not surprisingly, then, online delivery of services is growing very rapidly, with millions of new customers being added each year.

One of the most pressing EC issues relating to online services (as well as in marketing tangible products) is **disintermediation**. Intermediaries, also known as middlemen, have two functions: (1) they provide information and (2) they perform value-added services such as consulting. The first function can be fully automated and most likely will be assumed by e-marketplaces and portals that provide information for free. When this occurs, the intermediaries who perform only (or primarily) this function are likely to be eliminated. This process is called disintermediation.

In contrast, performing value-added services requires expertise. Unlike the information function, then, this function can be only partially automated. Thus, intermediaries who provide value-added services are not only likely to survive, but they may actually prosper. The web helps these employees in two situations: (1) when the number of participants is enormous, as with job searches, and (2) when the information that must be exchanged is complex.

In this section, you will examine some leading online service industries: banking, trading of securities (shares, bonds), job matching, travel services and online advertising.

Cyberbanking

Electronic banking, also known as **cyberbanking**, involves conducting various banking activities from home, at a place of business, or on the road instead of at a physical bank location. Electronic banking has capabilities ranging from paying bills to applying for a loan. For customers, it saves time and is convenient. For banks, it offers an inexpensive alternative to branch banking — for example, about 2 cents cost per transaction versus $1.07 at a physical branch. It also enables banks to attract remote customers. In addition to regular banks with added online services, **virtual banks**, which are dedicated solely to internet transactions, are emerging. An example of a virtual bank is ING Direct (**www.ingdirect.com.au**) (see figure 9.6).

FIGURE 9.6 ING Direct.

International banking and the ability to handle trading in multiple currencies are critical for international trade. Transfers of electronic funds and electronic letters of credit are important services in international banking. An example of support for EC global trade is provided by TradeCard, in conjunction with MasterCard. TradeCard is an international company that provides a secure method for buyers and sellers to make digital payments anywhere on the globe (see the demo at **www.tradecard.com**). In another example, banks and companies such as Oanda (**www.oanda.com**) provide conversions of more than 160 currencies.

Online securities trading

Australians continue to embrace online securities trading with several well-known securities companies, including ANZ's E*Trade, Westpac Online, CommSec, NAB Online's nabtrade and Bell Direct, offering only online trading. Market research company

Investment Trends estimates that in late 2012 there were more than 615 000 online share traders who made active trades over the preceding 12 months in Australia. Of the online share traders, 49 per cent were with CommSec, 18 per cent with E*Trade, 9 per cent with Westpac Online, 6 per cent with Bell Direct and 4 per cent with NAB Online. In Korea, more than half of stock traders are already using the internet for that purpose. Why? Because it is cheaper than a full-service or discount broker. On the web, investors can find a considerable amount of information regarding specific companies or mutual funds in which to invest (for example, money.cnn.com and **www.bloomberg.com**).

For example, let's say you have an account with Scottrade. You access Scottrade's website (**www.scottrade.com**) from your personal computer or your internet-enabled mobile device, enter your account number and password to access your personalised web page, and then click on 'stock trading'. Using a menu, you enter the details of your order — buy or sell, margin or cash, price limit, market order and so on. The computer informs you of the current 'ask' and 'bid' prices, much as a broker would do over the telephone. You can then approve or reject the transaction.

The online job market

The internet offers a promising new environment for job seekers and for companies searching for hard-to-find employees. Thousands of companies and government agencies advertise available positions, accept résumés, and take applications via the internet.

Job seekers use the online job market to reply online to employment ads, to place résumés on various sites and to use recruiting firms (for example, **www.seek.com.au**, **www.mycareer.com.au**, **www.linkedin.com.au** and **www.careerone.com.au**). Companies that have jobs to offer advertise these openings on their websites and they search the bulletin boards of recruiting firms. In many countries, governments must advertise job openings on the internet.

Travel services

The internet is an ideal place to plan, explore and arrange almost any trip economically. Online travel services allow you to purchase airline tickets, reserve hotel rooms and rent cars. Most sites also offer a fare-tracker feature that sends you email messages about low-cost flights. Examples of comprehensive online travel services are flightcentre.com.au, travelfactory.com.au and holidayplanet.com.au. Online services are also provided by all major airline holiday services, large conventional travel agencies, car rental agencies (**www.hertz.com.au**), hotels (e.g. **www.wotif.com**) and tour companies. In a variation of this process, webjet.com.au allows you to set a price you are willing to pay for an airline ticket or hotel accommodation. It then attempts to find a vendor that will match your price.

Online advertising

Advertising is the practice of disseminating information in an attempt to influence a buyer–seller transaction. Traditional advertising on TV or in newspapers is impersonal, one-way mass communication. In contrast, direct-response marketing, or telemarketing, contacts individuals by direct mail or telephone and requires them to respond in order to make a purchase. The direct-response approach personalises advertising and marketing. At the same time, however, it can be expensive, slow and ineffective. It can also be extremely annoying to the consumer.

Internet advertising redefines the advertising process, making it media rich, dynamic and interactive. It improves on traditional forms of advertising in a number of ways. First, internet ads can be updated any time at minimal cost and therefore can be kept current. In addition, these ads can reach very large numbers of potential buyers all over the world. Further, they are generally cheaper than radio, television and print ads. Finally, internet ads can be interactive and targeted to specific interest groups and/or individuals.

Advertising methods

The most common online advertising methods are banners, pop-ups and email. Banners are simply electronic billboards. Typically, a **banner** contains a short text or graphical message to promote a product or a vendor. It may even contain video clips and sound. When customers click on a banner, they are transferred to the advertiser's home page. Banner advertising is the most commonly used form of advertising on the internet.

A major advantage of banners is that they can be customised to the target audience. If the computer system knows who you are or what your profile is, it might send you a banner that is supposed to match your interests. A major disadvantage of banners is that they can convey only limited information because of their small size. Another drawback is that many viewers simply ignore them.

Pop-up and pop-under ads are contained in a new browser window that is automatically launched when you enter or exit a website. A **pop-up ad** appears in front of the current browser window. A **pop-under ad** appears underneath the active window; when users close the active window, they see the ad. Many users strongly object to these ads, which they consider intrusive. Modern browsers let users block pop-up ads, but this feature must be used with caution because some websites depend on pop-up capabilities to present content other than advertising. For example, when you log on to your Verizon email page, you also see a brief (one line each) summary of recent news stories. If you hover your mouse over one of them, you get a pop-up window with an extended summary (a few paragraphs) of that story. Another example is the Desire2Learn software for online instruction, where discussion group posts appear in pop-up windows. Blocking pop-ups would make the first of these two examples less useful and would eliminate important functionality from the second example.

Email is emerging as an internet advertising and marketing channel. It is generally cost-effective to implement and provides a better and quicker response rate than other advertising channels. Marketers develop or purchase a list of email addresses, place them in a customer database, and then send advertisements via email. A list of email addresses can be a very powerful tool because the marketer can target a group of people or even individuals.

As you have probably concluded by now, there is a potential for misuse of email advertising. In fact, some consumers receive a flood of unsolicited email, or *spam*. **Spamming** is the indiscriminate distribution of electronic ads without the permission of the receiver. Unfortunately, spamming is becoming worse over time.

Two important responses to spamming are permission marketing and viral marketing. **Permission marketing** asks consumers to give their permission to voluntarily accept online advertising and email. Typically, consumers are asked to complete an electronic form that asks what they are interested in and requests permission to send related marketing information. Sometimes, consumers are offered incentives to receive advertising.

Permission marketing is the basis of many internet marketing strategies. For example, millions of users periodically receive emails from supermarkets such as Coles or clothing retailers such as Barkers' online menswear telling them about special deals. Significantly, they can easily unsubscribe at any time. Permission marketing is also extremely important for market research (for example, search for 'Media Metrix' at www.comscore.com).

Viral marketing refers to online word-of-mouth marketing. The strategy behind viral marketing is to have people forward messages to friends, family members and other acquaintances suggesting they 'check this out'. For example, a marketer can distribute a small game program embedded with a sponsor's email that is easy to forward. The marketer releases only a few thousand copies, with the expectation that the recipients in turn will forward the program to many more thousands of potential customers. In this way, viral marketing enables companies to build brand awareness at a minimal cost without having to spam millions of uninterested users.

Issues in e-tailing

Despite e-tailing's increasing popularity, many e-tailers continue to face serious issues that can restrict their growth. Perhaps the two major issues are channel conflict and order fulfilment.

Clicks-and-mortar companies may face a conflict with their regular distributors when they sell directly to customers online. This situation, known as **channel conflict**, can alienate the distributors. Channel conflict has forced some companies to avoid direct online sales. For example, Myer, Kirkcaldie & Stains and Harvey Norman would rather have customers come to their stores. Therefore, although these companies maintain e-commerce websites, their sites place more emphasis on providing information — products, prices, specials and store locations — than on online sales.

Channel conflict can arise in areas such as pricing and resource allocation — for example, how much money to spend on advertising. Another potential source of conflict involves the logistics services provided by the offline activities to the online activities. For example, how should a company handle returns of items purchased online? Some companies have completely separated the 'clicks' (the online portion of the organisation) from the 'mortar' or 'bricks' (the traditional bricks-and-mortar part of the organisation). However, this approach can increase expenses and reduce the synergy between the two organisational channels. As a result, many companies are integrating their online and offline channels, a process known as **multichanneling**. IT's About Business shows how the online channel is causing problems for brick-and-mortar retailers. Alternatively, Wildfire sees great potential for incorporating social media tools, for primarily Facebook and Twitter, into the online/offline shopping experience, as you see in IT's About Business (opposite).

IT'S ABOUT BUSINESS

What to do about customer 'showrooming' practices?

In today's information rich and connected world, shoppers wielding smartphones can now browse online, while looking at the same physical item in any traditional 'bricks and mortar' retail store. Have you noticed customers browsing in store merchandise while looking at their mobile devices? Perhaps you have done this yourself? This practice is termed 'showrooming' and is becoming a concerning practice for physical retail stores.

Showrooming is the practice whereby customers physically examine or receive an in-store demonstration of products before going home to purchase the same item online. The reason behind this behaviour is that comparing the same or similar merchandise online can result in significant savings as the same merchandise is offered at discounted prices because they do not have the same physical overhead costs.

Typically consumer electronics and clothing stores are the most likely to have customers mobile showrooming their in-store products. However, in early 2013, a Queensland specialist store, Celiac Supplies, specialising in gluten-free groceries, unveiled an in-store policy notifying customers of a $5 store entry fee for in-store web browsing (the fee would be deducted from the cost of any in-store purchase). This approach was the manifestation of the store owner's frustration with mobile showrooming, but the backlash on social media reflected a sentiment of being ignorant, intolerant, self-defeating and hostile to prospective customers.

Not surprisingly retailers are struggling to deal with the practice of showrooming and are finding it more difficult to entice customers to make their purchases in-store. Yet Australian shoppers have always had the ability to compare prices and to choose where and from whom they purchase products. Smartphones and mobile devices are just like any other mode of communication, it is just that they give shoppers the ability to compare product and price offerings online, rather than physically travelling to different retail locations. The primary focus of shoppers has always been about achieving value for money and getting the right product or service at a decent price. With their mobile devices they are just doing the same thing, but with fewer limitations on where and when they can do it.

Retailers can likewise use customer smartphones as a means to present and engage with shoppers directly as they pass by or while they are within the store to encourage customers to purchase products in-store then and there. Retailers can facilitate the availability of information further via branded or partnered mobile apps, barcode scanning or adding a product to a wishlist. Retailers must listen and understand how customers are using their smartphones on shopping expeditions and develop effective strategies to meet the demand for information while on the move.

The issue remains as to how willing customers are to receive help, expert opinion or assistance via their mobile device in-store. For example, a well-informed sales assistant is indispensable, as it is often the immediacy of helpful information and the mix of customer service that can facilitate a sale then and there. Perhaps a virtual assistant, utilising 'always on' the mobile communication channel can offer promotional coupons, specials and discount information either via SMS or email, for those shoppers willing to sign up to the store's CRM database.

Overall mobile showrooming is neither a good nor a bad thing, it just depends on your view of whether it is another nail in traditional shopping or a chance to innovate and open up cross-channel e-commerce opportunities. Showrooming is forcing retailers to develop strategies to take advantage of the opportunities that mobile wielding customers present. Of course there is also the opposite of showrooming too, such as 'webrooming' and 'e-rooming', where customers initially search for and research products and retailers online, then physically go in-store to make their purchases in person.

Sources: A Kooser (2013), 'Store charges $5 "showrooming" fee to looky-loos', *CNET*, 26 March, www.news.cnet.com/store-charges-$5-showrooming-fee-to-looky-loos.html; R Kramer (2013), 'Facing up to showrooming', *Retail Biz*, www.retailbiz.com.au/2013/08/08/article/OPED-Facing-up-to-showrooming.html; S Murphy Kelly (2013), 'Retailers turn "showrooming" into innovation opportunity', *Mashable*, 20 May, www.mashable.com/2013/05/19/showrooming.html; E Ravenscraft (2013), 'Do you use retail stores for showrooming?', *Lifehacker Australia*, 17 June, www.lifehacker.com.au/2013/06/do-you-use-retail-stores-for-showrooming.html.

IT'S ABOUT BUSINESS

New Zealander starting a wildfire

Victoria Ransom was the co-founder of Wildfire, a social media strategy company. Victoria earned a reputation as one of the leading CEOs of a high-tech venture in Silicon Valley — a long way from her hometown of Bulls, New Zealand. From humble beginnings at the local primary school with just 25 other students, Victoria graduated at the top of her high school class, won a scholarship to attend college in the United States and progressed to complete a degree in psychology. After graduating, Victoria considered doing her PhD since she had a sense that practising psychology directly after her undergraduate training would not be satisfying. After some deliberation, she realised that she needed to get some real-world experience before continuing her studies. At that time she still had no intention of becoming an entrepreneur. Instead, after graduating Victoria spent two years working for Morgan Stanley Media in New York. This invaluable experience in the dotcom era was followed by the start-up of her adventure travel firm, Access Trips. Once that business was running itself, she went to Boston to complete an MBA at Harvard. That was when she and her boyfriend and business partner at that time (he was studying at Stanford) saw the opportunity to start a business riding the wave of the Facebook phenomenon.

Wildfire began as an application to enable a giveaway competition to be hosted on a Facebook business page, making the process simple for SMEs to run a competition without having to develop their own app first. In the early days, they gave their app away free of charge; later, they charged as little as 99 cents per day for small firms to access the technology. However, interest from larger organisations for more sophisticated tools and support soon broadened the depth and complexity of their business model. The product offering grew to include an integrated suite of tools to help businesses (without any programming capabilities) gather, energise and grow their online customer base using social media (primarily Facebook and Twitter). The business opened in 2008 and became profitable within its first year of operation. It has grown from 7 employees in that first year to nearly 400 staff by 2012, with 8 offices around the globe. The achievement is all the more spectacular because this expansion was effected using mainly internal cash flow with some initial start-up seed funding from Facebook and other investors. The business has attracted tens of thousands of clients — from small start-up businesses right up to Facebook itself, as well as other global big brands such as Pepsi, Unilever, Sony and AT&T.

What is just as remarkable is that Victoria has achieved all of this in the space of her young thirty-something years with no IT or computer training at all. It is no wonder she was named in the Forbes '40 under 40' list, and was the Ernst and Young New Zealand Entrepreneur of the Year in 2011. In what could only →

be described as a fairytale ending to this rapid growth story, the business was sold to Google in July 2012. Since the company's acquisition by Google, Victoria has assumed the role of Director of Product Management for Wildfire.

Sources: S Mitra (2012), 'From New Zealand to Silicon Valley: Victoria Ransom's Wildfire journey', 29 March, www.sramanamitra.com; J Constin (2012), 'Google acquires Wildfire, will now sell Facebook and Twitter marketing', *TechCrunch*, 31 July, techcrunch.com; V Ransom (2011), 'Victoria Ransom, founder and CEO of Wildfire', *Inc.*, 3 August, www.inc.com; Ernst & Young, 'Announcing the 2011 Ernst & Young Entrepreneur of the Year finalists', www.ey.com.

BEFORE YOU GO ON . . .

1 Describe electronic storefronts and malls.
2 Discuss various types of online services, such as cyberbanking, securities trading, job searches, travel services and so on.
3 Discuss online advertising, its methods and its benefits.
4 Identify the major issues relating to e-tailing.
5 What are spamming, permission marketing and viral marketing?

The second major issue confronting e-commerce is order fulfilment, which can create problems for e-tailers as well. Any time a company sells directly to customers, it is involved in various order fulfilment activities. It must perform the following activities: quickly find the products to be shipped; pack them; arrange for the packages to be delivered speedily to the customer's door; collect the money from every customer, either in advance, by COD, or by individual invoice; and handle the return of unwanted or defective products.

It is very difficult to accomplish these activities both effectively and efficiently in B2C, because a company has to ship small packages to many customers and do it quickly. For this reason, companies involved in B2C activities often experience difficulties in their supply chains.

In addition to providing customers with the products they ordered and doing it on time, order fulfilment provides all related customer services. For example, the customer must receive assembly and operation instructions for a new appliance. In addition, if the customer is not happy with a product, an exchange or return must be arranged. (Visit **www.fedex.com.au** to see how returns are handled via FedEx.)

In the late 1990s, e-tailers faced continuous problems in order fulfilment, especially during the holiday season. These problems included late deliveries, delivering wrong items, high delivery costs and compensation to unhappy customers. For e-tailers, taking orders over the internet is the easy part of B2C e-commerce. Delivering orders to customers' doors is the hard part. In contrast, order fulfilment is less complicated in B2B. These transactions are much larger, but they are fewer in number. In addition, these companies have had order fulfilment mechanisms in place for many years.

Apply the Concept

Background

At this point in your 'buying' career, you have probably bought something online, gone to an auction site and possibly won a bid, and engaged in some form of online banking. Your generation is very comfortable with the retail side of e-commerce. In the midst of this, you have probably created an account with a few vendors and received some email advertisements. No doubt you have also seen some pop-up ads promoting products when you search for certain items.

Another thing that has changed is that companies now want you to do their advertising for them. The text refers to this as viral marketing.

Activity

Go online and source a company that has effectively implemented a viral marketing campaign. Now imagine that you work for a restaurant that also has a catering business. The owner has never done much with email or Twitter and she is looking for you to help develop a viral marketing plan for the restaurant.

Deliverable

Write an email and/or Twitter content that the business owner can ask her patrons to share with others. Be sure to develop an incentive for the customers to share and for those who receive the email to share it with others. Put some thought into this based on your own experience. Try to create a 'use and share' feeling in your marketing collateral.

QUESTIONS

1. Would it make sense for The Nook to have a presence in an electronic mall? Why or why not?
2. How might The Nook use multichannelling as most of the club's online customers would also be in the same geographical area?

THE NOOK

9.3 Business-to-business (B2B) electronic commerce

In *business to business (B2B)* e-commerce, the buyers and sellers are business organisations. B2B comprises about 85 per cent of EC volume. It covers a broad spectrum of applications that enable an enterprise to form electronic relationships with its distributors, resellers, suppliers, customers and other partners. Organisations can use B2B to restructure their supply chains and their partner relationships.

B2B applications utilise any of several business models. The major models are sell-side marketplaces, buy-side marketplaces and electronic exchanges.

Sell-side marketplaces

In the **sell-side marketplace** model, organisations attempt to sell their products or services to other organisations electronically from their own private e-marketplace website and/or from a third-party website. This model is similar to the B2C model in which the buyer is expected to come to the seller's site, view catalogues and place an order. In the B2B sell-side marketplace, however, the buyer is an organisation.

The key mechanisms in the sell-side model are electronic catalogues that can be customised for each large buyer and forward auctions. Sellers such as Dell Computers (**www.dellauction.com**) use auctions extensively. In addition to conducting auctions from their own websites, organisations can use third-party auction sites, such as eBay, to liquidate items. Companies such as Ariba (**www.ariba.com**) are helping organisations to auction old assets and inventories.

The sell-side model is used by hundreds of thousands of companies. It is especially powerful for companies with superb reputations. The seller can be either a manufacturer (for example, Dell or IBM), a distributor (for example, **www.avnet.com**), or a retailer (for example, **www.bigboxx.com**). The seller uses EC to increase sales, reduce selling and advertising expenditures, increase delivery speed and lower administrative costs. The sell-side model is especially suitable to customisation. Many companies allow their customers to configure their orders online. For example, at Dell (**www.dell.com**), you can determine the exact type of computer that you want. You can choose the type of chip (for example, Itanium 2), the size of the hard drive (for example, 1 terabyte), the type of monitor (for example, 22-inch flat screen) and so on. Similarly, the Jaguar website (**www.jaguar.com**) allows you to customise the Jaguar you want. Self-customisation greatly reduces any misunderstandings concerning what customers want and it encourages businesses to fill orders more quickly.

Buy-side marketplaces

The **buy-side** marketplace is a model in which organisations attempt to buy needed products or services from other organisations electronically. A major method of buying goods and services in the buy-side model is the reverse auction.

The buy-side model uses EC technology to streamline the purchasing process. The goal is to reduce both the costs of items purchased and the administrative expenses involved in purchasing them. In addition, EC technology can shorten the purchasing cycle time. Procurement includes purchasing goods and materials as well as sourcing (finding goods), negotiating with suppliers, paying for goods and making delivery arrangements. Organisations now use the internet to accomplish all of these functions.

Purchasing by using electronic support is referred to as e-procurement. **E-procurement** uses reverse auctions, particularly group purchasing. In **group purchasing**, multiple buyers combine their orders so that they constitute a large volume and therefore attract more seller attention. In addition, when buyers place their combined orders on a reverse auction, they can negotiate a volume discount. Typically, the orders of small buyers are aggregated by a third-party vendor, such as the United Sourcing Alliance (**www.usa-llc.com**).

Electronic exchanges

Private exchanges have one buyer and many sellers. Electronic marketplaces (e-marketplaces), called **public exchanges** or just **exchanges**, are independently owned by a third party and connect many sellers and many buyers. Public exchanges are open to all business organisations. They frequently are owned and operated by a third party. Public exchange managers provide all the necessary information systems to the participants. Thus, buyers and sellers merely have to 'plug in' in order to trade. B2B public exchanges are often the initial point for contacts between business partners. Once the partners make contact, they may move to a private exchange or to private trading rooms provided by many public exchanges to conduct their subsequent trading activities.

Some electronic exchanges deal in direct materials and others in indirect materials. *Direct materials* are inputs to the manufacturing process, such as safety glass used in automobile windshields and windows. *Indirect materials* are those items, such as office supplies, that are needed for maintenance, repairs and operations (MRO). There are three basic types of public exchanges: vertical, horizontal and functional. All three types offer diversified support services, ranging from payments to logistics.

Vertical exchanges connect buyers and sellers in a given industry. Examples of vertical exchanges are **www.plasticsnet.com** in the plastics industry and **www.papersite.com** in the paper industry.

Vertical exchanges are frequently owned and managed by a *consortium*, a term for a group of major players in an industry. For example, Marriott and Hyatt own a procurement consortium for the hotel industry and ChevronTexaco owns an energy e-marketplace. The vertical e-marketplaces offer services that are particularly suited to the community they serve.

Horizontal exchanges connect buyers and sellers across many industries and are used primarily for MRO materials. Examples of horizontal exchanges are TradersCity (**www.traderscity.com**), Globalsources (**www.globalsources.com**) and Alibaba (**www.alibaba.com**).

In *functional exchanges*, needed services such as temporary help or extra office space are traded on an 'as-needed' basis. For example, Skilled (**www.skilled.com.au**) can find temporary labour by searching listed employees on its skill network.

BEFORE YOU GO ON . . .

1. Briefly differentiate between the sell-side marketplace and the buy-side marketplace.
2. Briefly differentiate among vertical exchanges, horizontal exchanges and functional exchanges.

Apply the Concept

Background

Many businesses today engage in both B2B and B2C. As is described in this text, in a B2B relationship the customer is another business, but in B2C the customer is the end consumer. The methodologies for managing and engaging these two different customers are very different. Therefore, the customer relationship management (CRM) tools used must serve different purposes on the B2C side (many customers) than the B2B side (few large customers).

Activity

Compare and contrast 'B2C' with 'B2B'. Once you feel like you have a good grasp on the difference, search online for some different CRM tools that support B2C and B2B.

Deliverable

Imagine that your senior marketing manager has created a task force to select a CRM tool. You operate in a B2C environment, but the options the manager has given the task force to choose between are all B2B software packages! Write an email that delicately shows the manager the difference between these two and that explains that the products he/she has selected will not work for your company. Be tactful in your response — managers do not like to hear that they are wrong!

THE NOOK

QUESTIONS

1 The Nook's suppliers have offered electronic data processing (EDP) for years. However, Malakai and Abbie have always placed their orders via the telephone. How might EDP help them?
2 Should they continue with B2B business as usual or go ahead and upgrade now? What data might be available for them via EDP that they do not currently have access to?

9.4 Ethical and legal issues in e-business

Technological innovation often forces a society to re-examine and modify its ethical standards. In many cases, the new standards are incorporated into law. In this section, you will learn about two important ethical considerations — privacy and job loss — as well as various legal issues arising from the practice of e-business.

Ethical issues

Many of the ethical and global issues related to IT also apply to e-business. Here you will learn about two basic issues: privacy and job loss.

By making it easier to store and transfer personal information, e-business presents some threats to privacy. First, most electronic payment systems know who the buyers are. It may be necessary, then, to protect the buyers' identities. Businesses frequently use encryption to provide this protection.

Another major privacy issue is tracking. For example, individuals' activities on the internet can be tracked by cookies (discussed in chapter 7). Cookies store your tracking history on your personal computer's hard drive and any time you revisit a certain website, the server recognises the cookie. In response, antivirus software packages routinely search for potentially harmful cookies.

In addition to compromising individual privacy, the use of EC may eliminate the need for some of a company's employees, as well as brokers and agents. The manner in which these unneeded workers, especially employees, are treated can raise ethical issues: How should the company handle the layoffs? Should companies be required to retrain employees for new positions? If not, how should the company compensate or otherwise assist the displaced workers?

Legal and ethical issues specific to e-commerce

Many legal issues are related specifically to e-commerce. When buyers and sellers do not know one another and cannot even see one another, there is a chance that dishonest people will commit fraud and other crimes. During the first few years of EC, the public witnessed many such crimes. These illegal actions ranged from creating a virtual bank that disappeared along with the investors' deposits to manipulating share prices on the internet.

Unfortunately, fraudulent activities on the internet are increasing. In the following section, you explore some of the major legal issues that are specific to e-commerce.

Fraud on the internet

Internet fraud has grown even faster than internet use itself. In one case, share promoters falsely spread positive rumours about the prospects of the companies they touted in order to boost the stock price. In other cases, the information provided might have been true, but the promoters did not disclose that they were paid to talk up the companies. Stock promoters specifically target small investors who are lured by the promise of fast profits.

Shares are only one of many areas where swindlers are active. Auctions are especially conducive to fraud, by both sellers and buyers. Other types of fraud include selling bogus investments and setting up phantom business opportunities. Because of the growing use of email, financial criminals now have access to many more people. The Australian Competition and Consumer Commission (ACCC, **www.scamwatch.gov.au**) in Australia and the Department of Internal Affairs (**www.dia.govt.nz**) in New Zealand provides information about how to recognise, avoid and report internet and email scams. Later in this section, you will see some ways in which consumers and sellers can protect themselves from online fraud.

Domain names

Another legal issue is competition over domain names. Domain names are assigned by central non-profit organisations that check for conflicts and possible infringement of trademarks. Obviously, companies that sell goods and services over the internet want customers to be able to find them easily. In general, the closer the domain name matches the company's name, the easier the company is to locate.

A domain name is considered legal when the person or business who owns the name has operated a legitimate business under that name for some time. Companies such as Christian Dior, Nike, Deutsche Bank and even Microsoft have had to fight or pay to get the domain name that corresponds to their company's name. Consider the case of Delta Air Lines. Delta originally could not obtain the internet domain name delta.com because Delta Faucet had purchased it first. Delta Faucet had been in business under that name since 1954 and therefore had a legitimate business interest in the domain name. Delta Air Lines had to settle for delta-airlines.com until it bought the domain name from Delta Faucet. Delta Faucet is now at deltafaucet.com. Several cases of disputed domain names are already in court.

Cybersquatting

Cybersquatting refers to the practice of registering or using domain names for the purpose of profiting from the goodwill or the trademark that belongs to someone else. The Anti-Cybersquatting Consumer Protection Act (1999) permits trademark owners in the United States to sue for damages in such cases.

However, some practices that could be considered cybersquatting are not illegal, although they may well be unethical. Perhaps the more common of these practices is 'domain tasting'. Domain tasting lets registrars profit from the complex money trail of pay-per-click advertising. The practice can be traced back to the policies of the organisation responsible for regulating web names, the Internet Corporation for Assigned Names and Numbers (ICANN) (**www.icann.org**) (see figure 9.7). In early 2013 the United Nations agency, World Intellectual Property Organization (WIPO) reported a 5 per cent increase in cases of alleged cybersquatting instances to a record 2884 cases in relation to 5084 internet domains for the year ending 2012. Since the year 2000 the WIPO has provided an arbitration service as means of resolving disputes over the rights to internet domain names as a mechanism to avoid potentially costly litigation. However, there is added complexity and complications when disputing parties reside in different countries, but arbitrators are empowered to award the disputed domain name if it is deemed that an accused party has acted nefariously or fraudulently in registering the domain name. For example, in 2013 in one case Donald Trump sought US$400 000 in damages from a Brooklyn man regarding four websites that were allegedly using the real estate mogul's name and brand.

The sites included trumpmumbai.com and trumpindia.com that were allegedly established after the Trump organisation had announced plans to build Trump-branded hotels and condominiums in Mumbai and Bangalore, India, in 2007.

Australian trademark holders who feel that their intellectual property may have been infringed upon or who wish to dispute internet domains should in the first instance consult the Australian equivalent dispute resolution policy (auDRP) of the .au Domain Administration Ltd organisation.[2]

FIGURE 9.7 Internet Corporation for Assigned Names and Numbers (ICANN) website.

Domain tasters exploit this policy by claiming internet domains for five days at no cost. These domain names frequently resemble those of prominent companies and organisations. The tasters then jam these domains full of advertisements that come from Yahoo! and Google. Because this process involves zero risk and 100 per cent profit margins, domain tasters register millions of domain names every day — some of them over and over again. Experts estimate that registrants ultimately purchase less than 2 per cent of the sites they sample. In the vast majority of cases, they use the domain names for only a few days to generate quick profits.

Taxes and other fees

In Australia, a goods and services tax (GST) came into effect on 1 July 2000, largely replacing the then embedded Commonwealth and State/Territory sales tax regimes of wholesale sales tax (WST), stamp duty on securities transactions, financial institutions duty (FID) and bank account debits (BAD) tax. The GST is a broad-based consumption tax of 10 per cent that is incorporated into the purchase price of various goods and services. Most goods and services consumed in Australia will attract GST, which is a multistage tax collected at each step along the supply chain.

Recent media coverage has highlighted the fact that e-commerce purchases made outside Australia that are below the $1000 mark do not attract GST. Some Australian retailers and their representative bodies have lobbied the Commonwealth government to lower the threshold, claiming that overseas retailers have an unfair commercial advantage over local retailers and suppliers via the online sales channel. However, the opportunity for Australian retailers to compete on a level playing field is unlikely to come about through any reduction in the low value importation threshold.

The area of e-commerce continues to grow as businesses look for ways to sell their products beyond the borders of their traditional domestic market. The issue of whether GST is payable on internet sales is fraught with risk given the complexity of the GST legislation, the Commissioner of Taxation public rulings and the administration cost of collecting the tax.

In-part other fees charged may incorporate postage and handling fees on top of the retail purchase price too. Then there is the jurisdictional issues about where — and in some cases, whether — electronic sellers should pay business license taxes, franchise fees, gross-receipts taxes, excise taxes, privilege taxes and utility taxes. Furthermore, how should tax collection be controlled?[3]

Copyright

Recall from chapter 6 that intellectual property is protected by copyright laws and cannot be used freely. This point is significant because many people mistakenly believe that once they purchase a piece of software, they have the right to share it with others. In fact, what they have bought is the right to *use* the software, not the right to *distribute* it. That right remains with the copyright holder. Similarly, copying material from websites without permission is a violation of copyright laws. Protecting intellectual property rights in e-commerce is extremely difficult, however, because it involves hundreds of millions of people in some 200 countries with differing copyright laws who have access to billions of web pages.

BEFORE YOU GO ON . . .

1. List and explain some ethical issues in EC.
2. Discuss the major legal issues of EC.
3. Describe buyer protection and seller protection in EC.

THE NOOK

QUESTIONS

1. What ethical and legal information can you find on PayPal's site?
2. If The Nook uses PayPal, who do you think would be responsible for any errors? What should Malakai and Abbie do if PayPal's Code of Ethics is different from what they consider ethical?

WHAT'S IN IT FOR ME?

FOR THE ACCOUNTING MAJOR

Accounting personnel are involved in several EC activities. Designing the ordering system and its relationship with inventory management requires accounting attention. Billing and payments are also accounting activities, as are determining cost and profit allocation. Replacing paper documents with electronic means will affect many of the accountant's tasks, especially the auditing of EC activities and systems. Finally, building a cost-benefit and cost-justification system to determine which products/services to take online and creating a chargeback system are critical to the success of EC.

FOR THE FINANCE MAJOR

The worlds of banking, securities and commodities markets, and other financial services are being re-engineered because of EC. Online securities trading and its supporting infrastructure are growing more rapidly than any other EC activity. Many innovations already in place are changing the rules of economic and financial incentives for financial analysts and managers. Online banking, for example, does not recognise state boundaries and it may create a new framework for financing global trades. Public financial information is now accessible in seconds. These innovations will dramatically change the manner in which finance personnel operate.

FOR THE MARKETING MAJOR

A major revolution in marketing and sales is taking place because of EC. Perhaps its most obvious feature is the transition from a physical to a virtual marketplace. Equally important, however, is the radical transformation to one-on-one advertising and sales and to customised and interactive marketing. Marketing channels are being combined, eliminated, or re-created. The EC revolution is creating new products and markets and significantly altering existing ones. Digitisation of products and services also has implications for marketing and sales. The direct producer-to-consumer channel is expanding rapidly and is fundamentally changing the nature of customer service. As the battle for customers intensifies, marketing and sales personnel are becoming the most critical success factor in many organisations. Online marketing can be a blessing to one company and a curse to another.

FOR THE PRODUCTION/OPERATIONS MANAGEMENT MAJOR

EC is changing the manufacturing system from product-push mass production to order-pull mass customisation. This change requires a robust supply chain, information support and re-engineering of processes that involve suppliers and other business partners. Suppliers can use extranets to monitor and replenish inventories without the need for constant reorders. In addition, the internet and intranets help reduce cycle times. Many production/operations problems that have persisted for years, such as complex scheduling and excess inventories, are being solved rapidly with the use of web technologies. Companies can now use external and internal networks to find and manage manufacturing operations in other countries much more easily. Also, the web is re-engineering procurement by helping companies conduct electronic bids for parts and subassemblies, thus reducing cost. All in all, the job of the progressive production/operations manager is closely tied in with e-commerce.

FOR THE HUMAN RESOURCES MANAGEMENT MAJOR

HR majors need to understand the new labour markets and the impacts of EC on old labour markets. Also, the HR department may use EC tools for such functions as procuring office supplies. Moreover, becoming knowledgeable about new government online initiatives and online training is critical. In addition, HR personnel must be familiar with the major legal issues related to EC and employment.

FOR THE MIS MAJOR

The MIS function is responsible for providing the information technology infrastructure necessary for electronic commerce to function. In particular, this infrastructure includes the company's networks, intranets and extranets. The MIS function is also responsible for ensuring that electronic commerce transactions are secure.

SUMMARY

1 Describe the six common types of electronic commerce.

In *business-to-consumer* (B2C) electronic commerce, the sellers are organisations and the buyers are individuals. In *business-to-business* (B2B) electronic commerce, the sellers and the buyers are businesses. In *consumer-to-consumer* (C2C) electronic commerce, an individual sells products or services to other individuals. In *business-to-employee* (B2E) electronic commerce, an organisation uses EC internally to provide information and services to its employees. *E-government* is the use of internet technology in general and e-commerce in particular to deliver information and public services to citizens (called government-to-citizen or G2C EC) and business partners and suppliers (called government-to-business or G2B EC). *Mobile commerce* refers to e-commerce that is conducted entirely in a wireless environment. We leave the examples of each type to you.

2 Describe the various online services of business-to-consumer (B2C) commerce, providing specific examples of each.

Electronic banking, also known as cyberbanking, involves conducting various banking activities from home, at a place of business, or on the road instead of at a physical bank location.

Online securities trading involves buying and selling securities over the web.

Online job matching over the web offers a promising environment for job seekers and for companies searching for hard-to-find employees. Thousands of companies and government agencies advertise available positions, accept résumés and take applications via the internet.

Online travel services allow you to purchase airline tickets, reserve hotel rooms and rent cars. Most sites also offer a fare-tracker feature that sends you email messages about low-cost flights. The internet is an ideal place to plan, explore and arrange almost any trip economically.

Online advertising over the web makes the advertising process media-rich, dynamic and interactive.

We leave the examples to you.

3 Describe the three business models for business-to-business electronic commerce.

In the *sell-side marketplace* model, organisations attempt to sell their products or services to other organisations electronically from their own private e-marketplace website and/or from a third-party website. Sellers such as Dell Computer (www.dellauction.com) use sell-side auctions extensively. In addition to auctions from their own websites, organisations can use third-party auction sites, such as eBay, to liquidate items.

The *buy-side marketplace* is a model in which organisations attempt to buy needed products or services from other organisations electronically.

E-marketplaces, in which there are many sellers and many buyers, are called *public exchanges*, or just exchanges. Public exchanges are open to all business organisations. They frequently are owned and operated by a third party. There are three basic types of public exchanges: vertical, horizontal and functional. *Vertical exchanges* connect buyers and sellers in a given industry. *Horizontal exchanges* connect buyers and sellers across many industries. In *functional exchanges*, needed services such as temporary help or extra office space are traded on an 'as-needed' basis.

4 Identify the ethical and legal issues related to electronic commerce, providing examples.

E-business presents some threats to privacy. First, most electronic payment systems know who the buyers are. It may be necessary, then, to protect the buyers' identities with encryption. Another major privacy issue is tracking, where individuals' activities on the internet can be tracked by cookies.

The use of EC may eliminate the need for some of a company's employees, as well as brokers and agents. The manner in which these unneeded workers, especially employees, are treated can raise ethical issues: How should the company handle the layoffs? Should companies be required to retrain employees for new positions? If not, how should the company compensate or otherwise assist the displaced workers?

We leave the examples to you.

>>> CHAPTER GLOSSARY

auction A competitive process in which either a seller solicits consecutive bids from buyers or a buyer solicits bids from sellers and prices are determined dynamically by competitive bidding.

banner Electronic billboards, which typically contain a short text or graphical message to promote a product or a vendor.

brick-and-mortar organisations Organisations in which the product, the process and the delivery agent are all physical.

business model The method by which a company generates revenue to sustain itself.

business-to-business electronic commerce (B2B) Electronic commerce in which both the sellers and the buyers are business organisations.

business-to-consumer electronic commerce (B2C) Electronic commerce in which the sellers are organisations and the buyers are individuals; also known as e-tailing.

business-to-employee electronic commerce (B2E) An organisation using electronic commerce internally to provide information and services to its employees.

buy-side marketplace B2B model in which organisations buy needed products or services from other organisations electronically, often through a reverse auction.

channel conflict The alienation of existing distributors when a company decides to sell to customers directly online.

clicks-and-mortar organisations Organisations that do business in both the physical and digital dimensions.

consumer-to-consumer electronic commerce (C2C) Electronic commerce in which both the buyer and the seller are individuals (not businesses).

cyberbanking Various banking activities conducted electronically from home, a business, or on the road instead of at a physical bank location; also known as *electronic banking*.

cybersquatting Registering domain names in the hope of selling them later at a higher price.

disintermediation Elimination of intermediaries in electronic commerce.

e-government The use of electronic commerce to deliver information and public services to citizens, business partners and suppliers of government entities, and those working in the public sector.

electronic business (e-business) A broader definition of electronic commerce, including buying and selling of goods and services, and servicing customers, collaborating with business partners, conducting e-learning and conducting electronic transactions within an organisation.

electronic commerce (EC or e-commerce) The process of buying, selling, transferring, or exchanging products, services, or information via computer networks, including the internet.

electronic mall A collection of individual shops under one internet address; also known as a *cybermall* or an *e-mall*.

electronic marketplace A virtual market space on the web where many buyers and many sellers conduct electronic business activities.

electronic payment systems Computer-based systems that allow customers to pay for goods and services electronically, rather than writing a cheque or using cash.

electronic retailing (e-tailing) The direct sale of products and services through storefronts or electronic malls, usually designed around an electronic catalogue format and/or auctions.

electronic storefront The website of a single company, with its own internet address, at which orders can be placed.

e-procurement Purchasing by using electronic support.

exchanges (see public exchanges)

forward auctions Auctions that sellers use as a selling channel to many potential buyers; the highest bidder wins the items.

group purchasing The aggregation of purchasing orders from many buyers so that a volume discount can be obtained.

mobile commerce (m-commerce) Electronic commerce conducted in a wireless environment.

multichanneling A process in which a company integrates its online and offline channels.

permission marketing Method of marketing that asks consumers to give their permission to voluntarily accept online advertising and email.

person-to-person payments A form of electronic cash that enables the transfer of funds between two individuals, or between an individual and a business, without the use of a credit card.

pop-under ad An advertisement that is automatically launched by some trigger and appears underneath the active window.

pop-up ad An advertisement that is automatically launched by some trigger and appears in front of the active window.

public exchanges (or exchanges) Electronic marketplaces in which there are many sellers and many buyers, and entry is open to all; frequently owned and operated by a third party.

reverse auctions Auctions in which one buyer, usually an organisation, seeks to buy a product or a service and suppliers submit bids; the lowest bidder wins.

sell-side marketplace B2B model in which organisations sell to other organisations from their own private e-marketplace and/or from a third-party site.

smart cards Cards that contains a microprocessor (chip) that enables the card to store a considerable amount of information (including stored funds) and to conduct processing.

spamming Indiscriminate distribution of email without the receiver's permission.

stored-value money cards A form of electronic cash on which a fixed amount of prepaid money is stored; the amount is reduced each time the card is used.

viral marketing Online word-of-mouth marketing.

virtual banks Banking institutions dedicated solely to internet transactions.

virtual (or pure play) organisations Organisations in which the product, the process and the delivery agent are all digital.

>>> DISCUSSION QUESTIONS

1. Discuss the major limitations of e-commerce. Which of these limitations are likely to disappear? Why?
2. Discuss the reasons for having multiple EC business models.
3. Distinguish between business-to-business forward auctions and buyers' bids for RFQs.
4. Discuss the benefits to sellers and buyers of a B2B exchange.
5. What are the major benefits of G2C electronic commerce?
6. Discuss the various ways to pay online in B2C. Which method(s) would you prefer and why?
7. Why is order fulfilment in B2C considered difficult?
8. Discuss the reasons for EC failures.
9. Should Mr Coffee sell coffeemakers online?
   Hint: Take a look at the discussion of channel conflict in this chapter.
10. In some cases, individuals engage in cybersquatting so that they can sell the domain names to companies expensively. In other cases, companies engage in cybersquatting by registering domain names that are very similar to their competitors' domain names in order to generate traffic from people who misspell web addresses. Discuss each practice in terms of its ethical nature and legality. Is there a difference between the two practices? Support your answer.

>>> PROBLEM-SOLVING ACTIVITIES

1 Assume you are interested in buying a car. You can find information about cars at numerous websites. Access five websites for information about new and used cars, financing and insurance. Decide which car you want to buy. Configure your car by going to the car manufacturer's website. Finally, try to find the car from www.autobytel.com. What information is most supportive of your decision-making process? Write a report about your experience.

2 Compare the various electronic payment methods. Specifically, collect information from the vendors cited in this chapter and find additional vendors using Google.com. Pay attention to security level, speed, cost and convenience.

3 Conduct a study on selling diamonds and gems online. Access such sites as www.bluenile.com, www.diamond.com, www.thaigem.com, www.tiffany.com and www.jewelryexchange.com.

   a What features do these sites use to educate buyers about gemstones?

   b How do these sites attract buyers?

   c How do these sites increase customers' trust in online purchasing?

   d What customer service features do these sites provide?

4 Access www.nacha.org. What is NACHA? What is its role? What is the ACH? Who are the key participants in an ACH e-payment? Describe the 'pilot' projects currently underway at ACH.

5 Access www.espn.com. Identify at least five different ways the site generates revenue.

6 Access www.queendom.com. Examine its offerings and try some of them. What type of electronic commerce is this? How does this website generate revenue?

7 Access www.ediets.com. Prepare a list of all the services the company provides. Identify its revenue model.

8 Access www.theknot.com. Identify the site's revenue sources.

9 Access www.mint.com. Identify the site's revenue model. What are the risks of giving this website your credit and debit card numbers, as well as your bank account number?

10 Research the case of www.nissan.com. Is Uzi Nissan cybersquatting? Why or why not? Support your answer. How is Nissan (the car company) reacting to the www.nissan.com website?

11 Enter www.alibaba.com. Identify the site's capabilities. Look at the site's private trading room. Write a report. How can such a site help a person who is making a purchase?

12 Enter www.grubhub.com. Explore the site. Why is the site so successful? Could you start a competing site? Why or why not?

13 Enter www.dell.com, go to 'Desktops' and configure a system. Register to 'My Cart' (no obligation). What calculators are used there? What are the advantages of this process as compared with buying a computer in a physical store? What are the disadvantages?

14 Enter www.checkfree.com and www.lmlpayment.com to identify their services. Prepare a report.

15 Access various travel sites such as www.travelocity.com, www.orbitz.com, www.expedia.com, www.kayak.com and www.pinpoint.com. Compare these websites for ease of use and usefulness. Note differences among the sites. If you ask each site for the itinerary, which one gives you the best information and the best deals?

16 Access www.outofservice.com and answer the musical taste and personality survey. When you have finished, click on 'Results' and see what your musical tastes say about your personality. How accurate are the findings about you?

17 **Tips for safe electronic shopping**

- Look for reliable brand names at sites such as Walmart Online, Disney Online and Amazon. Before purchasing, make sure that the site is authentic by entering the site directly and not from an unverified link.
- Search any unfamiliar selling site for the company's address and phone and fax numbers. Call up and quiz the employees about the seller.
- Check out the vendor with the local Chamber of Commerce or Better Business Bureau (www.bbbonline.org). Look for seals of authenticity such as TRUSTe.
- Investigate how secure the seller's site is by examining the security procedures and by reading the posted privacy policy.
- Examine the money-back guarantees, warranties and service agreements.
- Compare prices with those in regular stores. Too-low prices are too good to be true and some catch is probably involved.
- Ask friends what they know. Find testimonials and endorsements on community websites and well-known bulletin boards.
- Find out what your rights are in case of a dispute. Consult www.accc.gov.au, australia.gov.au, www.consumerlaw.gov.au, www.consumeraffairs.govt.nz and www.comcom.govt.nz.

>>> COLLABORATION EXERCISE

Background

Converting a business from bricks-and-mortar to e-business is a rather complicated task. At the turn of the 20th century (the early 1900s) Kirkcaldie & Stains was the pre-eminent department store in Wellington, New Zealand. This company's business model was founded on the principles of selling quality merchandise at a price that gave good value and service. Search their website at www.kirkcaldies.co.nz to read more about the history of this iconic New Zealand department store and view their online presence too.

Activity

Divide your team into the following positions: consumer, order processing, accounts receivable, product fulfilment, shipping, inventory and sales. Now given your responsibility, work through a catalogue order that includes five different items. To make it easier, imagine that full payment is received. Begin with the consumer and have each person write down on a piece of paper the information each needs at every stage. For example, the consumer will hand two pieces of paper to the order processing person: one will be the order and the other will be the payment. Then the order processing person will notify others in the group by creating a new piece of paper with new information. They will also keep a copy for themselves. As this order moves through the 'company', you will see how much paper and information is generated by traditional business.

Deliverable

As a team, write a summary of your experience that compares e-commerce to traditional commerce. Did anyone make a mistake when transferring the information? How could computer information systems (and therefore e-commerce) have helped make the process flow better?

Submit your paper to your instructor.

CLOSING CASE 1 >

The new virtual economy of Bitcoin

Bitcoin is a form of virtual cash used for online transactions across the internet that has recently come to prominence but it is not an official currency. Bitcoin functions as a consensus network that enables a digital payment system and is the first implementation utilising a concept call 'crypto-currency' that uses cryptography to control its creation and transactions. Bitcoin is a distributed digital online currency that operates through a person-to-person exchange, with no centralised monetary authority, like the Reserve Bank of Australia, to regulate it or government issuing authority responsible for issuing it. Although there is a Bitcoin community that can and has made changes as necessary, Bitcoins are owned by their users and Bitcoin value fluctuates like any other currency. All Bitcoin transactions are logged into a shared public ledger called the 'block chain' and it has become the underpinning currency for an internet-based virtual economy.

Fluctuations in the Bitcoin currency value remain volatile and have led to some economists suggesting that Bitcoin is just another speculative currency bubble that will soon crash. However, the beauty of the Bitcoin system is that it seems to have solved the 'double spending' problem, which has been the downfall of digital cash, where the money tokens can be duplicated and spent twice. So Bitcoin seems to be both an ingenious and possibly acceptable solution to digital cash with the added advantages of low exchange fees, no variation in value across international borders and user accounts that cannot be frozen.

Bitcoins are acquired through purchases via a Bitcoin exchange, through personal exchange or via person-to-person transactions for goods and services. However, unlike credit card transactions, Bitcoin transactions cannot be reversed and many exchanges do charge a small fee for conversion into dollars and euros too. Unlike governments that decide to issue or print paper money, Bitcoins are generated through users (referred to as 'miners').

Bitcoin is as virtual as credit cards and online banking that people use every day and is designed to allow users to send and receive payments with an acceptable level of privacy. Bitcoin is not anonymous; however, there are means of manipulating the network routing between the buyer and seller that can effect a high level of anonymity. One of the better known access tools is Tor, also known as 'The Onion Router'. It was developed by the US Navy to hide military communications. It is free browser and network software designed to provide users with an online presence away from surveillance. Tor works by concealing the user's internet address by routing the communication connection between user and merchant via multiple network servers that changes each time the user contacts the Tor server and no single server knows the complete connection path. Normally such connections are via a single server where the connection details back to the identities of the user and the merchant are easily identifiable.

As a consequence of the Tor capability, criminals and organised crime have been using the Tor approach as a means of maintaining anonymity while they plied their trade in illegal drugs, guns and pornography. One such example of this online black market site was Silk Road, which had a customer friendly website that displayed illicit drugs for sale. Silk Road utilised the Tor network to route customer transactions through at least three separate servers in an effort to disguise its users. Online customers from all over the world, including Australians, conducted business with Silk Road using Bitcoins and the site frequently assured its users that their illegal transactions were shrouded in layers of privacy.

Late in 2013, federal agents from the FBI (Federal Bureau of Investigation) and a number of other US law enforcement agencies were able to dismantle Silk Road using traditional investigatory techniques and high-tech cyber-sleuthing when the operator made some critical mistakes that enabled the agents to locate the website and link him to it. The investigators were able to locate six of Silk Road's supposedly 'off-the-grid' computer servers hidden in various locations around the world including Latvia and Romania, and copied the contents and observed buyers and sellers complete their illegal transactions. It shut down the website, seized its assets, including 26 000 Bitcoins belonging to Silk Road customers worth about $4 million, and arrested Ross Ulbricht, the alleged operator, in San Francisco on 1 October 2013. The FBI unsuccessfully attempted to claim the nearly 600 000 Bitcoins it estimates to be worth around $80 million, which Ulbricht himself is thought to be holding and equates to approximately five per cent of all Bitcoins in circulation. The FBI plans to hold on to the seized Bitcoins until the judicial process is over and then will probably just liquidate them.

So now consider that there exists an online crypto-currency, Bitcoin, which plays a part in the online virtual economy that is predicated on secrecy rather than on established currency payments. Online transactions can be conducted obscurely using network technologies designed to obfuscate detection and traceability. When you bring the two together, does this serve to further confound the perceived openness of the internet and associated communications? In part, the ethical considerations surrounding organisations and individuals using Bitcoin technology in this manner to conduct online transactions serves to illustrate that there are no established ethical boundaries, guidelines or expected behaviours to adhere to in the online world of e-commerce.

Therefore, from an ethical perspective there are always going to be individuals or organisations based on greed, poverty, extortion and corruption who will exploit whatever means at their disposal to make money illegally. It does not seem to matter what currency format or transaction environment is evident, there are always those with lesser ethical beliefs willing to exploit economies in this manner. So are Bitcoins any different? Are Bitcoins going to assuage or change any of these unethical practices? Bitcoin was deployed without business rules and is therefore open to exploitation by sites like Silk Road for illicit drug sales. Digital online payment processing is not the exclusive domain of new currencies like Bitcoin as banks and the dominant payment networks (Visa, MasterCard and American Express etc.) are almost 100 per cent digital, even if they are not quite as smart as Bitcoin. However, the incumbent banking services are governed by business rules and regulations to protect consumers, themselves and the economy. Even so, this does not necessarily make them ethical. So why are people not satisfied with current secure online payment methods as they are? Ultimately, ethical behaviour and practices are at the bequest of the individual and their interpretation of the ethical or unethical boundaries exist. Inherent implementation of Bitcoin lends itself to being exploited unethically due to its innate secrecy element.

Sources: Bitcoin Project 2009–2013, 'Bitcoin homepage', 2013, www.bitcoin.org/en.html; Bitcoin Project 2009–2013, 'Frequently asked questions — Bitcoin', 2013, www.bitcoin.org/en/faq#what-is-bitcoin.html; I Gillespie (2013), 'Cyber cops probe the deep web', *The Age, Digital Life*, 24 October, www.theage.com.au/digital-life/digital-life-news/cyber-cops-probe-the-deep-web.html; A Hern (2013), 'FBI struggles to seize 600 000 Bitcoins from alleged Silk Road founder', *The Guardian*, 7 October, www.theguardian.com/technology/2013/oct/07/fbi-bitcoin-silk-road-ross-ulbricht.html; K Hill (2013), 'The FBI's plan for the millions worth of Bitcoins seized from Silk Road', *Forbes*, 4 October, www.forbes.com/sites/kashmirhill/2013/10/04/fbi-silk-road-bitcoin-seizure.html; C Knaus (2013), 'Lessons in online ethics needed — expert', *The Age, Technology*, 24 October, www.theage.com.au/technology/technology-news/lessons-in-online-ethics-needed--expert.html; D Leinwand Leger (2013), 'How FBI brought down cyber-underworld site Silk Road', *USA Today*, 22 October, www.usatoday.com/story/news/nation/2013/10/21/fbi-cracks-silk-road.html; P Peyret (2013), 'Of Bitcoins and ethical banking', *The Huffington Post*, 7 October, www.huffingtonpost.com/patrice-peyret/of-bitcoins-and-ethical-banking.html; *USA Today* (2013), 'A briefing on Bitcoin', 21 October, www.usatoday.com/story/news/nation/2013/10/21/bitcoin-q-and-a.html.

QUESTIONS

1. What would doing business over the internet in this manner indicate? What conclusions can be drawn about those conducting online business transactions in this manner? Support your answer with other examples.
2. With increasing levels of online transactions being conducted. What are the advantages and disadvantages of using bitcoin technology to hide identity? Is it ethical or unethical to conduct online transactions in this manner,

rather than via conventional online payment channels?

3 What are the implications for free speech? Is using an amoral network like Tor to 'whistleblow' issues and reveal secrets ethically acceptable? Does the ends justify the means? Explain.

4 If you are using bitcoins and the Tor network to conduct online transactions, can you trust the bona fides of individuals on the internet if they are hiding behind technology in this manner? What actions and decisions might you take to protect yourself and your business?

CLOSING CASE 2 >

Two Australians on the 'up and up'

3Floorsup is a private web development company founded by Steven Quayle and Patrick O'Meara based in Melbourne, Australia. Steven and Patrick first met via their personal networks at ages 17 and 23 years respectively. Steven began working with Patrick on various ad-hoc consultancy opportunities and subsequently formed a partnership in 2006 to launch 3Floorsup. Steven has a degree in marketing and has always been self-employed. He started in business as a self-employed tennis coach and eventually turned his mind to creating a marketing consultancy. Patrick has a degree in design (multimedia systems) and has worked for some of Melbourne's leading web design companies. These partners possess a complementary array of skills and abilities that has served their fast-growing business well. The business name 3Floorsup relates to a frightening three-storey fall that Patrick survived during the formative period of their business. The fall had him relying heavily on the internet and mobile communications during the time he was recuperating. So, it seems that right from the beginning ICT was to play a significant role in their business.

In a spin-off division of the main business, 3Floorsup have developed a web-based management system for use by commercial wind farm operators to store and analyse wind turbine maintenance data called WTGservice.com. This has transformed what started as a quality focused home-based web development business into a rapidly expanding global opportunity via the world's fastest growing renewable energy source — wind power. Since developing this capability, their business has literally been swept around the world on the winds of change. The pair recognised that wind farms are high-tech capital intensive businesses that would benefit from a servicing system that manages assets, inventory, servicing schedules, reporting and quality in an integrated manner. Their software design achieves this at the same time as retaining the flexibility to allow application in varying markets and circumstances worldwide.

The fully developed product was launched and marketed under the new trading name and website WTGservice.com. At that time, it was the only commercially available 100 per cent web-based system specifically developed for wind farms. After an initial focus on the domestic market in Australia, further growth was targeted via international sales in the USA, India and China. The India–China roll-out proved a major breakthrough and was aided by a City of Melbourne innovation grant for A$25 000. The money helped 3Floorsup modify the software so that the program can be easily translated to any language, thus allowing a global sales focus. Comparing the e-commerce strategies reflected in the websites of the two businesses, the 3Floorsup.com.au website is a stylish (and somewhat minimalist) showcase of their web design capabilities, and WTGService.com is a clean, uncluttered site with a greater focus on information and technical content. Neither website attempts to sell a product online. Both aim to inform and then encourage a contact call for a later personal sales approach. Steven and Patrick do not want clients to confuse the two businesses during the initial sales pitch, so they have deliberately designed for this duel web persona.

The first international contract for WTGService.com came from India, signed with a world 'top ten' wind power producer. This deal took over four months of initial analysis, coupled with rigorous and frequent communications between employees, clients and third parties related to the power producer. Steven's experiences in India were typified by stories of exponential growth and a dynamic, even chaotic environment — very exciting times. In subsequent related dealings in mainland China, the pace was a little slower and Steven was often left trying to guess whether the local partners were happy with his approach. He has learned that it takes time and a great deal of close and prolonged communication to make progress with the Chinese division of the business. These international experiences have helped 3Floorsup to focus on implementing an e-commerce and ICT strategy that is capable of delivering accurate, relevant, timely and accessible information to internal and external users worldwide. WTG now has offices in Australia, Europe and the Americas, and Stephen has relocated to the United States to be closer to the growth markets for the business. Although born in Australia, the company is now a truly global business.

Because the WTGService.com business model involves a great deal of technical communications and sales-related international travel, Steven identified early on that ICT could assist with reliable and rapid communication. Information discussed between employees is recorded in digital format detailing all decisions made, as well as technical and operational aspects of these decisions. Steven initiated this system, which he refers to as 'project wiki', so data can be entered by owners and employees to produce an accessible online knowledge base. A wiki is a collaborative software tool that permits participants with access rights to collectively store, search, edit and access data online. The system allows employees to retrieve data 24/7, anywhere in the world. This capability has proven especially important in dealings with India, where there is a requirement to share information with the client's rapidly expanding workforce. In addition to this, while travelling Steven often finds himself communicating with the office via MSN (Microsoft Live Messenger) or Skype to clarify programming issues, confirm urgent requirements and make time critical decisions. Steven certainly agrees that he would not have been able to grow the business as quickly or as successfully without using a variety of ICT tools to do so.

Source: Case study prepared by Pamela Tan, based on interviews with Managing Director Steven Quayle.

QUESTIONS

1 As both the web design and wind turbine maintenance businesses grow, how do you think their respective information systems should evolve or devolve?

2 Do you think that 3Floorsup has a typical ICT implementation for its size, age and industry?

3 How would you describe and categorise Steven's attitude and management style as it relates to ICT adoption?

SPREADSHEET ACTIVITY **BUILDING CHARTS AND GRAPHS**

OBJECTIVE

Graphs and charts are helpful tools within most spreadsheet applications. This activity will place you in a business scenario where graphs and charts are extremely helpful in determining customer patterns and preferences.

Chapter connection

E-business and e-commerce are much more than simply buying and selling via the internet. Amazon.com is a perfect example of a company that has leveraged the power of the web to make product suggestions to customers and help them find the right product. This activity builds on this concept and applies spreadsheet tools to help provide this type of business data and make it useful even in a traditional bricks-and-mortar scenario.

ACTIVITY

Go to Amazon.com (or go to www.johnwiley.com.au/highered/rainer/ausnz/studentresources and click on the link to Amazon there) and search for a Coleman Sundome 10 X 10 tent. At the time of this writing, customers are shown items that are frequently purchased with the tent, items that customers often buy with it (but not as frequently as the other group) and finally a list of related products. This type of information is very helpful to consumers, especially when combined with customer ratings.

Another type of feedback provided by Amazon.com is the list of items that are most frequently purchased after shopping for a particular item. This type of information is invaluable to consumers and can only be provided in an online environment. Woolworths supermarket staff cannot tell customers what most people buy when they are standing in the aisle, so consumers are blind and have to make a choice based on either information they found before they arrived or what is said on the box.

Imagine that you work for a small bookstore. You would like to post a chart next to a book showing that it is one of the more popular books purchased or possibly to direct someone to a more popular book (that you also sell). Search Amazon.com for three books (pick your own genre) and find Amazon's 'Customers who bought this item also bought' section. You may have to search for more than three books to find this section because it is not listed on every page. Collect the 5-star rating and total number of ratings (4.5/5 stars by 1135 reviewers) for the main book and for the 5 competing books and place it in a spreadsheet. You will use different columns for each of these as shown in the table below. Be sure to also include the data from your original book.

	5-star rating	Total ratings
Main book 1	4.5	568
Customers also bought 1	3.5	789
Customers also bought 2	4.0	156
Customers also bought 3	2.7	45
Customers also bought 4	4.5	9
Customers also bought 5	5	12

Once your data collection is complete, you will have data for each of the three books in a spreadsheet. The table above illustrates what the data may look like for one of these books. Use the tools provided in Microsoft Excel to create at least three different types of charts based on your data. Take each chart and copy and paste it in a Word document that you could place on the shelf in your bookstore to help drive customers to the right product. If you need some help with charts, watch the tutorials that are linked at www.johnwiley.com.au/highered/rainer/ausnz/studentresources.

DELIVERABLE

The final product will be five separate Word documents that the owner of the small bookstore could place on the shelf in front of a product. The chart will show the percentage of Amazon.com customers who buy that product as well as what other books they purchase. The final documents demonstrate how traditional businesses can leverage the power of e-business and e-commerce in their stores with public information.

DISCUSSION QUESTIONS

1 Given the complexity of e-business and e-commerce, is it something that everyone should engage in? Is the future of business to have a website and sell everything online? Will there always be a place for traditional brick-and-mortar stores?

2 Online shopping provides many advantages to consumers. Other than the example provided in this exercise, what other ways can you think of that will help traditional businesses leverage the power of online tools for their in-store customers?

DATABASE ACTIVITY **FORMS II**

OBJECTIVE

In this activity, you will learn how to create a three-table form directly, using the Form Wizard, and how to improve the appearance of your forms. You were introduced to forms in the chapter 8 activity. There, you created three forms: one based on a single table, one based on two tables and one based on three tables where you had to create a subform yourself to deal with complex table relationships. Here, you will extend what you know to more complex form design issues.

Chapter connection

This chapter of the book is about electronic commerce. E-commerce runs on forms. With the knowledge you will gain here, you will be able to develop forms that need only be connected to the web and a database to be used in that area.

Prerequisites

Chapter 8 activity (Forms I).

ACTIVITY

In this activity, which you will find online at www.johnwiley.com.au/highered/rainer/ausnz/studentresources, you will work with a new database to create more advanced types of forms.

1 Download the **Ch 09 ItemSales** database from www.johnwiley.com.au/highered/rainer/ausnz/studentresources and open it. A store might use a database like this. It has data on items it sells, their manufacturers and the distributors from which it gets them. A distributor may supply items from several manufacturers. The relationship map, accessed via the Database Tools ribbon, shows the table relationships.

2 The first form will show all three tables. Open the Form Wizard. From DistTbl, select the distributor's name, city and state. (You should not have any trouble figuring out the correct column names for these.) From MfrTbl, select the manufacturer's name and country. From ProdTbl, select the item number, name, shipping weight, and selling price. Organise the form by DistTbl and specify 'Form with subform(s)'.

3 Finish creating the form as you did in the previous activity. Save the form as DistForm. Save its subforms as MfrSubform and ProdSubform. Open it to enter data.

4 You will see that there are two subforms inside the main form here. This is how the Form Wizard creates a three-table form. Although the lower one is not nested physically within the upper one, it behaves as though it is. When you move through the manufacturers supplied by the first distributor, in the upper subform, the lower subform changes to show each manufacturer's products.

5 This form looks exactly as the wizard created it. Now we will change its appearance. Repeat the form creation process, this time naming your form DistForm2, its subforms MfrSubform2 and ProdSubform2. Open it in Layout view to make changes.

   Usage hint: You might wonder, Why not just make a copy of the form? You could. You would have to make copies of the subforms, too. Then, you would have to open the forms and change their source data to refer to the copies. It is easier to create a new set.

6 Let's start with labels:

   a The form header shows the form's name in the database, DistForm2. Click on it to edit and change it to 'Distributors with Manufacturers and Products' (without quotation marks). This may make its box several lines deep. If it does, drag its right edge with your mouse far enough to the right to fit the header on one line. Then drag its bottom edge up as far as possible without covering any of the text.

   b Click in the field names in the top portion of the form and change them to 'Distributor', 'City' and 'State'. The original names were chosen for database developers. These names make more sense to the people who will use this form.

   c Shrink those fields vertically to one line each.

   d If you are used to an earlier version of Access, you may know that you cannot adjust one field without changing the others unless you remove the layout controls. This is no longer necessary in Access 2010. You can adjust the fields now. So, shrink the State field in width until it is about the right size for a few letters. Shrink the City field until it is long enough for a long city name. Then select the State field and its label (click one, then shift-click the other) together so they will move as a unit and position them to the right of the city field.

Usage hint: It can be hard to get the City and State fields to line up precisely. Design view has a grid to make this easier, but most things are easier done in Layout view. In that view, you can open the form's Property Sheet, under the Arrange ribbon tab. Click a field whose position is OK — say, the City field. Note the value of its Top attribute (under the Property Sheet's Format tab). To align other fields with it, select them and set their Top to that value.

Another option is to use the alignment tools in the Arrange ribbon in Design view. They are fine, but their behaviour can be non-intuitive. Try them if you want. There is an Undo button if you do not like the result.

e Edit the labels of the two subforms to read 'Manufacturer' and 'Product' in full. (This sometimes works better in Design view than in Layout view.) Using the Font tools under either the Format or the Home ribbon tab, make them bold and increase their size to 14 points.

f Shrink the fields ProdID and ProdPrice to reasonable widths for their contents. (You have to grab the column divider in the header row, not further down.) Then adjust the subform widths to what is now required. Also, move them up to use some of the space freed up when you put the distributor's city and state on a single line. (Forms that are unnecessarily spread out are hard to use and can take up an annoyingly large amount of screen space when several windows are open.)

g Find a picture on the web and download it. Click Logo in the Format ribbon, navigate to the picture and select it. It will appear in your form's header. Move it to the right of the text.

h Go to Design view if you are not already in it. Click the Rectangle tool in the Controls section of the Design ribbon. (You may have to scroll the set of icons down to see it.) You will see other tools that are not in Layout view, too. Draw a rectangle around all the distributor data at the top of the form.

i Switch back to Form view and admire your creation. At work, you might do more. You know about some of the tools you could use. Close the form, saving if prompted.

7 Your third form will be one that a firm could use to review customer orders. Download the **Ch 09 DaffyDonuts** database from www.johnwiley.com.au/highered/rainer/ausnz/studentresources. It has four tables: customers, products, orders and line items. You can see their relationships in the relationship map of the database. (It resembles the example in section 3.3 of the book, minus its supplier table. Its Line Item table is called Ordered Parts there.)

8 Open the Form Wizard and create a form using all four tables. Organise it by customer. Show all the customer information except CustomerID, order date and total, line item quantity, and product name and price. Use Tabular form for the Order subform (the first one), Datasheet form for the line item/product subform (the second).

9 Open the form in Layout view and improve its arrangement as you did earlier.

10 This form could be used by customers. Customers need instructions. To put them on the form, go to Design view. (Layout view will not do this.) Choose either the Label or the Text Box tool from the Design ribbon, the second or third item from the left in the Controls section. The mouse pointer becomes crosshairs. Draw a rectangle in any free space on the form. (You can move form elements to free up space.) Enter any text in it — we are not practising instruction writing. In Form view, confirm that your 'instructions' show up.

11 It can be hard to remember customer names or key them in without error. Access offers two ways to make it unnecessary. One, a *list box*, restricts selections to data in the list. We will use that here. The other, a *combo box*, lets users enter a new value in addition to those.

To begin, make room for the box where the CustName field is now. In Design view, delete it and its label. If any other fields move up to fill its space, select them and move them back down.

12 To create a list box, go to Design view and the Design ribbon. Click the downward triangle with the line over it at the right of the Controls section to confirm that Use Control Wizards is selected. If it is not, select it. Then click the List Box tool, shown in the figure, on the ribbon. (You may have to scroll the list up or down, or display the entire set via the same downward triangle with the line over it, to see this tool. You can also identify it by holding the mouse over it to see its tool tip.)

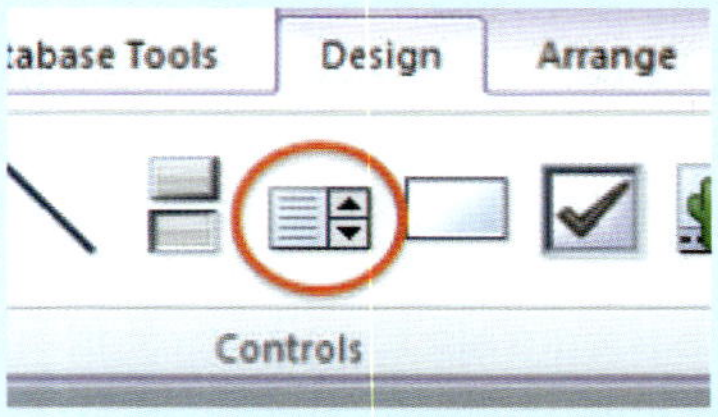

Draw a rectangle with the crosshairs where the customer name field used to be. Make it wide enough for a couple of data fields, deep enough for a few rows.

13 In the first step of the wizard, select 'Find a record on my form based on the value I selected in my list box', as this is what you want to do. Click Next.

14 Because you will pick a customer name, select CustTbl as the source of the values if it is not already selected. (This depends on your form design. Access may or may not have enough information to figure that out.) Click Next if necessary to advance to the next step.

15 Move CustID and CustName into the Selected Fields pane. You will need CustID to identify the correct record uniquely, CustName for people to read. Click Next.

16 Make sure the box to hide the key column is checked — your users do not need customer numbers — and expand the field width to permit longer names in the future. Click Next.

17 Choose the label Customer Name. Click Finish.

18 Go to Form view. You will see customer names in the list box, with scroll bar and arrows to move through the list. Select a customer name and his or her orders will appear below it. Select one of that customer's orders and its line items will appear in the bottom subform.

19 If necessary, move other fields out of the way of your list box. Close this form, saving if prompted. Name it CustOrderForm.

DELIVERABLE

The two databases, ItemSales and DaffyDonuts, with their new forms.

QUIZ QUESTIONS

1 True or false: In a list box, if you do not see the value you want, you can enter it.

2 To draw a new rectangle on a form, you would use
   a Form view
   b Layout view
   c Design view
   d Pivot chart view

3 True or false: In creating a form with subforms with the Form Wizard, all the data fields on the subforms must be in the tables that are chosen for the form.

4 In formatting data fields in Layout mode, the tools in the ribbon do all of the following *except*
   a Highlight text
   b Change text size
   c Change font
   d Put text in italics

DISCUSSION QUESTIONS

1 The last form above was described as being used to review customer orders. Therefore, its users do not need to be able to change order data. A company's order entry personnel, or customers directly, could use a similar form to enter new orders. They would first enter information such as date about a new order, then its line items. Discuss where one or more additional list boxes and/or combo boxes might be helpful for this new purpose. (Do not add them to the data base. Just discuss where you would and what they would do.)

2 Search the web for information on form usability. (The phrase 'ease of use' can be useful in your search strings.) Find four guidelines for easy-to-use forms. For each guideline, state whether the forms you developed here follow it, do not follow it, or it does not apply. (Your answers can differ for the two forms.) If they do not follow it, say what would have to change to follow it. If they do not apply, explain why.

3 If you were a market analyst for DaffyDonuts and wanted to analyse which of your products sell best in different stores and at different times, what additional data might you want that is not in the second form you developed here? Suggest three items. Do not limit your thinking to what is in the tables of this database but not on the form. Think more broadly. Discuss how you might use each of the additional data fields.

10 Wireless, mobile computing and mobile commerce

CHAPTER OUTLINE

10.1 Wireless technologies

10.2 Wireless computer networks and internet access

10.3 Mobile computing and mobile commerce

10.4 Pervasive computing

10.5 Wireless security

LEARNING OBJECTIVES

1. Identify advantages and disadvantages of each of the four main types of wireless transmission media.
2. Explain how businesses can use technology employed by short-range, medium-range and long-range networks, respectively.
3. Provide a specific example of how each of the five major m-commerce applications can benefit a business.
4. Describe technologies that underlie pervasive computing, providing examples of how businesses can utilise each one.
5. Explain how the four major threats to wireless networks can damage a business.

OPENING CASE >

Mobile technology changing IT service delivery in Queensland's outback

Footprint IT's history is not that different to a lot of other small IT companies around Australia. A skill developed as a user is called upon by friends who then recommend the service and it grows from there. Initially it was a part-time process, supplementing income from a job with a major telco. Over the period of 2005–07 the organisation went from an income of around $1500 per month to its current turnover of more than $400 000 per annum.

The initial accounting process used invoice books purchased from the newsagent with a stamp from the local office supply store, spreadsheets, manual tax returns, and an external bookkeeper and accountant, all trying to ensure enough income to support the CEO's family. Customers paid in cash or by cheque initially, but due to the amount of work coming in from new customers a new accounting process was required to enable invoicing and payment in real time.

From 2008–09 Footprint IT started using BankWest's mobile EFTPOS terminals, then became part of the XERO generation. This meant changing the manual process to doing all the accounts online, from invoicing, banking and reconciliation through to pay runs, timesheets, end of year reporting, profit and loss statements (P & Ls) and bank reconciliations.

Since the introduction of XERO into the Footprint IT accounting processes, all business data is electronically managed via the cloud on android devices, including tablets and mobile phones. Business banking is also conducted online from PCs and from mobile android devices. By adopting the XERO cloud accounting system, converting accounting processes into real-time payments, Footprint IT staff can now complete work at a client's premises, then before they leave the site, create an invoice in XERO, issue the invoice in a PDF format to the client's email account using android tablets and process the payment on the EFTPOS terminal onsite. Once the EFTPOS transaction has been completed the invoice can be marked as paid, which will then be ready for bank reconciliation the following day.

As a result of being able to process invoices and payments in real time, cheques have been phased out. This has reduced the expense of managing cheques from approximately $55 per cheque to zero. Additionally, bookkeeping and accounting

QUESTIONS

1. What other information and communication technologies (ICT) can Footprint IT use to promote their Footprints in the Outback mobile service?
2. What are the advantages to outback communities of this mobile ICT service?

costs to process business activity statements (BAS) and annual tax reports have been reduced from approximately $6000 pa to less than $2500 pa. This is due mostly to the reduction in bookkeeping staff costs, which have been reduced from 4 hours per week to 4 hours per quarter, when the BAS is due.

Discussing client feedback regarding Footprint IT no longer accepting client cheques, CEO Daemon Singer said, 'one customer, an NGO [non-governmental organisation], still pays by cheque, though the fees associated with those cheques have been waived as part of Footprint IT's community outreach program. This essentially allows a discount of $55 for the NGO on all jobs.'

With accounting processes manageable from anywhere at any time, Footprint IT is currently looking at ways of taking their IT services on the road to provide IT support to the outback of Queensland. Footprints in the Outback is an example of a real mobile business, with mobile, satellite based telephony and internet, a supply of parts, wireless, radio and phone communications and full accommodation, delivering services via a town to town circuit throughout Queensland — the ultimate mobile service.

Sources: Compiled from interview with Daemon Singer, CEO of Footprint IT, www.footprintit.com

3 What are the costs attributed to Footprint IT for servicing outback communities using this mobile ICT service?
4 What other technologies or solutions could Footprint IT use to provide ICT services to outback communities?
5 What would be the costs/benefits of establishing your new technologies or solutions to the outback community? To Footprint IT?

Introduction

The old, traditional working environment that required users to come to a wired computer was ineffective and inefficient. The solution was to build computers that are small enough to carry or wear and can communicate via wireless networks. The ability to communicate anytime and anywhere provides organisations with a strategic advantage by increasing productivity and speed and improving customer service. **Wireless** is a term used to describe telecommunications in which electromagnetic waves, rather than some form of wire or cable, carry the signal between communicating devices such as computers, smart phones and tablets.

Before you continue, it is important to distinguish between the terms *wireless* and *mobile*, because they can mean different things. The term *wireless* means exactly what it says: without wires. In contrast, *mobile* refers to something that changes its location over time. Some wireless networks, such as MiFi (discussed later in this chapter), are also mobile. Others, however, are fixed. For example, microwave towers form fixed wireless networks.

Wireless technologies enable individuals and organisations to conduct mobile computing, mobile commerce and pervasive computing. These terms are defined here, then each is discussed in detail later in the chapter.

Mobile computing refers to a real-time, wireless connection between a mobile device and other computing environments, such as the internet or an intranet.

THE NOOK

Imagine this scenario. A customer arrives at The Nook and is catching up with some friends. Rather than leaving the conversation and going to the bar, he gets out his smart phone, goes to The Nook's mobile site and places a drink order. Payment is made on PayPal's mobile site. The completed order information, including an order ID, is transmitted to the bartender and the customer at the same time. Customers also receive a reminder that they will have to show their ID when they pick up the order, or it will not be delivered and their money will not be refunded.

In just a few minutes, customers receive a text message that their drink is ready. They approach the 'web order' end of the bar, show their text message and their ID, and pick up their drink.

Is this feasible? What technology should The Nook use to deliver this wireless content? Malakai and Abbie have already discussed a wi-fi network, but they wonder what other alternatives might allow this type of interaction with their customers.

Mobile commerce — also known as m-commerce — refers to e-commerce (EC) transactions conducted with a mobile device. *Pervasive computing*, also called *ubiquitous computing*, means that virtually every object has processing power with wireless or wired connections to a global network.

Wireless technologies and mobile commerce are spreading rapidly, replacing or supplementing wired computing. A huge battle is underway to provide you with a mobile, digital wallet and to enable you to get rid of your physical wallet altogether, including all of the credit and debit cards you have in it. Billions of dollars are at stake, further highlighting the importance of wireless to you and your organisations.

Almost all (if not all) organisations utilise wireless computing. Therefore, when you begin your career, you will likely be assigned a company smart phone and a wirelessly enabled computer. Clearly, then, it is important for you to learn about wireless computing not only because you will be using wireless applications but also because wireless computing will be so important to your organisation. In your job, you will be involved with customers who conduct wireless transactions, with analysing and developing mobile commerce applications, and with wireless security. And the list goes on.

Simply put, an understanding of wireless technology and mobile commerce applications will make you more valuable to your organisation. When you look at 'What's In IT For Me?' at the end of this chapter, envision yourself performing the activities discussed in your functional area. An understanding of wireless technology can also help you start and grow your own business, as illustrated in the chapter opening case.

The wireless infrastructure upon which mobile computing is built may reshape the entire IT field. The technologies, applications and limitations of mobile computing and mobile commerce are the focus of this chapter. You begin the chapter by learning about wireless devices and wireless transmission media. You continue by examining wireless computer networks and wireless internet access. You then look at mobile computing and mobile commerce, which are made possible by wireless technologies. Next, you turn your attention to pervasive computing and conclude the chapter by familiarising yourself with a critical component of the wireless environment — namely, wireless security.

10.1 Wireless technologies

Wireless technologies include both wireless devices, such as smart phones and tablets, and wireless transmission media, such as microwave, satellite and radio. These technologies are fundamentally changing the ways organisations operate.

Individuals are finding wireless devices convenient and productive to use, for several reasons. First, they can make productive use of time that was formerly wasted — for example, while commuting to work on public transportation. Second, because they can take these devices with them, their work locations are becoming much more flexible. Third, wireless technology enables them to schedule their working time around personal and professional obligations.

Wireless devices

Wireless devices provide three major advantages to users.

- They are small enough to easily carry or wear.
- They have sufficient computing power to perform productive tasks.
- They can communicate wirelessly with the internet and other devices.

Modern *smart phones* provide capabilities that include mobile telephony, Bluetooth, wi-fi, a digital camera for images and video, global positioning system (GPS), an organiser, a scheduler, an address book, a calculator, access to email and Short Message Service (SMS, sending and receiving short text messages up to 160 characters in length), instant messaging, text messaging, an MP3 music player, a video player, light software applications (apps) and games, internet access with a full-function browser and a QWERTY touch or an alpha/number phone pad keyboard.

One downside of smart phones is that people can use them to copy and pass on confidential information. For example, if you were an executive at Intel, would you want workers snapping pictures of their colleagues with your secret new technology in the background?

Unfortunately, managers think of these devices as phones, not as digital cameras that can transmit wirelessly. New jamming devices are being developed to counter the threat. Some companies, such as Samsung (**www.samsung.com**), have recognised the danger and have banned the devices from their premises altogether. Regardless of any disadvantages, mobile phones, and particularly smart phones, have far greater impact on human society than most of us realise, as you see in the following example.

EXAMPLE The power of mobile banking in Australia

Although still an emerging technology, Australian bank customers are embracing mobile phones and tablets at an exponential speed. In 2013, St George Bank executive Travis Tyler expected the number of consumers dealing with their bank by smart phone or tablet apps to surpass the usage of the traditional ATM network. Australia's major banks report that the speed at which customers have adopted mobile banking is much more rapid than the initial uptake of internet banking despite some consumers' security and privacy concerns.

While most banking apps aim to enable customers to access account information, transfer funds and pay bills, arguably the most high profile mobile banking brand in Australia is Commonwealth Bank's Kaching app. Heavily marketed at the Gen Y segment, the app allows customers to pay anyone using the payee's mobile number, email address and Facebook contacts. Friends can even 'bump' funds to each other by physically tapping their iPhones together using the handsets' accelerometers and GPS to confirm the transaction. In the 11 months leading up to September 2012, 800 000 customers used Kaching to transfer or pay more than $1 billion.

The Kaching app was originally released only for iPhone before an Android version was subsequently made available, a common trend across the banking industry. National Australia Bank's group executive for group business services, Gavin Slater, implemented a different strategy, ensuring NAB took a 'device agnostic' development plan for their apps as opposed to giving Apple the first opportunity.

A recent Credit Suisse Australia report calibrated consumer feedback on the major banks' smart phone and tablet apps. The findings revealed that consumers essentially just wanted easy-to-use apps. It has generally been accepted that individual banks' apps are a source of competitive advantage, enabling new business opportunities and customer retention. Interestingly, the Credit Suisse report claimed the major banks are in fact overinvesting in mobile technology, and that despite the growth in customers accessing their finances on mobile devices, the benefits to the banks are still largely intangible. The Marketing Intelligence Strategy Centre cited that while mobile banking activity was made up of 40 per cent of all digital banking log-ons, it still accounted for only 9.6 per cent of total digital transactions.

Perhaps in response to this, the ANZ Bank is developing a new mobile platform they hope will 'leapfrog, not copy' its major competitors. ANZ chief information officer Anne Weatherston believes that banks will need to run their businesses like Amazon to stay competitive. As part of ANZ's $1.5 billion IT transformation programs, Weatherston led the ANZ board on a Silicon Valley trip. 'There can be no distinction between assisted and unassisted channels. Indeed in the future there will be no channels, there will simply be customer touchpoints.'

Sources: G Wilkins (2013), 'Mobile banking doesn't pay off: Credit Suisse', *The Sydney Morning Herald*, www.smh.com.au/business/banking-and-finance/mobile-banking-doesnt-pay-off-credit-suisse-20130626-2ox5e.html; B Ensor (2013), 'CBA's clever Kaching ambitions', Forrester Research in Business Spectator www.businessspectator.com.au/article/2013/4/29/technology/cbas-clever-kaching-ambitions; G Hutchens (2013), 'Customers take leap into mobile banking', *Sydney Morning Herald*, www.smh.com.au/business/customers-take-leap-into-mobile-banking-20130610-2o02o.html; P Smith (2013), 'Will mobile banking overtake ATMs in 2013?', Financial Review in *Business Review Weekly*, www.brw.com.au/p/tech-gadgets/will_mobile_banking_overtake_atms_Vc3no5vLSQ63RTNoKbxk8J; C Palmer (2013), 'ANZ looks to mobile to leapfrog competitors', *iTNews for Australian Businesses*, www.itnews.com.au/News/345871, anz-looks-to-mobile-to-leapfrog-competitors.aspx; S Burke, E Dart, K Allen, C Lindop, R Simpson, L Blockley, R Farmer and B Rolfe (2011), 'Customer led innovation: generation-Y and the need for customer service innovation in the Australian financial services sector', ipscape, Australian Information Industry Association, www.aiia.com.au/resource/dynamic/blogs/20110809_035545_28847.pdf; K Silva and A Tan (2010), 'Mobile banking rising globally, but Australia yet to fully embrace', KPMG Research Media release, www.kpmg.com/au/en/issuesandinsights/articlespublications/press-releases/pages/press-release-mobilebanking-12-aug-10.aspx; Apoorv Agrawal, 'Mobile banking in Australia', www.slideshare.net/ApoorvAgrawal2/mobile-banking-in-australia.

QUESTIONS

1 Discuss the importance of mobile banking apps.

2 What are the disadvantages of mobile banking apps to customers?

Yet smart phones can cause problems despite all their advantages. The following example demonstrates how smart phones can disrupt the court system.

EXAMPLE Smartphones in Australian courts

Real-time tweeting from NSW courtrooms could be a thing of the past since the NSW Government proposed a ban on smartphones and tablets in court. Currently there are already several jurisdictions around Australia that forbid recording instruments from being used in courts — except where judges expressly allow them — but the miniature size of modern recording devices has meant the rules are very difficult to enforce. Live tweeting and blogging directly from court proceedings has become a soaring trend in recent times.

In his address to the NSW Parliament, NSW Attorney-General Greg Smith stated that he proposed to amend the state's Court Security Act 'to prohibit the unauthorised use of any device, including a smart phone or tablet, to transmit sounds, images or information forming part of court proceedings from a room, or other place where a court is sitting, to another place. These amendments address recent security incidents in courts that have highlighted the fact that the existing legislation does not capture the capability of recent technology — for example, people in court transmitting witness evidence by smart phone to another witness waiting outside the court to give evidence', said Smith.

However, it is not a blanket ban on the use of technology in courts. Lawyers often use smartphones in court to reference legislation and other digital files, as well as to send emails to colleagues, staff and also their clients before the courts. The NSW Law Society and Bar association was consulted on the intended regulation, which may exempt lawyers and journalists — for the purposes of media reports on court developments — from the restrictions in the legislation.

Sources: R Crozier (2013), 'NSW Govt to ban smartphone, tablets in courts: wide net could kill live Tweeting, lawyer's communications', *iTNews for Australian Business*, www.itnews.com.au/News/328656,nsw-govt-to-ban-smartphone-tablets-in-courts.aspx; G Smith (2012), 'Courts and other legalisation further amendment bill 2012, Proof, 21 November 2012', Australian Federal Government, www.parliament.nsw.gov.au/prod/parlment/nswbills.nsf/0/ea0dcb6efe3fc1a8ca257abc0022588b/$FILE/2R%20COURTS%20.pdf; S Nicholls (2013), 'Laws may stop media blogging from court', *Sydney Morning Herald*, www.smh.com.au/technology/technology-news/laws-may-stop-media-blogging-from-court-20130113-2cnm1.html; J Emmett and J J Micholass (2011), *Roadshow Films Pty Limited v iiNet Limited [2011] FCAFC 23* (24 February 2011), Federal Court of Australia, www.austlii.edu.au/au/cases/cth/FCAFC/2011/23.html; Lawyers Weekly (2013), 'Lawyers excused from court tech ban', *Lawyersweekly.com.au*, www.lawyersweekly.com.au/the-new-lawyer/comment-debate/lawyers-excused-from-court-tech-ban.

Wireless transmission media

Wireless media, or broadcast media, transmit signals without wires. The major types of wireless media are microwave, satellite, radio and infrared. Table 10.1 lists the advantages and disadvantages of each type.

TABLE 10.1 Advantages and disadvantages of wireless media

Channel	Advantages	Disadvantages
Microwave	High bandwidth Relatively inexpensive	Must have unobstructed line of sight Susceptible to environmental interference
Satellite	High bandwidth Large coverage area	Expensive Must have unobstructed line of sight Signals experience propagation delay Must use encryption for security
Radio	High bandwidth Signals pass through walls Inexpensive and easy to install	Creates electrical interference problems Susceptible to snooping unless encrypted
Infrared	Low to medium bandwidth Used only for short distances	Must have unobstructed line of sight

Microwave

Microwave transmission systems transmit data via electromagnetic waves. These systems are used for high-volume, long-distance, line-of-sight communication. *Line-of-sight* means that the transmitter and receiver are in view of each other. This requirement creates problems because Earth's surface is curved rather than flat. For this reason, microwave towers usually cannot be spaced more than 48 kilometres apart.

Clearly, then, microwave transmissions offer only a limited solution to data communications needs, especially over very long distances. In addition, microwave transmissions are susceptible to environmental interference during severe weather such as heavy rain and snowstorms. Although long-distance microwave data communications systems are still widely used, they are being replaced by satellite communications systems.

Satellite

Satellite transmission systems make use of communication satellites. Currently, there are three types of satellites circling Earth: geostationary (GEO), medium-earth-orbit (MEO) and low-earth-orbit (LEO). Each type has a different orbit, with the GEO being farthest from Earth and the LEO the closest. In this section, you examine the three types of satellites and then discuss two major satellite applications: global positioning systems and internet transmission via satellites. Table 10.2 compares and contrasts the three types of satellites.

TABLE 10.2 Three basic types of telecommunications satellites

Type	Characteristics	Orbit	Number	Use
GEO	• Satellites stationary relative to point on Earth • Few satellites needed for global coverage • Transmission delay (approximately .25 second) • Most expensive to build and launch • Longest orbital life (many years)	35.4 km	8	TV signal
MEO	• Satellites move relative to point on Earth • Moderate number needed for global coverage • Requires medium-powered transmitters • Negligible transmission delay • Less expensive to build and launch • Moderate orbital life (6–12 years)	10 354.5 km	10–12	GPS
LEO	• Satellites move rapidly relative to point on Earth • Large number needed for global coverage • Requires only low-power transmitters • Negligible transmission delay • Least expensive to build and launch • Shortest orbital life (as low as 5 years)	644–1126.5 km	Many	Telephone

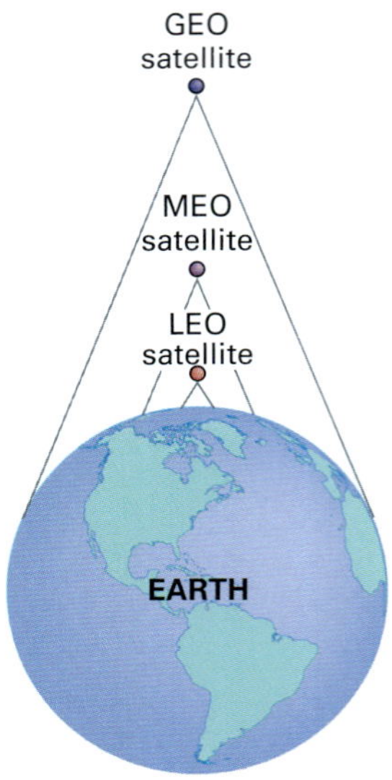

FIGURE 10.1 Comparison of satellite footprints.

As with microwave transmission, satellites must receive and transmit data via line-of-sight. However, the enormous *footprint* — the area of Earth's surface reached by a satellite's transmission — overcomes the limitations of microwave data relay stations. The most basic rule governing footprint size is simple: the higher a satellite orbits, the larger its footprint. Thus, medium-earth-orbit satellites have a smaller footprint than geostationary satellites and low-earth-orbit satellites have the smallest footprint of all. Figure 10.1 compares the footprints of the three types of satellite.

In contrast to line-of-sight transmission with microwave, satellites use *broadcast* transmission, which sends signals to many receivers at one time. So, even though satellites are line-of-sight like microwave, they are high enough for broadcast transmission, thus overcoming the limitations of microwave.

Types of orbits

Geostationary earth orbit (GEO) satellites orbit 35 888 kilometres directly above the equator. These satellites maintain a fixed position above Earth's surface because, at their altitude, their orbital period matches the 24-hour rotational period of Earth. For this reason, receivers on Earth do not have to track GEO satellites. GEO satellites are excellent for sending television programs to cable operators and for broadcasting directly to homes.

One major limitation of GEO satellites is that their transmissions take a quarter of a second to send and return. This brief pause, one kind of **propagation delay**, makes two-way telephone conversations difficult. Also, GEO satellites are large and expensive, and they require substantial amounts of power to launch.

Medium-earth-orbit (MEO) satellites are located about 9656 km above Earth's surface. MEO orbits require more satellites to cover Earth than GEO orbits because MEO footprints are smaller. MEO satellites have two advantages over GEO satellites: they are less expensive and they do not have an appreciable propagation delay. However, because MEO satellites move with respect to a point on Earth's surface, receivers must track these satellites. (Think of a satellite dish slowly turning to remain oriented to an MEO satellite.)

Low-earth-orbit (LEO) satellites are located 400 to 1126.5 km above Earth's surface. Because LEO satellites are much closer to Earth, they have little, if any, propagation delay. Like MEO satellites, however, LEO satellites move with respect to a point on Earth's surface and therefore must be tracked by receivers. Tracking LEO satellites is more difficult than tracking MEO satellites because LEO satellites move much more quickly than MEO satellites relative to a point on Earth.

Unlike GEO and MEO satellites, LEO satellites can pick up signals from weak transmitters. This characteristic makes it possible for satellite telephones to operate via LEO satellites, because they can operate with less power and smaller batteries. Another advantage of LEO satellites is that they consume less power and cost less to launch than GEO and MEO satellites.

At the same time, however, the footprints of LEO satellites are small, which means that many of them are required to cover the planet. For this reason, a single organisation often produces multiple LEO satellites, known as *LEO constellations*. Two examples are Iridium and Globalstar.

Iridium (**www.iridium.com**) has placed an LEO constellation in orbit that consists of 66 satellites and 12 in-orbit spare satellites. The company maintains that it provides complete satellite communications coverage of Earth's surface, including the polar regions. Globalstar (**www.globalstar.com**) also has an LEO constellation in orbit.

Global positioning systems

The **global positioning system (GPS)** is a wireless system that utilises satellites to enable users to determine their position anywhere on Earth. GPS is supported by 24 MEO satellites that are shared worldwide. The exact position of each satellite is always known because the satellite continuously broadcasts its position along with a time signal. By using the known speed of the signals and the distance from three satellites (for two-dimensional location) or four satellites (for three-dimensional location), it is possible to find the location of any receiving station or user within a range of 3 metres. GPS software can also convert the user's latitude and longitude to an electronic map.

Most of you are probably familiar with GPS in vehicles, which 'talks' to drivers when giving directions. Figure 10.2 illustrates two ways for drivers to obtain GPS information in a car: a dashboard navigation system and a GPS app (in this case, TomTom; **www.tomtom.com**) on an iPhone.

FIGURE 10.2 Obtaining GPS information in a vehicle.

Dashboard GPS

TomTom app on iPhone

Commercial use of GPS for activities such as navigating, mapping and surveying has become widespread, particularly in remote areas. Mobile phones in the United States now must have a GPS embedded in them so that the location of a person making an emergency call (for example, 911, known as wireless 911) can be detected immediately.

In Australia the mobile service provider can provide emergency services with location information in most cases if requested. The terrain of the New Zealand landscape and sparseness of the Australian outback mean mobile communications can be poor or non-existent due to the lack of network coverage, which can make an otherwise minor emergency into a major emergency. For example, a motor vehicle overheating would not be considered an emergency in many places; however, in the Australian outback people have died as a result of using drinking water in their overheated vehicle rather than keeping it for drinking.

Today mobile phones are developed with an inbuilt global system for mobile communications (GSM) which enables connection to local emergency operators when dialling 112. This is limited however due to service providers' coverage.[1]

Three other global positioning systems are either planned or operational. The Russian GPS, *GLONASS*, was completed in 1995. However, the system fell into disrepair with the collapse of the Soviet economy. In 2010, GLONASS achieved 100 per cent coverage of Russian territory. The European Union GPS, *Galileo*, has an anticipated completion date of 2015. China expects to complete its GPS, *Beidou*, by 2020.

Internet over satellite (IoS)

In many regions of the world, internet over satellite (IoS) is the only option available for internet connections because installing the necessary cables is either too expensive or physically impossible. IoS enables users to access the internet via GEO satellites from a dish mounted on the side of their homes. Although IoS makes the internet available to many people who otherwise could not access it, it has its drawbacks. Not only do GEO satellite transmissions entail a propagation delay, but they also can be disrupted by environmental influences such as thunderstorms.

Radio

Radio transmission uses radio-wave frequencies to send data directly between transmitters and receivers. Radio transmission has several advantages. First, radio waves travel easily through normal office walls. Second, radio devices are fairly inexpensive and easy to install. Third, radio waves can transmit data at high speeds. For these reasons, radio is increasingly being used to connect computers to both peripheral equipment and local area networks (LANs; discussed in chapter 4).

As with other technologies, however, radio transmission also has its drawbacks. First, radio media can create electrical interference problems. Also, radio transmissions are susceptible to snooping by anyone who has similar equipment that operates on the same frequency.

Another problem with radio transmission is that when you travel too far away from the source station, the signal breaks up and fades into static. Most radio signals can travel only 48 to 64 kilometres from their source. However, *satellite radio* overcomes this problem. **Satellite radio** (or **digital radio**) offers uninterrupted, near CD-quality transmission that is beamed to your radio, either at home or in your car, from space. In addition, satellite radio offers a broad spectrum of stations, including many types of music, news and talk.

XM Satellite Radio and Sirius Satellite Radio were competitors that launched satellite radio services. XM broadcasted its signals from GEO satellites, while Sirius used MEO satellites. In July 2008, the two companies merged to form Sirius XM (**www.siriusxm.com**). Listeners subscribe to the service for a monthly fee.

Infrared

The final type of wireless transmission is infrared transmission. **Infrared** light is red light that is not commonly visible to human eyes. Common applications of infrared light are found in remote control units for televisions, VCRs, and DVD and CD players. In addition, like radio transmission, infrared transceivers are used for short-distance connections between computers and peripheral equipment and local area networks. A *transceiver* is a device that can transmit and receive signals.

BEFORE YOU GO ON . . .

1. Describe the most common types of wireless devices.
2. Describe the various types of transmission media.

THE NOOK

QUESTIONS

1. What qualities of wireless transmission via radio waves would make it most ideal for The Nook?
2. Which business models would work best with satellite transmissions?

10.2 Wireless computer networks and internet access

You have learned about various wireless devices and how these devices transmit wireless signals. These devices typically form wireless computer networks and provide wireless internet access. Next, you will categorise wireless networks by their effective distance: short range, medium range and wide area.

Short-range wireless networks

Short-range wireless networks simplify the task of connecting one device to another, and they eliminate wires and enable users to move around while they use the devices. In general, short-range wireless networks have a range of 30.5 metres or less. In this section, you consider three basic short-range networks: Bluetooth, ultra-wideband (UWB) and near-field communications (NFC).

Bluetooth

Bluetooth (**www.bluetooth.com**) is an industry specification used to create small personal area networks. A **personal area network** is a computer network used for communication among computer devices — for example, telephones, personal digital assistants and smart phones — located close to one person. Bluetooth 1.0 can link up to eight devices within a 10-metre area with a bandwidth of 700 kilobits per second (Kbps) using low-power, radio-based communication. Bluetooth 2.0 can transmit up to 2.1 megabits per second (Mbps) and, at greater power, up to 100 metres. Ericsson, the Scandinavian mobile handset company that developed this standard, called it Bluetooth after the tenth-century Danish King Harald Blatan (*Blatan* means 'Bluetooth'). Ericsson named the standard after Blatan because he unified previously separate islands into the nation of Denmark.

Common applications for Bluetooth are wireless handsets for mobile phones and portable music players. Advantages of Bluetooth include low power consumption and the fact that it uses omnidirectional radio waves — that is, waves that are emitted in all directions from a transmitter. For this reason, you do not have to point one Bluetooth device at another for a connection to occur.

Ultra-wideband

Ultra-wideband (UWB) is a high-bandwidth wireless technology with transmission speeds in excess of 100 Mbps. This very high speed makes UWB a good choice for applications such as streaming multimedia from, say, a personal computer to a television.

Time Domain (**www.timedomain.com**), a pioneer in UWB technology, has developed many UWB applications. One interesting application is the PLUS Real-Time Location System (RTLS). An organisation can use PLUS to locate multiple people and assets simultaneously. Employees, customers and/or visitors wear the PLUS Badge Tag. PLUS Asset Tags are placed on equipment and products. PLUS is extremely valuable for health care environments, where real-time location of caregivers (e.g. doctors, nurses, technicians) and mobile equipment (e.g. laptops, monitors) is critical.

Near-field communications

Near-field communications (NFC) has the smallest range of any short-range wireless networks. It is designed to be embedded in mobile devices such as mobile phones and credit cards. For example, using NFC, you can swipe your device or card within a few centimetres of POS terminals to pay for items (see this chapter's Closing Case 1). NFC also has many other interesting uses. For example, IT's About Business shows how NFC technology helps travellers in Japan.

IT'S ABOUT BUSINESS

Near-field communications helps travellers in Japan

Japan's smart phones are called *keitai*. On their keitai, Japanese subscribers have a high-resolution camera, a projector and near-field communication (NFC) capability. For example, a Japanese woman uses her keitai to scan a QR code at a Tokyo bus stop. A timetable appears instantly on her screen, along with the estimated arrival time of the next bus. When her bus arrives, she uses her keitai to pay by simply waving it close to the payment terminal in the front of the bus.

Because the keitai are NFC equipped, they can function as boarding passes/tickets for trains, aeroplanes and events. They also allow users to check into hotels and will even serve as an electronic room key. Keitai also act as electronic wallets (e-wallets). With up to 50 000 yen credit input into a keitai over the internet, customers use their keitai to buy groceries at convenience stores, pay taxi drivers and purchase goods from Japan's ubiquitous vending machines.

Japan's leading airline, All Nippon Airways (ANA), has been using e-wallets to compete with the country's fast →

trains for several years. As one ANA spokesperson said, 'The major drawback of flying compared to train travel is, of course, the time spent at the airport.'

With ANA's all-in-one keitai ticket and boarding pass, passengers can arrive and board their planes within 15 minutes. This service, called SKiP, uses an e-wallet technology developed by communications company NTT.

Keitai are also equipped with GPS technology, which makes them very useful navigation tools. The Total Navigation site on a keitai shows three-dimensional maps and directions on the screen. If a user is holding the phone while navigating, it will vibrate to alert the driver to upcoming turns.

Keitai also help visitors cope with the Japanese language. For example, menus in Japanese restaurants are invariably only in Japanese. Using a keitai, a visitor can take a picture of a potential meal and the phone describes in English what the meal actually is. This is a valuable tool for many restaurants, because Japan looks to foreign tourists for needed revenue. Other applications allow users to bring up menus, reviews and translations by other users simply by focusing the phone's mobile camera at the restaurant itself.

In Kyoto, the Hyatt Regency offers an iPhone rental service that pinpoints guests' locations and beams target text, video and graphics to inform, help and guide them around the area. The hotel also augments this service with advice and suggestions from the concierge.

The keitai are also equipped with augmented reality (AR). AR apps know where users are and beam location-relevant information to their phones. This information is viewed superimposed on the camera viewfinder on the phone's screen. AR apps in Japan also add tagging and social networking. Like other AR apps, your keitai calculates your position, then, using the camera, displays location-specific information graphically on top of your real-world view.

Interestingly, individuals and businesses can add their own information to these AR apps. They point the phone's camera at the landscape, adding 'tags' that can include text, images and sound that can be picked up by others in the area later. Tags can translate into coupons from businesses or travel trips from friends and colleagues.

Sources: Compiled from M Fitzpatrick (2011), 'Near field communication transforms travel in Japan', *BBC News*, 28 April; S Clark (2010), 'NTT adds new mobile marketing capabilities to Japan's osaifu-keitai mobile wallet service', *Near Field Communications World*, 16 June; S Toto (2010), 'Separate keitai: meet Japan's sexiest new handset', *TechCrunch*, 5 February; 'Japanese cell phone culture', www.japaneselifestyle.com.au.

QUESTIONS

1. As the Japanese travel industry creates more applications of technology for travel, what assumptions is it making about tourists?
2. Which of these apps would you find most useful? Provide specific examples of the app(s) and the way(s) in which you would use them.
3. Do you see any problem with the social networking aspect of AR apps? Support your answer.

Medium-range wireless networks

Medium-range wireless networks are the familiar **wireless local area networks (WLANs)**. The most common type of medium-range wireless network is wireless fidelity, or wi-fi. WLANs are useful in a variety of settings, some of which may be challenging.

Wireless fidelity (wi-fi)

Wireless fidelity (wi-fi) is a medium-range WLAN, which is a wired LAN but without the cables. In a typical configuration, a transmitter with an antenna, called a **wireless access point**, connects to a wired LAN or to satellite dishes that provide an internet connection. Figure 10.3 displays a wireless access point. A wireless access point provides service to a number of users within a small geographical perimeter (up to 30 metres), known as a **hotspot**. Supporting a larger number of users across a larger geographical area requires multiple wireless access points. To communicate wirelessly, mobile devices, such as laptop PCs, typically have a built-in wireless network interface capability.

Wi-fi provides fast and easy internet or intranet broadband access from public hotspots located at airports, hotels, internet cafés, universities, conference centres, offices and homes. Users can access the internet while walking across a campus, to their office, or through their homes. In addition, users can access wi-fi with their laptops, desktops, or PDAs by adding a wireless network card. Most PC and laptop manufacturers incorporate these cards in their PCs.

The Institute of Electrical and Electronics Engineers (IEEE) has established a set of standards for wireless computer networks. The IEEE standard for wi-fi is the 802.11 family.

FIGURE 10.3 Wireless access point.

FIGURE 10.4 Wi-fi provides fast and easy internet or intranet broadband access from public hotspots such as internet cafés.

As of mid 2012, there were four standards in this family: 802.11a, 802.11b, 802.11g and 802.11n. In August 2013 the first shipments of 802.11ac were released, offering faster and more scalable opportunities than previous standards, coupling the 'freedom of wireless with the capacity of Gigabit Ethernet'.[2] Prior to the first shipments of the new chipset, ABI Research (2013) predicted that smartphones would account for almost half of the chipset shipment in 2018.[3] However, businesses need to be mindful that while the chipset in the laboratory may offer speeds of 1.3 gbps, devices can only deliver as much broadband as the slowest link in the network.[4]

Today, many WLANs use the 802.11n standard, which can transmit up to 600 Mbps and has a range of about 1287 km. There are many 802.11n products. One example is Netgear's (**www.netgear.com**) RangeMax Wireless-N router.

The major benefits of wi-fi are its low cost and its ability to provide simple internet access. It is the greatest facilitator of the wireless internet — that is, the ability to connect to the internet wirelessly.

Corporations are integrating wi-fi into their strategies. For example, Coffee Club, McDonald's and Starbucks offer customers wi-fi in many of their stores, primarily for internet access.

Search engines that focus specifically on locations for free wi-fi hotspots, such as JiWire[5] which uses Google maps and searches using postcodes as the location finders, make locating these hotspots quick and easy for the mobile business traveller. A list of these search engines also include the following.

- Wi-fi-freespot:[6] this directory is geared towards free hotspots. (Some of these otherwise free locations may require a store purchase, however.) Worldwide listings are organised both geographically and by business type.
- Free WiFi:[7] this directory includes user pay as well as free wi-fi hotspots in Australia but clearly differentiates between the two. Users enter a property name, state or post-code to find businesses offering wi-fi and are provided information about the businesses, including a map.
- CNET.com:[8] CNET.com provides a list of apps for a variety of mobile devices that enable you to locate free wi-fi hotspots from your mobile device. This is offered for a variety of operating systems including Android, iOS and Windows.[9]

Councils are also getting in on the wi-fi act, as you see in IT's About Business.

IT'S ABOUT BUSINESS

Free municipal wi-fi in Brisbane parks

Brisbane City Council, Australia's largest municipality, has rolled out free wi-fi at over 20 parks and public spaces at a cost of approximately $2 million. In the first two months of the initiative the service was used 34 300 times by 16 000 people, which equates to 636 daily users across all locations, sharing roughly 6500MB of data every 24 hours.

Brisbane Lord Mayor Graham Quirk believes the key benefits to residents and visitors is that 'people no longer have to lock themselves up at home' to experience their 'online lives'. Residents can find the free wi-fi using signs in each of the areas that indicate the 100 metre radius in which the service operates. The Council's objectives to promote active lifestyles, a smart economy and vibrant, creative city strategically align with the installation of a free public wi-fi system.

Easyweb Digital, the company behind the rollout, spent two months designing, building and installing the system. The project tied together several elements into a streamlined solution. Every location uses a unique service to provide internet access and the system features an intuitive info-portal which shows event information from the Council databases. Over a ten week period, coordination of engineers from infrastructure suppliers, Council and cabling experts was executed in line with network and graphic designers.

In terms of access controls, time and download limits can be set by BCC staff by location and instant deployments of additional SSIDs (network names) with different authentication and access controls. This enables BCC to cater for the needs of special events, for example, providing more comprehensive access for event staff. A control panel is available to Council through a secure internet portal that enables updates to info-portal content, adjustment of user access controls and live reporting on system usage. Real-time user statistics display downloads and uploads, device types, session times and dates by any date range for single or multiple locations allowing BCC to better understand usage and forward plan.

Beyond the lifestyle benefits of the program, it is yet to be seen if the rollout will successfully foster mobile commerce in Brisbane's local business sector. BCC would like wi-fi implemented in restaurants and cafes to demonstrate its credentials as a 'switched-on' city, but have only contributed $3000 worth of window stickers in support of the shift.

'These free wi-fi stickers give businesses another chance to say we're a friendly, digital business, come in and do some business with us. Why should ratepayers be up for the cost of those things when we can do it in partnership with business? I think that is the sensible way to go', Councillor Quirk said.

Sources: S Vogler (2012), 'Brisbane's free wifi network rolled out to 20 more locations', *The Courier-Mail*, 3 July, www.couriermail.com.au/news/brisbanes-free-wifi-network-rolled-out-to-20-more-locations/story-e6freon6-1226415560961; 'Brisbane WiFi in Parks', Easyweb Digital website, www.easywebdigital.com/projects/brisbane-wifi-in-parks; K Feeney (2012), 'Brisbane snaps up free wi-fi', *The Sydney Morning Herald*, 7 September, www.smh.com.au/it-pro/government-it/brisbane-snaps-up-free-wifi-20120907-25izr.html; K Feeney (2012), 'Council plan to spread WiFi comes at cafe's cost', *The Sydney Morning Herald*, www.smh.com.au/digital-life/council-plan-to-spread-wifi-comes-at-cafes-cost-20121204-2asj3.html.

Although wi-fi has become extremely popular, it is not without problems. Three factors are preventing the commercial wi-fi market from expanding even further: roaming, security and cost.

- At this time, users cannot roam from hotspot to hotspot if the hotspots use different wi-fi network services. Unless the service is free, users have to log on to separate accounts and, where required, pay a separate fee for each service.
- Security is the second barrier to greater acceptance of wi-fi. Because wi-fi uses radio waves, it is difficult to shield from intruders.
- The final limitation to greater wi-fi expansion is cost. Even though wi-fi services are relatively inexpensive, many experts question whether commercial wi-fi services can survive when so many free hotspots are available to users.

Wi-Fi Direct

Until late 2010, wi-fi required the presence of a wireless antenna at the centre of a hotspot and ad-hoc connections among individual computers or other devices were somewhat limited. Because of these limitations, organisations have typically used wi-fi for communications of up to about 240 metres and they have used Bluetooth for shorter, ad hoc connections.

Wi-Fi Direct is a new iteration of wi-fi. It enables peer-to-peer communications, so devices can connect directly. Wi-Fi Direct enables users to transfer content among devices, even without a wireless antenna. It can connect pairs or groups of devices at wi-fi speeds of up to 250 Mbps and at distances of up to 240 metres. Further, devices with Wi-Fi Direct can broadcast their availability to other devices just as Bluetooth devices can. Finally, Wi-Fi Direct is compatible with the more than 1 billion wi-fi devices currently in use.

Wi-Fi Direct will probably challenge the dominance of Bluetooth in the area of device-to-device networking. It offers a similar type of connectivity but with greater range and much faster data transfer.

MiFi

MiFi is a small, portable wireless device that provides users with a permanent wi-fi hotspot wherever they go. Thus, users are always connected to the internet. The range of the MiFi device is about 10 metres. Developed by Novatel, the MiFi device is also called an intelligent mobile hotspot. Accessing wi-fi through the MiFi device allows up to five persons to be connected at the same time, sharing the same connection.

MiFi provides broadband internet connectivity anywhere there is 3G cellular network coverage. MiFi also allows users to use voice-over-IP technology to make free (or cheap) calls, both locally and internationally. One drawback with MiFi is the cost, both for acquiring it and for using it.

Super Wi-Fi

Super Wi-Fi is a term coined by the US Federal Communications Commission (FCC) to describe a wireless network proposal that creates long-distance wireless internet connections. (The use of the trademark 'Wi-Fi' in the name has been criticised because Super Wi-Fi is not based on wi-fi technology.) Regardless, Super Wi-Fi uses the lower-frequency white spaces between television channel frequencies. These lower frequencies allow the signal to travel further and penetrate walls better than normal wi-fi frequencies.

Super Wi-Fi is already in use in the US. The technology threatens mobile phone carriers' 3G technology and it could be used to bring broadband wireless internet access to rural areas.

Wireless mesh networks

Mesh networks use multiple wi-fi access points to create a wide area network that can be quite large. Mesh networks could have been included in the long-range wireless section, but you see them here because they are essentially a series of interconnected local area networks.

Ips-Mesh wireless network community provides open nodes for people in the Ipswich community to access information without the need for internet access. In March 2013 Ips-Mesh and Briscomp (the Brisbane wireless network community), now sharing a wireless network, successfully tested embedded hardware out west to Marburg. The Ips-Mesh/Briscomp mesh network provides access to a variety of sites including weather, TV, radio, discount holiday sites, as well as other business and community sites.[10]

Around the United States, public wireless mesh programs have stalled and failed (for example, in Philadelphia, in Boston, and on Long Island, New York). Service providers that partnered with cities to maintain the systems are dropping out, largely because the projects' costs are escalating and the revenue models are unclear. However, San Jose, California, is building a new 'municipal wi-fi' network that shows promise.[11]

There are many examples of successful mesh network applications in Australia. However, there are important reasons for pursuing open wireless access (OWA) other than social networking.[12] Consider the following.

- Electronic Frontiers Australia believes open networks are crucial in cyclone-affected areas.
- Open wireless access provides opportunities for innovation.
- Emergency services providing a ready search site for do's and don'ts in emergency situations, such as resuscitating a person who has drowned, while waiting for emergency service staff to arrive. A quick guide could be available on any mobile device, including images to reduce translation issues.
- Uses for travellers, such as discount holiday packages (see Ips-Mesh.net).
- Reducing the digital divide by reducing access costs for lower socioeconomic groups. Additionally, OWA offers opportunities for community groups to communicate across distances, sharing ideas and collaborating on festivals and cultural activities.
- The benefits for businesses and economic development.[13]

Wide-area wireless networks

Wide-area wireless networks connect users to the internet over a geographically dispersed territory. These networks typically operate over the licensed spectrum — that is, they use portions of the wireless spectrum that are regulated by the government. In contrast, Bluetooth and wi-fi operate over the unlicensed spectrum and are therefore more prone to interference and security problems. In general, wide-area wireless network technologies fall into two categories: cellular radio and wireless broadband.

Cellular radio

Mobile telephones (mobile phones) provide two-way radio communications over a cellular network of base stations with seamless handoffs. Mobile telephones differ from cordless telephones, which offer telephone service only within a limited range through a single base station attached to a fixed landline — for example, within a home or an office.

The mobile phone communicates with radio antennas, or towers, placed within adjacent geographic areas called *cells* (see figure 10.5). A telephone message is transmitted to the local cell — that is, the antenna — by the mobile phone and then is passed from cell to cell until it reaches the cell of its destination. At this final cell, the message is either transmitted to the receiving mobile phone or it is transferred to the public switched telephone system to be transmitted to a wireline telephone. This is why you can use a mobile phone to call other mobile phones as well as standard wireline phones.

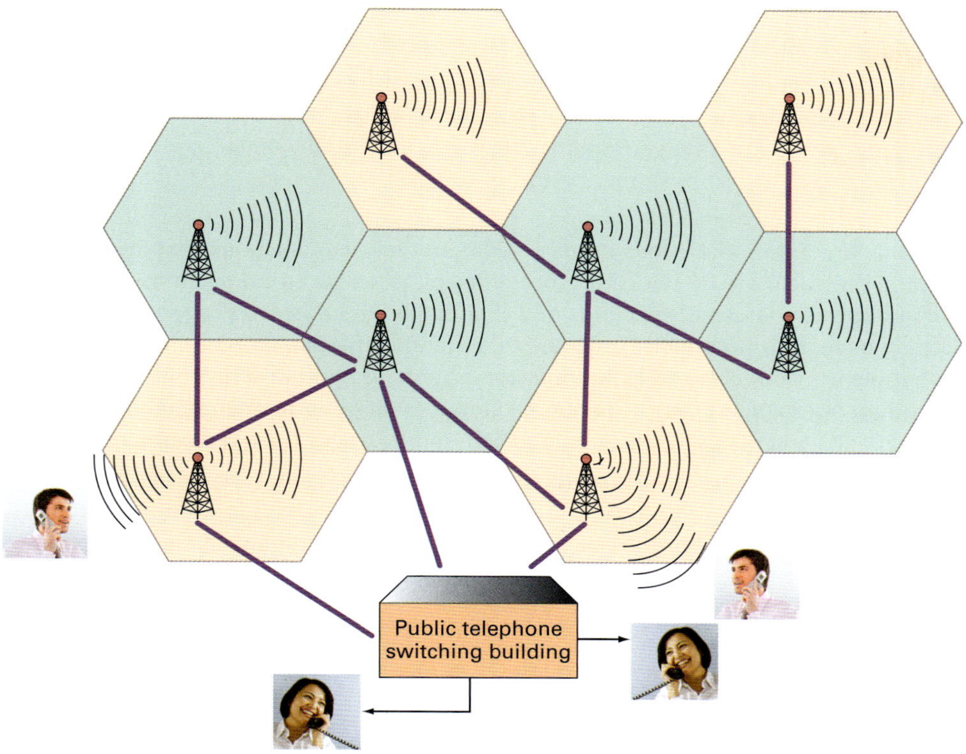

FIGURE 10.5 The mobile phone communicates with radio antennas, or towers, placed within adjacent geographic areas called *cells*.

Until early 2011, large cell towers were a 'given' for cellular technology. The following example introduces an exciting new technology from Alcatel-Lucent (**www.alcatel-lucent.com**) that aims to replace these towers.

Cellular technology is quickly evolving, moving towards higher transmission speeds and richer features. The technology has progressed through several stages.

- *First generation (1G)* cellular used analogue signals and had low bandwidth (capacity).
- *Second generation (2G)* uses digital signals primarily for voice communication; it provides data communication up to 10 Kbps.

EXAMPLE lightRadio

The global wireless industry is spending US $210 billion per year to operate its networks and $50 billion per year to upgrade them. Despite all that spending and pressure on consumers to curb their data usage, the networks are fighting a losing battle. Mobile data usage is expected to grow 30 times by 2015 and 500 times by 2020. The Australian Bureau of Statistics (2012) indicated that mobile wireless broadband accounted for 49 per cent of all connects in Australia. By December 2012 the number of subscribers to internet connections via a mobile handset had increased 7 per cent from 16.2 million to 17.4 million subscribers. While an increase in mobile broadband connectivity of 7 per cent sounds reasonable, within a three month period mobile broadband downloads had increased by 38 per cent to 13.7 thousand terabytes.

Understandably, wireless carriers are challenged with options to maintain support for mobile handset subscribers. With a combination of miniaturisation and cloud technology (discussed in Plug IT In 3), lightRadio might be able to help wireless carriers keep pace with their customers.

A lightRadio is a 5.8 centimetre cube that contains all of the components of a cell tower. Alcatel-Lucent's engineers stripped out all the heavy power equipment that controls mobile towers and moved it to centralised stations. Consequently, the lightRadio cubes are small enough to be deployed virtually anywhere and almost inconspicuously — for example, on top of bus station awnings, on the sides of buildings and on lampposts.

Not only are lightRadio cubes much smaller and less conspicuous than mobile towers, they also are 30 per cent more efficient. Wireless carriers can assess live data about who is using the cubes and then adjust the antennas' directional beams to maximise their potential. For example, antennas may be pointed in one direction as people are coming to work in the morning and in another direction when they are going home. In addition, the cubes contain multigenerational antennas that can relay 2G, 3G and 4G network signals (discussed next), all from the same cube.

Each lightRadio cube powers about a two-block radius, so in urban areas they can be deployed throughout the city and stacked in stadiums or other areas that need extra capacity. In rural areas, they can be deployed on top of existing mobile towers.

Sources: Compiled from S Portlock (2012), 'Bell Labs' lightRadio cube has big first year, wows crowds at Mobile Congress', *The Star Ledger* (www.nj.com/starledger), 29 February; D Goldman (2011), 'The tiny cube that could cut your phone bill', *CNNMoney*, 21 March; C Babcock (2011), 'Alcatel Lucent shrinks cell phone towers', *InformationWeek*, 7 February; www.alcatel-lucent.com; ACMA (2011), 'Towards 2020 — future spectrum requirements for mobile broadband', *Australian Communications and Media Authority*, www.acma.gov.au/webwr/_assets/main/lib312084/ifc13_2011_toward_2020-future_spectrum_requirements.pdf; ABS (2013), 'Mobile handset subscribers', Australian Bureau of Statistics, www.abs.gov.au/ausstats/abs@.nsf/Products/8153.0~December+2012~Chapter~Mobile+handset+subscribers?OpenDocument.

- *2.5G* uses digital signals and provides voice and data communication up to 144 Kbps.
- *Third generation (3G)* uses digital signals and can transmit voice and data up to 384 Kbps when the device is moving at a walking pace, 128 Kbps when it is moving in a car and up to 2 Mbps when it is in a fixed location. 3G supports video, web browsing and instant messaging.
- *Fourth generation (4G)* is still under development and is not one defined technology or standard. The International Telecommunications Union has specified speed requirements for 4G: 100 Mbps (million bits per second) for high-mobility communications such as cars and trains, and 1 Gbps (billion bits per second) for low-mobility communications such as pedestrians. A 4G system is expected to provide a secure all-IP (internet protocol)-based mobile broadband system to all types of mobile devices. Many of the current '4G' offerings do not meet the ITU specified speeds, but they call their service 4G nonetheless. See the 'IT's Personal' article opposite for more information.

BEFORE YOU GO ON . . .

1. What is Bluetooth? What is a WLAN?
2. Describe wi-fi, mobile service and WiMAX.

Wireless broadband or WiMAX

Worldwide interoperability for microwave access, popularly known as WiMAX, is the name for IEEE Standard 802.16. WiMAX has a wireless access range of up to 50 kilometres, compared to 91.5 metres for wi-fi. WiMAX also has a data-transfer rate of up to 75 Mbps. It is a secure system and offers features such as voice and video. WiMAX antennas can transmit broadband internet connections to antennas on homes and businesses kilometres away. The technology can therefore provide long-distance broadband wireless access to rural areas and other locations that are not currently being served.

IT'S PERSONAL

WIRELESS AND MOBILE

What the GSM3GHSDPA+4GLTE???

This chapter explains the many mobile platforms that are available to you as a consumer. Mobile, Bluetooth, wi-fi, satellite and other wireless options are available. That seems simple enough to understand. But within the mobile area, things get confusing because so many acronyms are used by the telecommunication companies these days. Have you ever wondered if Telstra 3G was equivalent to Optus 3G? What about 4G and 4G LTE? Of course, most people assume that 4G is faster than 3G, but how much so?

When in 2012 Apple released its new iPad in Australia, Apple claimed in its advertising and marketing materials that the iPad was 4G capable. The iPad was 4G capable in other countries, but not in Australia: it operated on the 700 MHtz and 2100 MHz bands, neither of which were available in Australia.

The ACCC commenced legal proceedings against Apple, alleging that Apple had misled consumers. In June 2012, the ACCC and Apple entered into a settlement agreement. Apple agreed to pay a fine of $2.25 million to the ACCC, and to pay $300 000 to cover the ACCC's legal costs.

Actual connection speeds are described in bit rates, meaning how many bits (1s or 0s) you can move in one second. If you see a speed described as 1.5 Mbps, this translates to 1.5 million bits per second. That sounds like a tremendous rate, but knowing the bits per second is only part of understanding the actual speed you will experience. This is because connection speed and throughput speed are different. Actual throughput will always be less than connection speed.

It works much like your car. Your car is probably capable of driving over 160 km per hour. However, you are 'throttled down' by various speed limits so much that you never reach your potential speed. Your actual speed varies depending on the route you take and the limits imposed along that route. So even though all Australian telecommunication companies boast incredible wireless speeds, they often say 'up to' because they know that you will never actually download a file at that rate.

The best way to see actual speeds of the networks is to run a speed test. This will give you first-hand experience of the actual throughput speed you can expect from their network. This number is much more realistic and will mean more to you than understanding the terms 3G, 4G, 4G LTE and so on.

Here is how you do the test: first, make sure the unit is only connected to a mobile network (not wi-fi). Then go to speedtest.net and click 'Begin Test'. These numbers are more informative than any name they are given (3G, 4G, etc.) because you see exactly what you can expect out of your wireless connection. Run this test at competing telecommunications stores and you will have real data to compare. As names change, you can always run a test to find the facts.

Source: D Fogarty (2012), 'Apple fined more than $2m over iPad claim', Australian Associated Press (Melbourne), 21 June.

Apply the Concept

Background

Many mobile phones today have multiple radios in them. Both the iPhone 5 and the Galaxy S3 have three different radio transceivers and one radio receiver. They are mobile (4G LTE, 4G, or 3G depending on your carrier), Bluetooth, wi-fi and GPS (the one that only receives). With all of these radios in a small mobile device, the possibilities of connectivity are nearly endless. For this activity, let's focus on Bluetooth.

As described in the chapter, it is used for short range, personal area networks. Many people use Bluetooth networks for sound via wireless headphones, speakerphones, car stereos, or speakers. The author personally uses an iPhone and four different radio transmitters to play music in his car. First, Optus and Telstra provide a 3G data connection. This 3G is shared with his iPhone over a wi-fi connection. This is done to stream Pandora music over Bluetooth to an FM transmitter that sends the signal to the factory FM radio. So at one time, the author is using mobile, wi-fi, Bluetooth and FM just to listen to Pandora radio.

However, Bluetooth can also be used to make the iPhone a remote for a keynote presentation, a display for a heart rate monitor, body activity monitor, sleep monitor, blood pressure monitor, or to connect to devices such as Google Glass (search Google for this — it's awesome!).

Activity

1 Research the different Bluetooth devices for business purposes. How many of these are viable? What industries are more likely to use them? What positions within the industries are likely to need small personal area networks for employees? How many devices can work with both Bluetooth and wi-fi?

2 Run a speed test on your home, office and mobile devices using ZDNet.com (**www.zdnet.com/broadband-speedtest**). What is the difference between the different connection types? Why are these connection speeds different? Does location make a difference? Does time of day accessed (when the test was undertaken) make a difference? Complete the test for at least three separate intervals during the day to test time usage influence (e.g. 6 am, 11 am, 2 pm, 5 pm, 6 pm and 9 pm). Explain why there is a difference.

Deliverable

1 Build a table that lists the different Bluetooth technologies you have found and that shows their potential applications. Try to find at least five different technologies and uses if you can. Submit your work to your instructor.

OR

2 Build a table that lists the different connection and device speed tests. Include connection type, device, location and time. Explain why there is a difference.

THE NOOK

QUESTIONS

1 For The Nook, what is a significant difference in the way Bluetooth operates compared to infrared transmission that would make it more feasible for Malakai and Abbie's choice of technology?

2 Obviously, Malakai and Abbie want to create a WLAN with some type of wireless technology. Based on the options discussed in section 10.2, which one do you think would be the most worthwhile? Keep in mind that to be useful to customers, devices must be compatible with the club's network.

10.3 Mobile computing and mobile commerce

In the traditional computing environment, users come to a computer, which is connected with wires to other computers and to networks. Because these networks need to be linked by wires, it is difficult or even impossible for people on the move to use them. In particular, salespeople, repair people, service employees, law enforcement officers and utility workers can be more effective if they can use IT while in the field or in transit. Thus, mobile computing was designed for workers who travel outside the boundaries of their organisations as well as for anyone travelling outside his or her home.

Mobile computing refers to a real-time connection between a mobile device and other computing environments, such as the internet or an intranet. This innovation is revolutionising how people use computers. It is spreading at work and at home; in education, health care and entertainment; and in many other areas.

Mobile computing has two major characteristics that differentiate it from other forms of computing: mobility and broad reach. *Mobility* means that users carry a device with them and can initiate a real-time contact with other systems from wherever they happen to be. *Broad reach* refers to the fact that when users carry an open mobile device, they can be reached instantly, even across great distances.

These two characteristics, mobility and broad reach, create five value-added attributes that break the barriers of geography and time: ubiquity, convenience, instant connectivity, personalisation and localisation of products and services. A mobile device can provide information and communication regardless of the user's location (*ubiquity*). With an internet-enabled mobile device, users can access the web, intranets and other mobile devices quickly and easily, without booting up a PC or placing a call via a modem (*convenience* and *instant connectivity*). A company can customise information and send it to individual consumers as a short message service (SMS) (*personalisation*). And, knowing a user's physical location helps a company advertise its products and services (*localisation*). Localisation is determined by your location provided to your service provider, or supplier when establishing your accounts; it does not mean that they know exactly where you are. The only time that real-time localisation is available is if you dial E112, which will connect you to the nearest emergency service office and provide your location. Mobile computing provides the foundation for mobile commerce (m-commerce).

Mobile commerce

In addition to affecting our everyday lives, mobile computing is also transforming the way organisations conduct business by allowing businesses and individuals to engage in mobile commerce. As you saw at the beginning of this chapter, **mobile commerce (or m-commerce)** refers to electronic commerce (EC) transactions that are conducted in a wireless environment, especially via the internet. Like regular EC applications, m-commerce can be transacted via the internet, private communication lines, smart cards and other infrastructures. M-commerce creates opportunities for businesses to deliver new services to existing customers and to attract new customers. To see how m-commerce applications are classified by industry, see **www.wirelessresearch.eu**. The development of m-commerce is driven by the following factors.

- *Widespread availability of mobile devices.* By mid 2012, more than 5 billion mobile phones were in use throughout the world. Experts estimate that within a few years about 70 per cent of mobile phones in developed countries will have internet access. Going further, as already discussed in this chapter, mobile phones are spreading even more quickly in developing countries. Thus, a potential mass market is developing for mobile computing and m-commerce.
- *Declining prices.* The price of wireless devices is declining and will continue to decline.
- *Bandwidth improvement.* To properly conduct m-commerce, you need sufficient bandwidth for transmitting text, voice, video and multimedia. Wi-fi, 4G mobile technology and WiMAX provide the necessary bandwidth.

Mobile computing and m-commerce include many applications. These applications result from the capabilities of various technologies. You will examine these applications and their impact on business activities in the next section.

Mobile commerce applications

Mobile commerce applications are many and varied. The most popular applications include location-based applications, financial services, intrabusiness applications, accessing information and telemetry. The rest of this section examines these various applications and their effects on the ways people live and do business.

An interesting twist on mobile applications has emerged, called a mobile extension. Mobile applications are internet applications that run on smart phones and other mobile devices. Mobile applications help users connect to internet services more commonly accessed on desktop or laptop computers. As you see in IT's About Business (overleaf), mobile extensions are different from mobile applications.

IT'S ABOUT BUSINESS

Xero to hero — floating on a NZ cloud

Known as the 'Apple of accounting', Xero is an online accounting software product designed specifically for small to medium sized businesses under a subscription based model (often referred to as 'SaaS', Software as a Service). Xero CEO and founder Rod Drury describes the cloud-based business as 'a global company that started in New Zealand'. The company spent its first five years in New Zealand, which was a highly effective strategy as it enabled Xero to gradually build a strong product while flying under the radar of its main competitors.

In October 2009 Xero was celebrating 12 000 customers, but they now have over 200 000 customers worldwide, surpassing the billion dollar mark in March 2013 with its value eventually rising above $NZ2 billion later that year. This rapid, exponential growth can be attributed to an audacious market entry strategy which had at its core the goal to make accountants and bookkeepers an endorsement channel for the software. Xero executed perfectly on this plan — up to 60 per cent of Xero licenses are sold through this channel.

According to its website, Xero is 'an easy-to-use but powerful online accounting platform designed from the ground up for the cloud, not adapted from desktop software'. The key features of Xero include automatic bank account feeds, invoicing, accounts payable, expense claims, fixed asset depreciation, and standard business and management reporting. Xero can automatically import bank statements from thousands of banks globally, including the major banks in the USA, UK, New Zealand and Australia.

Xero capitalised on their target market by recognising that small business were willing to pay for software applications but were not particularly well serviced by massive software companies Oracle and SAP. 'Some accountants are paying tens of thousands of dollars for tools to run their practice, what we are saying to them is come to Xero, bring your clients and we are going to let you run your practice on the cloud', said Xero's managing director Chris Ridd. The company is shaping as a serious threat to QuickBooks' and MYOB's market leading positions.

Sources: Sydney Morning Herald (2013), '*Xero value cracks $NZ2b mark*', www.smh.com.au/business/xero-value-cracks-nz2b-mark-20130704-2pd75.html; H McKenzie (2013), 'Xero: a billion-dollar software company that had five years in stealth at the bottom of the planet', *Pandodaily*, pandodaily.com/2013/05/01/xero-a-billion-dollar-software-company-that-had-five-years-in-stealth-at-the-bottom-of-the-planet; C Fitzsimmons (2013), 'Stuart McLean goes from Google to hero to Xero', *Business Review Weekly*, www.brw.com.au/p/tech-gadgets/stuart_mclean_goes_from_google_hero_w8FY4THYCU7LccKp5WWwdP; S Macpherson (2013), 'How Xero added 120 000 customers in three years', *Box Free IT*, boxfreeit.com.au/2013/03/29/how-xero-added-120000-customers-three-years; www.xero.com/au.

QUESTIONS

1. How do the add-on apps differ from mobile apps?
2. What are the advantages of a mobile accounting package such as Xero?
3. What add-on apps should small businesses use?
4. How could these add-on apps improve small business growth and profitability?

Location-based applications and services

M-commerce B2C applications include location-based services and location-based applications. Location-based mobile commerce is called **location-based commerce** (or **L-commerce**).

Location-based services provide information that is specific to a given location. For example, a mobile user can (1) request the nearest business or service, such as an ATM or a restaurant; (2) receive alerts, such as a warning of a traffic jam or an accident; and (3) find a friend. Wireless carriers can provide location-based services such as locating taxis, service personnel, doctors and rental equipment; tracking objects such as packages and train boxcars; finding information such as navigation, weather, traffic and room schedules; targeting advertising; and automating airport check-ins.

Consider, for example, how location-based advertising can make the marketing process more productive. Marketers can use this technology to integrate the current locations and preferences of mobile users. They can then send user-specific advertising messages concerning nearby shops, malls and restaurants to consumers' wireless devices.

Financial services

Mobile financial applications include banking, wireless payments and micropayments, money transfers, wireless wallets and bill-payment services. The bottom line for mobile financial applications is to make it more convenient for customers to transact business regardless of where they are or what time it is. Harried customers are demanding such convenience.

In many countries, banks increasingly offer mobile access to financial and account information. For example, Citibank (**www.citibank.com.au**) alerts customers on their digital mobile phones about changes in their account information.

If you took a taxi ride in Frankfurt, Germany, you could use your mobile phone to pay the taxi driver. Such very small purchase amounts (generally less than $10) are called *micropayments*.

Historically web shoppers have preferred to pay with credit cards. Because credit card companies sometimes charge fees on transactions, however, credit cards are an inefficient way to make very small purchases. The growth of relatively inexpensive digital content, such as music (for example, iTunes), ring tones, and downloadable games, is driving the growth of micropayments, as merchants seek to avoid paying credit card fees on small transactions.

Ultimately, however, the success of micropayment applications will depend on the costs of the transactions. Transaction costs will be small only when the volume of transactions is large. One technology that can increase the volume of transactions is wireless mobile wallets. Various companies offer **mobile wallet (m-wallet)** technologies that enable cardholders to make purchases with a single click from their mobile devices. Chapter Closing Case 1 discusses mobile wallets in detail.

In China, SmartPay allows users to use their mobile phones to pay their phone bills and utility bills, buy lottery tickets and airline tickets, and make other purchases. SmartPay launched 172.com, a portal that centralises the company's mobile, telephone and internet-based payment services for consumers. The portal is designed to provide a convenient, centralised source of information for all these transactions.

Intrabusiness applications

Although business-to-consumer (B2C) m-commerce gets considerable publicity, most of today's m-commerce applications actually are used *within* organisations. In this section, you will see how companies use mobile computing to support their employees.

Mobile devices are increasingly becoming an integral part of workflow applications. For example, companies can use nonvoice mobile services to assist in dispatch functions — that is, to assign jobs to mobile employees, along with detailed information about the job. Target areas for mobile delivery and dispatch services include transportation (e.g. delivery of food, oil, newspapers, cargo; courier services; tow trucks; taxis), utilities (e.g. gas, electricity, phone, water); field service (e.g. computer, office equipment, home repair); health care (e.g. visiting nurses, doctors, social services); and security (e.g. patrols, alarm installation).

Accessing Information

Mobile portals and voice portals are designed to aggregate and deliver content in a form that will work within the limited space available on mobile devices. These portals provide information anywhere and anytime to users.

A **mobile portal** aggregates and provides content and services for mobile users. These services include news, sports and email; entertainment, travel and restaurant information; community services; and stock trading. The world's best-known mobile portal — i-mode from NTT DoCoMo (**www.nttdocomo.com**) — has more than 40 million subscribers, primarily in Japan. Major players in Europe are Vodafone, O2 and T-Mobile. Some traditional portals — for example, Yahoo, AOL and MSN — have mobile portals as well.

A **voice portal** is a website with an audio interface. Voice portals are not websites in the normal sense because they can also be accessed through a standard phone or a mobile phone. A certain phone number connects you to a website, where you can request information verbally. The system finds the information, translates it into a computer-generated voice reply and tells you what you want to know. Most airlines provide real-time information on flight status this way.

An example of a voice portal is the voice-activated 511 travel information line developed by Tellme.com. It enables callers to inquire about weather, local restaurants, current traffic and other handy information. In addition to retrieving information, some sites provide true interaction. For example, iPing (**www.iping.com**) is a reminder and notification service that allows users to enter information via the web and receive reminder calls. This service can even call a group of people to notify them of a meeting or conference call.

Telemetry applications

Telemetry is the wireless transmission and receipt of data gathered from remote sensors. Telemetry has numerous mobile computing applications. For example, technicians can use telemetry to identify maintenance problems in equipment. As another example, doctors can monitor patients and control medical equipment from a distance.

Car manufacturers use telemetry applications for remote vehicle diagnosis and preventive maintenance. For instance, drivers of many General Motors cars use its OnStar system (**www.onstar.com**) in numerous ways. IT's About Business examines issues with ecosystems telemetry data collection in Australia.

IT'S ABOUT BUSINESS

Eco IT in Aus — animal telemetry data collection

The technological advancement of telemetry devices is enabling highly accurate and detailed recordings of animal movement and habitat selection. The telemetry equipment is, however, reasonably costly, considerable effort is required to attach the device and the process is stressful to the animal. With this in mind, are we as a research community making the most efficient use of these ecological data, and whether the findings from telemetry studies are being transferred into successful management actions for fisheries and wildlife?

Australia is the world's third largest producer of scientific publications pertaining to animal movement and location. Nearly all tertiary institutions have one or more groups utilising animal telemetry, and similarly, governmental natural resource departments and conservation NGOs are regularly carrying out wildlife tracking projects. Most of these research projects are undertaken to answer specific biological or management questions and the data is often redundant beyond its original application.

Moreover, the data are generally stored on personal hard drives and inaccessible to the wider scientific community. Assimilating these datasets and integrating them with environmental data has great potential for enhancing and accelerating our knowledge and understanding of Australian ecosystems. There are however, a number of analytical challenges associated with sharing and synthesising these data.

Spatial prioritisation analysis techniques are becoming widely used tools to protect areas for the preservation of biodiversity, but so far rely upon species presence data collected primarily by human observation.

Atlas of Living Australia rely on the community, community groups and environmental institutes to report sightings of individual species, including GPS location using a mobile application that can be downloaded onto any mobile device. While these are not telemetry data collection devises attached to an individual species they are improving the data collection knowledge and dissemination of Australia's species.

Sources: Australian Centre for Ecological Analysis and Synthesis, www.aceas.org.au/index.php?option=com_content&view=article&id=101&ltemid=103; ALA (2012), 'Three ways to get involved', The Atlas of Living Australia, www.ala.org.au/get-involved.

QUESTIONS

1. How can animal location data collected by different technologies and sampling regimes be integrated without introducing error?
2. What devices would you use to manage telemetry data?
3. How would you analyse and report your findings?

An interesting telemetry application for individuals is an iPhone app called Find My iPhone. Find My iPhone is a part of the Apple iCloud (**www.apple.com/icloud**). Find My iPhone provides several very helpful telemetry functions. If you lose your iPhone, there are two ways to see its approximate location on a map: you can sign into the Apple iCloud from any computer or you can use the Find My iPhone app on another iPhone, iPad, or iPod touch.

If you have left your iPhone somewhere you can't remember, you can write a message and display it on your iPhone's screen. The message might say, 'Left my iPhone. Please call me at 0443 551 211.' Your message appears on your iPhone, even if the screen is locked. And, if the map shows your iPhone is nearby — perhaps in your office under a pile of papers — you can tell Find My iPhone to play a sound that overrides the volume or silent setting.

If you left your iPhone in a public place, you may want to protect its contents. You can remotely set a four-digit passcode lock to prevent people from using your iPhone, accessing your personal information, or tampering with your settings.

You can initiate a remote wipe (erase all contents) to restore your iPhone to its factory settings. If you eventually find your iPhone, you can connect it to your computer and use iTunes to restore the data from your most recent backup.

If you have lost your iPhone and do not have access to a computer, you can download the Find My iPhone app to a friend's iPhone, iPad, or iPod touch and sign in to access all the Find My iPhone features.

BEFORE YOU GO ON . . .

1. What are the major drivers of mobile computing?
2. Describe mobile portals and voice portals.
3. Describe wireless financial services.
4. List some of the major intrabusiness wireless applications.

THE NOOK

QUESTIONS

1. Malakai and Abbie's idea for the mobile ordering of drinks is a form of location-based m-commerce. What other advantages (aside from mobile ordering and paying for drinks) can you think of that Malakai and Abbie can tap into?
2. Mobile commerce offers five value-added attributes that break the barriers of geography and time: ubiquity, convenience, instant connectivity, personalisation and localisation of products and services. Which of these do you think is most important for Malakai's idea of the mobile ordering system?

10.4 Pervasive computing

A world in which virtually every object has processing power with wireless or wired connections to a global network is the world of **pervasive computing** (or **ubiquitous computing**). Pervasive computing is invisible 'everywhere computing' that is embedded in the objects around us — the floor, the lights, our cars, the washing machine, our mobile phones, our clothes and so on.

For example, in a *smart home*, your home computer, television, lighting and heating controls, home security system and many appliances can communicate with one another via a home network. You can control these linked systems through various devices, including your pager, mobile phone, television, home computer, PDA and even your car. One of the key elements of a smart home is the *smart appliance*, an internet-ready appliance that can be controlled by a small handheld device or a desktop computer via a

Key fobs are a simple example of how wireless technologies have changed our lives.

home network, either wireline or wireless. Two technologies provide the infrastructure for pervasive computing: radio-frequency identification and wireless sensor networks.

Radio-frequency identification

Radio-frequency identification (RFID) technology allows manufacturers to attach tags with antennas and computer chips on goods and then track their movement through radio signals. There are many uses for RFID tags, as you see in IT's About Business.

IT'S ABOUT BUSINESS

BP uses wireless technologies

BP's 'Track and Trace' technology initiative involves deploying a web of networked RFID tags, mobile phones and GPS devices to monitor key assets around the world. Its goals were to improve safety and compliance. Another goal was to save money by reducing BP's asset loss and theft, employee downtime and material waste.

Track and Trace relies on a wide range of sensing technologies that had to be customised for the project. The technologies had to be safe to use around oil and gas and be able to survive harsh conditions — from Arctic cold to desert heat to Gulf humidity. For example, BP worked with a vendor partner to develop a GPS tracking device for pipeline inspectors, who often work alone in hazardous, remote conditions. The vendor had to shrink its standard device and ensure that it would not emit sparks, making it safe for use around combustible materials. Track and Trace technologies also had to be practical on a massive scale to influence the operations of a company with around 80 000 employees, thousands of facilities around the world and millions of pieces of field equipment.

When the Deepwater Horizon oil rig exploded in 2010, killing 11 people and spewing oil into the Gulf of Mexico for 87 days, BP faced one of the industry's biggest and costliest oil cleanups in history. When the incident occurred, Track and Trace enabled BP to respond quickly in managing the cleanup, primarily through alerting spill responders about what equipment they had to work with and what condition the rig was in. BP deployed RFID-tagged Wave Gliders (self-powered robots that float around collecting data on air and water quality) in the Gulf of Mexico, and tagged skimmers and other key assets across four US Gulf states.

Another example of Track and Trace's usefulness is the role it played when BP had to perform routine refinery maintenance at the firm's Gelsenkirchen (GSK) refinery in Germany. To accomplish this process, BP had to place RFID tags on 100 000 blinds at the refinery. GSK technicians must work section by section, sealing off one area before proceeding to the next. To do that, they use what is called a blind to close off pipe ends at the flange. Blinds must be inserted and removed in a precise sequence. Engineers use Track and Trace to track the blinds with handheld readers. SAP software analyses the data from Track and Trace automatically to determine which flanges should be blinded and when.

In another Track and Trace project, BP outfitted oil trucks in Alaska with cellular equipment that transmits data to BP through the AT&T cellular network or, as a backup, through Iridium's satellites. The system monitors driver activity and sends alerts through email and text about a suspected accident or unsafe activity such as speeding or hard braking. The system monitors about 900 trucks and generates roughly 500 000 messages per week.

Sources: Compiled from T Team (2012), 'BP goes for public relations makeover to get beyond Gulf spill', *Forbes*, 7 February; P McDougall (2011), 'Asset tracking aids huge BP cleanup', *InformationWeek*, 19 September; C Swedberg (2011), 'BP uses RFID sensors to track pipe corrosion', *RFID Journal*, 31 January; www.bp.com.

QUESTIONS

1. How did Track and Trace technologies help BP to effectively manage the catastrophic oil spill in the Gulf of Mexico?
2. What other uses might BP have for wireless sensor technologies?

RFID was developed to replace barcodes. A typical barcode, known as the *Universal Product Code (UPC)*, is made up of 12 digits that are batched in various groups. The first digit identifies the item type, the next 5 digits identify the manufacturer, and the next 5 identify the product. The last digit is a check digit for error detection. Barcodes have worked well, but they have limitations. First, they require a line of sight to the scanning device. This system works well in a store, but it can pose substantial problems in a manufacturing plant or a warehouse or on a shipping/receiving dock. Second, because barcodes are printed on paper, they can be ripped, soiled, or lost. Third, the barcode identifies the manufacturer and product but not the actual item. Two systems are being developed to replace barcodes: *QR* (for quick response) *codes* and RFID systems. Figure 10.6 shows barcodes, QR codes and an RFID tag.

FIGURE 10.6 QR codes, RFID tags and barcodes.

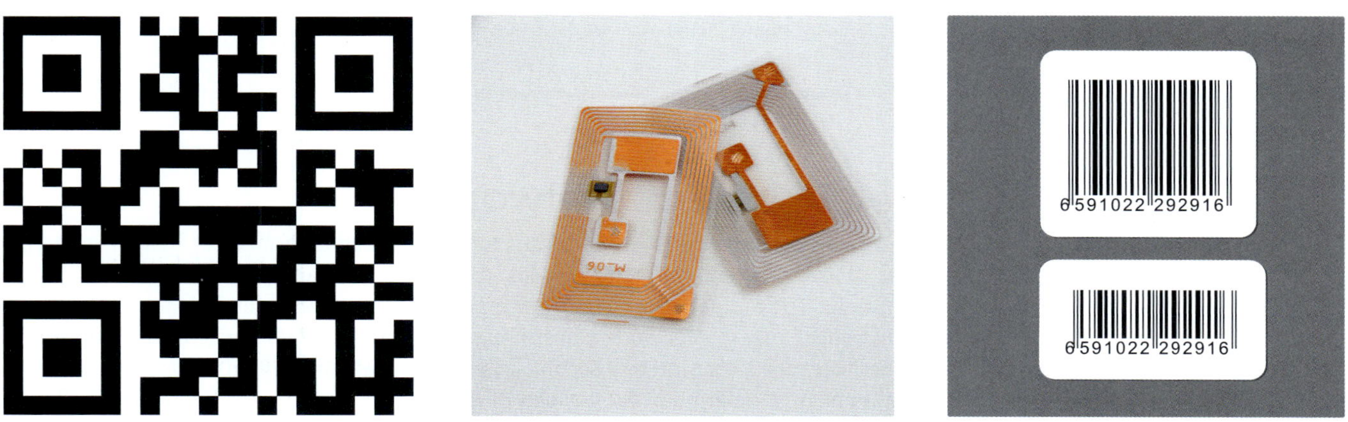

QR code | RFID tag | Barcodes

FIGURE 10.7 Small RFID reader.

A QR code is a two-dimensional code, readable by dedicated QR readers and camera phones. QR codes have several advantages over barcodes.

- QR codes can store much more information than barcodes.
- Data types stored in QR codes include numbers, text, URLs and even Japanese characters.
- The size of QR codes is small because these codes store information horizontally and vertically.
- QR codes are more resistant to damage than barcodes.
- QR codes can be read from any direction or angle, so the possibility of a failure in reading a QR code is reduced.

RFID systems use tags with embedded microchips, which contain data and antennas to transmit radio signals over a short distance to RFID readers. The readers pass the data over a network to a computer for processing. The chip in the RFID tag is programmed with information that uniquely identifies an item. It also contains information about the item such as its location and where and when it was made. Figure 10.7 shows an RFID reader.

There are two basic types of RFID tags: active and passive. *Active RFID tags* use internal batteries for power and they broadcast radio waves to a reader. Because active tags contain batteries, they are more expensive than passive RFID tags and can be read over greater distances. Active tags, therefore, are used for more expensive items. *Passive RFID tags* rely entirely on readers for their power. They are less expensive than active tags and can be read only up to 6 metres. They are generally applied to less-expensive merchandise. Problems with RFID include expense and the comparatively large size of the tags. RFID tags can also speed up grocery shopping, as the following example shows.

EXAMPLE

Woolworths and Coles have made self-service checkouts available to Australian consumers for years, but in the United States Ahold's Stop & Shop supermarkets have taken the self-service experience one step further with their 'Scan It' technology. Using this system, shoppers scan and bag their own groceries as they navigate the aisles, while a screen keeps a running total of their purchases. About a dozen times per shopping trip, the device lets out a 'Ka-ching' as an electronic coupon appears on the screen. When finished selecting items, Scan It shoppers either go to a self-checkout station to upload their bill and pay, or hand the scanner to a cashier. If shoppers scan an unwanted item by accident, they simply select 'Remove' from the menu option, scan the item again, and the item is removed from their cart and their total payment due.

Ahold has found that shoppers who use the Scan It system spend about 10 per cent more in its stores than the average customer. Therefore, the company is now testing ways for customers to download Scan It software directly into their smart phones. They are also exploring ways for customers to use their smart phones to pay.

Sources: Compiled from A Zimmerman (2011), 'Check out the future of shopping', *The Wall Street Journal*, 18 May; www.ahold.com.

Wireless sensor networks

Wireless sensor networks (WSNs) are networks of interconnected, battery-powered, wireless sensors called *motes* (analogous to nodes) that are placed into the physical environment. The motes collect data from many points over an extended space. Each mote contains processing, storage and radio-frequency sensors and antennas. Each mote 'wakes up' or activates for a fraction of a second when it has data to transmit. It then relays those data to its nearest neighbour. So, instead of every mote transmitting its data to a remote computer at a base station, the data are moved mote by mote until they reach a central computer where they can be stored and analysed. An advantage of a wireless sensor network is that if one mote fails, then another one can pick up the data. This process makes

WSNs very efficient and reliable. Also, if the network requires more bandwidth, it is easy to boost performance by placing new motes when and where they are required.

The motes provide information that enables a central computer to integrate reports of the same activity from different angles within the network. Therefore, the network can determine with much greater accuracy information such as the direction in which a person is moving, the weight of a vehicle and the amount of rainfall over a field of crops.

There are many applications of wireless sensors. Nest Labs (**www.nest.com**) produces a 'digital thermostat' that combines sensors and web technology. The thermostat senses not only air temperature, but also the movements of people in a house, their comings and goings, and adjusts room temperatures accordingly to save energy.

Placing sensors in all kind of products makes the products 'smart'. Smart equipment includes sensors in bridges and oil rigs that alert their human minders when they need repairs, before equipment failure occurs. Sensors in jet engines produce data in real time on the operating performance of the engines. Sensors in fruit and vegetable cartons can track location and 'sniff' the produce, warning in advance of spoilage, so shipments can be rerouted or rescheduled.

In Dubuque, Iowa, IBM has started on a long-term project with the local government to use sensors, software and the internet to improve the city's use of water, electricity and transportation. In a pilot project in 2011, digital water meters were installed in 151 homes, with software monitoring water use and patterns, informing residents about ways to consume less and alerting them to likely leaks. The savings in the pilot study translated into decreasing water use by 65 million gallons per year in the entire city.

In 2011, areas such as Tasmania that use only 2 per cent of the Derwent River for water supply were not happy about the introduction of digital water meters, as water had been free due to the low usage.

Lessons learned during IBM's Iowa project have opened opportunities for IBM to successfully work with city councils in Australia. IBM and the Townsville City Council have embarked on a similar project, which saw the two organisations win the 2013 Smart Infrastructure Award from Infrastructure Partnerships Australia. This project enables the capture and analysis of water use (big data) in real time, enabling the communities' water conservation drive as well as 'empowering residents with smart technology to assist with positive behavioural change'.[14]

A very useful application of sensors is to use them in smart electrical meters, thus forming a smart grid. Smart meters monitor the usage of electricity and transmit that data to the utility company. IT's About Business shows the advantages of smart meters in Brazil.

BEFORE YOU GO ON . . .

1. Define *pervasive computing, RFID* and *wireless sensor networks*.
2. Provide two specific business uses of RFID technology.

IT'S ABOUT BUSINESS

Brazil uses smart meters

Reading electricity meters can be a dangerous job in Brazil, as AES Electropaulo (www.aeselectropaulo.com.br) meter readers well know. Robson Dourado, a São Paulo meter reader, says residents of São Paulo's Morro do Indio slum watch him carefully as he makes his rounds, worried that he will see rogue wires siphoning away power illegally.

Electricity theft is rampant across much of Latin America, so much so that statisticians have devised a formula that uses the stolen wattage to measure the size of a country's informal economy. In some parts of Brazil, as much as 20 per cent of electricity is stolen. To combat the problem and avoid violent encounters, utilities are using smart meters. The devices, which cost $150 to $400 each, allow power companies to monitor power usage remotely and in real time. The meters can detect unusually heavy demand, which may signal an illegal hookup. They can also shut off service to households and businesses that do not pay their bills.

The devices remove the human factor from meter reading, so customers can no longer collude with dishonest meter readers to cheat the power company. Smart meters are the perfect solution, says the chief technology officer of a Rio de Janeiro-based utility that has installed more than 150 000 of the devices. He says, 'They save us money, they are easy to install and they require little maintenance'. One Brazilian government official believes the meters may save utility companies as much as $4.7 billion per year. →

Sales of smart meters in South America and Latin America are expected to generate $24 billion in revenue through 2020, two-thirds of it in Brazil. Estimates are that Brazilian utility companies may install as many as 63.5 million smart meters by 2020, while Mexico may install 22.4 million, Argentina 4.9 million and Chile 3.2 million over the same time.

In Rio de Janeiro, utility companies are taking advantage of preparations for the 2014 World Cup soccer championship and the 2016 Olympic Games to deploy the meters. Before August 2011, about 80 per cent of electricity in Tabajara and Morro dos Cabritos, two particularly violent slums, was stolen through illegal connections. After police established a constant presence in the slums in 2011, a utility company installed 50 000 smart meters. Electricity theft has dropped to zero since that time, proving the efficacy of the new technology.

Sources: Compiled from S Nielsen (2012), 'Smart meters help Brazil zap electricity theft', *Bloomberg BusinessWeek*, 8 March; 'Latin America's first smart grid project now complete' (2011), *SmartGridNews*, 22 December; 'Brazil will adopt smart meters' (2011), *Gulfnews.com*, 30 October; J St. John (2011), 'Echelon partners up to break into Brazil's smart meter market', *Greentechmedia*, 13 October; J St. John (2010), 'Brazil: the next hot smart meter market', *GigaOM.com*, 24 November; www.aeselectropaulo.com.br.

QUESTIONS

1. If smart meters are installed in large numbers, then what happens to the meter readers? Do you see problems with this scenario?
2. Besides deterring theft, what other advantages might a smart meter provide to a utility company? To a homeowner? To a business?

Apply the Concept

Background

Pervasive computing exists when the world around us becomes more connected in a digital manner. Refrigerators could text you if the door is not fully shut. The thermostat is connected to the internet so you can turn the temperature down after you leave home and realise you forgot to set it. The alarm system (this is not new) calls the police, fire department and you when there is a problem.

Activity

Visit **www.johnwiley.com.au/highered/rainer/ausnz/studentresources** and click on the link for Apply the Concept for chapter 10. This will take you to a video about 'sixth sense technology' by Pranav Mistry. Dr Mistry's research goes one step further than pervasive computing and attempts to completely blend the physical and digital world. Anything can be a screen, no keyboard or mouse is required, and information is automatically displayed when it recognises something in the physical world and has relevant information to share.

Deliverable

Describe a typical day for a paediatrician when this technology becomes a production scale reality. How will the office visit be handled? Will there be paper charts? Computerised charts? What about diagnosis? What if the computer system could see what the doctor sees and help with a diagnosis? What if the computer system could record the patient encounter so as to provide evidence in a malpractice situation? Would this be beneficial or would this 'pervasive' technology become 'invasive'? Submit your description to your lecturer.

THE NOOK

QUESTIONS

1. How might The Nook utilise telemetry to measure and account for its problem with shrinkage (the problem of a bartender pouring a little more alcohol than the customer paid for)?
2. Is there a mobile portal that could help Malakai and Abbie reach their customers?

10.5 Wireless security

Clearly, wireless networks provide numerous benefits for businesses. However, they also present a huge challenge to management — namely, their inherent lack of security. Wireless is a broadcast medium, and transmissions can be intercepted by anyone who is close enough and has access to the appropriate equipment. There are four major threats to wireless networks: rogue access points, war driving, eavesdropping and radio-frequency jamming.

A *rogue access point* is an unauthorised access point to a wireless network. The rogue could be someone in your organisation who sets up an access point meaning no harm but fails to inform the IT department. In more serious cases, the rogue is an 'evil twin' — someone who wishes to access a wireless network for malicious purposes.

In an evil twin attack, the attacker is in the vicinity with a wi-fi-enabled computer and a separate connection to the internet. Using a hotspotter — a device that detects wireless networks and provides information on them (see **www.canarywireless.com**) — the attacker simulates a wireless access point with the same wireless network name, or SSID, as the one that authorised users expect.

If the signal is strong enough, users will connect to the attacker's system instead of the real access point. The attacker can then serve them a web page asking for them to provide confidential information such as user names, passwords and account numbers. In other cases, the attacker simply captures wireless transmissions. These attacks are more effective with public hotspots (for example, McDonald's and Starbucks) than with corporate networks.

War driving is the act of locating WLANs while driving (or walking) around a city or elsewhere. To war drive or walk, you simply need a wi-fi detector and a wirelessly enabled computer. If a WLAN has a range that extends beyond the building in which it is located, then an unauthorised user might be able to intrude into the network. The intruder can then obtain a free internet connection and possibly gain access to important data and other resources.

Eavesdropping refers to efforts by unauthorised users to access data travelling over wireless networks.

In *radio-frequency (RF) jamming*, a person or a device intentionally or unintentionally interferes with your wireless network transmissions.

As you see, wireless systems can be difficult to secure. Plug IT In 6 discusses a variety of techniques and technologies that you should implement to help you avoid these threats.

BEFORE YOU GO ON . . .

1. Describe the four major threats to the security of wireless networks.
2. Which of these threats is the most dangerous for a business? Which is the most dangerous for an individual? Support your answers.

Apply the Concept

Background

For many of us, our life information lives within our smart phones — contacts, pictures, email, driving directions, entertainment, communication and soon even our wallets (probably the car keys too). However, as we put more and more information on our phones, we are also putting ourselves at risk for a dramatic loss of information.

Activity

Visit **www.johnwiley.com.au/highered/rainer/ausnz/studentresources** and click on the first link for Apply the Concept for chapter 10. This will provide some information about security issues for mobile phones. Then take a look at the article at the second link that illustrates how Google has committed to ensuring the safety of apps that are loaded onto Android devices. Finally, read over the article at the last link about the centralised database that the major phone system carriers have agreed to develop to help crack down on phone theft.

Deliverable

Build a table that shows the advantages and disadvantages of keeping lots of personal information on your phone. Additionally, describe the decision of locking the phone (and the convenience you give up for that) or leaving it unlocked. Consider the information that is available if it is left open. At the same time, consider how long it would take to keep it password protected. Once you develop your list, consider if you personally want to change any habits.

Submit your table to your tutorial group.

THE NOOK

QUESTIONS

1. Wireless security is going to be very important at The Nook. Malakai and Abbie only want customers who have paid the cover fee to be able to access the network. What ideas can you give them to help manage this need?
2. How do hotels and restaurants handle this problem? Would their model work for The Nook?

WHAT'S IN IT FOR ME?

FOR THE ACCOUNTING MAJOR

Wireless applications help accountants to count and audit inventory. They also expedite the flow of information for cost control. Price management, inventory control and other accounting-related activities can be improved with the use of wireless technologies.

FOR THE FINANCE MAJOR

Wireless services can provide banks and other financial institutions with a competitive advantage. For example, wireless electronic payments, including micropayments, are more convenient (anywhere, anytime) than traditional means of payment and they are less expensive. Electronic bill payment from mobile devices is becoming more popular, increasing security and accuracy, expediting cycle time and reducing processing costs.

FOR THE MARKETING MAJOR

Imagine a whole new world of marketing, advertising and selling, with the potential to increase sales dramatically. Such is the promise of mobile computing. Of special interest for marketing are location-based advertising as well as the new opportunities resulting from pervasive computing and RFIDs. Finally, wireless technology also provides new opportunities in sales force automation (SFA), enabling faster and better communications with both customers (CRM) and corporate services.

FOR THE PRODUCTION/OPERATIONS MANAGEMENT MAJOR

Wireless technologies offer many opportunities to support mobile employees of all kinds. Wearable computers enable off-site employees and repair personnel working in the field to service customers faster, better and less expensively. Wireless devices can also increase productivity within factories by enhancing communication and collaboration as well as managerial planning and control. In addition, mobile computing technologies can improve safety by providing quicker warning signs and instant messaging to isolated employees.

FOR THE HUMAN RESOURCES MANAGEMENT MAJOR

Mobile computing can improve HR training and extend it to any place at any time. Payroll notices can be delivered as SMSs. In addition, wireless devices can make it even more convenient for employees to select their own benefits and update their personal data.

FOR THE MIS MAJOR

MIS personnel provide the wireless infrastructure that enables all organisational employees to compute and communicate anytime, anywhere. This convenience provides exciting, creative, new applications for organisations to cut costs and improve the efficiency and effectiveness of operations (for example, to achieve transparency in supply chains). Unfortunately, as you saw earlier, wireless applications are inherently insecure. This lack of security is a serious problem with which MIS personnel must contend.

SUMMARY

1 Identify advantages and disadvantages of each of the four main types of wireless transmission media.

Microwave transmission systems are used for high-volume, long-distance, line-of-sight communication. One advantage is the high volume. A disadvantage is that microwave transmissions are susceptible to environmental interference during severe weather such as heavy rain and snowstorms.

Satellite transmission systems make use of communication satellites, and they receive and transmit data via line-of-sight. One advantage is that the enormous footprint — the area of Earth's surface reached by a satellite's transmission — overcomes the limitations of microwave data-relay stations. Like microwaves, satellite transmissions are susceptible to environmental interference during severe weather.

Radio transmission systems use radio-wave frequencies to send data directly between transmitters and receivers. An advantage is that radio waves travel easily through normal office walls. A disadvantage is that radio transmissions are susceptible to snooping by anyone who has similar equipment that operates on the same frequency.

Infrared light is red light that is not commonly visible to human eyes. Common applications of infrared light are in remote-control units for televisions, VCRs, and DVD and CD players. An advantage of infrared is that it does not penetrate walls and so does not interfere with other devices in adjoining rooms. A disadvantage is that infrared signals can be easily blocked by furniture.

2 Explain how businesses can use technology employed by short-range, medium-range and long-range networks, respectively.

Short-range wireless networks simplify the task of connecting one device to another, eliminating wires and enabling users to move around while they use the devices. In general, short-range wireless networks have a range of 30 metres or less. Short-range wireless networks include Bluetooth, ultra-wideband and near-field communications. A business application of ultra-wideband is the PLUS Real-Time Location System from Time Domain. Using PLUS, an organisation can locate multiple people and assets simultaneously.

Medium-range wireless networks include wireless fidelity (wi-fi) and mesh networks. *Wi-fi* provides fast and easy internet or intranet broadband access from public hotspots located at airports, hotels, internet cafés, universities, conference centres, offices and homes. *Mesh networks* use multiple wi-fi access points to create a wide area network that can be quite large.

Wide-area wireless networks connect users to the internet over geographically dispersed territory. They include mobile telephones and wireless broadband. *Mobile telephones* provide two-way radio communications over a cellular network of base stations with seamless handoffs. *Wireless broadband* (WiMAX) has a wireless access range of up to 50 kilometres and a data-transfer rate of up to 75 Mbps. WiMAX can provide long-distance broadband wireless access to rural areas and remote business locations.

3 Provide a specific example of how each of the five major m-commerce applications can benefit a business.

Location-based services provide information specific to a location. For example, a mobile user can (1) request the nearest business or service, such as an ATM or restaurant; (2) receive alerts, such as a warning of a traffic jam or an accident; and (3) find a friend. With *location-based advertising*, marketers can integrate the current locations and preferences of mobile users. They can then send user-specific advertising messages about nearby shops, malls and restaurants to wireless devices.

Mobile financial applications include banking, wireless payments and micropayments, money transfers, wireless wallets and bill-payment services. The bottom line for mobile financial applications is to make it more convenient for customers to transact business regardless of where they are or what time it is.

Intrabusiness applications consist of m-commerce applications that are used *within* organisations. Companies can use non-voice mobile services to assist in dispatch functions — that is, to assign jobs to mobile employees, along with detailed information about the job.

When it comes to *accessing information*, mobile portals and voice portals are designed to aggregate and deliver content in a form that will work within the limited space available on mobile devices. These portals provide information anywhere and any time to users.

Telemetry is the wireless transmission and receipt of data gathered from remote sensors. Company technicians can use telemetry to identify maintenance problems in equipment. Car manufacturers use telemetry applications for remote vehicle diagnosis and preventive maintenance.

4 Describe technologies that underlie pervasive computing, providing examples of how businesses can utilise each one.

Pervasive computing is invisible and everywhere computing that is embedded in the objects around us. Two technologies provide the infrastructure for pervasive computing: *radio-frequency identification* (*RFID*) and *wireless sensor networks* (*WSNs*).

RFID is the term for technologies that use radio waves to identify automatically the location of individual items equipped with tags that contain embedded microchips. WSNs are networks of interconnected, battery-powered, wireless devices placed in the physical environment to collect data from many points over an extended space.

5 Explain how the four major threats to wireless networks can damage a business.

The four major threats to wireless networks are rogue access points, war driving, eavesdropping and radio-frequency jamming. A *rogue access point* is an unauthorised access point to a wireless network. *War driving* is the act of locating WLANs while driving around a city or elsewhere. *Eavesdropping* refers to efforts by unauthorised users to access data travelling over wireless networks. *Radio-frequency jamming* occurs when a person or a device intentionally or unintentionally interferes with wireless network transmissions.

>>> CHAPTER GLOSSARY

bluetooth Chip technology that enables short-range connection (data and voice) between wireless devices.

global positioning system (GPS) A wireless system that uses satellites to enable users to determine their position anywhere on earth.

hotspot A small geographical perimeter within which a wireless access point provides service to a number of users.

infrared A type of wireless transmission that uses red light not commonly visible to human eyes.

location-based commerce (l-commerce) Mobile commerce transactions targeted to individuals in specific locations, at specific times.

mesh networks Networks composed of multiple Wi-Fi access points that create a wide area network that can be quite large.

microwave transmission A wireless system that uses microwaves for high-volume, long-distance, point-to-point communication.

mobile commerce (or m-commerce) Electronic commerce transactions that are conducted with a mobile device.

mobile computing A real-time connection between a mobile device and other computing environments, such as the internet or an intranet.

mobile portal A portal that aggregates and provides content and services for mobile users.

mobile telephones (mobile phones) Phones that provide two-way radio communications over a cellular network of base stations with seamless handoffs.

mobile wallet (m-wallet) A technology that allows users to make purchases with a single click from their mobile devices.

near-field communications (NFC) The smallest of the short-range wireless networks that is designed to be embedded in mobile devices such as mobile phones and credit cards.

personal area network A computer network used for communication among computer devices close to one person.

pervasive computing (or ubiquitous computing) A computer environment where virtually every object has processing power with wireless or wired connections to a global network.

propagation delay Any delay in communications from signal transmission time through a physical medium.

radio-frequency identification (RFID) technology A wireless technology that allows manufacturers to attach tags with antennas and computer chips on goods and then track their movement through radio signals.

radio transmission Uses radio-wave frequencies to send data directly between transmitters and receivers.

satellite radio (or digital radio) A wireless system that offers uninterrupted, near CD-quality music that is beamed to your radio from satellites.

satellite transmission A wireless transmission system that uses satellites for broadcast communications.

telemetry The wireless transmission and receipt of data gathered from remote sensors.

ubiquitous computing (see pervasive computing)

ultra-wideband (UWB) A high-bandwidth wireless technology with transmission speeds in excess of 100 Mbps that can be used for applications such as streaming multimedia from, say, a personal computer to a television.

voice portal A website with an audio interface.

wireless Telecommunications in which electromagnetic waves carry the signal between communicating devices.

wireless access point An antenna connecting a mobile device to a wired local area network.

wireless fidelity (wi-fi) A set of standards for wireless local area networks based on the IEEE 802.11 standard.

wireless local area network (WLAN) A computer network in a limited geographical area that uses wireless transmission for communication.

wireless sensor networks (WSNs) Networks of inter-connected, battery-powered, wireless sensors placed in the physical environment.

>>> DISCUSSION QUESTIONS

1 Discuss how m-commerce can expand the reach of e-business.

2 Discuss how mobile computing can solve some of the problems of the digital divide.

3 List three to four major advantages of wireless commerce to consumers and explain what benefits they provide to consumers.

4 Discuss the ways in which wi-fi is being used to support mobile computing and m-commerce. Describe the ways in which wi-fi is affecting the use of mobile phones for m-commerce.

5 You can use location-based tools to help you find your car or the closest petrol station. However, some people see location-based tools as an invasion of privacy. Discuss the pros and cons of location-based tools.

6 Discuss the benefits of telemetry in health care for the elderly.

7 Discuss how wireless devices can help people with disabilities.

8 Some experts say that wi-fi is winning the battle with 3G mobile service. Others disagree. Discuss both sides of the argument and support each one.

9 Which of the applications of pervasive computing do you think are likely to gain the greatest market acceptance over the next few years? Why?

>>> PROBLEM-SOLVING ACTIVITIES

1 Examine how new data-capture devices such as RFID tags help organisations accurately identify and segment their customers for activities such as targeted marketing. Browse the web and develop five potential new applications not listed in this chapter for RFID technology. What issues would arise if a

country's laws mandated that such devices be embedded in everyone's body as a national identification system?

2 Investigate commercial uses of GPS. Start with www.neigps.com. Can some of the consumer-oriented products be used in industry? Prepare a report on your findings.

3 Access www.bluetooth.com. Examine the types of products being enhanced with Bluetooth technology. Present two of these products to the class and explain how they are enhanced by Bluetooth technology.

4 Explore www.nokia.com. Prepare a summary of the types of mobile services and applications Nokia currently supports and plans to support in the future.

5 Enter www.ibm.com. Search for 'wireless e-business'. Research the resulting stories to determine the types of wireless capabilities and applications IBM's software and hardware support. Describe some of the ways these applications have helped specific businesses and industries.

6 Research the status of 3G and 4G cellular service by visiting the links available via www.johnwiley.com.au/highered/rainer/ausnz/studentresources. Prepare a report on the status of 3G and 4G based on your findings.

7 Enter Pitney-Bowes Business Insight (www.pbinsight.com). Click on 'MapInfo Professional', then click on the 'Resources' tab, then on the 'Demos' tab. Look for the location-based services demos. Try all the demos. Summarise your findings.

8 Enter www.packetvideo.com. Examine the demos and products and list their capabilities.

9 Enter www.onstar.com. What types of *fleet* services does OnStar provide? Are these any different from the services OnStar provides to individual car owners? (Play the movie.)

>>> COLLABORATION EXERCISE

Background

Greenway Medical Technologies sells electronic health record (EHR) software. Part of the company's product allows doctors to access patient records from their mobile devices. Many doctors love the flexibility of being able to share information quickly and easily with colleagues for a second opinion. They also appreciate the ability to catch up on charts from home, the road, the train and so on.

Activity

Divide your team into the following positions: patient, doctor, nurse, business administrator and IT director. Once your position is determined, do a little research on the idea of EHRs and mobile devices. Try to find and develop a 'platform' for a conversation about the advantages and disadvantages of this product. Once everyone has completed the research, meet as a team and have a conversation about implementing this at your local office. Stay in the role you were assigned and cast your vote for or against the implementation of the EHRs that allows mobile access.

Deliverable

Submit your team's voting results. Be sure to provide some background as to who voted which way and what the rationale was. Even if everyone agreed, explain yourselves so it is clear that you have had a serious discussion. Submit your team's vote and explanation to your instructor.

CLOSING CASE 1 >

A paperless airport

THE PROBLEM

Qantas (www.qantas.com) was running out of room at its large domestic terminal in Sydney, Australia, and needed to develop a new system to reduce frequent backups at its counters. The airline studied customer habits and worked on strategies to eliminate lines. The airline eventually decided to save customers time by eliminating 'pain points' in the airport, such as long check-ins, frustrating bag check and slow boarding lines.

THE IT SOLUTION

To eliminate these pain points, Qantas decided to invest in technology rather than adding floor space. Accordingly, Qantas built a system around radio-frequency ID (RFID) cards. Top-level frequent flyers received free ID cards that they can flash at a kiosk in the ticketing area. In seconds, the system can find the reservation for that day, assign a seat based on personal preferences if one was not preselected and check the passenger in. When everything is ready, a beacon illuminates. Paper itineraries, sticky luggage tags and boarding passes do not enter into the process at all.

With kiosks positioned in four V-shaped patterns, it is almost impossible for travellers to bunch up in long lines. There is still an old-fashioned check-in counter, but most of the baggage drop points are self-service.

To check luggage, passengers go to a baggage drop point, flash the frequent flyer card in front of a reader and drop luggage on a conveyor belt. The bag is then automatically weighed and lasers measure its dimensions to make sure it complies with limits.

Top-level frequent flyers have heavy-duty RFID tags called 'Q BagTags' for their bags that replace paper luggage tags. The technology reads the bag's 'identity' as it moves from luggage belts to carts to planes. This process ensures that luggage gets loaded on the same flight as its owner. Other travellers get a paper tag for their bags with an embedded RFID chip. (Customers who do not have top-level frequent flyer status can buy a Q BagTag for $51 at Qantas.com or from special vending machines in airports.) Finally, frequent flyers flash the ID card at the gate — no boarding pass needed — and agents there hand the traveller a receipt with the seat number printed on it.

THE RESULTS

Qantas's new system has created practically paperless airports, eliminated many long lines and sped up the flying process for passengers from check-in through to seating. Qantas is expanding its new system to its stations in New Zealand, which will be the first to incorporate passport information.

RFID systems are incredibly useful, but they are expensive. Although the cost of RFID-enabled baggage tags has decreased from more than $1 a piece to less than 20 cents, they are still more expensive than the paper tags currently used by airlines. On the other hand, Qantas notes that the new system could save them money by reducing the cost of reimbursing passengers for lost or delayed luggage. From January to October 2011, US airlines mishandled the bags of about 1.6 million passengers on domestic flights. That figure translates into 1 passenger out of every 287 on domestic flights who arrive without the luggage that person checked.

Qantas will not disclose data on the performance of the new system, such as the per cent reduction of mishandled baggage or the reduction in wait times for airport check-in. The company simply states that customer feedback has been 'overwhelmingly positive'. These superior services may well help Qantas gain market share and help make its operations more successful.

Sources: Compiled from S McCartney (2011), 'The trump card at check-in', *The Wall Street Journal*, 29 December; C Swedberg (2011), 'Tagsys ICM airport technics RFID bag tag to airlines', *RFID Journal*, 16 November; www.qantas.com.

QUESTIONS

1 What are the possible disadvantages of Qantas's RFID system?

2 How could Qantas measure the value of the RFID system? Provide specific examples of metrics that the airline could use to justify the cost of the system. Please also provide non-quantifiable measures that Qantas could use to justify its system.

CLOSING CASE **2 >**

The battle for the mobile wallet

THE PROBLEM

Customers today are in more of a hurry than ever before. To satisfy them and keep their business, retailers are looking for strategies to speed up the checkout process and improve the overall customer experience. One strategy is to use customers' smart phones as a replacement for credit and debit cards. Instead of swiping a plastic card at the checkout counter, consumers merely wave their phones a few inches above a payment terminal. This process uses a contact-free technology called near-field communications (NFC).

The technology described in the preceding paragraph, known as the mobile wallet, is already being installed on millions of phones. However, wide adoption of this technology in the United States is being hindered by a major battle among large corporations.

In one camp are the established credit card companies such as MasterCard, Visa and American Express, in alliance with the banks that actually issue the cards to customers. The goal of these businesses is to maintain their traditional position at the centre of any payment system and to continue to collect fees from merchants. However, they are facing intense competition from the other camp, which consists of technology companies such as Google and PayPal whose goal is to become major players in the new payment system. In addition, Apple and the mobile carriers such as Verizon, AT&T and T-Mobile form a third camp that wants to collect fees through its own control of the phones. Adding to the competitive mix are individual companies such as Starbucks that are developing proprietary mobile wallet technologies.

In the middle of this corporate battleground are the retailers, who may yet be the deciding factor in determining who wins the payment battle. Retailers have to install terminals that accept mobile payments in order to take advantage of mobile wallet technology. Additionally, consumer advocates are concerned that a mobile system would bring higher fees, which would ultimately be borne by the customers.

The stakes in this competition are enormous because the small fees generated every time consumers swipe their cards add up to tens of billions of dollars of annual revenue in the United States alone. This revenue, of course, goes straight into the pocket of whoever controls the payment system. Before any company makes money, all of them need to sort out what role each one will play and who will collect the lucrative transaction fees from retailers.

A VARIETY OF SOLUTIONS

Mobile phone carriers

In 2010, three of the four big mobile phone service providers in the United States— AT&T, T-Mobile and Verizon, but not Sprint — along with Discover (www.discovercard.com) and Barclays Bank (www.barclays.co.uk) — formed a joint venture named Isis. Their intention was to create a new payment network that included both credit card companies and card-issuing banks. Isis creates a digital wallet into which customers of card-issuing banks can easily move their accounts. Consumers would interface with Isis through a mobile app, which would give them access to multiple credit and debit accounts. Retailers would participate by offering targeted offers to loyal members through Isis, while product companies and brands could also offer discounts to customers who opt in.

Credit card issuers

All three-card issuers have mobile wallet applications: MasterCard has MasterCard PayPass (which is integrated into Google Wallet), Visa has the payWave mobile wallet and American Express has American Express Serve (with Sprint).

The credit card companies claim that their mobile applications enable consumers to make online payments quickly, without having to enter card numbers and billing addresses over and over. For example, a smart phone game could allow players to buy add-ons, such as new weapons or extra ammunition, by clicking a Visa logo. A caterer might be able to email a bill with a button that allows a client to pay with one click. Payers would authorise the transaction simply by entering a name and password.

Technology companies

In May 2011, Google released a free Android app called the Google Wallet. The wallet securely stores multiple credit cards or a Google prepaid card linked to your credit card. Google also introduced Google Offers, a location-based service that delivers daily, targeted, Groupon-like deals to the Google Wallet. The wallet also allows people to register their store loyalty cards and gift cards in the app.

Interestingly, if future models of the Apple iPhone incorporate NFC, the iPhone may route payments through Apple's iTunes store, which already has 200 million accounts tied to credit cards. Apple iTunes could therefore be transformed into mobile wallets. Both Google Wallet and Apple iTunes, however, would need access to smart phone chips and to merchants' terminals. Apple could solve this problem by manufacturing its own smart phone chips, but Google could not because it makes software only for Android smart phones, not the phones themselves.

PayPal demonstrated its Cloud Wallet in 2011, which does not use near-field communications. The only thing customers need to do to use the wallet is enter a phone number and PIN at the register. PayPal is also integrating check-in capabilities with its mobile application and location-based services, so that smart phone users can identify nearby stores or restaurants.

Individual companies

In January 2011, Starbucks (www.starbucks.com) announced that customers could use a barcode app on their phones to buy coffee in almost 7000 of its stores. This is the first major pay-by-phone initiative in the United States. Customers can download the free Starbucks Card app and hold their phones in front of a scanner at Starbucks cash registers. The money is subtracted from customers' Starbucks accounts, which they can connect to their credit cards or, on iPhones, to PayPal funds. Customers can also use the Starbucks app to check their balances, find nearby stores and earn stars to qualify for free drinks.

THE RESULTS

In December 2011, Verizon blocked its customers from installing Google Wallet on their smart phones. Verizon said that Google Wallet is not currently secure to use on its phones because of technical issues and they are working with Google to iron out those issues.

Despite this public statement, industry analysts say Verizon's move is likely related to its plan to team up with rival carriers AT&T and T-Mobile on the mobile payments venture Isis. Google is working with MasterCard, Citigroup and Sprint Nextel Corporation on its Google Wallet. Meanwhile, Visa is developing another digital wallet.

The battle for the transaction fees from your mobile wallet is ongoing and the results will be several years in arriving. However, the potential for large revenue streams is real, because mobile wallets have clear advantages. For example, which are you more likely to have with you at any given moment — your phone or your wallet? Also, keep in mind that if you lose your phone, it can be located on a map and remotely deactivated. Plus, your phone can be password protected. Your wallet cannot do these things.

Sources: Compiled from K Kelleher (2012), 'PayPal's bid for the digital wallet looks strong', *CNN Money*, 21 March; A Efrati and A Troianovski (2011), 'War over the digital wallet', *The Wall Street Journal*, 7 December; B Reed (2011), 'Verizon cites security issue for nixing Google Wallet', *Network World*,

6 December; D Goldman (2011), 'Verizon blocks Google Wallet,' *CNN Money*, 6 December; C Iozzio (2011), 'The cash killer', *Popular Science*, November; F Graham (2011), 'Will NFC make the mobile wallet work?' *BBC News*, 27 October; K Boehret (2011), 'Google mobile app aims to turn phones into wallets', *The Wall Street Journal*, 21 September; T Duryee (2011), 'PayPal's response to Google's payment plans', *AllThingsD.com*, 15 September; M Hachman (2011), 'Is Google Wallet what mobile payments need to succeed?' *PC Magazine*, 27 May; B Reed (2011), 'Google Wallet: five things you need to know', *Network World*, 26 May; R Kim (2011), 'Isis: respect the carriers; we'll be key to NFC success', *GigaOM*, 6 May; S Marek (2011), 'AT&T, Verizon Wireless and T-Mobile backpedal on Isis joint venture', *FierceWireless*, 4 May; R Sidel and S Raice (2011), 'Pay by phone dialed back', *Wall Street Journal*, 4 May; T Team (2011), 'American Express and Visa squeeze PayPal's crown jewels', *Forbes*, 4 April; A Efrati and R Sidel (2011), 'Google sets role in mobile payment', *Wall Street Journal*, 28 March; T Bernard and C Miller (2011), 'Swiping is the easy part', *New York Times*, 23 March; D Aamoth (2011), 'Pay phone', *Time*, 21 February; D MacMillan (2011), 'Turning smartphones into cash registers', *Bloomberg BusinessWeek*, 14–20 February; K Eaton (2011), 'The race is on to make NFC wireless credit card dreams come true (and win market share)', *Fast Company*, 2 February; M Hamblen (2011), 'NFC: what you need to know', *Computerworld*, 28 January; K Heussner (2011), 'Is your next credit card your cell phone?' *ABC News*, 26 January; S Greengard (2011), 'Mobile payment, please', *Baseline Magazine*, 26 January; E Zemen (2011), 'Will Apple, Google lead mobile payment revolution?' *InformationWeek*, 25 January; B Ellis (2011), 'The end of credit cards is coming', *CNNMoney*, 24 January; C Miller (2011), 'Now at Starbucks: buy a latte by waving your phone', *New York Times*, 18 January; O Kharif (2011), 'In the works: a Google mobile payment service?' *Bloomberg BusinessWeek*, 4 January; R King (2011), 'Wells Fargo to employees: leave wallets home, pay by phone', *Bloomberg BusinessWeek*, 4 January; H Shaughnessy (2010), 'Banking gets mobile and social', *Forbes*, 22 November; J Galante and P Eichenbaum (2010), 'Card companies are wooing programmers', *Bloomberg BusinessWeek*, 22–28 November; P Pachal (2010), 'US carriers create pay-by-phone system, for real this time', *PC Magazine*, 16 November; T Claburn (2010), 'Web 2.0: Google CEO sees android phones replacing credit cards', *InformationWeek*, 16 November; E Zeman (2010), 'Starbucks mobile pay now in NYC', *InformationWeek*, 1 November; www.iconcessionstand.com; www.paypal.com.

QUESTIONS

1 Given that you can lose a mobile phone as easily as a wallet, which do you feel is a more secure way of carrying your personal data? Support your answer.
2 If mobile computing is the next wave of technology, would you ever feel comfortable with handing a waiter or waitress your mobile phone to make a payment at a restaurant the way you currently hand over your credit or debit card? Why or why not?
3 What happens if you lose your NFC-enabled smart phone or it is stolen? How do you protect your personal information?
4 In your opinion, is the mobile wallet a good idea? Why or why not?

SPREADSHEET ACTIVITY **MOBILE SPREADSHEETS**

OBJECTIVE

Spreadsheets are powerful tools, but part of their power comes from the user interface (UI). This activity will use online demonstrations to allow you to experience spreadsheets in a mobile environment.

Chapter connection

This activity puts wireless spreadsheets into the palm of your hand. While the demonstrations used here are based on spreadsheet tools, the implications of mobile user interface will apply in many situations. While mobile tools are very useful, they are also limited. This activity will help you see the difference in interacting with spreadsheets based on the method used to connect to them.

Activity

Many online tools are available today. Microsoft has now released an online version of its Office Suite, though Google is by far the leader in online document creation. A single account with Google gives users access to email, calendars, documents, YouTube and much more. While online document creation, editing and storing offers lots of advantages, there are drawbacks, especially when these tools are used in a mobile environment.

There are three steps to this activity. First, you will create a Microsoft Excel spreadsheet that will track the amount of fuel your company vehicle uses. This sheet needs columns for the date, odometer reading, litres pumped and kilometres per litre. The last column will be calculated based on the difference in the previous and current odometer reading and the number of litres pumped. For this part of the exercise, you need at least five entries to be sure your spreadsheet is working properly.

Once you are satisfied that your spreadsheet is calculating appropriately, create a Google account and log into Google Drive in a web browser. Upload your spreadsheet and add five more entries online.

Finally, log into the mobile version of Google Drive on your mobile phone. If you do not have an internet-enabled phone, search Google for 'Opera Mini Demo,' and use the demo of Opera's mobile internet browser. Whether from your phone or the demo browser, add two more entries to your spreadsheet.

Keep a detailed diary of your experience, noting which method worked best. Be sure to explain the advantages and disadvantages of each method of accessing and editing the spreadsheet. Finally, open your Google spreadsheet in a browser and get the URL to share the document. Add this link to your diary and submit your document to your lecturer along with your original Excel spreadsheet.

Deliverable

You will submit both an Excel spreadsheet and a Word document. The spreadsheet should have at least five entries that calculate fuel used per kilometre. The document will be the diary detailing each of the three methods of accessing this spreadsheet.

DISCUSSION QUESTIONS

1 What do you think needs to change in the mobile and web-based environments for them to match the

traditional Excel experience? Or do they even need to match?

2 Recently it was reported that Google was going to release an operating system that ran in the 'cloud' that would bring us closer to a fully 'cloud-based' computing experience. Based on your diary thoughts, what improvements can you see that will need to be made in networks, computer interaction devices, storage speeds and so on for this to be successful?

DATABASE ACTIVITY **QUERIES I**

OBJECTIVE

In this activity, you will learn how to create a query based on more than one table, with multiple criteria. As you have seen, business questions often involve data from more than one table, so a query that can combine data from multiple tables is more useful than one that cannot.

In the chapter 6 activity, you selected records from a table by filtering. Sometimes selection criteria are too complex for that approach, especially if more than one table is involved. Or, perhaps you would like to set up a database so a user who is not familiar with Access can accomplish the same thing. Queries let you do that.

Chapter connection

You will see how queries can be useful in a mobile e-commerce situation.

Prerequisites

None, although the chapter 6 activity (Filters) will provide useful background.

ACTIVITY

In this activity, which you will find online at www.johnwiley.com.au/highered/rainer/ausnz/studentresources, you will create queries that combine data from more than one table to find information that, in the database, is spread across all of them.

1 Download and open the **Ch 10 DizzyDonuts** database from www.johnwiley.com.au/highered/rainer/ausnz/studentresources. It belongs to a chain of donut shops. Much of the company's business comes from people driving or walking by its stores. The company has a smart phone application that determines customer location from the phone's GPS data, lets a customer order online and pay by credit card, sends a barcode to the phone as a graphic, and then lets the customer pick up the order by holding the barcode up to a reader at the counter or drive-in window.

   The database you will work with here supports that application. It has five tables: stores, customers, products, orders and line items. You can see their relationships in the relationship map of the database. (This database resembles the Ch 09 DaffyDonuts database you may have used, plus a new store table with location information to support this app.)

2 The first query will be used to find out how often a given customer uses this service. We know the customer's name, but not his or her number, so we need to use both CustTbl and OrderTbl in this query. To start, click the Create ribbon tab, then Query Design in the Query section.

   Usage hint: In contrast to Design view for most other Access objects, Design view for queries is easy to use and adds important capabilities. Therefore, we will use it rather than a wizard here.

3 The first thing you see there is a Show Table box, similar to the one you may have used in creating the database relationship map in the chapter 2 activity. You use it to specify which tables you will use in this query. You must include three types of tables:
   - All tables that the query checks to select data to display in response to the query, even if no data from those tables will show up in the reply.
   - All tables that provide data to display in the reply to the query, even if no data from those tables is used in selecting records to display.
   - All tables that sit between any of the others in the database relationship map, because Access needs them to figure out how to connect the others.

   Usage hint: Selecting the wrong tables will cause a query to fail or return erroneous results. If your query has problems, this is one place to check. If the tables are not all connected to each other in the top pane of the query design window, you left one out or (less likely) your database does not have all the necessary table relationships.

   Here, add the Customer and Order tables. You will see a line between them. That means Access does not need any other tables to connect them. Close the Show Table window.

4 Click in the top row of the first column of the query design grid if it is not already selected. Enter Costae or select Costae from the pull-down list under the arrow. When you tab out of that field or click somewhere else, Access will fill in CustTbl as the table name directly underneath it.

   Usage hint: Easier: you can also drag a field name from any table in the upper pane of the design window into the grid. Even easier: double-click a field name in the upper pane and it will appear in the next empty grid column.

   By the way, this grid is sometimes referred to as the *Query by Example* or *QBE* grid because you use it to create an example of what you are looking for. The name is not very appropriate; it began at a time when the grid was a real example of data to be found, but it is still around.

5 In the Criteria row of that column, enter 'Adam' as the customer name. (The quotation marks are optional. If you leave them off, Access will supply them.) This will be the selection criterion for this query.

Usage hint (English usage, not Access): Criteria is the plural form. Use it only when there are two or more. If you only have one, it is a criterion.

6 In the top row of the next three columns, enter Order Date, Order Store and Order Total. Do not enter any selection criteria here. We want to see all of Adam's orders, no matter what date they were on or what store they were at.

7 Click Run, the large red exclamation point near the left of the ribbon, to see the result. It should be correct, but its structure and appearance leave a lot to be desired. If you do the Chapter 11 activity, you will see how to put this result into a better-organised, nicer-looking report.

If you got an empty table — no matching records — the most likely reason is an error in keying in 'Adam' as the selection criterion or entering it in the wrong column. Go back to Design view and check those.

Usage hint: The table-like results of a query are called a *dynaset*, for 'dynamic set'. When data in a table change, the dynaset changes dynamically, but records are not rescreened. If changes affect selection criteria, the affected records will not move in or out of the dynaset, but will show the new data. For example, if you select all items priced under $100, then change a price from $99.99 to $109.99, that item will still be displayed with its new, higher price. To update the selection for the new data, rerun the query. This item, which now costs over $100, will no longer be shown.

8 Return to Design view. Change the customer name to 'Belina'. Run the query again.

9 Close the query, saving it as 'CustOrderQry' when prompted.

10 The next query will find all customers who shopped at a given store. Create a new query in Design view. Enter CustTbl and StoreTbl into the upper pane of the query design window. You will see that they are not connected. The database relationship map shows why: they must be linked via the Order table. Reopen the Show Table box if you closed it (near the middle of the Design ribbon) and add OrderTbl to the query. The tables are now connected.

11 Select fields for this query: store city, customer name, order date and order total.

12 As a selection criterion, enter 'Boston' as the store city.

13 Run the query, showing all the orders for the Boston store.

14 Close the query, saving it as 'StoreOrderQry' when prompted.

15 The third query can be used to find out who orders expensive products. ('Expensive' is a relative concept. Nothing that a donut shop sells would be considered expensive at an art gallery.) As before, open a new query design window. This time you must connect products and customers. To do this, you will need to show additional tables in the query. Enter them in the upper pane from the Show Table list. You should see a total of four tables here. If you arrange them in a line with the Customer table at one end and the Product table at the other, the tables in that line should be connected from one end to the other.

16 In the first column of the query design grid, enter ProdPrice and a criterion of ' > 1.6' (without the quotation marks). Selection criteria can include comparisons, as well as other options. We will get to some of them later here and in future activities.

Usage hint: Criteria involving currency amounts must be entered as numbers. Access stores currency amounts that way. Specifying Currency data type controls how they are displayed, but does not affect the underlying data. Using a currency symbol in a query criterion will result in an error message. If this happens: dismiss the message, remove the dollar sign, remove the quotation marks that Access supplied because it thought you entered a character string and continue.

17 In the next two columns, enter ProdName and CustName. Run the query.

18 Close the query, saving it as 'ExpensiveProdQry' when prompted.

19 Make a copy of ExpensiveProdQry and open it in Design view. Add the Store table to the query. Add StoreCity to the first empty column of the query design grid. Enter a selection criterion of 'Boston' for it, in the same row as the price criterion. Run the query. The result shows customers who ordered expensive (that is, over $1.60) items from the Boston store.

Note: Criteria in the same row of the query grid, but in different columns, are combined via an implied 'And'.

20 Close the query, saving it as 'ExpensiveProdStoreQry' when prompted. (Depending on how you created the copy, you may have had a chance to name it earlier.)

21 Make a copy of ExpensiveProdStoreQry, which you just saved, and open it in Design view. Delete the Boston criterion from the grid cell it is in and re-enter it in the same column, one row down. Run the query. This time, you will see all the customers who ordered expensive products at any store and in addition all the customers who ordered anything at all from the Boston store.

Note: Criteria in different rows of the query grid are combined via an implied 'Or'.

22 Close the query, saving it as 'ExpensiveTestQry' when prompted. (Depending on how you created the copy, you may have had a chance to name it earlier.)

23 Close the database.

DELIVERABLE

Your database, with the preceding five queries.

QUIZ QUESTIONS

1 The relationship between Orders and Products in this database is
   a One-to-one
   b Many-to-one
   c Many-to-many
   d One-to-many
2 When criteria are entered on the same row of different columns in the query design grid:
   a The query will display result rows in which all criteria are true.
   b The query will display result rows in which at least one of the criteria is true.
   c The query will display result rows in which at least two of the criteria are true.
   d Something else.
3 The table pane of the query design grid should show:
   a Only tables whose values are tested by query criteria.
   b All tables in the database.
   c Only tables whose data we want to see in the query results.
   d None of the above answers is correct.
4 True or false: a query must use a minimum of two tables.

DISCUSSION QUESTIONS

1 Consider a three-table database of students, grades and courses, such as your university probably has. Suppose you want to display a student's grades. What would you put in the query design grid? (Make reasonable assumptions about the columns in the three tables.)
2 Suppose you are the director of business planning for Dizzy Donuts. You suspect that order patterns for the morning differ from those in the afternoon. (Access can compare times, though we did not use that here.) What sort of query could you design to help you confirm or deny this suspicion? Draw a sample page of how its results might look. You do not have to use real data from this database.
3 Some database management systems do not treat Currency as a data type when you define a table. Instead, currency amounts are first specified as Number. Currency formatting is available as an option for numeric data, but it is treated as a formatting option like the use of commas to separate groups of three digits. Do you prefer this approach or the Access approach? Why?

11 Information systems within the organisation

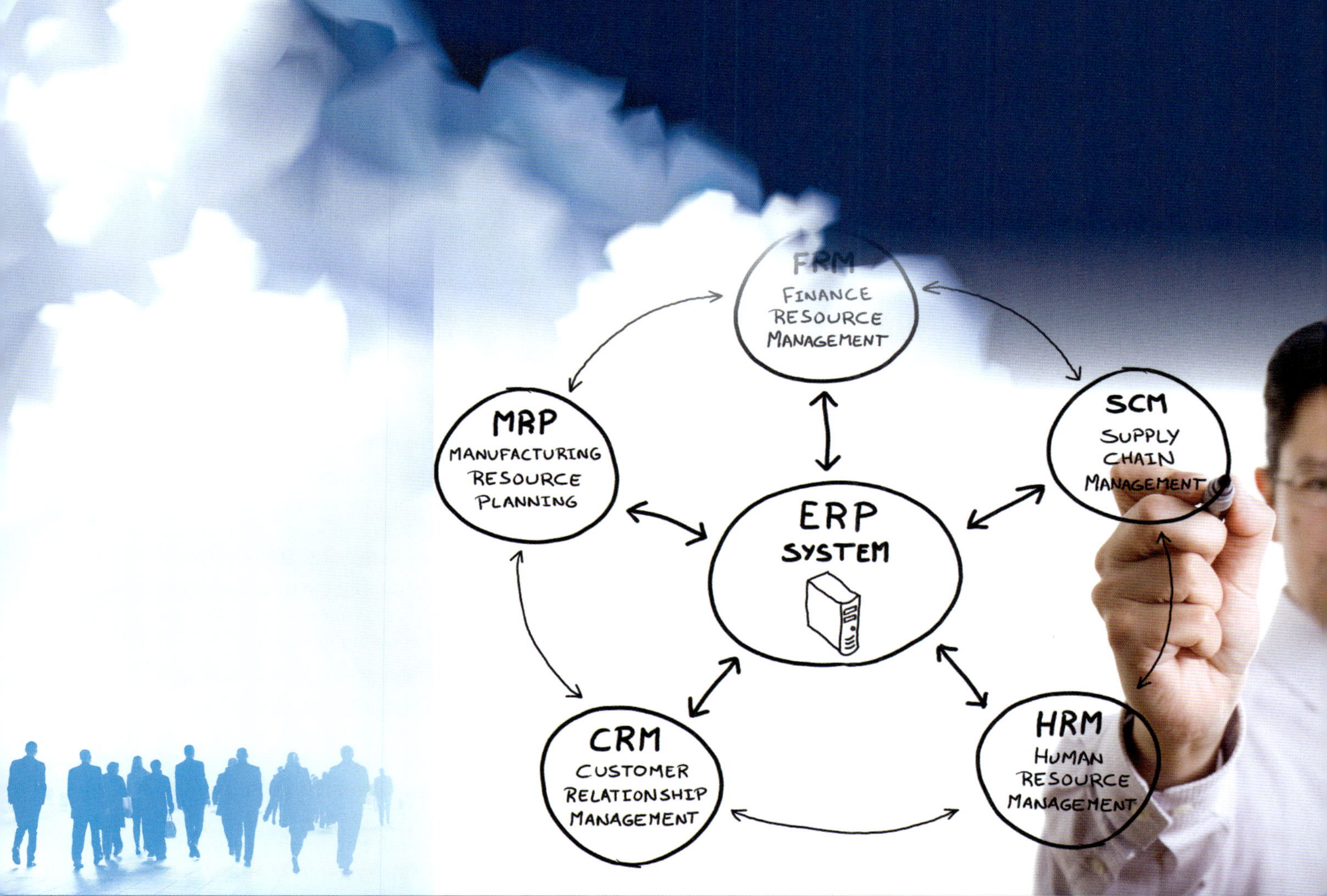

CHAPTER OUTLINE

LEARNING OBJECTIVES

1. Explain the purpose of transaction processing systems.
2. Explain the types of support information systems can provide for each functional area of the organisation.
3. Identify advantages and drawbacks to businesses implementing an enterprise resource planning system.
4. Discuss the three major types of reports generated by the functional area information systems and enterprise resource planning systems, providing examples of each type.

OPENING CASE >

Hog's Breath Cafe and Imagatec

When Hog's Breath Cafe opened in Australia and New Zealand they wanted to expand the business with the support of electronic information systems to replace paper-based systems and processes, which would make the business more efficient and productive. They turned to an Australian business, Imagatec, to provide a point of sale (POS) with a difference. Imagatec's POS is cloud based, called *i*POS.

*i*POS is a cloud database that is modular, allowing Hog's Breath Cafe to choose the base Warehouse system, then add any of the other modules that fit their business strategy. The Warehouse cloud database collects all sales data from their stores, providing hourly snapshots of data sent to a dashboard with full data collection happening in the background. All data for the day is verified against the store on a daily basis. This enables Hog's Breath Cafe management to have confidence that the sales being reported match the store daily balance.

Hog's Breath Cafe purchased the *i*Café module to manage restaurant seating, via a floorplan component that shows either a graphical floor plan or grid with colour coded status of every table. This enables the option for customers to have a single or split bill as ordered items are allocated to a seat at a table. This also reduces 'food auctions' when orders are delivered and billing distribution confusion at the end of the meal. The *i*Café solution also comprises a barcode scanner interface providing the ability to manage products, coupons, staff and loyalty cards in inventory or customer relationship management (CRM) systems as Hog's Breath Cafe expand their clientele service options.

Imagatec's director and software architect, Trevor Turnbull, pointed out that businesses such as Hog's Breath Cafe need to look carefully at their customer service policy and decide whether the systems fit their business objectives. For Hog's Breath Cafe the wireless solution was trialled, however this meant that their waiters were more focused on the technology and scrolling through Hog's Breath's 20 page menu, rather than focusing on the client. Therefore, while the technology demonstrated a good fit for a restaurant environment, it was not a good fit for Hog's Breath Cafe. Today, when customers walk into a Hog's Breath Cafe they are greeted by a friendly staff member interested in high quality customer service. While behind the counter their information systems support this priority, passing information back and forth seamlessly, ensuring an efficient, customer-focused service at the front and back of the counter.

Sources: Compiled from interview with T Turnbull, director, Imagatec Australia; 'Case study — Hog's Breath', www.imagatec.com.au/pages/pos/pos-case-study-hogsbreath.asp.

QUESTIONS

1. What other add-ons could Hog's Breath Cafe include in their organisation's information systems?
2. In what way and which information system would this add-on improve?

Introduction

As the opening case demonstrates, 'systems within organisations' do not have to be owned by the organisation itself. Instead, organisations can deploy very productive information systems that are owned by an external vendor. The important point here is that 'systems within an organisation' are intended to support internal processes, regardless of who actually owns the systems.

There is an astonishing variety of information systems (IS) that you will learn about in this chapter. ISs are everywhere and they affect organisations in countless ways. Who would have thought that an IS could help a large organisation such as a professional sport become more like a science? Information systems also influence small organisations, as illustrated by the chapter opening case.

It is important for you to have a working knowledge of IS systems within your organisation, for a variety of reasons. First, in your job you will be accessing corporate data that are largely supplied by your firm's transaction processing systems and enterprise resource planning systems. Second, you will have a great deal of input into the format and content of the reports that you receive from these systems. Third, you will use the information in these reports to perform your job more productively.

In this chapter, you will see the various systems within the organisation. You begin by considering transaction processing systems, the most fundamental information systems within organisations. You continue with the functional area management information systems and then with the enterprise resource planning systems.

11.1 Transaction processing systems

Millions (sometimes billions) of transactions occur in large organisations every day. A **transaction** is any business event that generates data worthy of being captured and stored in a database. Examples of transactions are a product manufactured, a service sold, a person hired and a payroll cheque generated. In another example, when you are checking out of IGA, Woolworths or Coles, each time the cashier swipes an item across the barcode reader is one transaction.

A **transaction processing system (TPS)** supports the monitoring, collection, storage and processing of data from the organisation's basic business transactions, each of which generates data. The TPS collects data continuously, typically in *real time* — that is, as soon as the data are generated — and it provides the input data for the corporate databases. The TPSs are critical to the success of any enterprise because they support core operations.

In the modern business world, TPSs are inputs to the functional area information systems and business intelligence systems, as well as business operations such as customer

THE NOOK

Each month, Malakai and Abbie sit down to a table of receipts. They know there is a lot of information in there, but they have a terrible time sorting their way through the piles to find it. They know there has to be a better way. This is part of the reason for integrating IT into their remodelled and restructured business. They hope that their new information systems will provide them with more accurate, timely, helpful information so they can go about making decisions.

Specifically, they hope their transaction processing system will capture and collect data on customers' entry and departure times, food and beverage items purchased, bands playing and so on to help them make plans for the future. As you read through this chapter, consider how The Nook could utilise the different information systems presented.

relationship management, knowledge management and e-commerce. TPSs have to handle both high and large variations in volume (for example, during peak times) of data efficiently. In addition, they must avoid errors and downtime, record results accurately and securely, and maintain privacy and security.

Figure 11.1 shows how TPSs manage data.

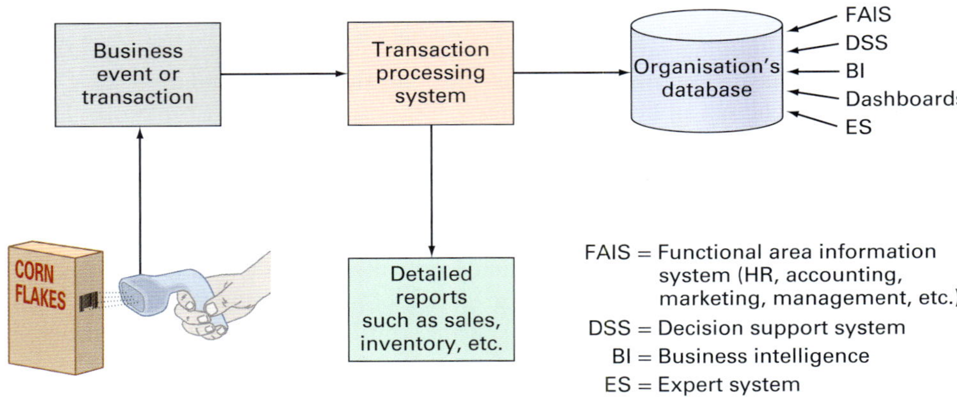

FIGURE 11.1 How transaction processing systems manage data.

Consider these examples of how TPSs manage the complexities of transactional data.

- When more than one person or application program can access the database at the same time, the database has to be protected from errors resulting from overlapping updates. The most common error is for the results of one of the updates to be lost.
- When processing a transaction involves more than one computer, the database and all users must be protected against inconsistencies arising from a failure of any component at any time. For example, if an error occurs at some point in an ATM withdrawal, the customer could receive cash while the bank's computer indicates that he did not. (Conversely, the customer might not receive cash while the bank's computer indicates that he did.)
- It must be possible to reverse a transaction in its entirety if it turns out to have been entered in error. It is also necessary to reverse a transaction when a purchased item is returned.
- It may be important to preserve an audit trail. In fact, for certain transactions an audit trail may be legally required.

These and similar issues explain why organisations spend millions of dollars on expensive mainframe computers. 'New mainframe hardware and software products are ideal for web transactions because they are designed to allow huge numbers of users and applications to rapidly and simultaneously access the same data without interfering with each other.'[1] In today's business environment, firms must have the dependability, reliability and processing capacity of these computers to handle their transaction processing loads.

Regardless of the specific data processed by a TPS, the actual process tends to be standard, whether it occurs in a manufacturing firm, a service firm, or a government organisation. First, data are collected by people or sensors and are entered into the computer via any input device. Generally speaking, organisations try to automate the TPS data entry as much as possible because of the large volume involved, a process called *source data automation.*

Next, the system processes data in one of two basic ways: batch processing and online processing. In **batch processing**, the firm collects data from transactions as they occur, placing them in groups or *batches*. The system then prepares and processes the batches periodically (say, every night).

In **online transaction processing (OLTP)**, business transactions are processed online as soon as they occur. For example, when you pay for an item at a store, the system records the sale by reducing the inventory on hand by one unit, increasing sales figures for the item by one unit and increasing the store's cash position by the amount you paid. The system performs these tasks in real time by means of online technologies.

BEFORE YOU GO ON . . .

1 Define TPS.
2 List the key functions of a TPS.

Apply the Concept

Background

This section has shown that transaction processing systems capture data and then automatically send that data on to different functional area systems. Most transaction processing systems are designed based on existing processes in an organisation. To better understand how this operates, you should consider the flow of data through the information system coming into, through and out of the organisation.

Activity

Visit the MIS iStudy and click on the link provided for Apply the Concept for chapter 11. This module will describe the process of creating data flow diagrams (DFDs).

After you read over the process of accepting and admitting students and are comfortable with the idea of a DFD, create a DFD for a transaction processing system that the Nook might use.

Deliverable

Submit your DFD to your tutorial group with an explanation of each step of the process.

QUESTIONS

1 How might The Nook benefit from a TPS that provides an audit trail?

2 Is The Nook subject to inconsistencies? Where might they come from and how could a TPS help protect the club from this problem?

3 Considering the processing methods of OLTP and batch processing, which seems most likely to be used at The Nook?

11.2 Functional area information systems

Each department or functional area within an organisation has its own collection of application programs, or information systems. Each of these **functional area information systems (FAIS)** supports a particular functional area in the organisation by increasing each area's internal efficiency and effectiveness. FAIS often convey information in a variety of reports, which you will see in section 11.4. Examples are accounting IS, finance IS, production/operations management (POM) IS, marketing IS and human resources IS.

As illustrated in figure 11.1, the FAIS access data from the corporate databases. In the following sections, you will study the support that FAIS provide for these functional areas.

Information systems for accounting and finance

A primary mission of the accounting and finance functional areas is to manage money flows into, within and out of organisations. This mission is very broad because money is involved in all organisational functions. Therefore, accounting and finance information systems are very diverse and comprehensive. In this section, you focus on certain selected activities of the accounting/finance functional area.

Financial planning and budgeting

Appropriate management of financial assets is a major task in financial planning and budgeting. Managers must plan for both acquiring and utilising resources.

- *Financial and economic forecasting.* Knowledge about the availability and cost of money is a key ingredient for successful financial planning. Cash flow projections are particularly important because they inform organisations what funds they need, when they need them and how they will acquire them.

- Funds for operating organisations come from multiple sources, including stockholders' investments, bond sales, bank loans, sales of products and services, and income from investments. Decisions concerning funding for ongoing operations and for capital investment can be supported by decision support systems, business intelligence applications (discussed in chapter 5) and expert systems (discussed in Plug IT In 4). In addition, numerous software packages for conducting economic and financial forecasting are available. Many of these packages can be downloaded from the internet, some of them for free.

- *Budgeting.* An essential part of the accounting/finance function is the annual budget, which allocates the organisation's financial resources among participants and activities. The budget allows management to distribute resources in the way that best supports the organisation's mission and goals.
  - Several software packages are available to support budget preparation and control and to facilitate communication among participants in the budget process. These packages can reduce the time involved in the budget process. Further, they can automatically monitor exceptions for patterns and trends.

Managing financial transactions

Many accounting/finance software packages are integrated with other functional areas. For example, MYOB (**www.myob.com.au**) offers a sales ledger, purchase ledger, cash book, sales order processing, invoicing, stock control, fixed assets register and more.

Companies involved in electronic commerce need to access customers' financial data (e.g. credit line), inventory levels and manufacturing databases (to see available capacity, to place orders). For example, Microsoft Dynamics GP (formerly Great Plains Software) offers 50 modules that meet the most common financial, project, distribution, manufacturing and e-business needs.

Organisations, business processes and business activities operate with, and manage, financial transactions. Consider the following examples.

- *Global stock exchanges.* Financial markets operate in global, 24/7/365, distributed electronic stock exchanges that use the internet both to buy and sell shares and to broadcast real-time share prices.
- *Managing multiple currencies.* Global trade involves financial transactions in different currencies. The conversion ratios of these currencies are constantly in flux. Financial and accounting systems take financial data from different countries and convert the currencies from and to any other currency in seconds. Reports based on these data, which used to take days to generate, now take seconds to produce. These systems manage multiple languages as well.
- *Virtual close.* Companies traditionally closed their books (accounting records) quarterly, usually to meet regulatory requirements such as business activity statements (BAS). Today, many companies want to be able to close their books at any time, on very short notice. Information systems make it possible to close the books quickly in what is called a *virtual close*. This process provides almost real-time information on the organisation's financial health.
- *Expense management automation.* Expense management automation (EMA) refers to systems that automate the data entry and processing of travel and entertainment expenses. EMA systems are web-based applications that enable companies to quickly and consistently collect expense information, enforce company policies and contracts, and reduce unplanned purchases as well as airline and hotel services. They also allow companies to reimburse their employees more quickly because expense approvals are not delayed by poor documentation.

Investment management

Organisations invest large amounts of money in shares, bonds, real estate and other assets. Managing these investments is a complex task, for several reasons. First, there are literally thousands of investment alternatives and they are dispersed throughout the world.

In addition, these investments are subject to complex regulations and tax laws, which vary from one location to another.

Investment decisions require managers to evaluate financial and economic reports provided by diverse institutions, including federal and state agencies, universities, research institutions and financial services firms. In addition, thousands of websites provide financial data, many of them for free.

To monitor, interpret and analyse the huge amounts of online financial data, financial analysts employ two major types of IT tools: (1) internet search engines and (2) business intelligence and decision support software.

Control and auditing

One major reason why organisations go out of business is their inability to forecast and/or secure a sufficient cash flow. Underestimating expenses, overspending, engaging in fraud and mismanaging financial statements can lead to disaster. Consequently, it is essential that organisations effectively control their finances and financial statements. Let us examine some of the most common forms of financial control.

- *Budgetary control.* Once an organisation has finalised its annual budget, it divides those monies into monthly allocations. Managers at various levels monitor departmental expenditures and compare them against the budget and the operational progress of the corporate plans.
- *Auditing.* Auditing has two basic purposes: (1) to monitor how the organisation's monies are being spent and (2) to assess the organisation's financial health. Internal auditing is performed by the organisation's accounting/finance personnel. These employees also prepare for periodic external audits by outside CPA firms.
- *Financial ratio analysis.* Another major accounting/finance function is to monitor the company's financial health by assessing a set of financial ratios. Included here are liquidity ratios (the availability of cash to pay debt), activity ratios (how quickly a firm converts noncash assets to cash assets), debt ratios (measure the firm's ability to repay long-term debt), and profitability ratios (measure the firm's use of its assets and control of its expenses to generate an acceptable rate of return).

Information systems for marketing

It is impossible to overestimate the importance of customers to any organisation. Therefore, any successful organisation must understand its customers' needs and wants and then develop its marketing and advertising strategies around them. Information systems provide numerous types of support to the marketing function. In fact, customer-centric organisations are so important that chapter 12 (Extending the organisation to customers) is devoted to this topic.

Information systems for production/ operations management

The production/operations management (POM) function in an organisation is responsible for the processes that transform inputs into useful outputs as well as for the overall operation of the business. Because of the breadth and variety of POM functions, you see only four here: in-house logistics and materials management, planning production and operation, computer-integrated manufacturing (CIM), and product life cycle management (PLM).

The POM function is also responsible for managing the organisation's supply chain. Because supply chain management is vital to the success of modern organisations, chapter 13 (Extending the organisation along the supply chain) covers this topic in detail.

In-house logistics and materials management

Logistics management deals with ordering, purchasing, inbound logistics (receiving) and outbound logistics (shipping) activities. Related activities include inventory management and quality control.

Inventory management

As the name suggests, inventory management determines how much inventory to maintain. Both excessive inventory and insufficient inventory create problems. Overstocking can be expensive, because of storage costs and the costs of spoilage and obsolescence. However, keeping insufficient inventory is also expensive, because of last-minute orders and lost sales.

Operations personnel make two basic decisions: when to order and how much to order. Inventory models, such as the economic order quantity (EOQ) model, support these decisions. A large number of commercial inventory software packages that automate the application of these models are available.

Inventory management is an important part of logistics management.

Many large companies allow their suppliers to monitor their inventory levels and ship products as they are needed. This strategy, called *vendor-managed inventory* (VMI), eliminates the need for the company to submit purchasing orders.

Quality control

Quality-control systems used by manufacturing units provide information about the quality of incoming material and parts, as well as the quality of in-process semifinished products and finished products. Such systems record the results of all inspections and compare the actual results to established metrics. These systems also generate periodic reports containing information about quality — for example, the percentage of defects and the percentage of necessary rework. Quality control data can be collected by web-based sensors and interpreted in real time, or they can be stored in a database for future analysis.

Planning production and operations

In many firms, POM planning is supported by IT. POM planning has evolved from material requirements planning (MRP), to manufacturing resource planning (MRP II), to enterprise resource planning (ERP). We briefly discuss MRP and MRP II here, and we examine ERP in detail later in this chapter.

Inventory systems that use an EOQ approach are designed for items for which demand is completely independent — for example, the number of identical personal computers a computer manufacturer will sell. In manufacturing operations, however, the demand for some items is interdependent. Consider, for example, a company that makes three types of chairs, all of which use the same screws and bolts. In this case, the demand for screws and bolts depends on the total demand for all three types of chairs and their shipment schedules. The planning process that integrates production, purchasing and inventory management of interdependent items is called *material requirements planning* (MRP).

MRP deals only with production scheduling and inventories. More complex planning also involves allocating related resources, such as money and labour. For these cases, more complex, integrated software, called *manufacturing resource planning* (MRP II), is available. MRP II integrates a firm's production, inventory management, purchasing, financing and labour activities. Thus, MRP II adds functions to a regular MRP system. In fact, MRP II has evolved into enterprise resource planning (ERP).

Computer-integrated manufacturing

Computer-integrated manufacturing (CIM; also called *digital manufacturing*) is an approach that integrates various automated factory systems. CIM has three basic goals: (1) to simplify all manufacturing technologies and techniques, (2) to automate as many of the manufacturing processes as possible, and (3) to integrate and coordinate all aspects of design, manufacturing and related functions via computer systems.

Product life cycle management

Even within a single organisation, designing and developing new products can be expensive and time consuming. When multiple organisations are involved, the process can become very complex. *Product life cycle management* (PLM) is a business strategy that enables manufacturers to share product-related data that support product design and development and supply chain operations. PLM applies web-based collaborative technologies to product development. By integrating formerly disparate functions, such as a manufacturing process and the logistics that support it, PLM enables these functions to collaborate, essentially forming a single team that manages the product from its inception through to its completion (see figure 11.2).

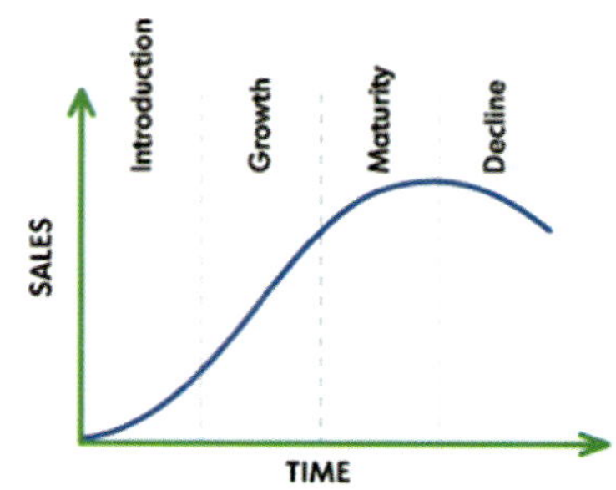

FIGURE 11.2 Product life cycle.

Information systems for human resource management

Initial human resource information system (HRIS) applications dealt primarily with transaction processing systems, such as managing benefits and keeping records of vacation days. As organisational systems have moved to intranets and the web, however, so have HRIS applications.

Many HRIS applications are delivered via an HR portal. For example, numerous organisations use their web portals to advertise job openings and conduct online hiring and training. In this section, you consider how organisations are using IT to perform some key HR functions: recruitment, HR maintenance and development, and HR planning and management.

Recruitment

Recruitment involves finding potential employees, evaluating them and deciding which ones to hire. Some companies are flooded with viable applicants; others have difficulty finding the right people. IT can be helpful in both cases. In addition, IT can assist in related activities such as testing and screening job applicants.

With millions of résumés available online, it is not surprising that companies are trying to find appropriate candidates on the web, usually with the help of specialised search engines. Companies also advertise hundreds of thousands of jobs on the web. Online recruiting can reach more candidates, which may bring in better applicants. In addition, the costs of online recruitment are usually lower than traditional recruiting methods such as advertising in newspapers or in trade journals.

Human resources development

After employees are recruited, they become part of the corporate human resources pool, which means they must be evaluated and developed. The cost for staff development is high, so organisations are constantly looking for solutions to support staff development. IT provides staff development support for these activities that can be completed anytime and anywhere.

Most employees are periodically evaluated by their immediate supervisors. Peers or subordinates may also evaluate other employees. Evaluations are typically digitised and are used to support many decisions, ranging from rewards to transfers to layoffs.

IT also plays an important role in training and retraining. Some of the most innovative developments are taking place in the areas of intelligent computer-aided instruction and the application of multimedia support for instructional activities. For example, companies conduct much of their corporate training over their intranet or via the web.

Human resources planning and management

Managing human resources in large organisations requires extensive planning and detailed strategy. The following three areas are where IT can provide support.

- *Payroll and employees' records.* The HR department is responsible for payroll preparation. This process is typically automated, with pay cheques being printed or money being transferred electronically into employees' bank accounts.
- *Benefits administration.* Employees' work contributions to their organisations are rewarded by wages, bonuses and other benefits. Benefits include health and dental care, pension contributions, wellness centres and child care centres.

BEFORE YOU GO ON . . .

1. What is a functional area information system? List its major characteristics.
2. How do information systems benefit the finance and accounting functional area?
3. Explain how POM personnel use information systems to perform their jobs more effectively and efficiently.
4. What are the most important HRIS applications?

Accounting and finance

Financial planning — and cost of money

Budgeting — allocates financial resources among participants and activities

Capital budgeting — financing of asset acquisitions

Managing financial transactions

Handling multiple currencies

Virtual close — ability to close books at any time on short notice

Investment management — managing organisational investments in shares, bonds, real estate and other investment vehicles

Budgetary control — monitoring expenditures and comparing against budget

Auditing — ensuring the accuracy and condition of financial health of organisation

Payroll

Marketing and sales

Customer relations — know who customers are and treat them like royalty

Customer profiles and preferences

Sales force automation — using software to automate the business tasks of sales, thereby improving the productivity of salespeople

Production/operations and logistics

Inventory management — how much inventory to order, how much inventory to keep and when to order new inventory

Quality control — controlling for defects in incoming material and defects in goods produced

Materials requirements planning — planning process that integrates production, purchasing and inventory management of interdependent items (MRP)

Manufacturing resource planning — planning process that integrates an enterprise's production, inventory management, purchasing, financing and labour activities (MRP II)

Just-in-time systems — principle of production and inventory control in which materials and parts arrive precisely when and where needed for production (JIT)

Computer-integrated manufacturing — manufacturing approach that integrates several computerised systems, such as computer-assisted design (CAD), computer-assisted manufacturing (CAM), MRP and JIT

Product life cycle management — business strategy that enables manufacturers to collaborate on product design and development efforts, using the web

Human resource management

Recruitment — finding employees, testing them and deciding which ones to hire

Performance evaluation — periodic evaluation by superiors

Training

Employee records

Benefits administration — retirement, disability, unemployment, etc.

FIGURE 11.3 Activities supported by functional area information systems.

Managing benefits is a complex task because of the multiple options offered and the tendency of organisations to allow employees to choose and trade off their benefits. In many organisations, employees can access the company portal to self-register for specific benefits.

- *Employee relationship management.* In their efforts to better manage employees, companies are developing *employee relationship management* (ERM) applications. A typical ERM application is a call centre for employees' problems.

Figure 11.3 opposite provides an overview of the activities that the FAIS support. Figure 11.4 diagrams many of the information systems that support these five functional areas.

FIGURE 11.4 Examples of information systems supporting the functional areas.

	ACCOUNTING	FINANCE	HUMAN RESOURCES	PRODUCTION/ OPERATIONS	MARKETING
STRATEGIC	Profitability planning	Financial planning	Employment planning, outsourcing	Product life cycle management	Sales forecasting, advertising planning
TACTICAL	Auditing, budgeting	Investment management	Benefits administration, performance evaluation	Quality control, inventory management	Customer relations, sales force automation
OPERATIONAL	Payroll, accounts payable, accounts receivable	Manage cash, manage financial transactions	Maintain employee records	Order fulfilment, order processing	Set pricing, profile customers

QUESTIONS

1 Do you think The Nook is big enough to need a different system for finance, accounting, HR and marketing? Or, would different views of the club's data suffice for Malakai and Abbie's small business?

2 How might Malakai and Abbie best tackle the difficulty of measuring shrinkage within their club (bartenders pouring more alcohol than the customer paid for)? With an inventory management system or a quality control system?

3 What are some benefits of replacing their old time-card system (they actually still use a card to 'clock in and clock out') with a newer HR system that tracks this data in a computer rather than on a card?

11.3 Enterprise resource planning systems

Historically, the functional area information systems were developed independently of one another, resulting in *information silos*. These silos did not communicate well with one another, and this lack of communication and integration made organisations less efficient. This inefficiency was particularly evident in business processes that involve more than one functional area.

Enterprise resource planning (ERP) systems are designed to correct a lack of communication among the functional area IS. ERP systems resolve this problem by tightly integrating the functional area IS via a common database. For this reason, experts credit ERP systems with greatly increasing organisational productivity. ERP systems adopt a business process view of the overall organisation to integrate the planning, management and use of all of an organisation's resources, employing a common software platform and database.

The major objectives of ERP systems are to tightly integrate the functional areas of the organisation and to enable information to flow seamlessly across them. Tight integration means that changes in one functional area are immediately reflected in all other pertinent functional areas. In essence, ERP systems provide the information necessary to control the business processes of the organisation.

It is important to understand here that ERP systems are an evolution of FAIS. That is, ERP systems have much the same functionality as FAIS and produce the same reports. ERP systems simply integrate the functions of the various FAIS.

Although some companies have developed their own ERP systems, most organisations use commercially available ERP software. The leading ERP software vendor is SAP (**www.sap.com**), which features its SAP R/3 package. Other major vendors include Oracle (**www.oracle.com**) and PeopleSoft (**www.peoplesoft.com**), now an Oracle company. (With more than 700 customers, PeopleSoft is the market leader in higher education.) For up-to-date information on ERP software, visit erp.ittoolbox.com.

Although ERP systems can be difficult to implement because they are large and complicated, many companies have done so successfully. IT'S About Business recounts a successful ERP deployment at Rigaku.

IT'S ABOUT BUSINESS

Burra Foods expansion required revamped ERP solution

Burra Foods is a South Gippsland–based business that produces dairy goods from 240 million litres of milk annually and employs about 100 people. Japan is now its biggest customer as the result of a partnership with Itochu Corporation in 2009, requiring its plant capacity to be increased by almost 100 per cent. However, Burra Foods was facing problems with an Excel-based planning tool that was becoming cumbersome as a result of the company's expansion.

Burra Foods engaged Fenwick Software to review and re-implement the latest version of Microsoft Dynamics NAV solution, with a revamped chart of accounts, for managing costs based on standard product specifications and plant efficiencies. Managing production and quality control were very important, but 'one of the ingredients costs 250 per cent more than another'. However, without an ERP that would help manage production costs and quality, more expensive products would be sent to clients without the ability to increase the charge to the client.

One of the recommendations by Fenwick Software was to re-engineer some of the milk purchasing and lab product clearance processes. A replenishment system that allowed Burra Foods to drive its supply chain more effectively was also recommended. This allowed Burra Foods to achieve optimum resource utilisation while generating essential business information.

The review and implementation enabled the discovery and elimination of a $200 000 loss in production costs. Additionally sales costs were separated from manufacturing, providing a revamped chart of accounts that provided:

- sales revenue
- cost of revenue
- revenue less cost (sales gross margin)
- production costs
- production cost margins, increasing Burra Foods transparency.

The implemented ERP solution has enabled more stringent quality controls and more efficient management of customer deliveries. The amount of time required to produce monthly reports has been halved.

Since implementation of the revamped ERP system, Clive Baldwin said 'the focus has now shifted from adding up the score at the end of the month to having much more of a feel for the business on a daily basis'.

Sources: Compiled from 'Industry specific solutions for this expanding dairy foods business', Fenwick Software, www.fenwicksoftware.com.au/erp-implementation-australia-burra-foods; 'Burra Foods reimplementation of Microsoft Dynamics NAV delivers immediate return on investment', Fenwick Software case study, www.fenwicksoftware.com.au/download/Case%20Study-Burra%20Foods5.pdf.

QUESTIONS

1. Describe why Burra Foods decided to revamp the Microsoft Dynamic NAV ERP system.
2. Describe the benefits that Burra Foods realised after deploying its revamped Microsoft Dynamic NAV ERP system.

Evolution of ERP systems

ERP systems were originally deployed to facilitate business processes associated with manufacturing, such as raw materials management, inventory control, order entry and distribution. However, these early ERP systems did not extend to other functional areas, such as sales and marketing. They also did not include any customer relationship management (CRM) capabilities that would allow organisations to capture customer-specific information. Further, they did not provide web-enabled customer service or order fulfilment.

Over time, ERP systems evolved to include administrative, sales, marketing and human resources processes. Companies now employ an enterprise-wide approach to ERP that utilises the web and connects all facets of the value chain. These systems are called ERP II.

ERP II systems

ERP II systems are interorganisational ERP systems that provide web-enabled links among a company's key business systems — such as inventory and production — and its customers, suppliers, distributors and others. These links integrate internal-facing ERP applications with the external-focused applications of supply chain management and customer relationship management. Figure 11.5 on the following page illustrates the organisation and functions of an ERP II system.

The various functions of ERP II systems are now delivered as e-business suites. The major ERP vendors have developed modular, web-enabled software suites that integrate:

- ERP
- customer relationship management
- supply chain management
- procurement
- decision support
- enterprise portals
- other business applications and functions.

Examples are Oracle's e-Business Suite and SAP's mySAP. The goal of these systems is to enable companies to operate most of their business processes using a single web-enabled system of integrated software rather than a variety of separate e-business applications.

ERP II systems include a variety of modules that are divided into core ERP modules — financial management, operations management and human resource management — and extended ERP modules — customer relationship management, supply chain management, business intelligence and e-business. If a system does not have the core ERP modules, then it cannot be called an ERP system. The extended ERP modules, in contrast, are optional. Figure 11.6 (overleaf) describes each of these modules.

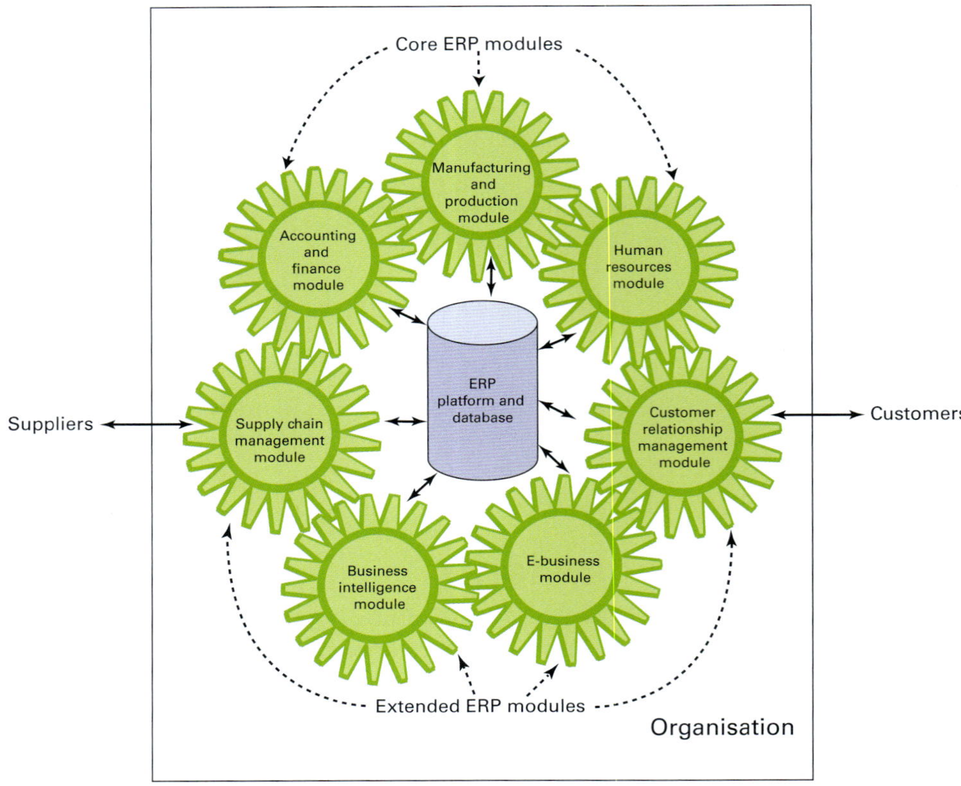

FIGURE 11.5 ERP II system.

Core ERP modules

Financial management. These modules support accounting, financial reporting, performance management and corporate governance. They manage accounting data and financial processes such as general ledger, accounts payable, accounts receivable, fixed assets, cash management and forecasting, product-cost accounting, cost-centre accounting, asset accounting, tax accounting, credit management, budgeting and asset management.

Operations management. These modules manage the various aspects of production planning and execution such as demand forecasting, procurement, inventory management, materials purchasing, shipping, production planning, production scheduling, materials requirements planning, quality control, distribution, transportation, and plant and equipment maintenance.

Human resource management. These modules support personnel administration (including workforce planning, employee recruitment, assignment tracking, personnel planning and development, and performance management and reviews), time accounting, payroll, compensation, benefits accounting and regulatory requirements.

Extended ERP modules

Customer relationship management. (Discussed in detail in chapter 12.) These modules support all aspects of a customer's relationship with the organisation. They help the organisation to increase customer loyalty and retention, and thus improve its profitability. They also provide an integrated view of customer data and interactions, enabling organisations to be more responsive to customer needs.

Supply chain management. (Discussed in detail in chapter 13.) These modules manage the information flows between and among stages in a supply chain to maximise supply chain efficiency and effectiveness. They help organisations plan, schedule, control and optimise the supply chain from the acquisition of raw materials to the receipt of finished goods by customers.

Business intelligence. (Discussed in detail in chapter 5.) These modules collect information used throughout the organisation, organise it and apply analytical tools to assist managers with decision making.

E-Business. (Discussed in detail in chapter 9.) Customers and suppliers demand access to ERP information including order status, inventory levels and invoice reconciliation. Further, they want this information in a simplified format that can be accessed via the web. As a result, these modules provide two channels of access into ERP system information — one channel for customers (B2C) and one for suppliers and partners (B2B).

FIGURE 11.6 ERP modules.

Benefits and limitations of ERP systems

ERP systems can generate significant business benefits for an organisation. The major benefits fall into the following categories.

- *Organisational flexibility and agility.* As you have seen, ERP systems break down many former departmental and functional silos of business processes, information systems and information resources. In this way, they make organisations more flexible, agile and adaptive. The organisations can therefore react quickly to changing business conditions and capitalise on new business opportunities.
- *Decision support.* ERP systems provide essential information on business performance across functional areas. This information significantly improves managers' ability to make better, more timely decisions.
- *Quality and efficiency.* ERP systems integrate and improve an organisation's business processes, resulting in significant improvements in the quality of customer service, production and distribution.

Despite all of their benefits outlined in the above list, ERP systems have a number of drawbacks. The business processes in ERP software are often predefined by the best practices that the ERP vendor has developed. *Best practices* are the most successful solutions or problem-solving methods for achieving a business objective. As a result, companies may need to change existing business processes to fit the predefined business processes of the software.

For companies with well-established procedures, this requirement can be a huge problem. It is important to note that best practices, by definition, are appropriate for *most* organisations. However, organisations differ. Therefore, a particular 'best practice' might not be the 'best' one for your company.

In addition, ERP systems can be extremely complex, expensive and time-consuming to implement. In fact, the costs and risks of failure in implementing a new ERP system are substantial. Quite a few companies have experienced costly ERP implementation failures. Large losses in revenue, profits and market share have resulted when core business processes and information systems failed or did not work properly. In many cases, orders and shipments were lost, inventory changes were not recorded correctly and unreliable inventory levels caused major stock outs to occur. Organisations such as the Queensland Health Department have sustained losses of up to hundreds of millions of dollars due to a failed ERP implementation.

In almost every ERP implementation failure, the company's business managers and IT professionals underestimated the complexity of the planning, development and training that were required to prepare for a new ERP system that would fundamentally change their business processes and information systems. Other typical causes of unsuccessful ERP projects included:

- failure to involve affected employees in the planning and development phases and in change management processes
- trying to do too much too fast in the conversion process.

Insufficient training in the new work tasks required by the ERP system and the failure to perform proper data conversion and testing for the new system also contributed to unsuccessful implementations. The cases at the end of this chapter highlight many of the difficulties involved in implementing and maintaining ERP systems.

BEFORE YOU GO ON . . .

1. Define ERP and describe its functionalities.
2. What are ERP II systems?
3. Differentiate between core ERP modules and extended ERP modules.
4. List some drawbacks of ERP software.

Enterprise application integration

For some organisations, ERP systems are inappropriate. This is particularly true for nonmanufacturing companies as well as manufacturing companies that find the process of converting from their existing system too difficult, time-consuming, or expensive.

Such companies, however, may still have isolated information systems that need to be connected with one another. To accomplish this task, some of these companies use enterprise application integration. An **enterprise application integration (EAI) system** integrates existing systems by providing layers of software that connect applications together.

These layers of software are called *middleware*. In essence, the EAI system allows existing applications to communicate and share data, thereby enabling organisations to use existing applications while eliminating many of the problems caused by isolated information systems.

Apply the Concept

Background

You have seen in this section that enterprise resource planning (ERP) works towards removing silos of information in an organisation by implementing a single system to support all functions. One example of this is SAP Business One. SAP is an industry-leading ERP solution. This activity will have you consider the impact of ERP for small- to medium-sized businesses.

Activity

Visit the MIS iStudy and click on the link provided for Apply the Concept for chapter 11. This module will explore SAP in action.

As you progress through the module, consider how many departments would have to be contacted to find the information that is presented in just a few short moments. If this organisation operated out of silos, the representative would have to take lots of notes, visit multiple departments and call the customer back at a later time with the answers.

Deliverable

Use Google Docs to create a drawing of the 'old' way OEC Computers would have done business. Imagine what it would have been like without the SAP system. Outline the steps that would need to be taken after the phone call, estimate the time it would have required for each step and then total the time of service. You will see a dramatic difference when information is in silos compared to the ERP.

Submit your outline to your tutorial group.

11.4 Reports

All information systems produce reports: transaction processing systems, functional area information systems, ERP systems, customer relationship management systems, business intelligence systems and so on. We discuss reports here because they are so closely associated with FAIS and ERP systems. However, the important point is that *all* information systems produce reports. These reports generally fall into three categories:

- routine
- ad-hoc (on-demand)
- exception.

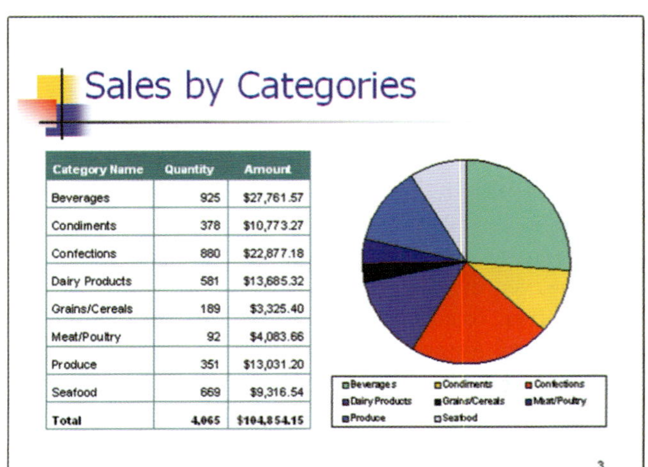

FIGURE 11.7 Monthly sales report.

Routine reports are produced at scheduled intervals. They range from hourly quality control reports to daily reports on absenteeism rates. Although routine reports, such as monthly sales reports (see figure 11.7), are extremely valuable to an organisation, managers frequently need special information that is not included in these reports. Other times they need the information but at different times ('I need the report today, for the last three days, not for one week').

Such out-of-the routine reports are called **ad-hoc (on-demand) reports**. Ad-hoc reports also can include requests for the following types of information.

- **Drill-down reports** display a greater level of detail. For example, a manager might examine sales by region and decide to 'drill down to more detail' to look at sales by store and then by salesperson.
- **Key-indicator reports** summarise the performance of critical activities. For example, a chief financial officer might want to monitor cash flow and cash on hand.
- **Comparative reports** compare, for example, performances of different business units or of a single unit during different times.

Some managers prefer **exception reports**. Exception reports include only information that falls outside certain threshold standards. To implement *management by exception*, management first creates performance standards. The company then sets up systems to monitor performance (via the incoming data about business transactions such as expenditures), compare actual performance to the standards and identify exceptions to the standards. The system alerts managers to the exceptions via exception reports.

Let us use sales as an example. First, management establishes sales quotas. The company then implements an FAIS that collects and analyses all of the sales data. An exception report would identify only those cases where sales fell outside an established threshold — for example, more than 20 per cent short of the quota. It would *not* report expenditures that fell *within* the accepted range of standards. By leaving out all 'acceptable' performances, exception reports save managers' time and help them focus on problem areas.

BEFORE YOU GO ON . . .

1 Compare and contrast the three major types of reports.

2 Compare and contrast the three types of on-demand reports.

Apply the Concept

Background

This section has discussed the different reports you can access from an ERP. These reports truly are the power of an ERP. Getting the right information to the right person at the right time to make the right decision is the purpose for the whole exercise of installing and running an ERP. If you recall from earlier in the text, managers need IT decision support tools because decisions are becoming more complex, there is less time to make decisions, there are more options and the cost of an incorrect decision is increasing.

Activity

Visit the MIS iStudy and click on the link provided for Apply the Concept for chapter 11. This module will introduce you to an effective dashboard tool with the ability for individual users to customise based on the information they need. This type of dashboard pulls together the many reports you have learned about in this chapter.

Imagine that you are in charge of human resources for a company that manufactures switches for Kia automobiles with this type of dashboard available. What information might you want available?

Deliverable

Sketch out a drawing of your dashboard. The main idea is for you to think about what information would be useful for an HR manager to see. What information outside of HR would be helpful for you to see? Anything from production? Anything from sales? What about information within your area?

THE NOOK

QUESTIONS

1. What types of report do you think Malakai and Abbie will benefit most from: routine, ad-hoc, drill-down, key-indicator, comparative, or exception? Why?
2. What would be some key indicators Malakai and Abbie should look for? Cover charges? Drinks? Food sold? What if they sell more food when there are fewer people and more drinks when there are more people? How could they use this data?

WHAT'S IN IT FOR ME?

FOR THE ACCOUNTING MAJOR

Understanding the functions and outputs of TPSs effectively is a major concern of any accountant. It is also necessary to understand the various activities of all functional areas and how they are interconnected. Accounting information systems are a central component in any ERP package. In fact, all large CPA firms actively consult with clients on ERP implementations, using thousands of specially trained accounting majors.

FOR THE FINANCE MAJOR

IT helps financial analysts and managers perform their tasks better. Of particular importance is analysing cash flows and securing the financing required for smooth operations. In addition, financial applications can support such activities as risk analysis, investment management, and global transactions involving different currencies and fiscal regulations.

Finance activities and modelling are key components of ERP systems. Flows of funds (payments), at the core of most supply chains, must be executed efficiently and effectively. Financial arrangements are especially important along global supply chains, where currency conventions and financial regulations must be considered.

FOR THE MARKETING MAJOR

Marketing and sales expenses are usually targets in a cost-reduction program. Also, sales force automation not only improves sales peoples' productivity (and thus reduces costs), but it also improves customer service.

FOR THE PRODUCTION/OPERATIONS MANAGEMENT MAJOR

Managing production tasks, materials handling and inventories in short time intervals, at a low cost and with high quality is critical for competitiveness. These activities can be achieved only if they are properly supported by IT. In addition, IT can greatly enhance interaction with other functional areas, especially sales. Collaboration in design, manufacturing and logistics requires knowledge of how modern information systems can be connected.

FOR THE HUMAN RESOURCES MANAGEMENT MAJOR

Human resources managers can increase their efficiency and effectiveness by using IT for some of their routine functions. Human resources personnel need to understand how information flows between the HR department and the other functional areas. Finally, the integration of functional areas via ERP systems has a major impact on skill requirements and scarcity of employees, which are related to the tasks performed by the HRM department.

FOR THE MIS MAJOR

The MIS function is responsible for the most fundamental information systems in organisations: the transaction processing systems. The TPSs provide the data for the databases. In turn, all other information systems use these data. MIS personnel develop applications that support all levels of the organisation (from clerical to executive) and all functional areas. The applications also enable the firm to do business with its partners.

SUMMARY

1 Explain the purpose of transaction processing systems.

TPSs monitor, store, collect and process data generated from all business transactions. These data provide the inputs into the organisation's database.

2 Explain the types of support information systems can provide for each functional area of the organisation.

The major business functional areas are production/operations management, marketing, accounting/finance and human resources management. Figure 11.3 provides an overview of the many activities in each functional area supported by FAIS.

3 Identify advantages and drawbacks to businesses of implementing an ERP system.

Enterprise resource planning (ERP) systems integrate the planning, management and use of all of the organisation's resources. The major objective of ERP systems is to tightly integrate the functional areas of the organisation. This integration enables information to flow seamlessly across the various functional areas.

The major benefits of ERP systems include the following.

- > Because ERP systems integrate organisational resources, they make organisations more flexible, agile and adaptive. The organisations can therefore react quickly to changing business conditions and capitalise on new business opportunities.
- > ERP systems provide essential information on business performance across functional areas. This information significantly improves managers' ability to make better, more timely decisions.
- > ERP systems integrate organisational resources, resulting in significant improvements in the quality of customer service, production and distribution.

The major drawbacks of ERP systems include the following.

- > The business processes in ERP software are often predefined by the best practices that the ERP vendor has developed. As a result, companies may need to change existing business processes to fit the predefined business processes of the software. For companies with well-established procedures, this requirement can be a huge problem.
- > ERP systems can be extremely complex, expensive and time-consuming to implement. In fact, the costs and risks of failure in implementing a new ERP system are substantial.

4 Discuss the three major types of reports generated by the functional area information systems and enterprise resource planning systems, providing examples of each type.

Routine reports are produced at scheduled intervals. They range from hourly quality control reports to daily reports on absenteeism rates.

Out-of-the routine reports are called *ad-hoc (on-demand) reports*. For example, a chief financial officer might want to monitor cash flow and cash on hand.

Exception reports include only information that falls outside certain threshold standards. An exception report might identify only those cases where sales fell outside an established threshold — for example, more than 20 per cent short of the quota.

>>> CHAPTER GLOSSARY

ad-hoc (on-demand) reports Non-routine reports that often contain special information that is not included in routine reports.

batch processing Transaction processing system (TPS) that processes data in batches at fixed periodic intervals.

comparative reports Reports that compare performances of different business units or times.

computer-integrated manufacturing (CIM) An information system that integrates various automated factory systems; also called *digital manufacturing*.

drill-down reports Reports that show a greater level of detail than is included in routine reports.

enterprise application integration (EAI) system A system that integrates existing systems by providing layers of software that connect applications together.

enterprise resource planning (ERP) systems Information systems that take a business process view of the overall organisation to integrate the planning, management and use of all of an organisation's resources, employing a common software platform and database.

ERP II systems Interorganisational ERP systems that provide web-enabled links among key business systems (such as inventory and production) of a company and its customers, suppliers, distributors and others.

exception reports Reports that include only information that exceeds certain threshold standards.

functional area information systems (FAIS) Systems that provide information to managers (usually midlevel) in the functional areas, in order to support managerial tasks of planning, organising and controlling operations.

key-indicator reports Reports that summarise the performance of critical activities.

online transaction processing (OLTP) Transaction processing system (TPS) that processes data after transactions occur, frequently in real time.

routine reports Reports produced at scheduled intervals.

transaction Any business event that generates data worth capturing and storing in a database.

transaction processing system (TPS) Information system that supports the monitoring, collection, storage and processing of data from the organisation's basic business transactions, each of which generates data.

>>> DISCUSSION QUESTIONS

1 Why is it logical to organise IT applications by functional areas?
2 Describe the role of a TPS in a service organisation.
3 Describe the relationship between TPS and FAIS.
4 Discuss how IT facilitates the budgeting process.
5 How can the internet support investment decisions?
6 Describe the benefits of integrated accounting software packages.
7 Discuss the role that IT plays in support of auditing.
8 Investigate the role of the web in human resources management.
9 What is the relationship between information silos and enterprise resource planning?

>>> PROBLEM-SOLVING ACTIVITIES

1 Finding a job on the internet is challenging as there are almost too many places to look. Visit the following sites: careerone.com.au, seek.com.au and seek.co.nz. What does each of these sites provide you as a job seeker?
2 Enter www.sas.com and access *revenue optimisation* there. Explain how the software helps in optimising prices.
3 Enter www.eleapsoftware.com and review the product that helps with online training (training systems). What are the most attractive features of this product?
4 Check out Microsoft Dynamics demos at www.johnwiley.com.au/highered/rainer/ausnz/studentresources. View three of the demos in different functional areas of your choice. Prepare a report on each product's capabilities.
5 Examine the capabilities of the following (and similar) financial software packages: Financial Analyser (from Oracle) and CFO Vision (from SAS Institute). Prepare a report comparing the capabilities of the software packages.
6 Surf the net and find free accounting software. (Try CNet's software at www.johnwiley.com.au/highered/rainer/ausnz/studentresources, www.rkom.com, www.tucows.com, www.passtheshareware.com and www.freeware-guide.com.) Download the software and try it. Compare the ease of use and usefulness of each software package.
7 Examine the capabilities of the following financial software packages: TekPortal (from www.tekknowledge.com), Financial Analyser (from www.oracle.com) and Financial Management (from www.sas.com). Prepare a report comparing the capabilities of the software packages.
8 Find Simply Accounting Basic from Sage Software (us.simplyaccounting.com). Why is this product recommended for small businesses?
9 Enter www.halogensoftware.com and www.successfactors.com. Examine their software products and compare them.
10 Enter www.iemployee.com and find the support it provides to human resources management activities. View the demos and prepare a report on the capabilities of the products.

>>> COLLABORATION EXERCISE

Background

Transaction processing systems, functional area systems and enterprise resource planning systems provide much of the basis for decision support within an organisation. All of the data often resides in a few databases or data warehouses and is then accessed by the various systems that provide support for making decisions.

Activity

Divide your team into the following positions based on major as much as possible (if you do not have enough majors to divide, then choose by preference): inventory, sales, production, labour and accounting. Imagine that you are a manufacturing company that sells widgets and that your top salesperson just closed a deal for 10 000 units.

For each of the systems mentioned above (transaction, function and enterprise), describe the information you think your area would need to capture, store, analyse and distribute for this transaction.

Once everyone has completed their list of data needs, meet as a team and have a conversation about how similar or different your needs are. Is there any overlap? How would you use the information to make decisions?

Deliverable

Write up a description of the data that is needed by different areas and how important data capture is for providing the correct data points to the enterprise system. Submit your description to your tutorial group.

CLOSING CASE **1** >

Information systems helping farmers manage emissions

THE PROBLEM

Dairy farmers in New Zealand face rising costs due to emissions that are produced in their land use. The impacts and incurred costs of these emissions are complex, as farmers need to take into consideration pricing, land use, business objectives, volatility of output prices, uncertainty of profit and uncertainty of these projections. Although managing land use can make emissions less volatile as emissions are a product of land use, understanding or modelling the impact of these decisions prior to changing land use can have a positive impact on the reduction of emissions. Consequently, managing land-use change helps the farmer also manage emissions from that land use.

Managing the cost of emissions through land-use change includes external factors such as social networks that influence decision making. Hence, there is a need to understand strategic decision making as a result of farmers' social networks. This is information that has not been collected or modelled in the past; thus the influence of these social networks on decision making is unclear. Therefore, collecting, analysing and disseminating this information through a software model that can demonstrate the impact of emissions of a proposed decision will help farmers in the decision-making process and the impacts of those decisions on emissions into the future.

The solution should provide New Zealand farmers with a multi-agent system (MAS) on the desktop, designed specifically for pastoralists to manage emissions production through land use management decisions that also incorporate information from social networking and business objectives. This system needs to include data collection from a number of areas, including graphic information system (GIS), industry mix (e.g. beef, sheep, dairy), biophysical data (input costs and outputs per hectare produced), other financial data (e.g. labour, overheads, depreciation and other farming expenses), economic data (e.g. income from milk, meat and timber) and social data (e.g. farmer's profile, behaviour characteristics, economic drivers and peer networks).

THE IT SOLUTION

A Desktop MAS was designed to be run for different *time step* of one year. The MAS requires farmers, interacting within the model, to input all decisions completely for the year before the model moves on to the next year. For every *time step*, the model executes pre-, main and post-processing, which calculates the pre-decision making based on the farmer's inputs about the farm's financial position. The main processing executes the farmer's decision making based on the farmer's social network and objectives. Therefore the system includes a section where the farmer can 'review what their peers have done over the last 3 years'. By being able to see a history and the results of other farmer's decisions, farmers modelling their own soil types and objectives can learn from their peers. When information from all farmers has been computed for the year, regional information, such as summaries of emissions across the region, can be calculated.

THE RESULTS

With farmers' information being shared across a whole region this information can inform further opportunities. These include estimating production levels under a range of different price projections. The MAS takes into consideration input and out prices that have been included in the information system, for instance, water, production or other supplements, and products including meat, milk and wood, as well as factoring in emissions and nitrates prices. By allowing the user to set the price paths of each of these parameters via a graphical user interface (GUI), the model outputs a wide range of information that can be viewed as a time series over the course of the simulation.

However, the Desktop MAS was probabilistic in that it was influenced by probabilities. Therefore, running the model many times trends the results towards the average probability of each decision, providing system level results that are an aggregate of individual results. To improve the probability and trending aspects of the system, it was recommended that further historic information about farmer's land-use decisions be included in the system.

The Desktop MAS system was able to model the impact of land use, social network and objectives on emissions, as well as providing a simulation on the results of changes in land use. They found that while changes in land use are relatively slow and economic factors were important to these decisions, non-economic external factors were important in the land-use decision-making process (e.g. social networks).

Source: C Schilling, B Kaye-Blake, E Post and S Rains (2012), 'The importance of farmer behaviour: an application of Desktop MAS, a multi-agent system model for rural New Zealand', Proceedings of the New Zealand Agricultural & Resource Economics Society (NZARES) Conference, Nelson, New Zealand, 30–31 August, ageconsearch.umn.edu/bitstream/136070/2/Schilling%202012%20 complete.pdf.

QUESTIONS

1 What objective do you think would influence a farmer's landuse change decision? Explain why you believe this is an important objective.
2 Do you think the Desktop MAS system would help farmers make more informed decisions? What type of impact would this have on the influence of the farmer's social network?
3 How important is collecting and understanding information shared in social networks, as they impact farmer's land-use decisions relating to emission costs?

CLOSING CASE **2 >**

Hilton embraces collaboration with information technology partners

THE PROBLEM

Hilton Worldwide (www.hilton.com) accommodates guests in more than 193 000 rooms in 540 hotels. Those hotels are located in 78 countries across six continents. Hilton had experienced years of rapid growth, several mergers and other business changes, all of which left them with a complex, fragmented information technology strategy that was completely inadequate to their needs. In addition, Hilton was expanding rapidly around the world and had outgrown its ability to support all of its internal technology services. Hilton executives, hotel managers, owners and customers faced daily problems and inconveniences when trying to accomplish simple tasks, such as accessing wi-fi or checking bookings at other properties in the company's portfolio.

THE IT SOLUTION

To correct these problems, Hilton adopted a new approach to its technology needs by creating the Hilton Worldwide Innovation Collaborative (HWIC). The mission of the HWIC is to deliver exceptional guest experiences while leveraging the skills, quality and scale of its technology partners to differentiate Hilton Worldwide brands from the competition. Partnering with technology firms who have experience in implementing systems development best practices, leveraging extensive research and development efforts, and delivering next-generation technology solutions leaves Hilton free to focus on its core competencies without the inconveniences and challenges of a flawed IT system.

Hilton selected five technology partners based on their global expertise and ability to deliver economies of scale in infrastructure, future development, application development and support services. The Hilton technology partners are Accenture (www.accenture.com), AT&T (www.att.com), IBM (www.ibm.com), Microsoft (www.microsoft.com) and Tata Consultancy Services (TCS; www.tcs.com).

- Accenture provides application development and support services for Hilton's property management systems and multibrand, transactional websites. Accenture also supports Hilton with a global service desk.
- AT&T provides a fully managed suite of wi-fi and internet services for Hilton Worldwide. The company also manages and operates Hilton's StayConnected program, which enables guests to access high-speed internet services in meeting spaces, public areas and their private hotel rooms.
- IBM hosts and manages the technology platforms that support Hilton's 10 brands, including, global email services, web hosting, data centre management and monitoring, and the central guest reservation system.
- Microsoft allowed Hilton to deploy its SharePoint 2010, Office 2010, Office Communications Server and Windows 7. Hilton also uses Microsoft's SQL Server and Visual Studio to power its proprietary property management system.
- TCS powers Hilton's corporate suite of applications, including learning management, quality assurance, business intelligence, financial systems and intranet applications.

THE RESULTS

Hilton has benefitted greatly from its technology partnerships in three key areas: improved project productivity, enhanced data centre efficiency and greater high-speed internet access. Specifically, the company's improved project productivity has allowed the hotel giant to accelerate its innovation and be the first to market with new technologies.

In the area of data centre efficiency, Hilton has a new Leadership in Energy and Environmental Design (LEED) gold-certified data centre. The data centre is an example of Hilton's commitment to sustainability, and includes energy-efficient and redundant power and cooling. These environment-saving technologies also lower the total cost of ownership for technology services. Hilton is using a cloud-computing environment at its data centre to enable greater technology flexibility, maintainability, scalability and overall system security.

Hilton has improved its high-speed internet access as well. The company has maintained best-in-class internet performance, reliability and consistency, while its cost per room is 60 per cent of the industry average. Improvements such as these have helped Hilton to considerably grow its customer base, increase confidence in its brands and lay the foundation for a successful, stable and growing business in the years ahead.

Sources: Compiled from R Webb (2011), 'Hilton IT partners for long stay', *Baseline Magazine*, 10 October; 'TCS, Hilton Worldwide ink agreement for IT services' (2010), Books *The Hindu*, 22 December; S O'Neill (2010), 'Hilton CIO: 4 reasons we're checking in SharePoint and Office 2010', *CIO*, 1 December; B De Lollis (2010), 'AT&T to take over internet services in most Hilton-brand Hotels', *USA Today*, 16 July; A Lorden (2010), 'Hilton's innovation acceleration', *Hospitality Technology*, 10 June; www.hilton.com.

QUESTIONS

1 Describe the reasons that Hilton decided to collaborate with IT partners rather than develop its own information systems in house.

2 What are the problems associated with collaborating with five large strategic IT partners? Provide specific examples to support your answer.

SPREADSHEET ACTIVITY **REGRESSION IN EXCEL**

OBJECTIVE

Microsoft Excel is powerful for more than just keeping up with numbers. With the right add-ins, you can run elaborate statistical analysis. This activity will introduce simple regression within Microsoft Excel.

Chapter connection

Transaction processing systems are just the beginning. They provide data to many systems throughout an organisation. Ultimately, the data they provide are used to plan and forecast for years ahead. This activity ties the spreadsheet tool to the data found in the various systems within the organisation.

ACTIVITY

Imagine that you work for a local restaurant/bar/club (the focus tends to change as it gets later in the evening). You have been asked to help the owners with a serious problem — managing their supply chain.

Forecasting has always been a problem for them. One week they are booming and another week things are dead. Really, they expect as much because most of their clientele are university students. But there are weekends when people should be in town and the establishment is not busy, and weekends when everyone should be gone and the place is packed.

The owners have put together a spreadsheet for you to use to help them understand their demand and how to better match their food and drink supplies to what the demand will be. For restaurant owners, there is nothing worse than telling customers that the kitchen is out of something or throwing away unsold goods that spoiled. They need better forecasting.

Go to www.johnwiley.com.au/highered/rainer/ausnz/studentresources and click on the videos for chapter 11. One describes an 'Add-In' you may have to install for Excel to run a regression and the other is about regression analysis itself. You will use this tool in Excel to help your employers better understand the situation they are in. Ultimately, you will complete your analysis to determine which variables have the most statistically significant impact on their demand. Finally, you will write a short memo to your employers (your professor) explaining your findings in a way they can understand it.

The spreadsheet you will download has lots of 1s and 0s in it. A 1 means an event was 'true'. For example, under 'Jazz' a 1 would mean that jazz was the genre of music playing that night in the club. A 0 would mean that jazz was not playing that night. Most of the variables are considered independent variables. This means that whether or not jazz was playing is not dependent on any other variables. You use these independent factors to help understand the *dependent* variables that you are most concerned about — cover sales, food sales and drink sales.

DELIVERABLE

Your work will include a spreadsheet that includes the regression analysis as well as a Word document that shows the interpretation of that analysis. The Word document will also (based on the interpretation) offer suggestions that will help the employers understand their demand and better schedule their food and drink purchases.

DATABASE ACTIVITY **REPORTS II**

OBJECTIVE

In this activity, you will learn how to create a report that uses a query, rather than tables, as its data source. The chapter 10 activity gave you the tools to create something like your grade report: the ability to combine data from more than one table, then to select the rows of combined data that you want. A real grade report, however, is formatted nicely and probably has summary calculations such as GPA. This activity adds those capabilities to your toolkit.

Chapter connection

Organisational information systems, such as those this chapter discusses, are a primary source of information for management. The methods used in this activity are how the information is organised and presented to them.

Prerequisites

Before starting this activity, you should complete the database activities for chapter 4 (Reports I) and chapter 10 (Queries I) activities.

ACTIVITY

In this activity, which you will find online at www.johnwiley.com.au/highered/rainer/ausnz/studentresources, you will combine the selection and table-joining capabilities of queries with the layout and summary capabilities of reports. This creates a powerful tool for presenting data to businesspeople who need to use it.

1 Download the Ch 11 DizzyDonuts database from www.johnwiley.com.au/highered/rainer/ausnz/studentresources and open it. It is the end product of the chapter 10 activity, with the queries described there. If you did that activity, you can use what you did there as the basis for this one.

2 Open StoreOrderQry. It shows all the orders placed at the Boston store. Go to Design view and add a column to the query for OrderStatus, because we want to ignore discarded orders in our analysis. Enter '<>Discarded' (without the quotation marks; Access will supply them around the character string part) for 'not equal to 'Discarded' in the Criteria section, on the same row as the store name. Run the query.

3 You will see that the result table is shorter and shows no orders with Discarded status. However, we do not need to display this column. Unnecessary content in user reports is clutter: it gets in the way of focusing quickly on the important parts. Go back to Design view and uncheck the Show box in the OrderStatus column. Rerun the query. It still excludes discarded orders, but no longer reminds us on every line. (If we cared about order status, we could leave that column in, but let us assume we do not.) Close the query, saving your changes.

4 Now click the Create ribbon tab and open the Report Wizard. The Tables/Queries menu in the first step includes both the tables and the queries in the database. We will base our new report on StoreOrderQry. Select it from the menu. Move CustName, OrderDate and OrderTotal into the Selected Fields panel. Then click Next.

   Usage hint: If we had left OrderStatus in the query results, we could choose not to move it to Selected Fields here. We would end up with exactly the same report.

5 Organise the report by CustTbl. That will group all the orders of each customer. Click Next twice, because you do not want to add any grouping levels.

6 In the next dialogue box, click Summary Options. Because OrderTotal is the only field that the Report Wizard knows how to summarise, only it will show. (Access can do more, as you may recall from the chapter 6 activity, but the Wizard cannot.) Check the Sum box to total each customer's orders. Select Detail and Summary at the right. Click OK, then Next.

7 Continue to click Next until the wizard finishes. If you are prompted to name your report, call it OrderSummaryRpt.

8 If you carried out all the above steps properly, the report will have the correct content. Its first few lines should look something like the following. Yours may not look exactly like this, depending on the design it uses. If you named it OrderSummaryRpt in the previous step, that name will show in the header instead of CustTbl.

   This appearance leaves a lot to be desired. So, switch to Layout view, and

   a Select the label that starts 'Summary for 'CustName ...' and delete it.

   b Select the sum fields (customer sum and overall sum) and move them to the left, closer to the data they are based on. If your chosen design has the order date and order total at the right, move them over to the left (as in the picture) too.

   c Edit the report heading to be more descriptive.

   d Edit the column headings to have meaningful labels, not database field names.

   e Change the word 'Sum' to 'Customer Total'.

9 Switch to Report view to make sure you are happy with the results. When you are, close the report. If you did not name it earlier, name it OrderSummaryRpt, renaming it in the navigation pane if necessary. (Right-click on its name for the Rename option.)

10 You realise that this report is just for one city. However, nothing about it identifies that city. Its name is only in the query design. To redo the report

to show that go back to step 4, this time moving all the fields into the Selected Fields pane. Organise the report by StoreTbl and click Next.

11 In the next dialogue box, add a grouping level by customer by selecting CustName and clicking >.

12 Continue as before, inserting a sum on OrderTotal, until you click Finish. Name this report 'ImprovedCityRpt' if you are prompted to name it when you create it.

Usage hint: If your report does not show the fields that should be at the right, revisit the Wizard and choose Landscape format.

13 You now have a report grouped by city. However, there is only one city in it, so that is not ideal. We would rather state the city in the header, with the report body much as it was before. This must be done in Design view, as Layout view does not allow moving report elements from one area to another. Change to that view.

14 Edit the report header to read 'Customers in City:' (without the quotation marks).

15 Delete the StoreCity column heading. Select the StoreCity data field. In the Home ribbon tab, click Cut (pair of scissors, near the left) or press control-X. Click in the Report Header section of the report design and click Paste (large icon with a sheet of paper sliding off a clipboard, in the same area) or press control-V. (If you are really good with your mouse or trackpad, you can avoid the cutting and pasting by selecting it and moving it while the mouse pointer is a four-headed arrow.)

16 Click the Format Painter in the Clipboard section of the Home ribbon tab or the Font section of the Format tab. (You may be familiar with it from other parts of Microsoft Office.) Click in the report header to copy its format, then in the StoreCity field you just moved to give it the same format. Move it to the right of the header text.

Usage hint: If you prefer, click in the report header. Note its font, size and colour in the Font section of the ribbon, under either the Home or the Format tab. Then select the StoreCity field and format it the same way. The result will be the same.

17 Format this report as you formatted the previous one. You can do most of the formatting in Layout view if you prefer. Also:

- **a** Drag CustName Header up to remove the space that the store city used to occupy. (This is easiest in Design view.)
- **b** Delete the heading for 'StoreCity' in the page header.
- **c** Move all the remaining column headings and data fields to the left, into the space that the city name used to occupy.
- **d** Delete the total at the city level. With just one city, it duplicates the grand total.

18 Close the report. Name it 'ImprovedCityRpt.'

19 Open StoreOrderQry, change the city to Chicago and close it, saving when prompted.

20 Open ImprovedCityRpt. It should say 'Chicago' in the header and reflect Chicago data.

DELIVERABLE

Your database with the modified query and two reports as described above.

QUIZ QUESTIONS

1 A report can display data from

- **a** more than one table.
- **b** more than one query.
- **c** a combination of tables and queries.
- **d** all of the above.

2 True or false: When a report is based on a query, the query is rerun with new selection criteria and the new query result is saved; opening the report will redisplay the original data.

3 Open any Access report (an existing one or a new one you create to play with — it does not matter) in Layout view. Try several Themes (near the left of the Design ribbon). Which of the following do Themes *not* modify?

- **a** Report fonts
- **b** Report column headings
- **c** Report font sizes
- **d** Report colours

DISCUSSION QUESTIONS

1 You are developing an information system for inventory management, which the book discusses in the 'Inhouse logistics and materials management' section of this chapter. You want to identify all items that are at 1.0 to 1.5 times their reorder point for human review. (If an item is below its reorder point, it has already been reordered, or someone decided not to reorder it.) You decide to do this with a query. Its selection criteria will specify these comparisons. Access will then create a report for the purchasing manager. Draw this report, with suitable data columns, groupings and summaries. Try to put yourself in the purchasing manager's position, asking what information this person needs to make reordering decisions and how that information can best be presented. Make any necessary assumptions about the content of your company's inventory database.

2 Section 4 of this chapter, 'Reports', discusses five types of reports: routine, drill-down, key-indicator, comparative and exception. Give an example of each, not repeating *examples* from that section, and discuss how a query could be used as the basis for it. If it cannot be, explain why.

3 You work in a university radio station. Your funding comes from several sources: the university, paid memberships, selling merchandise such as logo coffee mugs and drink can holders, and donations. Donations and merchandise sales often come from members and members often renew year after year. You have a database that stores this information, as well as results of surveys about favourite musicians and music genres. Many, but not all, of the surveys identify the respondent.

   a Draw an ERD for this database. If you did not study ER diagramming in chapter 3, draw an Access relationship map for it. Show its tables, their data fields (columns) and their relationships.

   b You want to use this information to help the station raise funds by matching its programming to what its supporters want and in other ways. How could you use query-driven reports to do this? Use your imagination. Be creative. Make any necessary assumptions about the content of the station's database.

12 Extending the organisation to customers

CHAPTER OUTLINE

12.1 Defining customer relationship management

12.2 Operational customer relationship management systems

12.3 Analytical customer relationship management systems

12.4 Other types of customer relationship management systems

LEARNING OBJECTIVES

1. Identify the primary functions of both customer relationship management (CRM) and collaborative CRM.
2. Describe how businesses might utilise applications used in each of the two major components of operational CRM systems.
3. Discuss the benefits of analytical CRM to businesses.
4. Explain the advantages and disadvantages of mobile CRM systems, on-demand CRM systems, and open-source CRM systems.

OPENING CASE >

Business consultant CRM in the cloud

Organisations come in all sizes, from micro, 0 to 4 person businesses; small, 0 to 19 person businesses (includes micro businesses for statistical purposes); medium, 20–199 person businesses; and large 200 and above person businesses, which can have an impact on how they manage their relationships with their customers. Managing customers in a micro or small business can mean the difference between a growing, thriving business or having to close your business. Therefore, it is important to maintain good customer relationships.

In the ever-changing technical environment of small business such as hairdressers, cafés and the corner store, the extent of the relationship tends to be built through frequency and recognition, where over time the business owner learns the customer's name, preferred products and services, and may learn their birth or anniversary dates but little else. In order to encourage frequency these same businesses may provide rewards cards or join larger rewards affiliations such as Lyoness that have established rewards systems donating part or all of the rewards to charities. For example, IGA stores offer rewards programs that donate the customer's reward to a charity of the customer's choice, helping the customer to 'feel good' about where their reward goes. Although organisations use these rewards systems, little is done with the information gathered about the customer, or the potential for gathering that information to understand the relationship that the customer has with the business. Approximately 8 per cent of small businesses in Australia could use these types of rewards systems integrated with a customer relationship management system; the other 80 per cent plus businesses are in the service area.

This case study explores a consultant, Heather Smith, who is in the service industry, looking at how she can use innovative technology to manage her customer relationships and expand her business, while maintaining a global presence and reducing costs. Heather's consultancy provides support for organisations using XERO accounting packages, as well as providing guidance to people planning or in the early stages of creating a business. Heather wrote the book *XERO for Dummies*, which also meant she could reach a wider audience as the Xero accounting package became internationally accepted.

Throughout Heather's travels and consultancies there has been demand for further information through conference presentations and books such as *Learn small business startup in 7 days*, which provide opportunities for her to expand her service to business, but removes her and her unique approaches from the relationship with her customers.

In order to maintain her relationship with her customers beyond the initial service, Heather provides her contact information in her publications and through social media including Facebook, Twitter, LinkedIn and her website. However, due to her limited time and the requests of so many clients needing her services, Heather uses a number of technologies, providing remote support over the internet. Due to the sensitivity of her clients' material, Heather provides support through cloud-based remote support software called GoToAssist, which offers 128 bit AES encryption end to end, providing the highest level of security. 'There are numerous free support solutions available on the market offering a similar service, however security of client's financial information is paramount'. GoToAssist enables ad hoc training via screen sharing, where the session is recorded and a copy of the recording is produced and provided to the client so they can refer to it afterwards. Ease-of-use for Heather's clients was important. 'It's super easy — even people who really struggle with computers have been successfully able to activate the secure remote connection on their computer. Once activated we both can control the mouse pointer; I can see exactly what they're seeing, and they are in the comfort of their own environment'. As the client has total control, they can terminate the session just by shutting the browser, so Heather can offer support from 5 to 50 minutes — whatever suits the client. The client is in complete control.

For customer relationship management Heather uses a number of software packages that integrate with her accounting system, ensuring a centralised system with reduced 'silos' of customer information. 'I track what I am doing with clients via the online solution MinuteDock, which has Task tracking capability and feeds into Xero seamlessly. I break down the services I offer across a detailed chart of accounts and set KPIs and benchmarks which are monitored utilising FathomHQ, another tool that integrates with Xero.' However, while Heather loves cloud computing and the opportunities that this technology offers, 'the speed of the internet is a concern'.

Sources: Compiled from interviews and emails with H Smith; ABS (2013), 'Key statistics: Australian small business', Department of Innovation, Industry, Science and Research, www.innovation.gov.au/smallbusiness/keyfacts/Documents/SmallBusinessPublication.pdf; H Smith (2013), 'Why choose Heather Smith?', heathersmithsmallbusiness.com.

QUESTIONS

1 What information can Heather collect from her CRM and how can this be used to improve her relationship with her customers?

2 Heather uses GoToAssist to support her clients remotely and securely. Identify at least two other remote assistance products, indicating the types of businesses each product would suit best and why.

THE NOOK

Malakai and Abbie realise that this generation is much more connected than any before. Facebook, Twitter, MySpace, text messaging, instant messaging and so on have all connected people anywhere, anytime. They also feel that they need to tap into this social market, but they are not sure how.

They know that many of their customers are on Facebook. However, they think that Facebook is more for personal use and do not want their customers to feel invaded by receiving advertisements from them on Facebook. Twitter seems more popular for business promotions, but they wonder how many of their customers are regulars on Twitter.

As you learn about customer relationship management, consider their dilemma. Maintaining customers is about balance. Communicate at the right time, place, and manner, and Malakai and Abbie can win with their customers. However, if they cross a boundary, they may lose the community atmosphere in their club because of a virtual communication.

Introduction

Before the supermarket, the shopping centre and the car, people went to their neighbourhood stores to purchase goods. The owner and employees recognised customers by name and knew their preferences and wants. For their part, customers remained loyal to the store and made repeated purchases. Over time, however, this personal customer relationship became impersonal as people moved from farms to cities, consumers became mobile, and supermarkets and department stores were established to achieve economies of scale through mass marketing efforts. Although prices were lower and products were more uniform in quality, the relationship with customers became nameless and impersonal.

The customer relationship has become even more impersonal with the rapid growth of the internet and the world wide web. In today's hypercompetitive marketplace, customers are increasingly powerful. If they are dissatisfied with a product and/or a service from one organisation, a competitor is often just one mouse click away. Further, as more and more customers shop on the web, an enterprise does not even have the opportunity to make a good first impression *in person*.

Customer relationship management (CRM) returns businesses to personal marketing. That is, rather than market to a mass of people or companies, businesses market to each customer individually. By employing this approach, businesses can use information about each customer — for example, previous purchases, needs and wants — to create offers that customers are more likely to accept. That is, the CRM approach is designed to achieve *customer intimacy*. This CRM approach is enabled by information technology in the form of a variety of CRM systems and applications.

Customer relationship management is not only about the software. Sometimes the problem with managing relationships is simply time and information. Old legacy systems may contain the information, but it may take too long to access it and the information may not be usable across a variety of applications. The result is reduced time to spend with customers. Heather Smith is emphasising a customer-centric approach to her business practices because she knows that sustainable value is found in long-term customer relationships that extend beyond today's business transaction.

However, you may be asking yourself this: Why should I learn about CRM? As you will see in this chapter, customers are supremely important to *all* organisations. Regardless of the particular job you perform, you will have either a direct or an indirect impact on managing your firm's customers. As you read the What's In IT For Me? feature, you will encounter a number of opportunities in which you can make immediate contributions on your first job. Therefore, it is important that you possess a working knowledge of CRM and CRM systems.

12.1 Defining customer relationship management

Customer relationship management (CRM) is an organisational strategy that is customer focused and customer driven. That is, organisations concentrate on satisfying customers by assessing their requirements for products and services and then providing high-quality, responsive service. CRM is not a process or a technology per se; rather, it is a way of thinking and acting in a customer-centric fashion. The focus of organisations today has shifted from conducting business transactions to managing customer relationships. In general, organisations recognise that customers are the core of a successful enterprise and the success of the enterprise depends on effectively managing relationships with them.

CRM builds sustainable long-term customer relationships that create value for the company as well as for the customer. That is, CRM helps companies acquire new customers, retain existing profitable customers and grow the relationships with existing customers. This last CRM function is particularly important because repeat customers are the largest generator of revenue for an enterprise. Also, organisations have long understood that getting a customer back after he or she has switched to a competitor is vastly more expensive than keeping that customer satisfied in the first place.

Figure 12.1 depicts the CRM process. The process begins with marketing efforts, where the organisation solicits prospects from a target population of potential customers. A certain number of prospects will make a purchase, thus becoming customers. Of the organisation's customers, a certain number will become repeat customers. The organisation then segments its repeat customers into low-value and high-value repeat customers. An organisation's overall goal is to maximise the *lifetime value* of a customer, which is that customer's potential revenue stream over a number of years.

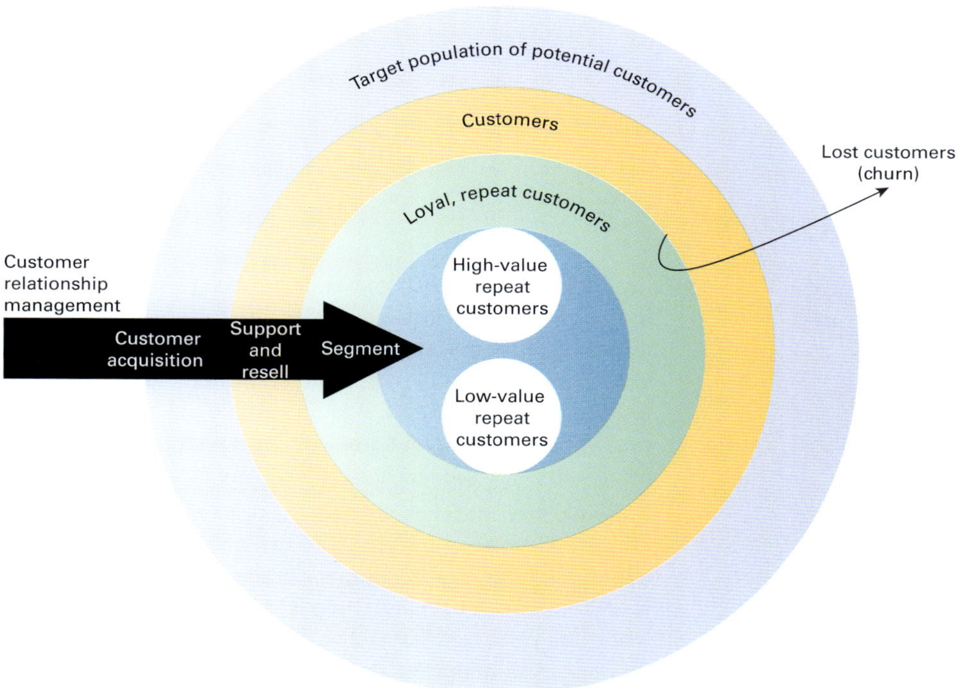

FIGURE 12.1 The customer relationship management process.

The organisation inevitably will lose a certain percentage of customers, a process called *customer churn*. The optimal result of the organisation's CRM efforts is to maximise the number of high-value repeat customers while minimising customer churn.

CRM is a simple idea: treat different customers differently because their needs differ and their value to the company may differ. A successful CRM strategy not only improves customer satisfaction, but it also makes the company's sales and service employees more productive, which in turn generates increased profits. In fact, researchers at the National Quality Research Centre at the University of Michigan found that a 1 per cent increase in customer satisfaction can lead to as much as a 300 per cent increase in a company's market capitalisation; defined as the number of shares of the company's stock outstanding multiplied by the price per share of the stock. Put simply, a minor increase in customer satisfaction can lead to a major increase in a company's overall value.

Up to this point, you have been looking at an organisation's CRM strategy. It is important to distinguish between a CRM *strategy* and CRM *systems*. Basically, CRM systems are information systems designed to support an organisation's CRM strategy. For organisations to pursue excellent relationships with their customers, they need to utilise CRM systems that provide the necessary infrastructure to support those relationships. Because customer service and support are essential to a successful business, organisations must place a great deal of emphasis on both their CRM strategy and their CRM systems.

Broadly speaking, CRM systems can be placed along a continuum, from low-end CRM systems — designed for enterprises with many small customers — to high-end CRM systems — for enterprises with a few large customers. An example of a low-end system is when Amazon uses its CRM system to recommend books to returning customers. An example of a high-end system is when Boeing uses its CRM system to coordinate staff activities in a campaign to sell its new 787 aircraft to Delta Airlines. As you go through the cases and examples in this chapter, consider where on the continuum a particular CRM system would fall.

There are many examples of organisations that have gone beyond what is merely expected in their efforts to be customer-centric. IT's About Business illustrates how 7-Eleven and Slurpee used Facebook to score new customers.

Although CRM varies according to circumstances, all successful CRM policies share two basic elements. First, the company must identify the many types of customer touch points. Second, it needs to consolidate data about each customer. Let us examine these two elements in more detail.

IT'S ABOUT BUSINESS

7-Eleven social media strategy

Anyone for a free Slurpee? Part of a customer relationship and engagement approach of the convenience store chain 7-Eleven is an annual 7-Eleven Day. In 2013 social media marketing group Thinktank Social managed 7-Eleven and Slurpee's 7-Eleven Day, promoting the Slurpee drink on both businesses' Facebook pages and websites. This added 28 000 new likes to the over 500 000 likes for the 7-Eleven Facebook page and 400 000 likes on the Slurpee Facebook page. Each site attracted new potential clients and then directed them to the respective organisations' websites. In order to claim the free Slurpee the customer was required to download a voucher, then go to their nearest 7-Eleven store to collect a free Slurpee. While liking each of the business Facebook pages enables these organisations to provide advertising on the individual's Facebook page, a good marketing strategy, they built their customer database by collecting further customer information from the website. In order to collect the voucher the new customer was required to complete a signup form that needed to be verified via an email, providing the organisations with validated customer information, as well as another avenue for marketing.

Building their databases in this way provides information about their customers they did not already know, such as age, gender, email contact details and location (postcode). Additionally, the customer is prompted to insert the date they expect to collect their free Slurpee. By collecting this data, customers are compelled to collect their free Slurpee on the selected date, enabling both Slurpee and 7-Eleven to gain a real perspective of the success of their campaign.

Sources: Compiled from Thinktank Social, '*7-Eleven & Slurpee*,' www.thinktanksocial.com.au/case-study/7-eleven; 7-Eleven Facebook Page, www.facebook.com/7ElevenAustralia; Slurpee Facebook Page, www.facebook.com/SlurpeeAustralia; Good Call, 7elevenday.com.au; K Yawised, P H Marshall and R Stockdale (2013), '*Social CRM: a review of academic and practitioner literatures and research agendas*', Proceedings of the Malaysian Conference on Information Systems MCIS2013, 13–16 February, Kota Kinbalu, Sabah, Malaysia, pp. 101–7.

QUESTIONS

1. How can 7-Eleven and Slurpee utilise this information to further build their customer relationship?
2. Should all organisations include a social media component in their CRM strategy? Why or why not? Support your answer.

Customer touch points

Organisations must recognise the numerous and diverse interactions that they have with their customers. These various types of interactions are referred to as customer touch points. Traditional **customer touch points** include telephone contact, direct mailings and actual physical interactions with customers during their visits to a store. However, organisational CRM systems must manage many additional customer touch points that occur through the use of popular personal technologies. These touch points include email, websites and communications via smart phones (see figure 12.2).

FIGURE 12.2 Customer touch points.

Data consolidation

Data consolidation is also critical to an organisation's CRM efforts. Customer data must be managed effectively by the organisation's CRM systems. In the past, customer data were located in isolated systems in different functional areas across the business. For example, it was not uncommon to find customer data stored in separate databases in the finance, sales, logistics and marketing departments. Even though all of these data related to the same customer, it was difficult to share them across the various functional areas.

As you saw in chapter 5, modern, interconnected systems built around a data warehouse now make all customer-related data available to every unit of the business. This complete data set on each customer is called a *360-degree view* of that customer. By accessing this 360-degree view, a company can enhance its relationship with its customers and ultimately make more productive and profitable decisions.

Data consolidation and the 360-degree view of the customer enable the organisation's functional areas to readily share information about customers. This information sharing leads to collaborative CRM. **Collaborative CRM systems** provide effective and efficient interactive communication with the customer throughout the entire organisation. That is, collaborative CRM systems integrate communications between the organisation and its customers in all aspects of marketing, sales and customer support. Collaborative CRM systems also enable customers to provide direct feedback to the organisation. As you read in chapter 4, web 2.0 applications such as blogs and Wikis are very important to companies that value customer input into their product and service offerings as well as into new product development.

BEFORE YOU GO ON . . .

1. What is the definition of customer relationship management?
2. Why is CRM so important to any organisation?
3. Define and provide examples of customer touch points.

A CRM system in an organisation contains two major components: operational CRM systems and analytical CRM systems. You learn about these components in the next two sections.

Apply the Concept

Background

This section has introduced the concept of a CRM system and suggested that it is better to focus on relationships than transactions. The idea is that relationships create transactions and therefore if you grow the relationship, you keep the customer!

Activity

Go to www.johnwiley.com.au/highered/rainer/ausnz/studentresources and click on the link to the video 'IBM DB2 data warehousing'.

As you watch the video, consider how it makes you feel as a customer to know that your experience is completely unique. Would you feel special knowing that your version of the REI website is different from anyone else's?

Now, click on the second link provided. This will take you to the REI homepage. If you see a general page, do you feel cheated? Do you feel like you should create an account, tell the company your preferences and then go back to the home page to see your custom content?

Deliverable

Write a short email to Julie Derry, the Director of Online Programs for REI, that explains how you feel about their CRM from your customer viewpoint. Watch the YouTube video again if you need help remembering the REI mission statement and what she hopes to accomplish through the CRM.

Submit your email to your tutorial group.

QUESTIONS

1. The Nook seeks to maintain customers. If CRM is not a technology but a way of thinking, then what role could technology play to support this way of thinking for Malakai and Abbie?
2. Look at figure 12.1, the CRM process. Ethically, when should The Nook begin marketing to students: at the beginning of their 3 to 6 years of university or only after they reach the age of 18?
3. If CRM were implemented at The Nook, would Malakai and Abbie need a low-end or high-end system?
4. What do you think are the most common touch points for The Nook customers? Mobile phones? Facebook? Email? Twitter? Telephone? USPS? Campus flyers?
5. Would Malakai and Abbie have a true 360-degree view of their customers if each order entry area operated on its own database? What would be the problem with having customer data spread over several computers?

12.2 Operational customer relationship management systems

Operational CRM systems support front-office business processes. Front-office processes are those that directly interact with customers — that is, sales, marketing and service. The two major components of operational CRM systems are customer-facing applications and customer-touching applications.

Customer-facing applications

Customer-facing CRM applications are those applications where an organisation's sales, field service and customer interaction centre representatives interact directly with customers. These applications include customer service and support, sales force automation, marketing and campaign management.

Customer service and support

Customer service and support refers to systems that automate service requests, complaints, product returns and requests for information. Today, organisations have implemented **customer interaction centres (CIC)**, where organisational representatives use multiple communication channels such as the web, telephone, fax and face-to-face interactions to support the communication preferences of customers.

One of the most well-known customer interaction centres is the *call centre*. A call centre is a centralised office used for the purpose of receiving and transmitting a large volume of requests by telephone. Call centres enable companies to respond to a large variety of questions, including product support and complaints.

Organisations use the CIC to create a call list for the sales team, whose members contact sales prospects. This type of interaction is called *outbound telesales*. Customers can communicate directly with the CIC to initiate a sales order, inquire about products and services before placing an order and obtain information about a transaction that they have already made. These interactions are referred to as *inbound teleservice*.

The CIC also provides the information help desk. The help desk assists customers with their questions concerning products or services and it processes customer complaints. Complaints generate follow-up activities such as quality-control checks, delivery of replacement parts or products, service calls, generation of credit memos and product returns.

Information technologies are extending the functionality of the traditional CIC to include email and web interaction. For example, Epicor (**www.epicor.com**) provides software solutions that combine web channels, such as automated email reply and web knowledge bases. The information the software provides is available to CIC representatives and field service personnel. Another technology, live chat, allows customers to connect to a company representative and conduct an instant messaging session. The advantage of live chat over a telephone conversation is the ability to show documents and photos (see **www.livechatinc.com** and **www.websitealive.com**). Some companies conduct the chat with a computer rather than a real person using natural language processing.

Social media are now providing methods that customers can use to get faster, better customer service. IT's About Business offers the example of Telstra's customer service and complaints response, integrating traditional and web 2.0 platforms to resolve customer complaints. Additionally, Telstra provides a proactive approach to social media by identifying and keeping their customers informed about issues as they become known.

IT'S ABOUT BUSINESS

Tweet for immediate customer service

In the 1980s and early 1990s, if customers were unhappy with the way they were treated by a business, they would call the manager or write an angry letter. With the advent of the internet and online comment forms, angry calls and letters gave way to tersely worded email responses. Soon these email responses gave way to customer call centres. Now customers have access to social media such as Facebook and Twitter.

Industry either chooses to ignore these social media platforms or embrace them, thereby improving their customer relationships and service reputation. One of Australia's large telecommunications organisations, Telstra, has embraced social media. While they offer a variety of options for complaints, including email, mail and 24/7 chat, they also have an active Facebook page, Twitter account and a discussion forum entitled Crowd Support. However, their approach to these social media customer support environments is to provide access through live Q&A sessions with their senior management team.

➜

This proactive approach to social media instils a feeling of being listened to; that the organisation cares about their clients and that the individual is being heard. In the Facebook Performance Report on Australian businesses, Telstra ranked in both first and second place for top post likes, post comments and post shares. The report also identified a significant 48 per cent of the share of engagement among the telecommunications industry. The report does not indicate counts by complaint posts, but the study shows that the posts that are trending the highest are Telstra's own promotional posts. While maintaining high positive trending posts, complaints are less likely to cause the organisation the negative public profile experienced by other organisations.

Customer service experts state that it is the public humiliation that sets Twitter complaints apart from other methods of communicating concerns. However, by having human resources staff dedicated to monitoring social media streams, any angry tweets, Facebook messages or Crowd Support tirades can be dealt with quickly. Social media such as Twitter has placed unprecedented power in the hands of customers. Companies beware!

Sources: Compiled from The Online Circle, theonlinecircle.com/wp-content/uploads/2013/10/OC_FBReport_October2013.pdf; Social Pulse, socialpulse.co/australian-facebook-performance-report; Telstra Crowd Support, crowdsupport.telstra.com.au/telstracon/board/crawl_message?board.id=Welcome&message.id=2; Telstra Complaints, www.telstra.com.au/help/contact-us/complaints; Telstra Facebook Page, www.facebook.com/Telstra24x7; Telstra Twitter page, twitter.com/Telstra.

QUESTIONS

1 What attributes of Twitter make the service so valuable for the resolution of customer complaints?

2 List a possible disadvantage of using Twitter to make a complaint about a company.

Sales force automation

Sales force automation (SFA) is the component of an operational CRM system that automatically records all of the components in a sales transaction process. SFA systems include a *contact management system*, which tracks all contacts that have been made with a customer, the purpose of each contact and any follow-up that might be necessary. This system eliminates duplicated contacts and redundancy, which in turn reduces the risk of irritating customers. SFA also includes a *sales lead tracking system*, which lists potential customers or customers who have purchased related products.

Other elements of an SFA system can include a *sales forecasting system*, which is a mathematical technique for estimating future sales, and a *product knowledge system*, which is a comprehensive source of information regarding products and services. More developed SFA systems also have online product-building features (called *configurators*) that enable customers to model the product to meet their specific needs. For example, you can customise your own running shoe at NikeID (**nikeid.nike.com**). Finally, many of the current SFA systems provide for remote connectivity for the salesperson in the field via web-based interfaces that can be displayed on smart phones.

Marketing

Thus far you have focused primarily on how sales and customer service personnel can benefit from CRM systems. However, CRM systems have many important applications for an organisation's marketing department as well. For example, they enable marketers to identify and target their best customers, to manage marketing campaigns and to generate quality leads for the sales teams. In addition, CRM marketing applications provide opportunities to sift through volumes of customer data — a process known as data mining — and develop *purchasing profiles* — a snapshot of a consumer's buying habits — that may lead to additional sales through cross-selling, up-selling and bundling.

Cross-selling is the practice of marketing additional related products to customers based on a previous purchase. This sales approach has been used very successfully by the world's largest online retailer, Amazon (**www.amazon.com**). For example, if you have purchased several books on Amazon, the next time you visit the website, Amazon will provide recommendations of other books you might like to purchase.

Up-selling is a sales strategy whereby the businessperson will provide to customers the opportunity to purchase higher-value related products or services as opposed to or along with the consumer's initial product or service selection. For example, if a customer goes into an electronics store to buy a new television, a salesperson may show him a 1080i high-definition LCD next to a plasma television in the hope of selling the more expensive set (assuming the customer is willing to pay the extra cost for a sharper picture). Other common examples of up-selling are warranties on electronics purchases and the purchase of a car wash after you purchased petrol at the petrol station.

Bundling is a form of cross-selling whereby a business sells a group of products or services together at a price that is lower than the combined individual prices of the products. For example, your cable company might offer a bundle price that includes basic cable TV, broadband internet access and local telephone service at a lower price than if you acquired each service separately.

Campaign management

Campaign management applications help organisations plan campaigns so that the right messages are sent to the right people through the right channels. Organisations manage their customers very carefully to avoid targeting people who have opted out of receiving marketing communications. Further, companies use these applications to personalise individual messages for each particular customer.

Customer-touching applications

Corporations have used manual CRM systems for many years. The term electronic *CRM* (or *e-CRM*) appeared in the mid-1990s, when organisations began using the internet, the web and other electronic touch points (e.g. email, point-of-sale terminals) to manage customer relationships. Customers interact directly with these technologies and applications rather than with a company representative as is the case with customer-facing applications. Such applications are called **customer-touching CRM applications** or **electronic CRM (e-CRM) applications**. Using these applications, customers are typically able to help themselves. There are many types of e-CRM applications. Some of the major applications are presented in this section.

Search and comparison capabilities

With the vast array of products and services available on the web, it is often difficult for customers to find what they want. To assist customers, many online stores and malls offer search and comparison capabilities, as do independent comparison websites (see **www.myshopping.com.au** in Australia or **www.shopbot.co.nz** in New Zealand). However, stores such as Harvey Norman also offer comparisons between different brands of products that they sell in an effort to keep customers from shopping elsewhere (see **www.harveynorman.com.au** where customers can compare different brands of similar products).

Technical and other information and services

Many organisations offer personalised experiences to induce a customer to make a purchase or to remain loyal. For example, websites often allow customers to download product manuals. One example is Samsung's website (**www.samsung.com.au**), which provides detailed technical and maintenance information. Another example is Goodyear's website (**www.goodyear.com.au**), which provides information about tyres and their use.

Customised products and services

Another customer-touching service that many online vendors use is mass customisation, a process in which customers can configure their own products. For example, Dell Computers (**www.dell.com**) allows customers to configure their own computer systems.

The Iconic (**www.theiconic.com.au**) allows customers to 'mix and match' an entire wardrobe. Websites such as Sanity (**www.sanity.com.au**) have partnered with bandit.fm's (**www.bandit.fm**) loyalty program to allow customers to pick individual music titles from a library to build points while downloading individual tracks, customising their listening for use on a variety of devices.

In November 2013, Australia Post added customisation to their express postal service by offering free 'video stamps' that enable personal video messages to be linked to a QR code placed on the parcel and posted anywhere in the world (**www.auspost.com.au**). In addition, customers can view their account balances or check the shipping status of their orders from their computers or smart phones at any time. If you order books from Fishpond, for example, you can look up the anticipated arrival date.

Personalised web pages

Many organisations permit their customers to create their own personalised web pages. Customers use these pages to record purchases and preferences, as well as problems and requests. For example, Qantas generates personalised web pages for each registered customer. From planning, booking, check-in and personalisation of all travel plans, airlines are giving customers control (**www.qantas.com.au/travel/airlines/home/au/en**). Jetstar have taken this one step further, providing a mobile app that enables real-time updates anywhere (**mobile.jetstar.com/s**).

FAQs

Frequently asked questions (FAQs) are a simple tool for answering repetitive customer queries. Customers who find the information they need by using this tool do not need to communicate with an actual person.

Email and automated response

The most popular tool for customer service is email. Inexpensive and fast, email is used not only to answer inquiries from customers but also to disseminate information, send alerts and product information, and conduct correspondence regarding any topic.

IT'S ABOUT BUSINESS

Google Helpout: real time customer relationship support

In 2013, Google released Helpout, a real-time service application that could enable consultant Heather Smith to advertise her services, indicating times that she is available to 'help out'. By setting a fee per minute of service, Heather's clients could contact her during these times if they are stuck on an issue, don't understand something in her books, or are international clients that don't want the expense of flights and accommodation for information that could be shared in 15 minutes to an hour. This also enables Heather to provide real-time classes for small business clients at times that might be outside the normal '9 to 5' working hours, which tend to be difficult for small businesses to manage, as they too require that time to service their own clients. Additionally, Helpout can be conducted over any device that has a browser and camera, therefore making the Helpout service available anywhere, any time.

Developing Helpout and other online training solutions that can be accessed anywhere, any time, Heather could expand her services to her customers and build stronger relationships. However, it is integrating the information about her customers from all these services into her customer relationship management system that helps her understand her clients. Identifying services that are in high demand and evaluating how to improve her service delivery, tailored to her clients, will give Heather the return clientele business that will continually expand her business.

Sources: helpouts.google.com; interviews and emails with H Smith, www.heathersmithsmallbusiness.com.

QUESTIONS

1. Do you see any disadvantages to Google's 'Helpout' service? Provide specific examples to support your answer.
2. How could an organisation manage customer service using Helpout?

Loyalty programs

Loyalty programs recognise customers who repeatedly use a vendor's products or services. Loyalty programs are appropriate when two conditions are met: a high frequency of repeat purchases and little product customisation for each customer.

The purpose of loyalty programs is not to reward past behaviour but to influence future behaviour. A study by Directivity and Citrus marketing technology firms found genuine brand loyalty was linked to loyalty programs that provide both transactional and emotional features in their program framework. Posner and Noble suggest loyalty programs that surprise members with unexpected rewards are highly sought after. Programs that offer 'surprise and delight' benefits will go a long way to overcoming consumers' belief that programs don't offer any real value. Creating the right loyalty program framework has become more important when taking into consideration the internet and social media.

'The internet and social media has shifted power to the consumer as the time cost of switching brands decreases, the number and visibility of competitors increase and the proliferation of channels means creating a consistent, remarkable customer experience is becoming more complex.' Interestingly, adults 55 years and above purchase more from companies that have loyalty programs but they do not believe that loyalty programs offer any real value. Eighty-one per cent of older adult respondents preferred personalised email communications from their loyalty programs and 80 per cent seek immediate price discounts when making purchases. One point of caution for these statistics is that less than 50 per cent of the 55 plus age group in Australia use computers and the internet. However, with technologies such as touch tablet computers becoming more prevalent with this age group, opportunities for business to utilise balance loyalty programs targeting specific age groups using social media could become the next marketing strategy.[1]

Operational CRM systems provide the following benefits:

- efficient, personalised marketing, sales and service
- a 360-degree view of each customer
- the ability of sales and service employees to access a complete history of customer interaction with the organisation, regardless of the touch point organisation.

BEFORE YOU GO ON . . .

1. Differentiate between customer-facing applications and customer-touching applications.
2. Other than the examples in the book, provide an example of cross-selling, up-selling and bundling.

Apply the Concept

Background

Section 12.2 has introduced you to the concept of customer-facing and customer-touching CRM applications. Many organisations use a combination of both types of systems to establish, develop and maintain relationships with consumers. This activity will help you learn to see these systems in action when you encounter a CRM on a website or in a brick-and-mortar business.

Activity

Visit a physical store where you like to shop (you do not have to buy anything for this exercise) and visit the shop's website. Be sure to pick a store that has both an internet site and a physical store so you can compare both approaches. As you walk through the store, look for cues that could tie a customer to a CRM. Does the business have any customer rewards programs? How does the store use them? Are you a member of these programs? Are there any significant advantages to joining the program?

Is the in-store membership tied to anything online? If so, how? Does it seem that the store has one in-store membership and another online?

Deliverable

List some recommendations for the store you visited on ways it can integrate online and in-store CRM systems. For a good example, visit your local Chemmart. To better service their customers, Chemmart provide a touch screen service that helps customers choose the right vitamin and mineral products, reducing confusion due to lack of information (see figure 12.3).[2] It demonstrates an attempt to bring part of the online customer-touching CRM into the physical store. Are there more ways than simply placing an internet-enabled touch screen near the products? Once you complete your list, submit it to your tutor.

FIGURE 12.3 This touch screen in a Chemmart store helps customers select the right vitamin and mineral products for their needs.

QUESTIONS

1. Do you think there would there be any legal or ethical issues with up-selling alcoholic beverages? What about cross-selling alcohol with food?
2. Campaign management seems to be the issue Malakai and Abbie are really concerned about. How do they touch their customer on the right touch point, at the right time, in the right way? What examples can you find online that show how other clubs/bars handle campaign management?
3. What type of loyalty club could Malakai and Abbie create? What advantages could they create for their customer with this type of club?

12.3 Analytical customer relationship management systems

Whereas operational CRM systems support front-office business processes, **analytical CRM systems** analyse customer behaviour and perceptions in order to provide actionable business intelligence. For example, analytical CRM systems typically provide information on customer requests and transactions, as well as on customer responses to an organisation's marketing, sales and service initiatives. These systems also create statistical models of customer behaviour and the value of customer relationships over time, as well as forecasts about acquiring, retaining and losing customers. Figure 12.4 illustrates the relationship between operational CRM systems and analytical CRM systems.

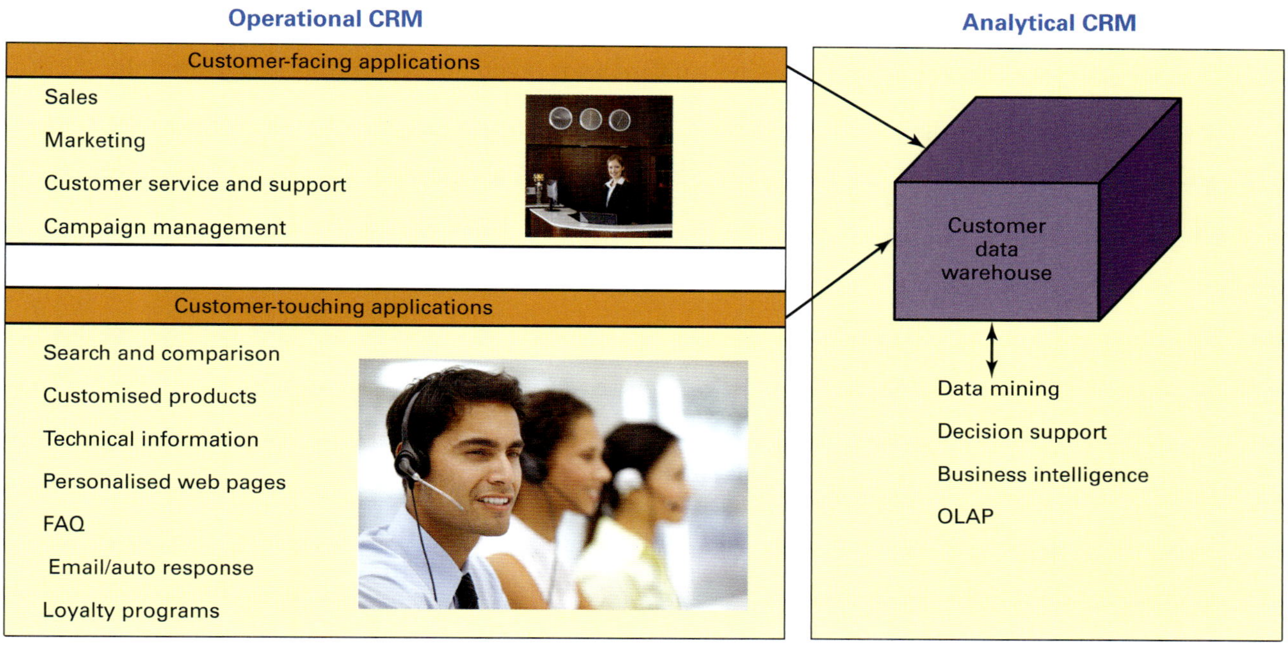

FIGURE 12.4 The relationship between operational CRM and analytical CRM.

Important technologies in analytical CRM systems include data warehouses, data mining, decision support and other business intelligence technologies. Once systems have completed the various analyses, information is available to the organisation in the form of reports and digital dashboards.

Analytical CRM systems analyse customer data for a variety of purposes, including these:

- designing and executing targeted marketing campaigns
- increasing customer acquisition, cross-selling and up-selling
- providing input into decisions relating to products and services (e.g. pricing and product development)
- providing financial forecasting and customer profitability analysis.

BEFORE YOU GO ON . . .

1. What is the relationship between operational CRM systems and analytical CRM systems?
2. What are some of the functions of analytical CRM systems?

Apply the Concept

Background

This section defined analytical CRM as systems that create statistical models of customer behaviour and the value of customer relationships over time, as well as forecasts about acquiring, retaining and losing customers. What that means is the more you shop on a website, the more it will learn about you. Google is a prime example.

Activity

Visit www.johnwiley.com.au/highered/rainer/ausnz/studentresources and click on the link provided for Apply the Concept for chapter 12. This is a case study that describes how 1-888-Trash-It uses its CRM system to enhance its business analytics. There is also a short video for you to watch. As you watch this, consider the integration and use of data across the organisation that helps make better decisions and serve customers.

Now, consider the following scenario. Analytical CRM provides senior management with a forecasts and trends model. Based on this model, management decides to run an ad in a local neighbourhood for a discounted service for new customers. The week after the ad is run headquarters uses the GPS location in the trucks to send the closest vehicle to the newest customer to provide efficient and quick service.

Deliverable

Draw a map that shows the locations for the activities in this system and ways this system is making a difference for both the business and the consumer in the scenario described above. At a minimum, you should have activities at headquarters, data at the truck locations, advertisements and new customers. This will help you see how a CRM influences many areas of business inside and outside the organisation.

Submit your map to your instructor.

12.4 Other types of customer relationship management systems

Now that you have examined operational and analytical CRM systems, you focus on other types of CRM systems. Three exciting developments in this area are:

- on-demand CRM systems
- mobile CRM systems
- open-source CRM systems.

On-demand CRM systems

Customer relationship management systems may be implemented as either *on premise* or *on demand*. Traditionally, organisations utilised on-premise CRM systems, meaning that they purchased the systems from a vendor and then installed them on site. This arrangement was expensive, time-consuming and inflexible. Some organisations, particularly smaller ones, could not justify the cost.

On-demand CRM systems became a solution for the drawbacks of on-premise CRM systems. An **on-demand CRM system** is a CRM system that is hosted by an external vendor in the vendor's data centre. This arrangement spares the organisation the costs associated with purchasing the system. In addition, because the vendor creates and maintains the system, the organisation's employees need to know only how to access and utilise it. The concept of on demand is also known as utility computing (see Plug IT In 2) or software-as-a-service (SaaS; see Plug IT In 3).

Despite their benefits, cloud computing CRM systems have potential problems.

1. The vendor could prove to be unreliable, in which case the company would have no CRM functionality at all.
2. Hosted software is difficult or impossible to modify and only the vendor can upgrade it.
3. Vendor-hosted CRM software may be difficult to integrate with the organisation's existing software.
4. Giving strategic customer data to vendors always carries risks.

These are issues that should be addressed when evaluating cloud computing solutions for your business.

Salesforce (www.salesforce.com/au/CRM) is the best-known on-demand CRM vendor. The goal of Salesforce is to provide a new business model that allows companies to rent the CRM software instead of buying it. The secret to Salesforce's success appears to be that CRM has common requirements across many customers.

Other vendors offering on-demand CRM software include Microsoft Dynamics CRM (www.microsoft.com/en-au/dynamics/crm.aspx); NetSuite Australia (www.netsuite.com.au) and CRM Online (www.crmonline.com.au). The following example demonstrates the advantages that McKesson Specialty (www.mckesson.com) gained from deploying the Oracle on-demand CRM application.

EXAMPLE

McKesson Specialty, a division of the McKesson Corporation (**www.mckesson.com**), delivers the approaches and solutions needed to ensure success in the evolving specialty pharmaceutical market. The division's services include reimbursement support services for patients and physicians, reimbursement strategies for pharmaceutical manufacturers, specialty distribution and pharmacy services, oncology services and patient support services, including clinical support and patient assistance programs.

McKesson Specialty wanted a CRM system that would enable it to perform the following functions:

- make sales activities and customer accounts more visible to the corporation
- standardise and automate sales and CRM processes
- track reported problems, inconsistent processes and resolution time.

In addition, the system had to be easy to use. McKesson Specialty ultimately implemented Oracle's CRM On Demand application to standardise the sales and marketing systems across all of its product lines. The new system enabled the company to consolidate reporting across product lines and it provided the necessary flexibility to accommodate multiple sales processes. Further, it allowed the organisation to monitor and track issues that arose in the resolution process.

In essence, Oracle's CRM On Demand application provided McKesson Specialty with a 360-degree view of customer account information across the entire organisation, which has proved to be very useful. In addition, McKesson Specialty was able to deploy the system in less than 90 days.

Sources: Compiled from 'McKesson Specialty: Oracle customer snapshot', www.oracle.com; 'McKesson Specialty standardises sales and marketing processes and increases customer visibility', techrepublic.com.

Mobile CRM systems

A **mobile CRM system** is an interactive CRM system that enables an organisation to conduct communications related to sales, marketing and customer service activities through a mobile medium for the purpose of building and maintaining relationships with its customers. Put simply, mobile CRM systems involve interacting directly with consumers through their own portable devices, such as smart phones. Many forward-thinking companies believe mobile CRM systems hold tremendous promise as an avenue to create a personalised customer relationship that may be accessed anywhere and at any time. In fact, the potential opportunities provided through mobile marketing appear so rich that a host of companies have already identified mobile CRM systems as a cornerstone of their future marketing activities.

Open-source CRM systems

As explained in Plug IT In 2, the source code for open-source software is available at no cost to developers or users. An **open-source CRM system**, therefore, is a CRM system whose source code is available to developers and users.

Open-source CRM systems do not provide more or fewer features or functions than other CRM software and they may be implemented either on premise or on demand. Leading open-source CRM vendors include:

- SugarCRM (**www.sugarcrm.com**)
- Concursive (**www.concursive.com**)
- vtiger (**www.vtiger.com**)
- My IMS (**www.myims.com.au**).

BEFORE YOU GO ON . . .

1. Define on-demand CRM.
2. Define mobile CRM.
3. Define open-source CRM.

IT'S ABOUT BUSINESS

CRM risk/return

The benefits of open-source CRM systems include favourable pricing and a wide variety of applications. In addition, these systems are very easy to customise. This is an attractive feature for organisations that need CRM software designed for their specific needs. Finally, updates and bug fixes (software errors) for open-source CRM systems occur rapidly and extensive support information is available free of charge.

Like all software, however, open-source CRM systems have certain risks. The most serious risk involves quality control. Because open-source CRM systems are created by a large community of unpaid developers, sometimes there is no central authority responsible for overseeing the quality of the product.

Further, for best results, companies must have the same information technology platform in place as the platform on which the open-source CRM system was developed.

Apply the Concept

Background

This section has outlined the different types of CRM systems — not operational or analytical, but the ways you can actually implement a CRM system. For example, you can purchase industry standard CRM, customised CRM, open-source CRM, on-demand CRM (cloud) and more. In reality, you just about have this many options with any system you plan to implement!

Activity

Visit www.johnwiley.com.au/highered/rainer/ausnz/studentresources and click on the links provided for Apply the Concept for chapter 12. One will take you to a YouTube video describing an on-demand CRM (Salesforce). Another will take you to a video describing an open-source CRM (Sugar CRM).

These represent quite extreme approaches. In one instance (Salesforce), the company that is providing the CRM assumes responsibility for all major hardware and software components. In the other, the company buying the CRM assumes all major hardware and software components.

Deliverable

Build a table that illustrates the advantages and disadvantages of each approach. Are they in offerings of the software? Or does this present a more strategic issue of hardware and software ownership? Does one system provide more flexibility than another? Is customisation sacrificed for flexibility? What about data security?

Submit your table to your tutor.

WHAT'S IN IT FOR ME?

FOR THE ACCOUNTING MAJOR

CRM systems can help companies establish controls for financial reporting related to interactions with customers in order to support compliance with legislation.

CRM systems can also track document flow from a sales opportunity, to a sales order, to an invoice, to an accounting document, thus enabling finance and accounting managers to monitor the entire flow. CRM systems that track sales quotes and orders can be used to incorporate process controls that identify questionable sales transactions. CRM systems can provide exception-alert capabilities to identify instances outside defined parameters that put companies at risk.

FOR THE FINANCE MAJOR

CRM systems allow companies to track marketing expenses, collecting appropriate costs for each individual marketing campaign. These costs can then be matched to corporate initiatives and financial objectives, demonstrating the financial impact of the marketing campaign.

Pricing is another key area that influences financial reporting. For example, what discounts are available? When can a price be overridden? Who approves discounts? CRM systems can put controls into place for these issues.

FOR THE MARKETING MAJOR

CRM systems are an integral part of every marketing professional's work activities. CRM systems contain the consolidated customer data that provide the foundation for making informed marketing decisions. Using this data, marketers develop well-timed and targeted sales campaigns with customised product mixes and established price points that enhance potential sales opportunities and therefore increase revenue.

CRM systems also support the development of forecasting models for future sales to existing clients through the use of historical data captured from previous transactions.

FOR THE PRODUCTION/OPERATIONS MANAGEMENT MAJOR

Production is heavily involved in the acquisition of raw materials, conversion and distribution of finished goods. However, all of these activities are driven by sales. Increases or decreases in demand for goods results in a corresponding increase or decrease in a company's need for raw materials.

Integral to a company's demand is forecasting future sales, an important part of CRM systems. Sales forecasts are created through the use of historical data stored in CRM systems.

This information is critically important to a production manager who is placing orders for manufacturing processes. Without an accurate future sales forecast, production managers may face inventory problems (discussed in detail in this chapter). The use of CRM systems for production and operational support is critical to efficiently managing the resources of the company.

FOR THE HUMAN RESOURCES MAJOR

As companies try to enhance their customer relationships, they must recognise that employees who interact with customers are critical to the success of CRM strategies. Essentially, CRM will be successful based on the employees' desire and ability to promote the company and its CRM initiatives. In fact, research analysts have found that customer loyalty is largely based on employees' capabilities and their commitment to the company.

As a result, human resource managers know that if their company desires valued customer relationships, then it needs valued relationships with its employees. Therefore, HR managers are implementing programs to increase employee satisfaction and are providing training for employees so that they can execute CRM strategies.

FOR THE MIS MAJOR

The IT function in the enterprise is responsible for the corporate databases and data warehouse, and the correctness and completeness of the data in them. That is, the IT department provides the data used in a 360-degree view of the customer. Further, IT personnel provide the technologies underlying the customer interaction centre.

SUMMARY

1 Identify the primary functions of both customer relationship management (CRM) and collaborative CRM.

Customer relationship management (CRM) is an organisational strategy that is customer focused and customer driven. That is, organisations concentrate on satisfying customers by assessing their requirements for products and services and then providing high-quality, responsive service. CRM functions include acquiring new customers, retaining existing customers and growing the relationships with existing customers.

Collaborative CRM is an organisational CRM strategy whereby data consolidation and the 360-degree view of the customer enable the organisation's functional areas to readily share information about customers. The functions of collaborative CRM include integrating communications between the organisation and its customers in all aspects of marketing, sales and customer support processes, and enabling customers to provide direct feedback to the organisation.

2 Describe how businesses might utilise applications used in each of the two major components of operational CRM systems.

Operational CRM systems support the front-office business processes that interact directly with customers (i.e. sales, marketing and service). The two major components of operational CRM systems are customer-facing applications and customer-touching applications.

Customer-facing CRM applications include customer service and support, sales force automation, marketing and campaign management. *Customer-touching applications* include search and comparison capabilities, technical and other information and services, customised products and services, personalised web pages, FAQs, email and automated response, and loyalty programs.

3 Discuss the benefits of analytical CRM to businesses.

Analytical CRM systems analyse customer behaviour and perceptions in order to provide business intelligence. Organisations use analytical systems for many purposes, including designing and executing targeted marketing campaigns; increasing customer acquisition, cross-selling, and up-selling; providing input into decisions relating to products and services (e.g. pricing and product development); and providing financial forecasting and customer profitability analysis.

4 Explain the advantages and disadvantages of mobile CRM systems, on-demand CRM systems and open-source CRM systems.

On-demand CRM systems are CRM systems hosted by an external vendor in the vendor's data centre. Advantages of on-demand CRM systems include lower costs and a need for employees to know only how to access and utilise the software. Drawbacks include possibly unreliable vendors, difficulty in modifying the software and difficulty in integrating vendor-hosted CRM software with the organisation's existing software.

Mobile CRM systems are interactive CRM systems whereby communications related to sales, marketing and customer service activities are conducted through a mobile medium for the purpose of building and maintaining customer relationships between an organisation and its customers. Advantages of mobile CRM systems include convenience for customers and the chance to build a truly personal relationship with customers. A drawback could be difficulty in maintaining customer expectations. That is, the company must be extremely responsive to customer needs in a mobile, near-real-time environment.

Open-source CRM systems are CRM systems whose source code is available to developers and users. The benefits of open-source CRM systems include favourable pricing, a wide variety of applications, easy customisation, rapid updates and bug (software error) fixes, and extensive free support information. The major drawback of open-source CRM systems is quality control.

>>> CHAPTER GLOSSARY

analytical CRM systems CRM systems that analyse customer behaviour and perceptions in order to provide actionable business intelligence.

bundling A form of cross-selling whereby an enterprise sells a group of products or services together at a lower price than the combined individual price of the products.

campaign management applications CRM applications that help organisations plan marketing campaigns so that the right messages are sent to the right people through the right channels.

collaborative CRM systems CRM systems in which communications between the organisation and its customers are integrated across all aspects of marketing, sales and customer support processes.

cross-selling The practice of marketing additional related products to customers based on a previous purchase.

customer-facing CRM applications Areas where customers directly interact with the organisation, including customer service and support, sales force automation, marketing and campaign management.

customer interaction centres (CIC) CRM operations where organisational representatives use multiple communication channels to interact with customers in functions such as inbound teleservice and outbound telesales.

customer relationship management (CRM) A customer-focused and customer-driven organisational strategy that concentrates on satisfying customers by addressing their requirements for products and services, and then by providing high-quality, responsive service.

customer-touching CRM applications (or electronic CRM or e-CRM applications) Applications and technologies with which customers interact and typically help themselves.

customer touch points Any interactions between a customer and an organisation.

electronic CRM (e-CRM) (see customer-touching CRM applications)

loyalty programs Programs that offer rewards to customers to influence future behaviour.

mobile CRM system An interactive CRM system where communications related to sales, marketing and customer service activities are conducted through a mobile medium for the purpose of building and maintaining customer relationships between an organisation and its customers.

on-demand CRM system A CRM system that is hosted by an external vendor in the vendor's data centre.

open-source CRM system CRM software whose source code is available to developers and users.

operational CRM systems Components of CRM that support the front-office business processes that directly interact with customers (i.e. sales, marketing and service).

sales force automation The component of an operational CRM system that automatically records all the aspects in a sales transaction process.

up-selling A sales strategy whereby the organisational representative will provide to customers the opportunity to purchase higher-value related products or services as opposed to or along with the consumer's initial product or service selection.

>>> DISCUSSION QUESTIONS

1 How do customer relationship management systems help organisations achieve customer intimacy?
2 What is the relationship between data consolidation and CRM systems?
3 Discuss the relationship between CRM and customer privacy.
4 Distinguish between operational CRM systems and analytical CRM systems.
5 Differentiate between customer-facing CRM applications and customer-touching CRM applications.
6 Explain why web-based customer interaction centres are critical for successful CRM systems.
7 Why are companies so interested in e-CRM applications?
8 Discuss why it is difficult to justify CRM applications.
9 You are the CIO of a small company with a rapidly growing customer base. Which CRM system would you use: on-premise CRM system, on-demand CRM system, or open-source CRM system? Remember that open-source CRM systems may be implemented either on premise or on demand. Discuss the pros and cons of each type of CRM system for your business.

>>> PROBLEM-SOLVING ACTIVITIES

1 Enter www.annaandboy.com, www.sassandbide.com and www.alexperry.com.au. Compare and contrast the customer service activities offered by these companies on their websites. Do you see marked similarities? Differences?
2 Access your university's website. Investigate how your university provides for customer relationship management. (*Hint:* First decide who your university's customers are.)
3 Access www.sugarcrm.com and take the interactive tour. Prepare a report on SugarCRM's functionality to the class.
4 Enter the Teradata Student Network (www.johnwiley.com.au/highered/rainer/ausnz/studentresources) and find the First American Corporation case (by Watson, Wixom and Goodhue), which focuses on CRM implementation. Answer the questions at the end of the case.

>>> COLLABORATION EXERCISE

Background

Customer relationship management (CRM) tools generally provide information to the marketing department. However, as you have seen in other chapters, the information in one department will affect the activities in another department. For example, when a decision is made about how much to produce over the next quarter, labour is updated, suppliers are updated and information from that decision is shared with many others who make decisions within the organisation so that they can make appropriate plans.

Activity

Visit www.johnwiley.com.au/highered/rainer/ausnz/studentresources and find the links provided for the collaboration exercise for chapter 12. You will find a list of open-source and proprietary CRM solutions. Look over these and choose one that your team will research.

Imagine that you are an car manufacturer. Your vehicles are priced at the lower end of new vehicle prices. The majority of your customers always have a car payment (meaning they trade before they pay one off), work by the hour, live pay cheque to pay cheque, and have an average of $10 000 in credit card debt. They like cash rebates, sales, high trade values and typically give in to 'gimmicks' that sell cars.

With this in mind, divide your team into the following positions based on major as much as possible (if you do not have enough majors to divide, then choose by preference): inventory, sales, production, labour and accounting. Each team member will research the CRM solution from their position (major or functional area) to make note of the information each could use from the CRM.

Once everyone has completed the list of data needs, meet as a team and have a conversation about the type of data you would find useful from a CRM within the context of the automobile manufacturing environment.

Deliverable

Work with your team to write up a summary of the software package you reviewed. Be sure to include the various areas that are supported by this CRM even though it is generally targeted to marketing and sales.

CLOSING CASE **1** >

Competitive advantage using a concierge app

THE PROBLEM

Luxury hotels are known for their concierge services that cater discreetly to every guest. Managed by Starwood Hotels & Resorts Worldwide, the SLS Hotel in Beverly Hills, California, is part of the Luxury Collection Hotel brand owned by SBE Entertainment Group LLC. Debuting in 2008 following a $230 million renovation of the former Le Meridien Beverly Hills, the 297-room SLS Hotel is all about delighting the senses. French modern designer Philippe Starck oversaw the $100 million décor. Competition in the luxury hotel industry is fierce, with the requirement to personalise luxury experiences becoming a client expectation.

THE IT SOLUTION

In Australia the luxury Conrad Hotel chain, owned by Hilton, developed a mobile app that is available on all platforms. Called the Conrad Concierge, the app was updated in January 2013, enabling guests to book then customise their booking for their individual needs. Guests who are looking for a late-night snack, an extra bottle of shampoo or valet service no longer need to pick up their room phone, search for the correct button and then interact with a hotel employee. They can request any service they need within seconds or minutes just by clicking an icon on their smart phones or computers. The app's about page tells clients that it helps staff understand their needs — 'This app aims to make guests' visits more intimate and tailored to suit their specific needs'. This includes booking rooms, transportation and when the guest would like their hot meal delivered to their room.

There are 20 Conrad hotels and resorts worldwide, with a further four hotels opening in 2016 throughout Asia, and two more currently under construction (due to open in 2019 and 2020). This means Australian guests planning visits to these destinations can book spa treatments, arrange transportation, schedule wake-up calls and make room amendments down to the choice of pillow, room service times and bathroom amenities packages — just some of the requirements to personalise the guest's luxury experience. Understanding their guests' requirements at one location are transferable to other locations makes a luxury experience a little more special.

Concierge apps provide a significant competitive advantage for the luxury hotel industry, therefore the security of the mobile app is a major concern for hotel customers. GoSLSHotel guests sign in with their room number and name, and are not required to swipe their credit card for any purchase, thus easing the security fear factor. Conrad Hotel guests sign in with either their hotel confirmation number or their Hilton Honors user name. GoSLSHotel states that its app has generated 'overwhelmingly positive comments'.

THE RESULTS

As mentioned above, GoSLSHotel has driven new business, generated additional revenue and given SLS Hotel a crucial competitive advantage over its competitors. However, the app's return on investment is just as much about the 'intangibles' as it is about revenue generation. The level of convenience added by the app generates good customer feelings, which boost the hotel's reputation and ensure future business growth and stability.

Interestingly, of the Hilton Honors hotel chain, which includes Waldorf Astoria, Conrad, Hilton, DoubleTree, Embassy Suites Hotels, Hilton Garden Inn, Hampton, Homewood Suites, Home2 Suites and Hilton Grand Vacations, only the Conrad hotels have a concierge app, adding to the exclusivity of the Conrad brand. They market the Conrad brand in the following way: 'Smart luxury is at the core of everything Conrad Hotels & Resorts does. We offer our guests one-of-a-kind experiences, service that's intuitive and connects to people and places near or far. We're the destination of a new generation of global travellers for whom life, business and pleasure seamlessly intersect. People who know that the greatest luxury is the luxury of being yourself' (hiltonworldwide.com/portfolio/conrad). However, as competition for hotel guests increases, apps such as the Conrad Concierge could provide a competitive edge for the Hilton Worldwide.

Sources: Compiled from E Savitz (2012), 'Rushing mobile apps out means ushering hackers in', *Forbes*, 26 February; E Savitz (2012), 'The growing problem of privacy-invading mobile apps', *Forbes*, 23 February; L Tucci (2012), 'Hotel app pockets revenue by putting concierge service in your pocket', *SearchCIO.com*, 23 February; P Dailey (2010), 'SLS Hotel adds personal touch to guest visits with custom mobile app', *Hospitality Technology*, 13 May; 'Runtriz delivering mobile guest facing app for SLS Hotel at Beverly Hills' (2010), Hospitalitynet.com, 3 February; www.goslshotel.com; eTravel Business News, australia.etbnews.com/135512/conrad-concierge-3; Conrad Hotels, conradhotels3.hilton.com/en/explore/exclusively/iphoneapp.html; Hilton Worldwide, hiltonworldwide.com/portfolio/Conrad.

QUESTIONS

1 Why does GoSLSHotel give the hotel such a competitive advantage? Is this competitive advantage likely to be long-lived? Why or why not?

2 What are the privacy implications of the GoSLSHotel app?

CLOSING CASE 2 > British Gymnastics

THE PROBLEM

Originally established as the British Amateur Gymnastics Association in 1888, British Gymnastics (www.british-gymnastics.org) is responsible for the promotion, development and management of gymnastics in the United Kingdom. Its mission is to promote the practice of gymnastics, secure more funding for the sport, improve the quality of coaching and promote the popularity of gymnastics internationally.

These different organisational missions mean that British Gymnastics needs to efficiently accomplish a wide range of tasks. Among other things, the organisation operates 150 to 200 events per year and coaches gymnasts across a broad range of disciplines and abilities. The organisation also engages with members and clubs on many levels, including managing membership subscriptions, running courses, distributing awards and sending out news updates to their membership.

In the past, the organisation accomplished all these tasks using either paper-based systems or disparate databases and spreadsheets. This process was slow, expensive to administer and prone to errors. With London winning the bid to host the 2012 Olympic Games, British Gymnastics realised that updating its membership management system was necessary in order to accommodate an increased public interest in gymnastics and provide more professional and efficient service to its existing members.

British Gymnastics' new member management system automated all of the processes that used to be run manually. Therefore, the organisation decided to deploy a customer relationship management (CRM) system to form closer, more targeted relationships with its members.

THE IT SOLUTION

British Gymnastics selected Sage CRM. They chose this product because it was intuitive and browser based, and could be accessed via the internet without having to install any new software. Sage CRM is also highly customisable, a crucial feature for British gymnastics as their requirements are very different from that of the average commercial environment.

To install the Sage CRM solution, British Gymnastics chose Concentrix (www.concentrix.com), a systems integrator and Sage specialist. This proved to be a good choice, as British Gymnastics was very pleased by the amount of effort Concentrix undertook to understand the organisation's particular organisational needs and requirements.

THE RESULTS

One key benefit of the Sage CRM system was its integration with the British Gymnastics website. After the integration was completed, users were able to log on to view and update their details, register for events and renew their membership. Another key benefit of Sage CRM was that it was web based, so users and managers were able to obtain information and reports from anywhere with an internet connection. Sage CRM also gave British Gymnastics an efficient way to accommodate growing numbers of members.

In addition to the above front-end benefits, Sage CRM also provided advanced reporting capabilities. These capabilities allowed British Gymnastics to measure and analyse key performance indicators, make informed decisions about operations, then report on those decisions to their three crucial sources of funds: UK Sport, Sport England and the UK's Sports Councils.

Finally, Sage CRM stored data on all gymnasts, including their membership and demographic information, the club with which they are associated, their training history and their list of previously attended events. British Gymnastics can use this information to generate ad hoc reports on, for instance, the success of a particular event or membership mailing.

The Sage CRM system allowed British Gymnastics to accomplish several important goals: to identify community needs and initiate programs to meet these needs; to increase its membership; and to maintain closer relationships with gymnasts at every level of expertise. By meeting these goals, British Gymnastics hopes to secure additional funding with an eye on improving the country's success on an international level.

Sources: Compiled from 'Sage CRM and British Gymnastics CRM case study', *SageCRM*, 2012; www.british-gymnastics.org, www.sagecrm.com, www.concentrix.com.

QUESTIONS

1 Why is it so important for British Gymnastics to stay in close touch with its membership?

2 Why do you think British Gymnastics hired Concentrix to install the Sage CRM system? Why did they not just install the system themselves?

THE NOOK

Excel is a spreadsheet and it can be used to support CRM efforts. Recently, Malakai and Abbie teamed up with one of their university lecturers and created a survey to find out about student use of different media. Visit www.johnwiley.com.au/highered/rainer/ausnz/studentresources to find the survey results and a video that will describe the data in the spreadsheet.

For your analysis, Malakai and Abbie want you to look specifically for the social networks used by students with three or more free nights a week. Their idea is that if they can get the people with more free time as customers, those people will become regulars and bring their friends. So Malakai and Abbie want to connect with their potential customers on the right social network and establish loyalty through that channel.

You can accomplish this search by using filters and/or a pivot table. When you are confident that you have found the right target market for Malakai and Abbie, write them a letter describing what you have discovered.

SPREADSHEET ACTIVITY **MAIL MERGE AS CRM**

OBJECTIVE

Customer relationship management (CRM) is very important in today's market. Competition is reaching new frontiers with global companies doing business in rural areas that have traditionally been served by small mum-and-dad companies. How, exactly, can these smaller companies survive without the complex CRM tools available to the 'big-box' companies? Although some tools are free (open-source), they do not come with customer support or instruction manuals. It is good to be aware of some of the tasks that CRM tools can help with that can also be accomplished in an Excel spreadsheet. This activity will walk you through the steps of automating and customising customer engagement based on recent activity.

Chapter connection

CRM is an excellent use of technology. It is easy to understand because the students are often on the 'receiving' end of this particular system. However, students also experience many of its flaws because they receive invitations and coupons that they do not use. This money ends up being wasted because it did not bring its target customer into the store. This activity teaches students how they can utilise a simple spreadsheet to create their own basic CRM. Although it is a very basic function and a poor example of a CRM solution, it does show how simple tools such as Excel and Word can be utilised to create helpful systems.

ACTIVITY

A year ago, Dustin was very busy in his shop. That was before Woolworths opened its Tyre & Lube Express. Now a lot of Dustin's customers have switched to Woolworths for the convenience of having their vehicle serviced while they shop. However, Dustin has an idea. He has created a spreadsheet of data from everyone who has brought their car to him on a regular basis. He wants to contact them with a personal letter to try to win back their service.

Dustin wants to thank his customers for past business and draw on their home town emotions to pull them back to him in spite of Woolworths' convenience and lower price. Although he cannot afford an expensive CRM tool, he does remember something about Microsoft Excel having a mail-merge feature that would allow him to rapidly produce customised letters for the mail.

Visit www.johnwiley.com.au/highered/rainer/ausnz/studentresources and click on the first link provided for chapter 12. This will take you to Microsoft's website and an explanation of how the Mail Merge process works. It is a simple process and it is explained in just a couple of pages. Once you feel comfortable with the concept, visit www.johnwiley.com.au/highered/rainer/ausnz/studentresources again and click on the second link provided. Here you can download the files required for chapter 12. There will be an Excel spreadsheet and the Word document that Dustin plans to mail out. Your activity is to connect the two such that the letters will be automatically created for multiple customers at one time. After you connect the files, produce a batch of letters ready to send out to customers.

DELIVERABLE

Submit your spreadsheet and Word document, which are linked such that your work can be checked. Your instructor will choose how many letters need to be submitted.

DISCUSSION QUESTIONS

1 CRM does not have to be complicated; it is simply an effort to reach out to the customer to develop and/or maintain loyalty. As such, simple tools like Mail Merge can be used to touch customers on a personal basis. In what other ways could this tool be used in place of a more complex and more expensive CRM?

2 What do you think should be the determining factor regarding the type of CRM to use? Given that simple Excel tools can be used to reach customers, why would a company spend lots of time and energy implementing a system that may not reach more customers than the Excel tools would? What creates the 'breaking point' of when things need to change?

DATABASE ACTIVITY **QUERIES II**

OBJECTIVE

In this activity, you will learn how to use parameters to simplify entering query selection criteria. When you needed Adam's orders from DizzyDonuts, you entered his name in the query design grid. That is not ideal for casual users. This activity will show you how using query parameters avoids this step.

Chapter connection

People who work with customer information must often specify whose information they need to review. Queries can do that, but a customer service agent should not have to modify the query design for each question!

Prerequisites

Before starting this activity, you should complete the database activity for chapter 10 (Queries I).

ACTIVITY

In this activity, which you will find online at www.johnwiley.com.au/highered/rainer/ausnz/studentresources, you will provide a simple interface to enter data for a query. For example, a database user could ask for information on sales between 1 June and 31 August one time, and 1 and 30 September another time, without needing to alter the query itself.

1 Download and open the Ch 12 DizzyDonuts database from www.johnwiley.com.au/highered/rainer/ausnz/studentresources. This is a fresh copy of the database you used in the chapter 10 activity.

2 The first query you developed there was to find out how often a given customer uses the mobile ordering service. This one will be similar. Create a new Query Design with Customer, Order and Store tables. Enter CustName, StoreCity, OrderDate and OrderTotal in the grid.

3 In the chapter 10 activity, you entered 'Adam' as the CustName selection criterion. Here, we will use a parameter instead. A parameter in Access is a user-entered value that determines what data a query returns. Each time the query is run, Access will prompt the user to enter a value. No fixed value, Adam or anything else, is built into the query.
To specify that a query will ask for a parameter when it is run, instead of entering the desired value in the Criteria section of the grid, enter a *prompt string* there between square brackets, like this:

Field:	CustName	OrderDate	StoreCity
Table:	CustTbl	OrderTbl	StoreTbl
Sort:			
Show:	✓	✓	✓
Criteria:	[Enter customer name]		

4 Run the query. You will see a dialogue box like this:

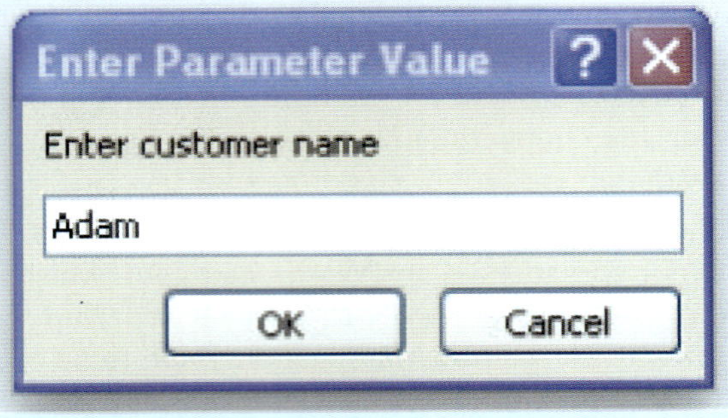

into which you can enter a customer name. The text above the data entry box is between the brackets in the query design grid. There is a box in which the user can enter any desired parameter value. Enter 'Adam', as shown, and click OK. You should see a list of all Adam's orders, with cities, dates and totals.

Usage hint: There are a few rules about what you put in a prompt string. It must fit on one line (about 40 characters), it cannot be a field name and it cannot use '.' (full stop), '!' (exclamation mark), '&' (ampersand), or '[' or ']' (square brackets).

If your query uses multiple criteria, you can have parameters in several of them. Here, you could look for all the orders from a specific customer (one parameter) after a specific date (a second parameter) at a specific store (a third one).

5 To rerun the query, select Refresh All from the middle of the Home ribbon. (If the icon reads 'Refresh', click the down-arrow for other options and select Refresh All.) You will see the dialogue box for entering a parameter value again. Now, enter Belina to see her orders.

6 Close the query, saving it as CustOrderParamQry.

7 Parameters are not limited to finding exact matches. Any type of comparison that can be done in a query criterion can use parameters. Before Access does the comparison, it gets values for all the parameters in it and replaces the parameter indicators with those values. Entering a parameter value 'Adam' is the same as entering 'Adam' in the query design grid.

Re-create ExpensiveProdQry from chapter 10. As the query's only criterion, however, do not use the earlier ' > 1.6'. Instead, enter '> [Products over what amount?]' (without the quotation marks).

Usage hint: Comparison operators include, besides '>' for 'greater than', these:

< less than

>= greater than or equal to

<= less than or equal to

>< not equal to

= equal to (assumed if no comparison sign is entered)

IN followed by a list of text strings separated by commas, will match anything in the list

BETWEEN ... AND ... does what you would expect. This, by the way, is an example of where you might want to use two parameters in the same criterion — for example, a starting and an ending date when you want all dates between two user-specified limits.

There are more, but this is enough for now. You know enough to understand and use what you will find in a web search for more in this area.

8 Run this query twice: first with a cutoff of $1.50, then with a cutoff of $5.

Usage hint: If you use a dollar sign when you enter a currency amount in a parameter entry box, Access is smart enough to ignore it.

9 Close the query, saving it as ExpensiveProdParamQry.

10 Queries can calculate a column based on other data in the same row. This can be data you choose not to show, as long as it comes from a table in the query. Let's create a query to help our staff price out orders for more than one of an item. (In a real store, this would be done electronically, but the query is still a good example.) Open a new query in Design view, select ProdTbl as its data source, and enter ProdName and ProdPrice into the design grid.

11 In the top row of the first empty column, enter '2*ProdPrice' (without quotation marks), make sure that column's Show box is checked and run the query. You will see something like this:

ProdName	ProdPrice	Expr1
Plain Donut	$1.19	$2.38
Blueberry Muffin	$1.29	$2.58
Sm Coffee	$1.29	$2.58

The calculated values are in the column where you entered the expression.

12 Return to Design view and look at the expression again. Access changed it in two ways:

1 Access created the name we saw as its column name, Expr1. It precedes the expression, separated by a colon. If we do not like this name, we can change it. If we know what we want ahead of time, we can enter it when we define the calculated field.

2 Access put square brackets around the field name. These are only required when there are spaces in the field name, but Access plays it safe and puts them in every time.

13 Change the column name 'Expr1' to read '2x'.

14 Enter expressions for 3x, 4x and 5x. (It may be easier to copy and paste the 2x column, then edit its column name and the multiplier in its calculation, than to key in each one from scratch. It is definitely less error-prone.)

15 Run the query to confirm that it works. Then close it, saving it as ProdPriceQry.

This query did not use selection criteria and did not combine tables, but it is still useful. We would not want to store this information in the Product table because it can lead to data errors: When a price changes, someone might forget to update the other columns or might make an error in one of them. (A specialist would say such a table violates normalisation rules by having columns whose value depends only on other columns of the same table.)

16 It is easier to build complicated expressions with the Expression Builder. Create a new query, using the same two fields from ProdTbl as above. In Design view, click the top row of the first empty column and then Builder in the Query Setup section of the Design ribbon. The Expression Builder will open. It has two main sections:

- A: a window in which to build an expression.
- B: a series of three areas to select expression elements without keying them in. (Keying them in is always an option, however.) If you click '<< Less', this area is hidden and the button changes to 'More >>' so you can display it again.

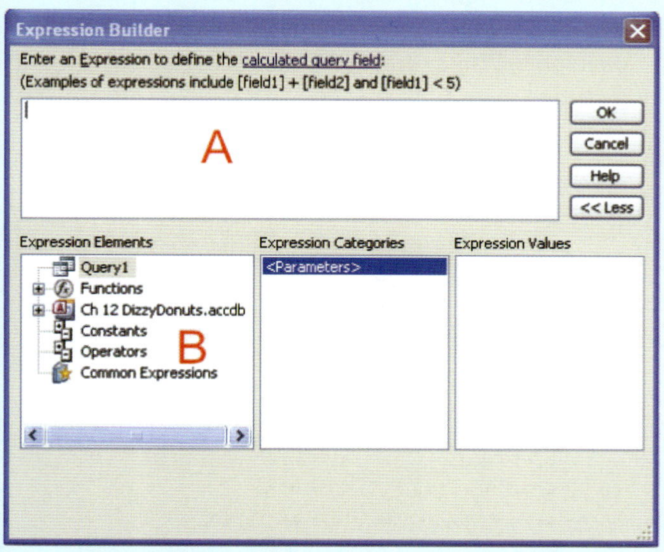

17 We will create an expression to round up each product price to the next whole dollar. Expand Functions in the left pane of the bottom area and select Built-In Functions.

18 In the middle pane, double-click Math as the type of function.

19 In the right pane, double-click Int. The Int function takes the integer part of a number: Given 1.79, it will return 1. It appears in the top pane, with a placeholder for the number.

20 Click the placeholder to select it. Then expand the database name in region B, expand Tables, select ProdTbl in the list of tables that drops down and double-click ProdPrice in the list of fields for that table in the middle pane. It will replace «Number» in the expression.

21 Because Int gives the integer below the price and we want the next whole dollar above it, we must add 99¢ to the value it takes the Int of. (If we added $1, a price in whole dollars such as $2.00 would become the next higher dollar amount, in this case $3.00. We do not want that to happen.) With the insertion point between ProdPrice and the right parenthesis of Int, select Operators in Region B. In the middle pane, select either < All > or Arithmetic. In the right pane, double-click the plus sign. It will show up in your expression where the insertion point was. «Expr» shows where it needs something to add. Click «Expr» to select it and type '0.99' (without the quotation marks). Then click OK.

Usage hint: In this case it would probably have been easier to just key in '+0.99' rather than going to the list of operators and then replacing 'Expr'. However, it's important to know where to find the full process and how to go through it, because it's often the best way to get something done.

22 Back in the design grid, replace the name of this column, which Access has set to its default of Expr1, to 'Rounded Up'. (It may be easier to do this if you widen the column.)

23 Run the query. It shows 2 for every item priced from $1.01 to $2.00 and so on.

24 The new column would look better formatted as currency. Return to Design view, select the expression and open the query's Property Sheet (at the right end of the ribbon, in the Show/Hide section, under the Design tab). Under the General tab of the property sheet, click in the Format row (the second one down). Select Currency formatting from the list.

Usage hint: You may have read in earlier activities that the Property Sheet is the 'go-to place' for most things that do not have ribbon icons. This is an example. We could have used Expression Builder's formatting functions instead, but they are more work.

25 Run the query again to confirm that the formatting is correct, close and save it. Name it ProdPriceRoundUpQry if you did not do so previously.

DELIVERABLE

Your database, with the above three queries.

QUIZ QUESTIONS

1 True or false: Access always names calculated fields as Expr1, Expr2, etc.

2 Which of the following is *not* a capability of Access queries?

a Combining data from three tables.

b Choosing all records that have a date field with a value after June 6, 1944.

c Displaying the cosine of a number that the query finds.

d None of the above; Access can do all of them.

3 True or false: You can set the formatting of a calculated field to Currency by clicking the $ sign in the ribbon.

4 A parameter, in the context of an Access query, is

a a characteristic of an Access object on the screen, such as font, height, or colour.

b a distance of slightly less than 2 metres, scaled to the window size.

c a query criterion data item that a user can enter.

d the fraction of available RAM that the currently open database is using.

DISCUSSION QUESTIONS

1 At the end of every semester, you probably read your grade report online. As you now understand, it is produced by a database query. What are that query's two parameters?

2 If you develop a database in Access, anyone who uses it can see everything in it. In some situations, this is unacceptable. Other database management systems, including some from Microsoft, allow database designers to restrict access to certain rows (for example, only you can see your grade data, other students cannot) or columns (a faculty advisor can see your academic information, but not your medical or financial information). Suppose you are designing a query for a software company's technical support staff. They receive emails and phone calls from customers with questions about this company's products. The support staff may need to know something about the customer, such as the version of a product he or she has. Asking would be time-consuming and should not be necessary, because the company already has the information in its customer database. Discuss the row-level and column-level restrictions you might place on a query that they were to use for this purpose. Make any reasonable assumptions about the content and organisation of their database.

3 The DizzyDonuts database has a field in the Order table that stores the total amount of each order. This could be calculated each time the order is displayed: a calculated field will multiply price × quantity for each line item and the Sum function of the report could add them up. When asked why they designed the database this way, the DizzyDonut database designers explained that they wanted to store what orders cost when they are placed, not what they might cost when a report is run later if prices changed in the meantime. Do you agree with their logic? Why or why not?

13 Extending the organisation along the supply chain

CHAPTER OUTLINE

LEARNING OBJECTIVES

1. Describe the three components and the three flows of a supply chain.
2. Identify popular strategies for solving different challenges of supply chains.
3. Explain the utility of each of the three major technologies that supports supply chain management.

OPENING CASE >

The Kimberly Clark Australia supply chain story

Kimberly Clark (KC) brands — including Kleenex, Huggies, Scott, Pull-Ups, U by Kotex and Depend — are known to 175 countries globally, and are heavily relied upon by Australian consumers in businesses, hospitals and government departments. KC is considered the leader in supply chain management and their service is unique in the market, given their standards increase accuracy and reduce time, cost and inventory, and improve customer service levels among various KC stakeholders.

In the 21st century, organisations like KC must integrate smarter technology solutions in their strategy to meet competition, globalisation, environmental, political and health and safety challenges.

Supply chain management considers the process of a product from vendor, to manufacturer, to wholesale, to a retailer and finally to the consumer. To improve organisational performance, most large corporations use software applications like ERP or SAP, which provide an integrated real-time view of its core business processes such as production, order processing and inventory management.

To improve supply chain management performance and operation, KC implemented GS1 standards. GS1 is an international non-profit association dedicated to the development and implementation of global specifications to management of supply and demand chains across multiple sectors, primarily through a barcoding system.

Kimberly Clark Australia recently initiated Project DANE (Distribution and Network Excellence) to improve the footprint, velocity, efficiency and service capability of its finished goods supply chain. The goals of the project included streamlining processes and systems, and accelerating 'speed to market' by standardising common procedures used at multiple sites.

Kimberly Clark Australia is also a network partner of the WWF (World Wide Fund for Nature). Poor forest governance, weak law enforcement, unclear land rights and other problems mean that forest products imported to Australia from many parts of the world may be linked to habitat loss, community conflicts and climate change.

Kimberly Clark Australia has committed to removing unknown sources from their supply chain, in an effort to preserve threatened, biodiversity-rich tropical forests.

Sources: GS1 (n.d.), 'The Kimberly-Clark supply chain story', www.gs1au.org/assets/documents/info/case_studies/GS1-Australia-Kimberly-Clark-Supply-Chain-Story.pdf; Kimberly-Clark (2013), 'About us — Kimberly-Clark', www.kimberly-clark.com.au/en/our-company/; Kimberly-Clark (2013), 'Overview Kimberly-Clark', www.kimberly-clark.com/ourcompany/overview.aspx; J A Leeman (2010), *Supply chain management*, Germany: Institute for Business Process Management; Techtarget (2013), 'Supply chain management (SCM)', searchmanufacturingerp.techtarget.com/definition/supply-chain-management; Worldwide Fund for Nature (2013), *Working with business: Kimberly Clark*, www.wwf.org.au/about_us/working_with_business/gftn_partnerships/kimberly_clark/.

QUESTIONS

1. List and discuss the advantages and disadvantages of GS1 standards.
2. Discuss the dissimilarity and similarity of supply chain management software.

13.1 Supply chains

Modern organisations are increasingly concentrating on their core competencies and on becoming more flexible and agile. To accomplish these objectives, they are relying on other companies to supply necessary goods and services, rather than owning these companies themselves. Organisations recognise that these suppliers can perform these activities more efficiently and effectively than they themselves can. This trend towards relying on an increasing number of suppliers has led to the concept of supply chains. A **supply chain** refers to the coordinated flow of materials, information, money and services from raw material suppliers, through factories and warehouses, to the end customers. A supply chain also includes the *organisations* and *processes* that create and deliver products, information and services to end customers.

Supply chains improve trust and collaboration among supply chain partners, thus improving supply chain visibility and inventory velocity. **Supply chain visibility** is the ability for all organisations in a supply chain to access or view relevant data on purchased materials as these materials move through their suppliers' production processes and transportation networks to their receiving docks. In addition, organisations can access or view relevant data on outbound goods as they are manufactured, assembled, or stored in inventory, and then shipped through their transportation networks to their customers' receiving docks. The sooner a company can deliver your products and services after receiving the materials required to make them — that is, the higher the *inventory velocity* — the more satisfied the company's customers will be.

Supply chains are a vital component of the overall strategies of many modern organisations. To utilise supply chains efficiently, a business must become tightly integrated

THE NOOK

Malakai and Abbie always have trouble scheduling their inventory. It is especially difficult in a student housing hub where their customers pour in one week and leave a ghost town behind the next week. It seems that many factors influence their customer base on any given night. Obviously, the university schedule is a big factor, as are community events, athletic events and more, but how much does each of these factors influence the number of customers they will have?

More than once Malakai and Abbie have had to throw away perishable goods because they were not able to use all that they had ordered before the expiration date, or they ran out of food when they had more customers than they expected. Neither of these situations is desirable because both mean lost profits.

Malakai and Abbie know they must do a better job of planning. They need to know the key factors that really drive the fluctuations in their customers. They remember some courses about supply chain management, logistics and statistics, but are not sure how to apply it to their situation in order to determine these key factors. As you learn these concepts, consider their situation. In your final exercise, you will be given some data to analyse in light of this chapter to help Malakai and Abbie make better planning decisions.

with its suppliers, business partners, distributors and customers. One of the most critical components of this integration is the use of information systems to facilitate the exchange of information among the participants in the supply chain.

You might ask why you need to study supply chain management. The answer is that supply chains are critical to modern organisations. Therefore, regardless of your position within an organisation, you will be involved with some aspect of your company's supply chain.

The structure and components of supply chains

The term *supply chain* comes from a picture of how the partnering organisations are linked together. Figure 13.1 illustrates a typical supply chain. Recall that figure 1.8 also illustrated a supply chain in a slightly different way. Note that the supply chain involves three segments.

1 *Upstream*, where sourcing or procurement from external suppliers occurs. In this segment, supply chain (SC) managers select suppliers to deliver the goods and services the company needs to produce its product or service. Further, SC managers develop the pricing, delivery and payment processes between a company and its suppliers. Included here are processes for managing inventory, receiving and verifying shipments, transferring goods to manufacturing facilities and authorising payments to suppliers.

2 *Internal*, where packaging, assembly or manufacturing takes place. SC managers schedule the activities necessary for production, testing, packaging and preparing goods for delivery. SC managers also monitor quality levels, production output and worker productivity.

3 *Downstream*, where distribution takes place, frequently by external distributors. In this segment, SC managers coordinate the receipt of orders from customers, develop a network of warehouses, select carriers to deliver their products to customers and develop invoicing systems to receive payments from customers.

FIGURE 13.1 Generic supply chain.

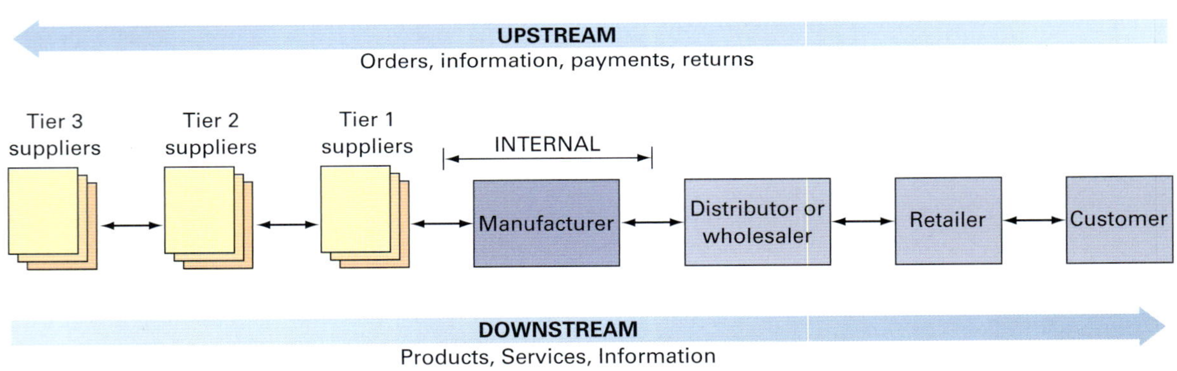

The flow of information and goods can be bidirectional. For example, damaged or unwanted products can be returned, a process known as *reverse logistics*. Using the retail clothing industry as an example, reverse logistics would involve clothing that customers return, either because the item had defects or because the customer did not like the item.

Tiers of suppliers

If you look closely at figure 13.1, you will notice several tiers of suppliers. As the diagram shows, a supplier may have one or more subsuppliers, the subsupplier may have its own subsupplier(s), and so on. For example, with a car manufacturer, tier 3 suppliers produce basic products such as glass, plastic and rubber. Tier 2 suppliers use these inputs to make windshields, tyres and plastic mouldings. Tier 1 suppliers produce integrated components such as dashboards and seat assemblies.

The flows in the supply chain

There are typically three flows in the supply chain:

- material
- information
- financial.

Material flows are the physical products: raw materials, supplies and so forth that flow along the chain. Material flows also include *reverse* flows (or reverse logistics) — returned products, recycled products and disposal of materials or products. A supply chain thus involves a *product life cycle* approach, from 'dirt to dust'.

Information flows consist of data that are related to demand, shipments, orders, returns and schedules, as well as changes in any of these data. Finally, *financial flows* involve money transfers, payments, credit card information and authorisation, payment schedules, e-payments and credit-related data.

Significantly, different supply chains have different numbers and types of flows. For example, in service industries there may be no physical flow of materials, but frequently there is a flow of information, often in the form of documents (physical or electronic copies). In fact, the digitisation of software, music and other content may create a supply chain without any physical flow. Notice, however, that in such a case there are two types of information flows: one that replaces material flow (for example, digitised software) and one that provides the supporting information (for example, orders and billing). To manage the supply chain an organisation must coordinate all of these flows among all of the parties involved in the chain.

BEFORE YOU GO ON . . .

1. What is a supply chain?
2. Describe the three segments of a supply chain.
3. Describe the flows in a supply chain.

THE NOOK

QUESTIONS

1. Upstream from Malakai and Abbie are grocery providers. What type of information might flow upstream to their suppliers while the materials flow downstream?
2. The Nook has some internal issues to deal with regarding their supplies. The food in the cooler is used in no particular order and sometimes it goes bad. This situation is not from a lack of customers but, rather, poor planning. What policies could be put in place to help remedy this situation?

13.2 Supply chain management

Supply chain management (SCM) is an activity in which the leaders of an organisation provide extensive oversight for the partnerships and processes that comprise the supply chain and leverage these relationships to provide an operational advantage. The function of supply chain management is to plan, organise and optimise the various activities performed along the supply chain. Like other functional areas, SCM utilises information systems. The goal of SCM systems is to reduce the problems, or friction, along the supply chain. Friction can involve increased time, costs and inventories as well as decreased customer satisfaction. SCM systems, then, reduce uncertainty and risks by decreasing inventory levels and cycle time while improving business processes and customer service. All of these benefits make the organisation more profitable and competitive.

Significantly, SCM systems are a type of interorganisational information system. An **interorganisational information system (IOS)** involves information flows among two or more organisations. By connecting the information systems of business partners, IOSs enable the partners to perform a number of tasks:

- reduce the costs of routine business transactions
- improve the quality of the information flow by reducing or eliminating errors
- compress the cycle time involved in fulfilling business transactions
- eliminate paper processing and its associated inefficiencies and costs
- facilitate the transfer and processing of information for users.

The push model versus the pull model

Many supply chain management systems use the push model. In the **push model**, also known as *make-to-stock*, the production process begins with a forecast, which is simply an educated guess as to customer demand. The forecast must predict which products customers will want as well as the quantity of each product. The company then produces the amount of products in the forecast, typically by using mass production, and sells, or 'pushes', those products to consumers.

Unfortunately, these forecasts are often incorrect. Consider, for example, a vehicle manufacturer that wants to produce a new car. Marketing managers conduct extensive research, including customer surveys and analyses of competitors' cars, and they provide the results to forecasters. If the forecasters are too high in their prediction — that is, they predict that sales of the new car will be 200 000 and actual customer demand turns out to be 150 000 — then the vehicle maker has 50 000 cars in inventory and will incur large carrying costs. Further, the company will probably have to sell the excess cars at a discount.

From the opposite perspective, if the forecasters are too low in their prediction — that is, they predict that sales of the new car will be 150 000 and actual customer demand turns out to be 200 000 — then the vehicle maker will probably have to run extra shifts to meet the demand and thus will incur large overtime costs. Further, the company risks losing customers to competitors if the car the customer wants is not available. Using the push model in supply chain management can cause problems, as you see in the next section.

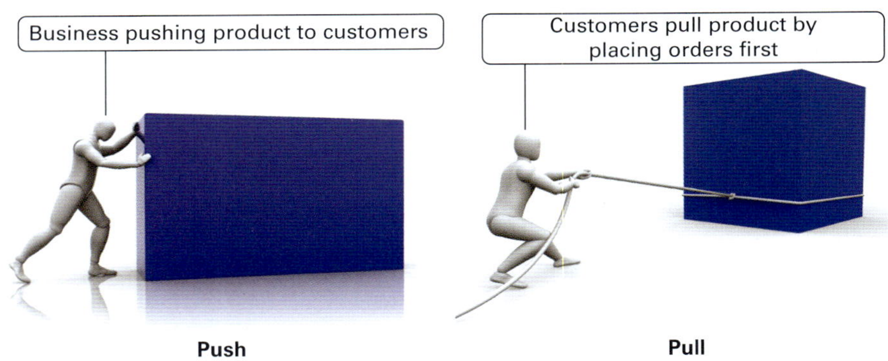

To avoid the uncertainties associated with the push model, many companies now use web-enabled information flows to employ the pull model of supply chain management. In the **pull model**, also known as *make-to-order*, the production process begins with a customer order. Therefore, companies make only what customers want, a process closely aligned with mass customisation.

IT'S ABOUT BUSINESS

Energizer supply chain and technology

Energizer Holdings is considered one of the world's largest manufacturers of primary batteries. In Australia, Energizer Holdings products are distributed from households through to warehouses and offer solutions in portable power, lighting and skin care machines.

Delivering products between companies, partners and users requires efficient and effective collaboration, communication and technology. Energizer recently experienced a challenge by a number of claims of inaccurate orders from partners and users. To resolve these challenges, Energizer used new technologies — EDI (electronic data interchange) and GS1net data to accurately deliver an effective service to their partners and users.

These smart new technologies assisted Energizer Holdings to enter, validate and maintain all products, pricing and other related information in one location. GS1net is an

Australian and New Zealand data synchronisation solution for data. Using GS1 and EDI technologies allows Energizer to share information with partners and users in Australia and around the world in an extraordinary way.

Adopting GS1net data and EDI allows Energizer to minimise data entry errors and duplication, and prevent the use of various formats for data entry. This move allowed Energizer partners to receive automatic and updated data for all their products and needs. Moreover, EDI enabled Energizer to communicate electronic documents and business data rapidly with their partners. As a result, adopting this technology in Energizer's strategy provided faster response times, outstanding invoicing processes, reduced claims, cost savings and most importantly saved their supply chain process, which is now well-organised, profitable and effective.

Sources: Bizcaps Software (n.d.), 'GS1-Australia-Bizcaps-Energizer-Case-Study', www.gs1au.org/assets/documents/info/collaterals/GS1-Australia-Bizcaps-Energizer-Case-Study.pdf; Energizer (2013), 'About Energizer Holdings Inc.', www.energizer.com/about-energizer/pages/enr-energizer-holdings.aspx; GS1 (n.d.), 'Australian supply chain professionals: competencies, use of technologies and future challenges', www.gs1au.org/assets/documents/info/case_studies/case_sc_professionals.pdf.

QUESTIONS

1. List and discuss the advantages of GS1 and EDI technologies.
2. In your opinion, are there any other industries that might benefit from GS1 and EDI technologies? Why? List the industries and the types of apps that would be useful.

Not all companies can use the pull model. Cars, for example, are far more complicated and more expensive to manufacture than computers, and companies require longer lead times to produce new models. Car companies use the pull model, but only for specific cars that specific customers order.

Problems along the supply chain

As noted, friction can develop within a supply chain. One major consequence of ineffective supply chains is poor customer service. In some cases, supply chains do not deliver products or services when and where customers — either individuals or businesses — need them. In other cases, the supply chain provides poor-quality products. Other problems associated with friction are high inventory costs and loss of revenues.

The problems along the supply chain arise primarily from two sources: (1) uncertainties and (2) the need to coordinate multiple activities, internal units and business partners. A major source of supply chain uncertainties is the *demand forecast*. Demand for a product can be influenced by numerous factors such as competition, prices, weather conditions, technological developments, overall economic conditions and customers' general confidence. Another uncertainty is delivery times, which depend on factors ranging from production machine failures to road construction and traffic jams. In addition, quality problems in materials and parts can create production delays, which also generate supply chain problems.

One of the major challenges that managers face in setting accurate inventory levels throughout the supply chain is known as the bullwhip effect. The **bullwhip effect** refers to erratic shifts in orders up and down the supply chain (see figure 13.2, overleaf). Basically, the variables that affect customer demand can become magnified when they are viewed through the eyes of managers at each link in the supply chain. If each distinct entity that makes ordering and inventory decisions places its interests above those of the chain, then stockpiling can occur at as many as seven or eight locations along the chain. Research has shown that in some cases such hoarding has led to as much as a 100-day supply of inventory that is waiting 'just in case', versus 10 to 20 days under normal circumstances.

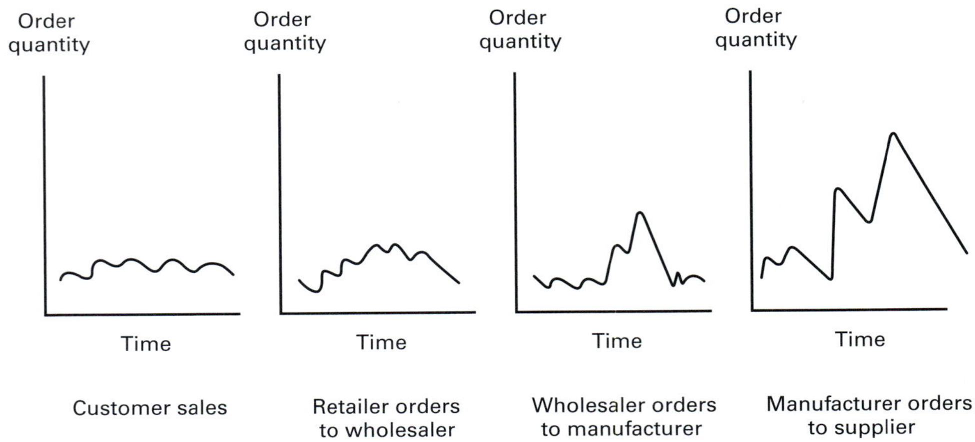

FIGURE 13.2 The bullwhip effect.

Solutions to supply chain problems

To reduce supply chain problems in the 21st century, supply chain organisations integrated smart technology in their strategy to reduce cost and manage competition, globalisation and environmental, political, health and safety challenges. By adopting smart technology in supply chain business, organisations become unique, exclusive and exceptional globally and locally.

In 2001, Health Purchasing Victoria (HPV) was established with an endorsement from the Victorian State Government to assist public hospitals and other health services to purchase goods and services on best-value terms. Currently, HPV contracts can be assessed by several public hospitals and healthcare services that provide healthcare to Victorian residents. To enhance the service between Victorian healthcare stakeholders, the NPC (National Product Catalogue) is used by HPV to access accurate and validated data, as the NPC is a single repository of product, pricing and healthcare data for all health industry product categories.[1]

Using inventories to solve supply chain problems

Undoubtedly, the most common solution to supply chain problems is *building inventories* as insurance against supply chain uncertainties. As you have learned, some costs are associated with holding too much inventory. Thus, companies make major attempts to optimise and control inventories. IT's About Business (opposite) illustrates how Airbus is using a 'smart' supply chain to manage its parts inventory.

A well-known initiative to optimise and control inventories is the **just-in-time (JIT) inventory system**, which attempts to minimise inventories. That is, in a manufacturing process, JIT systems deliver the precise number of parts, called *work-in-process* inventory, to be assembled into a finished product at precisely the right time.

Although JIT offers many benefits, it has certain drawbacks as well. To begin, suppliers are expected to respond instantaneously to requests. As a result, they have to carry more inventory than they otherwise would. The inventory has not gone away in JIT; rather, it has just shifted from customer to supplier. This process can result in an overall improvement if the supplier can spread the increased inventory over several customers, but that is not always possible.

In addition, JIT replaces a few large supply shipments with a large number of smaller ones. This process is less efficient in terms of transportation.

Information sharing

Another common way to solve supply chain problems, and especially to improve demand forecasts, is *sharing information* along the supply chain. Information sharing can be facilitated by electronic data interchange and extranets, topics you will read about in the next section.

One of the most notable examples of information sharing occurs between large manufacturers and retailers.

Woolworths Supermarkets is one of Australia's largest food retailers and the nation's second biggest private employer. Woolworths offers produce in more than 850 locations across Australia. To improve business performance and efficiency, Woolworths worked closely with Logica (**www.logica.com.au/**) to maintain and sustain hardware mobility to track and manage stock movement across Woolworths' distribution centres. Logica implemented Intermec mobile devices linked to a warehouse management system to enable staff to capture and retrieve stock information quickly through the distribution centre.[2] These devices were linked with a radio frequency network as well as wireless network technology. Using this technology in Woolworths' warehouse management to provide more efficient, reliable and faster service also reduced time and cost.

BEFORE YOU GO ON . . .

1. Differentiate between the push model and the pull model.
2. Describe various problems that can occur along the supply chain.
3. Discuss possible solutions to problems along the supply chain.

IT'S ABOUT BUSINESS

Airbus moves to a smart supply chain

Supply chain information that was previously generated manually will now increasingly be generated by sensors, RFID tags, meters, GPS and other devices and systems. What does this mean for supply chain managers? For one thing, it means they will have real-time information on all products moving through their supply chains. Supply chains will therefore need to rely less on labour-based tracking and monitoring, because the new technology will allow shipping containers, trucks, products and parts to report on their own status.

Airbus is one of the world's largest commercial aircraft manufacturers, producing over half of the world's new aircraft with more than 100 seats per plane. With its suppliers becoming more geographically dispersed, Airbus was finding it increasingly difficult to track parts, components and other assets as it moved from the warehouses of various suppliers to its 18 different manufacturing sites.

To improve the overall visibility of its supply chain, Airbus created a smart sensing solution capable of detecting any deviations of inbound shipments from their intended path. Here is how the sensing solution works: as parts move from suppliers' warehouses to the Airbus assembly line, they travel in smart containers fitted with RFID tags that hold important information (RFID is discussed in detail in chapter 10). At each stop along the supply chain, RFID readers communicate with each tag. If shipments end up at the wrong location or do not contain the correct parts, the RFID readers alert employees early so they can fix the problem before it disrupts production.

Airbus's supply chain solution, the largest of its kind in manufacturing, has significantly reduced the incidence and severity of incorrect parts delivery orders and the costs associated with correcting such problems. Reducing the number of incorrect shipments and deliveries has allowed Airbus to reduce the number of overall travel containers by 8 per cent, avoid significant inventory carrying costs and increase the overall efficiency of its parts flow.

Sources: Compiled from 'At Airbus, it's clear skies and high visibility', *The Smarter Supply Chain of the Future* (IBM Corporation), 2012; www.airbus.com.

QUESTIONS

1. Discuss the value to Airbus of supply chain transparency (i.e. knowing where every part is in real time).
2. What are potential problems with using RFID tags throughout Airbus's parts supply chain?

THE NOOK

QUESTIONS

1 Based on your understanding of The Nook's business model, do you think it is in a push or pull scenario?

2 Do you think The Nook would begin the bullwhip effect, or do you think it would have problems because someone else started it?

3 Is JIT realistic for The Nook? Should The Nook invest in alcohol and grocery distribution businesses?

13.3 Information technology support for supply chain management

Clearly, SCM systems are essential to the successful operation of many businesses. As you have seen, these systems — and interorganisational information systems in general — rely on various forms of IT to resolve problems. Three technologies in particular provide support for interorganisational information systems and supply chain management systems: electronic data interchange, extranets and web services. You learn about web services in Plug IT In 3. You examine the other two technologies in this section.

Electronic data interchange (EDI)

Electronic data interchange (EDI) is a communication standard that enables business partners to exchange routine documents, such as purchasing orders, electronically. EDI formats these documents according to agreed-upon standards — for example, data formats. It then transmits messages using a converter, called a *translator*. The message travels over the internet.

EDI provides many benefits compared with a manual delivery system. To begin, it minimises data entry errors because each entry is checked by the computer. In addition, the length of the message can be shorter and the messages are secured. EDI also reduces cycle time, increases productivity, enhances customer service, and minimises paper usage and storage. Figure 13.3 contrasts the process of fulfilling a purchase order with and without EDI.

EDI does have some disadvantages. Business processes must sometimes be restructured to fit EDI requirements. Also, many EDI standards are in use today. As a result, one company might have to use several standards in order to communicate with multiple business partners.

In today's world, where every business has a broadband connection to the internet and where multimegabyte design files, product photographs and PDF sales brochures are routinely emailed, the value of reducing a structured e-commerce message from a few thousand XML bytes to a few hundred EDI bytes is negligible. As a result, EDI is being replaced by XML-based web services. (You will learn about XML in Plug IT In 2.)

Extranets

To implement IOSs and SCM systems, a company must connect the intranets of its various business partners to create extranets. **Extranets** link business partners to one another over the internet by providing access to certain areas of one another's corporate intranets (see figure 13.4, overleaf).

The primary goal of extranets is to foster collaboration between and among business partners. An extranet is open to selected business-to-business (B2B) suppliers, customers and other business partners. These individuals access the extranet through the internet.

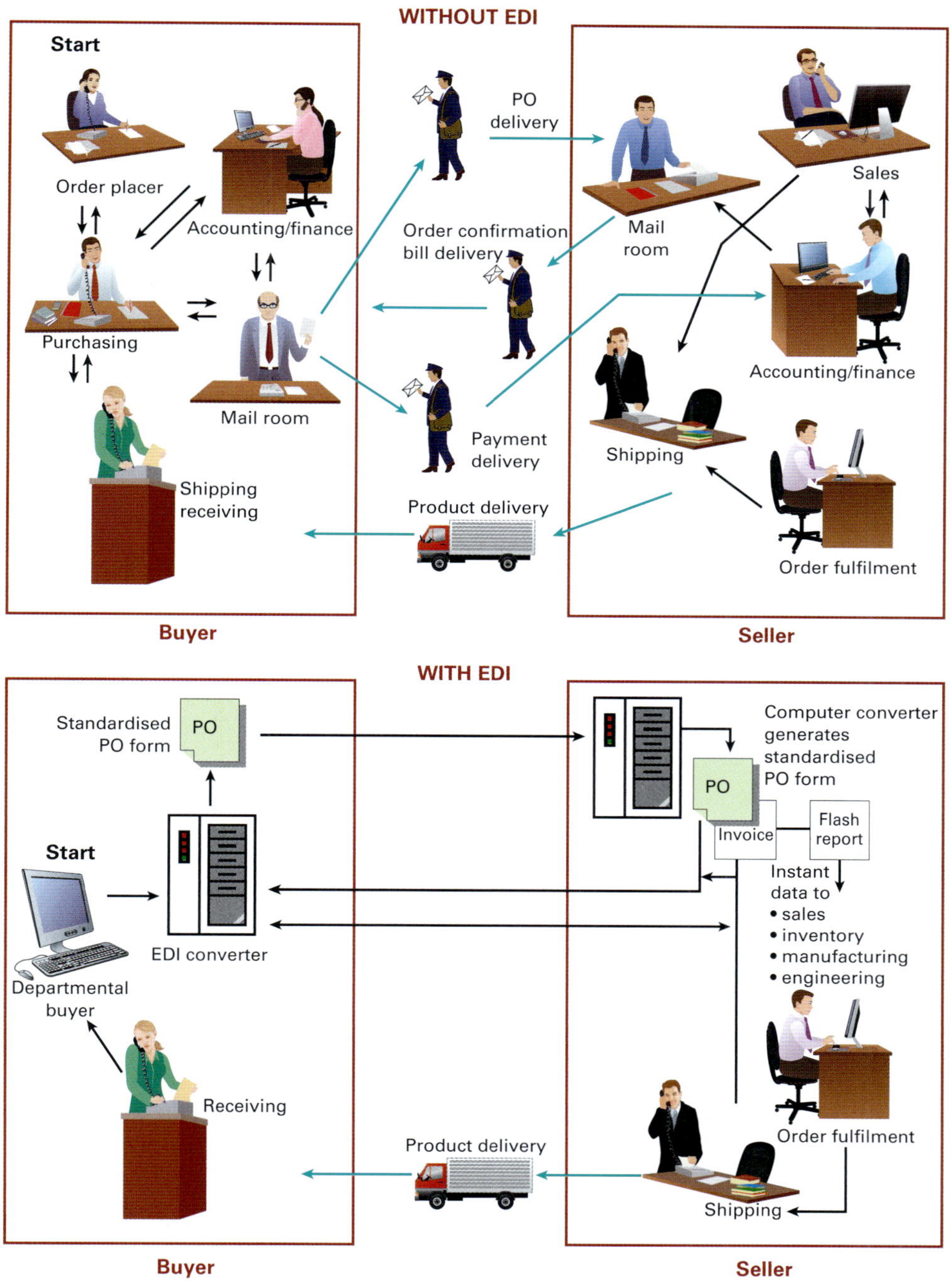

FIGURE 13.3 Order fulfilment with and without EDI.

Extranets enable people who are located outside a company to work together with the company's internally located employees. An extranet also allows external business partners to enter the corporate intranet, via the internet, to access data, place orders, check the status of those orders, communicate and collaborate. It also enables partners to perform self-service activities such as checking inventory levels.

Extranets use virtual private network (VPN) technology to make communication over the internet more secure. The major benefits of extranets are:

- faster processes and information flow
- improved order entry and customer service
- lower costs (for example, for communications, travel and administrative overhead)
- an overall improvement in business effectiveness.

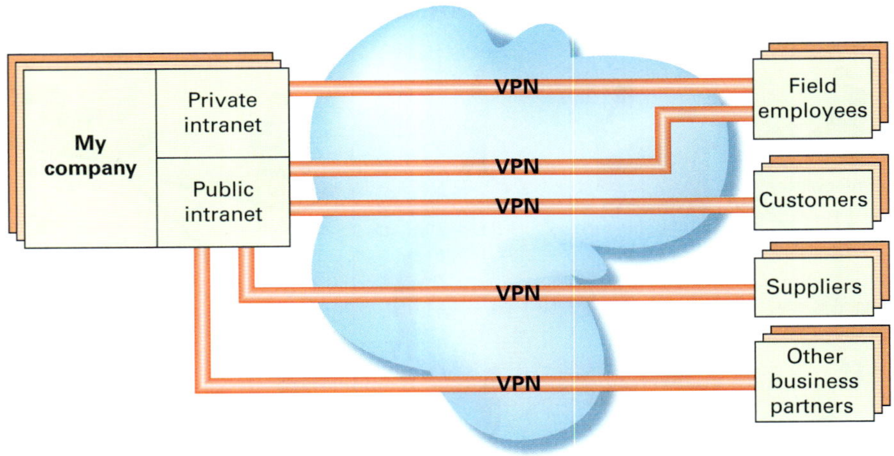

FIGURE 13.4 The structure of an extranet.

There are two major types of extranets. Companies choose a particular type depending on the business partners involved and the purpose of the supply chain. Each type, along with its major business applications, is described in the following subsections.

A company and its dealers, customers or suppliers

This type of extranet is centred on a single company. An example is Australia Post, which allows customers to track the status of a delivery via various devices such as mobiles (iPhone), portable devices (iPad via the Australia Post app), laptops and workstations. To do so, customers use the Australia Post website (intranet) by entering the tracking number (or article ID) and clicking search. A tracking summary appears, listing delivery information about the location of a package. Australia Post saves the cost of having a human operator perform that task over the phone.

An industry's extranet

Just as a single company can set up an extranet, the major players in an industry can team up to create an extranet that will benefit all of them. For example, Australia IBM provides B2B cloud service solutions between partners and communities. B2B service solutions ranged from on demand to fully managed solutions, since this service provides flexibility and mobility to match business needs. Adoption of this service will increase the profile, reduce costs, enhance service and be more sustainable.

BEFORE YOU GO ON . . .

1. Define EDI and list its major benefits and limitations.
2. Define an extranet and explain its infrastructure.
3. List and briefly define the major types of extranets.
4. Differentiate between procurement portals and distribution portals.

Portals and exchanges

As explained in chapter 4, corporate portals offer a single point of access through a web browser to critical business information in an organisation. In the context of B2B supply chain management, these portals enable companies and their suppliers to collaborate very closely.

The two basic types of corporate portals are procurement (sourcing) portals for a company's suppliers (upstream in the supply chain) and distribution portals for a company's customers (downstream in the supply chain).

Procurement portals automate the business processes involved in purchasing or procuring products between a single buyer and multiple suppliers. For example, Boeing has deployed a procurement portal called the Boeing Supplier Portal through which it conducts business with its suppliers.

Distribution portals automate the business processes involved in selling or distributing products from a single supplier to multiple buyers. For example, Dell services its business customers through its distribution portal at **premier.dell.com**.

Apply the Concept

Background

Electronic data interchange (EDI) is defined in this section as a communication standard that enables business partners to exchange routine documents, such as purchasing orders, electronically. There is a need for electronic sharing of information.

Activity

Search for the YouTube video titled 'What is EDI' by user hitekequipment. There is also an article that defines EDI and discusses some of its standards.

As you watch the video, pay attention to the important pieces that are necessary to share information between two organisations. Then consider the fact that rarely does a supplier only operate in one supply chain. Suppliers often have multiple customers, which means they are sharing information with many organisations with EDI.

Deliverable

Create a list of the top five reasons EDI needs a standard to operate today. Perhaps it will help you to consider what EDI would be like if there were no standard for everyone to use.

IT'S ABOUT BUSINESS

Concrete ideas for sustainable business

Sustainability was coined by Gro Harlem Brundtland from the World Commission on Environment and Development meetings in 1983. This report urged businesses to be sustained without destroying the natural resources of the environment. Erek et al. define sustainability as 'a survival assurance meaning that an economical, ecological or social system should be preserved for future generations and, thus, necessary resources should only be exploited, to a degree, where it is possible to restore them within a regeneration cycle'. Based on this, it suggests that businesses, organisations and individuals must protect the current substructure so that it can be reclaimed by the next generation.

Sustainability is a complex and challenging exercise, but considered significant in the 21st century. Usage by businesses and individuals requires some thinking in terms of delivering 'solutions rather than products, and seek to define their markets in terms of customer activities and outcomes rather than products and services'.[3]

Sustainability is a core element in any organisation's strategy to reduce costs, preserve resources and make businesses more unique. Implementing sustainability in business is a challenging exercise that demands communication, collaboration, information and management strategies, guidelines, procedures and policies between organisations, vendors, manufacturers and consumers. Supply chain management is one of the business processes that enable a meaningful integration of sustainable practices.

The supply chain in the concrete industry is particularly complex given that numerous stakeholders are involved and the potential for wasted energy — from initially taking the minerals from the Earth through to a completed structure — is massive. There is a demand to introduce sustainability in this industry since it is estimated that cement accounts for five per cent of the world's carbon dioxide emissions.[4]

To solve this problem, a collaborative working group was established comprising a group of property companies including Bovis Lend Lease, Stockland and Landcom. These companies started to develop a sustainable strategy team for supply chain management in the concrete industry, by examining the risks and opportunities as well as informing the key stakeholders behind the barriers and the potential of change.

The sustainability team aims to raise suppliers' awareness of greenhouse gas emissions via the supply chain in the concrete industry. The team identifies policies and standards which are required in order to change existing behaviour and reduce greenhouse gas emissions and energy use, as well as provide design and delivery options.

→

The OECD's Pressure State Response (RSR) model was implemented to change the mindset of the supply chain in the concrete industry's delivery. The elements adopted were: pressure (the environmental, social or economic impacts), state (production of concrete and the use of concrete in building and infrastructure), response (lower carbon in product) and finally, strategy (strategy to reduce the carbon emission by concrete supply chain management). Using this model in the concrete industry is a challenging exercise given the vastly differing expectations of stakeholders and the influence of lobbyists whose own goals are misaligned with sustainable best practice. The future of supply chain management is a collaborative model based on information sharing, warehouse, logistics and suppliers.

Effective communication along the concrete supply chain is essential in order reduce carbon emissions, reduce costs and preserve resources for the next generation. The primary challenge remains to ensure that sustainability considerations are embedded within all sourcing processes in the concrete industry.[5]

Sources: S Benn, A Woodhead & T Capon (2009), 'Guidelines for sustainability in supply chains', aries.mq.edu.au/projects/SupplyChain/pdf/supply_chain_guidelines.pdf; K Erek, Nils-Holger Schmidt, R Zarnekow & L M Kolbe (2009), *Sustainability in information systems: assortment of current practices in IS organisations*, paper presented at the Americas Conference on Information Systems (AMCIS); C Gunn (2010), 'Sustainability factors for e-learning initiatives', *ALT-J Research in Learning Technology 18*(2), 89–103; T Issa, V Chang & T Issa (2010), *The impact of cloud computing and organisational sustainability*, paper presented at Cloud Computing and Virtualization 2010, Singapore; P Jeffers (2009), 'Embracing sustainability — information technology and the strategic leveraging of operations in third-party logistics', *International Journal of Operations & Production Management, 30* (3), 260–287; P Smith & C Sharicz (2011), 'The shift needed for sustainability', *The Learning Organisation 18* (1), 73–86; United Nations Global Compact (n.d.), 'Supply chain sustainability', www.unglobalcompact.org/issues/supply_chain, accessed 25 August 2013; C-Y Wong & K-L Goh (2012), 'The sustainability of functionality development of science and technology: papers and patents of emerging economies', *Journal of Informetics*, *6*(1), 55–65.

QUESTIONS

1. What is the nature of the relationship between sustainability and the supply chain management process?
2. List both the opportunities and risks of integrating sustainability in the supply chain management process. Do the opportunities outweigh the risks? Provide a rationale for your answer.

THE NOOK

QUESTIONS

1. How might information sharing be the answer to The Nook's problems? What specific information should be shared with Malakai and Abbie's suppliers to move as close as possible to a JIT system?
2. Would it make sense for alcohol or grocery distributors to allow businesses to connect to them via an extranet to share information and place orders via the web?

WHAT'S IN IT FOR ME?

FOR THE ACCOUNTING MAJOR

For the accounting major, accounting in a supply chain is part of the supply chain management sector. Students who are planning to work in this sector need planning, monitoring, management and information skills to understand the supply chain process. The accounting major aims to understand the flow of information and accounting, and prepare the necessary reports and documents for top management decision making.

FOR THE FINANCE MAJOR

The finance major in the supply chain management sector is responsible for analysing, creating and sharing information and data among top management and supply chain management stakeholders. This major is essential in the supply chain management process, since his/her job is dealing with purchasing, materials management, legal matters, inventory control, distribution, warehousing and managing stakeholders' expectations.

FOR THE MARKETING MAJOR

For the marketing major, supply chain management is essential to market supply chain activities; therefore, the marketing student should have specific skills from transportation, purchasing, warehousing, inventory and understand the retailing sector linkage with government and public and private sectors.

FOR THE PRODUCTION/OPERATIONS MANAGEMENT MAJOR

The production/operations management major plays a significant role in the supply chain development process. In any organisation, this major is essential since employees need to use the latest technology to meet the challenges from competition, globalisation and sustainability. This sector will examine the quality and inventory management, as well as using supply chain management tools and techniques to reduce cash flow throughout the supply chain management process.

FOR THE HUMAN RESOURCES MANAGEMENT MAJOR

The human resources management major is essential in the supply chain management process, since this major organises the interaction and communication between organisations, suppliers, partners and stakeholders, including customers. The HR manager must be able to address supply chain management process issues from job descriptions and staffing. In addition, the HR manager must provide training to employees who are planning to work outside their home country in relation to cultural differences.

FOR THE MIS MAJOR

Currently, the MIS major is crucial in the supply chain management process, since managing information from both supply and demand supply is important. This major will assist the supply chain to design, develop and prepare the necessary reports and information for various stakeholders in the supply chain management for making decisions and delivery. The MIS major will bring tools, techniques, models, framework and methodology to link between information technology/ systems and supply chain management.

SUMMARY

1 Describe the three components and the three flows of a supply chain.

A *supply chain* refers to the flow of materials, information, money and services from raw material suppliers, through factories and warehouses, to the end customers. A supply chain involves three segments: upstream, where sourcing or procurement from external suppliers occurs; internal, where packaging, assembly, or manufacturing takes place; and downstream, where distribution takes place, frequently by external distributors.

The three flows in the supply chain are *material flows*, which are the physical products, raw materials, supplies and so forth; *information flows*, which consist of data that are related to demand, shipments, orders, returns and schedules, as well as changes in any of these data; and *financial flows*, which involve money transfers, payments, credit card information and authorisation, payment schedules, e-payments and credit-related data.

2 Identify popular strategies for solving different challenges of supply chains.

Two major challenges in setting accurate inventory levels throughout a supply chain are the *demand forecast* and the *bullwhip effect*. Demand for a product can be influenced by numerous factors such as competition, prices, weather conditions, technological developments, economic conditions and customers' general confidence. The bullwhip effect refers to erratic shifts in orders up and down the supply chain.

The most common solution to supply chain problems is *building inventories* as insurance against supply chain uncertainties. Another solution is the *just-in-time* (JIT) inventory system, which delivers the precise number of parts, called work-in-process inventory, to be assembled into a finished product at precisely the right time.

3 Explain the utility of each of the three major technologies that supports supply chain management.

Electronic data interchange (EDI) is a communication standard that enables the electronic transfer of routine documents, such as purchasing orders, between business partners.

Extranets are networks that link business partners to one another over the internet by providing access to certain areas of one another's corporate intranets. The main goal of extranets is to foster collaboration among business partners.

Corporate portals offer a single point of access through a web browser to critical business information in an organisation. In the context of business-to-business supply chain management, these portals enable companies and their suppliers to collaborate very closely.

>>> CHAPTER GLOSSARY

bullwhip effect Erratic shifts in orders up and down the supply chain.

distribution portals Corporate portals that automate the business processes involved in selling or distributing products from a single supplier to multiple buyers.

electronic data interchange (EDI) A communication standard that enables the electronic transfer of routine documents between business partners.

extranets Link business partners to one another over the internet by providing access to certain areas of one another's corporate intranets.

interorganisational information system (IOS) An information system that supports information flow among two or more organisations.

just-in-time (JIT) inventory system A system in which a supplier delivers the precise number of parts to be assembled into a finished product at precisely the right time.

procurement portals Corporate portals that automate the business processes involved in purchasing or procuring products between a single buyer and multiple suppliers.

pull model A business model in which the production process begins with a customer order and companies make only what customers want, a process closely aligned with mass customisation.

push model A business model in which the production process begins with a forecast, which predicts the products that customers will want as well as the quantity of each product. The company then produces the amount of products in the forecast, typically by using mass production, and sells, or 'pushes', those products to consumers.

supply chain Coordinated flow of materials, information, money and services from raw material suppliers, through factories and warehouses, to the end consumers.

supply chain management (SCM) An activity in which the leaders of an organisation provide extensive oversight for the partnerships and processes that comprise the supply chain and leverage these relationships to provide an operational advantage.

supply chain visibility The ability for all organisations in a supply chain to access or view relevant data on purchased materials as these materials move through their suppliers' production processes.

sustainability To manage resources so that there is enough left for the next generation.

>>> DISCUSSION QUESTIONS

1 Explain how a supply chain approach may be part of a company's overall strategy.
2 Explain the important role that information systems play in supporting a supply chain strategy.
3 Would Rolls-Royce Motorcars (www.rolls-roycemotorcars.com) use a push model or a pull model in its supply chain? Support your answer.
4 Why is planning so important in supply chain management?

>>> PROBLEM-SOLVING ACTIVITIES

1 Enter the Teradata Student Network (at www.johnwiley.com.au/highered/rainer/ausnz/studentresources) and find the podcasts that deal with supply chains (by Jill Dyche). Identify the benefits cited in the podcasts.
2 Access www.ups.com and www.fedex.com. Examine some of the IT-supported customer services and tools provided by the two companies. Write a report on how the two companies contribute to supply chain improvements.
3 Enter www.supply-chain.org, www.cio.com, www.findarticles.com, and www.google.com and search for recent information on supply chain management.
4 Surf the web to find a procurement (sourcing) portal, a distribution portal and an exchange (other than the examples in this chapter). List the features they have in common and those features that are unique.

>>> COLLABORATION EXERCISE

Background

Supply chain management is very important to organisations because it helps them to manage inventory. Managing inventory is key to reducing costs and increasing profits. However, much of supply chain management also deals with quality, legal contracts, deliveries, production schedules, forecasts and more.

Activity

Divide into teams and visit local businesses in different industries. Have one group visit a car dealership, gas station, restaurant, vehicle parts store, doctor's office, or other local businesses that require a supply chain. Visit with the manager and discuss the business's supply chain. Some stores may operate out of a regional warehouse, others may have multiple suppliers. Ask about the products that are shipped, the frequency of the shipping, the information that is shared and anything else your lecturer asks you to enquire about.

Deliverable

Draw up a model of the supply chain for the company your team visited. Be sure to include upstream and downstream flows of material, information and money. Bring your team's work to class and discuss the differences in supply chains for businesses in different industries. Finally, submit your team's supply chain model to your tutorial group.

CLOSING CASE **1 >**

The computer that could cut fatality rates for truckies

There are plenty of accusations levelled at our supermarket duopoly, but none more serious than they are complicit in the killing of truck drivers. The fatality rate for truckies is 11 times higher than the average Australian worker, according to a new Safe Work Australia report, and the Transport Workers Union (TWU) says more than 300 people in the transport industry die on our roads each year. The TWU isn't shy about apportioning blame for these tragic statistics. It says the traditional competitiveness of the road freight industry has been compounded by the price war between two of its biggest customers — Coles and Woolworths — to stretch the supply chain dangerously thin.

'The fact is, $1 a loaf means you're buttering your bread with the blood of truck drivers', TWU general secretary Tony Sheldon told *BRW* in February. In terms much less vivid, the big supermarkets consistently reject such claims. 'Coles recognises the importance of road safety', a spokesperson for the Wesfarmers subsidiary told *The Australian Financial Review* in July [2013]. 'The TWU's ongoing claims about Coles are baseless and they consistently fail to produce evidence to support these claims. In no way do our contracts force drivers into unsafe or illegal practices.'

ONE DAY, 18 HOURS

The war of words has been ignited by the new Road Safety Remuneration Tribunal, created by Workplace Relations minister Bill Shorten after TWU lobbying, which is now considering submissions from all sides of the industry on what truckie pay rates and legal working hours should be. In his submission, owner–driver Craig Ballinger, from Serpentine in Western Australia, claimed he had to drive 18 hours in one day to meet a deadline for a Coles delivery. Another driver, Bill Bihas, said deliveries for Woolworths were not accepted if they were 30 minutes late.

In conflicts where emotions run high, facts are the best arbitrator and that's what Tom Scahill, the Australian head of the transport and logistics division of multinational Trimble, says he can provide. The US-based Trimble's transport and logistics division provides integrated onboard computing and mobile communications technology that aims to get fleets operating more efficiently, and importantly, more safely. Trimble's technology claims to pinpoint unsafe driving practices within fleets by monitoring aggressive driving manoeuvres, such as hard acceleration, braking and turns, as well as excessive driving duration.

Scahill says drivers receive real-time feedback via spoken messages alerting them if they are exceeding predetermined speed maximums, or if their braking or accelerating behaviour doesn't conform to preset values. The technology also helps businesses gain insight into what went on in the seconds before an accident — and there were 185 of those involving heavy vehicles on Australia's roads in the 2011–12 financial year.

KNOWLEDGE IS PEACE

The TWU campaign is a sensitive one for Scahill. Linfox, which competes with Toll Holdings to be Australia's largest transport and logistics firm and therefore handles plenty of supermarket work, is among Trimble's biggest clients in this market. 'There's pressure on all sides. Port to supermarket is a highly competitive space — there's 42 000 trucking businesses in Australia — and it's no secret the logistics business has small margins in it', he says. However he sees a big role for the data provided by companies like Trimble — 'the autonomous players in all this' — in lowering the temperature of the debate.

This is especially the case because a new national regulator for the heavy vehicle industry — called, fittingly enough, the National Heavy Vehicle Regulator — will, from September 1, be administering a single rule book for trucks Australia-wide. At the same time the use of electronic work diaries will soon be mandated to replace the paper logbooks still widely in use. The form the diaries will take is still up for debate. Linfox favours what's used in Europe, a tachograph that allows the regulator to literally drive alongside a truck and scan the vehicle itself to assess the driver's data. Regardless of what form the electronic work diary ends up taking, Scahill says the data will be seen by regulators and legislators, and hopefully shared between all stakeholders in the supply chain itself, leading to a better-informed rule-setting process.

CLEAR EXPECTATIONS

'Drivers want to drive safe and negotiate their wages from that position', he says. 'They can use our technology to prove they were doing what they were supposed to be doing, and if the expectations of them are unrealistic, that should be pretty clear.' Scahill admits that the basic data such as that collected for electronic work diary purposes is now the 'commoditised' end of the telematics industry. However, there is growing demand for the enterprise software and analytics required to turn that data into better productivity. He says a typical Trimble installation — the in-vehicle hardware plus the software-as-a-service fee that includes access to the data — can be run for under $2 per truck per day.

'Our clients will have got payback on that within the first year' of a three year contract, he says, given what analysing can produce in terms of optimised routes, reduced fuel costs, more kindly treated engines and fewer accidents. The telematics industry has been transformed in the last five years by the rise of the mobile phone as a computer, Scahill says. 'That's lifted the level of expectation for our customers' customers. They want to see where a delivery is at all points, and they want to know it's safe.'

Source: M Bailey, *BRW*, www.brw.com.au/p/business/the_computer_that_could_cut_fatality_NRZHX87zf9YhKV9ASvhDuJ, 14 August 2013.

QUESTIONS

1. How is Trimble using data to 'lower the temperature of the debate' between unions, the trucking industry and Australia's supermarket duopoly?
2. Suggest a different industry in which this technology could be successfully implemented along the supply chain to enhance workplace health and safety.

CLOSING CASE **2 >**

Information technology helps Cannondale manage its complex supply chain

THE PROBLEM

Cannondale (www.cannondale.com) is a pioneer in the engineering and manufacturing of high-end bicycles, apparel, footwear and accessories for independent dealers and distributors in more than 66 countries. Cannondale designs, develops and produces bicycles at its factory in Bedford, Pennsylvania, and it operates subsidiaries in Holland, Switzerland, Japan and Australia.

As a leading custom bicycle manufacturer with an extensive and impressive customer list — including Olympic athletes, professional racing teams and Tour de France competitors — Cannondale realises that meeting customer demands and expectations is critical to its success.

Cannondale produces more than one hundred different bicycle models annually, 60 per cent of which are newly introduced lines. Working in a cyclical business that is affected by market and weather conditions, coupled with the international nature of its business, Cannondale is faced with highly complex and volatile consumer demand. In addition to constantly shifting demand and a rapidly changing product portfolio, Cannondale has a global supply chain that must integrate global manufacturing, assembly, and sales and distribution sites.

Cannondale manufactures both make-to-order and make-to-stock models. Consequently, the company needs to manage a range of product batch sizes, sometimes including one-of-a-kind orders. A typical bicycle requires a 150-day lead time with a 4-week manufacturing window and some bicycles have more than 250 parts in their bills of materials (BOMs). (A bill of materials specifies the raw materials, assemblies, components and parts needed to manufacture a final product, along with the quantities of each one.) Cannondale has to manage more than 1 million BOMs and more than 200 000 individual parts. Adding to Cannondale's manufacturing complexity, some of these parts are supplied by specialty vendors who require long lead times and have only limited production capacity. This complexity significantly challenged Cannondale's capacity to quickly deliver complex and custom products to meet its customers' high expectations.

To manage parts availability and varying customer demands, Cannondale's manufacturing operations must be highly flexible. Therefore, the company needed a global system that allowed managers to access all plant inventory levels and supply schedules to better manage shifts in product and customer demand.

Cannondale had been using a legacy material requirements planning system (MRP II) that generated weekly reports. Because Cannondale's manufacturing environment is so dynamic, however, by Tuesday afternoon Monday's reports were so outdated that they were useless. The supply chain team had to substitute parts in order to meet demand, causing an ever-increasing parts flow problem. Cannondale's primary objective was to find an IT solution that would improve the accuracy of the company's parts flow, support the company's need for flexibility and operate within the confines of its existing business systems — all at an affordable cost.

THE SOLUTION

Cannondale selected the Kinaxis RapidResponse (www.kinaxis.com) system for its integrated demand and supply planning and monitoring. RapidResponse provides users with necessary information in minutes, as opposed to 8 hours with the previous system. RapidResponse generates accurate and detailed supply chain information with an easy-to-use spreadsheet user interface, employing data supplied from the company's existing MRP II systems.

RapidResponse has transformed Cannondale's entire supply chain. Buyers, planners, master schedulers, sourcers (people who procure products), product managers, customer service personnel and financial managers use the system for sales reporting, forecasting, monitoring daily inventory availability and providing production schedule information to the MRP II and order-processing systems. Supply chain participants located around the world can now instantly simulate, share and score what-if scenarios to evaluate and select the actions they need to take to respond to changing supply and demand conditions.

Company managers now receive up-to-date visibility of global operations. In addition, the management team uses RapidResponse daily to examine the company's manufacturing backlog. Having access to current information enables the team to compare old forecasts with new ones.

THE RESULTS

Today, Cannondale responds to customer orders quickly and it has significantly reduced its inventory, with its associated costs. In addition, the company has benefited from higher inventory turns, reductions in safety stock, improvement in cycle times, reduced lead times and more accurate promise dates. As a result, customer satisfaction has improved. All of these benefits have provided Cannondale with a competitive advantage in a highly competitive industry.

Sources: Compiled from B Ferrari (2010), 'Kinaxis RapidResponse — much more than a planning application', *Supply Chain Matters*, 8 January; Kinaxis Corporation, 'Cannondale improves customer response times while reducing inventory using RapidResponse', *Kinaxis Customer Spotlight*, 2010; www.kinaxis.com, www.cannondale.com.

QUESTIONS

1 Describe Cannondale's complex manufacturing environment and identify some of the problems this environment created.

2 Describe the RapidResponse system's impact on Cannondale's global supply chain management.

SPREADSHEET ACTIVITY **PROJECT MANAGEMENT IN EXCEL**

OBJECTIVE

Supply chain management is a vital operation for organisations — so much so that if one supplier fails to do its job, the entire operation may be shut down. Microsoft Excel is often used to assist in this basic planning. Logic and algebra can be applied in a spreadsheet to make simple calculations that apply within the supply chain scenario.

Chapter connection

At one time, Dell realised it had almost perfected the assembly process within its plant. The only way to improve its product was to improve the entire supply chain. So Dell began working with its suppliers to streamline its processes. Although its supply chain system is too complex for a spreadsheet, the principle applies to many situations. This activity will take a simpler scenario and introduce the concept of planning for the supply chain and using spreadsheet tools to improve the process.

ACTIVITY

Mr Stephens works in construction. Specifically, he builds custom homes. He always gets complaints about his work being late, even though his customers are generally happy with the final product. To try to deal with the complaints and to give his customers a better understanding of when their home will be complete, he wants to build a spreadsheet that will lay out the entire process of building the home, specify the amount of time each part will take and build in time for bad weather, corrections and other issues that always arise.

Mr Stephens compiled the following data for his next construction job. Although he ultimately wants to create a universal spreadsheet, for now he just wants to work on the concept and get it to work for this next job. Use the data and build him a spreadsheet that has the job description in one column and other columns for start date, earliest end date and latest end date. Unless otherwise noted, these steps are performed in order and one cannot begin until the previous step is completed.

1. Groundwork will take 3 to 4 days.
2. Footers will take 2 to 3 days.
3. Block work for crawl space will take 7 to 10 days.
4. Foundation will take 3 to 4 days. Timber should be ordered a week in advance.
5. Remaining frame will take 2 to 3 weeks. Home should be dried-in at this time.
6. Exterior oriented strand board (OSB) and house wrap will take 7 to 10 days.
7. Electrical work may begin at this point. It will take 8 to 12 days to complete the rough-in wiring for the home.
8. Rough-in plumbing work may begin when the exterior OSB is complete. Rough-in plumbing will take 5 to 7 days.
9. Insulation and dry wall may go up at this time when both electrical and plumbing are roughed in. It will take 17 to 21 days to complete the installation of exterior and interior walls insulation as well as the drywall work.
10. Cabinetry and final electrical work may begin at this point. Cabinetry will take 1 to 3 days and the finish work on electrical items will take 7 to 10 days. Cabinets should be ordered a month in advance.
11. The final plumbing work may begin when the cabinets are complete and will take 3 to 5 days to complete.
12. All work on the rest of the house may begin at this time. Paint, trim and flooring typically take 2 to 3 weeks.

Given this description from Mr Stephens, build a spreadsheet that will allow him to demonstrate to his customers how long it takes to build a home. Use a start date of 1 February and allow 2 weeks for weather delays. Given this information, determine the projected end date if everything finishes as early as possible and the projected end date if everything takes as long as possible.

DELIVERABLE

Submit your spreadsheet along with a Word document that answers the questions listed above.

DISCUSSION QUESTIONS

1. Supply chain management is extremely important in today's business environment. Look up some supply chain management tools and compare them to your Excel activity. Discuss the advantages and disadvantages of these systems. What do they provide that the spreadsheet example does not?
2. Given that some refer to supply chains as a web rather than a chain, what type of problems do you see arising from the parent company's need to share information with so many others at the same time? Also, what complications arise from the suppliers needing to share information? Which company should determine the platform and methods of sharing data?

DATABASE ACTIVITY **QUERY BY FORM**

OBJECTIVE

Forms and queries have a two-sided relationship. Forms can be an easy-to-use way to provide the input to a query. Query results can also be used in place of tables to drive forms. In this activity, you will see how a form drives a query, increasing your understanding of both.

Chapter connection

Supply chain integration, as you read in this chapter, is complex. One company's supplier is another company's customer and so on, all the way up to raw material extraction and down to individual end users. The database applications that are needed to manage this supply chain are correspondingly complex. It can take a mix of database features to get the entire job done. This activity shows how two database capabilities interact with each other.

Prerequisites

Before starting this activity, you should complete the database activities for chapter 9 (Forms II) and chapter 10 (Queries I) activities.

ACTIVITY

In this activity, which you will find online at www.johnwiley.com.au/highered/rainer/ausnz/studentresources, you will take what you know about queries and forms, and combine them to improve the usability of your queries.

1 Download and open the Ch 13 CarlaComputerStores database from www.johnwiley.com.au/highered/rainer/ausnz/studentresources. (You may be familiar with it from the chapter 5 activity.) It contains sales data for a chain of computer stores.

2 We will use a querying method called Query By Form, QBF for short. It lets us replace a series of parameter entry dialogue boxes with a single form while allowing us to create a more attractive user interface. To use it, we must create both the query and the form. It is easiest to do this in a few stages.

3 First, we will create the part of the query that returns results, adding criteria later because they will come from a form we have not created yet. We do this so that, when we create the form, we will be able to tell it which query to run. So, start with Query Design in the Other section of the Create ribbon.

   Usage hint: This query-form-query sequence is not strictly necessary. However, methods that do the job in two steps are more complicated, because they require referring to Access objects that do not exist yet.

4 We want this query to tell us which customers ordered products in a chosen category from a chosen store and exactly what products they ordered. So, first show all five database tables in the upper pane of the query design window. Then, double-click on four fields to enter them into the query design: StoreCity from StoreTbl, ProdCategory from ProductTbl, CustName from CustomerTbl, and ProdDescrip from ProductTbl. Run the query to test it. You should see an unsorted list of all 312 purchases. If you do not, review the previous steps to find the error. Then close it, saving it as CS_Qry when prompted.

   Usage hint: Testing is a vital part of information system development. Test often. If anything does not work, the reason is usually in what you did since the previous test. You can fix it while what you just did is still fresh in your mind.

5 Now that CS_Qry exists, we can create the form that will activate it. Click the Form Design tool in the Forms section of the Create menu.

6 First, we will create a field to enter the store we want information about. Click the Text Box tool in the Controls section of the Design ribbon. The mouse pointer becomes crosshairs in the form design grid. Drag to create a text-size area somewhere in the upper right part of this grid. (You use the right side to leave room for a label at the left.)

7 The label to the left of the text box will read 'Text0'. Edit it in place to read 'Store City'. Its enclosing box will expand to hold its new, longer contents.

8 The text inside the text box reads 'Unbound'. However, that is not the name of the text box. That says where its data comes from. 'Unbound' means it does not come from the database — that is, it has not been 'bound' to a database item. We want to give the text box a name so we can refer to it in our query. To do that, open the Property Sheet of the form if it is not already open. (Click the Property Sheet tool in the Tools section of the Design ribbon, or press F4.) Find Name in either the Other or the All tab of the property sheet. Replace it with the name 'StoreField'.

9 Create another text box named 'CatField' in the same way, with its label reading 'Product Category'. Line up the two fields and labels, one below the other, as closely as you can.

   Usage hint: You can line them up exactly by selecting both boxes and using the tools in the Control Alignment section of the Arrange ribbon. For more precision, open the Property Sheet and set their Left property to any desired value. If you do this while both are selected, they will both take on this value. You can set any desired property of several controls at the same time this way.

10 Enter a form header above the text fields by clicking on Title in the Header/Footer area of the Design ribbon. Enter 'Store and Category Search' in the label box. Select the entire box and use the formatting tools in the Home ribbon to enlarge the type, make it bold, change its colour and give the label box a light-coloured background.

11 Now, we will create the button that starts the search. Make sure Use Control Wizards is highlighted in the Controls section of the Design ribbon. (Expand that area using the down-pointing triangle with the line above it at the right to see the wizard.) Then click the Button tool. (It is in the top row of controls, fourth from the left.) Drag it over a rectangular area below your text boxes to create the button shape. The wizard will start.

12 We want it to run a query. Select this action from the Miscellaneous category. Click Next.

13 Select the query you created earlier, CS_Qry, from the list of available queries. Click Next.

14 Click 'Text' as what you want to see on the button, and enter 'Search' into the text field next to that option button. Click Next.

15 Optionally name the button anything you want and click Finish.

16 To test what you have done so far, switch to Form view and click your button. You should see the same datasheet you saw when you test ran the query in step 4. If you do, the form is finished. Return to it and save it as CS_Qry_Frm. Now, we will continue with the query design.

17 With the query open in Design view, specify a sort order for the data. Click in the Sort row of the StoreCity column in the design grid. Select Ascending from the pull-down menu at the right. Repeat for CustName and ProdCategory. Test again by running the query. You should see all 312 purchases again, but this time they should be sorted.

18 To add a selection to the query, return to Design view and click in the StoreCity column, in the first Criteria row. Next, select the Builder tool from the Query Setup section of the Design ribbon. (Its icon looks like the Use Control Wizards icon.) Your criteria will be based on CS_Qry_Form, so expand the database name, then Forms, then its All Forms sub-folder. Select CS_Qry_Form. In the second column, double-click StoreField.

19 You will see 'Forms![CS_QueryForm]![StoreField]' in the upper portion of the dialogue box. This is Access's internal way to identify the form field we want. Click OK. It will appear in the Criteria section of the query design.

Usage hint: If you know Access well, you can also key criteria directly into the query design grid. For short criteria that can be faster, but it is also more error-prone.

20 To check your work, close the query, saving when prompted. Open CS_Qry_Frm. On the form, enter Chicago into the Store field and click Search. You should get 78 records of Chicago sales. Close the query and enter Miami. You should get a blank datasheet, because Carla's has no store there. (You will get the same result if you spell 'Chicago' wrong.)

Usage hint: You could have checked your work a bit earlier by running the query directly, without the form. If you do that, you will get a parameter box with an odd-looking prompt string: the name of the form field. It should work, however.

21 Repeat steps 18 and 19 for ProdCategory. Test by entering Denver and Storage into the two form fields. Your query should retrieve ten records.

22 You may want to find data about all Storage sales, or some other category, without regard for city. Enter Storage in the category field, leaving the Store field blank. Run the query. Nothing comes up. You realise the reason: No data records match a blank StoreCity! This must be fixed. You want the query to select a record if either (a) its StoreCity matches what is in the form or (b) if the field in the form is blank. Fortunately, that is not hard.

23 Return to query Design view. Click in the StoreCity criterion field and reopen the Expression Builder. Put the insertion point after the field name that is already there. Then either key in the word 'Or' or follow Operators > Logical and double-click 'Or' in the lower part of the Expression Builder window. You will see the word 'Or' appear in the Expression Builder box after the field name. Then select StoreField again and after it type the words 'is null' (without the quotation marks). This means that the query will select a record if it matches what is in the field, OR if the field is null — that is, there is nothing in it. That is exactly what we want.

Usage hint: Instead of keying in 'is null', we could have found the IsNull function in Expression Builder. In this case, the words are so short that keying them in is easier.

24 Modify the CatField test criterion in the same way.

25 Test again: Close the query, enter Storage in the Category field of the form and leave the City field blank. You should see 66 storage sales in all four stores, starting with Alice's purchase of a 1TB disk in Atlanta.

26 Test to confirm that entering a city, but no category, works too.

27 Test to confirm that leaving both blank shows all 312 rows of the full table.

28 Look at the query in Design view. Access has rearranged your criteria, turning them into four and adding two columns that do not show up in the query results. (Their 'Show' boxes are unchecked.) It sometimes does this to reduce a complex query to several simpler ones. That is not a problem. We mention it here only so it does not faze you if you see it.

29 Close your database, saving if prompted.

DELIVERABLE

Your database, with the form and query.

QUIZ QUESTIONS

1 True or false? A form is the only way a user can specify search criteria (without opening a query in Design view, which most end users are not up to).

2 How many portable computers did the Atlanta store sell in the period covered by this database? Who bought more than anyone else? How many did this person buy?

3 Look at the Property Sheet of either text box in CS_Qry_Form. It allows you to specify many properties of these boxes. (Some can be specified through ribbon tools or in other ways as well.) In particular, it lets a form designer choose all of the following *except*
   a font size in points.
   b background colour of the box.
   c which sides of the box will show borders.
   d colour of the box borders.

4 The condition 'IS NULL' in a database query is satisfied if the field in question

a has a numeric value of 0 (zero).

b has an incorrect data type — for example, letters where numbers are required.

c violates validation tests — for example, a month number that is not from 1 to 12.

d is empty — that is, it contains no data.

DISCUSSION QUESTIONS

1 This activity used a form to drive a query. The two can also work together in the opposite direction: using queries as input to a form, where we used only tables until now. Use the form and query you created in this activity to select sales of Display products in all stores. With the query results showing, create a form using the Form tool in the Create ribbon. How does what you created resemble, and how does it differ from, a form you could have created from the tables that underlie this query?

2 In step 25 of the activity, you saw that Access turned your two criteria, each of which contained two elementary conditions combined by OR, into four criteria. Try to figure out the conditions under which each of the four would apply.

3 Query criteria can use hundreds of built-in functions. They are listed under Functions, then Built-In Functions, in the Builder dialogue box. Many of these resemble functions you are familiar with from Excel formulas, including 13 financial functions such as internal rate of return (IRR) and loan payments (PMT) that one might not initially think of when one thinks of database applications. Discuss how a query might use such financial functions.

14
Acquiring information systems and applications

CHAPTER OUTLINE

14.1 Planning for and justifying IT applications

14.2 Strategies for acquiring IT applications

14.3 The traditional systems development life cycle

14.4 Alternative methods and tools for systems development

14.5 Vendor and software selection

LEARNING OBJECTIVES

1. Discuss the different cost/benefit analyses that companies must take into account when formulating an IT strategic plan.
2. Discuss the four business decisions that companies must make when they acquire new applications.
3. Enumerate the primary tasks and importance of each of the six processes involved in the systems development life cycle.
4. Describe alternative development methods and tools that augment development methods.
5. Analyse the process of vendor and software selection.

OPENING CASE >

Learning from the Queensland Health payroll fiasco

The torturous implementation of Queensland Health's payroll system will almost certainly be remembered as one of the most disastrous IT projects in our country's history. What began as a $6.19 million contract between the state of Queensland and IBM Australia to replace Queensland Health's ageing payroll system eventually led to over 35 000 payroll anomalies and will ultimately cost taxpayers $1.25 billion.

The project has been subjected to numerous reviews and a commission of inquiry that saw a number of key IBM and QLD State Government personnel take the stand.

A GROSS UNDERESTIMATION

The stunted progress of the implementation project that the state had spent two years trying to roll out had a direct impact on Queensland Health, which was originally scheduled to receive the new SAP-based system in 2006 and was using a decade-old LATTICE payroll system at the time. With the supplier ending support for the LATTICE payroll system in July 2008, a decision was made in late 2007 by Queensland Health and CorpTech to escalate the implementation of the Queensland Health payroll system. That's where IBM came into the picture, in what would be its first project in a prime contractor role.

The contract price negotiated for the design and implementation of the new payroll system was $6.19 million. It was to be delivered in July 2008, the same month that the support for the existing payroll system was scheduled to expire.

The fact that Queensland Health, CorpTech and IBM agreed to a seven month timeframe to deliver a payroll system with complex award structures that spanned 13 awards and multiple industrial agreements, and contained in excess of 24 000 different combinations of pay for 80 000 employees shows a gross underestimation of the project at hand. What is even more alarming is that according to the original project documentation, a timeframe of only two weeks was allocated to determine the business requirements and solution scope of the complex payroll project.

To put this in context, a similar payroll project took 12 months to scope and three years to rollout at the privately run Mater hospital, which incidentally finished on time and on budget. It's no wonder then that the Queensland Health project soon started to groan under the weight of scope creep, with a recorded 47 submitted change requests signed off by CorpTech in a space of just two months after the contracts were signed.

CUTTING CORNERS AND IBM'S DUTY OF CARE

While the time-strapped state government was allegedly responsible for setting the timeframe, it almost certainly raises a duty of care issue on IBM's part. Independent expert, Dr David Manfield, who was engaged by the Commission of Inquiry into the payroll rollout, said in his report that IBM must have recognised the complexity and size of the solution required well before they were awarded the prime contractor role.

However, IBM continued to operate under the varying scope and the state government kept signing off on the change requests. By the time the system finally went live in March 2010, 20 months after the original start date, the bill had already ballooned to $101 million. The project documentation also reveals that prior to the payroll system going live the project underwent four revised go live dates and four separate stages of change requests, often done at the last minute.

The cost of going live with a premature system resulted in more than 35 000 payroll anomalies and to date has cost the state in excess of $400 million, just to operate the system. KPMG has estimated that the cost of making the system function for the next five years will be another $836 million.

QUESTIONABLE PROCUREMENT PROCESSES

One of the areas closely scrutinised by the inquiry has been the procurement processes that led to IBM being appointed as the prime contractor. It's certainly an area worth examining. The fact that a former IBM executive, Terry Burns, had been tasked with running the bidding process, should have immediately sent alarm bells ringing over the credibility of the entire procurement process.

Burns has since admitted to having let IBM have a 'dry run' of its bid for the prime contractor role, a luxury not afforded to the other bidding vendors, Accenture and Logica. The inquiry has also revealed the leaking of a competitive bid and alleged modification of scoring during the final selection process.

LESSONS LEARNT?

Questionable procurement practices aside, delivering an ICT project of this complexity and scale is not a joke. And the task was made harder by basing

THE NOOK

It is time for Malakai and Abbie to begin discussing the implementation of the systems they have decided on. Specifically, they need some help determining the best method for developing, implementing, running and maintaining this mobile ordering system.

They realise that having the idea for a system is only the beginning. They need to know about development methodologies and which ones make the most sense for them. Remember, their strategy is to provide a relaxing, community-type atmosphere and they think this ordering system will support that mission by making it easier for people to continue with their socialising and not take time away to order drinks and food.

As you read through this chapter, consider the end-of-section questions in light of this case. Although there are more possibilities to think about, these will give you some direction to help develop your final report to them at the end of the chapter.

QUESTIONS

1 Compare and contrast the risks and opportunities of ICT use within an organisation.

2 List and discuss the advantages and disadvantages of ICT use in health and education sectors.

implementation on loosely defined business requirements within an impossible timeframe. A project blowout was always on the cards. The system failed critical user acceptance testing (UAT) processes but instead of addressing the issues, the bar for testing was simply lowered and less stringent guidelines adopted in an effort to get the system out the door to meet a time imperative.

There is little doubt that the state government should have acted to address the underlying issues instead of ignoring the risks and letting a flawed system go into production. A system that left thousands of Queensland Health employees underpaid, overpaid or not paid at all.

Source: K Sharma (2013), 'Learning from the Queensland Health payroll fiasco', *Technology Spectator*, 20 June, www.businessspectator.com.au/article/2013/6/20/technology/learning-qld-health-payroll-fiasco.

Introduction

Competitive organisations move as quickly as they can to acquire new information technologies or modify existing ones when they need to improve efficiencies and gain strategic advantage. Today, however, acquisition goes beyond building new systems inhouse, and IT resources go beyond software and hardware. The old model in which firms built their own systems is being replaced with a broader perspective of IT resource acquisition that provides companies with a number of options. Thus, companies now must decide which IT tasks will remain inhouse, and even whether the entire IT resource should be provided and managed by outside organisations. Regardless of which approach an organisation chooses, however, it must be able to manage IT projects adeptly.

Even for a small business, IS upgrades present a complex problem. Small organisations must select vendors based on a number of factors, particularly (1) the ability of the vendor's product(s) to meet the organisation's current business needs, (2) the viability of the vendor as a whole (you do not want to sign a contract with someone who might go into bankruptcy), and (3) the relationship between the two companies. After the organisation has selected a vendor, the two parties must decide on the contract and clear it with their lawyers. Finally, the organisation must acquire the hardware to support the new software. Even for a small business, these decisions are very important because of the lasting impact of this investment. Although the right information systems may not 'make or break' the organisation, they can definitely help it become more competitive.

In this chapter, you learn about the process of acquiring IT resources from a managerial perspective. This means from *your* perspective, because you will be closely involved in all aspects of acquiring information systems and applications in your organisation. In fact, when we mention 'users' in this chapter, we are talking about you. You will also study the available options for acquiring IT resources and how to evaluate the options. Finally, you will learn how organisations plan and justify the acquisition of new information systems.

14.1 Planning for and justifying IT applications

Organisations must analyse the need for applications and then justify each purchase in terms of costs and benefits. The need for information systems is usually related to organisational planning and to the analysis of its performance vis-à-vis its competitors. The cost–benefit justification must look at the wisdom of investing in a specific IT application versus spending the funds on alternative projects. This chapter focuses on the formal processes of large organisations. Smaller organisations employ less formal processes, or no processes at all. It is important to note that even if a small organisation does not have a formal process for planning and justifying IT applications, the steps of a formal process exist for a reason and they have value. At the very least, decision makers in small organisations should consider each step when they are planning changes in their information systems.

When a company examines its needs and performance, it generates a prioritised list of both existing and potential IT applications, called the **application portfolio**. These are the applications that have to be added, or modified if they already exist.

IT planning

The planning process for new IT applications begins with analysis of the *organisational strategic plan*, which is illustrated in figure 14.1. The organisation's strategic plan identifies the firm's overall mission, the goals that follow from that mission and the broad steps required to reach these goals. The strategic planning process modifies the organisation's objectives and resources to match its changing markets and opportunities.

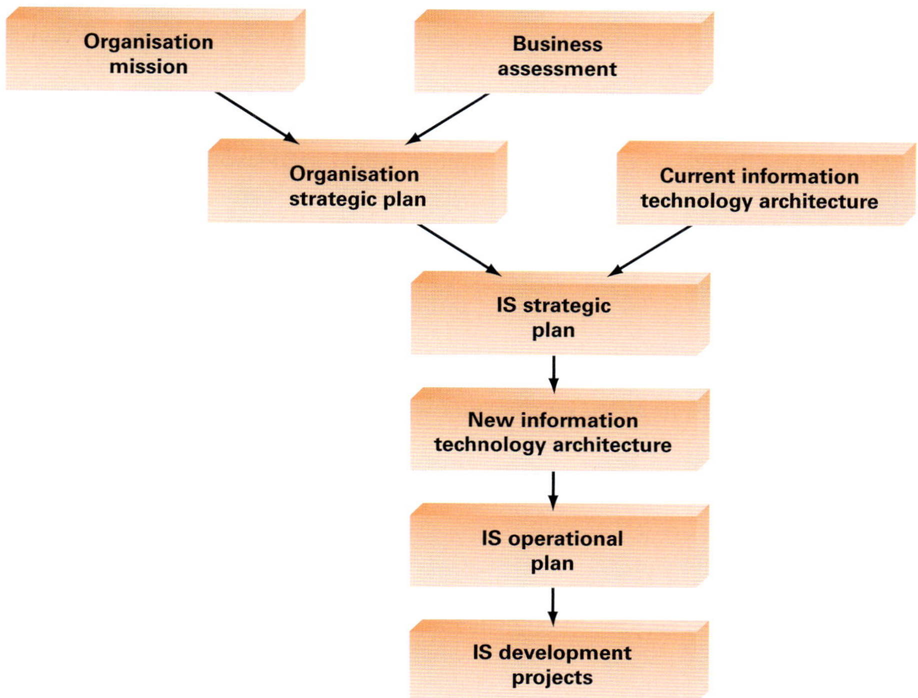

FIGURE 14.1 Analysis of the organisational strategic plan.

The organisational strategic plan and the existing IT architecture provide the inputs in developing the IT strategic plan. The *IT architecture* (see figure 14.2) delineates the way an organisation's information resources should be used to accomplish its mission. It encompasses both the technical and the managerial aspects of information resources.

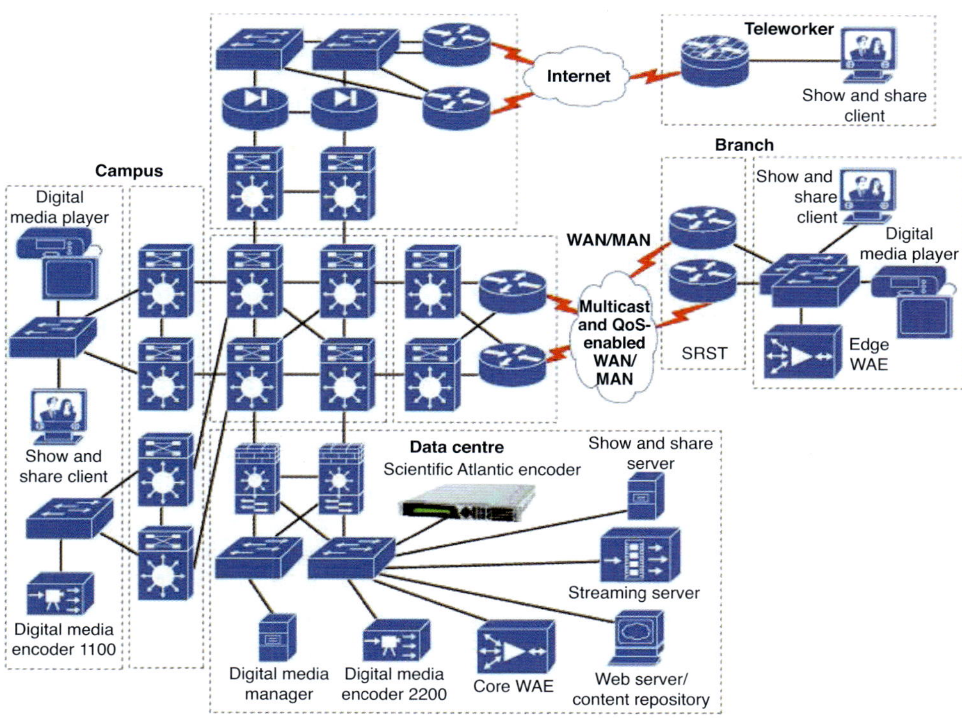

FIGURE 14.2 IT architecture.

The technical aspects include hardware and operating systems, networking, data management systems and applications software. The managerial aspects specify how the IT department will be managed, how the functional area managers will be involved and how IT decisions will be made.

The **IT strategic plan** is a set of long-range goals that describe the IT infrastructure and identify the major IT initiatives needed to achieve the organisation's goals (see this chapter's Closing Case 2). The IT strategic plan must meet three objectives.

1 ***It must be aligned with the organisation's strategic plan.*** This alignment is critical because the organisation's ISs have to support the organisation's strategies. (Recall the discussion of organisational strategies and information systems in chapter 2.)

Consider an application that improves customer service at a small cost. It would be considered favourably at a high-end department store, but it would be rejected at a low-cost chain store. The reason is that the application would fit in favourably (i.e. align) with the high-end department store's service-at-any-cost strategy. However, it would not fit in well with the low-cost chain store's low-cost strategy. You see two department stores, same application, same cost and benefits — but different answers to the question 'Should we develop the application?'

2 ***It must provide for an IT architecture that seamlessly networks users, applications and databases.***

3 ***It must efficiently allocate IS development resources among competing projects so the projects can be completed on time and within budget and still have the required functionality.***

The existing IT architecture is a necessary input into the IT strategic plan because it acts as a constraint on future development efforts. It is not an absolute constraint, however, because the organisation can change to a new IT architecture. Companies prefer to avoid this strategy, however, because it is expensive and time-consuming.

Consider this example. You have a Mac (Apple) system and you need a new software application. You search and find several such packages for both Mac and MS Windows. Unfortunately, the best package runs only on Windows. How much better would this package have to be for you to justify a switch to a new system?

One critical component in developing and implementing the IT strategic plan is the **IT steering committee**. This committee, comprised of a group of managers and staff who represent the various organisational units, is created to establish IT priorities and to ensure that the MIS function is meeting the organisation's needs. The committee's major tasks are to link corporate strategy with IT strategy, to approve the allocation of resources for the MIS function, and to establish performance measures for the MIS function and ensure that they are met. The IT steering committee is important to you because it ensures that you get the information systems and applications that you need to do your job.

After a company has agreed on an IT strategic plan, it next develops the **IS operational plan**. This plan consists of a clear set of projects that the IS department and the functional area managers will execute in support of the IT strategic plan. A typical IS operational plan contains the following elements:

- *mission:* the mission of the IS function (derived from the IT strategy)
- *IS environment:* a summary of the information needs of the functional areas and of the organisation as a whole
- *objectives of the IS function:* the best current estimate of the goals of the IS function
- *constraints on the IS function:* technological, financial, personnel and other resource limitations on the IS function
- *the application portfolio:* a prioritised inventory of present applications and a detailed plan of projects to be developed or continued during the current year
- *resource allocation and project management:* a listing of how and when who is going to do what.

Evaluating and justifying IT investment: benefits, costs and issues

Developing an IT plan is the first step in the acquisition process. Because all companies have limited resources, they must justify investing resources in some areas, including IT, rather than in others. Essentially, justifying IT investment involves calculating the costs, assessing the benefits (values) and comparing the two. This comparison is frequently referred to as cost–benefit analysis. Cost–benefit analysis is not a simple task.

Assessing the costs

Placing a dollar value on the cost of IT investments is not as simple as it may seem. One of the major challenges that companies face is to allocate fixed costs among different IT projects. *Fixed costs* are those costs that remain the same regardless of any change in the activity level. For IT, fixed costs include infrastructure costs and the costs associated with IT services and IT management. For example, the salary of the IT director is fixed and adding one more application will not change it.

Another complication is that the costs of a system do not end when the system is installed. Rather, costs for maintaining, debugging and improving the system can accumulate over many years. This is a critical point because organisations sometimes fail to anticipate these costs when they make the investment.

A dramatic example of unanticipated expenses was the Year 2000 (Y2K) reprogramming projects, which cost organisations worldwide billions of dollars. In the 1960s, computer memory was very expensive. To save money, programmers coded the 'year' in the date field 19_ _, instead of _ _ _ _. With the '1' and the '9' hard-coded in the computer program, only the last two digits varied, so computer programs needed less memory. However, this process meant that when the year 2000 rolled around, computers would display the year as 1900. This programming technique could have caused serious problems with financial applications, insurance applications and countless other apps.

This Y2K example illustrates the point that database design choices tend to affect the organisation for a long time. As the 21st century approached, no one still used hardware or software from the 1960s (other than a few legacy applications). Database design choices made in the 1960s, however, were often still in effect.

Assessing the benefits

Evaluating the benefits of IT projects is typically even more complex than calculating their costs. Benefits may be harder to quantify, especially because many of them are intangible — for example, improved customer or partner relations or improved decision making. As an employee, you will probably be asked for input about the intangible benefits that an IS provides for you.

The fact that organisations use IT for multiple purposes further complicates benefit analysis. In addition, to obtain a return from an IT investment, the company must implement the technology successfully. In reality, many systems are not implemented on time, within budget, or with all the features originally envisioned for them. Also, the proposed system may be 'cutting edge'. In these cases, there may be no basis for identifying the types of financial payback the company can expect.

Conducting the cost–benefit analysis

After a company has assessed the costs and benefits of IT investments, it must compare them. You have studied, or will study, cost–benefit analyses in more detail in your finance courses. The point is that real-world business problems do not come in neatly wrapped packages labelled 'this is a finance problem' or 'this is an IS problem'. Rather, business problems span multiple functional areas.

There is no uniform strategy for conducting a cost–benefit analysis. Rather, an organisation can perform this task in several ways. Here you see four common approaches: (1) net present value, (2) return on investment, (3) breakeven analysis and (4) the business case approach.

- Analysts use the *net present value (NPV)* method to convert future values of benefits to their present-value equivalent by 'discounting' them at the organisation's cost of funds. They can then compare the present value of the future benefits to the cost required to achieve those benefits to determine whether the benefits exceed the costs.
- *Return on investment (ROI)* measures management's effectiveness in generating profits with its available assets. ROI is calculated by dividing the net income generated by a

BEFORE YOU GO ON . . .

1. What are some problems associated with assessing the costs of IT?
2. What difficulties accompany the intangible benefits from IT?
3. Describe the NPV, ROI, breakeven analysis and business case approaches.

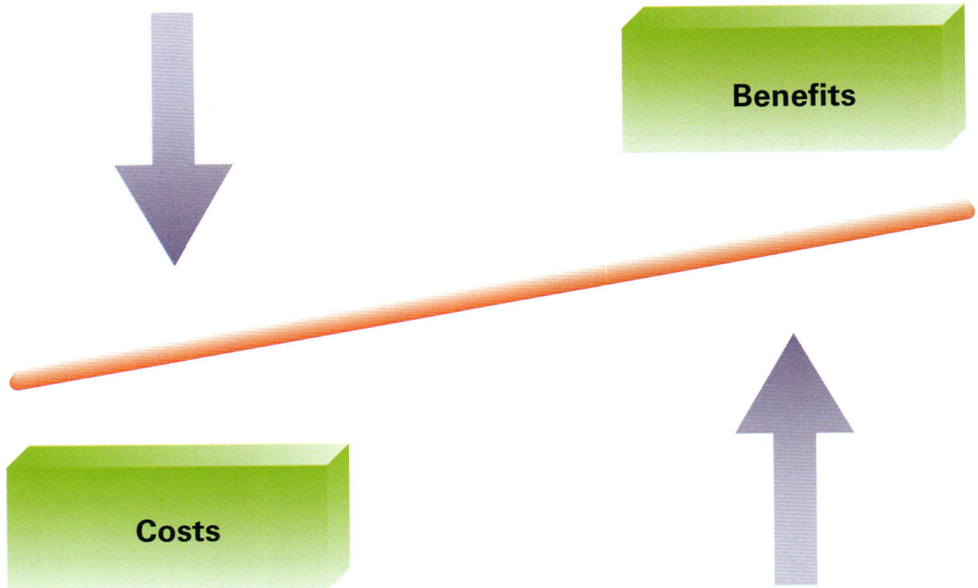

FIGURE 14.3
Cost–benefit analysis.

project by the average assets invested in the project. ROI is a percentage and the higher the percentage return, the better.

- *Breakeven analysis* determines the point at which the cumulative dollar value of the benefits from a project equals the investment made in the project.
- In the *business case approach*, system developers write a business case to justify funding one or more specific applications or projects. IS professionals will be a major source of input when business cases are developed because these cases describe what you do, how you do it and how a new system could better support you.

THE NOOK

QUESTIONS

1. Based on what you have learned about The Nook in this book, what do you think Malakai and Abbie's strategic plan is? Do you think they could accomplish their plan without the use of technology?
2. If the purpose of this system is to collect orders and serve as the transaction processing system (TPS) for their other information systems, what level of accuracy and reliability do you believe Malakai and Abbie need? At what point does a system failure become a problem to customers?

14.2 Strategies for acquiring IT applications

After a company has justified an IT investment, it must then decide how to pursue it. As with cost–benefit analyses, there are several options for acquiring IT applications. To decide on which option to choose, companies must make a series of business decisions. The fundamental decisions are these.

- *How much computer code does the company want to write?* A company can choose to use a totally prewritten application (to write no computer code), to customise a prewritten application (to write some computer code), or to custom-write an entire application (write all new computer code).
- *How will the company pay for the application?* Once the company has decided how much computer code to write, it must decide how to pay for it. Companies can buy or lease

prewritten applications or customised prewritten applications. Companies use internal funding to purchase custom applications.
- *Where will the application run?* The next decision is whether to run the application on the company's platform or on someone else's platform. In other words, it can employ either a software-as-a-service vendor or an application service provider. (You will examine these options later in this chapter.)
- *Where will the application originate?* Prewritten applications can be open-source software or they can come from a vendor. The company may choose to customise prewritten open-source applications or prewritten proprietary applications from vendors. Further, it may customise applications inhouse or outsource the customisation. Finally, it can write totally custom applications inhouse or outsource this process.

In the following sections, you will find more detail on the variety of ways that companies can acquire applications. A good rule of thumb is that an organisation should consider all feasible acquisition methods in light of its own business requirements. You will learn about the following acquisition methods.
- Purchase a prewritten application.
- Customise a prewritten application.
- Lease the application.
- Use application service providers and software-as-a-service vendors.
- Use open-source software.
- Use outsourcing.
- Employ custom development.

Purchase a prewritten application

Many commercial software packages contain the standard features required by IT applications. Therefore, purchasing an existing package can be a cost-effective and time-saving strategy compared with custom-developing the application inhouse. Nevertheless, a company should carefully consider and plan the buy option to ensure that the selected package contains all of the features necessary to address the company's current and future needs. Otherwise, these packages can quickly become obsolete. Before a company can perform this process, it must decide which features a suitable package must include.

In reality, a single software package can rarely satisfy all of an organisation's needs. For this reason, a company sometimes must purchase multiple packages to fulfil different needs. It then must integrate these packages with one another as well as with its existing software. Figure 14.4 summarises the advantages and limitations of the buy option.

FIGURE 14.4 Advantages and limitations of the buy option.

Advantages
Many different types of off-the-shelf software are available.
Software can be tried out.
The company can save much time by buying rather than building.
The company can know what it is getting before it invests in the product.
The company is not the first and only user.
Purchased software may eliminate the need to hire personnel specifically dedicated to a project.
Disadvantages
Software may not exactly meet the company's needs.
Software may be difficult or impossible to modify, or it may require huge business process changes to implement.
The company will not have control over software improvements and new versions.
Purchased software can be difficult to integrate with existing systems.
Vendors may discontinue a product or go out of business.
Software is controlled by another company with its own priorities and business considerations.
Intimate knowledge in the purchasing company is lacking about how and why the software works as it does.

Customise a prewritten application

Customising existing software is an especially attractive option if the software vendor allows the company to modify the application to meet its needs. However, this option may not be attractive in cases where customisation is the only method of providing the necessary flexibility to address the company's needs. It is also not the best strategy when the software is either very expensive or is likely to become obsolete in a short time. Further, customising a prewritten application can be extremely difficult, particularly for large, complex applications.

Lease the application

Compared with the buy option and the option to develop applications inhouse, the lease option can save a company both time and money. Of course, leased packages (like purchased packages) may not exactly fit the company's application requirements. However, as noted, vendor software generally includes the features that are most commonly needed by organisations in a given industry. Again, the company will decide which features are necessary.

It is common for interested companies to apply the 80/20 rule when evaluating vendor software. Put simply, if the software meets 80 per cent of the company's needs, then the company should seriously consider changing its business processes so it can utilise the remaining 20 per cent. Many times this is a better long-term solution than modifying the vendor software. Otherwise, the company will have to customise the software every time the vendor releases an updated version.

Leasing can be especially attractive to small- to medium-size enterprises (SMEs) that cannot afford major investments in IT software. Large companies may also prefer to lease packages in order to test potential IT solutions before committing to major investments. In addition, a company that does not employ sufficient IT personnel with the appropriate skills for developing custom IT applications may choose to lease instead of developing software inhouse. Even those companies that employ inhouse experts may not be able to afford the long wait for strategic applications to be developed inhouse. Therefore, they lease (or buy) applications from external resources to establish a faster presence in the market.

Leasing can be executed in one of three ways. The first way is to lease the application from a software developer, install it and run it on the company's platform. The vendor can assist with the installation and frequently will offer to contract for the support and maintenance of the system. Many conventional applications are leased this way.

The other two options involve leasing an application and running it on the vendor's platform. Organisations can accomplish this process by using an application service provider or a software-as-a-service vendor.

Application service providers and software-as-a-service vendors

An **application service provider (ASP)** is an agent or a vendor who assembles the software needed by enterprises and packages the software with services such as development, operations and maintenance. The customer then accesses these applications via the internet. Figure 14.5 illustrates the operation of an ASP. Note that the ASP hosts an application and a database for each customer.

Software-as-a-service (SaaS) is a method of delivering software in which a vendor hosts the applications and provides them as a service to customers over a network, typically the internet. Customers do not own the software; rather, they pay for using it. SaaS eliminates the need for customers to install and run the application on their own computers. Therefore, SaaS customers save the expense (money, time, IT staff) of buying, operating and maintaining the software. For example, Salesforce (**www.salesforce.com**), a well-known SaaS provider for customer relationship management (CRM) software solutions, provides these advantages for its customers.

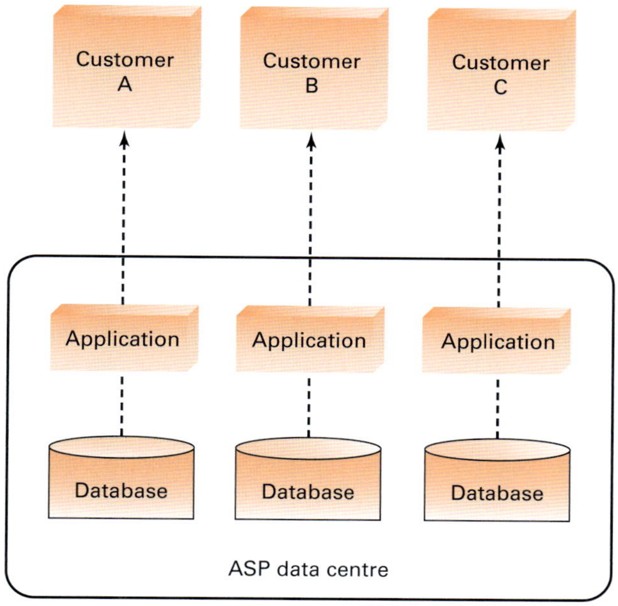

FIGURE 14.5 Operation of an application service provider (ASP).

Figure 14.6 displays the operation of a SaaS vendor. Note that the vendor hosts an application that multiple customers can use. Further, the vendor hosts a database that is partitioned for each customer to protect the privacy and security of each customer's data.

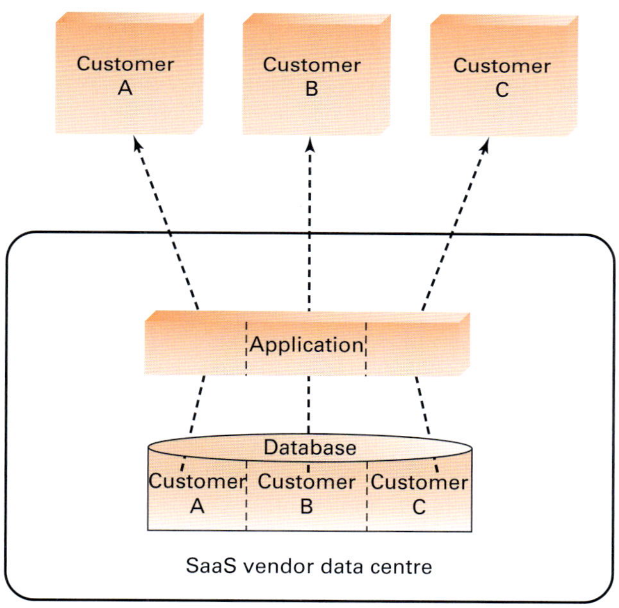

FIGURE 14.6 Organisation of a SaaS provider.

At this point, companies have made the first three decisions and must now decide where to obtain the application. Recall that in general, for prewritten applications, they can use open-source software or obtain the software from a vendor. For customised prewritten applications, they can customise open-source software or customise vendor software. For totally custom applications, they can write the software inhouse or outsource this process.

Use open-source software

Organisations obtain a license to implement an open-source software product and either use it as is, customise it, or develop applications with it. Unless the company is one of the few that want to tinker with their source code, open-source applications are, basically, the same as a proprietary application except for licensing, payment and support. Open-source is really an alternative source of applications rather than a conceptually different development option. (Open-source software is discussed in Plug IT In 2.)

Outsourcing

Acquiring IT applications from outside contractors or external organisations is called **outsourcing**. Keep in mind that outsourcing can be used in many situations. Companies may choose this strategy in certain circumstances. For example, they might want to experiment with new IT technologies without making a substantial up-front investment. They also might use outsourcing to protect their internal networks and to gain access to outside experts. One disadvantage of outsourcing is that a company's valuable corporate data may be under the control of the outsourcing vendor.

Several types of vendors offer services for creating and operating IT systems, including e-commerce applications. Many software companies, from IBM to Oracle, offer a range of outsourcing services for developing, operating and maintaining IT applications. IT outsourcers, such as EDS, offer a variety of services. Also, the large CPA companies and management consultants — for example, Accenture — offer outsourcing services.

As the trend to outsource is on the rise, so is the trend to relocate these operations offshore, particularly in India and China. *Offshoring* can save money, but it includes risks as well. The risks depend on which services are being offshored. If a company is offshoring application development, then the major risk is poor communication between users and developers.

Custom development

Companies may also decide to custom-build an application. They can either perform this operation inhouse or outsource the process. Although custom development is usually more time-consuming and costly than buying or leasing, it often results in a better fit with the organisation's specific requirements.

The development process starts when the IT steering committee (discussed previously in this chapter), having received suggestions for a new system, decides it is worth exploring. These suggestions come from users (who will be you in the near future). Understanding this process will help you get the systems that you will need. Not understanding this process will reduce your chances, because other people who understand it better will make suggestions that use up available resources.

As the company goes through the development process, the mindset changes. In systems investigation, the organisation is trying to decide whether to build something. Everyone knows it may or may not be built. In later stages of the development process, the organisation is committed to building the application. Although a project can be cancelled at any time, this change in attitude is still important.

The basic, backbone methodology for custom development is the systems development life cycle (SDLC), which you will read about in the next section. Section 14.4 examines the methodologies that complement the SDLC: prototyping, joint application development, integrated computer-assisted systems development tools and rapid application development. You will also consider four other methodologies: agile development, end-user development, component-based development and object-oriented development.

BEFORE YOU GO ON . . .

1. Describe the four fundamental business decisions that organisations must make when acquiring information systems.
2. Discuss each of the seven development methods in this section with regard to the four business decisions that organisations must make.

Apply the Concept

Background

This section has discussed the many possibilities available to acquire information systems. One of the more popular methods today is software-as-a-service (SaaS). This method is popular because it removes the need for the company using the software to maintain the hardware that the software will run on. They simply need an internet connection to access the software from the host company.

Activity

Visit **www.johnwiley.com.au/highered/rainer/ausnz/studentresources**. There are two videos linked there that illustrate SaaS. As you watch these videos, think about what hardware is required on both sides of the relationship. Also, consider the legal nature of the relationship given that data will likely reside with the service provider.

Deliverable

Draw an illustration that shows where the software resides, where it can be accessed and what is required to access the software. Include a few points that discuss the importance of the legal relationship as well.

THE NOOK

QUESTIONS

1. Review figure 14.4 and see if the buy option is truly the best option for Malakai and Abbie's mobile ordering system. Which aspects of the buy option will create the most problems for them?
2. Should Malakai and Abbie consider software-as-a-service as an option for their mobile ordering system, or is the information that they track too sensitive to entrust to another company?

14.3 The traditional systems development life cycle

The **systems development life cycle (SDLC)** is the traditional systems development method that organisations use for large-scale IT projects. The SDLC is a structured framework that consists of sequential processes by which information systems are developed. For our purposes (see figure 14.7), you identify six processes, each of which consists of clearly defined tasks:

- systems investigation
- systems analysis
- systems design
- programming and testing
- implementation
- operation and maintenance.

FIGURE 14.7 A six-stage systems development life cycle (SDLC) with supporting tools.

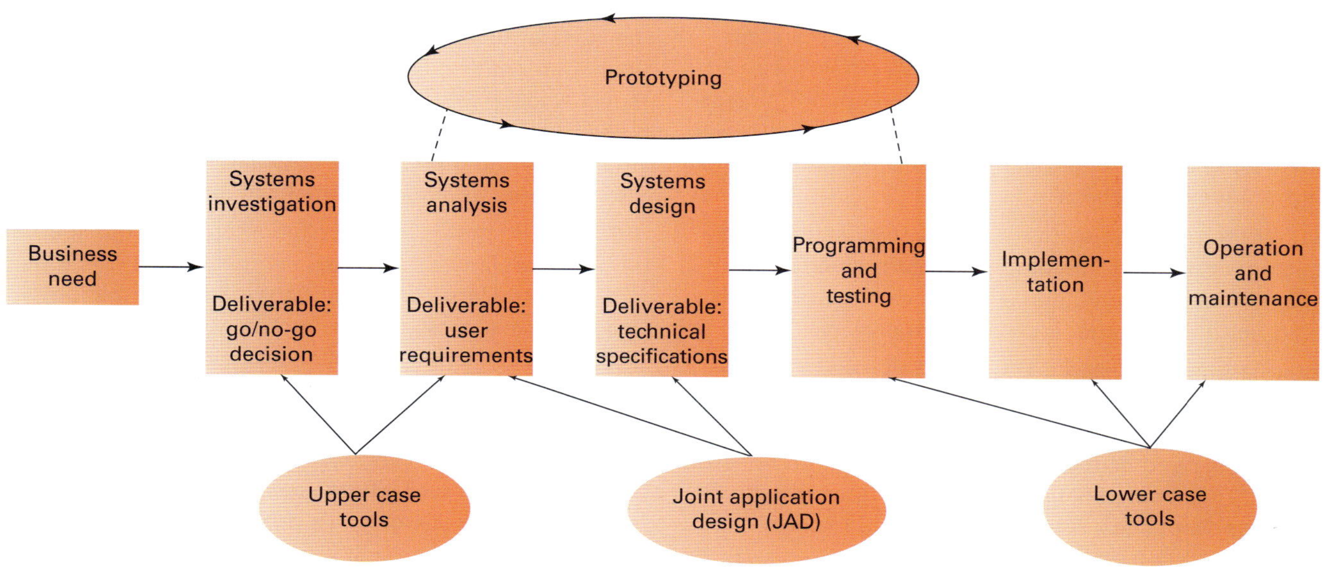

Other models for the SDLC contain more or fewer than the six stages presented here. The flow of tasks, however, remains largely the same. When problems occur in any phase of the SDLC, developers often must go back to previous phases.

Systems development projects produce desired results through team efforts. Development teams typically include users, systems analysts, programmers and technical specialists. *Users* are employees from all functional areas and levels of the organisation who interact with the system, either directly or indirectly. **Systems analysts** are IS professionals who specialise in analysing and designing information systems. **Programmers** are IS professionals who either modify existing computer programs or write new programs to satisfy user requirements. **Technical specialists** are experts on a certain type of technology, such as databases or telecommunications. The **systems stakeholders** include everyone who is affected by changes in a company's information systems; for example, users and managers. All stakeholders are typically involved in systems development at various times and in varying degrees. IT's About Business shows how Atlassian helps companies apply collaborative software development with large projects.

IT'S ABOUT BUSINESS

Atlassian helps manage large software projects

Inhouse software development was once the sole responsibility of companies' IT departments. Today, the process is also of concern to business managers and executives. Companies' business leaders are now involved in discussions about how well software projects are delivering. These discussions increasingly need to be open and global, as the work of development, implementation, bug fixes and upgrades is more divided than ever across different areas of expertise around the world. This process of cross-company discussion around software project development is called collaborative software development.

One example of a company successfully using collaborative software development is Lancôme, a division of L'Oréal that owns brands such as YSL Beauty. In 2010, Lancôme wanted to revamp its websites, electronic commerce and online marketing efforts. In order to do this, the company had to figure out some way to coordinate the work of inhouse employees, freelance web developers and creative staff in Chicago, India and elsewhere. The company needed to figure out how to use software to manage its product development and production process.

Rather than assign this task to its overworked IT staff, Lancôme turned to Atlassian (www.atlassian.com). Atlassian sells an online application called Jira, which can track and manage large software projects.

Atlassian helped speed up Lancôme's projects and made each step of the development process visible to anyone on the team. The software also decreased the number of meetings and back-and-forth emails required for each project. These benefits translated into more sales on Lancôme's websites. After this successful experience, the company is now looking at implementing Jira in other divisions of the company.

Another company that made good use of Atlassian's product is NYSE Euronext. NYSE Euronext wanted to improve its collaboration and speed up the development process of its software projects. The firm also wanted to revamp its website and its mobile and e-commerce data products. When NYSE Euronext deployed Atlassian, some employees who used to jealously guard their code did not like the openness and collaboration of the new tools. These employees no longer work at NYSE Euronext. The CIO notes that the firm experienced a lot of attrition among their developers, but that it was 'good attrition'. Productivity in software development improved from 30 to 50 per cent in just the first 6 months.

Research shows that when a company uses one Atlassian product, it will often also end up using another because of its tight integration. For example, a data management firm called Cloudera uses Jira to track bugs. Additionally, all 150 of Cloudera's employees use Atlassian's Confluence collaboration software to share information on sales, personnel issues, business development and bug reports from Jira.

Atlassian is serious about collaboration and transparency in how people work and how companies are run. It posts an unusually large amount of company information for employees to see on an internal website, including financials, sales performance and pretty much everything except employee salaries.

Atlassian applies different community collaboration rules for different kinds of content. Developer documentation is managed in a wiki where anyone with an account can post or edit content. This process works well for generating code samples and usage examples. For the core product documentation, Atlassian gives editing abilities to some members of the community, but requires those editors to first undergo a vetting process. Furthermore, individuals with editing capabilities are required to sign an agreement detailing their rights and responsibilities. Users that lack editor rights can also post comments on the formal documentation and the editors are responsible for monitoring those comments to see if there are items that they need to add or change.

Once per quarter, Atlassian hosts its 'FedEx Days', which are competitions in which employees compete to produce a product in 24 hours (typically fuelled by pizza and beer). Atlassian uses a social event, rather than any promise of monetary reward, to spur innovation and creativity. FedEx the company has nothing to do with this competition, other than to be a source of inspiration. The name of the competition references FedEx's tradition of being the delivery company to choose 'when it absolutely, positively has to be there overnight'.

Atlassian adopted the trend of pricing web software so cheaply that small firms are able to purchase their products. Atlassian then grows virally through companies that adopt its software. Atlassian posts all its prices on its website — typically $10 per month for up to 10 users for each product and up to $1000 per month for up to 2000 users per product. The firm invites customers to sign up with no negotiation necessary. This business model has proved its worth to Atlassian — the company now has 24 000 customers across 138 countries, including Microsoft, Oracle, Facebook, Twitter, LinkedIn, L'Oréal and NYSE Euronext, and are growing rapidly despite competition from IBM, Microsoft, MindTouch and Jive. Atlassian's revenue was up more than 40 per cent in 2011.

Sources: Compiled from T Geron (2012), 'We're all coders', *Forbes*, 12 March; D Carr (2012), 'Atlassian boosts JIRA social features, social integration', *InformationWeek*, 22 February; D Carr (2012), 'How social media changes technical communication', *InformationWeek*, 4 January; D Carr (2011), 'How to create a new product in 24 hours', *InformationWeek*, 2 December; T Taulli (2011), 'Atlassian: $100M + M business with no sales people?', *Forbes*, 14 June; www.atlassian.com.

QUESTIONS

1 Why are collaboration and transparency so important in the software development process?

2 What potential problems could arise when using Atlassian to manage software development? Provide specific examples to support your answer.

3 Provide an example of a software development project for which it would not be advisable to use Atlassian.

Figure 14.8 indicates that users have high involvement in the early stages of the SDLC, lower involvement in the programming and testing stage, and higher involvement in the later stages. Figure 14.9 (overleaf) discusses the advantages and disadvantages of the SDLC.

FIGURE 14.8 Comparison of user and developer involvement over the SDLC.

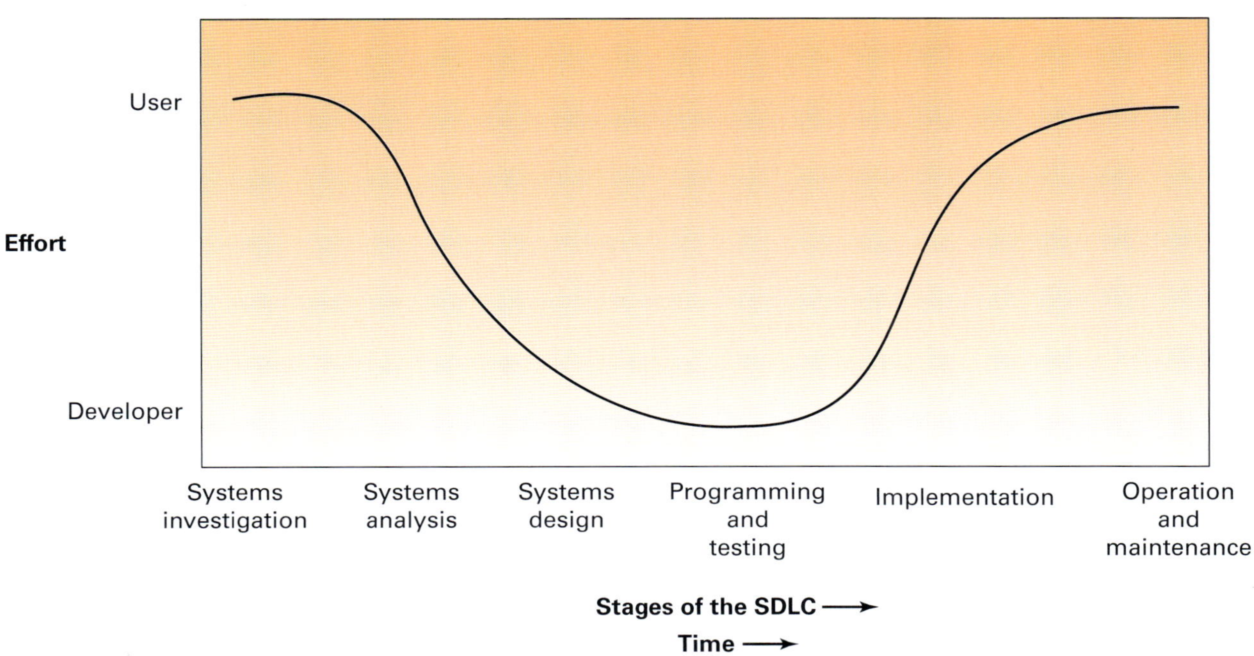

FIGURE 14.9 Advantages and disadvantages of system acquisition methods.

Traditional systems development (SDLC)

Advantages
- Forces staff to systematically go through every step in a structured process.
- Enforces quality by maintaining standards.
- Has lower probability of missing important issues in collecting user requirements.

Disadvantages
- May produce excessive documentation.
- Users may be unwilling or unable to study the approved specifications.
- Takes too long to go from the original ideas to a working system.
- Users have trouble describing requirements for a proposed system.

Prototyping

Advantages
- Helps clarify user requirements.
- Helps verify the feasibility of the design.
- Promotes genuine user participation.
- Promotes close working relationship between systems developers and users.
- Works well for ill-defined problems.
- May produce part of the final system.

Disadvantages
- May encourage inadequate problem analysis.
- Not practical with large number of users.
- User may not give up the prototype when the system is completed.
- May generate confusion about whether the system is complete and maintainable.
- System may be built quickly, which may result in lower quality.

Joint application design

Advantages
- Involves many users in the development process.
- Saves time.
- Greater user support for new system.
- Improved quality of the new system.
- New system easier to implement.
- New system has lower training costs.

Disadvantages
- Difficult to get all users to attend JAD meeting.
- JAD approach has all the problems associated with any group meeting.

Integrated computer-assisted software engineering

Advantages
- Can produce systems with a longer effective operational life.
- Can produce systems that closely meet user requirements.
- Can speed up the development process.
- Can produce systems that are more flexible and adaptable to changing business conditions.
- Can produce excellent documentation.

Disadvantages
- Systems often more expensive to build and maintain.
- Require more extensive and accurate definition of user requirements.
- Difficult to customise.

Rapid application development

Advantages
- Can speed up systems development.
- Users intensively involved from the start.
- Improves the process of rewriting legacy applications.

Disadvantages
- Produces functional components of final systems, but not final systems.

End-user development
Advantages • Bypasses the IS department and avoids delays. • User controls the application and can change it as needed. • Directly meets user requirements. • Increased user acceptance of new system. • Frees up IT resources. • May create lower-quality systems.
Disadvantages • May eventually require maintenance from IS department. • Documentation may be inadequate. • Poor quality control. • System may not have adequate interfaces to existing systems.
Object-oriented development
Advantages • Objects model real-world entities. • May be able to reuse some computer code.
Disadvantages • Works best with systems of more limited scope (i.e. with systems that do not have huge numbers of objects).

Systems investigation

The initial stage in a traditional SDLC is systems investigation. Systems development professionals agree that the more time they invest in (1) understanding the business problem to be solved, (2) specifying the technical options for the systems and (3) anticipating the problems they are likely to encounter during development, the greater the chances of success. For these reasons, systems investigation addresses *the business problem* (or business opportunity) by means of the feasibility study.

The main task in the systems investigation stage is the feasibility study. Organisations have three basic solutions to any business problem relating to an information system:

1 do nothing and continue to use the existing system unchanged
2 modify or enhance the existing system
3 develop a new system.

The **feasibility study** analyses which of these three solutions best fits the particular business problem. It also provides a rough assessment of the project's technical, economic and behavioural feasibility, as explained below.

- *Technical feasibility* determines whether the company can develop and/or acquire the hardware, software and communications components needed to solve the business problem. Technical feasibility also determines whether the organisation can use its existing technology to achieve the project's performance objectives.
- *Economic feasibility* determines whether the project is an acceptable financial risk and, if so, whether the organisation has the necessary time and money to successfully complete the project. You have already learned about the commonly used methods to determine economic feasibility: NPV, ROI, breakeven analysis and the business case approach.
- *Behavioural feasibility* addresses the human issues of the systems development project. Clearly, you will be heavily involved in this aspect of the feasibility study.

After the feasibility analysis is completed, a 'go/no-go' decision is reached by the steering committee if there is one, or by top management in the absence of a committee. The go/no-go decision does not depend solely on the feasibility analysis. Organisations often have more feasible projects than they can fund. Therefore, the firm must prioritise the feasible projects and pursue those with the highest priority. Unfunded feasible projects may not be presented to the IT department at all. These projects therefore contribute to the *hidden backlog*, which are projects that the IT department is not aware of.

If the decision is no-go, then the project either is put on the shelf until conditions are more favourable or is discarded. If the decision is go, then the project proceeds and the systems analysis phase begins.

Systems analysis

Once a development project has the necessary approvals from all participants, the systems analysis stage begins. **Systems analysis** is the examination of the business problem that the organisation plans to solve with an information system.

The main purpose of the systems analysis stage is to gather information about the existing system in order to determine the requirements for an enhanced system or a new system. The end product of this stage, known as the *deliverable*, is a set of *system requirements*.

Arguably, the most difficult task in systems analysis is to identify the specific requirements that the system must satisfy. These requirements are often called *user requirements*, because users (meaning you) provide them. When the systems developers have accumulated the user requirements for the new system, they proceed to the systems design stage.

Systems design

Systems design describes how the system will resolve the business problem. The deliverable of the systems design phase is the set of *technical system specifications*, which specifies the following:

- system outputs, inputs and user interfaces
- hardware, software, databases, telecommunications, personnel and procedures
- a blueprint of how these components are integrated.

When the system specifications are approved by all participants, they are 'frozen'. That is, they should not be changed. Adding functions after the project has been initiated causes **scope creep**, which endangers the project's budget and schedule. Because scope creep is expensive, successful project managers place controls on changes requested by users. These controls help to prevent runaway projects.

Programming and testing

If the organisation decides to construct the software inhouse, then programming begins. **Programming** involves translating the design specifications into computer code. This process can be lengthy and time consuming, because writing computer code is as much an art as a science. Large systems development projects can require hundreds of thousands of lines of computer code and hundreds of computer programmers. These large-scale projects employ programming teams. The teams often include functional area users, who help the programmers focus on the business problem.

Thorough and continuous testing occurs throughout the programming stage. Testing is the process that checks to see if the computer code will produce the expected and desired results. It is also intended to detect errors, or bugs, in the computer code.

Implementation

Implementation (or *deployment*) is the process of converting from an old computer system to a new one. The conversion process involves organisational change. Only end users can manage organisational change, not the MIS department. The MIS department typically does not have enough credibility with the business users to manage the change process. Organisations use three major conversion strategies:

- direct
- pilot
- phased.

In a **direct conversion**, the old system is cut off and the new system is turned on at a certain point in time. This type of conversion is the least expensive. It is also the most risky because, if the new system does not work as planned, there is no support from the old system. Because of these risks, few systems are implemented using direct conversion. IT's About Business on the opposite page demonstrates the risks of a direct conversion.

BEFORE YOU GO ON . . .

1. Define *feasibility* study.
2. What is the difference between systems analysis and systems design?
3. Describe structured programming.
4. What are the four conversion methods?

IT'S ABOUT BUSINESS

Virgin Australia's reservation system

Virgin Australia, co-founded by Sir Richard Branson in 2000, is Australia's second largest airline. Based in Brisbane, Virgin serves 29 cities in Australia, using Boeing and Embraer jets as well as Airbus aircraft.

On 26 September 2010, Virgin's online booking system went down due to hardware failure, impacting the airline's internet, booking, reservations and check-in and boarding systems. The outage interrupted Virgin for 11 days, affecting more than 50 000 passengers and 400 flights, and costing more than $20 million.

To solve this problem, Virgin implemented the Sabre reservation system. Sabre global distribution system, owed by Sabre Holdings, is used by more than 350 000 travel agents worldwide, with more than 400 airlines and 100 000 hotels. Sabre claims that Sabre systems are used by '25 car rental brands, 50 rail providers, 13 cruise lines and other global travel suppliers. More than 300 million people purchase airline tickets through this channel annually.'

However, in August 2013, the Sabre airline reservation system went down, causing a major problem in several airports in Australia. Virgin cancelled more than 30 flights on that day and many were delayed after the booking and check-in system went down. Virgin confirmed that their IT team and the Sabre airline reservation system managed to resolve the problem within two hours, compared to 2010 when it took more than 11 days.

Using technology in an organisation enhances work performance and productivity, improves communications and collaboration between employees and stakeholders, better stores and protects information, and improves an organisation's efficiency by developing automated processes. However, a slight problem or error will cause a huge problem to an organisation in relation to profit as well as reputation. It is imperative that the IT team has enough knowledge and skills in solving problems and decision making promptly and efficiently.

Sources: ABC News (2010), 'Virgin ill-prepared for system crash, experts say', www.abc.net.au/news/2010-09-27/virgin-ill-prepared-for-system-crash-experts-say/2276192; ABC News (2013), 'Virgin Australia check-in system crash causes flight delays and cancellations', www.abc.net.au/news/2013-08-06/virgin-flights-hits-by-check-in-system-crash/4869022; F Foo (2010), 'Virgin system crash may spark multi-million-dollar payout', www.theaustralian.com.au/technology/virgin-system-crash-may-spark-multi-million-dollar-payout/story-e6frgakx-1225930251112; E Harvey (2010), 'Computer glitch causes Virgin Blue delays', www.smh.com.au/travel/travel-news/computer-glitch-causes-virgin-blue-delays-20100926-15s0k.html; M O'Sullivan (2013), 'Virgin Australia flight delays after check-in system crashes worldwide', www.theadvocate.com.au/story/1687204/virgin-australia-flight-delays-after-check-in-system-crashes-worldwide; Sabre (2013), 'About us', www.sabre.com/home/about/our_businesses/sabre_travel_network; B Sandilands (2013), 'Virgin Australia put to the Sabre by IT stuff up', blogs.crikey.com.au/planetalking/2013/08/06/virgin-australia-put-to-the-sabre-by-it-stuff-up/?wpmp_switcher=mobile; SBS News (2013), 'Slow take-off after Virgin system crashes', www.sbs.com.au/news/article/2013/08/06/slow-take-after-virgin-system-crashes.

QUESTIONS

1 List and discuss two reservations online systems in the market.

2 From your perspective, why is using technology in an organisation essential?

Apply the Concept

Background

The systems development life cycle uses a very systematic approach where each stage is built from work done at an earlier stage. It is an excellent model to follow, assuming the right decision is made in the feasibility study. The feasibility study looks at three different aspects of the organisation. First is technical feasibility (Can it be done?), then financial feasibility (Can we afford it?) and last is behavioural feasibility (Will the people use it?). If the answer to any of these is 'No', then the new system must be seriously reconsidered.

Activity

Consider the following scenario. A customer pulls up to a petrol station and chooses to pay at the bowser. After he has swiped his card, he begins pumping petrol. While standing at the bowser, he is asked if he would like to add a drink to the petrol bill he has already paid. Or, he may choose a $5 credit that would print so he could take it inside and redeem for merchandise. If he chooses the drink, it would simply be added to the bill and a receipt printed. If he chooses the dollar amount, he would take the credit slip into the store and redeem it for goods. The next time you fill up your car, go inside and speak to the manager about this idea. How did he respond? Do they think it is technically feasible? Would it be financially beneficial to set this up? Would people use it or would customers just pay at the bowser and leave?

Deliverable

Build a table that has your assumed answers and the manager's answers. Your table will look like the one below.

Feasibility area	Personal thoughts	Manager's thoughts
Technical		
Financial		
Behavioural		

QUESTIONS

1. Have Malakai and Abbie already engaged in any stages of the SDLC?
2. Do you think there is enough time to devote to this type of system development?
3. Who should Malakai and Abbie include in their behavioural feasibility analysis? Does anyone outside of The Nook's employment need special consideration?

14.4 Alternative methods and tools for systems development

Alternative methods for systems development include joint application design, rapid application development, agile development and end-user development.

Joint application design

Joint application design (JAD) is a group-based tool for collecting user requirements and creating system designs. It is most often used within the systems analysis and systems design stages of the SDLC. JAD involves a group meeting attended by the analysts and all of the users. It is basically a group decision-making process that can be conducted manually or via the computer. During this meeting, all users jointly define and agree on the systems requirements. This process saves a tremendous amount of time. Figure 14.9 (p. 468) lists the advantages and disadvantages of the JAD process.

Rapid application development

Rapid application development (RAD) is a systems development method that can combine JAD, prototyping and integrated computer-assisted software engineering (ICASE) tools (discussed later in this section) to rapidly produce a high-quality system. In the first RAD stage, developers use JAD sessions to collect system requirements. This strategy ensures that users are intensively involved early on. The development process in RAD is iterative, similar to prototyping. That is, requirements, designs and the system itself are developed and then undergo a series, or sequence, of improvements. RAD uses ICASE tools to quickly structure requirements and develop prototypes. As the prototypes are developed and refined, users review them in additional JAD sessions. RAD produces the functional components of a final system, rather than prototypes. To understand how RAD functions and how it differs from SDLC, see figure 14.10. Figure 14.9 (p. 468) highlights the advantages and disadvantages of the RAD process.

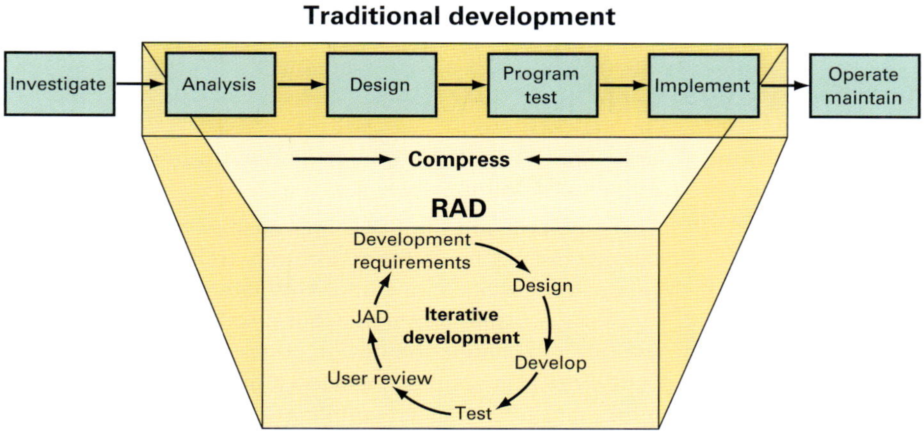

FIGURE 14.10 A rapid prototyping development process versus SDLC.

Agile development

Agile development is a software development methodology that delivers functionality in rapid iterations, which are usually measured in weeks. To be successful, this methodology requires frequent communication, development, testing and delivery. Agile development focuses on rapid development and frequent user contact to create software that addresses the needs of business users. This software does not have to include every possible feature the user will require. Rather, it must meet only the user's more important and immediate needs. It can be updated later to introduce additional functions as they become necessary. The core tenet of agile development is to do only what you have to do to be successful right now.

One type of agile development uses the *scrum approach*. A key principle of scrum is that during a project users can change their minds about what they want and need. Scrum acknowledges that a development problem cannot be fully understood or defined from the start. Therefore, scrum focuses on maximising the development team's ability to deliver iterations quickly and to respond effectively to additional user requirements as they emerge.

Scrum contains sets of practices and predefined roles. The primary roles are these:

- the *scrum master*: maintains the processes (typically replaces a project manager)
- the *product owner*: represents the business users and any other stakeholders in the project
- the *team*: a cross-functional group of about seven people who perform the actual analysis, design, coding, implementation, testing and so on.

Scrum works this way: During each sprint, which is typically a two to four week period, the team creates a potentially shippable product increment, such as working and tested software. The set of features that goes into each sprint comes from the product backlog, which is a prioritised set of high-level work requirements to be completed.

The sprint planning meeting determines which backlog items will be addressed during a sprint. During this meeting, the product owner informs the team of the items in the product backlog that he or she wants completed. The team members then determine how many of these projects they can commit to during the next sprint and they record this information in the sprint backlog.

During a sprint, no one is allowed to change the sprint backlog, which means that the requirements are frozen for the sprint. Each sprint must end on time. If the requirements are not completed for any reason, they are left out and returned to the product backlog. After each sprint is completed, the team demonstrates how to use the software. IT's About Business (overleaf) illustrates how GE Healthcare moved from the systems development life cycle to agile development.

End-user development

End-user development is an approach in which the organisation's end users develop their own applications with little or no formal assistance from the IT department. Figure 14.9 lists the advantages and disadvantages of end-user development.

IT'S ABOUT BUSINESS

GE Healthcare switches from Waterfall to Agile

GE Healthcare (www.gehealthcare.com) is a $17 billion business unit of General Electric (www.ge.com) that manufactures products designed to help clinicians be more productive. These technologies, which range from high-definition CT scanners to diagnostic pharmaceutical devices, are developed by the company's Imaging Solutions unit. Imaging Solutions employs 375 engineers who support 18 high-tech products. Unfortunately, this unit has experienced several difficulties.

First, Imaging Solutions struggled with the predictability of its systems development project execution. The cycle time on projects was too long to begin with (from 12 to 24 months) and often experienced significant delays beyond the already-long cycle time. These long cycle times frequently caused the business to add features beyond the initial user requirements, reflecting concerns that customers could not wait for a new system to have these features. This coping mechanism, in turn, often increased a project's scope, causing further delays and increasing the project cycle time even more. Longer cycle times increase the risk that the user requirements gathered at the beginning of the project will be out-of-date by the time the product reaches the market.

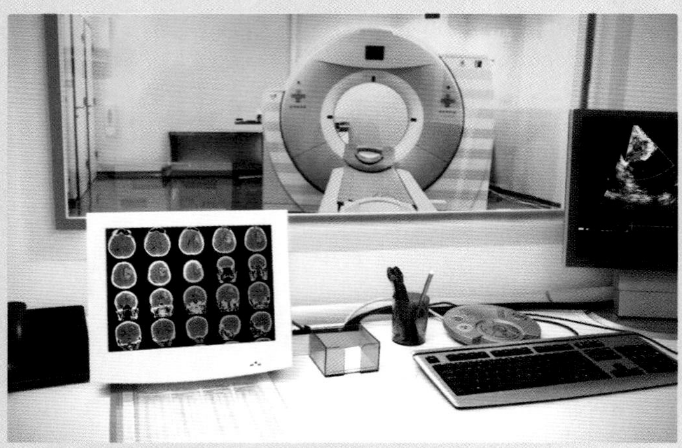

In addition, Imaging Solutions' systems development process followed the systems development life cycle (SDLC) approach. In other words, Imaging Solutions began its process with investigation, systems analysis and systems design. After completing these steps, the unit then conducted a formal design review. After obtaining the various approvals for the design, the engineers began programming new systems.

Programming at Imaging Solutions typically took several months, after which the development team would release the new system into a test environment to collect user feedback. This point in the process was usually the first time that users came into contact with the new system. After the team accumulated and incorporated user input, it continued the testing effort prior to implementing the new system.

The problem with the SDLC approach was that the system did not have the opportunity to incorporate user-requested modifications until very late in the project cycle. As a result, any significant errors could require the team to change the design completely — in effect, to start over. This approach wasted a great deal of time and effort, and often caused significant delays in projects.

To address these issues, Imaging Solutions replaced its SDLC approach with an agile-based scrum initiative. Scrum (discussed in detail in this chapter) focuses on maximising the development team's ability to deliver iterations quickly and respond effectively to additional user requirements as they emerge. In contrast to SDLC, agile development involves adding functionality in a series of phases and then testing the product after each phase is completed. The Imaging Solutions unit particularly liked the idea of demonstrating each phase's functionality to users and then receiving immediate feedback. This approach was much more economical and efficient than receiving feedback at the point when the system was nearing completion.

Imaging Solutions launched its move to agile development with a single development team and a pilot project that had a manageable scope and a luxurious four month deadline. The project was substantial enough that the team could learn scrum skills while delivering a valuable product, but manageable enough to be a good first test run. The team also established clear criteria by which to measure its success so that team members could objectively evaluate whether they had achieved their goals.

The pilot project was concluded successfully and contained all of the correct features and functionality. The release, however, was one month past the desired roll-out date, so Imaging Solutions is still working on its predictability of delivery.

This pilot project informed Imaging Solutions that the company could adopt agile development, but only with certain limitations. Specifically, the rigours of operating in a regulated industry required it to deploy a hybrid development process that involved more initial planning and testing than would be found in other agile organisations.

Following the resolution of the pilot project, Imaging Solutions formed 10 scrum teams of seven to nine people each. Every two weeks, the teams met on Wednesday mornings to conduct increment reviews and on Wednesday afternoons to hold their planning meetings for the next increment. This process ensured that teams were sharing knowledge with their fellow team members and were aware of what was being done outside of their own particular team.

To obtain maximum benefits from the agile system, Imaging Solutions had to transform its culture somewhat by modifying the role of managers and individual contributors on scrum teams. For example, Imaging Solutions managers can no longer use a command-and-control style of management and must instead concentrate on assembling empowered teams.

These cultural and process changes have resulted in positive results for Imaging Solutions. Obtaining user feedback early and often has enabled Imaging Solutions to prioritise features correctly. For instance, in one example, the new system helped a team identify a clinical workflow it previously was not aware of. Insights such as this one will continue to allow Imaging Solutions to develop products that will be successful in the market and release those products in a timely manner, thereby growing profitability and credibility as a company.

Sources: Compiled from K Liang (2012), 'What jobs are available for software engineers who want to advance medical research?', *Forbes*, 2 March; J Hammond (2011), 'Customer-centric development: it's now or never for IT shops', *InformationWeek*, 26 April; S Denning (2011), 'Six common mistakes that Salesforce.com didn't make', *Forbes*, 18 April; A Deitsch and R Hughes (2010), 'GE Healthcare goes agile', *InformationWeek*, 6 December; J Vijayan (2010), 'The grill: John Burke,' *Computerworld*, 13 September; J Kobelius (2010), 'Agile data warehousing: do you scrum?', *InformationWeek*, 21 July; www.ge.com; www.gehealthcare.com; www.rallydev.com.

QUESTIONS

1 Compare and contrast the risks and benefits of digitising medical records, especially the private information. What risks can you think of that are associated with digitising such private information? Do you feel more comfortable with your medical records in a paper file on a shelf or in a computer?

2 Search for the phrase *scope creep* and relate your findings. How would this phenomenon cause a problem in the acquisition and implementation of information systems?

Tools for systems development

Several tools can be used with various systems development methods. These tools include prototyping, integrated computer-assisted software engineering (ICASE), component-based development and object-oriented development.

Prototyping

The **prototyping** approach defines an initial list of user requirements, builds a model of the system, then refines the system in several iterations based on users' feedback. Developers do not try to obtain a complete set of user specifications for the system at the outset and they do not plan to develop the system all at once. Instead, they quickly develop a smaller version of the system known as a **prototype**. A prototype can take two forms. In some cases, it contains only the components of the new system that are of most interest to the users. In other cases, it is a small-scale working model of the entire system.

Users make suggestions for improving the prototype, based on their experiences with it. The developers then review the prototype with the users and use their suggestions to refine the prototype. This process continues through several iterations until the users approve the system or it becomes apparent that the system cannot meet the users' needs. If the system is viable, then the developers can use the prototype to build the full system. One typical use of prototyping is to develop screens that a user will see and interact with. Figure 14.9 (p. 468) describes the advantages and disadvantages of the prototyping approach.

A practical problem with prototyping is that a prototype usually looks more complete than it is. It may not use the real database, it usually does not have the necessary error checking and it almost never includes the necessary security features. Users who review a prototype that resembles the finished system may not recognise these problems. Consequently, they might have unrealistic expectations about how close the actual system is to completion.

Integrated computer-assisted software engineering tools

Computer-aided software engineering (CASE) is a group of tools that automate many of the tasks in the SDLC. The tools that are used to automate the early stages of the SDLC (systems investigation, analysis and design) are called upper CASE tools. The tools used to automate later stages in the SDLC (programming, testing, operation and maintenance) are called lower CASE tools. CASE tools that provide links between upper CASE and lower CASE tools are called **integrated CASE (ICASE) tools**. Figure 14.9 (p. 468) lists the advantages and disadvantages of ICASE tools.

Component-based development

Component-based development uses standard components to build applications. Components are reusable applications that generally have one specific function, such as a shopping cart, user authentication, or a catalogue. Component-based development is closely linked with the idea of web services and service-oriented architectures, which you see in Plug IT In 3.

Many startup companies are pursuing the idea of component-based application development, or less programming and more assembly. An example of these companies is Ning (www.ning.com), which allows organisations to create, customise and share their own social network.

Object-oriented development

Object-oriented development is based on a different view of computer systems to the perception that characterises traditional development approaches. Traditional approaches can produce a system that performs the original task but may not be suited for handling other tasks. This observation applies even when these other tasks involve the same real-world entities. For example, a billing system will handle billing but probably cannot be adapted to handle mailings for the marketing department or to generate leads for the sales force. This is true even though the billing, marketing and sales functions all use similar data, including customer names, addresses and purchases. In contrast, an *object-oriented (OO) system* begins not with the task to be performed but with the aspects of the real world that must be modelled to perform that task. Therefore, in our example, if the firm has a good model of its customers and its interactions with them, then it can use this model equally well for billings, mailings and sales leads.

The development process for an object-oriented system begins with a feasibility study and an analysis of the existing system. Systems developers identify the *objects* in the new system — the fundamental elements in OO analysis and design. Each object represents a tangible, real-world entity, such as a customer, bank account, student, or course. Objects have *properties*, or *data values*. For example, a customer has an identification number, a name, an address, an account number(s) and so on. Objects also contain the *operations* that can be performed on their properties. For example, operations that can be performed on the customer object may include obtain-account-balance, open-account, withdraw-funds and so on. Operations are also referred to as *behaviours*.

This approach enables OO analysts to define all the relevant objects needed for the new system, including their properties and operations. The analysts then model how the objects interact to meet the objectives of the new system. In some cases, analysts can reuse existing objects from other applications (or from a library of objects) in the new system. This process saves the analysts the time they otherwise would spend coding these objects. In most cases, however, even with object reuse, some coding will be necessary to customise the objects and their interactions for the new system.

You have studied many methods that can be used to acquire new systems. Figure 14.9 (p. 468–9) provides an overview of the advantages and disadvantages of these methods.

BEFORE YOU GO ON . . .

1. Describe the tools that augment the traditional SDLC.
2. Describe the alternate methods that can be used for systems development, other than the SDLC.

Apply the Concept

Background

Prototyping is a method of systems development that allows an idea to get into a testable form very quickly. Often, ideas can go from discussion to prototype at the dinner table in a simple sketch on a napkin.

Activity

Visit www.johnwiley.com.au/highered/rainer/ausnz/studentresources. This will show you a Vimeo video about prototyping.

Imagine that you are an app developer for iPhone apps. At lunch the other day someone mentioned a very cool idea for a new camera app that would allow you to take pictures by opening the app and saying 'click' rather than pushing a button. This would also allow you to take remote pictures when you are ready rather than using a timer.

What should this app look like? Draw up a sketch of at least two screens. First, the camera screen, second the options screen. Discuss this with a couple of your friends and see what they think. Ask someone who has an iPhone their ideas on your prototype.

Deliverable

Based on your friends' reviews, write up a revision plan for your app. Submit your sketches and your plan for revisions to your lecturer.

THE NOOK

QUESTIONS

1. Do any of the prototyping methods of development seem to fit well within Malakai and Abbie's needs?
2. After reviewing figure 14.9, which method do you feel is most suited to the needs of this mobile ordering system?

14.5 Vendor and software selection

Few organisations, especially small- to medium-size enterprises, have the time, financial resources, or technical expertise required to develop today's complex IT or e-business systems. For this reason, business firms increasingly rely on outside vendors to provide software, hardware and technical expertise. Consequently, selecting and managing these vendors and their software offerings has become a major aspect of developing an IT application. The following six steps in selecting a software vendor and an application package are useful.

Step 1: Identify potential vendors

Companies can identify potential software application vendors through various sources:

- software catalogues
- lists provided by hardware vendors
- technical and trade journals
- consultants and industry analysts experienced in the application area
- peers in other companies
- web searches.

These sources often yield so many vendors and packages that the company must use some evaluation criteria to eliminate all but the most promising ones from further consideration. For example, it can eliminate vendors that are too small or have a questionable reputation. Also, it can eliminate packages that do not have the required features or are not compatible with the company's existing hardware and/or software.

Step 2: Determine the evaluation criteria

The most difficult and crucial task in evaluating a vendor and a software package is to select a detailed set of evaluation criteria. Some areas in which a customer should develop detailed criteria are these:

- characteristics of the vendor
- functional requirements of the system
- technical requirements that the software must satisfy

- amount and quality of documentation provided
- vendor support of the package.

These criteria should be set out in a **request for proposal (RFP)**. An RFP is a document that is sent to potential vendors inviting them to submit a proposal that describes their software package and explains how it would meet the company's needs. The RFP provides the vendors with information about the objectives and requirements of the system. Specifically, it describes the environment in which the system will be used, the general criteria that the company will use to evaluate the proposals, and the conditions for submitting proposals. The RFP may also request a list of current users of the package whom the company may contact. Finally, it can require the vendor to demonstrate the package at the company's facilities using specified inputs and data files.

Step 3: Evaluate vendors and packages

The responses to an RFP generate massive volumes of information that the company must evaluate. The goal of this evaluation is to determine the gaps between the company's needs (as specified by the requirements) and the capabilities of the vendors and their application packages. Often, the company gives the vendors and packages an overall score by (1) assigning an importance weight to each of the criteria, (2) ranking the vendors on each of the weighted criteria (say 1 to 10) and then (3) multiplying the ranks by the associated weights. The company can then shorten the list of potential suppliers to include only those vendors who achieved the highest overall scores.

Step 4: Choose the vendor and package

Once the company has shortened the list of potential suppliers, it can begin negotiations with these vendors to determine how their packages might be modified to remove any discrepancies with the company's IT needs. Thus, one of the most important factors in the decision is the additional development effort that may be required to tailor the system to the company's needs or to integrate it into the company's computing environment. The company must also consider the opinions of both the users and the IT personnel who will have to support the system.

Several methods are commonly used for selecting software. For a list of general criteria, see figure 14.11.

FIGURE 14.11 Criteria for selecting a software application package.

Functionality (Does the package do what the organisation needs?)
Cost and financial terms
Upgrade policy and cost
Vendor's reputation and availability for help
Vendor's success stories (Visit the vendor's website, contact clients.)
System flexibility
Ease of internet interface
Availability and quality of documentation
Necessary hardware and networking resources
Required training (check if provided by vendor)
Security
Learning (speed of) for developers and users
Graphical presentation
Data handling
System-required hardware

Step 5: Negotiate a contract

The contract with the software vendor is very important. It specifies both the price of the software and the type and amount of support that the vendor agrees to provide. The contract will be the only recourse if either the system or the vendor does not perform as expected. It is essential, then, that the contract directly references the proposal, because this is the vehicle that the vendor used to document the functionality supported in its system. Furthermore, if the vendor is modifying the software to tailor it to the company's needs, the contract must include detailed specifications (essentially the requirements) of the modifications. Finally, the contract should describe in detail the acceptance tests that the software package must pass.

Contracts are legal documents and they can be quite tricky. For this reason, companies might need the services of experienced contract negotiators and lawyers. Many organisations employ software-purchasing specialists who assist in negotiations and write or approve the contract. These specialists should be involved in the selection process from the start.

Step 6: Establish a service-level agreement

Service-level agreements (SLAs) are formal agreements that specify how work is to be divided between the company and its vendors. These specifications are based on a set of agreed-upon milestones, quality checks and what-if situations. They describe how quality checks will be made and what is to be done in case of disputes. SLAs accomplish these goals by:

1 defining the responsibilities of both partners
2 providing a framework for designing support services
3 allowing the company to retain as much control as possible over its own systems.

SLAs include such issues as performance, availability, backup and recovery, upgrades, and hardware and software ownership. For example, the SLA might specify that the application service provider have its system available to the customer 99.9 per cent of the time.

BEFORE YOU GO ON . . .

1 List the major steps of selection of a vendor and a software package.
2 Describe a request for proposal (RFP).
3 Explain why SLAs play an important role in systems development.

QUESTIONS

THE NOOK

1 What information would Malakai and Abbie need to include in an RFP?
2 Search the web for SLAs and see if you can find some key words that Malakai and Abbie will need to include in their document.

WHAT'S IN IT FOR ME?

FOR THE ACCOUNTING MAJOR

Accounting personnel help perform the cost–benefit analyses on proposed projects. They may also monitor, control and manage ongoing project costs to keep them within budget. Currently, the internet and social networking sites help the accounting sector to share and exchange information between businesses, suppliers and stakeholders. Accounting personnel undoubtedly will find themselves involved with systems development at various points throughout their careers.

FOR THE FINANCE MAJOR

Finance personnel are frequently involved with the financial issues that accompany any large-scale systems development project (for example, budgeting). They also are involved in cost–benefit and risk analyses. To perform these tasks they need to stay abreast of the emerging techniques used to determine project costs and ROI. Information technology use in the finance major will assist users to exchange financial transactions, information internally or externally. Currently, the finance major relies on information technology, including the online services such as the internet and other facilities. Finally, because they must manage vast amounts of information, finance departments are also common recipients of new systems.

FOR THE MARKETING MAJOR

In most organisations, marketing, like finance, involves massive amounts of data and information. Like finance, then, marketing is also a hotbed of systems development. Marketing personnel will increasingly find themselves participating on systems development teams. Such involvement increasingly means helping to develop systems, especially web-based systems that reach out directly from the organisation to its customers.

Overall, technology plays a major role in any major, including the marketing major. Technology use will allow a user to do more with less time; productivity and performance will be improved via business processes and metrics. As well, technology will manage and monitor the marketing aspects from inventory, shipping, receiving, logistics and advertising. Finally, adoption technology in the marketing major will create a unique and niche market for competition and cooperation.

FOR THE PRODUCTION/OPERATIONS MANAGEMENT MAJOR

Participation on development teams is also a common role for production/operations people. Manufacturing is becoming increasingly computerised and integrated with other allied systems, from design to logistics to customer support. Production systems interface frequently with marketing, finance and human resources. In addition, they may be part of a larger, enterprise-wide system. Also, many end users in POM either develop their own systems or collaborate with IT personnel on specific applications.

Finally, technology use within an organisation will improve the service networking internally and externally, and employees can receive prompt feedback from their managers. Furthermore, technology plays a major role in the POM, to organise and monitor the business process. However, integrating technology in an organisation's strategy requires a lot of planning due to technology infrastructure, including the online services.

FOR THE HUMAN RESOURCES MANAGEMENT MAJOR

The human resources department is closely involved with several aspects of the systems acquisitions process. Acquiring new systems may require hiring new employees, changing job descriptions, or terminating employees. Human resources staff perform all of these tasks. Further, if the organisation hires consultants for the development project, or outsources it, the human resources department may handle the contracts with these suppliers. Finally, technology use in a human resources management major includes each aspect from financial resources, inventory, human skills, production resources or information technology. Technology needs plenty of skills and knowledge to perform efficient and effective results; therefore, staff should and must have enough knowledge to perform the tasks and resolve the problems in a productive way.

FOR THE MIS MAJOR

Regardless of the approach that the organisation adopts for acquiring new systems, the MIS department spearheads it. If the organisation chooses either to buy or to lease the application, the MIS department leads in examining the offerings of the various vendors and in negotiating with the vendors. If the organisation chooses to develop the application inhouse, then the process falls to the MIS department. MIS analysts work closely with users to develop their information requirements. MIS programmers then write the computer code, test it and implement the new system. Currently, technology use in the MIS major is essential and crucial to achieve the information technology strategy as well as to meet organisation and stakeholders needs. Technology adoption will enhance organisation performance and operation. Finally, to ensure that technology use will reduce the environmental impact, these days, MIS starts to adopt smart technology (i.e. cloud computing and virtualisation) in an organisation to reduce cost, maintenance and energy, and this will lead to reduced carbon emission as well.

SUMMARY

1 Discuss the different cost/benefit analyses that companies must take into account when formulating an IT strategic plan.

The four common approaches to cost–benefit analysis are these.

> The *net present value (NPV)* method converts future values of benefits to their present-value equivalent by 'discounting' them at the organisation's cost of funds. They can then compare the present value of the future benefits to the cost required to achieve those benefits to determine whether the benefits exceed the costs.

> *Return on investment (ROI)* measures management's effectiveness in generating profits with its available assets. ROI is calculated by dividing net income attributable to a project by the average assets invested in the project. ROI is a percentage and the higher the percentage return, the better.

> *Breakeven analysis* determines the point at which the cumulative dollar value of the benefits from a project equals the investment made in the project.

> In the *business case approach*, system developers write a business case to justify funding one or more specific applications or projects.

2 Discuss the four business decisions that companies must make when they acquire new applications.

> *How much computer code does the company want to write?* A company can choose to use a totally prewritten application (to write no computer code), to customise a prewritten application (to write some computer code), or to customise an entire application (write all new computer code).

> *How will the company pay for the application?* Once the company has decided how much computer code to write, it must decide how to pay for it. With prewritten applications or customised prewritten applications, companies can buy them or lease them. With totally custom applications, companies use internal funding.

> *Where will the application run?* Companies must now decide where to run the application. The company may run the application on its own platform or run the application on someone else's platform (use either a software-as-a-service vendor or an application service provider).

> *Where will the application originate?* Prewritten applications can be open-source software or come from a vendor. Companies may choose to customise prewritten open-source applications or prewritten proprietary applications from vendors. Companies may customise applications inhouse or outsource the customisation. They can also write totally custom applications inhouse or outsource this process.

3 Enumerate the primary tasks and importance of each of the six processes involved in the systems development life cycle.

The six processes are these.

> *Systems investigation:* Addresses the business problem (or business opportunity) by means of the feasibility study; main task in the systems investigation stage is the feasibility study.

> *Systems analysis:* Examines the business problem that the organisation plans to solve with an information system; main purpose is to gather information about the existing system in order to determine the requirements for the new system; end product of this stage, known as the 'deliverable', is a set of system requirements.

> *Systems design:* Describes how the system will resolve the business problem; deliverable is the set of technical system specifications.

> *Programming and testing:* Programming translates the design specifications into computer code; testing checks to see if the computer code will produce the expected and desired results and detects errors, or bugs, in the computer code; deliverable is the new application.

> *Implementation:* The process of converting from the old system to the new system via three major conversion strategies: direct, pilot and phased; deliverable is properly working application.

> *Operation and maintenance:* Types of maintenance include debugging, updating and adding new functions when needed.

4 Describe alternative development methods and tools that augment development methods.

These are the *alternative* methods.

> *Joint application design (JAD)* is a group-based tool for collecting user requirements and creating system designs.

> *Rapid application development (RAD)* is a systems development method that can combine JAD, prototyping and ICASE tools to rapidly produce a high-quality system.

> *Agile development* is a software development methodology that delivers functionality in rapid iterations, which are usually measured in weeks.

> *End-user development* refers to an organisation's end users developing their own applications with little or no formal assistance from the IT department.

These are the tools.

> The *prototyping* approach defines an initial list of user requirements, builds a model of the system and then improves the system in several iterations based on users' feedback.
> *Integrated computer-aided software engineering (ICASE)* combines upper CASE tools (automate systems investigation, analysis and design) and lower CASE tools (programming, testing, operation and maintenance).
> *Component-based development* uses standard components to build applications. Components are reusable applications that generally have one specific function, such as a shopping cart, user authentication, or a catalogue.
> *Object-oriented development* begins with the aspects of the real world that must be modelled to perform that task. Systems developers identify the *objects* in the new system. Each object represents a tangible, real-world entity, such as a customer, bank account, student, or course. Objects have *properties*, or *data values*. Objects also contain the *operations* that can be performed on their properties.

Figure 14.9 shows advantages and disadvantages of alternative methods and tools.

5 Analyse the process of vendor and software selection.

The process of vendor and software selection is composed of six steps:

> Identify potential vendors.
> Determine evaluation criteria.
> Evaluate vendors and packages.
> Choose the vendor and package.
> Negotiate a contract.
> Establish service-level agreements.

>>> CHAPTER GLOSSARY

agile development A software development methodology that delivers functionality in rapid iterations, measured in weeks, requiring frequent communication, development, testing and delivery.

application portfolio The set of recommended applications resulting from the planning and justification process in application development.

application service provider (ASP) An agent or vendor who assembles the software needed by enterprises and packages them with outsourced development, operations, maintenance and other services.

component-based development A software development methodology that uses standard components to build applications.

computer-aided software engineering (CASE) Development approach that uses specialised tools to automate many of the tasks in the SDLC; upper CASE tools automate the early stages of the SDLC and lower CASE tools automate the later stages.

direct conversion Implementation process in which the old system is cut off and the new system is turned on at a certain point in time.

end-user development Approach in which the organisation's end users develop their own applications with little or no formal assistance from the IT department.

feasibility study Investigation that gauges the probability of success of a proposed project and provides a rough assessment of the project's feasibility.

implementation The process of converting from an old computer system to a new one.

integrated CASE (ICASE) tools CASE tools that provide links between upper CASE and lower CASE tools.

IS operational plan Consists of a clear set of projects that the IS department and the functional area managers will execute in support of the IT strategic plan.

IT steering committee A committee, comprised of a group of managers and staff representing various organisational units, set up to establish IT priorities and to ensure that the MIS function is meeting the needs of the enterprise.

IT strategic plan A set of long-range goals that describe the IT infrastructure and major IT initiatives needed to achieve the goals of the organisation.

joint application design (JAD) A group-based tool for collecting user requirements and creating system designs.

object-oriented development A systems development methodology that begins with aspects of the real world that must be modelled to perform a task.

outsourcing Use of outside contractors or external organisations to acquire IT services.

programmers IS professionals who modify existing computer programs or write new computer programs to satisfy user requirements.

programming The translation of a system's design specifications into computer code.

prototype A small-scale working model of an entire system or a model that contains only the components of the new system that are of most interest to the users.

prototyping An approach that defines an initial list of user requirements, builds a prototype system, and then improves the system in several iterations based on users' feedback.

rapid application development (RAD) A development method that uses special tools and an iterative approach to rapidly produce a high-quality system.

request for proposal (RFP) Document that is sent to potential vendors inviting them to submit a proposal describing their software package and how it would meet the company's needs.

scope creep Adding functions to an information system after the project has begun.

service-level agreements (SLAs) Formal agreements regarding the division of work between a company and its vendors.

software-as-a-service (SaaS) A method of delivering software in which a vendor hosts the applications and provides them as a service to customers over a network, typically the internet.

systems analysis The examination of the business problem that the organisation plans to solve with an information system.

systems analysts IS professionals who specialise in analysing and designing information systems.

systems design Describes how the new system will resolve the business problem.

systems development life cycle (SDLC) Traditional structured framework, used for large IT projects, that consists of sequential processes by which information systems are developed.

systems stakeholders All people who are affected by changes in information systems.

technical specialists Experts on a certain type of technology, such as databases or telecommunications.

>>> DISCUSSION QUESTIONS

1 Discuss the advantages of a lease option over a buy option.
2 Why is it important for all business managers to understand the issues of IT resource acquisition?
3 Why is it important for everyone in business organisations to have a basic understanding of the systems development process?
4 Should prototyping be used on every systems development project? Why or why not?
5 Discuss the various types of feasibility studies. Why are they all needed?
6 Discuss the issue of assessing intangible benefits and the proposed solutions.
7 Discuss the reasons why end-user-developed information systems can be of poor quality. What can be done to improve this situation?

>>> PROBLEM-SOLVING ACTIVITIES

1 Access the Australia Post website (www.auspost.com.au). Read and review the e-commerce payment solutions of Australia Post.
2 Use an internet search engine to obtain information on CASE and ICASE tools. Select several vendors and compare and contrast their offerings.
3 Access australianwebdesign.net.au. Observe how the site provides components to design, promote and host an online business.
4 Enter www-01.ibm.com/software/au/websphere. Find its Web Sphere product. Read recent customers' success stories. What makes this software so popular?
5 Enter the websites of The Australian (www.theaustralian.com.au/technology), Computer World Australia (www.computerworld.com.au) and CIO (www.cio.com.au). Search for recent material about ASPs and outsourcing, and prepare a report on your findings.
6 Shopify (www.shopify.com.au) is a an e-commerce platform that enables organisations and users to develop online stores. At its site, the company provides demonstrations illustrating the types of store fronts used to create a store.
   a Go to www.shopify.com.au/examples and try the demonstration trial.
   b What features does Shopify provide?
   c Does Shopify support smaller or larger stores?
   d What other products does Shopify offer for creating online stores? What types of stores do these products support?

>>> COLLABORATION EXERCISE

Background

System acquisition and implementation is as important to the life of an information system as anything else. The right decision could be made about what is needed, but if the implementation of that system is not successful, the whole exercise is in vain. This chapter has covered many techniques for developing and implementing information systems, all of which apply to different needs and situations.

Activity

If you completed the Collaboration Exercise for chapter 13, assemble that same group and complete this exercise. If you did not, please review the requirements for that activity. You will visit a local business and learn about its supply chain management systems. Once you have done this (no matter if it was for chapter 13 or not), imagine that this company is going to develop and implement a new supply chain management system. The business has chosen to use the SDLC and has created a team of employees (your team) to layout the plan of attack. For this particular business situation, imagine how the SDLC would play out. Ultimately, provide feedback as to whether or not the SDLC was the best pick for that business in that industry.

Deliverable

Work with your group to lay out the steps of the SDLC for the project implementation you have learned about. Submit your outline and your recommendation on acquisition methods to your tutorial group.

CLOSING CASE 1 >

Tweak or trash?

THE PROBLEM

Chief information officers (CIOs) face a continuing dilemma. When the time comes to upgrade information technology equipment and systems, is it better to repair what you already have by patching and tweaking systems and software to keep them operating, or is it better to replace (a.k.a. trash) your old technology and start with an entirely new system?

The 'tweak or trash' problem is extremely complicated. The main directive of every IT department is to ensure uptime and avoid downtime at all costs, which creates a bias towards risk avoidance and therefore towards tweaking. Usually, tweaking seems to be far less risky than implementing an entirely new system. However, tweaking nurtures a growth of hybrid IT environments in which multiple systems coexist, making system documentation and qualified programmers hard to find. Additionally, tweaking often makes programmers feel that it is safer and cheaper to make tiny patches rather than risk transformational change, which can limit a company's IT capability and result in inefficiencies that cost the company time and money.

In 2000, Accenture (www.accenture.com) was a new company that had only recently gone live to the public. The company had inherited legacy systems from its former parent company and needed to build separate technology capabilities. Accenture had ambitious growth strategies and knew that it needed appropriate IT infrastructure to support that growth.

THE IT SOLUTION

When Accenture started the process of revamping its IT infrastructure in the early 2000s, the company did not consciously pursue a total replacement policy of the systems that were already in place. However, managers generally did not want to be encumbered by old technology. They knew that conflicts between different IT systems could impose huge burdens on performance. Therefore, they consistently got rid of old systems in favour of new systems. In other words, they chose to trash rather than to tweak.

Accenture kicked off the replacement process by first establishing a coherent IT strategy and building its own independent IT capabilities. Then, it concentrated on operating the IT department just as any other business would be operated, with a focus on efficiency. Accenture centralised and standardised its IT function. The company cut its total number of global applications from 600 globally to just 267 and decreased its total number of local applications from 1500 down to 255. An example of this application-cutting process was Accenture's migration from multiple country-specific platforms to a single global enterprise resource planning (ERP) system from SAP (www.sap.com).

By the middle of the decade, Accenture had its IT function in order and began to address larger changes. These changes included a complete network transformation, which gave the company the bandwidth to construct one of the world's largest high-definition video conferencing networks and enabled it to introduce an entire suite of powerful collaboration tools. These technologies enable Accenture professionals to travel less, thereby saving money and time while providing enormous benefits for family life.

THE RESULTS

Accenture invested a grand total of approximately $1 billion in its IT infrastructure from 2001 to 2011. These investments resulted in $3 billion in savings.

Each of the IT changes that Accenture achieved took time to implement and caused disruption to the business. For example, the company moved to its global SAP platform in a single 'big-bang' implementation. The downside risks were huge, but so was the upside potential. When the company implemented SAP successfully, it was able to achieve a 'single version of the truth' across its entire global enterprise more quickly than before. (A 'single version of the truth' means that everyone in a company operates from the same data and information, at the same time.)

Accenture's internal customers are pleased with the results of the IT transformation. The percentage of 'satisfied sponsors' (sponsors being the pool of senior executives who work closely with the IT department on new initiatives) increased from 67 to 92 per cent between 2001 and 2011.

Accenture's IT transformation led to a dramatic increase in operational efficiency over a 10-year period. The amount spent on IT in total dropped 22 per cent over this period and IT expense as a percentage of Accenture's net revenue decreased by 59 per cent. IT expense per employee decreased by 70 per cent, even though Accenture had made massive IT investments throughout the decade to equip its professionals with the most advanced technology tools possible.

So, what was the final result of Accenture's decision to trash not tweak? Today, Accenture is a global company with more than 244 000 employees and revenues of over $25 billion.

Sources: Compiled from D Carr (2012), 'Accenture CIO vision emphasizes social, contextual IT', *InformationWeek*, 27 February; F Modruson (2012), 'Debate: remaking IT at Accenture', *Baseline Magazine*, 27 February; S Overby (2011), '5 things Accenture's CIO has learned about cloud computing', *CIO*, 15 March; J King (2008), 'The grill: to Kishore Swaminathan, CIO means "Chief Intelligence Officer"', *Computerworld*, 15 September; 'CIO 100 2008 winner profile: Accenture', *CIO*, 2008; www.accenture.com.

QUESTIONS

1 What are the risks associated with throwing out old information systems and replacing them with new information systems? Provide examples to support your answer.

2 Provide examples of a situation in which it would be better for an organisation to tweak an existing information system rather than replace it with a new system.

CLOSING CASE **2 >**

Smart technology in Western Australia information security group

THE PROBLEM

Information Security Group (ISG), now known as Central Data Systems, is a security provider based in Western Australia. ISG mainly focuses on network and desktop management, hardware and software support as well as consultancy services. ISG also provides a substantial role in IT procurement, installation, security and remote access solutions to real estate, engineering, mining sectors, medical, legal and other manufacturing and construction industry areas.

ISG faced a significant challenge a few years ago when they set high revenue targets for their business using a break–fix business model. This situation was difficult to achieve due to the non-billable time technical staff were spending travelling to and from customer sites. To resolve this problem ISG integrated a new smart technology to make support and service more profitable.

THE SOLUTION

ISG integrated Kaseya's IT managed service solution into their information technology strategy to support remote control and support, patch management, network monitoring and alerts, software upgrades and help desk policy enforcement. This solution allowed ISG to provide service to their customers from one product set. By using Kaseya's IT managed service solution, the ISG business became more efficient and unique in the marketplace, and within the short term the company saw increased profits. Kaseya is a global provider of information technology automation software for information technology solution providers and public and private sector IT organisations. Kaseya's software allows IT teams to manage and monitor IT infrastructure remotely and easily with one integrated web-based platform.

THE RESULTS

Integrating Kaseya's IT solution enabled ISG to satisfy client needs, since Kaseya gives ISG the opportunity to manage more clients in less time. Employees are spending 15 hours a week on tasks that would previously have taken 40 hours.

Recently, ISG purchased endpoint security, back-up and disaster recovery and user state management to meet the organisational strategy and satisfy their clients' needs. The company's CIO, Matt Lansdown, stated that Kaseya's IT solution in ISG generates more revenue, and 'we are in a stronger position to hold onto our clients'. Finally, integrating Kaseya's IT solution in ISG's IT strategy allows business to become unique compared to other IT companies since their support and services targets were managed and achieved well because client and computer numbers are increased with no need to raise staffing levels.

Sources: Central Data Systems (2013), 'About us', www.central-data.net/about-us; Kaseya Automating IT (n.d.), 'Case study — information security', www.kaseya.com.au/download/en-US/MSP_case_studies/Information.Security.Group.cs.kaseya.pdf.

QUESTIONS

1 List and discuss the advantages and disadvantages of web-based platform technology use in ISG.

2 List and discuss information technology team skills within an organisation.

3 What are the advantages and disadvantages of Kaseya IT use in ISG's IT strategy?

SPREADSHEET ACTIVITY **IF-THEN STATEMENTS**

OBJECTIVE

This activity will introduce the 'if-then' statement within the context of making a decision. It will help students take criteria from a situation and build it into a spreadsheet.

Chapter connection

Acquiring an information system should be an easy task, right? Wrong! Sometimes the method of acquiring the system is as complex as the system itself. Although most situations would require a much more complicated decision support system, in this situation a spreadsheet formula can help make the decision by using formulas to narrow down the top contenders and provide a score/ranking for the companies under consideration.

ACTIVITY

It is time for the university to upgrade its website. This decision is very important because it will affect current and potential students, faculty and the community at large. The university has graded 50 different vendors on 10 criteria and the weight given to each. The 10 criteria and their weights are given below.

1 Customisability (15%)

2 Expandability (15%)

3 Faculty tutorials (5%)

4 Student tutorials (5%)

5 Mobile access (10%)

6 Video support (10%)

7 File system (5%)

8 Course migration (15%)

9 Faculty user interface (10%)

10 Student user interface (10%)

Visit www.johnwiley.com.au/highered/rainer/ausnz/studentresources and download the spreadsheet provided for chapter 14. Then create two formulas. One will calculate a final grade based on the weights provided above and the work already done by the university. Once you have the final grade, you will then create an if-then formula to find those vendors that rank worthy of an 'A' and those who 'fail' to meet the stated criteria. If you are not familiar with if-then statements, please see the Help material in Microsoft Excel under the formulas area of the program. Basically, your statement will say 'If the score is greater than a 90, then say 'Yes', otherwise, 'No'.

DELIVERABLES

Prepare a written summary of your findings. Is there a clear winner? Or does it depend on what the university favours in the rankings?

DISCUSSION QUESTIONS

1 Acquisition of information systems is a complicated affair. Decisions to build inhouse, outsource, or purchase off-the-shelf software can sometimes be the greatest asset or the Achilles heel of a company. Given the complexity, what roles can a spreadsheet play in this process other than the one illustrated by this case?

2 Implementation strategies vary as much as the acquisition decision. Considering products like the Google Spreadsheet Flow Chart, how can spreadsheets assist with the planning of software implementation?

DATABASE ACTIVITY **FORMS III**

OBJECTIVE

In this activity, you will learn how to create a menu interface (a 'navigation form' in Access terminology) that will allow users with no training to reach important elements of a system easily. Consider what happens when you launch Access. You get an easy-to-navigate screen that asks questions such as 'Do you want to open an existing database, start a blank one, or ...?' We should design databases for the same ease of entry. Navigation forms are how.

Chapter connection

In this chapter, you read how organisations acquire their information systems. Often, they develop IS internally. The result has to look as professional as if the application had been purchased. That includes interfaces such as you will develop here.

Prerequisites
None.

ACTIVITY

In this activity, which you will find online at www.johnwiley.com.au/highered/rainer/ausnz/studentresources, you will take an existing database with forms and reports, develop menus for using it and set your database to launch with these menus.

A finished navigation form, which you will end up with at the end of this activity, might look like the figure below. One does not have to be an Access expert, or even an experienced Access user, to use it. Each button is labelled with its function. Such an interface is planned in the System Design stage of the SDLC development process, which you read about in this chapter. Putting it together, as you will do here, is part of the Programming and Testing stage.

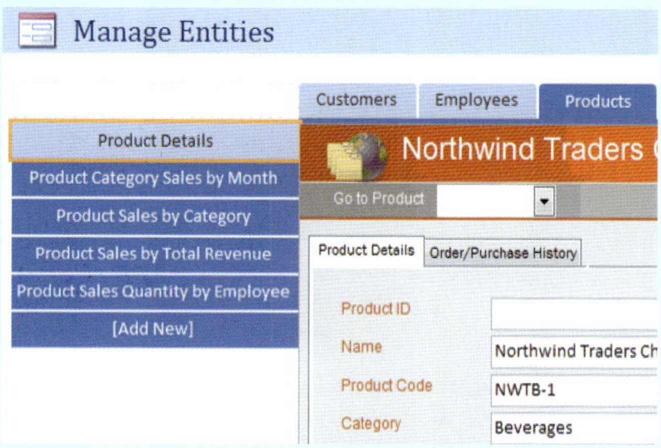

1 Download the Ch 14 DandyDonuts database from www.johnwiley.com.au/highered/rainer/ausnz/studentresources. (It resembles the donut store databases you may have worked with in earlier activities.) It has four tables: stores, customers, orders, line items (each item in an order) and products. It also includes a few forms and reports. These are not intended as good examples of form or report design. They are there only so your switchboards will have something to open.

2 To create a navigation form, go to the Create ribbon tab and pull down the list of navigation forms via the triangle to its right. Select the first layout, Horizontal Tabs.

3 You will see a blank navigation form in Design view. The space where the tabs will go, across the top, is empty except for a placeholder that reads '[Add New].'

4 If your navigation pane is not showing, as it is at the left of the screen shot above, open it by clicking the .>>. at the top.

5 Drag the four reports into the Add New area, one at a time. As each one comes in, you will see a tab created for it.

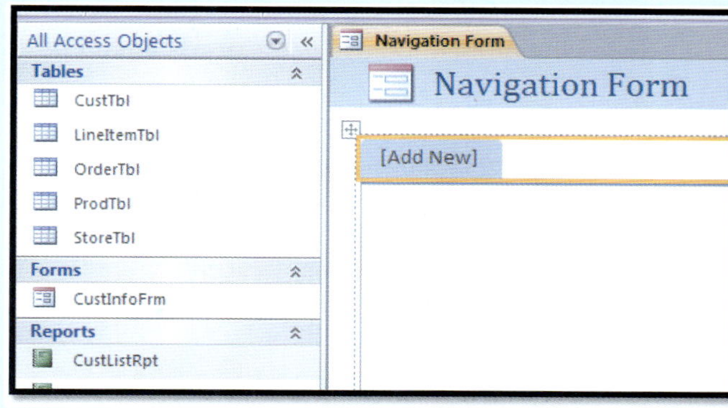

6 Go to Form view. The '[Add New]' has gone away. Click on each tab to see the corresponding report.

7 Return to Layout view. To clean up the form design, edit the top line to read 'Reports' instead of 'Navigation Form'. Edit the four tabs to read, respectively, 'Customer List', 'Customer Orders', 'Orders by Date' and 'Orders by Store'. You will probably have to widen some of the tabs for the new names to fit on a single line.

8 Save your new navigation form as 'Report List'.

9 Create a new navigation form, but this time use Vertical Tabs Left layout.

10 Enter CustInfoFrm and your new Report List into the tab area.

11 Change the header of this form to read 'Main Menu' and the name 'CustInfoFrm' to read 'Cust. Info'.

12 Confirm in Form view that everything works.

13 Now we will add an 'Exit' button to our main menu. Go to Design mode and make sure Use Control Wizards is highlighted in the Controls section of the Design ribbon. (Expand that area using the down-pointing triangle with the line above it at the right to see the wizard.) Then click the Button tool. (It is in the top row of controls, fourth from the left.) Drag it over a rectangular area in the form header, to the right of the words 'Main Menu', to create the button shape. The wizard will start.

Usage hint: You can create buttons in Layout mode, but in that mode, if you try to put them in the navigation tab area, Access will insist on turning them into new tabs. In Design view, you can create freestanding buttons.

14 Choose the Application category, then Quit Application (the only item in it). Click Next.

15 Select Text for the button content type, then enter 'Exit' into the text field.

16 Name the button 'ExitButton' so you will know what it is later and click Finish.

17 Adjust the size and location of your button if you wish.

18 Go to Form view and confirm that your new button works. If it does not, the easiest fix is probably to start over rather than figuring out why. If your second

attempt to create it fails too, it is time to try to diagnose the problem. Close your form, naming it 'Main Menu'.

19 Users would like the application to open with this menu, instead of having to open it from the navigation pane. To make this happen, go to the File tab and click Options near the bottom. Select Current Database at the left, then select your main switchboard from the pull-down menu for Display Form. It should look like this:

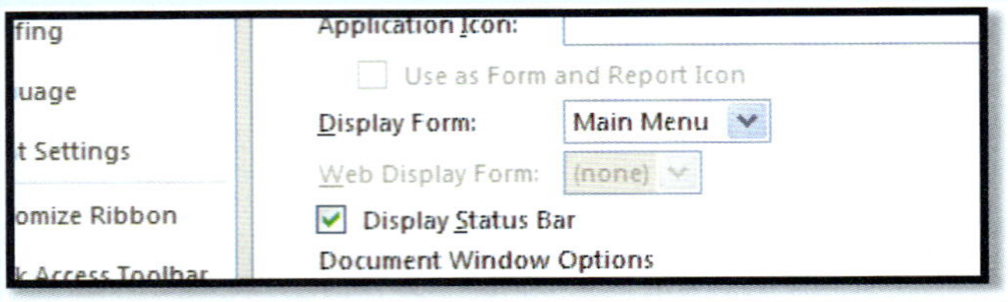

20 Close the database (as you will be told to do for this option to take effect), reopen it and confirm that it opens with your main menu.

DELIVERABLES

The above database, with its two navigation forms.

QUIZ QUESTIONS

1. How many tabs can a standard Access navigation form can have?
2. A navigation form can do the following:
   - **a** Open a form or a report.
   - **b** Open a report or a table.
   - **c** Open another navigation form.
   - **d** It can do all of the above.
3. True or false: A navigation form is a specialised type of report.
4. When a user clicks a button linked to the Quit Application action,
   - **a** the database closes, but Access remains active.
   - **b** the computer shuts down.
   - **c** Access closes.
   - **d** the computer goes into Sleep mode.

DISCUSSION QUESTIONS

1. Open the Main Menu navigation form in Design view. Click on Cust. Info. and change something in the customer information form. Then close the navigation form. What happened? Do you think it is a good idea for Access to work this way, or not? Explain why you feel this way.
2. In the second part of this activity, you created the Main Menu navigation form after you created the Reports form. Could you have done this in the other order? If not, why not?
3. Search the web for images of Access 2007 switchboards. You will find that many look more or less like this, with only cosmetic changes:

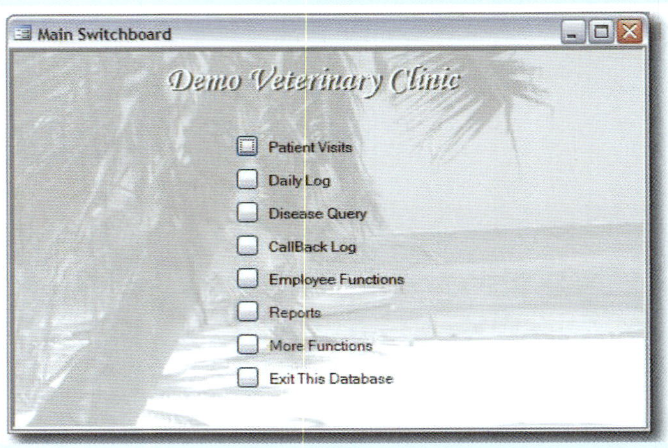

This menu, called a *switchboard*, was created with Access 2007 or an earlier version. Find three such switchboards. In your opinion, are they more attractive and/or easier to use (as far as you can tell without trying them out) than the navigation forms of Access 2010? Explain why you feel this way. (Paste the three switchboards' images into the answer you submit to your instructor.)

ACKNOWLEDGEMENTS

The author and publisher would like to thank the following copyright holders, organisations and individuals for their permission to reproduce copyright material in this book.

Images

• © Shutterstock: **1**, **415** (left, second from top)/Monkey Business Images; **5**/Dmitry Kalinovsky; **6**/Peter Bernik; **8**/XiXinXing; **9**/Maridav; **12** (bottom)/Nils Petersen; **12** (right)/DavidEwingPhotography; **12** (top)/wavebreakmedia; **13** (centre)/Michael Pettigrew; **27**/Syda Productions; **37**/Boris Sosnovyy; **38**/Rob Wilson; **45**/wavebreakmedia; **47**/guentermanaus; **49**/JuliusKielaitis; **71**/Zurijeta; **72**/ChameleonsEye; **95**/EcoPrint; **111**/White78; **118** (middle left)/Igor Klimov; **118** (middle right)/Digital Genetics; **118** (top left)/Christopher Meder; **118** (top right)/michaeljung; **120** (right)/Datskevich Aleh; **130**/Jeff Skopin; **134**/gemphoto; **153**/NAN728; **157**/Pablo Calvog; **184**/graphixmania; **186**/1000 Words; **191**/Gajus; **206**/mangostock; **209**/Kekyalyaynen; **213**/Jim Pruitt; **216**/Swill Klitch; **218**/Rob Kints; **248**/Gts; **256**/Kheng Guan Toh; **257**/Denphumi; **264**/nito; **282**/dencg; **295**/bloomua; **305**/Markus Gann; **312**/gpointstudio; **333**/Tyler Olson; **334**/Modfos; **337**/Oleksiy Mark; **338**/Xufang; **341** (left)/katix; **343**/SeanPavonePhoto; **345** (bottom)/Hasloo Group Production Studio; **345** (top)/Natalia Siverina; **346**/wang song; **354**/Pichugin Dmitry; **358**/ARENA Creative; **359** (bottom left)/Nicemonkey; **359** (bottom middle)/Albert Lozano; **359** (bottom right)/Grounder; **362**/Pi-Lens; **382**/Michal Kowalski; **401**/Rafal Olechowski; **402**/Gemenacom; **407** (left)/dotshock; **407** (centre)/Art Allianz; **407** (right)/joyfull; **407** (top left)/Maxx-Studio; **415** (top left)/Robert Kneschke; **429**/Ian Holland; **437**/James A. Harris; **442**/photobank.ch; **453**/Arjuna Kodisinghe; **454**/Maridav; **474**/sfam_photo • © Newspix: **2**/News Ltd/Stuart McEvoy; **182**/Rob Baird; **376**/Ian Munroe • © iStockphoto: **13** (far left middle)/René Mansi; **17**/sturti; **22** (left)/pengpeng; **22** (right)/lisafx; **119** (bottom left)/zwolafasola; **119** (bottom right)/piotr_malczyk; **119** (top left)/deepspacedave; **119** (top right)/dzidzileyla; **120** (left)/SKashkin; **168** (bottom)/NAN104; **249**/pkline; **375**/hjalmeida; **434**/Milan Zeremski; **435**/Kevin Landwer-Johan • © Alamy Limited: **23**/Daniel Santos Megina; **169** (top)/Richard Levine; **254**/AKP Photos; **264**/incamerastock; **267**/NetPhotos; **341** (right)/Alex Segre; **360**/kolvenbach; **406**/© ZUMA Press, Inc.; **410** (top left)/NetPics; **434**/Milan Zeremski • © Microsoft Corporation: **35** (top and bottom), **68** (top left), **152**, **177**, **178** (middle of right column, bottom of left column, top of left and right column), **245**/Screenshot(s) reprinted by permission from Microsoft Corporation; **68** (top and bottom right), **247**, **292** (bottom right, top right and left), **330**, **399**, **426** (left, second from top and top left), **427**, **487** (left and right), **488** (left and right), **178** (bottom of right column), **179** (top and bottom of right column), **179** (left column) • © Fairfax Syndications (Photos): **112**/NBN /AFR /Glenn Hunt; **181**/Fairfax Photo Library/*The Age*/Angela Wylie; **205**/Fairfax Photos /Katherine Griffiths; **430**/Fairfax Photos/AFR /Louie Douvis • © Creative Commons: **129** • © Google Inc.: **130** (top), **169** (bottom), **255**/ Google.com • © Industry Capability Network: **133** • © Getty Images: **138**/Gary Dineen/NBAE; **154**/David Jones; **266**/Bloomberg; **304** (centre)/AFP • © Erika Fish: **221** • © Heather Grey: **250** • © TransLink Transit Authority: **260**/Translink Division, Transport and Main Roads © Department of Transport and Main Roads • © Freelancer.com: **296** • © Public Transport Victoria: **304** (bottom)/Public Transport Victoria. Myki is a trademark of Public Transport Victoria, registered in Australia • © ING Direct: **309** • © Internet Corporation for Assigned Names and Numbers (ICANN): **319**/ICANN, with permission, Internet Corporation for Assigned Names & Numbers • © Sumo Visual Group: **414**.

Text

• © Adam Brown: **56** • © Copyright Agency Limited: **147–8**/ACCC takes aim at ISPs' BitTorrent slowdowns, *BRW*, James Hutchinson, 12 February 2013; **221**/Plotting likely plan of cyberattack at QUT, *The Australian*, Jennifer Foreshew, 25 June 2013; **445–6**/The computer that could cut fatality rates for truckies, *BRW*, Michael Bailey, 14 August 2013 • ©Esri Australia: **170–1**/Esri Australia • Creative Commons: **189–90**/© Office of the Australian Information Commissioner; **190**/© Electronic Frontiers Australia Inc.; **356**/ This work was supported by the Australian Centre for Ecological Analysis and Synthesis, a facility of the Australian Government-funded Terrestrial Ecosystem Research Network (http://www.tern.org.au/), a research infrastructure facility established under the National Collaborative Research Infrastructure Strategy and Education Infrastructure Fund—Super Science Initiative • © Business Spectator **240–1**/Originally published at Business Spectator, www.businessspectator.com.au/article/2013/6/10/technology/inside-look-governments-cyber-security-plans; **454–6**/Originally published at Business Spectator, www.businessspectator.com.au/article/2013/6/20/technology/learning-qld-health-payroll-fiasco • © Ernst & Young—Sydney: **296**/Extracts from 'Free Agent' from *Exceptional Australia*, 2012, p. 12. Text updated by Matt Barrie. Reproduced with permission from Ernst & Young • © Victoria Ransom: **313–14**/© Victoria Ransom, www.wildfireapp.com/company/leadership • © Steven Quale: **327–8**.

Every effort has been made to trace the ownership of copyright material. Information that will enable the publisher to rectify any error or omission in subsequent editions will be welcome. In such cases, please contact the Permissions Section of John Wiley & Sons Australia, Ltd.

ENDNOTES

CHAPTER 1

1. P Ruthven (2012), 'A snapshot of Australia's digital future to 2050', *IBISWorld*, Sydney, NSW, www.ibm.com/au.
2. Hudson (2012), 'Salary & employment insights 2012: information, communication & technology Australia/New Zealand', *Hudson ICT*, au.hudson.com.
3. ACS (2012), *2012 Australian ICT statistical compendium*, Australian Computer Society, Sydney, NSW, www.acs.org.au.
4. AIIA (2013), *App purchases by Australian consumers on mobile and handheld devices, issues paper by Consumer Affairs Advisory Council*, Australian Information Industry Association, ccaac.gov.au.
5. M M Mackay (2012), *Australian mobile phone lifestyle index. 8th edition — special topic: impact of tablets on mobile phone use*, AIMIA, www.aimia.com.au.
6. A Bender & B Connolly (2013), 'CIO insights 2013: leading CIOs share their thoughts on cloud computing and mobility applications', *CIO*, www.cio.com.au.
7. ibid.
8. 'Using mobile apps to build your business' (2013), Queensland Government business and industry portal website, www.business.qld.gov.au.
9. Department of Primary Industries and Regions South Australia website, www.pir.sa.gov.au.
10. Fujitsu (2013), *Case study: Department of Primary Industries and Regions (PIRSA)*, www.fujitsu.com/au.
11. FA (2008), *Fishing and aquaculture: final report, Government of South Australia, Department of Trade and Economic Development*, www.competitivesa.biz.
12. National Museum of Australia website, www.nma.gov.au.
13. J Foreshew (2013), 'Robots find themselves at home on the farm', *The Australian*, 19 February, www.theaustralian.com.au.
14. P Stafford (2012), 'Australia's top 20 online retailers', *Smart Company*, www.smartcompany.com.au.
15. 'Why buy from Booktopia?', Booktopia website, www.booktopia.com.au.

CHAPTER 2

1. L Tay (2012), 'Yarra Valley Water brings IT in-house', *iTnews*, 5 December, www.itnews.com.au.
2. ibid.
3. Antares Solutions website, www.antaressolutions.com.au.
4. Microsoft (2012), 'Kennards adopts business intelligence', *Microsoft case studies*, www.microsoft.com/casestudies.
5. H Barwick (2012), 'Deploying Windows Server 2012', *CIO*, www.cio.com.au.
6. Microsoft (2012), 'Kennards adopts business intelligence', *Microsoft case studies*, www.microsoft.com/casestudies.
7. R Mulcahy, 'Business intelligence definition and solutions', *CIO*, www.cio.com.au.
8. Microsoft (2012), 'Kennards adopts business intelligence', *Microsoft case studies*, www.microsoft.com/casestudies.
9. ibid.
10. C Martin (2013), 'New iPad Air 5th generation release date, specs and new features', *PC Advisor*, 22 October, www.pcadvisor.co.uk.
11. E Pineda (2013), 'iPad 5, iPad Mini 2 release date update: 5 power specs & killer features Apple will likely unveil on Oct 15', *International Business Times*, 21 September, au.ibtimes.com.
12. Department of the Environment (2010), *Australian government ICT Sustainability Plan 2010–2015*, www.environment.gov.au.
13. ibid.
14. L Tay (2011), 'Parliament passes e-waste legislation', *iTnews*, 23 June, www.itnews.com.au.
15. ibid.
16. EPA NSW (2013), 'Computer and electronic waste (e-waste)', *New South Wales Environment Protection Authority*, Sydney, NSW, www.epa.nsw.gov.au.
17. EPA NSW (2014), 'Waste: e-waste', *New South Wales Environment Protection Authority*, Sydney, NSW, www.epa.nsw.gov.au.
18. 'Digital Regions Initiative' (2013), Department of Broadband, Communications and the Digital Economy website, www.archive.dbcde.gov.au.
19. 'Broadband for seniors' (2014), Department of Social Services website, www.dss.gov.au.
20. 'Indigenous communications program', Department of Communications website, www.communications.gov.au.
21. 'Commercial electronic messaging', Australian Communications and Media Authority website, www.acma.gov.au.
22. 'Key elements of the Spam Act' (2013), Australian Communications and Media Authority website, www.acma.gov.au/industry.
23. IKEA website, www.ikea.com.
24. M E Porter (1985), *Competitive advantage*, New York: Free Press.
25. ibid.
26. M E Porter, 'Strategy and the internet', *Harvard Business Review*, March 2001, pp. 62–78.
27. 'Admission to practice', The College of Law website, www.collaw.edu.au.
28. D Friedlos (2012), 'Cotton On lets you "try on your sound"', *RFiD Journal*, www.rfidjournal.com.
29. 'Results — what our clients are saying', GRA website, www.gra.net.au.
30. G Robinson (2007), 'Do you remember our first ATM?', *Brisbane Times*, 17 September, www.brisbanetimes.com.au.

31. Teachers Mutual Bank (2011), 'Queensland Teachers' Credit Union unveiling a new brand as QT Mutual Bank', 4 October, www.tmbank.com.au.
32. ALDI website, corporate.aldi.com.au.
33. C Webb (2008), 'Aldi's simple recipe for success', *The Age*, 26 July, www.theage.com.au.
34. ALDI website, corporate.aldi.com.au.
35. B Speedy (2013), 'Aldi eyes $2bn expansion as chain outperforms rivals', *The Australian*, 30 March, www.theaustralian.com.au.
36. McKinsey & Company (2008), 'McKinsey global survey results: IT's unmet potential', *McKinsey Quarterly*, November, pp. 1–9, www.mckinsey.com.

CHAPTER 3

1. S Siewert (2013), 'Big data in the cloud: data velocity, volume, variety, veracity', *IBM developerWorks*, www.ibm.com.
2. Globe News Wire (2013), 'Peak 10 poised for big data growth trend with Atlanta expansion', 18 October, www.globenewswire.com.
3. PR Web (2013), 'Big data market 2014–2019: business case, industry analysis, size, share, growth, trends and forecasts', 12 September, www.prweb.com.
4. 'Big data: what information, if you had it, would change the way you run your business?', Gartner, Inc. website, www.gartner.com/technology.
5. A Fisher (2013), '7 benefits of cloud accounting systems — as noted in my book Connected Technology — how to transform your business with cloud accounting', *Barrington accountants & advisors*, 30 April, www.barringtonpractice.com.au.
6. V Hernandez (2012), 'Cloud Accounting Australia estimates $625B savings for business over 5 years', *International Business Times*, 17 August, au.ibtimes.com.
7. 'Small business owners miss opportunities for growth in the cloud' (2013), BDO Australia website, www.bdo.com.au.
8. ibid.
9. S Macpherson (2013), 'Early AccountRight Live reviews pit features versus slow speed', *Box Free IT*, 7 January, boxfreeit.com.au.
10. 'MYOB AccountRight Live — are you ready to work within the cloud?' (2013), Rubiix business accountants website, www.rubiixbusinessaccountants.com.au.
11. MYOB website, www.myob.com.au.
12. S Slisar (2013), 'Case study: using MYOB for expenses in real time with cloud accounting software', *EzyLearn*, 16 August, www.ezylearn.com.au.
13. P Madytianos (2013), 'MYOB client case study: McRose Caravan Park', *2 Peas Pty Ltd*, 27 September, www.twopeas.com.au.
14. *The Privacy Act 1988*, Office of the Australian Information Commissioner website, www.oaic.gov.au.
15. 'Case study: NSW Police Force business process digitisation program for accounts payable', NSW Government website, www.records.news.gov.au.
16. Australian Tourism Data Warehouse website, www.atdw.com.au.
17. eTravel Business News (2013), 'Independence and industry perspectives to drive ATDW's future', 19 September, australia.etbnews.com.
18. 'Australian Tourism data warehouse API', Programmable Web website, www.programmableweb.com.
19. 'Industry news: edition 110' (2013), Tourism Victoria website, www.tourism.vic.gov.au.
20. 'Renew your ATDW listing', Brisbane Marketing website, www.brisbanemarketing.com.au.
21. 'Version 11 of the Tourism 3 kit now available!' (2013), Australian Tourism Data Warehouse website, www.atdw.com.au.
22. P Kazanjy (2013), 'Source hidden software engineers on Quora', *SourceCon*, 20 June, www.sourcecon.com.
23. K Yeung (2013), 'Quora expands into a blogging platform, promises rich text mobile editing soon', *The Next Web*, 23 January, www.thenextweb.com.
24. A Jeffries (2013), 'No longer just questions and answers, Quora introduces user blogs', *The Verge*, 23 January, www.theverge.com.
25. P Kazanjy (2013), 'Source hidden software engineers on Quora', *SourceCon*, 20 June, www.sourcecon.com.
26. A Jeffries (2013), 'No longer just questions and answers, Quora introduces user blogs', *The Verge*, 23 January, www.theverge.com.
27. J Xu (2013), 'Are you using Quora in your social strategy? 8 tips to do it right', *The Daily Egg*, 5 October, blog.crazyegg.com.

CHAPTER 4

1. 'Australian internet traffic to grow fivefold by 2016' (2013), *iTnews* , 21 June, www.itnews.com.au.
2. 'What is the National Broadband Network?', Department of Communications website, www.communications.gov.au.
3. StatCounter website, www.statcounter.com.
4. M Butler (2012), 'Search engine market share November 2012', *Search Engine Journal*, 16 December, www.searchenginejournal.com.
5. Karma Snack (2013), 'Search engine market share', 23 August, www.karmasnack.com.
6. 'About us', Industry Capability Network website, www.icn.org.au.
7. E Cho (2012), 'Skype: CNET editor's review', *Download.com*, 31 October, www.download.cnet.com.
8. University of South Australia (2013), 'Thank you for your wonderful collaboration in the world's first university jam', www.unisa.edu.au; P Jump (2013), '"Unijam" strikes mass chord at University of South Australia', *Times Higher Education*, 23 May, www.timeshighereducation.co.uk.
9. Open Universities Australia website, www.open.edu.au.

CHAPTER 5

1. H-G Kemper, P Rausch & H Baars (2013), 'Business intelligence and performance management: introduction', in P Rausch (Ed.), *Business intelligence and performance management: theory, systems and industrial applications (advanced information and knowledge processing)*, pp. 3–10, London, Springer-Verlag.
2. H Mintzberg (1973), *The nature of managerial work*, New York, Harper & Row.
3. H A Simon (1977), *The new science of management decision making*, Upper Saddle River, NJ, Prentice Hall.
4. G A Gorry & M S Scott Morton (1971), 'A framework for management information systems', *Sloan Management Review*, vol. 13, no. 1, pp. 55–70.

CHAPTER 6

1. Australian Computer Society website, www.acs.org.au.
2. R Monem (2011), 'The One.Tel collapse: lessons for corporate governance', *Australian Accounting Review*, vol. 21, no. 4, pp. 340–51; SAI Global website, www.saiglobal.com.
3. 'About privacy', Office of the Australian Information Commissioner website, www.oaic.gov.au.
4. 'Who is covered by privacy', Office of the Australian Information Commissioner website, www.oaic.gov.au.
5. 'What is covered by privacy', Office of the Australian Information Commissioner website, www.oaic.gov.au.
6. 'Surveillance Devices Bills 2004', Electronic Frontiers Australia website, www.efa.org.au.
7. 'Surveillance laws and powers', Electronic Frontiers Australia website, www.efa.org.au.
8. 'Platform for privacy preferences (P3P) project', World Wide Web Consortium website, www.w3.org/P3P.
9. Association of Chartered Certified Accountants (ACCA) website, www.accaglobal.com; CPA Australia website, www.cpaaustralia.com.au; Institute of Public Accountants (IPA) website, www.publicaccountants.org.au; Institute of Chartered Accountants Australia website, www.charteredaccountants.com.au.
10. 'CLERP 9: corporate reporting and disclosure laws', Australian Securities & Investments Commission website, www.asic.gov.au.

CHAPTER 7

1. D Ball & G Waters (2013), 'Cyber defence and warfare', *Security Challenges*, 9(2), pp.91–8; 'Cyber Security Operations Centre', Department of Defence website, www.asd.gov.au; C Joye & J Kerin (2013), 'Australia developing offensive cyber capabilities', *The Australian Financial Review*, 6 May, www.afr.com.
2. Australian Government ComLaw website, www.comlaw.gov.au; 'Intellectual property and copyright', Attorney-General's Department website, www.ag.gov.au; 'Short guide to copyright', Attorney-General's Department website, www.ag.gov.au; 'Software & Apps information sheet' (2012), Australian Copyright Council website, www.copyright.org.au.
3. Enterprise Data Corporation website, www.enterprisedata.com.au.
4. 'Forensic Accounting', Institute of Chartered Accountants Australia website, www.charteredaccountants.com.au.
5. 'Auditing and forensic accounting', CPA Australia website, www.cpaaustralia.com.au.

CHAPTER 8

1. C Porter (2013), 'Customers outraged over Myer's NDIS comments', *news.com.au*, 2 May, www.news.com.au.
2. W Gordon & E Limer (2013), 'The best Google Reader alternatives', *Lifehacker Australia*, 14 March, www.lifehacker.com.au.
3. N Barber (2013), 'How to migrate RSS feeds from Google Reader', *PC World*, 19 March, www.pcworld.com.
4. 'Social business', IBM website, www.ibm.com.
5. Dialog (2012), 'Griffith University has gone Google', *Dialog Information Technology*, www.dialog.com.au.
6. R LeMay (2011), 'Griffith Uni dumps Lotus for Gmail', *Delimiter*, 18 October, www.delimiter.com.au.
7. G Baldassarre (2013), 'Social shopping website gives cash back', *Dynamic Business*, 18 April, www.dynamicbusiness.com.au.
8. Capital Wines (2011), 'How 29 tweets per day has grown our wine business', *Capital Wines Grazing in the vines*, 5 January, blog.capitalwines.com.au.

CHAPTER 9

1. Public Transport Victoria website, ptv.vic.gov.au.
2. AFP (2013), 'Cyber-squatting cases reach record high', *The Sydney Morning Herald*, 29 March, www.smh.com.au; Domain Registration Services (2013), '2012 a record-breaker for cybersquatting cases', 1 April, www.domainregistration.com.au; .au Domain Administration Ltd (2010), '.au Dispute Resolution Policy (auDRP)', *.auDA*, 13 August, www.auda.org.au.
3. 'Understanding the basics of GST', GST Start-up Assistance Office website, gst.nusystems.com.au; 'Australian e-commerce and GST' (2010), Deloitte website, www.deloitte.com; 'GST and internet sales', Herbert Geer website, www.herbertgeer.com.au.

CHAPTER 10

1. 'Calling the Emergency Call Service from a mobile phone: FAQs', Australian Communications and Media Authority website, www.acma.gov.au; 'Calling triple zero from a mobile', Australian Communications and Media Authority website, www.acma.gov.au, 'Emergency communications', Bushwalkers Wilderness Rescue Squad website, www.bwrs.org.au.
2. CISCO (2014), *802.11ac: the fifth generation of wi-fi: technical white paper*, Cisco, www.cisco.com.
3. S L Khin (2013), 'Smartphones will account for nearly half of both 802.11ac and 802.11ad chipset shipments in 2018', *ABI Research Technology Market Intelligence*, 11 June, www.abiresearch.com.
4. S Vaughan-Nichols (2013), 'High-speed 802.11ac wi-fi finally taking off', *ZD Net*, 8 August, www.zdnet.com.

5. JiWire Wi-Fi finder website, v4.jiwire.com.
6. The Wi-Fi-FreeSpot Directory website, www.wififreespot.com.
7. Hotspot Heaven website, www.hotspot-heaven.com.
8. 'Search results for "wi-fi finder"', Download.com website, www.download.cnet.com.
9. 'Free online wi-fi hotspot locators', About.com Computing Wireless and Networking website, www.compnetworking.about.com.
10. Ips-Mesh Wireless Network Community website, www.ips-mesh.net.
11. 'Brisbane WiFi in Parks', Easyweb Digital website, www.easywebdigital.com.
12. A Kamdar (2012), 'Why we have an Open Wireless Movement', *Electronic Frontier Foundation*, 30 October, www.eff.org.
13. 'Reasons for Open Wireless', Open Wireless Movement website, www.openwireless.org.
14. ABC News (2011), 'Water meter fury', 7 January, www.abc.net.au/news.

CHAPTER 11

1. 'Who uses mainframes and why do they do it?', IBM website, www.ibm.com.

CHAPTER 12

1. Customer Loyalty Conference (2013), 2–3 December, Melbourne, Victoria, Australia, www.customerloyaltysummit.com.au; A Posner & P Noble (2013), *For love or money? 2013 consumer study into Australian loyalty programs*, The Loyalty Point, www.theloyaltypoint.com.au; C philips (2013), 'Loyalty programs in Australia: Coles Flybuys takes first place', *Power Retail*, 20 May, www.powerretail.com.au/multichannel/australian-loyalty-programs-research/.
2. 'Featured case study: Adairs', Sumo Visual Group website, www.sumovisualgroup.com.au.

CHAPTER 13

1. T Truman (2010–11), 'Health procurement leader turns to Australia's National Product Catalogue to improve tendering', *GS1*, www.gs1.org.
2. 'Case study: Woolworths Supermarkets', Logica website, www.logica.com.au.
3. P Jeffers (2009), 'Embracing sustainability — information technology and the strategic leveraging of operations in third-party logistics', *International Journal of Operations & Production Management*, vol. 30, no. 3, pp. 260–87.
4. A Woodhead (2009), 'Guidelines for sustainability in supply chains: thinking systems for business sustainability', *The Australian Research Institute in Education for Sustainability*, www.aries.mq.edu.au.
5. 'Supply chain sustainability', United Nations Global Compact website, www.unglobalcompact.org.

INDEX

N

O

P

Q

R